Corporatisation in Local Government

Marieke Van Genugten
Bart Voorn • Rhys Andrews
Ulf Papenfuß • Harald Torsteinsen
Editors

Corporatisation in Local Government

Context, Evidence and Perspectives from 19 Countries

palgrave
macmillan

Editors
Marieke Van Genugten
Institute for Management Research
Radboud University
Nijmegen, The Netherlands

Bart Voorn
Institute for Management Research
Radboud University
Nijmegen, The Netherlands

Rhys Andrews
Cardiff Business School
Cardiff University
Cardiff, UK

Ulf Papenfuß
Zeppelin University
Friedrichshafen, Germany

Harald Torsteinsen
Department of Social Sciences
UiT The Arctic University of Norway
Tromsø/Harstad, Norway

ISBN 978-3-031-09984-7 ISBN 978-3-031-09982-3 (eBook)
https://doi.org/10.1007/978-3-031-09982-3

This Palgrave Macmillan imprint is published by the registered company Springer Nature Switzerland AG.
The registered company address is: Gewerbestrasse 11, 6330 Cham, Switzerland

Contents

List of Contributors

Rhys Andrews is Professor of Public Management in Cardiff Business School. His research interests focus on the management and performance of public organisations. He is the co-author of *Strategic Management and Public Service Performance* and *Public Service Efficiency: Reframing the Debate.*

Germà Bel is a Full Professor in the School of Economics at Universitat de Barcelona. His research interests focus on public sector reform, with special emphasis on local government. His more than 120 articles have been appeared in *JCR* journals, and he has also published several books. He is the editor of *Local Government Studies.*

Pedro J. Camões is a member of the Research Centre in Political Science at the University of Minho. His articles have appeared in some of the best ranked journals in public administration and political science. He coordinated several externally funded research projects on municipal efficiency, public procurement, and public sector design.

Simone Cocciasecca successfully completed his PhD in "corporate governance of state-owned enterprises in Italy" at the University of Chieti and Pescara, Italy. His main research interests concern appointment of public sector organisations and governance of public enterprises.

Marc Esteve is Full Professor in the School of Public Policy at University College London and a visiting professor at ESADE-Ramon Llull University. His primary research interests focus on understanding how individual characteristics influence decision making. His articles have been published in the *Journal of Public Administration Research and Theory, Public Administration Review, PlosOne, and Public Administration.*

Laurence Ferry is Professor and Head of Accounting in Durham University Business School and a Parliament Academic Fellow 2018/19 at the UK House of Commons reporting on arrangements for audit and inspection of local authorities in England. His research interests focus on accounting, performance, and fairness of public organisations, especially local public bodies. He is the co-author of *Public Service Accountability: Rekindling a Debate.*

Juan Carlos Garrido-Rodríguez is PhD Lecturer in Accounting at the Universidad de Granada. His research interests focus on local government, public administration, and transparency of local governments. Several of his articles have been published in international scholarly journals on these topics.

Giuseppe Grossi is Research Professor of Accounting at Nord University, Norway, and Professor of Public Management and Accounting at Kristianstad University, Sweden. His research interests concern hybrid organisations, smart cities and public budgeting. He is the editor-in-chief of *Journal of Public Budgeting, Accounting and Financial Management* (Emerald), guest editor, and the editorial board member of several journals.

György Hajnal is Professor and the director of the Institute of Economic and Public Policy, Corvinus University of Budapest, and a research professor at the ELKH Centre for Social Sciences. His research interests extend to public management reforms, the structural dynamics of government bureaucracy, and the bureaucratic implications of illiberal transformation.

Anna Hazan teaches at the School of Political Sciences, University of Haifa, and at the Department of Public Administration and Policy, Sapir Academic College. She served for many years as the director of the Local Development Department of Israel's Ministry of Interior and has authored numerous publications on local government in Israel.

Claire Kaiser is a research associate at the Institute of Public Management at the ZHAW School of Management and Law (Switzerland). After completing her MSc, she worked at the Competence Center for Public Management at the University of Bern, where she also obtained her PhD in administrative sciences. Her research focuses on local governance and public sector reforms.

Jan Erling Klausen is Associate Professor of Political Science at the University of Oslo, Norway. His research focuses mainly on municipal policy and management, local government reform and local democracy. Klausen co-authored a study about corporate governance and democratic accountability (*Journal of Public Policy*, 2021) and a recent comparative study of *Municipal Territorial Reforms of twenty-first Century in Europe* (2022).

Sanja Korać is Full Professor of Public Management at the University of Speyer, Germany, and a lecturer at the University of Klagenfurt, Austria. Her main research interests are performance management in public sector entities, governmental financial management and accounting, resilience in public organisations, and public personnel management and leadership.

Joanna Krukowska (PhD) is Assistant Professor in the Department of Local Development and Policy, Faculty of Geography and Regional Studies, University of Warsaw. Her research interest is local and regional development policy, democracy, and local leadership. She has been working at the Ministry of Regional Development, in the media, and for NGOs.

Bence Kucsera is a PhD candidate at Political Science Doctoral School of the Corvinus University of Budapest. His PhD research relates to describing and explaining the changes in Hungarian municipally owned corporations. In addition, he is conducting research related to the evolution of Hungarian business associations.

Marta Lackowska is Professor at the University of Warsaw, working in the Department of Local Development and Policy, at the Faculty of Geography and Regional Studies. Her research interests are inter-municipal cooperation, central-local relations, metropolitan governance, and Europeanisation. She is a board member of European Urban Research Association.

Gwenaël Leblong-Masclet is a territorial administrator and deputy general officer in Brest Metropole (West of France, 210,000 inhabitants). He is an associate expert in a research programme about Territories and Public Action Changes, in Sciences Po Rennes (CNRS-ARENES).

Andrej Christian Lindholst is Associate Professor of Public Management at the Centre for Organisation, Management, and Administration,

Department of Politics and Society at Aalborg University, Denmark. His research addresses public sector issues related to public sector reforms, marketisation and contract management.

Julita Łukomska (PhD) is Assistant Professor in the Department of Local Development and Policy, Faculty of Geography and Regional Studies, University of Warsaw. Her research and publications have focused on local politics (recently, local public service provision) and local government finance.

Joseph Lyons is Assistant Professor and Director of the Local Government Program in the Department of Political Science at Western University in Ontario, Canada. His research and teaching interests are in the areas of multilevel governance, local government, and public administration and policy.

Jana Machljankin is a research associate and a PhD candidate at the Institute of Public Management in the ZHAW School of Management and Law (Switzerland) and the University of Lausanne (Switzerland). Prior to this, she worked for the Deutsche Gesellschaft für Internationale Zusammenarbeit (GIZ) GmbH. Her research interests include local governance and public sector reform.

Irmak Özer is a PhD student in the Urban Policy Planning and Local Governments programme at the Middle East Technical University in Turkey. Her main research interests are municipally owned corporations, local government, governance reforms and state-owned corporations.

Ulf Papenfuß is Professor of Public Management and Public Policy at Zeppelin University Friedrichshafen. His research focuses on sustainable public corporate governance and integrated governance of public administrations and public organisations with legal or managerial independence in the context of corporatised public service provision.

Eran Razin is Professor of Geography and Urban and Regional Studies at The Hebrew University of Jerusalem, Israel, and holds the Leon Safdie Chair in Urban Studies. He specialises in comparative local government, urban planning and development, and he has published/coedited eight books and numerous journal articles in these fields.

Iris Saliterer is Full Professor of Public and Nonprofit Management at the University of Freiburg, Germany, and a lecturer at the University of

Klagenfurt, Austria. Her research focuses on performance management and the implementation of accounting reforms in public entities, and she frequently publishes on governmental resilience from a comparative perspective.

Emília Sičáková-Beblavá (PhD) is the director of the Institute of Public Policy at the Faculty of Social and Economic Sciences, Comenius University (Bratislava, Slovakia). Here she conducts research, manages graduate and PhD programmes on public policy, and teaches courses related to the public sector. Emília has attended post-gradual programs at Georgetown University, Yale University, and Harvard University.

Matúš Sloboda (PhD) is a researcher at the Institute of Public Policy at the Faculty of Social and Economic Sciences, Comenius University (Bratislava, Slovakia). His recent works focus on behavioural public administration, regulatory quality, public sector innovation, municipal corporatisation—service characteristics, organizational, political, and regulatory settings.

Zachary Spicer is Associate Professor in the School of Public Policy and Administration at York University in Ontario, Canada. His research focuses on local government, public administration and innovation policy.

Reto Steiner is Professor of Public Management and the Dean of the ZHAW School of Management and Law (Switzerland). His articles have been published extensively on the management of agencies, digital transformation, state-owned enterprises, decentralisation, and local governance. Steiner serves on various international academic boards and held academic positions at universities in Europe and Asia.

Paweł Swianiewicz is Professor at the Division of Social and Economic Research, Institute of Spatial Management, Wrocław University of Environmental and Life Sciences. Until 2021 he was a professor at the University of Warsaw. His research concentrates on local governments and decentralisation both in Poland and in comparative European perspective.

Katarzyna Szmigiel-Rawska is Associate Professor in the Department of Local Development and Policy, Faculty of Geography and Regional Studies, University of Warsaw. She is a coordinator and a participant of research and consulting projects for governmental organisations. Also she is an author and editor of numerous articles, book chapters, and books on local government and strategic public management.

Evrim Tan is a postdoctoral researcher at the KU Leuven Public Governance Institute. His research focuses on different fields under political and social sciences including decentralisation, local government, public governance, and e-government. He is the author of *Decentralisation and Governance Capacity: The Case of Turkey* (Palgrave Macmillan).

António F. Tavares is Associate Professor of Habilitation in Political Science and a member of the Research Centre in Political Science at the School of Economics and Management of the University of Minho in Braga, Portugal. His research interests include local public service delivery arrangements, land use management, and civic engagement and political participation.

David Taylor is an instructor of municipal law in the Local Government Program in the Department of Political Science at Western University in Ontario, Canada. He is also the Director at Legal Services for the Municipality of Chatham-Kent, Ontario, Canada.

Anna Thomasson is Associate Professor at the School of Economics and Management, Lund University. In her research Anna mainly focuses on issues related to governance and organisation of public sector services, among them innovation, digitalisation, collaboration, and corporatisation.

Harald Torsteinsen is Professor of Political Science/Public Management at UiT The Arctic University of Norway, Tromsø/Harstad. His research interests include organisational and political innovation and reform in local government, especially corporatisation of service provision. His articles have been recently published in *Public Administration* (2021), *Local Government Studies* (2021) and *Public Money & Management* (2019) journals.

Athanasia Triantafyllopoulou is Professor of Local Development Institutions at the University of the Peloponnese. Her main research interests are local government, local development, and local policy making.

Theodore N. Tsekos is Professor of Public Administration at the University of the Peloponnese and Director of the Institute of Political Research at the National Centre for Social Research in Greece. His main research interests are public policy, public management, and organisational design.

Marieke Van Genugten is Associate Professor of Public Administration at the Institute for Management Research, Department of Public Administration at Radboud University, The Netherlands. Her main research interests are local public management and governance, in particular arm's length governance and corporatisation, and the design of municipal organisations.

Bart Voorn is Assistant Professor of Public Administration at the Institute for Management Research, Department of Public Administration at Radboud University, The Netherlands. His main research interests are local public management and governance, in particular causes and consequences of different local public service delivery options.

José Luis Zafra-Gómez is Full Professor of Accounting at the Universidad de Granada, Spain. His research interests focus on local government. His articles have been recently published in journals, including the *Journal of Public Administration Research and Theory*, *Public Administration*, *Regional Studies*, *Urban Studies*, *European Journal of Operational Research*, and *OMEGA*.

List of Figures

List of Tables

CHAPTER 1

Corporatisation in Local Government: An Introduction

Harald Torsteinsen, Rhys Andrews, Ulf Papenfuß, Marieke Van Genugten, and Bart Voorn

1.1 The Changing Face of Local Government Service Provision

During the past 25 years or so, corporatisation has emerged as one of the most important and characteristic trends in local government, not least in Europe (Andrews et al. 2020; Grossi et al. 2015; Papenfuß and Keppeler 2020; Van Genugten et al. 2020). Although not a completely new

H. Torsteinsen (✉)
Department of Social Sciences, UiT The Arctic University of Norway, Tromsø/Harstad, Norway
e-mail: harald.torsteinsen@uit.no

R. Andrews
Cardiff Business School, Cardiff University, Cardiff, UK
e-mail: andrewsr4@cardiff.ac.uk

U. Papenfuß
Zeppelin University, Friedrichshafen, Germany
e-mail: ulf.papenfuss@zu.de

M. Van Genugten et al. (eds.), *Corporatisation in Local Government*, https://doi.org/10.1007/978-3-031-09982-3_1

phenomenon—signs appear already in the late nineteenth and early twentieth centuries in some countries (e.g. Voorn 2021)—the recent prevalence and the scope of this development have often been interpreted by both practitioners and scholars as an example of New Public Management (NPM) ideas being implemented in local public administration. The practical outcome of this process is the creation of municipally owned corporations—or MOCs as we denote them in this book—entities operating at some distance from their owner municipalities as arm's length bodies (Van Genugten et al. 2020). To the extent that local government institutions or organisations own or control, directly or indirectly, more than 50% of a corporation, we consider it as a MOC (Grossi et al. 2015; Papenfuß and Keppeler 2020; Voorn et al. 2017).

Corporatisation is the process by which governments convert an existing public service into a majority-owned corporate entity or create a new service (Andrews 2022; Papenfuß and Schmidt 2021). It serves as a supplement or an alternative to other forms of local government service delivery: traditional in-house provision by municipal entities, contracting out—often combined with legal tendering procedures—and finally, various cooperative arrangements with other municipalities, regional and national public organisations, private business companies or non-profit civic organisations. All of these service delivery forms have their advantages and disadvantages, and these questions cut to the heart of local politics, as they can affect what services are received by citizens (Bel and Gradus 2018; Hefetz et al. 2012; Schoute et al. 2017; Zafra-Gómez et al. 2013).

Corporatisation may but does not necessarily mean commercialisation and profit-seeking (Papenfuß 2020; Papenfuß and Schmidt 2021). It may just as well serve as an approach aimed at enhancing quality, efficiency, and effectiveness in public service provision. Furthermore, it may serve as a vehicle for economic and social development of a community and "represents an excellent example of the systemic or corporate public entrepreneurship" (Andrews et al. 2020, p. 482).

Corporatisation implies opportunities and challenges. On the one hand, corporatisation may improve the performance in public service

---

M. Van Genugten • B. Voorn
Institute for Management Research, Radboud University,
Nijmegen, The Netherlands
e-mail: marieke.vangenugten@ru.nl; bart.voorn@ru.nl

provision by enhancing autonomy, flexibility, specialisation, and professionalism by introducing more business techniques and incentives for good public service delivery in the public sector. It may further increase effectiveness, efficiency, and service quality (Andrews et al. 2020; Papenfuß and Schmidt 2021; Van Genugten et al. 2020; Voorn et al. 2017), and it can help to solve competence and capacity challenges for the public sector.

On the other hand, corporatisation may fragment and complicate the local democratic and bureaucratic governance system, obfuscating or weakening the traditional chain of command and control (Berge and Torsteinsen 2021a; Papenfuss 2020; Pierre 2009; Voorn and Van Genugten 2021). In addition, the mismatch between the rapid growth in MOCs and the development of appropriate corporate governance mechanisms in local government signifies an institutional lag, which aggravates these problems (Papenfuß 2020; Papenfuß and Schmidt 2021). Further, local politicians are not always aware about what corporatisation means in practice, how it influences their roles as ombudsmen, shareholders, principals and stewards, how it increases their overall strategic responsibility for the MOCs, and how it reduces their power over MOCs' daily operations (Klausen and Winsvold 2019; Papenfuß 2020; Papenfuß and Schmidt 2021; Voorn and Van Genugten 2021). The saying "out of sight, out of mind" also has some relevance here in the sense that local politicians may lose interest in their MOCs, weakening the attention and vigilance that is necessary for effective public corporate governance. An associated challenge is lack of accountability and heightened risk of corruption (e.g. Bergh et al. 2021). For municipal chief executive officers (CEOs), MOCs represent a deviation from the traditional political-administrative chain of governance, confusing or even interrupting their line of authority and accountability. Therefore, CEOs often perceive corporatisation as a problematic development, but they seldom express their frustrations openly. The anonymity of research interviews, however, gives them an opportunity to speak their minds more freely.

Interviews with two municipal Norwegian CEOs may exemplify how some of them experience and evaluate effects of corporatisation. In the first interview, an experienced CEO gave graphic descriptions of some of the challenges she met. Some years earlier, the municipality had set up an in-house MOC for managing all its properties, that is, schools, kindergartens and elderly homes. Although this meant more professional property management and better facilities, it also led to a steep rise in the rents service providing entities had to pay, infuriating the managers of these entities with tight budgets. According to the CEO, the property MOC tended to "gold-plate" its maintenance and investments, that is, spending more money than what she deemed necessary. At the same time, as the MOC was able to accumulate funds, the municipality was hit by economic austerity and had to cut several budget items, for example, to pay the increased property rents for its service entities. When asked if it would be better to transform the MOC into a limited liability company, she responded: "That would be much, much worse!" The problem is, she explained, "I do not have control over the municipal properties on which I depend to provide municipal services". She added: "This company and our other MOCs tend to become too narrow-minded, too commercial. They stop seeing themselves as complementary parts of the larger municipal organisation". During the interview she became more and more upset, using rather explicit and harsh language about some of the MOCs, including their managers and boards. In the second interview, we met a newly appointed CEO. Still, she shared many of the evaluations of her older colleague, but at the same time she underlined some benefits of corporatisation. She wondered: "Is it ok to allow a MOC to live its own life and make its own priorities at the expense of all other services?". She further reflected about "what would happen if the municipality corporatised all attractive, profit-oriented services and was only left with the burdensome, budget-dependent services for which the demand seems insatiable?". Her own answer was that "the municipality then loses opportunities, a tool to provide revenues for financing our service provision. This is perhaps the greatest risk". On the other hand, however, both she and the senior CEO acknowledge that corporatisation may improve the quality of the local public services. MOCs tend to become more professional and task-oriented, their performance is often easier to observe and measure, and mandatory annual reporting may enhance their transparency. Although ideographic, these examples highlight some typical ambiguities and tensions that may arise between owner municipalities and MOCs.

Nonetheless, in summing up, it seems obvious that corporatisation raises several dilemmas which make the balancing of benefits and costs a difficult task. The calculation also affects principles of democracy, rule of law, justice, and common good that carry more weight than individual consumer-oriented interests, petty technicalities or minor economic gains (Moore 2014). Finally, national political culture and context will most certainly influence the weights and values ascribed to specific benefits and costs, and in the end, Lasswell's classical question, "Who gets What, When, How", is still relevant (Lasswell 1936).

1.2 Aim of the Book

The aim of this book is to provide an in-depth cross-country comparison of corporatisation in local government. While we are understanding more about causes (Andrews et al. 2020; Tavares 2017) and effects (Voorn et al. 2017) of the trend of corporatisation at the local level, we know little about cross-country differences in what MOCs look like, what legislation applies to them and how they are governed. Multiple researchers have called for more extensive research into MOCs (Cambini et al. 2011; Ferry et al. 2018; Lidström 2017; Papenfuß and Keppeler 2020; Torsteinsen 2019; Voorn 2021; Voorn et al. 2018).

Knowledge of cross-country differences in municipal corporatisation is critical for various reasons. For academics, the differences between countries lead to misunderstandings and make it difficult to generalise findings from one country to another. For practitioners, understanding differences between countries allows policy learning, particularly in governance and legislation, as governance of MOCs continues to be difficult. Therefore, the key objective of the book is to go beyond the national context to give an overview of what unites all countries in terms of the trend towards MOCs, and what differentiates them, in order to bridge this gap in the literature.

1.3 MOCs: A Definition

To make cross-country comparison possible, we established one broad definition of MOCs. In this book we define MOCs as corporations and enterprises that are under the control of a municipality either by majority ownership by one or more municipalities or otherwise by exercising an equivalent degree of control (Andrews et al. 2020; Grossi et al. 2015; Papenfuß and Keppeler 2020; Voorn et al. 2017). More specifically, MOCs are organisations that are (Voorn et al. 2017, based on Tavares and Camoes 2007):

1. Structurally separated from their owner municipalit(y/ies) and with independent corporate status (i.e. with *legal autonomy*)
2. Managed by an executive board appointed primarily by the municipal owners (with *managerial autonomy*)
3. With *majority public ownership*

The term "MOC" covers all other typical terms used for arm's length bodies at the local level such as state-owned enterprises, corporations, government-owned companies, public enterprises, local corporations,

Table 1.1 Typology of arm's length bodies at the local level

Type	*Definition*	*Types of bodies at the local level*
1	Semi-autonomous body, unit or body without legal independence but with considerable managerial autonomy	In-house delivery by "autonomised" units
2	Legally independent body with managerial autonomy (in principle public law based)	Inter-municipal companies, public bodies, statutory bodies
3	Body established by or on behalf of the local government such as a foundation, corporation, company or enterprise (private law based)	Limited companies and foundations

Source: Based on Papenfuß and Keppeler (2020); Torsteinsen and Van Genugten (2016); Van Genugten et al. (2020)

government-sponsored enterprises, mixed enterprises, and indirect or direct holdings of government (Bernier et al. 2020; Grossi et al. 2015). Moreover, in the typology of arm's length bodies at the local level, MOCs can be understood as type 2 and type 3 arm's length bodies (Papenfuß and Keppeler 2020; Torsteinsen and Van Genugten 2016; Van Genugten et al. 2020), and in some instances also as a hybrid of type 1 and type 2 (see Table 1.1).

Note that this is still a very broad definition and categorisation, and that MOCs can have many different shapes and forms depending on the country. For instance, in some countries, MOCs are primarily based in public (government) law; in others, they are primarily based in private (commercial) law. In some countries, MOCs are multi-purpose, delivering multiple services at once, while in others they are more fragmented, instituted for the delivery of a single service. In some countries, MOCs (can) have multiple owners or shareholders, whereas in others that is much rarer. In some countries, MOCs may develop into complex enterprises, comprising cross ownerships and subsidiaries of different types, while in other countries this is less common. In some countries, municipalities administer and control their MOCs with a unit in the core administration and hold the shares of these corporations directly, whereas in other countries municipalities outsource these tasks to a holding management company with a municipality as 100% shareholder. Therefore, the term "MOC" encompasses all these empirical forms: all direct (first-degree) and indirect majority (second- or third-degree; at least 50% majority) corporations.

1.4 MOCs in Historical and Political Context

During much of public administration history, local public services were administered directly by the government bureaucracy or by the private sector, with few alternatives. With the growing task portfolio and size of the public sector combined with increasing austerity, this "binary" choice between public and private service delivery became unsatisfactory for practitioners over time. Since the 1980s, public and academic concerns about inefficiency of government bureaucracy caused reconsideration of such public "bureaucratic" forms of public service delivery (Dunleavy and Hood 1994), and since the 1990s, academics and the public recognise that private forms of public service delivery do not always increase efficiency either, especially at the local level, where frequent market concentration and information advantages for incumbents can cause competitive tendering procedures to trend towards monopoly rather than competition (Dijkgraaf and Gradus 2007; Ohemeng and Grant 2008).

Starting especially in the 1990s, local governments began to seek alternatives. Municipally owned corporations offered one such alternative. MOCs offer a "middle ground" in the "pendulum shift" between public and private service provision (cf. Warner and Aldag 2021; Wollmann and Marcou 2010) and allow policymakers to strike a balance between public interests and private efficiency by introducing private sector behaviour under public ownership (Leavitt and Morris 2004; Voorn et al. 2020).

MOCs began to rapidly increase in popularity throughout the 1990s and 2000s, for both good and bad reasons. On the negative side, practitioners found that MOCs offered a way to circumvent financial constraints faced by municipalities (Bernier et al. 2020; Citroni et al. 2013; Ferry et al. 2018), as expenditures in MOCs are not always visible in municipal bookkeeping, and user fees charged by MOCs are not counted as taxes (Tavares 2017; Tavares and Camões 2007). Politically, policymakers found the user fees that MOCs could levy easier to justify than taxation (Voorn et al. 2021), and also that they could shift the blame to MOCs' professional managers in case things went wrong (Bourdeaux 2007). On the more positive side, MOCs can be seen as an innovation to reduce red tape (Blom et al. 2021), can bring benefits through hybridity (Torsteinsen 2019) and can help avoid labour restraints in situations where that is economically sensible (Voorn et al. 2017). All this brought a rise in the number of MOCs in Europe, which has been described as a "field-level change" (Ferry et al. 2018).

1.5 MOCs: Connection to Overarching Public Administration Themes

As outlined earlier, MOCs are of particular importance to the state and society as well as state and public administration modernisation. In several countries, a high proportion of employees in local government do not work in the core administration; instead, they work in MOCs. MOCs often undertake a high percentage of the public sector's investments, and the debt ratio of MOCs is often even higher than that of the administration (Bernier et al. 2020; Papenfuß and Keppeler 2020; Papenfuß and Schmidt 2021).

Furthermore, in the debate on sustainable services of general interest, the United Nations Sustainable Development Goals (SDGs) such as climate protection, reduction of poverty and unemployment, sustainable city development, digital transformation, and equality of living conditions, the role of MOCs may become a crucial future topic.

The same is true for issues of sustainable digitisation, digital transformation, smart city and integrated city/urban development for which public authorities in many countries have formulated ambitious goals. To meet these goals integrated management of the core public administrations and MOCs may become more relevant, meaning avoiding unnecessary duplication of effort and promoting development in individual areas by meeting regularly, sharing experiences and taking effective measures. Other examples of integrated management are the development of coherent digital strategies by municipalities and MOCs, and the creation of MOCs serving as specialised competence and service centres for digitisation of one or several municipalities. Moreover, exchange of data between administrations and MOCs in the form of a comprehensive strategic information system may be vital for smart city and integrated urban development.

Also, from a theoretical point of view, MOCs are a relevant research object as they lie on a continuum between the core public administration and private firms. Therefore, research on MOCs promises to generate valuable insights for several theoretical debates, on overriding public administration issues, for instance on performance of public services, accountability, control and trust in steering relations, competing institutional logics, public corporate governance, corruption and (de-)politicisation (Berge and Torsteinsen 2021b; Grossi et al. 2015; Klausen and Winsvold 2019; Papenfuß 2020; Van Genugten et al. 2020; Verhoest et al. 2012).

Overall, corporatisation of local government and MOCs have very high relevance and potential for overarching public administration themes.

1.6 Contribution of the Book

As the following country chapters demonstrate, MOCs can differ greatly in legal form, size, purpose, ownership structure, autonomy and corporate governance practices. Moreover, the motivations that lie behind the use of MOCs often vary from country to country, with economic rationales predominating in some countries and political or organisational rationales in others. These cross-country variations highlight that the corporatisation of local government is a public sector reform that merits especially careful contextual analysis and interpretation. By systematically presenting the distinctive approaches to the use of MOCs in multiple countries, this book aims to further develop scholarly understanding of the nature of corporatisation of local government in several important ways.

First, we develop a common analytical framework for understanding similarities and differences in the use of MOCs in different contexts. In doing so, we seek to illustrate the typical challenges and opportunities confronted by municipalities that corporatise their public services. The framework we use has been inspired by the so-called COBRA survey conducted among agencies at the national level (Verhoest et al. 2012). Second, by using our analytical framework to pinpoint important differences in the approaches to corporatisation in different countries, we are able to trace out how dissimilar administrative traditions, local government systems and politics exert a major influence on reforms to the public sector at the local level. Public administration scholars have long compared and contrasted the varying rationales for reorganisations of local government across multiple countries (e.g. Baldersheim and Rose 2010; Kuhlmann and Bouckaert 2016), but the corporatisation of local government and the use of arms-length bodies by municipalities, more generally, remain areas ripe for comparative analysis and insights. Third, our cross-country approach highlights the varying ways in which the logic of managerialism and the corporation has now penetrated local governance. As a result, we are able to cast invaluable light on alternative approaches to steering and managing the hybrid forms of organisation that are increasingly responsible for providing public services (Brandsen and Karré 2011; Vakkuri et al. 2021).

In addition to contributing to the burgeoning scholarship on the changing nature of the local state, the book is intended to make a direct contribution to research dealing with corporatisation of local public services and the use of MOCs, specifically. Through the collection, presentation and analysis of high-quality data capturing key facets of MOCs, the contributors to the book provide a unique and detailed insight into the dynamics of corporatisation within their countries. Each country chapter represents a major contribution to our knowledge about contemporary developments in local governance, how those developments can be evaluated and the limits to, and possibilities for, further research on the use of MOCs within and across countries. To date, much of the ground-breaking research on corporatisation is based on data that was collected prior to the global financial crisis (see Tavares 2017; Voorn et al. 2017). The up-to-date information on MOCs presented in the book can form the foundation for an array of new research projects. At the same time, the significant cross-country variations in the theory and practice of corporatisation demonstrate the need for a community of international scholars dedicated to taking research on the topic forward into the future.

Finally, as well as making a significant contribution to academic research, the book contains unique insights and evidence that will be of value to policymakers and practitioners at the local, regional and national levels. The discussion of corporatisation in each country chapter provides valuable background information for policymakers seeking to learn from the positive and negative experiences of municipalities in other countries. Better understanding of the varying legal forms, ownership structures and corporate governance practices present in different countries can potentially inform debates about appropriate national legislation, regulatory actions and local policy choices pertaining to the management and performance of MOCs. Likewise, the analysis of the mechanisms for holding MOCs accountable to their parent organisation(s) presented in the country chapters could potentially inform deliberations about the best approach to steering MOCs within municipalities themselves. While the book may not present off-the-shelf solutions to the dilemmas of governance, accountability and performance posed by corporatisation, at the very least it provides much-needed context for discussions amongst local government policymakers and practitioners about the prospective directions that further reforms could and, potentially, should take.

1.7 Our Approach

1.7.1 General Methodology

To achieve a genuinely comparative approach to understanding the corporatisation of local government and the use of MOCs, we invited a series of academic experts in local governance to contribute book chapters describing corporatisation and MOCs within their country. The experts were identified on the basis of their publication history in the field of local public administration and through personal networks. We received positive responses to our invitations from research teams working in nineteen countries. These countries provide a good mix of different administrative traditions for the book: Anglo-Saxon (Canada, England, Israel, Wales), Central Eastern European (Hungary, Poland, Slovakia), Central European Federal (Austria, Germany, Switzerland), Napoleonic (France, Greece, Italy, Portugal, Spain, Turkey) and Nordic (Denmark, the Netherlands, Norway, Sweden).

To ensure that a common approach was adopted by all contributors, we developed an analytical framework capturing the main facets of MOCs that we believed to be most important (see next). The framework also formed the proposed structure of the contents for each country chapter. Contributors were given a detailed checklist on the information that should be presented in their chapter along with the order in which it should be reported. This checklist was then used by the editorial team to evaluate the extent to which each country chapter included information on each of the main facets of MOCs, and to summarise the information that was provided. The process of revising the chapters went through two iterations before the final draft of the book was submitted to the publishers.

1.7.2 Facets of MOCs

In order to compare the extent of corporatisation in local government and the similarities and differences in the application of MOCs within different countries, we developed a framework that could guide the production of each country chapter based around five key facets relating to the creation and operation of MOCs.

First, we asked contributors to report on and discuss trends in the numbers of MOCs within their country. This would provide a basis for evaluating the degree to which the corporatisation of local government had taken place within each country and whether it had become more or less prevalent in recent years. Second, we asked contributors for an overview of the main legal forms that MOCs take within their country. Prior research suggests that the legal form of MOCs has major implications for their management and performance (Papenfuß and Schmidt 2021; Van Genugten et al. 2020; Voorn et al. 2017). Third, contributors were requested to report on the typical policy sectors, ownership structure and size of MOCs within their country. Again, previous studies indicated that these background characteristics could have important implications for the management and performance of MOCs. Fourth, contributors were asked to discuss the relative autonomy of MOCs—freedom for professional managers to manage being a rationale that is often advanced in favour of corporatised public services (Bourdeaux 2008; Papenfuß and Schmidt 2021). Each chapter therefore includes commentary on the extent to which MOCs in each country can set their own goals and make their own financial and employment decisions, along with reflections on the accountability regimes and corporate governance regulations that may be present. Fifth, to explore corporate governance issues and prevailing debates (Papenfuß 2020; Papenfuß and Schmidt 2021) in more depth, we requested that contributors explain the type of board systems for MOCs, and to discuss the typical composition of those boards. Contributors were then given the further option of exploring the background and compensation of MOC executive directors in more depth.

1.7.3 Local Government Typology

In this book we apply one of the most recent typologies used for classifying local governments in Europe (Schwab et al. 2017). The typology builds on a previous classification of public administration systems in Europe shaped by different historical, institutional and cultural forces (Kuhlmann and Wollmann 2019). These systems constitute the contexts within which local governments develop and operate in the different countries covered by this volume. In Table 1.2 we briefly describe the typology of Schwab et al. (2017).

The typology has several limitations. First, it is primarily based on Western European history, institutions and culture. Swianiewicz (2014), among others, has criticised the tendency to classify all East-European countries into one (or as in this case two) type(s) despite the huge variation within this group. This does not, however, make the presented typology completely irrelevant, not even outside Europe, since needs and solutions for political and administrative organisation at the local level is a generic phenomenon. Second, although path dependencies certainly influence the formation of local government systems, ideas and practices travel across boundaries and may therefore blend with other traditions. Third, the present features of specific countries do not always fit neatly into the broad local government types presented. Over time, these

Table 1.2 Local government typology

Type	*Dimensions*						
	History		*Institutions*			*Culture*	
	Western Weberian bureaucracy	*Post-communist*	*Unitary centralised*	*Unitary decentralised*	*Federal*	*Rule of law Legalism*	*Public law Common law*
Napoleonic	X		X			X	
Belgium, *France*, *Greece*, *Italy*, *Portugal*, *Spain*, *Turkey*	Comprehensive codification and strong centralisation		Central state and bureaucracy very strong and accepted, functionally weak local governments			South European countries: politicisation, clientelism and party patronage trends particularly visible	
Central European Federal	X				X	X	
Austria, *Germany*, *Switzerland*			Central government weaker and leaner, local government and subsidiarity of higher importance than in CEN. Influential mayors			Strong legalistic and "Rechtsstaat" culture	
Nordic	X			X		X	
Denmark, Finland, Iceland, *the Netherlands*, *Norway*, *Sweden*	Open civil service recruitment, transparency, clearly influenced by managerialism and to some degree marketisation		Politically and functionally strong local government, highly decentralised and autonomous			Consensual, cooperative, pragmatic and open political culture	
Anglo-Saxon	X		X		X[a]		X
Canada, Cyprus, *England*, Ireland, *Israel*, Scotland, *Wales*	Open civil service recruitment, transparency. Strongly influenced by managerialism and marketisation		Local government functionally strong, politically weak.			Market-oriented, public interest culture, liberal state philosophy	
Central East European		X		X		X	

(*continued*)

Table 1.2 (continued)

Type	*Dimensions*						
	History		*Institutions*			*Culture*	
	Western Weberian bureaucracy	*Post-communist*	*Unitary centralised*	*Unitary decentralised*	*Federal*	*Rule of law Legalism*	*Public law Common law*
The Czech Republic, Estonia, *Hungary*, Latvia, Lithuania, ***Poland***, *Slovakia*	Scepticism towards centralised government, territorial fragmentation		Decentralised public administration, functionally strong local government, varying fiscal autonomy, Baltic states lean towards the Nordic model				
South-East European		X	X			X	
Albania, Croatia, Romania, Slovenia			Local government functions limited, low fiscal discretion, strong local leadership			Similarities to South European countries	

Note: Names in italic—countries represented in this book

[a]Canada: federal system

features may develop and give rise to diverging or converging tendencies. Finally, other typologies for comparing local government systems exist (Lidström 1998; Swianiewicz 2014), which could have drawn our attention to additional or other features. However, for our purpose the typology of Schwab et al. (2017) works sufficiently well.

1.8 Outline of the Book

The typology of local government systems presented in the previous section provides the structure of the book. In five parts five sets of country studies are presented, in alphabetical order: Anglo Saxon countries (Canada, England and Wales, Israel) in Part I, Central East European countries (Hungary, Poland, Slovakia) in Part II, Central European Federal countries (Austria, Germany, Switzerland) in Part III, Napoleonic countries (France, Greece, Italy, Portugal, Spain, Turkey) in Part IV, and Nordic countries (Denmark, the Netherlands, Norway, Sweden) in Part V. All country chapters discuss the five key facets relating to the creation and operation of MOCs. The concluding chapter in Part VI summarises key similarities and differences. Furthermore, we derive some general conclusions and perspectives for the future of MOCs and present a research agenda.

References

Andrews, R. (2022). Organizational publicness and mortality: Explaining the dissolution of local authority companies. *Public Management Review, 24*(3), 350–371.

Andrews, R., Ferry, L., Skelcher, C., & Wegorowski, P. (2020). Corporatization in the public sector: Explaining the growth of local government companies. *Public Administration Review, 80*(3), 482–493.

Baldersheim, H., & Rose, L. (Eds.). (2010). *Territorial choice: The politics of boundaries and borders*. Palgrave Macmillan.

Bel, G., & Gradus, R. (2018). Privatisation, contracting-out and inter-municipal cooperation: New developments in local public service delivery. *Local Government Studies, 44*(1), 11–21.

Berge, D. M., & Torsteinsen, H. (2021a). Governance challenges of different institutional logics and modes of organising: A Norwegian case study of municipal water supply. *Local Government Studies*. https://doi.org/10.1080/03003930.2021.1942853

Berge, D. M., & Torsteinsen, H. (2021b). Corporatization in local government – Promoting cultural differentiation and hybridity? *Public Administration*. https://doi.org/10.1111/padm.12737.

Bergh, A., Erlingsson, G. Ó., & Wittberg, E. (2021). What happens when municipalities run corporations? Empirical evidence from 290 Swedish municipalities. *Local Government Studies.* https://doi.org/10.1080/03003930.2021.1944857

Bernier, L., Bance, P., & Florio, M. (2020). *The Routledge handbook of state-owned enterprises.* Routledge.

Blom, R., Borst, R. T., & Voorn, B. (2021). Pathology or inconvenience? A meta-analysis of the impact of red tape on people and organizations. *Review of Public Personnel Administration, 41*(4), 623–650.

Bourdeaux, C. (2007). Reexamining the claim of public authority efficacy. *Administration & Society, 39*(1), 77–106.

Bourdeaux, C. (2008). Politics versus professionalism: The effect of institutional structure on democratic decision making in a contested policy arena. *Journal of Public Administration Research and Theory, 18*(3), 349–373.

Brandsen, T., & Karré, P. M. (2011). Hybrid organizations: No cause for concern? *International Journal of Public Administration, 34*(13), 827–836.

Cambini, C., Filippini, M., Piacenza, M., & Vannoni, D. (2011). Corporatization and firm performance: Evidence from publicly-provided local utilities. *Review of Law & Economics, 7*(1), 191–213.

Citroni, G., Lippi, A., & Profeti, S. (2013). Representation through corporatisation: Municipal corporations in Italy as arenas for local democracy. *European Political Science Review, 7*(1), 63–92.

Dijkgraaf, E., & Gradus, R. (2007). Collusion in the Dutch waste collection market. *Local Government Studies, 33*(4), 573–588.

Dunleavy, P., & Hood, C. (1994). From old public administration to new public management. *Public Money & Management, 14*(3), 9–16.

Ferry, L., Andrews, R., Skelcher, C., & Wegorowski, P. (2018). New development: Corporatization of local authorities in England in the wake of austerity 2010–2016. *Public Money & Management, 38*(6), 477–480.

Grossi, G., Papenfuß, U., & Tremblay, M. (2015). Corporate governance and accountability of state-owned enterprises: Relevance for science and society and interdisciplinary research perspectives. *International Journal of Public Sector Management, 28*(4), 274–285.

Hefetz, A., Warner, M. E., & Vigoda-Gadot, E. (2012). Privatization and intermunicipal contracting: The US local government experience 1992–2007. *Environment and Planning C: Government and Policy, 30*(4), 675–692.

Klausen, J. E., & Winsvold, M. (2019). Corporate governance and democratic accountability: Local state-owned enterprises in Norway. *Journal of Public Policy, 41*(1), 161–184.

Kuhlmann, S., & Bouckaert, G. (Eds.). (2016). *Local public sector reforms in times of crisis.* Palgrave Macmillan.

Kuhlmann, S., & Wollmann, H. (2019). *Introduction to comparative public administration. Administrative systems and reforms in Europe* (2nd ed.). Edward Elgar.

Lasswell, H. D. (1936). *Politics: Who gets what, when, how*. Whittlesey House.
Leavitt, W. M., & Morris, J. C. (2004). In search of middle ground: The public authority as an alternative to privatization. *Public Works Management & Policy, 9*(2), 154–163.
Lidström, A. (1998). The comparative study of local government systems—a research agenda. *Journal of Comparative Policy Analysis: Research and Practice, 1*(1), 97–115. (Published online 2007).
Lidström, A. (2017). Public authorities and intermunicipal cooperation in a European context. *Urban Affairs Review, 53*(2), 403–409.
Moore, M. H. (2014). Public value accounting: Establishing the philosophical basis. *Public Administration Review, 74*(4), 465–477.
Ohemeng, F. K., & Grant, J. K. (2008). When markets fail to deliver: An examination of the privatization and de-privatization of water and wastewater services delivery in Hamilton. *Canada. Canadian Public Administration, 51*(3), 475–499.
Papenfuß, U. (2020). Corporate governance of state-owned enterprises: Conceptualization, challenges and perspectives for the public corporate governance field. In L. Bernier, P. Bance, & E. Florio (Eds.), *The Routledge handbook of state-owned enterprises* (pp. 433–444). Routledge.
Papenfuβ, U., & Keppeler, F. (2020). Does performance-related pay and public service motivation research treat state-owned enterprises like a neglected Cinderella? A systematic literature review and agenda for future research on performance effects. *Public Management Review, 22*(7), 1119–1145.
Papenfuß, U., & Schmidt, C. (2021). Personnel governance of corporatized public services: Effects of executive resources and corporation forms on turnover. *Public Administration*. https://doi.org/10.1111/padm.12752
Pierre, J. (2009). Reinventing governance, reinventing democracy. *Policy and Politics, 37*(4), 591–609.
Schoute, M., Budding, T., & Gradus, R. (2017). Municipalities' choices of service delivery modes: The influence of service, political, governance, and financial characteristics. *International Public Management Journal, 21*(4), 502–532.
Schwab, C., Bouckaert, G., & Kuhlmann, S. (Eds.). (2017). *The future of local government in Europe. Lessons from research and practice in 31 countries*. Nomos.
Swianiewicz, P. (2014). An empirical typology of local government systems in Eastern Europe. *Local Government Studies, 40*(2), 292–311.
Tavares, A. F. (2017). Ten years after: Revisiting the determinants of the adoption of municipal corporations for local service delivery. *Local Government Studies, 43*(5), 697–706.
Tavares, A. F., & Camoes, P. (2007). Local service delivery choices in Portugal: A political transaction costs framework. *Local Government Studies, 33*(4), 535–553.
Torsteinsen, H. (2019). Debate: Corporatization in local government – The need for a comparative and multi-disciplinary research approach. *Public Money & Management, 39*(1), 5–8.

Torsteinsen, H., & Van Genugten, M. (2016). Waste management in the Netherlands and Norway – From in-house provision to inter-municipal cooperation. In S. Kuhlman & G. Bouckaert (Eds.), *Local public sector reforms in times of crisis: National trajectories and international comparisons* (pp. 205–220). Palgrave.

Vakkuri, J., Johanson, J.-E., Feng, N. C., & Giordano, F. (2021). Governance and accountability in hybrid organizations–past, present and future. *Journal of Public Budgeting, Accounting & Financial Management, 33*(3), 245–260.

Van Genugten, M., Van Thiel, S., & Voorn, B. (2020). Local governments and their arm's length bodies. *Local Government Studies, 46*(1), 1–21.

Verhoest, K., Van Thiel, S., Bouckaert, G., & Lægreid, P. (Eds.). (2012). *Government agencies: Practices and lessons from 30 countries*. Palgrave Macmillan.

Voorn, B. (2021). Debate: Shadow government—A note for European corporatization research. *Public Money & Management, 41*(7), 561–562.

Voorn, B., Borst, R. T., & Blom, R. (2020). Business techniques as an explanation of the autonomy-performance link in corporatized entities: Evidence from Dutch Municipally owned corporations. *International Public Management Journal*. https://doi.org/10.1080/10967494.2020.1802632

Voorn, B., & Van Genugten, M. (2021). Dealing with multiple principals in at arm's length organisations: A qualitative study of Dutch municipally owned corporations. *Public Administration*. https://doi.org/10.1111/padm.12746

Voorn, B., Van Genugten, M., & Van Thiel, S. (2017). The efficiency and effectiveness of municipally owned corporations: A systematic review. *Local Government Studies, 43*(5), 820–841.

Voorn, B., Van Genugten, M., & Van Thiel, S. (2021). Re-interpreting re-municipalization: Finding equilibrium. *Journal of Economic Policy Reform, 24*(3), 305–318.

Voorn, B., Van Thiel, S., & Van Genugten, M. L. (2018). Debate: Corporatization as more than a recent crisis-driven development. *Public Money & Management, 38*(7), 481–482.

Warner, M. E., & Aldag, A. M. (2021). Re-municipalization in the US: A pragmatic response to contracting. *Journal of Economic Policy Reform, 24*(3), 319–332.

Wollmann, H., & Marcou, G. (2010). Introduction. In H. Wollmann & G. Marcou (Eds.), *The provision of public services in Europe: Between state, local government and market* (pp. 1–14). Edward Elgar.

Zafra-Gómez, J. L., Prior, D. P., Díaz, A. M., & López Hernández, A. M. (2013). Reducing costs in times of crisis: Delivery forms in small and medium sized local governments' waste management services. *Public Administration, 91*(1), 51–68.

PART I

Anglo Saxon Countries

CHAPTER 2

Municipally Owned Corporations in Canada

Joseph Lyons, Zachary Spicer, and David Taylor

2.1 Introduction and Context

Municipalities in Canada are established and defined by their respective provincial governments. A common refrain in Canada is that municipalities are "creatures of the provinces", meaning that the authority, decision-making power, and very existence of municipalities are the product of provincial legislation. Each provincial government has at least one piece of general enabling legislation for municipal governments (Sancton 2021).[1] Some provinces also have legislation in place for specific cities, such as Ontario's City of Toronto Act (2006). An important fact to note,

[1] Some provincial governments have more than one Act respecting different aspects of municipal activities, such as a general Municipal Act as well as others governing municipal elections, municipal finance or municipal law. For more information on the Canadian municipal system, see Sancton (2021).

J. Lyons (✉)
Department of Political Science, Western University, London, ON, Canada
e-mail: jlyons7@uwo.ca

Z. Spicer
School of Public Policy and Administration, York University, Toronto, ON, Canada
e-mail: zspicer@yorku.ca

M. Van Genugten et al. (eds.), *Corporatisation in Local Government*, https://doi.org/10.1007/978-3-031-09982-3_2

especially given the focus of this book, is that these provincial statutes refer to municipal governments as municipal corporations. As such, for the purposes of this chapter, we will use the terms municipality or municipal government, to refer to general-purpose local governments and municipally owned corporations (MOCs) as a catch-all term to refer to specialised local corporate bodies tasked with some public purpose by either a municipality or provincial government and governed by a board with some measure of legal autonomy.

With each province having its own statute or set of statutes addressing municipal government, it should come as no surprise that there is variation in municipal authority and autonomy throughout the country. This is true as well when it comes to MOCs. Municipalities in Canada generally have the ability to establish corporations. However, there are differences concerning the types of corporations that can exist, whether municipalities can create corporations autonomously, and the authority vested in specific types of MOCs (see Taylor and Dobson 2020). Some municipalities also make more use of MOCs than others, even when the legislative environments are similar. Although Canadian research exists on the use of specialised jurisdictions in keeping with this book's definition of MOCs (see Lucas 2016; Lyons 2021), we are lacking a coherent classification system to capture the types and extent of local corporatisation in Canada. An aim of this chapter is to use the typology developed by Van Genugten et al. (2020) to make a meaningful start towards the creation of such a system.

What follows is divided into six sections. First, we take a national-level overview of the use of MOCs in Canada by exploring local service delivery in the largest city in each of Canada's ten provinces. Here we make a first attempt at adapting the typology developed by Van Genugten et al. (2020) to classify Canadian MOCs and observe national-level trends. Second, we explore the use of MOCs in Canada's largest and most populous province: Ontario. One trend observed in the national-level overview is that MOCs are more heavily used in larger cities. Ontario is home to most of Canada's largest cities and focusing on a single province allows us to keep the legislative environment constant. We remain with Ontario for the next section on legal status for this same rationale. The legal status of MOCs varies by type and by province. But given the level of detail needed to fully

---

D. Taylor
Municipality of Chatham-Kent, ON, Canada

understand and appreciate within province variation, a full national level exploration is beyond the scope of this chapter. This is an avenue for future work on this topic. In the next two sections that follow, we revert to our national-level perspective. First, to explore the commonalities and differences with respect to the level of autonomy granted to MOCs in Canada. And second, to make some observations about the organisational structures of Canadian MOCs as well as the role of executive directors. The final section concludes the chapter.

2.2 Municipally Owned Corporations in Canada: Background and Trends

2.2.1 Background and Observations on Municipal Service Delivery

MOCs in Canada go by different names, including agencies, boards, commissions, corporations, non-profit corporations, and special-purpose bodies. There is also no census of governments in Canada to classify and track the various types of MOCs that do exist. Apart from contributing to the broader discussion about cross-country differences in the use of MOCs, this chapter will also be the first attempt to adopt a coherent classification scheme for MOCs in Canada. In this section we begin the task by exploring and describing the use of MOCs in the largest city in each Canadian province before moving onto a discussion about observable trends. First, as this book is intended for an international audience, we provide some additional context regarding the different types of Canadian municipalities that exist in Canada and the mainly non-partisan nature of municipal politics in Canada.

Apart from documenting the use of MOCs by the largest city in each province, from West to East, Table 2.1 also includes information about population size and type of municipality.[2] The population numbers in Tables 2.1 and 2.2 are from the 2016 Canadian Census of Population

[2] In this chapter, we are focusing only on municipalities in Canada's provinces. We are excluding Canada's North, which consists of the territories of Nunavut, Northwest Territories, and Yukon Territory. The territories are geographically vast but sparsely populated and do not have the same degree of constitutional authority as provincial governments. Only a small percentage of the land in the territories is organised municipally. Municipalities in Canada's North tend to have very small populations and are separated from each other by large geographical distances.

Table 2.1 Local service delivery in largest city in each Canadian province

	Vancouver, BC	*Calgary, AB*	*Saskatoon, SK*	*Winnipeg, MB*	*Toronto, ON*	*Montreal, QC*	*Halifax, NS*	*Moncton, NB*	*Charlottetown, PEI*	*St. John's, NFLD*
Population (000s)	630	1200	246	705	2700	1700	403	70	36	109
Municipal type	Lower tier	Lower tier	Single tier	Single tier	Single tier	Lower tier	Single tier	Single tier	Single tier	Single tier
Service										
Economic development	MOC-T3	MD + NPC/A	NPC/A	J-M/ POC-T3	MD, MOC-T2 + 2MOC-T3	MD + J-NPC	NPC/A	MD + J-NPC	J-M/POC-T3	MD
Electricity	P	MOC-T3	MOC-T3	P	MOC-T3	P	P	P	N/G	P
Library	MOC-T2	MOC-T2	MOC-T2	MD	MOC-T2	MD	MOC-T2	MOC-T2	P	P
Natural gas	P	MOC-T3 + NG	P	P	N/G	N/G	N/G	N/G	N/A	N/A
Parking	MOC-T3	MOC-T2	MD	MOC-T2	MOC-T2	MD + MOC-T2	MD	MD	MD	MD
Police	MOC-T2	MOC-T2	MOC-T2	MOC-T2/MD	MOC-T2	MD	MOC-T2	P	MD	P
Public health	P	P	P	P	MOC-T2	P	P	P	P	P
Sewer	MD + RMD	MD	MD	MD	MD	MD	MOC-T3	MD	MD	MD

Social/public housing	MOC-T3	MD + MOC-T3	P	MOC-T3	MD + MOC-T3	MD + MOC-T3	P	P	P	MD
Tourism	DMO	DMO	DMO	J-M/ POC-T3	MD + DMO	NPC	DMO	MD	MD + DMO	MD
Transit	P	MD	MD	MD	MOC-T2	MOC-T2	MD	MD	MD	MOC-T2
Water	MD + RMD	MD	MD	MD	MD	MD	MOC-T3	MD	MD	MD

MOC-T2 Type 2 MOC, *MOC-T3* Type 3 MOC, *MD* Municipal Department, *R* Regional, that is, upper-tier municipal government, *J* Joint, that is, partnership with province and/or other municipal governments, *DMO* Destination Marketing Organisation, *NPC* Non-profit Corporation, *NPC/A* Non-profit Corporation with service agreement, *P* Province, *N/G* provided by non-government entity

Table 2.2 Local service delivery in ten largest municipalities in Ontario

	Toronto	*Ottawa*	*Mississauga*	*Brampton*	*Hamilton*	*London*	*Markham*	*Vaughan*	*Kitchener*	*Windsor*
Population (000s)	2700	934	705	594	537	384	329	306	233	217
Municipal type	Single tier	Single tier	Lower tier	Lower tier	Single tier	Single tier	Lower tier	Lower tier	Lower tier	Single tier
Service										
Economic development	MD, MOC-T2 + 2MOC-T3	MD + NPC/A	MD	MD	MD	MD + NPC/A	MD + RMD	MD + RMD	MD + RNPC/A	MD + JNPC/A
Electricity	MOC-T3	MOC-T3	J-MOC-T3	J-MOC-T3	J-MOC-T3	MOC-T3	J-MOC-T3	J-MOC-T3	J-MOC-T3	MOC-T3
Library	MOC-T2	MOC-T2	MOC-T2	MOC-T2	MOC-T2	MOC-T2	MOC-T2	MOC-T2	MOC-T2	MOC-T2
Natural gas	N/G	N/G	N/G	N/G	N/G	N/G	N/G	N/G	MD	N/G
Parking	MOC-T2	MD	MD	MD	MD	MD	MD	MD	MD	MD
Police	MOC-T2	MOC-T2	RMOC-T2	RMOC-T2	MOC-T2	MOC-T2	RMOC-T2	RMOC-T2	RMOC-T2	MOC-T2
Public health	MOC-T2	MOC-T2	RMOC-T2	RMOC-T2	MOC-T2	JMOC-T2	RMOC-T2	RMOC-T2	RMOC-T2	JMOC-T2
Sewer	MD	MD	RMD	RMD	MD	MD	MD + RMD	MD+RMD	MD+RMD	MD
Social/public housing	MD + MOC-T3	MD + MOC-T3	RMD + RMOC-T3	RMD + RMOC-T3	MOC-T3 and MD	MD+RMOC -T3	RMD + RMOC-T3	RMD + RMOC-T3	RMD + MOC-T3/ NPC	MD + MOC-T3
Tourism	MD and DMO	DMO	DMO (MOC-T3)	MD	DMO (MD)	DMO (MOC-T3)[a]	DMO	DMO (MOC-T3)	RDMO (RMOC-T3)	RDMO (JMOC-T3)
Transit	MOC-T2	MOC-T2 and MD	MD	MD	MD	MOC-T2	RMD	RMD	RMD	MD
Water	MD	MD	RMD	RMD	MD	MD + 2JMOC-T2	MD + RMD	MD + RMD	MD + RMD	MOC-T2 + MOC-T3

MOC-T2 Type 2 MOC (Local Board), *MOC-T3* Type 3 MOC (Municipal Services Corporation), *MD* Municipal Department, *R* Regional, that is, upper-tier municipal government, *J* Joint, i.e., partnership with province and/or other municipal governments, *DMO* Destination Marketing Organisation, *NPC* Non-profit Corporation, *NPC/A* Non-profit Corporation with service agreement, *P* Province, *N/G* provided by non-government entity

[a]Incorporated federally

(Statistics Canada 2017b). Regarding municipal type, there are three basic types of municipalities in Canada: single tier, lower tier, and upper tier. Single tier meaning that there is only one municipality with jurisdiction in the defined territory. Lower-tier and upper-tier municipalities exist concurrently with two or more lower-tier municipalities being constituent municipalities of an upper-tier municipality. The division of labour between upper-tier and lower-tier municipalities varies both within and across provinces where they exist. In general, though, local services like firefighting and neighbourhood parks are provided by lower-tier municipalities, while regional services such as regional roads and trunk water and sewer lines are provided by the upper-tier. In single-tier systems all these services are provided by one municipality.

Information on partisanship is not included in Table 2.1, but for comparative purposes it is important to note that British Columbia (BC) and Quebec (QC) are the only two provinces in Canada where municipal political parties are encouraged and supported through provincial legislation. In Vancouver, BC, the conservative leaning Non-Partisan Association is the longest standing political party. Parties more to the left, such as the Coalition of Progressive Electors and Vision Vancouver, have experienced more competition and volatility. In Montreal, QC, political parties tend to coalesce around specific candidates for mayor, meaning that party names and identities are even more fluid than they are in Vancouver. Despite having overlapping ideological orientations, local political parties in Canada are not directly linked to provincial and federal political parties. With better understanding of Canadian municipalities, we now turn our attention to municipal functions and the use of MOCs as listed in Table 2.1. As this is a novel attempt to classify municipal corporations in Canada, we started by reviewing how municipal services are delivered by the largest city in each Canadian province. To do this, we used existing lists of common municipal service areas developed by Lucas and Smith (2019) and a research team from Western University's Centre for Urban Policy and Local Governance (Horak and Taylor 2021). We identified 12 functional areas in which at least one of our sample municipalities used an MOC in keeping with the book's definition. These functions appear as rows under the heading 'Service' in Table 2.1.

As evident in Table 2.1, municipalities in Canada are primarily charged with functions related to protecting, maintaining, and enhancing the built environment (Sancton 2021, p. 24). Though municipalities in Canada, and especially the larger municipalities included in this study, are branching out into areas such as immigrant settlement, poverty reduction, and climate change, their capacity is restricted by their geographical and jurisdictional limitations and reliance on property-based taxes and fees. Other common municipal services not listed in Table 2.1, because we found no evidence of the use of MOCs in these areas, include emergency management, planning, roads, highways, bridges, and waste collection and disposal. Parks and recreation is not included either; however, this service is provided by an MOC in Vancouver, the Vancouver Board of Parks and Recreation, which is the only such body in Canada (Vancouver Board of Parks and Recreation 2018). Elsewhere, this service is provided by municipal departments.

The 12 services included vary in their characteristics, with some like public health and policing resembling public goods, and others like water, sewer, and electricity being toll goods. Other functions like economic development and tourism promotion are more difficult to classify, but the private sector is often involved in various aspects of service delivery. There is also considerable variation in how these 12 services are delivered across these 10 municipalities. The legend included in Table 2.1 explains what each label and label combination mean. Regarding MOCs, in keeping with Van Genugten et al.' (2020) typology, we distinguish between Type 2 and Type 3 MOCs: MOC-T2 and MOC-T3, respectively. Type 2 MOCs align nicely with what are often referred to as local boards in Canada. Local boards are created as "bodies corporate" through a municipal by-law or provincial statute but do not have their own incorporation documents. Type 3 MOCs, on the other hand, take the process one step further and are formally incorporated as either business or not-for-profit corporations. This distinction between local boards and MOCs plays out differently in each province and is a dynamic that we will explore more fully in relation to municipalities in Ontario after making national-level observations about each service included in Table 2.1.

One other note about our labelling scheme is that it does not necessarily tell the full story with respect to how each individual service is provided. What we have tried to identify in Table 2.1 is the functional lead for each service in each municipality. However, where two or more entities share significant responsibilities such that it is difficult to determine which is the lead, we have included multiple entries in individual cells. Nevertheless, Table 2.1 still does not capture all forms of alternative service delivery such as contracting out or franchises—Type 4 agencies according to Van Genugten et al. (2020). In many instances where a municipal department (MD or RMD) or MOC is the lead, certain aspects of the service may still be provided by a private company or non-profit group under contract. It is also important to note that by using function or service as our unit of analysis, we are leaving unexplored the often complicated public–private partnerships involved in designing, building, operating, and maintaining facilities such as sports venues, performance-art theatres, and convention centres. In short, the more complex minutiae of local alternative service delivery in Canada are not fully covered in this chapter. The intent is to flush out MOCs with autonomous decision-making responsibilities. The functions will be addressed alphabetically, as they are listed in Table 2.1.

Functions and Policy Leads Economic development is delivered in varied ways across the ten municipalities in Table 2.1. St. John's, Newfoundland is the only municipality on the list that delivers this service solely through a municipal department. Municipal departments are involved in economic development to a degree in most other cities, given the importance of this policy area for municipal politicians (see Lucas and Smith 2019), but an MOC or non-profit corporation is often heavily involved as well. MOCs are created by the municipal governments themselves, sometimes in concert with the province or other neighbouring municipalities, whereas separate, non-profit economic development corporations are usually incorporated by industry partners and provide services to the municipality through a purchase of service agreement (NPC/A in Table 2.1). These non-profit corporations do not meet the book's definition of a MOC because they are not publicly owned. But they are similar in most other respects. Either way, when it comes to municipally owned or non-profit economic development agencies, the intent is to insulate economic development activity from political interference and to include industry representatives in governance and decision making.

Only three municipalities are involved in providing electricity to their residents: Calgary, Saskatoon, and Toronto. All three do so through a Type 3 MOC. In most other places it is provided by provincial-level utilities.

Libraries are governed and managed by local library boards in most municipalities. Except in Winnipeg and Montreal, where they are run by municipalities, and Charlottetown and St. John's where they are run by the province. In many ways, the smaller provinces in Atlantic Canada are more involved in certain aspects of service delivery than their larger peers to the West. Libraries are a good example of this phenomenon.

Natural gas is mostly provided through provincial-level or private utilities, except in Calgary, where it is provided by ENMAX, the municipality's electricity and energy corporation as well as several other private providers. So, there is competition in Calgary's natural gas market and consumers have some choice.

Parking is managed by a Type 3 MOC in Vancouver and a local board in Calgary,[3] Winnipeg, Toronto, and Montreal. Everywhere else by a municipal department.

Police services are governed by a local board in all the municipalities listed, except in Montreal and Charlottetown where they are delivered by municipal departments, and Moncton and St. John's where they are delivered by provincial-level police services. Winnipeg and Montreal both have unique arrangements worthy of mention. In Winnipeg, the police board sets policy and hires the chief of police but the City of Winnipeg is the employer for all Winnipeg police service members, including the chief (City of Winnipeg n.d.). In Montreal, police services are provided through a municipal department, but the province appoints the chief of police.

Public health is a provincial responsibility in all municipalities, except Toronto, where this service is delivered by a public health board, a Type 2 MOC.

Only the five largest municipalities in this list are involved in social housing in any way: Vancouver, Calgary, Winnipeg, Toronto, and Montreal. The lead affordable housing provider in all five cities is a Type 3 MOC. But municipal departments are still often involved in the financing and construction of new affordable housing units.

Tourism delivery varies considerably throughout the municipalities reviewed. Some municipalities deliver this service through internal departments, but most municipalities have entered into agreements with non-profit corporations known as destination marketing organisations (DMOs), which provide tourism and promotion activities on behalf of the local community. While DMOs can be MOCs, most are arms-length organisations created by partners in the local tourism industry, such as hotels, restaurants, convention centres, sports venues, and other

[3] As of September 2021, the Calgary Parking Authority will be integrated into the municipal structure such that it may no longer qualify as a Type 2 MOC moving forward (The City of Calgary Newsroom 2021).

attractions. Like the non-profit economic development agencies with service agreements described earlier, these DMOs do not fit the definition of an MOC for the purpose of this book, because they are not publicly owned. The exception to the rule appears to be Winnipeg where the same Type 3 MOC, jointly owned by the province and the city, provides economic development and tourism services (KPMG 2018).

Transit is provided by local boards in Toronto, Montreal, and St. John's. In most other municipalities it is provided by a municipal department. Public transit in Vancouver, and indeed across the entire Vancouver metropolitan region, is provided by Translink, an agency of the provincial government.

Water and sewer services are delivered under the auspices of a single municipal department in all municipalities, except for Vancouver and Halifax. In Vancouver there is a wholesale/retail relationship established whereby Metro Vancouver, the upper-tier municipality, wholesales bulk water and sewer services to its local municipalities, which retail water and sewer services directly to residents. In Halifax, these services are provided by Halifax Water, which is a Type 3 MOC.

2.2.2 National-Level Trends

We can observe three trends from this national-level overview. The first is that MOCs are not a widely used tool among Canadian municipalities. This is a subset of only 12 municipal functions where we could find evidence of local corporatisation, yet where the province is not involved, provision through a municipal department remains common. Such that it is more difficult to make a strong claim about whether MOCs are increasingly being used for service provision in Canada than it may be for the United States and across Europe (Voorn et al. 2017). This is especially true for Saskatoon and the smaller Atlantic Canada municipalities: Moncton, Charlottetown, and St. John's. Indeed, there is a long history of providing services like water and electricity through arm's-length boards and commission in Canada, so these are not new inventions (see Lucas 2016).

Larger municipalities use more MOCs, which is the second observable trend. A part of this can be explained by path dependency and provincial legislative requirements. Local police services predate the creation of many provincial and municipal governments, for example, and have long fought to maintain their independence from municipal governments (see Sancton

2021, pp. 54–60 for a fuller discussion). Other likely explanations relate to population size and density, as well as organisational scale, scope, and sophistication. This is most evident in relation to services like parking, public transit, and social housing. The Toronto Transit Commission, for example, has an operating budget of more than 1.5 billion USD, which greatly exceeds the budgets of all but the largest Canadian municipalities. The smaller municipalities included in Table 2.1 either do not provide these services or do so only at a basic level.

Though Montreal and Vancouver both have local political parties, it is difficult to draw any conclusions about the independent effects of local political parties on local corporatisation. Vancouver's use of MOCs is roughly in line with its size, whereas Montreal uses fewer MOCs than its peers. Probing the more limited use of MOCs in Montreal would require additional research that is beyond the scope of this chapter. As Canada's only predominantly French speaking province, Quebec's political culture is distinct from the rest of Canada but in ways that are likely to have indeterminate effects on the use of MOCs (see Anderson 2010). It may also be the case that there is little appetite for the coordination challenges that would arise from adding even more autonomous actors to an already fragmented and complicated system of local government in the city (Bherer and Hamel 2012).

Economic development is the one area where there is a consistent use of either a MOC or non-profit corporation with a sole-sourced service agreement to provide economic development services to the municipality. Such that we can identify this as the third trend. Municipalities also face very little in the way of provincial restrictions when it comes to how this service is delivered, so there is room for discretion. We explore these trends more fully in the next section by focusing on the use of MOCs in Canada's largest and most populous province: Ontario.

2.3 Municipally Owned Corporations in Ontario

2.3.1 Background and Observations on Service Delivery

Ontario was selected as the province for further inquiry into the use of MOCs for two inter-related reasons. First, focusing on a single province allows us to hold the legislative environment constant. As mentioned earlier, because Canadian municipalities owe their existence to provincial legislation, the rules around MOCs vary by province. This explains some of the evident variations in Table 2.1. Second, as this relates more specifically to the choice of Ontario rather than other provinces, as discussed, a trend evident in Table 2.1 is that larger municipalities appear to make greater use of MOCs than smaller municipalities. Of the 24 municipalities in Canada with populations greater than 200,000, ten are in Ontario (Statistics Canada 2017a). Focusing on any other province would likely mean uncovering fewer MOCs. Ontario, then, was not chosen as a case study because it is representative of the rest of the country, but instead because we expect to find more MOCs here than in any other province.

Functions and Policy Leads As is the case nationally, there is considerable variation when it comes to the provision of economic development in Ontario. Recall that economic development is an area where municipalities have considerable flexibility when it comes to service delivery structure in Canada. The alternative service delivery option of choice in Ontario appears to be a non-profit corporation with agreement (NPC/A). But municipal departments tend to remain involved. When it comes to the lower-tier municipalities of Mississauga, Brampton, Markham, Vaughan, and Kitchener, they all deliver economic development at least partly through a local municipal department. Mississauga and Brampton are both in Peel Region (immediately West of the City of Toronto) and apart from planning, the regional government does not play an active role in economic development. Markham and Vaughan are in York Region (immediately North of the City of Toronto) and the regional government has its own economic development department. Kitchener, which is a lower-tier municipality in Waterloo Region, has its own economic development department, but a regional-level non-profit corporation has also been tasked with economic development responsibilities.

Next, we can discuss the single-tier municipalities of Toronto, Ottawa, Hamilton, London, and Windsor. Of these, Ottawa, London, and Windsor have similar structural arrangements with shared responsibilities between municipal departments and non-profit corporations. The non-profit corporations typically focus on attracting and retaining investment and talent, whereas the municipal departments are involved in licensing, regulations, real estate, and development approvals. Hamilton is unique among the single-tier municipalities in providing economic development solely through a municipal department. Toronto is unique, too, in that it has a municipal department with economic responsibilities, as well as a local board called Create TO which manages the City's real estate holdings and also oversees two Type 3 MOCs involved in economic development and real estate, the Toronto Economic Development Corporation, and Build Toronto. The former owns, manages, and promotes the development of Toronto's Port Lands, the latter owns, manages, develops, and markets the City's surplus land (City of Toronto 2018a, b).

There is a noticeable difference from Table 2.1 with respect to electricity. Across the board, electricity is provided by Type 3 MOCs in Ontario. As explained further, this is a provincial requirement in Ontario. It is worth noting that the same, jointly owned MOC, Alectra Utilities, provides electricity to Mississauga, Brampton, Hamilton, Markham, and Vaughan, as well as other municipalities in the broader urbanised area surrounding the city of Toronto.

Libraries, parking, and policing are straightforward to explain so they are grouped together here. Public Libraries are provided by local boards in all municipalities. This is much the same for policing. However, policing is an upper-tier service in Peel and York Region. Toronto is the only municipality in Table 2.2 that provides parking services through a local board.

Natural gas is mostly provided by privately owned utilities in Ontario, except for Kitchener, which delivers natural gas through the same municipal department as it does water and sewer services. The provision of natural gas, where the service exists by private utilities, was observed among several municipalities in Table 2.1 as well. The exceptions being Vancouver, Saskatoon, and Winnipeg, where it is delivered by provincial utilities, and Calgary where a municipal corporation competes with private utilities.

Public health is provided by local boards across the province of Ontario, known as public health units. Historically, public health has been delivered at a scale spanning multiple municipalities. However, health unit boundaries are now coterminous with the municipalities of Toronto, Ottawa, and Hamilton, which were all created in their current forms in the late 1990s and early 2000s as the result of amalgamations of all the lower-tier municipalities in former two-tier systems. Public health is provided by regional level boards in two-tier systems. Mississauga and Brampton are covered by Peel Public Health, Markham and Vaughan are covered by York Region Public Health, and Kitchener is covered by the Region of Waterloo Public Health. London and Windsor are single-tier municipalities that escaped the creation of regional governments in the 1960s and 1970s and the amalgamation wave at the turn of the millennium. They are part of health units that include their neighbouring municipalities.

Social housing can be divided between housing administration, and housing facility operation. Administration of housing, such as rent supplements and determining eligibility for housing, is delivered by municipal departments. Housing facility operation is consistently delivered by municipally owned corporations in Ontario. These corporations are created under specific provincial legislation for this purpose, which is discussed further in the legal status section.

Sewers are provided by municipal departments across the board, usually with some upper-tier involvement in two-tier systems. The same can mostly be said for water, except in London and Windsor. In London, two joint-local boards treat and wholesale water to several municipalities in the region. One board manages a system originating in Lake Erie, the other does the same for a system originating in Lake Huron. In Windsor, a local board, the Windsor Utilities Commission owns the infrastructure that serves Windsor and two neighbouring municipalities and contracts ENWIN, a Type 3 MOC, to operate and maintain the water system (ENWIN n.d.; Windsor Utilities Commission n.d.). ENWIN also owns Windsor's electricity distribution system.

Transit is provided by local boards in Toronto, Ottawa, and London. Elsewhere it is provided either by a municipal department or an upper-tier municipal department.

Destination Marketing Organisations (DMOs) are involved in tourism in every municipality except Bampton, with varying levels of municipal involvement. The proliferation of DMOs in Ontario can be partly explained by the introduction of the optional municipal accommodation tax in 2017 and the requirement that municipalities that levy the tax must share the revenues equally with a local tourism promotion organisation (City of Vaughan 2019). In Toronto and Ottawa, the DMOs are independent non-profit corporations governed by industry partners and do not meet the public ownership criterion. Mississauga's, Vaughan's, Kitchener's, and Windsor's DMOs, however, are non-profit municipal services corporations (City of Mississauga 2020; City of Vaughan 2019; Explore Waterloo Region n.d.; Tourism Windsor Essex Pelee Island n.d.). London's DMO is incorporated federally (Government of Canada 2021) and the City of Hamilton has taken on the role of a DMO as Tourism Hamilton (City of Hamilton 2021).

2.3.2 *Provincial-Level Trends in Ontario*

As was expected, we do observe greater use of MOCs among these Ontario municipalities than we did in our national-level overview. This can be partly attributed to size, as all the municipalities included have populations of at least 200,000. Size is likely only an important factor with respect to transit and economic development, though, and parking in the case of Toronto. But several large cities like Mississauga, Brampton, and Hamilton still provide transit through a municipal department, so size is not the only explanatory factor. There may be some threshold effects at play with respect to size as well, as, apart from transit, we do not observe a noticeable drop off in the use of MOCs in Kitchener and Windsor, the two smallest municipalities listed. Municipal type likely matters here as well. This is evident when it comes to water for London and Windsor as local boards provide some of the functions that upper-tier municipal departments provide elsewhere. When it comes to economic development, a municipal department is at least one of the policy leads in all of the municipalities listed but four also employ a non-profit corporation, and the City of Toronto uses a local board and two MOCs.

In other service areas, provincial requirements are the main explanatory factor. This applies for electricity, libraries, policing, public health, and social housing. These requirements will be explored more fully in the next section on the legal status of MOCs and local boards.

2.4 Legal Status

Staying with Ontario for further detailed study of the legal status of MOCs, we find two broad categories of subsidiary organisations that can be used by Ontario municipalities to deliver services that meet the book's definition of a MOC: local boards (Type 2 MOCs) and municipal services corporations (Type 3 MOCs). Local boards are established through municipal by-laws or provincial legislation as independent "bodies corporate" with certain powers and responsibilities granted through the Municipal Act, 2001.

A local board is the legal category for subsidiary organisations such as transit commissions, library boards, boards of health, police services boards, and similar boards, commissions, and committees, exercising any power with respect to the affairs or purposes of one or more municipalities (Municipal Act, 2001, s. 1(1)). In Table 2.2, we see the local board structure used for delivering public transit in Toronto, Ottawa, and London, while this service is provided directly by municipal departments in the remaining municipalities. There is considerable flexibility in using a local board for service delivery as the composition, processes, procedures, relationship, and powers of a municipal service board are determined by municipal councils (Municipal Act, 2001, ss. 196(1), and 198) subject to some restrictions.[4]

Some local boards are created under subject area specific legislation, such as the Police Services Act (1990), while others are created under the broad municipal powers to establish local boards under the Municipal Act, 2001 (Municipal Act, 2001, s. 196(1). Local boards are defined as "bodies corporate" (Municipal Act, 2001, s. 196(1)),[5] unless council provides otherwise when creating the board, and is deemed to be an agent of the municipality (Municipal Act, 2001, s. 197). Due to this status as a "body corporate," local boards can do most of those things a corporation could do, including buying and selling property, entering into contracts, and having employees, unless specifically restricted by the municipality or other legal restrictions imposed in legislation applicable to that board.

There is no need for a formal incorporation process to be followed for creation of a local board; rather, municipal councils can establish a new local board by passing a by-law (Municipal Act, 2001, ss. 196(1) and 198). In this way, local boards are established under public law; specifically, through broad powers provided to municipalities by the province for these purposes. Where a local board is created and regulated under area-specific legislation, such boards of health (Health Protection and Promotion Act, 1990, s. 52), planning boards (Planning Act, 1990, s. 11), police services boards (Police Services Act, 1990, s. 30), and public library boards (Public Libraries Act, 1990, s. 3), these, too, do not get established through a formal private law incorporation process, but rather are created through public law processes.

Similar to local boards, municipal services corporations can be created by municipal councils through subject area specific legislation, such as the Electricity Act (1998), or under broad municipal powers to establish

[4] See for example Municipal Act, 2001, s. 4 regarding the term of the appointment for board members, or s. 23.2, which provides some restrictions on which powers municipal councils can delegate.

[5] Similar legislative provisions also establish Boards of Health, Planning Boards, Police Services Boards and Public Libraries Act as "bodies corporate".

municipal services corporations for municipal purposes in section 203 of the Municipal Act, 2001. Permissions and limitations on these MOCs are outlined in a regulation under that Act, Municipal Services Corporations (Ontario Regulation 599/06). For example, extra steps or limitations apply to economic development corporations (Ontario Regulation 599/06, s. 9), holding corporations (Ontario Regulation 599/06, s. 10), and public utility companies (Ontario Regulation 599/06, s. 19(5)), while there are also certain core municipal services which the province prohibits municipalities from delivering through a municipal services corporation. These relate to aspects of emergency services, children's services, public health, long-term care, courts, libraries, and certain benefits services (Ontario Regulation 599/06, s. 11).

To create a municipal services corporation, a municipality must adopt an asset transfer policy and cannot transfer assets to a corporation until this is done (Ontario Regulation 599/06, s. 7). However, the details of what must be included in such a policy is not outlined in the Act or regulation. As a result, considerable latitude is granted to municipalities regarding the details of such a policy. A municipality must also consult with the public before establishing a corporation (Ontario Regulation 599/06, s. 8), but similarly the scope of that consultation is left to councils' discretion. Following these processes, municipal services corporations are incorporated as either business corporations or not-for-profit corporations under the Ontario Business Corporations Act (1990) following the same manner as private corporations, including filing of corporate documents with the province. Municipal services corporations may also be limited in their functions in the same manner as a private company, such as limits in authority through the articles of incorporation, corporate by-laws, or a unanimous shareholder's direction to the board. In these ways, municipal services corporations are created through a mix of public law and private law.

Two areas that we see consistent use of municipal services corporations by Ontario municipalities are in the social/public housing and electricity distribution areas. Local housing corporations were initially created by provincial legislation on behalf of a particular municipality (Social Housing Reform Act, 2000, s. 23). This process did not require formal private law incorporation, but rather was a public law creation of a housing corporation by the province. Rules regarding organisation, operation, financial matters, share ownership and funding of local housing corporations are outlined under the now Housing Services Act (2011) and regulations

(Ontario Regulation 367/11). In comparison, electricity distribution companies[6] owned by municipalities are formally incorporated under the Ontario Business Corporations Act (1990) in the same manner as any other private company. The consistent use of corporations for electricity distribution is the result of a requirement in the Electricity Act (1998) which mandated municipalities to convert former municipal divisions into separate corporations for electricity transmission and related services (Electricity Act, 1998, s. 142).

If we look at the total number of MOCs that are created by municipalities in Ontario, the vast majority falls within the local board (or MOC-T2) category. This use of local boards has a long history in Ontario municipalities, through public utilities commissions, transit commissions, and various other special-purpose bodies. Municipal services corporations, which are formally created through private law processes, are fewer in number but do have some use by Ontario municipalities. The choice of which model to use, and the powers delegated to the board or corporation varies and provides municipalities with considerable flexibility; municipalities can exert direct control, can choose to delegate some aspects of a service delivery, or can establish a fully independent board or corporation.

With a better understanding of how MOCs are used across Canada, in Ontario, and of Ontario's legal environment for MOCs, we return to national-level observations and comparisons of the autonomy, accountability, and organisation of MOCs in Canada.

2.5 Autonomy

As discussed earlier in the chapter, there is considerable variation in the use, function, and scope of MOCs in Canada. This variation extends to autonomy as well. However, the general trend in Canada is that most MOCs have general autonomy to act on labour issues, set salary and benefit structures, manage their fiscal health, and attend to day-to-day operational issues. The scope of many of these organisations is far too large to micromanage by municipal (or provincial) authorities. However, this does not necessarily mean that MOCs do not fall under administrative or political scrutiny by municipal decision-makers or, as we will see, provincial

[6] Electricity generation is primarily a provincial function in Ontario, but significant portions of electricity transmission are performed by local distribution companies (LDCs), which are often owned by local municipalities.

authority. Most MOCs have an appointed board, which often includes several municipal politicians (see below). Senior staff in these organisations report directly to the board, providing an outlet for stewardship, scrutiny, and indirect control by municipal decision-makers. However, if needed, municipalities have been shown to step in more forcefully on rare occasions to disrupt organisations or correct their course.

MOCs generally find themselves subject to local and provincial regulations on transparency and disclosure, which provides pathways for the public to understand the operations of these corporations and govern their relationship. Generally falling into the broad categories of "public bodies", MOCs with some autonomy from a municipality would be subject to similar transparency regulations as the municipal government itself. For instance, the City of Winnipeg is included in the Province of Manitoba's Freedom of Information and Protection of Privacy Act (1997). Municipalities, local government districts, and a variety of other "local government bodies", such as planning bodies or watershed management councils, fall under the Act, as would other "local government bodies", which could also include MOCs. Other provinces, including Nova Scotia, British Columbia, and Alberta extend the same provisions to local bodies.

Some provinces, such as Ontario, have separate freedom of information acts established for local governments and public bodies. Ontario's Municipal Freedom of Information and Protection of Privacy Act (1990) extends to all municipalities and any agencies, boards, and commissions. As a result of a municipal legislation review undertaken in 2016 and 2017, all municipalities in the province are required to have an Integrity Commissioner, who is empowered to investigate complaints into the conduct of members of council, as well as most municipal agencies and commissions. Ontario's City of Toronto Act (2006) also enshrines a number of accountability and transparency requirements in legislation for the City. The Act requires the City of Toronto to have an Integrity Commissioner, an Ombudsman, a Lobbyist Registry, and an Auditor General. The powers of most of these offices extend towards the City's various agencies and commissions.

Through such accountability and oversight measures the public and the media have some (albeit limited in certain cases) means to understand the operations and mandate of local corporations. Such measures often include some ability to seek remedy from public office holders, if needed. When necessary, however, municipalities have been shown to step in and provide more concrete direction of municipal corporations. A good illustration of this is the City of Toronto's long and often troubled relationship with Toronto Community Housing (TCH), a MOC tasked with providing social housing in the city. For many years, TCH suffered from accusations of mismanagement, resulting in the dismissal of several senior executives and a ballooning repair backlog of 2.01 billion USD. In 2015, Mayor John Tory established an expert task force to provide recommendations on how to improve the agency.

In 2016, the task force returned with 29 recommendations, including the creation of a new non-profit housing provider which would put more emphasis on direct support for tenants (Pagliaro 2016). None of the recommendations included new funding for the organisation but did include a recommendation of decentralisation of staff from the central office to facilitate more interaction with tenants, direction to seek out more external partnerships and a call for more funding from the provincial and federal governments (Pagliaro 2016). Most importantly, however, the report called for the organisation to exist at greater reach from the city and be "off the city's books" to the point where it would become another of more than 240 other non-profits providing housing throughout the city (Pagliaro 2016).

MOCs in Canada are generally free to operate on a day-to-day basis and to set organisational direction as long as they adhere to their broad mandate. They often must follow a general set of accountability and transparency mechanisms prescribed by the province and sometimes enforced locally by municipal decision-makers. The aforementioned example with TCH illustrates, however, that while municipalities are satisfied to allow arm's-length corporations to operate independently to a certain degree, they will step in if decision-makers feel it necessary. TCH had suffered from a number of high-profile challenges and accusations of mismanagement followed suit. Pressure built to address many of these issues both from residents and the public. Mayor Tory responded with an expert working group whose recommendations would have dramatically transformed the organisation's relationship with the city. This example also illustrates that day-to-day tensions are more likely to arise between MOCs and their municipalities rather than the province. The province is likely to only get involved if there are larger sectoral issues at play, such that a change in enabling legislation is contemplated.

2.6 Organisational Structure and the Role of the Executive Director

Most MOCs in Canada typically have a one-tier board, but generally use several standing committees to govern the organisation. Fairly standard board committees include a governance committee and an audit or finance committee. The board is the main decision-making body and usually includes the executive director or CEO in a non-voting role. The executive director or CEO holds operational control of the organisation and in most cases reports directly to the board, which would be responsible for evaluating the performance of the organisation and leadership team, identifying long-term opportunities and threats and carrying out a general stewardship role for the organisation in a similar way as private sector boards.

The professional background of the executive director depends on the type of organisation. For instance, most hydro and electricity organisations do have executives who have extensive work experience in that sector, often joining the organisation from senior roles in other hydro and electricity firms. Similar trends tend to be exhibited in transit, where most senior executives have ascended to these positions through many years of experience in the transit sector. These are, of course, very technical and demanding positions, where industry experience is key to success. Public sector experience tends to be prized in local corporations with a more direct linkage to core government services. For instance, the heads of housing corporations tend to have public policy or land use planning backgrounds and often served as municipal staff earlier in their careers, while the CEOs of library boards often have many years' experience in senior roles in different library systems.

MOC executives tend to be quite well compensated by public sector standards. The Province of Ontario has a public sector salary requirement, which provides us with a general understanding of how these types of executives are compensated. Most heads of MOCs, such as the Toronto Transit Commission or Toronto Community Housing, can expect compensation in the range of 232,000–309,000 USD (as of 2020). This is in line with many other public sector executives, such as the managers of large cities or the presidents of post-secondary institutions. For comparison, the Mayor of Toronto and the Premier of Ontario earn around 150,000 USD. The exception to this trend is found in hydro and electricity, where CEOs can expect to earn around 460,000 USD a year or more.

The overarching trend in this area, however, is a merit-based hiring process. Very rarely would a political appointment who had little qualifications be inserted as the executive director or CEO of an MOC. Most of those appointed have spent many years building their careers and gaining experience in the public or private sector. Controversy generally follows in the rare cases where political interference occurs. For instance, in early 2020, a highly publicised case occurred where the head of New Brunswick's library system resigned abruptly amid accusations of incompetence (Mackinnon 2020). Those involved with the library service argued that several qualified internal candidates were passed over by a direct appointment made by the provincial government, which led to a slew of poor decisions and mismanagement (Mackinnon 2020). There is a general expectation of merit-based hiring throughout Canada's public sector, which carries through to MOCs.

While senior administrators in these organisations are hired based upon merit, municipalities do tend to populate the board with some municipal appointments. Looking back at the data collected and displayed earlier in Tables 2.1 and 2.2, most MOCs tend to have some representation from municipal councils. Councillors often have the majority of the representation on the board of Type 2 MOCs. For instance, the Toronto Transit Commission has ten representatives, six of which are councillors. Some, such as Montreal's transit board are balanced between local politicians and members of the public. Type 3 MOCs tend to have fewer council appointees. The Calgary Housing Company is one such board, with only two councillors represented on the 12-member board. Of note, the board chair is a municipal councillor, however. Hydro and electricity companies tend to have independent board members. For instance, Calgary's utility, ENMAX, has a board entirely free of municipal politicians. Where municipal councillors are included on hydro boards, they tend to be in the minority. For example, Toronto Hydro's 18-member boards include only three councillors. Tourism boards tend to come in the form of destination marketing organisations. Of those, the boards of the vast majority are composed of private sector appointments, mainly representatives from the local tourism industry, such as hotel, restaurant, and transportation firms.

Municipal staff do appear on boards occasionally as well. For instance, Metrobus, St John's Newfoundland's transit system, has the city manager and deputy city manager (Finance) on its board, alongside three councillors and four members of the public. Another rare example is the Vancouver Economic Commission, where the board is composed entirely of three senior City of Vancouver Staff members—namely the acting city manager and two deputy city managers.

Throughout our study, we notice several trends in the organisational design of local corporations in Canada. For the most part, local corporations have a professional, merit-based staff. Those at the senior level are generally compensated handsomely. These executives report directly to a board. The composition of these boards change based upon the service area and type of MOC in question, but many include local politicians. Hydro and tourism organisations tend to have the least amount of municipal representation.

2.7 Conclusion

This chapter began with several aims. The first was to take the opportunity to develop a classification for Canadian MOCs. This is accomplished in Tables 2.1 and 2.2 and provides a novel understanding of local corporatisation in Canada for both domestic and international audience. The second was to illustrate and make sense of trends in the creation and management of MOCs in Canada. In this, we have observed several key trends. The first, and likely most important, is that MOCs are not a widely used tool among Canadian municipalities. Size appears to be part of the explanation for why some municipalities employ more MOCs than others, but this applies only to select big-city functions like public transit, social housing, and parking. Provincial requirements and path dependency are also important explanatory factors, especially in Ontario for functions like electricity, libraries, policing, and public health. Local political parties, where they exist, do not appear to have a significant effect on the use of MOCs. We found no evidence of MOCs as functional leads in the areas of emergency management, planning, roads, highways and bridges, and waste collection and disposal.

More broadly, where local corporations are established, they generally employ merit-based hiring and report to an appointed board. In many cases, these boards have municipal councillors on them and generally act in a stewardship role. Aside from municipal decision-makers on their boards, these organisations tend to operate free from political interference. In rare instances—one of which was highlighted above—municipalities will disrupt the organisation and become directly engaged in their affairs. For the most part, however, these organisations operate in the public interest and are subject to high standards of transparency and accountability.

Acknowledgements The authors would like to thank Andrew Sancton and Sandra Breux for their assistance with identifying MOCs for Montreal, Quebec. We retain responsibility for any errors or omissions.

References

Anderson, C. (2010). Regional heterogeneity and policy preferences in Canada: 1979-2006. *Regional and Federal Studies, 20*(4–5), 447–468.

Bherer, L., & Hamel, P. (2012). Overcoming adversity, or public action in the face of new urban problems: The example of Montreal. In M. Horak & R. Young (Eds.), *Sites of governance: Multilevel governance and policy making in Canada's big cities*. McGill-Queen's University Press.

City of Hamilton. (2021). *Tourism development profile*. Accessed August 23, 2021, from https://www.hamilton.ca/government-information/trust-and-confidence-report/tourism-development-profile

City of Mississauga. (2020). *Tourism Mississauga announces new board of directors*. Accessed August 23, 2021, from https://www.mississauga.ca/city-of-mississauga-news/news/tourism-mississauga-announces-new-board-of-directors/

City of Toronto. (2018a). *Revised shareholder direction – Build Toronto*. Accessed August 23, 2021, from https://www.toronto.ca/legdocs/mmis/2017/ex/bgrd/backgroundfile-109169.pdf

City of Toronto. (2018b). *Revised shareholder direction – Toronto Port Lands Company*. Accessed August 23, 2021, from https://www.toronto.ca/legdocs/mmis/2017/ex/bgrd/backgroundfile-109170.pdf

City of Vaughan. (2019). *Report no. 1 of the Finance, Administration and Audit Committee*. Accessed July 27, 2021, from https://pub-vaughan.escribemeetings.com/filestream.ashx?DocumentId=9524

City of Winnipeg. (n.d.). *About the Winnipeg police board*. Accessed July 27, 2021, from https://winnipeg.ca/clerks/boards/WpgPoliceBoard/aboutpoliceboard.stm

ENWIN. (n.d.). *Welcome to ENWIN*. Accessed August 20, 2021, from https://enwin.com/about/

Explore Waterloo Region. (n.d.). *About explore Waterloo region*. Accessed August 23, 2021, from https://explorewaterloo.ca/about-ewr/

Government of Canada. (2021, June 28). *Federal corporation information – 330976-2*. Accessed August 23, 2021, from https://www.ic.gc.ca/app/scr/cc/CorporationsCanada/fdrlCrpDtls.html?corpId=3309762&V_TOKEN=null&crpNm=Tourism%20London&crpNmbr=&bsNmbr=

Horak, M., & Taylor, Z. (2021). *Canadian municipal attributes portal (C-MAP)*. Working documentation for on-line database of local government institutions in selected Canadian cities.

KPMG. (2018). *Financial statements of economic development.* Winnipeg Inc. Accessed August 20, 2021, from https://www.economicdevelopmentwinnipeg.com/uploads/document/2018_12_31_economic_development_winnipeg_fs.t1556030735.pdf

Lucas, J. (2016). *Fields of authority: Special purpose governance in Ontario, 1815-2015.* University of Toronto Press.

Lucas, J., & Smith, A. (2019). Which policy issues matter in Canadian municipalities? A survey of municipal politicians. *University of Calgary SPP Research Paper, 12*(8), 1–25.

Lyons, J. (2021). The democratic dimensions of specialized governments. In C. Anderson & L. Stephenson (Eds.), *What is democracy and how do we study it?* (pp. 145–166). University of Toronto Press.

Mackinnon, B. J. (2020, July 6). Head of public library service resigns after controversy over qualifications. *CBC News.* Accessed August 24, 2021, from https://www.cbc.ca/news/canada/new-brunswick/kevin-cormier-new-brunswick-library-executive-director-trevor-holder-1.5639313

Pagliaro, J. (2016, January 26). Mayor's task force recommends shakeup at Toronto Community Housing. *Toronto Star.* Accessed August 24, 2021, from https://www.thestar.com/news/city_hall/2016/01/26/mayors-task-force-recommends-shakeup-at-toronto-community-housing.html

Sancton, A. (2021). *Canadian local government: An urban perspective* (3rd ed.). Oxford University Press.

Statistics Canada. (2017a). *Census in brief: Municipalities in Canada with the largest and fastest-growing populations between 2011 and 2016.* Accessed August 20, 2021, from https://www12.statcan.gc.ca/census-recensement/2016/as-sa/98-200-x/2016001/98-200-x2016001-eng.cfm

Statistics Canada. (2017b). *Population and dwelling count highlight tables, 2016 Census.* Accessed August 20, 2021, from https://www12.statcan.gc.ca/census-recensement/2016/dp-pd/hlt-fst/pd-pl/Table.cfm?Lang=Eng&T=301&S=3&O=D

Taylor, Z., & Dobson, A. (2020). *Power and purpose: Canadian municipal law in transition.* IMFG Papers on Municipal Finance and Governance, No. 47. Institute of Municipal Finance and Governance. Accessed August 24, 2021, from https://tspace.library.utoronto.ca/bitstream/1807/99780/1/IMFG_Paper_No47_Power_and_Purpose_Taylor_Dobson.pdf

The City of Calgary Newsroom. (2021, September 16). *The City of Calgary welcomes the Calgary Parking Authority (CPA) into our organization.* Accessed September 22, 2021, from https://newsroom.calgary.ca/the-city-of-calgary-welcomes-the-calgary-parking-authority-cpa-into-our-organization/

Tourism Windsor Essex Pelee Island. (n.d.). *About us.* Accessed August 23, 2021, from https://visitwindsoressex.com/about-us/

Vancouver Board of Parks and Recreation. (2018). *Vanplay: Imagine parks and recreation*. Accessed August 24, 2021, from https://vancouver.ca/files/cov/vanplay-report-2-goals-to-shape-the-next-25-years.pdf

Van Genugten, M., Van Thiel, S., & Voorn, B. (2020). Local governments and their arm's length bodies. *Local Government Studies, 46*(1), 1–21.

Voorn, B., Van Genugten, M., & Van Thiel, S. (2017). The efficiency and effectiveness of municipally owned corporations: A systematic review. *Local Government Studies, 43*(5), 820–841.

Windsor Utilities Commission. (n.d.). *Welcome to WUC*. Accessed August 20, 2021, from https://enwin.com/wuc-corporate-information/

CHAPTER 3

Municipally Owned Corporations in England and Wales: A Tale of Two Countries

Rhys Andrews and Laurence Ferry

3.1 Introduction

Municipally owned corporations (MOCs) have long been used by local governments in the UK to provide the infrastructure required to support economic development (Skelcher 2017). However, during the past few decades they have become an increasingly prominent vehicle for delivering the full range of local public services (Grant Thornton 2018). In England, this development has emerged at the same time as a wider demand to develop alternative service delivery models in response to fiscal austerity (Sandford 2016) and is emblematic of the resilience of local governments (John 2014), and their capacity to innovate in response to external pressures (Skelcher 2017). Nevertheless, comparatively little is known about

R. Andrews (✉)
Cardiff Business School, Cardiff University, Cardiff, UK
e-mail: andrewsr4@cardiff.ac.uk

L. Ferry
Durham University Business School, Durham University, Durham, UK
e-mail: laurence.ferry@durham.ac.uk

M. Van Genugten et al. (eds.), *Corporatisation in Local Government*, https://doi.org/10.1007/978-3-031-09982-3_3

the dynamics of corporatisation across the different constituent countries of the UK, or the organisational characteristics of MOCs or their corporate governance practices.

To understand trends in the use of MOCs in England and Wales, their legal status, background characteristics and corporate governance, this chapter focuses on MOCs operated by the main types of local government in the two countries for the financial years 2009/10–2019/20. In England, there were 123 single-tier local governments in operation during this period: 32 London boroughs (e.g. Westminster), 36 metropolitan boroughs (e.g. Manchester) and 55 unitary authorities (e.g. Bristol), operating mostly in urban areas; while a two-tier system covers rural areas: 27 county councils (e.g. Kent) in the upper-tier; 201 district councils in the lower-tier (e.g. Forest of Dean). In Wales, the local government system is composed of 22 single-tier unitary authorities covering urban and rural areas (e.g. Cardiff and Pembrokeshire). English and Welsh local governments are very large by international standards: England—London boroughs (mean population of 255,205); metropolitan boroughs (mean population of 318,741); unitary authorities (mean population of 220,193); county councils (mean population of 787,075); district councils (mean population of 105,726); Wales—unitary authorities (mean population of 139,248).[1] The large size of the local governments reflects successive amalgamations implemented by UK central government aimed at generating economies of scale within the local government system (Andrews 2013). During the past ten years, the average expenditure of English and Welsh local governments ranged from more than £1500 per capita in London boroughs to about £300 per capita in district councils. Most local governments in England are controlled by either the main right-wing political party, the Conservative Party, or the main left-wing party, Labour, with the centrist Liberal Democrats being less influential. In Wales, Plaid Cymru, the Welsh nationalist party, is also important.

Local governments in England and Wales manage more than a quarter of the total UK public services budget (HM Treasury 2018), and are heavily dependent upon grants and transfer payments from central government, which, on average, account for more than two-thirds of their expenditure. They are elected bodies usually with a Westminster-style cabinet system of political management made up of senior members of the ruling political party. The politicians implement national policy

[1] Based on UK national census figures for 2011.

frameworks on the advice of professional local government managers led by a CEO and a team of appointed senior corporate and functional service directors. Single-tier governments in both countries provide education (e.g. primary and secondary schooling); social care (e.g. services for young and older people); environmental services (e.g. waste management); highways, economic development social housing (e.g. sheltered accommodation and rent subsidies); and public health and leisure and culture services (e.g. sports centres, libraries). In the two-tier system present in rural England, county councils provide all of the above services, except for waste collection, social housing, public health and leisure services, which are provided by district councils.

To identify the MOCs operated by local governments in England and Wales, the audited annual statements of account for each local government were scrutinised in detail, with particular attention given to the ownership structure of all the corporate entities in which local governments registered an interest. This extensive search procedure revealed the existence of more than 1200 separate corporations of varying kinds during the study period, of which 945 were majority owned. To construct an MOC-level dataset for the purposes of the chapter, the registered company number for each of the majority-owned entities was searched using the UK Companies House database and then imported into the FAME database from Bureau Van Dijk to extract the MOC-level information necessary for the analysis presented further in the chapter. This process revealed that a small number of MOCs (mostly charitable bequests) lacked separate legal status, so the final sample consisted of 930 MOCs.

Based on the information collected, this chapter begins by describing trends in corporatisation in England and Wales, reflecting on explanations for the different trends in each country. Following that, the legal status of MOCs in both countries is examined, and trends in the growth of profit-making forms of MOC are discussed. Next, the policy sectors in which MOCs are predominately found are assessed, along with their use as vehicles for joint service delivery and their typical size and purpose. Thereafter, the corporate governance of MOCs is explored, in particular, the relationships between MOCs and their parent organisations, accountability to higher levels of government, and board structure and composition. Finally, the chapter concludes with some reflections on future research directions and the challenges confronting the policy-makers responsible for overseeing MOCs.

3.2 Municipal Corporatisation in England and Wales

Corporatisation is the process by which governments create a new service or convert an existing one into either a wholly or partly owned corporate entity (Clifton and Díaz-Fuentes 2018). Previous research suggests that this process of corporatisation has grown rapidly amongst single- and upper-tier local governments in England (Ferry et al. 2018), largely in response to difficulties meeting increased service demands in a context of declining budgets (Andrews et al. 2020). While district councils in the lower-tier of the local government system covering rural England have not experienced the same degree of fiscal stress as their larger counterparts in urban areas (see Gray and Barford 2018), they have not been protected from budget cuts (National Audit Office 2018) and have been devoting ever more attention to the development of innovative new models of service delivery (Andrews et al. 2021). For this reason, it seems reasonable to anticipate that a similar trend towards corporatisation may be present across all parts of the English local government system. Nevertheless, a full picture of its dynamics across the whole of UK local government has yet to emerge, despite on-going calls for more cross-national comparisons of public policy within Britain (see Paun et al. 2016).

Several studies point to the presence of different approaches to public service delivery across the local government systems in England, Scotland and Wales (e.g. Martin et al. 2016; Entwistle et al. 2016). However, to date, little systematic attention has been paid to local policy variations across the constituent countries of the UK. Comparative analysis of corporatisation in different nations of the UK can therefore shed valuable light on whether the apparently dramatic growth of MOCs in England represents a wider trend towards corporatisation across the UK or whether it represents a form of English exceptionalism. Comparison of the trends in corporatisation amongst English and Welsh local governments, in particular, can help us to better understand these issues because there is less divergence between the legal frameworks for local public services in these two countries, and because both countries have been governed by opposing political parties with contrasting ideologies during the past ten years.

Analysis of the data on the number of MOCs operated by English and Welsh local governments suggests that there has been a substantial growth in the number of MOCs operated by English local governments nearly trebling from 312 in 2009 to 803 in 2019. By contrast, the number of

MOCs in Wales has grown much more slowly with only 28 in operation in 2009 and 37 in 2019.[2] These changes are illustrated in Fig. 3.1, which contrasts the growth in the number of MOCs operated by single/upper-tier and lower-tier local governments in England, with the trend for Welsh unitary authorities.

Figure 3.1 underlines that between 2009 and 2019 the numbers of MOCs in all English local governments grew dramatically, especially among single-tier and upper-tier governments, whereas numbers of MOCs increased more slowly in Wales. There are two principal explanations for this striking divergence.

Firstly, the approach to managing budget cuts in the wake of austerity by the Welsh government has meant that locally provided public services in Wales have received nearly as much protection as those provided by the National Health Service (NHS). In particular, by making small targeted cuts to local services and allowing local governments to raise more income from the council tax—a property tax that is the principal local source of revenue for British local governments—the Welsh government has

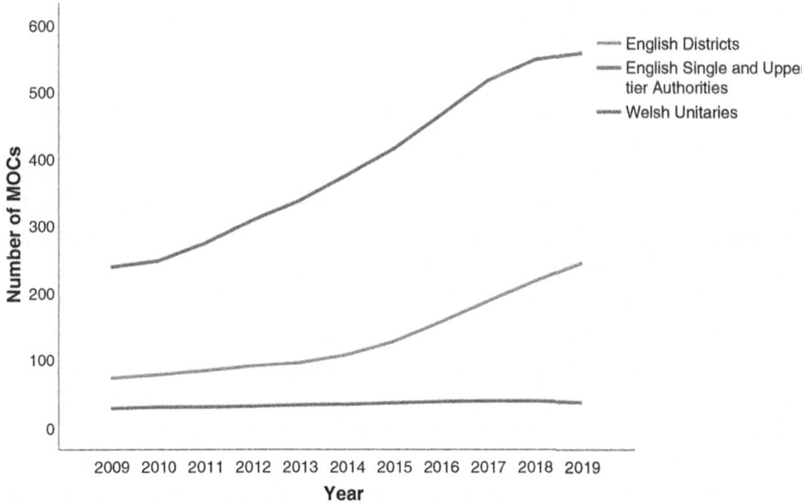

Fig. 3.1 Number of MOCs in England and Wales

[2] It is important to note that Wales accounts for only 5% of the population of both countries.

facilitated the protection of front-line services (Ogle et al. 2017). By contrast, in England, UK central government enacted swingeing cuts to the grants allocated to local governments and aggressively capped council tax rises, while increasing expenditure on the NHS. As a result, local governments in England have experienced much greater fiscal pressure than their Welsh counterparts (Gray and Barford 2018), and have been under more pressure to find alternative ways of providing and funding services than local governments in Wales. Indeed, research suggests that public sector austerity has led English local governments to borrow large sums of money to invest in the corporatisation of local public services (Andrews et al. 2020), as well as a range of other risky commercial propositions (De Widt 2021).

Secondly, in the wake of devolution there has been a concerted effort in Wales to distinguish a Welsh approach to providing, co-ordinating and supporting public services from that adopted in England (Moon 2013). Ever since the second First Minister Rhodri Morgan declared in a speech at Swansea University in 2002 that there was "clear red water" between his Labour administration in Cardiff and Tony Blair's in Westminster, there has been a strong ideological presupposition in favour of state-led service provision in Wales. Moreover, there has also been a broader recognition that due to the comparatively small size of local governments in Wales (see above), they typically lack the capacity for far-reaching structural innovations, but benefit from a stronger sense of ownership amongst local communities (Moon 2013). These idiosyncratic ideological and political features of the Welsh public service delivery system have continued to inform the thinking of the Labour Party administrations in Wales (Moon 2017), and have therefore remained an important constraint on the adoption of more commercially-orientated approaches to public services in the country.

Despite the sharply divergent rates of corporatisation in England and Wales, there are many similarities in the ways in which MOCs are created and used by local governments in each country. To deepen our understanding of the tale of these two countries, we next examine the legal provisions that have facilitated the creation of MOCs by English and Welsh local governments along with the typical legal forms that they take.

3.3 The Legal Status and Form of MOCs in England and Wales

Historically, local governments in England and Wales have been authorised to charge for the activities that they undertake in any of their areas of specific competence, albeit on a cost-recovery basis (Holden 2013). The ability of local governments to undertake wider commercial activities (to "trade" in the UK legal parlance) can only be carried out in accordance with their functions via a private company form—something that was formalised in the Local Government Act of 2003. The aim of these commercial constraints was to ensure that MOCs would be subject to the same regulations as private businesses and therefore unable to gain an unfair advantage over them in the competition for contracts. To address the restrictions on the scope of MOC operations in England, the Localism Act of 2011 opened up a wider power of general competence, which established in law the right to trade across core functions and territorial boundaries. This general power of competence was only introduced by the Welsh government in the Local Government and Elections (Wales) Act 2021 and may in part explain the diverging trends in corporatisation between the two countries between 2009 and 2019. That said, it is important to note that there are still many similarities in the legal frameworks underpinning the creation of MOCs in England and Wales. In particular, in both countries, all of the MOCs created and operated by local governments must be incorporated under private company law.[3] As such, they are Type 3 arms-length bodies as defined in Van Genugten et al. (2020).

3.3.1 The Legal Form of MOCs

Although MOCs must operate under UK private company law, that law does permit the incorporation of a wide variety of different kinds of for-profit and not-for-profit entities. In England and Wales, the most common form of profit-making company is the company limited by shares, and this is undoubtedly the most popular legal form of MOC in both countries (see next). Companies limited by shares are owned by individual shareholders with the right to receive dividend payments and to vote on company matters, with corresponding liability for the full value of their

[3] Inter-municipal shared services arrangements are typically operated as joint committees, and therefore are not accorded independent legal corporate status.

shares in the event of dissolution. Another more recently permitted company form is the Limited Liability Partnership (LLP), which establishes collective rather than individual responsibility for liabilities, and is exempt from corporation tax because it treats partners as self-employed persons with responsibility for their own tax affairs. Due to their tax advantages, LLPs have become attractive vehicles for local governments seeking to establish MOCs in partnership with private companies. A similar corporate form, the Limited Partnership, has also been adopted in a few cases.

In addition to profit-making forms of companies, there are an array of different non-profit corporate forms that MOCs can take. The most common of these is the company limited by guarantee, which is owned by legal guarantors who commit an agreed amount of money in the event that a company cannot meet its financial obligations. Critically, companies limited by guarantee must retain any gained income for reinvestment in the company itself, and, as such, can be accorded registered charity status if they provided a public benefit. Other common forms of non-profit organisation adopted by local governments include "pure" charitable incorporated organisations, industrial and provident societies (a type of mutual organisation) and community interest companies, which must have a social object but, unlike charities, are not subject to an annual audit of their public benefit statement along with their financial accounts.[4]

Analysis of the data on the legal form of the MOCs operated by English and Welsh local governments indicates that there has been a substantial growth in the number of profit-making MOCs operated by local governments in both countries. In England, the number of MOCs that were companies limited by shares or limited liability partnerships soared from 131 in 2009 to 604 in 2019. In Wales, the number of MOCs that were companies limited by shares increased only gradually from 17 in 2009 to 26 in 2019. Figure 3.2 depicts the dramatic nature of the changes in the use of different legal forms of MOC in England.

Figure 3.2 highlights the extraordinary growth in the creation and use of companies limited by shares by English local governments since 2009. It also shows how there was a gradual increase in the use of LLPs, whilst

[4] Registered charities are responsible for preparing a trustees' report that incorporates a public benefit statement: 'A statement confirming whether the charity trustees have complied with their duty to have due regard to the guidance on public benefit published by the commission in exercising their powers or duties' (https://www.gov.uk/government/publications/charity-reporting-and-accounting-the-essentials-cc15b/charity-reporting-and-accounting-the-essentials).

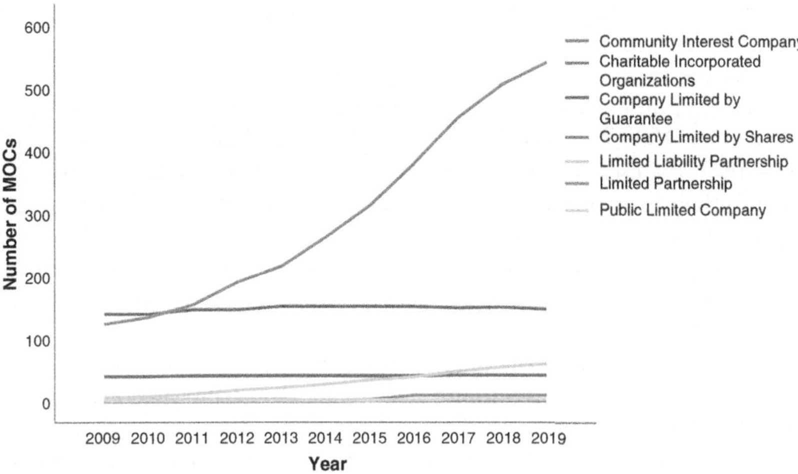

Fig. 3.2 Legal form of MOCs in England

the use of different non-profit forms of MOC remained virtually static. Further analysis of the service areas in which different forms of MOC are present can more fully illustrate the dynamics of corporatisation in England.

3.3.2 *Services Provided by MOCs*

Prior to the 1990s, MOCs in England and Wales tended to take two main forms: (i) profit-making entities providing transportation services, such as airports, ports and buses; and (ii) not-for-profit trusts organising cultural activities or preserving historical buildings, parks and monuments. Then, from the late 1980s onwards, housing companies and leisure trusts in England were created in response to policies requiring local authorities to market-test their services (Compulsory Competitive Tendering [CCT] and Best Value). In Wales, several profit-making waste disposal companies were established in response to those policies and the 1990 Environmental Protection Act, requiring local governments to create Local Authority Waste Disposal Companies if they wished to compete with private contractors in the waste management market (Davies 2007). Corporatisation in this context could therefore be used as a tool to enable local governments to retain unionised front-line staff who were previously directly employed by them—something of particular importance to the many Labour-led local governments present across Wales, as well as the Labour Party politicians in the Welsh and UK parliaments.

The data on the service areas in which English MOCs have been operating since 2009 is shown in Fig. 3.3. The figure indicates that the rapid growth in the creation of companies limited by shares is mostly attributable to their increased use to provide economic development, central services (i.e. HR and IT) and social housing. Such service areas offer more commercial possibilities and can be seen to represent new revenue streams, which can potentially raise money for reinvestment in statutory services suffering from funding shortfalls, such as adults' and children's social care. Fine-grained analysis of the data reveals that LLPs are being used almost exclusively to provide economic development, usually in collaboration with large private construction firms. By contrast, the use of a non-profit legal form for English MOCs is more common for the provision of human services, such as social housing, social care, education and leisure. However, the number of non-profit MOCs has recently begun to decrease in the social housing area as local governments increasingly seek to generate revenue through hybrid companies that build and operate mixed-use housing developments.

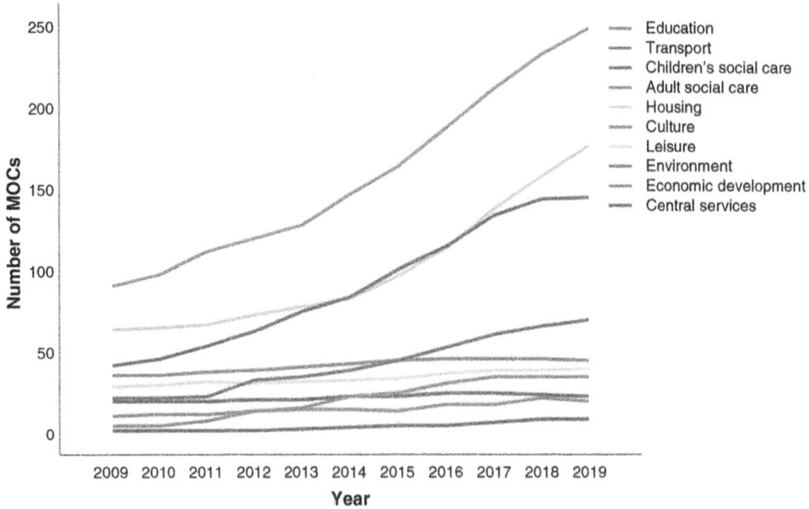

Fig. 3.3 Type of service provided by MOCs in England

In Wales, MOCs are still primarily employed for the purpose of waste management (10 in 2009, 12 in 2019), with economic development being the next most common service provided by MOCs (6 in 2009, 8 in 2019). The overwhelming majority of the Welsh waste management MOCs (ten) were established during the 1990s (as indeed were several of the other MOCs), which points to significant path dependency in the dynamics of corporatisation in Wales. Reflecting their origins as a reaction to the CCT legislation introduced in the 1980s, nearly all of the Welsh MOCs are companies limited by shares.

Although there is convergence towards the use of profit-making MOCs in both England and Wales, the differences in the purposes to which MOCs are put again reflect the divergent national fiscal and political environments in which they operate. Nevertheless, it is also clear that the different legal frameworks regulating local government commercial activities across England and Wales may also be an important influence on the use of MOCs. We turn next to examine the extent to which the MOCs that have been established by English and Welsh local governments share similar organisational characteristics.

3.4 MOC Ownership Structure and Size

In many European countries MOCs are used as vehicles for inter-municipal cooperation (Van Genugten et al. 2020), and are less frequently undertaken in partnership with private firms or minority owned by municipalities (Voorn et al. 2017). However, in England and Wales, examples of multiple municipal owners of MOCs are less common, while corporatised forms of partnerships with the private sector generally take the form of minority-owned companies limited by shares or LLPs. This pattern of ownership is apparent within the data on English and Welsh MOCs for 2009–19. For example, in England, 83% of MOCs were owned by a single local government in 2009, rising to 88% in 2019. This emphasis on wholly owned MOCs reflects a growing desire to generate and retain revenues specific to a single local government, along with sector-wide learning about the improved lines of control and accountability associated with full ownership (Grant Thornton 2018). Furthermore, wholly owned companies are exempt from full procurement processes when seeking government contracts under EU regulations, which can reduce the transaction costs associated with corporatisation of an in-house service. In Wales, the proportion of MOCs owned by a single local government remained virtually unchanged between 2009 (86%) and 2019 (87%), pointing once more to the path dependency in corporatisation in the country.

In terms of partnerships with private firms, only 16% of MOCs in England involved a private partner in 2009, a figure which grew to 19% in 2019, reflecting the increasing popularity of LLPs. Although local governments in Wales have been slightly less reluctant to partner with private firms when establishing majority-owned corporations than their English counterparts, the proportion of Welsh MOCs involving the private sector remained the same at 21% from 2009 to 2019. Hence, while there are some subtle differences in the trends in the ownership structure adopted for MOCs in England and Wales, the overall pattern is remarkably similar across both countries. Nevertheless, when we explore the organisational size of MOCs in each country in more detail, some intriguing differences begin to emerge.

The amount of assets held by an organisation is a commonly used measure of organisational size in the business management literature (see Dang et al. 2018), and can provide a good proxy for understanding a MOC's scale of operations. Although the data capturing the assets held by English and Welsh MOCs is incomplete,[5] that which is available paints an interesting picture of divergence between and within the two countries. Single- and upper-tier local governments in England operate the largest MOCs by far (average assets of £13 million in 2009 and £24 million in 2019), while Welsh unitary authorities operate MOCs that are of a similar size (average assets of £5.9 million in 2009 and £6.2 million in 2019) to those operated by the district councils in the lower-tier of England's rural local government system (average assets of £4.6 million in 2009 and £6.3 million in 2019). These differences in organisational size undoubtedly reflect differences in the population size for different types of local government, and in Wales may also be indicative of the weaker market for public services to which Welsh Labour Party politicians have regularly alluded (Moon 2013). Nevertheless, the huge standard deviations for the assets held by MOCs in both countries indicate that there is considerable diversity in the kinds of MOCs in operation throughout England and Wales. The trends in organisational size though, again point to divergence.

As the aforementioned figures suggest, the average size of MOCs has grown considerably among those operated by single- and upper-tier local governments in England. This expansion in the size of MOCs occurred in

[5] Data on assets was available for a maximum of 687 MOCs between 2009 and 2019.

the years immediately following the Localism Act in 2011, when the average assets jumped from £11.1 million in 2012 to £23.3 million in 2013. It seems likely that this reflects the expanded general power of competence for English local governments to engage in commercial 'trading' activities. Some of the largest MOCs in England are profit-making entities that co-ordinate the provision of several different public services, and that operate in multiple geographical areas across the country. For instance, MOCs, such as the Norse Group owned by Norfolk County Council, Corserv owned by Cornwall Council and Tricuro owned by Dorset, Bournemouth and Poole councils. To date, local governments in Wales have not set up the kind of multi-purpose MOCs that are becoming increasingly common in England. It will be interesting to observe whether such MOCs emerge in the wake of the general power of competence being extended to Welsh local governments in 2021.

Aside from multi-purpose MOCs, other English MOCs that hold a large amount of assets include the companies limited by shares that are responsible for managing regional airports (e.g. Birmingham and Manchester) and the companies limited by guarantee that provide children's social care services in large urban boroughs (e.g. Achieving for Children owned by Kingston and Richmond-upon-Thames councils and the Sandwell Children's Trust). Historically, the largest MOC in Wales has been Cardiff City Transport Services, which is responsible for bus transportation within the capital city and is more than twice as large as any other longstanding MOC. In 2018 though, CSC Foundry, an economic development partnership between ten of the local governments in South Wales,[6] started operating using £40 million from the Cardiff Capital Region's £1.2 billion city deal with UK central government. The smallest MOCs in both England and Wales are the charitable incorporated organisations that are responsible for managing small-scale leisure facilities (e.g. swimming pools) and museums, especially those charities for which a local government acts as the sole trustee.

As discussed earlier, although there are some similarities in the ownership structure for MOCs in England and Wales, there are considerable differences in their size and scope. In particular, Welsh MOCs resemble those that have been established by district councils, even though Welsh unitary authorities have a much wider portfolio of service responsibilities,

[6] The councils of Bridgend, Cardiff, Blaenau Gwent, Caerphilly, Merthyr, Monmouthshire, Newport, Rhondda Cynon Taff, Torfaen and Vale of Glamorgan.

and, unlike the MOCs established by their single-tier counterparts in England, MOCs in Wales are all single-purpose organisations. Despite the divergent application of the general power of competence, local governments in both England and Wales are subject to a very similar legal framework. We might therefore anticipate that the corporate governance of MOCs in both countries will exhibit fewer differences than the organisational characteristics considered here.

3.5 Corporate Governance of English and Welsh MOCs

To undertake commercial activities (or 'trade'), local governments are required to set up a corporate entity, which by definition is then subject to private company law rather than municipal administrative law. As a result of this movement into a private regulatory environment, there are three key aspects of the corporate governance of MOCs that mark them out as autonomous from their parent organisations, and the municipal administrative law and regulations to which local governments adhere.

3.5.1 Accountability of MOCs

Firstly, private companies in the UK are guided by the UK corporate governance code, which lays down a series of recommendations for relationships between executive boards and owners, along with guidance on board meetings, structure and composition (Financial Reporting Council 2018). Reporting on application of the code in their annual financial reports is only mandatory for organisations listed on the stock exchange. Nevertheless, all corporate entities covered by company law are generally expected to have a one-tier board structure composed of a chairperson, chief executive, company secretary and an appropriate balance of other executive and nonexecutive directors. The data collected on the composition of MOC boards in England and Wales indicates that nearly all of them adhere to these expectations, apart from those that are LLPs or are very small, typically charitable incorporated organisations managing leisure or heritage facilities. Although directors of MOCs are not required by law to adhere to the *Code of Conduct for Board Members of Public Bodies* (Cabinet Office 2019), which applies to national public corporations, advisory bodies increasingly recommend that MOC directors should adopt the ethical standards stipulated by the code (Local Partnerships 2021).

Secondly, despite being responsible for upholding the public interest,[7] MOCs are subject to a less stringent annual financial audit process than those organisations that are designated 'public sector bodies' in England and Wales, such as central government departments, NHS trusts and local authorities. Because they are subject to public sector audit, designated bodies are expected to demonstrate that effective value for money arrangements are in place (Public Audit Forum 2016)—something that does not apply to MOCs, as they are covered solely by private rather than public sector accounting and auditing standards. In particular, MOCs are not required to adhere to the Code of Audit Practice, which regulates the accounting of local governments. Instead, like other corporate entities, they are required to prepare independently audited accounts each financial year, showing money received and expended, plus assets and liabilities (unless they qualify for an exemption due to small size).[8] As noted earlier, MOCs that are registered charities are also required to include a public benefit statement for audit along with their annual accounts.

Thirdly, MOCs are not subject to the performance regimes that apply to designated public sector bodies in England and Wales, which are expected to collect an array of statutory performance indicators that are subsequently evaluated by central government departments and regulatory agencies (Martin et al. 2016). Although some MOCs do report on their service performance in their annual financial statements, they are not required to do so and are not subject to any centrally mandated performance standards against which their achievements could be judged. The achievements of MOCs contribute to the aggregate performance data that is collected and published at the local government level, but MOCs will not be held corporately responsible for those achievements by UK central government. Nonetheless, given the long-established importance of performance measurement and management in the UK public sector (Hood

[7] The "arrangements put in place to ensure that the intended outcomes for stakeholders are defined and achieved" (International Federation of Accountants and Chartered Institute of Public Finance and Accountancy 2014).

[8] The most recent UK government guidance indicates that companies can qualify for an audit exemption, provided that their articles of association or shareholders do not demand one, when they have at least two of: i) an annual turnover of no more than £10.2 million; ii) assets worth no more than £5.1 million; iii) 50 or fewer employees on average. https://www.gov.uk/audit-exemptions-for-private-limited-companies

2006), the performance of MOCs will typically be measured and monitored internally by their parent organisations as part of their routine practices of oversight and financial control.

3.5.2 Autonomy of MOCs

All of the three features of MOC governance discussed earlier point towards the significant autonomy that MOCs in England and Wales have in their relations with UK central government, especially when compared with the relations between local governments and central government (John 2014). They also indicate that MOCs should in principle be insulated from undue political interference by local governments. However, given the absence of centrally mandated corporate governance requirements specific to MOCs, the ways in which they are controlled, operated and held accountable by their parent organisations will exhibit a certain degree of practice variation, which reflects the different political management approaches adopted within individual local governments.

Like all other local government-led initiatives in England and Wales, MOCs are typically set up through a process of negotiation between the ruling political party and the public managers responsible for designing and implementing appropriate policies. As a result, the relationship between political and administrative leaders within local governments ultimately determine the dynamics of corporatisation within particular governments. Nevertheless, the inspiration for establishing a MOC is most likely to originate with the senior managers (e.g. the chief executive and the chief financial officer), who are responsible for designing and implementing the policies that will enable a local government to achieve the aims of its political leadership. At the same time, the MOCs that are created by English and Welsh local governments are likely to be monitored and controlled by senior public managers with comparatively little political involvement, aside from the presence of a few local councillors on the boards of directors (see below).

Political accountability for public service provision in British local governments operates through a series of service-specific committees that are chaired by a cabinet member with responsibility for oversight of the specific service and to whom the administrative head of that service is accountable. The most important business dealt with by these service-based committees is then discussed at regular cabinet meetings, along with strategic matters relating to major central government policy initiatives, large-scale changes in land use and the financial position of the government as a whole. The frequency of the service-specific committee and cabinet meetings can vary from government to government, but they usually tend to occur on a monthly basis. However, given the sheer scope of the responsibilities of local governments, those meetings cover an extremely wide range of issues in a very short period (approximately two hours), and, consequently touch upon the management and performance of the MOCs within their service remit only sporadically. At cabinet level, even large strategically important MOCs may merit detailed consideration on little more than an annual basis (Alonso and Andrews 2021). Although the financial management of MOCs will be scrutinised by politicians and auditors at audit committee meetings, MOCs are largely held accountable for their service performance by the public managers who lead the service departments under whose umbrella they operate.[9] Such oversight is only occasionally intensive or intrusive, so the autonomy of MOCs in England and Wales is constrained mainly by the original purposes laid out by the local government and by the presence of local government managers on the boards of directors.

3.5.3 MOC Boards of Directors

Like private companies, strategic decisions in MOCs are made by the board of directors who are also responsible for supervising the managers charged with implementing those decisions. While the board may need to be mindful of statutory guidance relating to the provision of certain public services (especially for social care), they generally confront the same legal regulations and constraints as the private sector. In theory, MOCs therefore have considerable autonomy over HR, finance and operational matters. However, in practice, they are likely to be restricted by normative pressures from the local government to adopt certain policies and processes, which accord with the government aims and objectives. For example, research has highlighted that MOCs may be expected by local governments to remunerate employees at a similar rate to their directly employed counterparts, even though they are not legally required to do so (Ferry et al. 2020). Moreover, as owners, local governments retain the

[9] In a small number of cases, local governments appoint a dedicated commercial services manager who monitors the management and performance of all the MOCs operated by an organisation.

right to appoint new directors, change the articles of association, alter the budget and, ultimately, re-municipalise or sell MOCs. Such pressures within the local governance of MOCs are likely to be more acute where the political leader, chief executive or another senior politician or manager sits on the board of directors, especially if they occupy the chairperson's role, as is sometimes the case. Given the potential for local government control over MOCs to be exerted through a strategy of board influence, it is therefore important to understand the composition of MOC boards in more detail.

As noted earlier, the boards of directors for English and Welsh MOCs are one-tier boards, upon which politicians and senior local government managers may sit, subject to the principles of board independence laid down in the UK corporate governance code. In 2019, the average size of MOC boards was similar across all the different types of local government in England and Wales, with about six directors in place. However, board size has dropped considerably in England, as in 2009 there were on average about ten directors on each MOC board. This decline in the number of MOC directors is largely attributable to the increase in the use of profit-making MOCs, which are less likely to have local political or community representation on their boards than non-profit MOCs. While many MOCs do not have any politicians on the board, a large number do, though this varies by type of local government. Amongst MOCs with politicians on the board, those that are run by English district councils have lower political representation (on average approximately 1.6 politicians per board) than all other types of local government (about 2.5 politicians per board). This number has remained fairly static at the same time as the average board size has fallen, implying that political control over MOCs in England and Wales has increased slightly during the past decade or so, albeit only for those MOCs with politicians on their boards of directors.

In addition to guidelines relating to board independence, the UK corporate governance code stipulates that appointments to corporate boards should be mindful of gender, social and ethnic diversity. Although there are currently no quotas for representation on company boards, information on gender representation can be garnered from company financial reports to assess whether equality in the boardroom is improving or deteriorating in MOCs. Based on the available data,[10] Fig. 3.4 illustrates the

[10] Data on women's representation on the board was available for a maximum of 858 MOCs between 2009 and 2019.

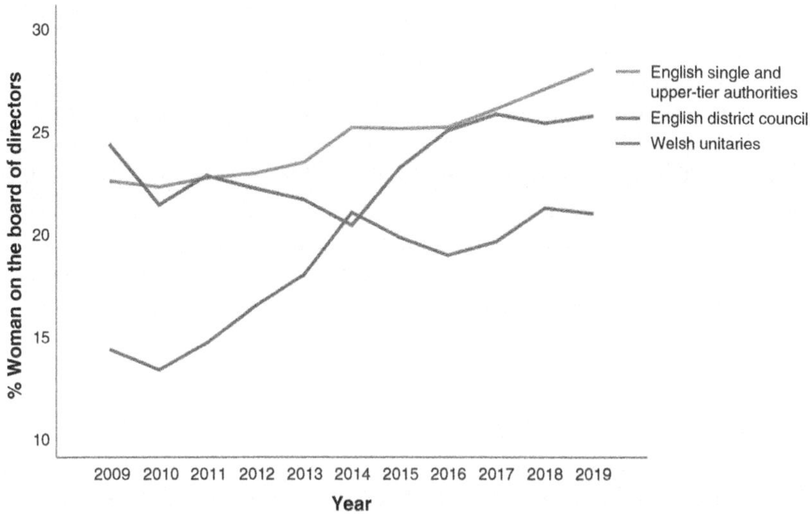

Fig. 3.4 Women's representation on MOC boards in England and Wales

proportion of women MOC directors in each of the main types of local government in England and Wales.

Figure 3.4 highlights that the representation of women on MOC boards has been increasing in England and Wales from 22% on average in 2009 to 27% in 2019. This represents a significant achievement since it has occurred at a time when the average board size has been decreasing. Nevertheless, it is quite clear that Welsh MOCs are lagging behind English MOCs in promoting gender equality at director level, something which may reflect the dominant male political culture throughout much of local government in Wales (Farrell and Titcombe 2016). Analysis of the very small number of MOCs for which salary data is available[11] also suggests that there is a negative correlation between total board remuneration and women's representation on a MOC board.[12] This negative relationship is especially strong for the MOCs operated by single- and upper-tier local

[11] Data on total board compensation was only available for a maximum of 173 MOCs between 2009 and 2019.

[12] Although a similar negative correlation is observed between women's representation and CEO pay, this should be interpreted with even greater caution because the data for CEO pay is only available for a maximum of 58 MOCs between 2009 and 2019.

governments in England where women are more likely to be board members, and which, according to the scant available data, have experienced a dramatic increase in the total amount of compensation paid annually to board members rising from an average of £200,000 per board in 2009 to £350,000 per board in 2019. By contrast, average boardroom compensation in MOCs operated by English districts fell from £160,000 to £83,000 per board, and in Welsh MOCs stayed relatively static at around £125,000 per board. All of the aforementioned variations in gender representation and pay are likely to reflect the dramatic trend towards the use of larger, profit-making entities by single- and upper-tier local governments in England.

3.6 Conclusion

This chapter has explored the dynamics of municipal corporatisation in England and Wales, along with the legal status, ownership structure, size and corporate governance of the MOCs that are operated by the local governments in both countries. Important differences in the nature of corporatisation have emerged that reflect the diverging legal frameworks and politics of public administration in the two countries. In England, the imposition of drastic cuts to public sector budgets and the introduction of the general power of competence have led local governments to set up an array of profit-making MOCs. In Wales, devolution has insulated Welsh local governments from some of the fiscal pressures experienced by their English counterparts, and this coupled with the absence of a general power of competence and a wider resistance to alternatives to state-led provision has meant that a drive to corporatise local public services has been absent. Hence, the evidence presented here tells a tale of two countries, which has important implications for researchers and policy-makers alike.

Firstly, the drive to corporatise local public services in England raises an important question about the financial sustainability and resilience of this model of service delivery in general. In the wake of austerity, numerous large English local governments have been at risk of bankruptcy, with Northamptonshire County Council being abolished and reorganised into North Northamptonshire and West Northamptonshire by UK central government after it issued two Section 114 notices—a legal restriction on the scope of permissible expenditures. Problems with financial resilience amongst local governments in England have been linked to the use of MOCs, as well as the myriad other commercial activities that they have been undertaking in order to improve their financial position. For example, the auditors of Nottingham City Council issued a Public Interest Report relating to their management of Robin Hood Energy, a MOC supplying electricity, which resulted in the council closing the company down and selling its assets to British Gas, the main private energy supplier in the UK (Murphy and Lakoma 2021). In addition, there are deep concerns about the financial resilience of the many property development MOCs that have sprung up recently.

Brick-by-Brick, an MOC established by Croydon London Borough council to build new homes and to operate social housing, is regarded as the main source of the financial problems that led the council to issue a Section 114 notice in 2020. To prop up the company, the council wrote off loans of more than £200 million to keep it in business and has received no payments in return (Rudgewick 2021). The granting of soft loans to English and Welsh MOCs is permissible and not uncommon, but when coupled with ambitious investment plans can have a potentially dramatic impact on the finances of local governments if the projected returns are not achieved. All of which belies a pressing need for researchers and policymakers in the UK to gain a better understanding of the dynamics of financial management and performance of MOCs. Aside from large-scale quantitative analyses and qualitative case studies, practitioners could potentially learn lessons from long-established MOCs in both England and Wales. At the same time, there could be an important role for sector-led support networks, alongside central government monitoring of value-for-money arrangements in large-scale MOCs.

Secondly, although the financial condition of MOCs in England and Wales is gradually becoming a focus of attention within policy and practice networks, their service performance and responsiveness to local citizens more generally remains something of a black box. Some organisations have been in operation for many years now, which implies that they are achieving the purposes set out for them, but we need to know more about whether the services provided by MOCs are better or worse than those provided in-house or by private contractors. Aside from empirical studies comparing different delivery models, it would also be valuable to understand more about public perceptions of those models. While corporatisation is an increasingly important policy issue within England, the wider public in England (and Wales) seems uninterested in whether services are provided by local governments or arms-length organisations. Research investigating attitudes towards different service delivery models and levels of satisfaction with different types of MOC would therefore shed invaluable light on the wider public value created by MOCs.

Finally, the financial and service performance of MOCs in England and Wales is likely to have been affected by the restrictions on public movements aimed at preventing transmission of the Covid-19 virus. Public transportation, airports, leisure and cultural services and civic amenities of all kinds have experienced dramatic falls in usage. Alongside the stalling of many housing development projects, service decline is likely to undermine the financial resilience of both MOCs and the local governments that operate them. It is conceivable that in England, where the income from MOCs is increasingly important, many of the assets held by MOCs will either be sold to private companies or brought back in-house to re-establish them on a sounder financial footing. Indeed, inspection of the unaudited accounts of English local governments for 2019/20 already points towards a slowdown in corporatisation, which could be hastened by the financial fallout from the pandemic. In Wales, the granting of the general power of competence in 2021 may conceivably encourage greater levels of corporatisation, which could initiate a wider debate regarding the long-term strategic choices for the management of local public services in the country. Future studies comparing the English and Welsh approaches to corporatisation before and after the recovery from the Covid-19 pandemic would therefore further illuminate the politics of public administration in the devolved UK, especially if supplemented with analysis of corporatisation in Northern Ireland and Scotland.

References

Alonso, J. M., & Andrews, R. (2021). Government-created non-profit organizations and public service turnaround: Evidence from a synthetic control approach. *Journal of Public Administration Research and Theory, 31*(2), 346–362.

Andrews, R. (2013). Local government amalgamation and financial sustainability: The case of England and Wales. *Public Finance & Management, 13*(2), 124–141.

Andrews, R., Bello, B., Downe, J., Martin, S., & Walker, R. M. (2021). The motivations for the adoption of management innovation by local governments and its performance effects. *Public Administration Review, 81*(4), 625–637.

Andrews, R., Ferry, L., Skelcher, C., & Wegorowski, P. (2020). Corporatization in the public sector: Explaining the growth of local government companies. *Public Administration Review, 80*(3), 482–493.

Cabinet Office. (2019). *Code of conduct for board members of public bodies*. Cabinet Office.

Clifton, J., & Díaz-Fuentes, D. (2018). The state and public corporations. In A. Nolke & C. May (Eds.), *Handbook of the international political economy of the corporation* (pp. 106–119). Edward Elgar.

Dang, C., Li, Z., & Yang, C. (2018). Measuring firm size in empirical corporate finance. *Journal of Banking & Finance, 86*, 159–176.

Davies, S. (2007). *Politics and markets: The case of UK municipal waste management*. Working Paper 95. School of Social Sciences, Cardiff University.

De Widt, D. (2021). The impact of demographic trends on local government financial reserves: Evidence from England. *Local Government Studies, 47*(3), 405–428.

Entwistle, T., Guarneros-Meza, V., Martin, S., & Downe, J. (2016). Reframing governance: Competition, fatalism and autonomy in central–local relations. *Public Administration, 94*(4), 897–914.

Farrell, C., & Titcombe, S. (2016). Gender and the experiences of local elected members–a focus on Wales. *Local Government Studies, 42*(6), 867–884.

Ferry, L., Andrews, R., Skelcher, C., & Wegorowski, P. (2018). Corporatization of local authorities in England in the wake of austerity 2010-2016. *Public Money and Management, 38*(6), 477–480.

Ferry, L., Andrews, R., & Wegorowski, P. (2020). *Hybrid organizing, conflicting institutional logics and corporatization of social care*. Working paper.

Financial Reporting Council (FRC). (2018). *The UK corporate governance code*. FRC.

Grant Thornton. (2018). *In good company: Latest trends in local authority trading companies*. Grant Thornton.

Gray, M., & Barford, A. (2018). The depths of the cuts: The uneven geography of local government austerity. *Cambridge Journal of Regions, Economy and Society, 11*(3), 541–563.

HM Treasury. (2018). *Public expenditure: Statistical analysis 2018*. HM Stationery Office.

Holden, N. (2013, December 17). Charging and trading – a new dawn. *Local Government Lawyer*. Accessed March 30, 2022, from https://www.localgovernmentlawyer.co.uk/governance/314-governance-a-risk-articles/39680-charging-and-trading-a-new-dawn

Hood, C. (2006). Gaming in targetworld: The targets approach to managing British public services. *Public Administration Review, 66*(4), 515–521.

International Federation of Accountants and Chartered Institute of Public Finance and Accounting. (2014). *International framework for good governance in the public sector*. IFAC.

John, P. (2014). The great survivor: The persistence and resilience of English local government. *Local Government Studies, 40*(5), 687–704.

Local Partnerships. (2021). *Local authority company review guidance.* Local Partnerships.

Martin, S., Nutley, S., Downe, J., & Grace, C. (2016). Analysing performance assessment in public services: How useful is the concept of a performance regime? *Public Administration, 94*(1), 129–145.

Moon, D. S. (2013). Rhetoric and policy learning: On Rhodri Morgan's 'clear red water' and 'made in Wales' health policies. *Public Policy and Administration, 28*(3), 306–323.

Moon, D. S. (2017). Red Dragon FM: Carwyn Jones's 'Welsh Labour rhetoric'. In J. Atkins & J. Gaffney (Eds.), *Voices of the UK left: Rhetoric, ideology and the performance of politics* (pp. 123–146). Palgrave Macmillan.

Murphy, P., & Lakoma, K. (2021). Debate: Public audit, the Redmond review, and the use of public interest reports. *Public Money & Management, 41*(2), 150–151.

National Audit Office (NAO). (2018). *Financial sustainability of local authorities 2018.* Report by the Comptroller and Auditor General. : NAO.

Ogle, J., Luchinskaya, D., & Trickey, M. (2017). *Austerity and local government in Wales: An analysis of income and spending priorities, 2009-10 to 2016-17.* Wales Public Services 2025.

Paun, A., Rutter, J., & Nicholl, A. (2016). *Devolution as a policy laboratory. Evidence sharing and learning between the UK's four governments.* Alliance for Useful Evidence, Carnegie UK Trust, Institute for Government.

Public Audit Forum. (2016). *Statement of recommended practice – Practice note 10: Audit of financial statements of public sector bodies in the United Kingdom.* National Audit Office.

Rudgewick, O. (2021, January 14). Croydon set to lend more to troubled housing company. *Public Finance.* Accessed March 30, 2022, from https://www.publicfinance.co.uk/news/2021/01/croydon-set-lend-more-troubled-housing-company

Sandford, M. (2016). *Local government: Alternative models of service delivery.* House of Commons Library Briefing Paper Number 05950.

Skelcher, C. (2017). An enterprising municipality? Municipalisation, corporatisation and the political economy of Birmingham City Council in the nineteenth and twenty-first centuries. *Local Government Studies, 43*(6), 927–945.

Van Genugten, M., Van Thiel, S., & Voorn, B. (2020). Local governments and their arm's length bodies. *Local Government Studies, 46*(1), 1–21.

Voorn, B., Van Genugten, M. L., & Van Thiel, S. (2017). The efficiency and effectiveness of municipally owned corporations: A systematic review. *Local Government Studies, 43*(5), 820–841.

CHAPTER 4

Municipally Owned Corporations in Israel: Local Initiative and the Pursuit of Flexibility in a Centralised Context

Eran Razin and Anna Hazan

4.1 Introduction

Municipally owned corporations (MOCs) of all classifications—municipal companies, public benefit companies, municipal associations and water and sewage corporations—account for an estimated 17% of the total financial turnover of Israel's local government (2017–2018 data). MOCs advanced to the forefront of the municipal arena in the late 1980s and 1990s. Local governments have been hard pressed to compete with each other over local economic development and quality of life, beyond their formal obligations, in a context of diminishing effectiveness of central

E. Razin (✉)
Department of Geography, The Hebrew University, Jerusalem, Israel
e-mail: msrazin@mail.huji.ac.il

A. Hazan
School of Political Sciences, University of Haifa, Haifa, Israel

Department of Public Administration and Policy, Sapir Academic College, Sderot, Israel

M. Van Genugten et al. (eds.), *Corporatisation in Local Government*, https://doi.org/10.1007/978-3-031-09982-3_4

state role. The establishment of companies engaged in local development became widespread amid growing disparities—disadvantaged and managerially weak municipalities failed to join the trend. A parallel trend, since the 1990s, consisted of strengthened regulation of MOCs by the Ministry of Interior. Moreover, municipalities have been compelled since the early 2000s to transfer their water and sewage systems from municipal departments to autonomous municipal water and sewage corporations, regulated by the central state Water Authority.

The main policy challenge of Israeli MOCs consists of regulating them effectively, without crippling their business-like project-based orientation as flexible municipal arms. In the context of neoliberal prominence in the early 2000s, central state legal and economic gatekeepers frequently expressed ambivalent attitudes towards MOCs, preferring privatisation over transferring functions to MOCs. However, the aftermath of the 2020 Covid-19 crisis is likely to strain municipal tax bases and end a prolonged period of readily available cheap finance, signalling the necessity to resort to mechanisms such as public-private partnerships (PPP) and the development of income-producing properties, in which municipal companies play a vital role.

This chapter discusses attributes and challenges of Israel's MOCs, in the context of tensions between their fundamental rationale of being the flexible arm of local government, acting at arm's length from the municipality, and the traditional path-dependent centralism of Israeli political system. We focus in particular on municipal companies (termed 'urban companies' in Israel), emphasizing their dual nature, being subject to both private and municipal laws, the contrasting arguments on over- or under-regulation, and their vital role in local development and service provision.

4.2 A Centralised Context

Israel is a rather centralised unitary state, with only two tiers of government: central and local (OECD 2020; Razin 2004; Beeri 2020). Israel's local government included 257 local authorities (in 2020), with an average size of about 35,000 inhabitants (excluding two local industrial councils). The largest were Jerusalem (950,000 inhabitants) and Tel Aviv (465,000 inhabitants), while 34% had a population of less than 10,000. Local government expenditures stood at a modest 16% of total public spending in 2018.

Israeli municipalities are responsible for mandatory tasks in infrastructural, environmental and social services; the latter—education and social services—are formally provided on behalf of the central state and consist of more than half of local recurrent expenditures. Municipalities also perform voluntary tasks, primarily cultural and recreational services and local economic development. Centralisation is evident in the minimal engagement of local government in public security and public housing, the limited autonomy in education and land use planning, and the extensive regulation of local decisions through a-priori approvals by central state regulators to a wide host of local decisions, including land deals and contracts (Razin et al. 2020).

Mayors have been directly elected since 1978, generating a shift towards a de facto more decentralised strong mayor system. Israel has passed a substantial neoliberal transition since the late 1980s. A sharp increase in the dependency of municipalities on self-generated revenues, particularly non-residential property taxes, occurred as a consequence of steps to curb inflation in 1985, leading to an increased competition over business land uses. Local government reforms aimed at greater fiscal discipline and cost efficiency were implemented during the 2003–2004 economic crisis, associated with the second Palestinian *Intifada* (uprising). These changes amplified inter-municipal fiscal disparities, associated with Israel's socio-ethnic and religious diversity, marked core-periphery spatial structure, and reliance of municipal budgets on unequally distributed non-residential property taxes.

4.3 Trends in the Evolution of Municipal Corporations: Rapid Growth Followed by Increasing Regulatory Constraints

4.3.1 Growth in the Number of Companies

Municipal companies were established since the pre-statehood British mandate period, first by the city of Tel Aviv in the 1930s, followed by several other cities. The pace of their establishment somewhat accelerated in the decades following the founding of the State of Israel in 1948, but their major surge occurred in the late 1980s and 1990s, when more than 150 new companies were founded. A 1990 survey identified about 150 companies, among them 28 of Tel Aviv, 16 of Jerusalem and 11 of Haifa

(Megama 1990). Ten years later, a 2000 survey identified 250 municipal companies (Idea 2004). Of 239 companies fully controlled by municipalities in 2012, 78% were established after 1980, mostly in the 1990s (State Comptroller 2012).

The surge in popularity of municipal companies in the late 1980s and 1990s was associated with the diminishing effectiveness of the central state in promoting local development (Razin 1990). Municipal entrepreneurialism was further stimulated by a sharp increase in the dependency of local authorities on non-residential property taxes since 1985. New municipal companies were established mainly in medium sized and small local authorities that hardly utilised this tool in earlier years, engaging in local development and management of municipal assets. Performing municipal tasks by municipal companies provided tax benefits and flexibility, lifting constraints of public tender regulations and unionised labour, and serving as a bypass to municipal manpower caps imposed by the central state.

4.3.2 *Stabilisation amid Regulatory Constraints*

The pace of establishment of municipal companies slowed down thereafter, apparently due to the 2001–2004 economic recession, which was followed by stricter regulations that made the establishment of such companies less beneficial. The regulatory framework of MOCs evolved since the 1980s, along with the increase in their number and financial turnover. It moved from the lack of any specific provisions, except for being subject to the 1929 British Mandate Companies Ordinance and the 1909 Ottoman Law of Associations, with their amendments, to a complex set of provisions specified in the Municipal Ordinance, orders and procedures set by the Ministry of Interior, in addition to the Companies and Associations Laws.

Particular legal provisions for MOCs were first set in the 1964 update of the 1934 British mandate Municipal Ordinance, which explicitly stated that municipalities are permitted to establish companies and associations and to purchase stock of such entities, as long as they perform tasks permitted by the Municipal Ordinance. A 1980 ministerial order required the approval of the Minister of Interior for the establishment of such corporations and included additional regulations, followed by more detailed provisions defined in subsequent years, mainly as non-statutory procedures published as Ministry's circulars between 2003 and 2014. The 2011 procedures were a particular milestone in forming a comprehensive regulatory framework for MOCs.

As lax regulations tightened, the benefits of not being bound by public sector regulations have diminished, leaving one major rationale for the establishment of MOCs: their integrative, less bureaucratic, project-based orientation. Remaining justifications for performing municipal tasks through MOCs have included specialisation in particular tasks, greater operational flexibility and ability to financially isolate tasks from the municipal budget.

Requests to set up new MOCs have faced tight scrutiny of the Ministry of Interior since the 2000s, also encouraging inactive corporations to formally close down. Some companies, for example, of the city of Tel Aviv, were merged with others to improve cost efficiency. The number of municipal companies hence remained stagnant throughout the first two decades of the twenty-first century, standing at 249 in 2020. To those can be added 316 municipal non-profits—33 public benefit companies and 283 municipal associations—as well as 56 water and sewage corporations (Table 4.1). Water and sewage corporations are not usually counted with other 'urban companies'. They are not regulated by the Ministry of Interior and rather than serving as flexible municipal arms, are subject to the 2001 Water and Sewage Corporations Law, intended to constrain municipal autonomy, mainly by limiting the transfer of their revenues to other municipal tasks (Tevet and Talit 2021).

4.3.3 *Ownership Structure, Revenues, and Representative Organisation*

The vast majority of municipal companies (91%) are fully owned by local authorities (Table 4.2), also because of the negative attitude of the Ministry of Interior towards jointly owned municipal-private corporations, and the complete rejection of requests for the establishment of new companies in which municipalities hold a minority of the shares. However, control of non-profit municipal associations is more diverse—the municipality holds at least 50% of the board in only 44% of these associations (Table 4.2), mainly because municipalities have only minority representation in boards of many community centres, most of the rest held by a state-owned non-profit.

Revenues of MOCs of all types stood at about 17.7 billion Shekels (US$4.9 billion) in 2017/8: 8.54 billion Shekels in companies ($2.36

Table 4.1 MOCs in Israel by type and field of activity, 2020

Field	*Companies*	*Public benefit companies*	*Associations*	*Water and sewage corporations*
Infrastructure and economic development	151	1	3	0
Business and industrial parks	29	0	0	0
Community centres and administrations	0	0	142	0
Education, culture and sport	24	31	92	0
Welfare	4	0	35	0
Water and sewage	17	0	0	56
Tourism	9	1	5	0
R & D	1[a]	0	6	0
Renewal and public housing	5	0	0	0
Environmental services	4	0	0	0
Municipal bonds	3	0	0	0
Transportation	1	0	0	0
Agriculture	1	0	0	0
Total	249	33	283	56

Source: Data of the Ministry of Interior and the Water Authority

Note: The table includes all corporations with majority and minority share of the municipality

[a]Partnership

Table 4.2 MOCs in Israel (excluding water and sewage corporations) by type and level of municipal control, 2020

Field	*Companies*[a]	*Public benefit companies*	*Associations*
Majority municipal share	226	28	124
Minority municipal share	23	5	159
Total	249	33	283

Source: Data of the Ministry of Interior and the Water Authority

[a]Including one partnership

billion), 4.54 Shekels in non-profits ($1.26 billion), and 4.6 billion Shekels in water and sewage corporations ($1.27 billion). The financial turnover was somewhat higher, because a few companies included only their overheads for some projects in their financial reports, while the full expense was included in the development budget of the municipality.

The Association of the CEOs of Urban Corporations in Local Government was established in the mid-1990s—the decade of their major expansion in Israel—as an initiative of the person who engaged in developing municipal companies in the city of Petah Tikva, with the support of the person in charge of urban corporations in the Ministry of Interior. It emphasised training programmes, later on becoming the Urban Corporations in Local Government Association, engaged in promoting the cause of MOCs, also through the organisation of high-profile annual conventions. A major challenge of the Association is to lobby for the vital role of these MOCs as the flexible arm of local government. It aims to promote professionalism and good governance, and to eradicate negative images of corruption and obscure unregulated corners of local government.

MOCs were indeed occasionally regarded as the mayor's hidden backyard, used for political appointments, bypassing manpower caps, hiding deficits and improper sub-contracts with affiliates; hence the distrust of the Ministries of Justice and the Interior in these corporations. Efforts to improve corporate governance have gained the support of the Urban Corporations Association, opting for a compulsory appointment of an internal auditor (perhaps also in order to reduce the intensity of external monitoring), and for raising the qualifications of CEOs and members of the board. The Association not only supports closing down corporations lacking a clear mission but also complains about excessive constraints set by the Ministry on the establishment of new corporations that champion a sound economic rationale. These constraints practically prevent the establishment of corporations in fiscally weak municipalities by rejecting loan requests of corporations owned by municipalities that are unable to borrow by themselves.

4.4 Legal Status: Duality (an 'Androgynous') In-Between Private and Municipal Laws

4.4.1 The Loyalty Contradiction in Municipal Companies

MOCs are subject to both private and municipal laws and regulations, hence referred to as hybrid, dual entities or 'androgynous'. They are subject to the 1999 Companies Law that replaced the 1929 Ordinance, managed as private limited companies, or the 1980 Associations Law that replaced the 1909 Ottoman Law, but also to the stricter regulations of the Municipal Ordinance and the orders and regulations associated with it.

The stated objectives of MOCs can only be within the tasks defined for municipalities in the Municipal Ordinance, because Israel formally adheres to the ultra vires principle.

Being subject to two different sets of regulations and regulators creates a major conflict of loyalty for members of the board of municipal companies who represent the municipalities. Whereas the fidelity of members of the boards according to the Companies Law is to the company and its profitability, the loyalty of municipal representatives according to the Municipal Ordinance, since 1987, is to the municipality. This deviation has been deliberately set to prevent MOCs from acting against the public interest in order to serve the interest of the company itself. Nevertheless, it fundamentally contradicts the principle of 'separate legal personality' of a limited company, embedded in the Companies Law. The loyalty deviation concerns only companies whose majority shares are held by the municipality; hence the Ministry of Interior rejects the establishment of companies in which municipalities are a minority and all members of the board are thus accountable to the company.

There are two exceptions to the loyalty contradiction. The first concerns municipal companies established in order to issue municipal bonds, which singularly used a 2004 legal amendment that enabled the establishment of special municipal companies in which the loyalty of all members of the board is to the company. This has obviously been done to assure the ability of the company to repay bond holders. The second concerns water and sewage corporations that were intentionally established to prevent excessive diversion of revenues to other municipal tasks.

The enactment of a municipal corporations law, similar to the 1975 Governmental (central state) Companies Law, never took off, because of disagreements between the central and local states over a complex set of regulations, rejected by local government leaders. It was debated in the late 2010s, but as of early 2021 only partial agreements have been reached and political instability at the central state level has hampered any practical progress.

4.4.2 *Legal Status of Non-profits*

Municipal associations are subject to both the 1980 Associations Law and the Municipal Ordinance and regulatory powers of the Ministry of Interior over MOCs. A major advantage of municipal associations is their ability to collect donations. Unlike companies, municipalities are a minority on the board of most municipal associations; hence, associations are more difficult to regulate, even to be identified, by the Ministry of Interior. Nevertheless, regulation on these associations has tightened in the 2010s (State Comptroller 2020b).

A major reform of the private sector regulatory framework, which applies also to MOCs, consisted of the legislation of a new Companies Law in 1999, followed by a 2007 amendment that updated rules for the establishment of non-profit public benefit companies, as an alternative to the long-standing option of non-profit associations. Public benefit companies are a unique type of non-profit corporations that can act within specific public objectives defined by the law. The Ministry of Interior prefers public benefit companies over associations, because of their more effective internal auditing and external supervision and regulation. However, the share of public benefit companies among MOCs has remained small and even decreased in the late 2010s.

4.4.3 *The Unique Status of Water and Sewage Corporations*

Water and sewage corporations are subject to dedicated regulation based on the 2001 Water and Sewage Corporations Law that overrides the regulatory powers of the Ministry of Interior. The 2001 law encouraged the transfer of water and sewage services to municipal water and sewage corporations, aimed to prevent involvement of the municipality in their day-to-day operation and to ensure that revenues are routed to investment in water and sewage infrastructure, rather than to subsidizing other municipal tasks. Water tariffs for all water users are set nationally by the Governmental Council for Water and Sewage and the Israel Water Authority was established in 2007 to regulate the MOCs. A 2004–2006 legal amendment compelled all municipalities, except for rural regional councils, to join regional corporations, composed of several municipalities, by 2008 (Marin et al. 2017; Tevet and Talit 2021). However, by 2020, 24 urban municipalities, mainly small ones, such as Omer (7500 inhabitants), have still refused to corporatise their water and sewage services, and many more refused to join a regional corporation. Hence, 158 municipalities provide water and sewage services through 56 corporations, 27 of which are owned by a single municipality, despite the incentives to join regional corporations, 13 include 2 or 3 municipalities and 16 include 4 municipalities or more (State Comptroller 2020c).

Whereas total expenditures of municipal companies and non-profits have been higher than their revenues (State Comptroller 2017), the total figures for water and sewage corporations showed a surplus (State Comptroller 2020c). Municipalities have pressed to relax restrictions on collecting dividends from water and sewage corporations, also fearing that accumulating surpluses beyond needed investments would be eventually seized by the state. In 2011 such dividends to local authorities were granted a tax break for five years. A few cities collected substantial dividends from their water and sewage corporations between 2010 and 2018, particularly Rishon LeZion, Netanya and Eilat (Koren 2019), but dividends remained subject to the approval of the Water Authority, based on specific criteria. The requirement for a regulatory approval reduced substantially the ability to divert funds to other municipal uses, but a problematic aspect identified by a 2019 Water Authority report was that dividends were backed in some cases by loans taken by the corporations, rather than by budget surpluses. In the case of the water corporation of Kiryat Gat, these loans were higher than the dividends allocated to the city in the years 2010–2018 (Koren 2019). The report called to reduce such leak of resources through the amalgamation/regionalisation of corporations. It should be noted that ordinary municipal companies rarely distribute dividends, even when profitable, because these dividends are taxed.

Corporatisation of municipal water and sewage services that first emerged as a local initiative (Ben Eliah 1998) was viewed by the Ministry of Finance in the 1990s and early 2000s as a first step towards partial or full privatisation of these services (Shapira Bar-Or 2009). Privatisation failed to materialise: its appeal faded with the accumulating experience of failed privatised water supply in Europe and mounting political opposition within Israel. Instead, the Ministry has opted to reduce the number of corporations from 56 to about 30 and eventually to only 11 regional ones, with the aim of eliminating small inefficient corporations and reducing the ability of municipalities to draw substantial dividends from unprofitable corporations. A 2013 legal amendment required all municipalities, except regional councils, to join regional corporations according to a map imposed by the Water Authority. This step encountered fierce opposition of sound municipalities, backed by the Federation of Local Authorities in Israel. Sound municipalities refused to cooperate with managerially and economically disadvantaged ones and consolidation failed to be implemented by 2021. Moreover, of the ten corporations that ended 2018 with financial loses, six were regional ones, indicating that regional corporations were not necessarily more efficient than single-municipality ones, although the losses of the former apparently reflected also the refusal of sound municipalities to join them (State Comptroller 2020c). A fundamental impact of the proposed regionalisation is further centralisation and nationalisation of water and sewage services, because municipalities may lose meaningful influence on large inter-municipal corporations that are strictly regulated by the central state.

4.5 Diverse Activities: A Flexible Arm with Project-Based Orientation

MOCs in Israel are typically single-purpose, established to perform an explicit task, sometimes to manage a particular project. Their activities can eventually expand and diversify but within predefined objectives set in their constitutional documents. These are more broadly defined in companies engaged in economic development or in urban infrastructure development, but even these companies usually engage in multiple projects within one field, because focused specialisation is the major rationale for corporatisation.

The dominant sector among municipal companies was infrastructure and economic development: 61% of all municipal companies in 2020 (Table 4.1). This included primarily economic development companies of municipalities of all sizes and companies engaged with infrastructure development. The latter have been characterised by the largest financial turnout, including Moriah—the largest of them all—acting as the infrastructure development arm of Jerusalem. Moriah is owned by the city but mainly carries out transportation projects (72% of the revenues in 2018) and other urban infrastructure projects funded by the central state. It also develops parks and educational facilities at the neighbourhood scale, having a total projected expenditure of 1.8 billion Shekels (more than US$0.5 billion) in 2020, and 2.2 billion Shekels (US$0.67 billion) in 2021 (70% funded by the Ministry of Transportation and the rest by the city, but most of it apparently originating at other central state ministries).

Additional, 12% of the companies engage in developing and managing business and industrial parks (Table 4.1), bringing the share of companies engaged in local development to nearly 75%. Most are owned by more than one municipality, established since 1992 to manage joint industrial parks, mainly in Israel's periphery. Two companies, jointly owned by a private sector company and a city (minority share), engage in high-technology parks. Additional companies engage in education, culture and sport, tourism and water and sewage. The 17 latter companies are owned by regional councils that have not been compelled to establish or join the differently regulated water and sewage corporations, whereas the 56 water and sewage corporations are subject to unique rules and regulations.

Three companies were specifically established to enable municipalities to issue bonds. They are unique companies in which the loyalty of the municipal representatives on the board is to the company, rather than to the municipality. One partnership of two regional councils and an agricultural-industrial association owned by kibbutzim in these regional councils engages in R & D.

In contrast to companies, the vast majority (84%) of municipal non-profits of both types engage in community centres and administrations, education, culture and sport (Table 4.1). In 93% of the community centres and administrations, the municipality holds only a minority position on the board (Tables 4.1 and 4.3). Most community centres are non-profit associations jointly owned by the Israel Association of Community Centres—a state-owned public benefit company—and the local authority.

Table 4.3 MOCs with majority municipal share (at least 50% municipal ownership) in Israel by type and field of activity, 2020

Field	*Companies*[a]	*Public benefit companies*	*Associations*	*Water and sewage corporations*
Infrastructure and economic development	139	1	2	0
Business and industrial parks	26	0	0	0
Community centres and administrations	0	0	10	0
Education, culture and sport	21	26	73	0
Welfare	4	0	30	0
Water and sewage	16	0	0	56
Tourism	7	1	5	0
Other	13	0	4	0
Total	226	28	124	56

Source: Data of the Ministry of Interior and the Water Authority

[a]Including one partnership

Each has a 40% representation on the board, the rest are outside directors (State Comptroller 2020a). Nearly all municipal public benefit companies engage in culture and sport. A substantial number of associations also engages in welfare.

An unusual municipal association of the city of Jerusalem—The Association for Urban Planning, Development and Conservation Jerusalem—is a statutory framework for Jerusalem's Transportation Masterplan Team that practically serves as a metropolitan transportation authority for planning and development, jointly operated by the municipality and the Ministry of Transportation; funded by the latter through the Association. The Masterplan Team manages the BOT contract signed between the Israeli government and the private concessionaire for the construction and operation of Jerusalem's light rail system, whereas the Moriah municipal company is in charge of the publicly funded (by the Ministry of Transportation) work.

Total expenditures were highest in infrastructure and economic development corporations (close to US$1.65 billion in 2017), followed by water and sewage corporations and education and culture. Community centres also had expenditures of about US$0.3 billion in 2017. Infrastructure development companies increasingly engaged in neighbourhood development and urban renewal in the late 2010s, implementing large-scale infrastructure projects funded by the central state in the context of umbrella agreements. According to these agreements, the state made a commitment for substantial investment in urban infrastructure and public facilities in return for a commitment of the municipality to support large-scale residential projects needed to alleviate the housing crisis.

MOCs are diverse in their size. Some, particularly in the largest cities, have expenditures of over US$100 million, whereas others are very limited in scope and may even be inactive, although the Ministry of Interior attempts not to count inactive corporations. In 2017, 7% of MOCs had annual expenditures of over US$28 million, 21% had expenditures of between 5.5 to 28 million, 38% had expenditures of 1.4 to 5.5 million and 34% had expenditures of less than US$1.4 million.

Setting up MOCs has largely been a privilege of municipalities with medium to high financial and managerial capacity, whereas disadvantaged ones, particularly Arab, and small municipalities, had limited ability to use this tool, except for having a share in community centres. Operation of economic development companies in small municipalities has been likely to produce deficits.

Several large cities—Tel Aviv, Haifa, Beer Sheva and recently also Rishon LeZion and Holon—have gained a reputation for experienced corporate governance. Tel Aviv has a long-operating Municipal Corporations Bureau, focusing on the implementation of proper norms of governance, coordination, promotion of the cause of the MOCs, and appointment of members of the boards and their training. Haifa and Ramat Gan also operate such bureaus. A few municipal companies have subsidiary companies, essential in cases such as the private-municipal company that develops and manages a prominent high-tech park in Haifa (Matam), owned jointly by the private company Gav-Yam (50.1%) and Haifa's municipal economic corporation (49.9%). The Ministry of Interior discourages such joint corporations and 'pyramids' of MOCs, because of the difficulty to regulate them.

4.5.1 MOCs and Inter-municipal Cooperation

MOCs serve as a tool of inter-municipal cooperation. The statutory form of inter-municipal cooperation—municipal unions—has failed to gain popularity, due to their bureaucratic inflexible nature and dependency on transfers from member municipalities (Heinelt et al. 2011). Instead, in the infrequent cases of bottom-up cooperation, municipalities opted to cooperate through jointly owned MOCs. Only five municipal associations had representatives of more than one municipality on their boards in 2020, none of the public benefit companies were jointly owned, but 23 companies were owned by more than one municipality; 18 of them engaged in developing and managing joint industrial parks. The first such company was a 1992 bottom-up initiative (ZHR—jointly owned by Zefat, Hazor, and Rosh Pinah), followed by many others (Razin 2016) and becoming the most substantial type of inter-municipal cooperation through MOCs. These joint companies, established as local initiatives, also involved the redistribution of property tax revenues, opting to moderate the drive for 'fiscal zoning' and municipal boundary conflicts over tax-generating businesses.

A 2006 amendment to the Municipal Ordinance, intended to reduce the burden of equalisation grants on the central state and to promote distributive justice, enabled the Minister of Interior to impose such cooperation and redistribution between adjacent municipalities. This step paradoxically led to a freeze on the establishment of such new joint corporations (Razin 2016). The Minister managed to execute these new powers for the first time only in 2014, and at a broader scale since late 2020, with a focus on redistribution of property taxes rather than on cooperation. Moreover, in the case of the flagship joint company YS Gat Ltd—where a large Intel semiconductor plant is located and property tax revenues are substantial—persisting pressures by the mayor of the city of Kiryat Gat, who perpetually disrupted payments to the neighbouring regional councils, led Minister of Interior Deri in 2020 to practically end meaningful inter-municipal cooperation by letting Kiryat Gat retain nearly all future property tax revenues of the industrial park. This was done only a few years after Minster of Interior Saar in 2014 imposed a revenue redistribution formula between Kiryat Gat and its neighbours in an attempt to end the decade-long conflict. The transformation of bottom-up inter-municipal cooperation through municipal companies into a top-down imposed tool aimed to serve distributional justice, and arguably political inclinations of central state ministers, demonstrates the limits of this mode in the Israeli context.

A newer mode of cooperation-termed regional clusters was also initiated through local initiative in 2009. It was adopted as state policy in 2012, encouraging the establishment of more regional clusters as a form of multifunctional voluntary regional cooperation (Arieli 2019). The regional clusters were established as joint municipal companies—the only multi-purpose MOCs in Israel. However, a 2016 legislation mandated their transformation into more bureaucratic municipal unions, in order to enable the transfer of statutory municipal powers from the municipalities to the regional clusters. Finally, 29 of the 56 water and sewage corporations are owned by more than one municipality, being at the centralised top-down end of the spectrum; i.e. cooperation imposed by the central state.

4.5.2 Public-Private Partnerships and Municipal Companies

Municipal companies usually serve as the municipal arm in public-private partnerships (PPP). These include primarily Build-Operate-Transfer (BOT) contracts to finance, build, operate, and maintain public infrastructure, and a few joint municipal-private corporations, and projects that leverage municipally owned land to promote local development (Razin et al. 2020). Regulatory hurdles restrict the engagement of municipalities in PPP. BOT contracts are subject to several layers of regulatory approvals that increase the burden of transaction costs, particularly because municipal projects are rather small. BOT contracts lost appeal in the 2010s, particularly among fiscally sound cities and water and sewage MOCs, not because of an ideological rejection, but largely due to low interest rates that eliminated their financial motive. However, the post-2020 Covid-19 pandemic realities of escalating public deficits could lead municipalities to resort to BOT as a local development tool at a much greater scale than in the 2010s.

The Ministry of Interior discourages the establishment of new corporations jointly owned by municipalities and private or third sector entities. The law permits such corporations, but the Ministry discourages their establishment and categorically does not approve corporations in which the municipality holds a minority share, because of its own inability to regulate them. This negative attitude stems from the fear of bankruptcy of the private partner, in which case debts would be rolled on to the deep pocket of the municipality, who, albeit not necessarily responsible for the deficit, cannot simply vanish. The Ministry is also ill at ease with the loyalty of municipal representatives on the board to the joint company rather than to the municipality. Conversely, representatives of Israel's Urban Corporations Association emphasise the need to ease restrictions on the establishment of municipal-private corporations for tasks such as cultural enterprises or student dormitories, in which they partake in control and management and do not cede their powers and flexibility for many years to a BOT concessionaire (Razin et al. 2020).

Finally, PPPs in the form of leveraging municipal land for private investment beneficial for the local economy proliferated in the 1990s (Hasson and Hazan 1997). The urban development company has been usually responsible for the tender and subsequent work with the private developer on behalf of the municipality, such as in the case of the Ashkelon marina in the 1990s. The significance of this form of PPP was modest in scale in the 2010s, largely consisting of a public facility, such as a new city hall, and commercial uses. The developer received municipal land at reduced or no cost, and the right to build and operate the commercial uses as a BOT project, in return for building the public facility. Such projects were administered by the urban development company, such as in the case of Umm al-Fahm in the 2010s (Razin et al. 2020).

4.5.3 *Urban Foundations: An Unregulated Corner?*

Urban development philanthropic foundations were established by mayors of several cities as non-profit associations. Best known are the Jerusalem Foundation, established by mayor Teddy Kollek in 1966, and the Tel Aviv

Foundation, established by Tel Aviv's mayor Shlomo Lahat in 1977. Other mayors followed, initiating the establishment of foundations to raise funds for urban development and social welfare projects. Whereas some foundations have functioned as MOCs, many opted to avoid being defined as MOCs, in order to enable their donors to utilise charity tax-breaks. While mayors were nearly always the founders of the foundations, municipal representatives have either been a minority on the board—with the mayor usually acting as the chair of the board—or a complete formal separation between the foundation and the municipality has been strictly adhered to, such as in the case of Jerusalem (State Comptroller 2010).

Regardless of the formal structure, close ties with the municipality have been the norm. Foundations performed functions for the municipalities, sometimes with municipal rather than philanthropic funds, practically steered by senior municipal leaders and officials. The Jerusalem Foundation served as a role model for a visionary initiative of a prominent mayor that had a major contribution to Jerusalem's development, active for decades beyond the long term of its founding mayor, and maintaining complete formal separation between the municipality and the foundation. Complaints on mismanagement proliferated in some other foundations that escaped the regulatory framework of the Ministry of Interior (State Comptroller 2010). Growing difficulties in collecting substantial donations from abroad have in any case led to the decline of some of these foundations in the 2010s.

4.6 Internal Structure and Autonomy: Over-regulation?

4.6.1 *The Management Hierarchy*

Governance of MOCs demonstrates growing regulatory requirements, beyond those that apply to non-governmental companies and associations. The municipal council acts as the general shareholders assembly of corporations fully owned by the municipality. It is responsible for appointing the board of directors, making changes in the constitutional documents, increasing share capital and distributing dividends.

Boards of directors of MOCs (termed governing boards in associations) determine the corporation's policy and decide on specific projects. The composition of boards fully owned by municipalities has been regulated only since 1996. Boards include between 6 and 15 members, one-third are elected council members, roughly representing the composition of parties in the council, one-third are senior municipal bureaucrats, such as the municipal treasurer, and one-third are outside directors. The bureaucrats and outside directors should have an appropriate representation of women and, since 2006, their appointment requires the approval of a committee at the Ministry of Interior, established in 2008—a procedure not always kept. The mayor, or in a few cases a deputy mayor or another council member, chairs the board.

The CEO and the chairman of the board (the mayor) are usually the prominent figures in municipal companies. The CEO is expected to implement the policies determined by the board of directors, and in practice usually works closely with the mayor who is likely to be more dominant than the board. The CEO is in charge of day-to-day operations: manpower management, tenders, and sub-contracting. According to the Companies Law, CEOs are appointed by the board. However, the Ministry of Interior published in 2004 a circular that requires public sector standards for these appointments in MOCs. A search committee should be appointed, composed of three members who represent the board of directors, the Ministry of Interior, and a CEO of another municipal corporation of similar size. The call for applicants should include relevant higher education and experience requirements and the chosen applicant has to be approved by a vote on the board. A final approval of the Ministry of Interior regulator is also required. In practice, the mayor usually has a major say in appointing the CEO, but the Ministry of Interior has the authority to block appointments that seem inappropriate. Before 2004, a call for a CEO position of an urban corporation could include minimal requirements, such as high school education and ten years of any managerial experience, but at present a higher education degree, usually a second degree, is required, in addition to relevant experience.

Salaries of CEOs of MOCs are regulated since 2003 by Ministry of Interior procedures that follow Ministry of Finance directives. Salaries are capped at between 65% and 90% of the salary of the municipality's general director, depending on the size of the corporation: expenditures and balance sheet. Salaries of deputy CEOs and other senior executives are defined as a proportion of the salary of the CEO. These salaries are reasonable, but not on par with those of senior executives at private sector companies; expectedly, local government representatives call for greater autonomy, such as in paying bonuses to senior executives for achieving pre-defined objectives. Salaries of senior employees are included in the annual report of salaries in public organisations, published by the Ministry of Finance.

Assuring the qualifications of thousands of persons who serve on the boards of MOCs is a challenge. In addition to the Ministry of Interior's committee in charge of scrutinizing outside directors on the board, the Municipal Corporations Association organises training for members of the board as well as for CEOs. Outside directors are unpaid and it has been argued that securing a financial reward for them is essential to assure their active participation.

4.6.2 *Internal and External Monitoring*

Internal monitoring of MOCs follows the requirements of the Companies Law and Associations Laws. Appointment of an internal auditor is not required, except for rare circumstances, and MOCs are only subject to auditing by the internal auditor of the municipality. Whereas the Urban Corporations Association calls for adding such a requirement, state agencies are not enthusiastic and the regulatory policy in recent decades has been to focus on external regulatory mechanisms.

The Ministry of Interior regards MOCs as less transparent than municipal departments, hence the steps undertaken since the 1980s and particularly in the late 1990s and early 2000s to equate regulatory measures imposed on these corporations to the ones in effect for municipalities. In particular, the Urban Corporations Department of the Ministry of Interior rejects, since its setup in 2008, the establishment of new corporations in which the municipality holds a minority share, except for community centres, which are nearly impossible to regulate through orders and circulars of the Ministry. These increasing regulatory burdens constrain the autonomy of MOCs and their ability to serve as a flexible municipal arm.

External regulation has been partial and weak in its early years. The 1980 order that required the approval of the Minister of Interior for the establishment of MOCs did not apply to corporations established prior to 1980. The Ministry of Interior even lacked a complete list of MOCs and a full stock of their financial reports. A rather reliable database was compiled by the Urban Corporations Department of the Ministry of Interior only in the 2010s.

A 2012 report of the State Comptroller revealed that the national Companies' Registrar did not seek the required approval of the Minister of Interior before registering new municipal companies—such coordination has apparently improved later on. The report also identified numerous breaches in appointments to boards of municipal companies:

nominations that were not submitted for approval of the appointments committee of the Ministry of Interior and boards that did not conform to the required size and composition.

A 2002 amendment to the Mandatory Tenders Law made tenders compulsory also for urban corporations. However, the Minister of Interior rejected the detailed regulations prepared by his legal councillor that required approval within 90 days, regarding them as too burdensome; hence, the tender requirement did not formally take effect. Consequently, the General Director of the Ministry published in 2004 a rule stating that approval for the establishment of new urban corporations would be contingent upon including tender requirements, based on the Municipal Ordinance, in their constitutional documents. Nevertheless, many existing corporations have not changed their constitutional documents accordingly, not rejecting the need for tenders, but refusing to be subject to regulations imposed on municipalities that are tighter than those imposed on state-owned corporations (State Comptroller 2012).

Among the more defiant corporations are those of Israel's capital and largest city—Jerusalem—particularly its largest corporation—Moriah—established in 1987. Projects implemented by Moriah are mainly funded by central state ministries—primarily the Ministry of Transportation—and the company claims the right to operate according to more lenient rules of central state-owned companies, supported by the legal fuzziness of the requirement to act according to the stricter Municipal Ordinance and Ministry of Interior regulations. For example, it claims the right to perform 'best and final' practices, that is, a second-round tender in which the top bidders are asked to improve their offers. The Ministry of Interior rejects this practice, fearing that it can be used to encourage a priori chosen bidders to improve their offer in order to win, but municipal companies see it as a vital tool to save costs. In addition to tenders, disputes between companies and the Ministry surround approvals required for manpower recruitment, salaries and required credit approvals.

Disagreements between the Ministry of Interior regulator and local government representatives over the rationale for approving joint municipal-private corporations have not been resolved. The Ministry rejects categorically the establishment of new corporations in which the municipality has minority shares or representation on the board and even proposes to compel municipalities to sell their shares in such corporations or to find a legal solution to conflicts of interest of municipal representatives on their boards. It aims to impose a minimal municipal share of 70%

in joint companies and 51% in non-profits, permitting a minority municipal share only when the central state has part ownership, which together with the municipality totals more than 50%, such as the case of community centres. Local governments oppose these rigid requirements that are not backed by legislation, arguing that private partners, who are expected to secure most of the financing for the project, would not compromise on minority shares.

There is no MOCs law, defining a unique corporate governance code, except for water and sewage corporations discussed earlier. The regulatory measures developed by the Ministry of Interior include reference to a broad spectrum of financial, labour, and organisational issues, largely aimed at binding MOCs to similar regulations imposed on municipalities. Contracts for a period of three years and more, loans and issuing bonds require the approvals of the Ministries of Interior and Finance. These requirements serve as a leverage to demand adherence to the Ministry's regulatory policy, such as making changes in the constitutional documents and to submit audited financial reports, in addition for business plans for projects to be funded by requested loans.

A reform in the regulation of MOCs had been negotiated in the late 2010s, opting for a MOCs law. It proposed a differential approach: categorisation of MOCs into three groups—sound, ordinary and 'under recovery'—based on financial and proper administration parameters. Such a distinction between sound and other municipalities was defined in a 2014 amendment to the Municipal Ordinance. Sound municipalities have been granted exemptions from various regulatory requirements of the Ministry of Interior, such as approvals for land transactions, contracts and various budgetary actions. The status of sound MOCs would be based on their performance rather than on that of the owning municipality, and they would be exempt from various approvals of the Ministry. The proposed reform addresses also corporate governance, human capital and additional aspects, but as of early 2021, consensus has not been achieved between the Ministry and local government representatives.

4.7 Conclusions

MOCs in Israel are indeed considered as long municipal organs for local development, acting at arm's length from the municipality. They expanded rapidly during the late twentieth century—a period characterised by unstable post-Fordism, economic globalisation and glocalisation that enhanced local entrepreneurialism. Their financial turnover has also substantially grown in the early twenty-first century, particularly that of infrastructure and economic development companies.

However, a simultaneous shift, from a regulatory vacuum to an extensive dual regulatory system based on both private and municipal laws, has occurred. The evolving regulatory framework covered most aspects of their functioning. These included their establishment, rejection of joint private-municipal corporations, composition of the board and loyalty of its members, constitutional documents, labour recruitment, including the CEO and salaries of senior employees, tenders, loans, public-private partnerships and even tax revenue redistribution of MOCs owned by several municipalities that engage in managing industrial parks.

Hence, MOCs faced the contradictory logic of being committed to the interests of the corporation versus the overriding commitment to the municipality, and the contradiction between the aim to serve as a flexible project-oriented municipal arm and the aim to avoid using these corporations as regulatory bypasses by making corporations subject to the full range of regulations that apply to municipalities. Corporatisation of water and sewage services has been explicitly intended to constrain local autonomy and semi-nationalise the service. These tensions are at the heart of the policy pursuit for a regulatory framework that balances the desire for local autonomy and the path-dependent centralisation embedded in Israeli politics.

Despite tightening regulation, MOCs are expected to become an increasingly essential municipal tool. MOCs engaged in culture and sports were hard hit by the 2020/21 Covid-19 pandemic: revenues dived while central state support was targeted at private sector corporations. However, inevitable public sector budget deficits and financing difficulties in the years following the Covid-19 crisis will make municipal companies crucial at least in two respects. First, public-private partnerships, in which municipal companies act as the municipal partner, will become increasingly essential because of expected public sector financing difficulties. Second, the development of income-generating municipal properties, to fill the gap caused by decreasing property tax revenues from retail, office and tourism-based uses, will also be performed by municipal companies.

References

Arieli, T. (2019). Intermunicipal cooperation and ethno-social disparity in peripheral regions. *Regional Studies, 53*, 183–194.

Beeri, I. (2020). Lack of reform in Israeli local government and its impact on modern developments in public management. *Public Management Review, 23*, 1423–1435.

Ben Eliah, N. (1998). *The privatization of water and sewage infrastructure, between local initiative and government policy.* Floersheimer Institute for Policy Studies. (Hebrew).

Hasson, S., & Hazan, A. (1997). *Municipal-private partnership: Opportunities and risks.* The Floersheimer Institute for Policy Studies. (Hebrew).

Heinelt, H., Razin, E., & Zimmerman, K. (2011). *Metropolitan governance, different paths in contrasting contexts: Germany and Israel.* Campus.

Idea – Economic management and consulting. (2004). *A study of urban corporations.* Ministry of Interior. (Hebrew).

Koren, O. (2019, April 2). Municipalities milked 760 million Shekels from the water bills at the expense of the residents. *TheMarker Haaretz.* (Hebrew).

Marin, P., Tal, S., Yeres, J., & Ringskog, K. (2017). *Water management in Israel.* World Bank Group.

Megama. (1990). *Municipal corporations survey.* Submitted to the Ministry of Interior. Megama. (Hebrew).

OECD. (2020). Reducing socio-economic differences between municipalities. In *OECD economic surveys Israel* (pp. 71-107). Paris: OECD.

Razin, E. (1990). Urban economic development in a period of local initiative: Competition among towns in Israel's southern coastal plain. *Urban Studies, 27*, 685–703.

Razin, E. (2004). Needs and impediments for local government reform: Lessons from Israel. *Journal of Urban Affairs, 26*, 67–109.

Razin, E. (2016). Inter-municipal cooperation in the development of industrial parks and tax redistribution: The road to hell is paved with good intentions. *Quaestiones Geographicae, 35*(2), 83–90.

Razin, E., Hazan, A., & Elron, O. (2020). The rise and fall (?) of public-private partnerships in Israel's local government. *Local Government Studies.* https://doi.org/10.1080/03003930.2020.1832892

Shapira Bar-Or, E. (2009). Privatizing Israel's water-supply services: On the route of total privatization. *Hukim, A*, 319–348. (Hebrew).

State Comptroller. (2010). Activities of foundations beside local authorities. In *Reports on Local Government Auditing 2009* (pp. 453–503). Jerusalem. (Hebrew)

State Comptroller. (2012). Regulation and supervision of urban corporations in local government. In *Reports on Local Government Auditing 2012* (pp. 325–410). Jerusalem. (Hebrew)

State Comptroller. (2017). Board of directors of municipal corporations. In *Reports on Local Government Auditing 2017* (pp. 3–72). Jerusalem. (Hebrew)

State Comptroller. (2020a). Activities of local authorities through community centres. In *Reports on Local Government Auditing 2020* (pp. 325–410). Jerusalem. (Hebrew)

State Comptroller. (2020b). Activities of local authorities through urban associations. In *Reports on Local Government Auditing 2020* (pp. 411–473). Jerusalem. (Hebrew)

State Comptroller. (2020c). Water and sewage corporations – regulation, management and supervision. In *Annual Report 71a* (pp. 1391–1501). Jerusalem. (Hebrew)

Tevet, E., & Talit, G. (2021). Regulation of water and sewage corporations: Impact on prices and services. In E. Tevet, V. Shiffer, & I. Galnoor (Eds.), *Regulation in Israel: Values, effectiveness, methods* (pp. 77–94). Palgrave Macmillan.

PART II

Central East European Countries

CHAPTER 5

Municipally Owned Corporations in Hungary

György Hajnal and Bence Kucsera

5.1 Introduction

Practically, the historical epoch that ended in 1989/1990 was characterised by an exclusive reliance on state-owned corporations in every sector of the economy. The private sector only accounted for 10% of GDP in 1980, increasing to 24% in 1990 (Árvay & Vértes, 1994/2006, p. 219), effectively rendering the concept of government/state-owned companies redundant and obsolete. Although less than some other communist countries, Hungary allowed a larger-than-typical share of the private sector in its economy, with over 80% being under state ownership. Most of these corporate assets were controlled by the central government, usually

G. Hajnal (✉) • B. Kucsera
Institute of Economic and Public Policy, Corvinus University of Budapest, Budapest, Hungary
e-mail: gyorgy.hajnal@uni-corvinus.hu; bence.kucsera@stud.uni-corvinus.hu

M. Van Genugten et al. (eds.), *Corporatisation in Local Government*, https://doi.org/10.1007/978-3-031-09982-3_5

sectoral ministries and their agencies. However, some companies were established and run by territorial or local organs of the state (the so-called councils), which can be regarded as the historical antecedents of the current municipally owned corporations (hereinafter: MOCs[1]). A noteworthy difference was that many communist-era companies (including state- and council-owned) would clearly be classified as private in a market economy, producing goods (services) such as repairing household equipment or offering mover services.

The systemic change that occurred between 1989 and 1990 involved a radical downscaling of the pre-existing stock of state-owned (including council-owned) corporations. This partly happened through privatising all (or part) of these corporations using various mechanisms, and partly by liquidating them as economically unsustainable (Mihályi, 1996). By the mid-1990s, this resulted in a governmental share of corporations that was comparable with most European countries (Engerer, 2001, p. 255). Spectacularly and somewhat controversially, the enterprises owned by central government, which represented modern and prospective instruments of governance, featured only marginally among the research agendas of relevant disciplines in Hungary. This is even more characteristic for MOCs, which have been somewhat omitted as self-contained research focus areas over the past decades. The few exceptions to this phenomenon predominantly focused on the legal aspects of the problem field, as highlighted by Auer et al. (2018) and Lehoczki (2019). In addition, MOCs mainly appeared in studies that only focused on selected, individual sectors (typically, public utility). The current work represents the first comprehensive attempt to describe Hungary's MOC landscape from a longitudinal perspective, focusing on its role in local public service provision.

In the following sections, we first provide a brief overview of Hungary's local government, with a particular emphasis on the broad re-shaping of the field between 2010 and 2020. This is indispensable for contextualising and appreciating the transformation of the MOC sector. Then, we examine the role of MOCs in the service provisions of local government, followed by a discussion of the steering and governance arrangements of MOCs. The chapter concludes with a brief discussion of the results.

[1] Municipally owned enterprises/corporations are "[…] autonomous organisations owned by municipalities, used to produce or deliver local public services outside the local bureaucracy." (Voorn et al., 2017, p. 820).

It is important to note the non-existence of scholarly work describing Hungary's contemporary MOCs and the unavailability of systematic data and registries on MOCs. Prior to 2010, some national-level surveys of local self-governments could be carried out, which resulted in some important empirical data and analytical results regarding the role and operation of MOCs (see, e.g. Péteri, 2007). After 2010, such endeavours became largely unfeasible because central government agencies (or political actors) discouraged local self-governments from responding to surveys or from collaborating with researchers. This lack of information and evidence constitutes a major stumbling block for the current research, causing our observations regarding recent developments to be based on expert interviews and anecdotal evidence. We interviewed four senior experts as part of this research, each of whom had several decades of partly practitioner and partly research experience related to MOCs.[2]

5.2 Local Governments in Hungary

5.2.1 *The 'Heydays' of Local Autonomy (1990–2010)*

Hungary created its modern, democratic local government system at an early stage of its post-communist transformation. The 1990 Act on Local Self-Government established a credible and fully fledged local-territorial dimension of representative, democratic governance. The foundation of the new system was rooted in the reform ideas developed in relation to the Communist council system from the mid-1980s (Verebélyi, 1988). It was based on the principle that every local community (irrespective of size) has a fundamental right of self-governance, manifesting as an independent and elected local government.

As a consequence of the Act, the 1586 Soviet-type local councils transformed into autonomous local governmental units between 1990 and 1991. Another important feature of the Act was replacing the hierarchical chain of administrative and the political network of relationships among settlements and tiers of self-government. This spanned from Budapest and the county centres to the sub-regional level (until 1981) and each village, with legally guaranteed equal status of local and territorial (i.e. county)

[2] Our expert interviewees, indicatively of the sensitive nature of the topic, all wished to remain anonymous. We acknowledge their contribution and express our gratitude for their invaluable insights.

self-governments. Accordingly, the new framework abolished any hierarchical relationships between intermediary and municipal governments. Two types of local governments were legislated: municipal (first tier) governments having equal rights (albeit, with diverse functions) and county (second tier) governments with regional functions. The territory of Hungary constitutes an area of 93,030 km^2, which was divided into 19 counties and the metropolitan area of Budapest at the regional tier of self-governance, and 3047 local self-governments at the lowest (settlement level) of self-governance.

Measured according to international standards, the average size of basic local governmental units created in 1990 was quite small, which remains the case (see Table 5.1). If we consider the large extent of municipal autonomy and the wide spectrum of municipal tasks and responsibilities, the extent of decentralisation in the Hungarian local governmental system was extremely large. Moreover, the distribution of tasks and responsibilities among territorial and local self-governments was based purely on the spatial characteristics of public (including administrative) services provided. Thus, basic services (e.g. educational and medical) were assigned to local self-governments, whereas institutions providing higher-level services for a larger mass of users were administered by county (or Budapest) self-governments.

Table 5.1 Number of local self-government units by population size

Population size (citizens)	*Number of settlements*
0–199	429
200–499	715
500–999	664
1000–1999	604
2000–4999	475
5000–9999	124
10,000–19,999	86
20,000–49,999	43
50,000–99,999	25
100,000–	12
Total	3177

Source: Hungarian Central Statistical Office (2020)

Note: As of 1 January 2020 the capital city of Budapest has a population of 1.76 million and is recorded here as 23 district-level self-governments

Until its fundamental re-shaping between 2010 and 2020, the central problems of the new local government system resulted from the tension between its fragmented nature and the broad autonomies and tasks assigned to local self-governments. These problems were continually exacerbated by a long-term pattern of central government policy, which cumulatively undermined the financial sustainability of the (already over-burdened) local self-governments. Indeed, tax revenues and central government transfers continued to decrease throughout the 1990s and 2000s. From the mid-2000s, the central government made recurrent efforts to induce an extent of amalgamation (or cooperation between) local services. However, this initiative was not directed at the self-governments and only achieved limited success (Hegedűs & Péteri, 2015).

5.2.2 *Orbán Era Reforms and the Radical Cutting Back of Local Autonomy (2010–2020)*

The increasing tensions and rapidly growing debts of local self-governments were exacerbated by the economic and fiscal crisis from 2008 onwards, justifying extensive reform of the system. There was an idealist enthusiasm in the 1990s regarding markets and (in the context of municipal operations) corporate and privatised service provision. However, this enthusiasm had already waned by the second half of the 2000s due to the bitter experiences of the unfolding economic and fiscal crises.

This was the justification for the broad local government reforms used by the second Orbán government after its landslide victory in 2010. Importantly, this transformation took place in the context of an extensive wave of radical changes, which was explicitly acknowledged as 'illiberal' by the reformers themselves. The result was a transformation of the entire state machinery (including its constitutional foundations), which also manifested in the broader spheres of the economy and the state–society and state–economy relationships (Hajnal, 2021; Hajnal & Csengődi, 2014; on the local dimension see Hajnal & Rosta, 2019).

The process that resulted in the adoption of a new constitution in 2011 was indicative of the unconstrained nature of Hungary's transformation, which we do not intend to describe in detail here. After the inauguration of the second Orbán government in 2010, nine amendments to the old constitution and several amendments to the new one were instigated, almost immediately after its adoption. In many cases, these changes were triggered by the day-to-day political needs of the government. The institutions of checks and balances have been cumulatively weakened, such as the constant diluting of the powers of the Constitutional Court in response to their negative decisions on government policies. There has also been radical weakening of the role of such formally autonomous actors as parliamentary ombudsmen and the budgetary council.

Organisational structures were undergoing far-reaching centralisation, and in the ensuing tightly controlled top-down system, (almost) all issues became politicised. The process of politicisation was also explicitly enacted in the civil service legislation. This was partly achieved by eliminating some of its (already weak) merit-based elements and partly by making political/ideological loyalty a formal criterion of (continued) employment. Further, horizontal communication and accountability as well as consultative forums have been abolished (or reduced) to symbolic levels.

Central-local relations became radically rebalanced in favour of the central government. Whereas the fragmentation of local self-governments has not changed and the number of local units has remained constant (3178 local self-governments; see Hungarian Central Statistical Office, 2018), their de jure and de facto autonomy radically decreased. Key elements of this local governmental reform included a radical reduction of local self-governments task portfolio, including education, primary and secondary health care services, and a broad range of administrative tasks, which were all taken over by central authorities. Further, there was a parallel decrease in local self-governments' administrative apparatuses and financial resources. Accordingly, county self-governments were deprived of practically all of their earlier functions, such as secondary education, culture and health services. In summation, the weight of local self-governments reduced from its previous share (12%–13% of GDP) to approximately 8%, which was a characteristic of the 1990s and 2000s (Hegedűs & Péteri, 2015). Moreover, local self-government operations (e.g. financial autonomy) were subjected to very tight central governmental regulatory and control regimes.

The ongoing COVID-19 pandemic elicited additional pressures and political opportunities for further restricting local autonomy (Hajnal et al., 2021). Whereas some measures affected all municipalities, the most significant ones were selective and only impacted larger cities, including Budapest. Importantly, these municipalities became strongholds for opposition parties or independent civic organisations during the 2019 local governmental elections. The main tool employed to weaken them was the deprivation of important revenue sources. This included vehicle tax

(1%–5% of municipal revenue) and car parking fees (possibly 6% of revenue in city self-governments). Further, business taxes (constituting the most significant own-source revenue) were halved and earmarked. Furthermore, a number of local development projects (typically social) were cancelled, predominantly in opposition-led municipalities. Whereas some of the measures were allegedly temporary, others constituted permanent and institutionalised restrictions of local autonomy.

5.3 The Role of MOCs in Local Public Service Provision

5.3.1 Historical Preliminaries

As mentioned previously, the predecessors (pre-1990) of contemporary MOCs were the so-called council companies (*tanácsi vállalat*). These were transformed into legal entities compatible with the market economy in several stages as part of the process of transforming the entire production and service spheres of the country. This is broadly (and somewhat vaguely) referred to as privatisation, which began in the late 1980s. The successive stages could be characterised as spontaneous privatisation, mass privatisation, and revenue-oriented privatisation (Mészáros & Tátrai, 2009; also see Boóc, 2005).

When the new local government system was created, former councils, their agencies (including council companies) and other assets (such as state-owned real estate, forests, water, and monetary assets) fell into the hands of the newly formed local self-governments. Moreover, assets used for locally provided services were transferred to municipal ownership. Subsequently, local self-governments privatised companies by equalising shares to the value of land in the former state entities (Péteri, 2003). By the mid-1990s, local self-governments became legally entitled to create new budgetary organisations, corporate entities, and non-profit and other organisations to carry out tasks of local public interest. Moreover, they were entitled to exercise all ownership rights over these entities, such as nominating managers.

5.3.2 MOCs Between 2010 and 2020

To gain a fuller understanding of the role of MOCs, we briefly sketch the rapidly changing landscape of local governmental provision of public services between 2010 and 2020. According to the classification of Horváth (2019), local self-governments have four organisational options through which they can provide local public services: budgetary organisations; public benefit companies (these could be established only until 2006); corporate enterprises (limited liability or joint stock companies); and holding type corporate organisations (operating as umbrella companies owning other companies).

Our focus is the last two structural solutions, which fall into the conceptual category of MOCs. The population of MOCs underwent significant changes between 2010 and 2020, as a result of sweeping central governmental policy changes. In the following sections, we provide a short overview of these changes by describing how (and through what factors) the distribution of public service provision changed within the above fourfold classification.

Public budget organisations are predominantly used within human public services (e.g. schooling and health services) and are sometimes employed to conduct asset management tasks. Public benefit companies and corporate enterprises are typically used in physical, infrastructural services. For example, 86% of the water supply, 89% of communal waste, 95% of district heating, and nearly 100% of local public transport services were supplied by municipally owned corporate enterprises in 2006 (Péteri, 2007). Since the mid-2000s, public benefit companies have become increasingly criticised for the opacity of their finances (Horváth, 2019; Sárközy, 2006). Accordingly, new public benefit companies were, from 2006 on, not allowed to be established, and their proportion gradually diminished in favour of 'regular' MOCs.

The most significant (some would say shocking) policy affecting local self-governments' organisational landscape happened to the MOC sector. From 2010, a vast array of local and regional public utility services became subject to consecutive central government measures, eventually leading to municipalisation, mergers and eventual nationalisation (takeovers). This was conducted directly or indirectly by the central government (Hegedűs & Péteri, 2015). Whereas the re-municipalisation of public services (counteracting earlier trends of privatisation) had been a trend that was observable internationally in broadly varying contexts, this new nationalisation thrust is unique to the Hungarian governmental landscape (Horváth, 2016a). It is not our purpose to identify the intentions, conflicts and dynamics that resulted in this outcome, because the practical significance extended far beyond a mere organisational re-shuffling of public tasks. Here, it is sufficient to note the following: reversing the previous (socialist-liberal) governments' pro-privatisation policies (favouring financially powerful foreign [Western] public utility operators) and fighting their supposedly monopolistic pricing practices (and the resulting exploitation of Hungarian households) were key rhetorical, ideological and political messages of consecutive Orbán governments between 2010 and 2020 (cf. Horváth, 2016b; Horváth & Bartha, 2018; Horváth & Péteri, 2013, 2015).

According to the informed judgement of our interviewees, some of the regulatory and other policy changes, especially those involving the initial re-municipalisation and amalgamation of service providers, could be justified by technical and economic arguments to a certain extent. For example, the extensive fragmentation of the water supply sector resulted in deficiencies in economies of scale. Moreover, despite explicit legal prohibition, most of the water supply infrastructure was privatised between 1990 and 2010 (for more details of the transformation of the water sector, see Horváth, 2016c, 2018, 2019; Ungvári & Koskovics, 2011).

Private (mostly foreign) operators were aggressively removed from the water utility and other sectors, such as solid waste disposal. However, according to our interviewees, in this latter case the economies-of-scale argument was much less of a valid justification than for the water sector, since the spontaneous amalgamation of service providers had already started in the 2000s. Although local utility companies had been criticised for many reasons (such as the opacity of their accountability mechanisms), the newly and artificially (legislatively) created service regions sometimes resulted in a decrease in operational efficiency.

The re-municipalisation of the public utilities sector, meaning the creation of larger corporate entities that were solely (or majority owned) by municipalities, was only the first stage of the transformation. As part of the much broader move towards centralisation described previously, the central government then limited the ownership rights of the previously municipalised utility companies and centralised, in its hands, local regulatory powers (e.g. tariff setting).

The fourth type of local governmental agencies (holding type organisations) is mainly employed in larger cities, where they primarily operate public utility (water, sewage, and solid waste) companies. The holding company exercises the municipality's ownership rights and performs direct management tasks over these service companies, with the original structures only retaining their supervisory (not management) boards. Accordingly, the joint management board of the holding company is able to oversee the interconnections between the operations of member companies. The main motivation for creating holdings would appear to be a distancing of service operations from direct political oversight. The board of directors of holding companies oversees service operations and typically consists of technocrats (not politicians), enabling them to serve as a buffer. For example, the elaboration and approval of business plans is controlled by this board instead of being decided by local councils. Typically, local politicians are only members of these holding company supervisory boards, affording them somewhat limited influence.

With regard to voluntary municipal tasks, several are predominantly supplied through MOCs. These include cultural services (e.g. theatre operations and local broadcasting), servicing public areas, operating local markets, and controlling sporting facilities (cf. ÁSZ, 2019a, 2019b, 2019c). These MOCs can be non-profit or for-profit companies.

In summation, most of the impetus affecting the organisational facets of local self-governments' public service provision emanated from central government. These changes predominantly affected companies operating in the public utility sector, such as chimney sweeping, district heating, electricity, natural gas pipelines and sewage (in addition to those previously mentioned). Unfortunately, describing the trends of the past decade in terms of how the available organisational types featured in municipal service provision cannot be based on national-level data, because there are no relevant systematic data or information available. However, based on expert interviews, we were able to identify a few additional, typical patterns and factors that shaped local self-governments' organisational choices. These included the following:

- Public utilities run by MOCs are, especially in larger cities, increasingly organised into holdings.
- Other local services where user fees predominantly cover operational costs (e.g. thermal baths and sporting facilities) can be provided by enterprises, either municipally owned or privately owned and operating on a contracted-out basis.
- Public services where user charges do not fully cover operational costs can only be administered by enterprises when municipal tasks

are obligatory (e.g. local public transport). For non-obligatory municipal tasks (e.g. elderly care centres), the municipality does not have sufficient legal grounds for providing subsidies to its enterprise, meaning the MOC format is not usually applicable. Consequently, financially loss-making elective services are typically provided by public budget organisations.

- Public services requiring significant investment often induce local self-governments to invite private investors, implying a reliance on MOCs/corporate enterprises with mixed public and private ownership. Given the policy changes after 2010, this motivation only played a role between 2000 and 2010.

The portfolio of self-governments' tasks has reduced significantly compared to 1990–2010. Predominantly, this has occurred in public service areas that are typically supplied by public budget organisations, such as health, social care, and education. However, this trend has also manifested in the public utilities sector, having been characterised by MOCs prior to 2010. Here, the typical scenario was that centrally imposed price and service regulations (e.g. stricter procurement rules for non-publicly owned entities) rendered utilities operated by private (and subsequently, municipal) owners increasingly unsustainable in terms of economics. Municipal owners had to some extent been compensated through standardised general central governmental transfers. However, in the absence of such compensation, foreign private operators were increasingly forced to exit these sectors. With nationalisation and the reshuffling of service provisions, their roles were taken over by either government-friendly 'crony' business groups or publicly owned (politically controlled) operators that benefitted from central governmental support (Hegedűs & Péteri, 2015).

These trends manifested somewhat differently in the different subsectors of local public utility services. In the water utilities sector, Act CCIX of 2011 required operators to achieve a minimum operational size. Initially, this was 50,000, which was subsequently increased to 100,000 and 150,000 user equivalents in 2014 and 2016, respectively (Horváth & Péteri, 2013). This reduced the former market of more than 400 providers to 50 by the end of 2012 and 30 by 2016. In the solid waste sector, the original 100 waste management companies were reduced to approximately 60 companies by the mid-2010s. These became subcontractors, which were managed by 19 government-controlled regional waste management companies. The district heating sector was an exception to this general trend, as no such process took place in this area. In cities with a district heating network (n = 100–110), municipalities typically inaugurated their own MOCs to provide the service, which were occasionally under private market ownership (some of which were foreign).

As a result of the processes outlined earlier, the proportion of central to local public services provision changed from approximately 1:1 (characterising the 2000s) to approximately 4:1 in favour of the central government. Nevertheless, the similarly significant reduction of MOCs' weight in local government, characterised by an approximate 80% share in water, solid waste, and district heating sectors previous to 2010, cannot be assessed quantitatively based on available information.

The reports produced by the State Audit Office (ÁSZ) are the only source of quantitative information on MOCs (in particular, see ÁSZ, 2018, 2021). According to ÁSZ (2021, p. 7), there were 1440 MOCs in Hungary at the end of 2018. Further, a non-representative survey conducted by the State Audit Office (ÁSZ, 2018) revealed that more than 70% of MOCs belonged to the micro-enterprise category (featuring a balance sheet total of less than HUF 100 million (~270 thousand euros). Similarly, more than two-thirds of MOCs had less than 50 employees.

The weights of public service provisions in MOCs' functions are listed in Table 5.2. For comparative purposes, we provide similar data on government-owned enterprises.

Table 5.2 Distribution of state and municipally owned corporations by public service provision

	State-owned corporations		*Municipally owned corporations*	
	Number	*Proportion*	*Number*	*Proportion*
Corporations without public service provision	165	63%	158	32%
Corporations with exclusively public service provision	10	4%	44	9%
Corporations with public service provision and tasks that do not qualify as a public service provision	85	33%	290	59%
Σ[a]	260	100%	492	100%

Source: ÁSZ (2018, p. 9)

[a] $n = 752$

5.4 The Governance of MOCs

Existing literature on the internal operation and autonomy of Hungarian municipal companies is scarce, mostly focusing on legal regulations. However, actual practices do not strictly follow regulations, as suggested by our expert interviews. Legal regulations only allow self-governments to own corporate entities having limited liability, which reduces the available legal-organisational formats to limited liability and joint stock companies.

5.4.1 Municipal Oversight

Formally and practically, the ownership rights of local self-governments are exercised by the elected municipal councils, which are, generally, the main decision-making bodies of MOCs. Their functions incorporate the following (see ÁSZ, 2021; Lehoczki, 2019):

- Approving the business plans and accounts of companies
- Determining the qualitative and quantitative parameters of the service to be provided (typically, through a municipal decree)
- Approving and amending the articles of association
- Appointing members of the board of directors and supervisory board
- Exercising employer rights over these entities and approving their rules of procedure
- Appointing (typically) executive directors (administrative heads) and their deputies

The rules pertaining to the exercise of ownership rights are defined by municipal councils in their rules of procedure. Key strategic decisions are typically exercised by the council as such. However, certain decisions—such as nominating top managers, or approving the yearly business plan—are frequently delegated to the mayor or, possibly, to a council sub-committee. In the case of holding type arrangements, however, the ownership rights over individual MOCs overseen by the holding entity are exercised by the holding (and not the municipal council). In such cases municipal oversight works indirectly, by controlling the operation of the holding company.

In MOCs' founding documents, municipal councils determine the public tasks to be performed by municipally owned companies and any requirements pertaining to the performance of such tasks. There are no special legal regulations with regard to the creation of MOCs. Accordingly, local self-governments create MOCs within the general frameworks regulating the financial and structural aspects of their operation, which is at their own discretion.

5.4.2 *The Autonomy and Board Structure of MOCs*

In privately owned enterprises, the establishment of a supervisory board is compulsory for certain, but not all, companies. By comparison, supervisory boards—structurally separated from the operative management of companies—are mandatory for all MOCs (Lehoczki, 2019, p. 119). Further, the supervisory board is the ex-ante control body of the MOCs, with the special task of commenting on annual MOC reports. These are, in turn, approved by the municipal council.

The structural features of the operative management of MOCs depend on the legal format and size of the corporation. Moreover, MOCs operating as limited companies may be overseen by one or more chief executives. In some cases, a unified management body performs the statutory tasks of operative management and those of the supervisory board. These are created instead of having separate supervisory boards and boards of directors. Similarly, MOCs limited by shares are typically overseen by a single chief executive. However, it is possible to establish a board of directors, especially for larger MOCs (Lehoczki, 2019, p. 118). The board of directors has direct responsibility for overseeing the company's operations and defines its rules of procedure autonomously. However, it should be noted that Hungarian legal regulations and corporate practice do not include an overarching concept of the board of directors that applies to all organisation types and contexts. Therefore, we use the term more generally when referring to collective entities overseeing and directing MOC operations, rather than in a strictly legal sense.

Companies enjoy a significant extent of formal autonomy regarding strategic and (to a variable but significant extent) routine operations. However, owners have crucial de facto influence through both council and municipality executives. According to our interview evidence, the internal management procedures of MOCs adhere to the following guidelines (especially in larger localities).

As noted previously, the municipal council has the final say in the operation of MOCs from a legal perspective. However, the board of directors and supervisory board frequently make operational decisions during informal consultations with each other, and their decisions are typically accepted by municipal councils. According to our key informants, the municipal council (and mayor) rarely exert direct influence on specific operational decisions.

Typically, boards of directors and supervisory boards convene once a month. Agendas are prepared by the company's operative management, including items such as business plans, reports, contractual tasks, and planned or actual investments. Although supervisory boards bear no direct responsibility (or tangible decision competences) over corporate operations, they can request reports from operational management and formulate proposals for the owner. However, in some rare cases, it is not possible to refer an item to the board of directors without preliminary approval of the supervisory board. Moreover, supervisory boards have the right to convene general meetings of the public limited company when a serious violation threatens operative management. Thus, despite the lack of hard decision competences, the supervisory board's concerns are typically taken seriously by the board of directors. When there is a disagreement, the heads of the two boards frequently attempt to reach an informal agreement. The task of operative management (consisting of the executive(s) of the company) is to ensure the company's operations in terms of economics and efficiency. This echoes a general municipal requirement for companies to be managed in such a way that they do not make a loss.

Formally, MOCs' operative management makes decisions autonomously with respect to employment issues (e.g. hiring, redundancies and promoting personnel). Regarding company finances, major decisions (e.g. arranging and repaying significant loans) should be planned and justified in advance and approved by the owner. Similarly, the approval of corporate investments (with some variations and to a certain amount) resides under the operational management's decision competencies. More significant investments usually require the owner's approval, as do applications for EU funding. Finally, matters pertaining to internal organisation are regulated by the MOC's internal rules of procedure, which can only be modified with owner approval.

5.5 Concluding Remarks

In these pages, we attempted to explore the changing landscape of Hungary's municipally owned corporations in the broader context of local self-governance and local public service provision. Until now, systematic scholarly work on MOCs has been scarce and has focused on other aspects, such as applicable legal regulations or municipal agencies operating in the local utilities sector. Thus, MOCs have not featured as a stand-alone topic in Hungarian research agendas.

The lack of publicly available data at local/regional and national levels renders systematic quantitative descriptions unfeasible. Based on available evidence, it would appear that the past decade of rapid transformation of the local government arena has progressively weakened local autonomies and local institutions, augmented by a parallel build-up of central political, administrative and financial governmental control. This has also had a serious impact on the MOC sector, particularly regarding their role in the local utilities sector, which has diminished significantly compared to the early 2010s. However, it would appear that the overall weight of MOCs in local public service provision has not changed dramatically, as the presence of MOCs in other service areas has strengthened (to an extent).

Any such hypothesis regarding the impact of macro policy and institutional transformations on MOCs and on their role in local public service provision needs refining (and subsequently testing) based on systematic empirical evidence. This constitutes a central and prerequisite task for any further progress in this field of academic research.

Acknowledgement We thankfully acknowledge the comments and suggestions received from Petra Reszkető (Corvinus University of Budapest).

References

Auer, Á., Boros, A., & Szólik, E. (2018). *Az önkormányzati vagyongazdálkodás aktuális kérdései [Current issues of municipal asset management]*. Dialóg Campus Kiadó.

Árvay, J., & Vértes, A. (1994). A magángazdaság [The private sector]. In R. Andorka, T. Kolosi, & G. Vukovich (Eds.), *Társadalmi riport 1994* (pp. 218–247). TÁRKI.

ÁSZ. (2018). *Elemzés a köztulajdonú gazdasági társaságok 2017. évi integritási helyzetéről [Analysis of the integrity situation of publicly owned corporations in 2017]*. Állami Számvevőszék.

ÁSZ. (2019a). *Elemzés az önkormányzati tulajdonú, város- és piacüzemeltetési feladatokat ellátó gazdasági társaságok ellenőrzési tapasztalatairól [Analysis of the audit experience of municipally owned corporations performing urban and market management tasks]*. Állami Számvevőszék.

ÁSZ. (2019b). *Elemzés az önkormányzati tulajdonú, sporttal kapcsolatos feladatokat ellátó gazdasági társaságok ellenőrzési tapasztalatairól [Analysis of the audit experience of municipally owned corporations performing sports-related tasks]*. Állami Számvevőszék.

ÁSZ. (2019c). *Elemzés a kultúra és média területén tevékenykedő önkormányzati tulajdonú gazdasági társaságok ellenőrzési tapasztalatairól [Analysis of the audit experience of municipally owned corporations operating in the field of culture and media]*. Állami Számvevőszék.

ÁSZ. (2021). *A tulajdonosi joggyakorlási tevékenység megerősítése [Strengthening the exercise of ownership]*. Állami Számvevőszék.

Boóc, Á. (2005). A short review of the history of the Hungarian privatization. *Acta Juridica Hungarica, 46*(1), 115–236.

Engerer, H. (2001). *Privatization and its limits in Central and Eastern Europe. Property rights in transition*. Palgrave Macmillan.

Hajnal, G. (2021). Illiberal challenges to mainstream public management research: Hungary as an exemplary case. *Public Management Review, 23*(3), 317–325.

Hajnal, G., & Csengődi, S. (2014). When crisis hits superman: Change and stability of political control and politicization in Hungary. *Administrative Culture, 15*(1), 39–57.

Hajnal, G., & Rosta, M. (2019). A new doctrine in the making? Doctrinal foundations of sub-national governance reforms in Hungary (2010-2014). *Administration and Society, 51*(3), 404–430.

Hajnal, G., Jeziorska, I., & Kovács, É. M. (2021). Understanding drivers of illiberal entrenchment at critical junctures: Institutional responses to COVID-19 in Hungary and Poland. *International Review of Administrative Sciences, 87*(3), 612–630.

Hegedűs, J., & Péteri, G. (2015). Közszolgáltatási reformok és a helyi önkormányzatiság [Public services reforms and local self-governance]. *Szociológiai Szemle, 25*(2), 90–119.

Horváth, M. T. (2016a). A szépség és a szörnyeteg – közigazgatás és vállalat. [The beauty and the beast: Public administration and corporate enterprises]. *Állam- és Jogtudomány, 57*(1), 24–39.

Horváth, M. T. (2016b). A fáraó varázsol. A rezsicsökkentés beágyazottsága. [The pharaoh is charming. The embeddedness of the utility fee reduction]. *Politikatudományi Szemle, 25*(3), 135–146.

Horváth, M. T. (2016c). From municipalisation to centralism: Changes to local public services delivery in Hungary. In H. Wollmann, I. Kopric, & M. Gérard (Eds.), *Public and social services in Europe. From public and municipal to private sector provision* (pp. 185–199). Palgrave Macmillan.

Horváth, M. T. (2018). Evaluation of anti-monopoly programme in Hungarian public utilities. In I. Kopric, W. Hellmut, & M. Gérard (Eds.), *Evaluating reforms of local public and social services in Europe. More evidence for better results* (pp. 279–296). Palgrave Macmillan.

Horváth, M. T. (2019). Állami vállalattulajdonlás piacgazdaságokban [State ownership of corporations in market economies]. In V. Szikora (Ed.), *Állami vállalatok nemzetközi összehasonlításban* (pp. 459–485). Magyar Közlöny Lap- és Könyvkiadó.

Horváth, M. T., & Bartha, I. (2018). EU-compatible state measures and member states interests in public services: Lessons from the case of Hungary. *International Public Administration Review, 16*, 137–159.

Horváth, M. T., & Péteri, G. (2013). Nem folyik az többé vissza. Az állam szerepének átalakulása a vízközmű-szolgáltatásban. [It is not going to flow back. The changing role of the state in the water utility services]. In P. Valentiny, F. L. Kiss, & C. I. Nagy (Eds.), *Verseny és szabályozás* (pp. 177–189). MTA KRTK Közgazdaság-tudományi Intézet.

Hungarian Central Statistical Office. (2020). *8.1.2.8. A települések száma és népessége népességnagyság kategóriák szerint, 2020. január 1. [8.1.2.8. Number and population of settlements by population size categories, 1 January 2020]*. Accessed September 21, 2021, from https://www.ksh.hu/stadat_files/fol/hu/fol0013.html

Hungarian Central Statistical Office. (2018). *Magyarország Közigazgatási Helynévkönyve 2018. január 1. [Gazetteer of Hungary 1 January 2018]*. Központi Statisztikai Hivatal.

Lehoczki, Z. Z. (2019). Az önkormányzati tulajdonban lévő gazdasági társaságok jellegzetességei [The main characteristics of companies owned by local governments]. *Pro Publico Bono – Magyar Közigazgatás, 3*, 112–129.

Mészáros, T., & Tátrai, M. (2009). A privatizáció 20 éve Magyarországon [Twenty years of privatisation in Hungary]. In P. Sánor, A. Stumpf, & L. Vass (Eds.), *Magyarország politikai évhuszadkönyve: Kormányzati rendszer a parlamenti demokráciában 1988-2008 (n.p.)*. Demokrácia Kutatások Magyar Központja Közhasznú Alapítvány.

Mihályi, P. (1996). Privatisation in Hungary: Now comes the "hard core". *Communist Economics & Economic Transformation, 8*(2), 205–216.

Péteri, G. (2003). *From usage to ownership: Transfer of local government property in Central Europe*. Central European University Press.

Péteri, G. (2007). Nagyobb felelősség, átalakuló feladatok, új szerepek. Helyi közszolgáltatások és döntéshozatal változása a polgármesterek véleménye alapján (1991–2006) [Greater responsibilities, transforming functions, new roles. Changes in local service provision and in decision making, according to the mayors (1991-2006)]. In M. T. Horváth (Ed.), *Piacok a főtéren. Helyi kormányzás és szolgáltatásszervezés* (pp. 19–68). Budapest.

Sárközy, T. (2006). *Államszervezetünk potenciazavarai. A betegség okai, a beteg állapota, a gyógyulás útjai. [Potency disorders of the state machinery. Causes of the disease, the status of the patient, possible therapies]*. HVG-ORAC.

Ungvári, G., & Koskovics, É. (2011). Áttekintés a magyar víziközmű-ágazatról. [An overview of the water utilities sector]. In P. Valentiny, F. L. Kiss, & C. I. Nagy (Eds.), *Verseny és szabályozás* (pp. 305–328). MTA KRTK Közgazdaság-tudományi Intézet.

Verebélyi, I. (1988). Korszerűsítés – önkormányzati reform. [Modernisation – local government reform]. In A. Bőhm (Ed.), *Lehet-e a közélet a lakóhelyen? A helyi társadalom önkormányzati esélyei* (pp. 41–63). Kossuth Könyvkiadó.

Voorn, B., Van Genugten, M. L., & Van Thiel, S. (2017). The efficiency and effectiveness of municipally-owned corporations: A systematic review. *Local Government Studies, 43*(5), 820–841.

CHAPTER 6

Municipally Owned Corporations in Poland: Delivery of Local Public Services

Julita Łukomska, Paweł Swianiewicz, Katarzyna Szmigiel-Rawska, Marta Lackowska, and Joanna Krukowska

6.1 Introduction

Recent years have brought an increasing number of municipally owned corporations (MOCs) created in Poland. In the 1990s they were established mainly by medium-sized and big cities, but recently the trend has involved also smaller municipalities. On average, there is 1.1 MOC per municipality in Poland (approximately 2800 private-law based MOCs in total in 2020). In big cities there are mainly single-purpose MOCs, whereas multi-purpose MOCs are more often created by small municipalities.

J. Łukomska (✉) • K. Szmigiel-Rawska • M. Lackowska • J. Krukowska
Department of Local Development and Policy, Faculty of Geography and Regional Studies, University of Warsaw, Warsaw, Poland
e-mail: j.lukomska@uw.edu.pl; k.szmigiel@uw.edu.pl; m.lackowska@uw.edu.pl; jkrukowska@uw.edu.pl

P. Swianiewicz
Section of Social and Economic Studies, Institute of Spatial Management, Wrocław University of Environmental and Life Sciences, Wroclaw, Poland
e-mail: pawel.swianiewicz@upwr.edu.pl

M. Van Genugten et al. (eds.), *Corporatisation in Local Government*, https://doi.org/10.1007/978-3-031-09982-3_6

MOCs have a two-tier structure regardless of service type: an executive board and a supervisory board (whose members are appointed by the owner). Most Polish MOCs operate in technical services sectors, while there are very few in social and culture services. The majority of MOCs are companies with 100% municipal ownership. The MOCs dependency from the municipal executive is significant and still growing due to the direction of legal changes in Poland. Even if MOCs operate under private law and are relatively independent of the owner in their day-to-day operations, since executive directors can be dismissed by the supervisory board at any time, in practice we observe his/her dependence on the mayor.

In this chapter, we follow the definition of MOCs adopted in this book, describing them as structurally separated from their owner municipalit(y/ies) and with independent corporate status, managed by an executive board appointed primarily by the municipal owners, and with majority public ownership (Voorn et al., 2017). In Poland, there is no detailed specific register or database on MOCs, so we have to use estimations based on various partial sources. That is why the chapter is based on several sources of empirical data. The essential five are as follows:

1. The databases build on information collected in the National Court Register in which data on Polish companies are gathered. Unfortunately, the data provided in this register is not complete. The Register is not precise and the large set analysis is difficult since the accessibility of data is low. Therefore, we complemented them with datasets collected empirically by research projects and other sources. In the case of the water and sewage sector and local transport, we supplemented the database by own desk-research. As a result, we managed to obtain 1760 MOCs in the database. This is not complete information, because we know from other sources (information on transformations and privatisation of municipal property provided by the Polish Ministry of Treasury, data based on Dolewka, 2017), that there were about 2700 MOCs in total in 2018. In this way, we have detailed information on approximately 65% of all Polish MOCs. We refer to this source as National Court Register 2018 and in case of MOCs in inter-municipal cooperation: National Court Register 2014 (see point 3).
2. A survey of Polish municipalities. The questionnaire was designed based on a pilot study consisting of in-depth interviews, and of a similar survey previously carried out in Portugal (Rodrigues et al.,

2012). About 2478 questionnaires were sent by traditional post and by email to every Polish municipality in 2018. The link to the computer-assisted questionnaire was also provided by email. The response rate was over 40% (1089) and it was representative of different Polish regions, different municipality sizes, and urban and rural areas.[1] We refer to this source as Survey 2018.

3. The inter-municipal companies' (IMCs) data was collected within a project on inter-municipal cooperation. The research involved financial data, National Court Register 2014, a survey conducted with inter-municipal companies (IMCs) in 2017 and information gathered during the interviews in 2017–2019. In this chapter, we also use materials collected in 2018 during interviews with the directors of executive boards in Polish MOCs as part of the 'Fees for Local Public Services—Financial and Political Importance' research project.[2] We refer to these two sources in the text as Interviews on MOCs.
4. Survey data on debt and investment expenditures collected over the years by the Polish local government magazine *Wspólnota*. Usually, the survey was sent to the largest Polish cities (cities with county status, $N = 66$); in some years the survey also covered medium-sized cities (capitals of counties, $N = 267$). The rate of return ranged from 52% (in the case of mid-sized cities) to 97% (in the case of cities with county status).
5. Data on the size of executive boards and supervisory boards of MOCs collected by students of the Faculty of Geography and Regional Studies at the University of Warsaw as part of field research. The study included MOCs in the biggest Polish cities that are regional capitals (there are 18 such cities) operating in the area of 5 sectors of communal services: water supply and sewage services, waste management, public transport, social housing, heating ($N = 110$). We refer to this source as Field Research 2020.

We begin our chapter with a presentation of the Polish local government system and the history of corporatisation in Poland. Then, we

[1] The questionnaire study was conducted under research project supported by the Polish National Science Centre, entitled 'Determinants of local public service provision model in the context of transaction costs economy, market characteristics and political costs' under grant agreement number UMO-2016/23/B/HS4/03148.

[2] The project was funded by the Polish National Science Centre, grant agreement number UMO-2015/19/B/HS4/02898.

discuss the legal framework, autonomy and management structures of private-law based MOCs. That section is followed by the description of the main characteristics and trends illustrating the role of MOCs in the delivery of selected local services in Poland. The next part of the chapter focuses on the ownership of MOCs and their role in inter-municipal cooperation. The conclusions and prospects for the future are given in the final section of the chapter.

6.2 Local Government System in Poland and the Origins of Municipal Corporatisation

The contemporary history of democratic sub-national governments in Poland goes back to the political turn-over of 1989/1990. The first post-communist government-initiated decentralisation reform granted a considerable amount of autonomy in service delivery management to almost 2500 municipal (*gmina*) governments (for details see Swianiewicz, 1992). A few years later, at the end of 1998, the territorial system of elected governments was supplemented by two new tiers: 315 counties (*powiat*) and 16 regions (*województwo*). The same 1998 reform has created the concept of cities of county status (*miasta na prawach powiatu*) which allowed the 66 largest cities' governments to combine functions allocated to municipal and county tiers.

In our chapter, we focus on the municipal tier. The main reason is that this is the tier responsible for a wide range of services, and its budget spending comprises ca. 75% of all sub-national public expenditures. The corporations owned by sub-national authorities operate on other tiers of sub-national governments as well (e.g. regional railway corporations owned by some of the regional governments or agencies aimed to promote regional development), but the scale of corporatisation is by far the highest on the municipal level. Municipal governments are responsible both for social services (nurseries, kindergartens and primary schools as well as a large part of social protection services) and technical services (water and sewage, waste management, street cleaning, central heating systems, local roads and streets, local public transport, parks and green areas) as well as land-use regulations. In addition, cities of county status are responsible for secondary schools, a wider range of social protection services, and maintenance of main roads going through their territory. The wide range of services provided and considerable autonomy in their organisation is reflected in the value of the Polish Local Autonomy Index, which belongs to the highest in Europe, after Switzerland and the Nordic countries (Ladner et al., 2019).

During the first years of decentralisation reform, local governments faced decisions on choosing the organisational form of service delivery. Possibilities or even incentives towards corporatisation through the establishment of MOCs were present already in the first years of the last decade of the twentieth century. Before 1990, municipal services were provided by budgetary units and enterprises operating based on public law. The 1990 Law implementing a new system of municipal government required local governments to decide on selecting a new form of service delivery. Available options included a transformation of old enterprises into budgetary units integrated with the local budget, various forms of privatisation or outsourcing of service provision or creation of the corporation (operating on the commercial law basis) which majority (usually 100%) of shares would be owned by the municipal government. In the absence of own experience of functioning within the frame of market economy, local politicians and bureaucrats were open to follow the advice of numerous foreign consultants working in Poland (as well as in other countries of Central and Eastern Europe) funded by the World Bank, or American and Western European agencies for international development. Those consultants together with a group of domestic experts were bringing ideas of New Public Management advocating for privatisation or corporatisation of municipal services (Aziewicz, 1994; Swianiewicz, 2007). They argued that the delivery of services by municipal companies would help to separate management from politics, making it more technocratic and effective. In the absence of home-grown experiences, this advice was often taken for granted by inexperienced local government officials. As a result, almost one-fourth of municipal entities responsible for service delivery were transformed into MOCs already by 1993, and in 1995, this proportion had grown to almost one third (Aziewicz, 1994, 1998; Swianiewicz, 1997).

After 1990, legal regulations obligated municipalities to choose a new legal-organisational form of providing services. There were two main options for the transformation of a state-owned enterprise: MOCs or units such as budgetary enterprises (see definition below) (Aziewicz, 1998). Currently, there are the following major possible forms of providing local services in Poland:

- In-house—when a service is organised and provided by local bureaucracy through one of the units of municipal office.
- In-house budgetary unit (*jednostka budżetowa*)—according to Polish legal rules, it is an organisational unit of the public finance sector without legal personality, which covers its expenses directly from the budget, and transfers the collected revenues to the account of respective revenues of the state budget or the budget of a local government unit. It operates based on the statute specifying, in particular, its name, seat and subject of activity, and the basis of financial management is the income and expenditure plan, known as the "financial plan of a budgetary unit" (Act on Public Finance, August 27, 2009, Journal of Laws of 2019, item 869, as amended).
- Budgetary enterprise (*zakład budżetowy*)—it does not have a legal personality that is separate from the local government, but it is financially semi-independent. It keeps revenues from the sale of services and may use them to finance current operations. Where its revenues do not cover the full cost of a service, it may receive a transfer (subsidy) from the local government budget, but according to the law, this subsidy cannot exceed 50% of annual operating costs. It is an organisation operating under the full control of local government and administrative law. The manager of the budgetary establishment is appointed and dismissed by the mayor (Act on Public Finance, August 27, 2009, Journal of Laws of 2019, item 869, as amended).
- MOCs including inter-municipal forms—it is a private-law based actor. It operates based on a company agreement or statute preceded by a relevant resolution of the municipal council. It is a separate legal entity, even if 100% owned by a single local government. It has assets separated from local government ownership and operates freely in the course of trade, bearing legal responsibility for it. It is financially self-dependent, that is, it finances its operation from its own revenues (mostly sell of services), it may apply for the bank credit, issue bonds, or apply for external funding, for example, by the EU funds.
- Contracting out (with a private agent or non-governmental organisation)—purchase of services based on contracts executed in line with public procurement law.
- Inter-municipal contract/agreement (*międzygminne porozumienie administracyjne*)—one local government agrees to provide a service on behalf of the other municipality, financial compensation is agreed

by provisions of the contract; the contract is executed in line with public law.

- Inter-municipal union (*związek komunalny*)[3]—special purpose and legal grounds association of two or more municipalities. It is a separate legal entity of the public law character for specified functions (one or more, but not for general purpose), which may be financed by contributions of member municipalities and by revenues from services.

There are also many cases of multi-layered service provision forms like an inter-municipal corporation co-owned by a MOC or by an inter-municipal union.

Data collected in the recent survey of mayors in over twenty European countries (Heinelt et al., 2018) demonstrate that the idea of marketisation of public service delivery brought by New Public Management is still very popular in Poland, much above the European median (Swianiewicz, 2017). Wide support for MOCs is a part of this trend, and the role of the corporations in the provision of local public services remains unchallenged.

6.3 Legal Framework and Autonomy of MOCs

Municipalities in Poland may establish limited liability companies (*spółki z ograniczoną odpowiedzialnością*) by drawing up a company agreement (*umowa spółki*) or joint-stock companies (*spółki akcyjne*)—the founding act takes the form of a company's statute (*statut spółki*).[4]

[3] According to the definition of MOC used throughout the book, we could consider inter-municipal union as a type of public-law based MOC. However, in this chapter we decided to focus on private-law (commercial code) based MOCs, which are most similar to private corporations operating on the market, so their corporate status is undoubtful. In addition, the importance of inter-municipal unions in the provision of services is marginal compared to private-law based MOCs. In 2020 there were only 142 active inter-municipal unions in Poland, which submitted their financial reports, their total expenditure amounted to PLN 2.6 billion, which is only 1% of total municipal budget spending. Unfortunately, current and complete data on the finances of private-law based MOCs are not available. From our incomplete data, covering just nearly half of MOCs, their turn-over in 2012 was already several times bigger than in case of inter-municipal unions, exceeding PLN 12 billion (National Court Register 2018).

[4] The vast majority of MOCs in Poland are a limited liability company. Establishing a joint-stock company requires significant financial outlays, and the process of its formation is more complex in comparison with a limited liability company. The share of joint-stock companies among MOCs in Poland has been around 10–15% in recent years (Dolewka, 2017).

There is no single legal act in Poland regulating the overall functioning of MOCs. The corporations operate based on private law, that is, the Act—Code of Commercial Companies. But the regulation of the principles of establishing, joining or operating MOCs is dispersed in many legal acts, such as the Municipal Economy Act and derivative laws, regulations on the principles of managing state property or shaping the remuneration of people managing certain corporations (i.e. State Treasury and local government corporations). Consequently, corporatisation in Poland is based on private law, but creation, liquidation and re-organisation of MOCs by municipalities is possible due to specific regulation in public law. It is worth noting that MOC's employees are not counted as public employees in official statistics.[5]

Since MOCs are separate legal entities, they are separate from the municipality VAT payer—they settle this by themselves. The debt of the municipal company does not count against the legally stipulated debt limit of the local governments. These two arguments are often the reasons for MOCs in Poland to be entrusted with the implementation of many municipal investments (unlike municipalities, MOCs have the possibility of VAT re-claims on the investment, and the incurred debt is not included in the municipal debt). Moreover, corporations do not undergo public procurement law, which was also often mentioned as a big procedural simplification when compared to municipal actions (Interviews on MOCs). MOCs can benefit from subsidies in the form of municipal contributions to share capital, tax reliefs, preferential loans, cancellation of tax receivables or donation of property (in this way, they function under more favourable terms than those offered on the market).

The MOCs in Poland operate in a two-tier system. They are managed by an executive board (*zarząd spółki*) and a supervisory board (*rada nadzorcza*). The owners are represented by a general assembly of stakeholders (*zgromadzenie wspólników*).[6]

The executive director manages the company and has no formal restrictions on labour and financial issues. However, he/she is indirectly dependent on the owner (general assembly, in the case of companies 100% owned by one municipality: the mayor) who appoints and dismisses

[5] For this reason, data on employment in MOCs is not available on country level in Poland.

[6] If no other source is indicated, the source of information on the described bodies of MOC is the Act – Code of Commercial Companies, September 15, 2000, Journal of Laws of 2020, item 1526, as amended.

members of the supervisory board. The owner can dismiss the executive director at any time even without giving a reason (Swianiewicz et al., 2019).

At the same time, this "absolute" power of a mayor (owner) often does not refer to the daily routines of a MOC. The legal construction of MOCs is quite far from day-to-day municipal affairs and local democratic procedures. The separation of the executive board from municipal councillors and the mayor creates a relatively high level of autonomy in everyday activities (Interviews on MOCs). Strategic decisions are made by the general assembly of stakeholders, but all current routine tasks are implemented by the board, with no need for consultations. This makes the management in the corporations smoother and quicker than in the bodies that undergo the rules of local bureaucracy. Comparing MOCs with other legal forms of service delivery beyond in-house available in Poland, the corporations reveal the highest number of features of market-based actions. On the other hand, respondents of the project on IMCs, who have experience in municipal and private companies, do notice that the first ones are less free, and slower in decision-making than the private ones (interviews on MOCs). This seems to be a good illustration of the character of MOCs, as entities stretched between municipal (public) and private law (both hard law and soft law).

In 2018, the change in law was passed, according to which mayors are not allowed to take place in supervisory boards of MOCs. Our respondents were critical about this decision, claiming that up till then, the supervisory board composed of mayors was a decisive, strong body, who cooperated very effectively with the boards. Mayors as members of the supervisory board had a clear democratic mandate. Now, accountability of the body seems much more limited. There is a possibility that new supervisory boards will only be able to "make notes for the mayors", not to negotiate and make decisions with the governing board (Interviews on MOCs).

The exclusive competence of the municipal council is to pass resolutions on municipal property matters, exceeding the scope of ordinary management, regarding 'the creation, liquidation and re-organisation of MOC' (Act on Local Government, March 8, 1990, Journal of Laws of 2020, item 713, as amended). The procedure is carried out based on the provisions of the Act—Code of Commercial Companies and the minimum deadlines indicated therein. The sale of the MOCs assets requires a resolution of the owners unless the articles of the company agreement provide otherwise.

The municipality approves the establishment of the MOC in a resolution of the municipal council, specifying its name and purpose. Detailed management goals (for the executive board) are determined by the general assembly of stakeholders and the supervisory board of the MOC, examples of management objectives are indicated in the central law (Act on the Principles of Shaping the Remuneration of Persons Managing Certain Companies, September 9, 2016, Journal of Laws of 2020, item 1907, as amended).

Given MOCs' relatively high organisational and financial independence from the municipality, it would seem that autonomy and freedom of the executive director are high in Poland. In practice, however, this is not the case due to the fact that his/her contract can be terminated at any time without cause by the supervisory board (appointed by the owner). In this way, the autonomy of MOCs is only apparent or illusory. Neither the mayor nor a councillor can sit on both the executive and supervisory board of MOCs. Supervisory board members are usually politically elected. Although they must meet certain requirements (e.g. state examination and relevant education), these functions are often held by former or current civil servants from the local administration. Most Polish municipalities do not establish any guidelines and procedures for monitoring the activities of MOCs. Ownership supervision is typically limited to formal activities consisting of appointing and dismissing members of the MOCs' bodies and approving annual activity reports. Only in the case of larger cities there are rules of supervision of MOCs introduced by the owner-city, which are not only formal but also substantive and economic-financial in nature. The municipal councils are most often not involved in the control of MOCs (although they are not forbidden to do so by law). It is usually the mayor (who is a member of the general assembly of stakeholders) or employees from the municipal office (designated by the mayor) who are responsible for the control and monitoring of MOCs. Polish MOCs (usually in bigger cities) have something like a 'corporate governance code', which is written in the company's by-laws. To have it is not imposed by the central law, so many MOCs (usually in smaller municipalities) do not have such regulations (Żabski, 2017).

6.4 The Bodies of MOCs

The executive board may consist of one or more members. The term of office by a member of the board may not exceed five years in the case of joint-stock companies or depends solely on the provisions of the company agreement in the case of limited liability companies. Since 2016, MOCs' executive board members have been employed based on the so-called management contract, that is, the corporation enters with them into management contracts.[7] The competencies and tasks of the executive board include managing the company's affairs and representing it in external matters, reporting, as well as communicating with the supervisory board and the owner of the company. A member of the board is appointed and dismissed (re-called) by a resolution of the supervisory board[8] but neither councillors nor the mayor may be a member of the executive board. A board member can be dismissed at any time. Legal regulations contain a mechanism forcing the determination of the amount of remuneration in a manner dependent on the current situation of the company, its size and the scale of the conducted activity. The total remuneration of an executive board member consists of a fixed part, which is the basic monthly salary,[9] and a changing part, which is supplementary remuneration for the company's financial year (this part may not exceed 50% of the basic salary of a member of the board in the previous financial year). The remuneration of members of the board is public, but it is not shared in the aggregate database. This information can be obtained by contacting the specific company directly.

In slightly more than half of the MOCs in the largest Polish cities, the executive board consists of only one member (executive director). In one-third of the corporations, the executive board is constituted by two members. In the remaining corporations, there are three to five members of the executive boards. Water supply and sewage corporations have the most numerous boards (over 70% of them have more than one member of the executive board), while the boards of corporations dealing with social housing and central heating are the least numerous (over 60% of them consist only of the executive director). Taking into consideration the

[7] Prior to 2016, they were employed based on an employment contract. The legislation applies to newly hired managers, thus it does not make it mandatory to transfer previously employed executives from full-time positions to management contracts.

[8] Unless the company's agreement or statute provide otherwise; in the case of corporations in which the municipality holds more than 50% of the share, the supervisory board has the exclusive competence to appoint and dismiss executive board members.

[9] It depends on the average monthly salary in the enterprise sector without the payment of bonuses from profit in the fourth quarter of the previous year (currently this value has been retained since 2016). This base amount is multiplied by a factor depending on the size of the company, its turnover and assets.

example of the water and sewage sector (we use this sector further in the text as an exemplar since these services are available in all Polish local governments in contrast to e.g. public transportation, and take up an important part of the municipal activity), we know that supervisory boards of MOCs operating in this sector consist of three to nine members (most often it is five members) (Field research 2020).

The supervisory board is an obligatory body, so Polish MOCs have mandatory two-tier boards. The term of office of a supervisory board member is three years. The board is composed of at least three members (in joint-stock companies that are listed on the stock exchange, the minimum number is five members). Supervisory board members are appointed by the general assembly of stakeholders (i.e. in the case of companies 100% owned by one municipality—directly by the mayor), but neither councillors nor the mayor may be elected to this position. Members of the supervisory board must have appropriate education or qualifications specified by law (including higher education and passing the relevant exam).[10] They may be dismissed by a stakeholders' resolution at any time. The supervisory board performs the main role of the constant supervisory and control body of the company's operations in all areas of its activity. It performs its supervisory functions by adopting relevant resolutions, expressing opinions and evaluations (a quorum is required to adopt resolutions). The main tasks and powers of the board include: appointing and dismissing members of the executive board, financial and HR matters, conclusion of contracts, resolutions of the executive board and the general assembly. The company's management board is obliged to provide the supervisory board with all necessary documents and information. Moreover, at the request of the board, it should prepare and present all materials and analyses within the time limit set by it and provide detailed (reliable and exhaustive) explanations in all matters related to the indicated area of the company's operations. Supervisory board members express their will by voting on relevant resolutions. The supervisory board should periodically assess the executive board and, if possible, advise on the management of

[10] Reports of the control bodies (the Supreme Audit Office) indicate, however, that in some cases the election of supervisory board members is discretionary, no qualification procedures are carried out, or persons who do not meet statutory requirements are appointed (NIK, 2016).

the company's affairs.[11] When announcing a competition for an executive board member, the supervisory board may formulate its own evaluation criteria over and above those provided for in commercial law.

In the corporations with full ownership by one local government, the function of the general assembly of stakeholders is performed by the executive body of the municipality (mayor),[12] while in the case of corporations in which a municipality holds more than 50% of the share, the exercise of ownership rights is carried out by the manner of representation indicated in the statute or the Act—Code of Commercial Companies. The general assembly delegates its representatives to the supervisory board and votes the draft resolution on the remuneration of the executive board members. The assembly is obliged to take steps to define, by resolution or in the company's statute/agreement, the requirements to be met by a candidate for a member of the executive board.

6.5 Role of MOCs in Service Delivery in Chosen Service Sectors: Basic Characteristics and Trends

6.5.1 Popularity and Trends

The number of private-law based MOCs in Poland has been stable at the beginning of the twenty-first century and accounted for around 2000. As Fig. 6.1 shows, we have been observing a clear increase in the number of these entities since 2010. At that time, the legislator significantly limited the scope of activities of budgetary enterprises—providing services in this form has been limited only to selected sectors. This resulted in the transformation of some of these entities into MOCs which significantly increased

[11] Currently, an intensive work is underway in Poland on the amendment to the Act – Code of Commercial Companies, precisely in terms of increasing the efficiency of supervisory boards (the regulations are to enter into force in 2021), whose activities so far have been assessed as not active enough. Municipalities do not develop clear rules for exercising corporate governance, including the method of conducting substantive economic-financial supervision over their companies, often limiting supervision to formal activities consisting in appointing and recalling members of company bodies and approving annual reports on activities (Chyb, 2015).

[12] Some municipalities (mainly larger ones) have units in their organisational structure that deal with ownership supervision over subordinate companies. In the case of rural municipalities, organisational units in the office are usually not created, but an employee responsible for supporting the mayor in exercising the rights of the company owner is appointed (Żabski, 2017).

the overall number of MOCs in Poland. Most of the new corporations have been limited liability companies. Establishing a joint-stock company requires significant financial resources, and the process of its formation is more complex than that of a limited liability company. This form is more appropriate for a large-scale operation. As a result, the number and share of joint-stock companies in the MOCs population are relatively low (share is approximately 14%). Often, local governments decide to establish these entities with the participation of third parties (Dolewka, 2017). However, this form was relatively popular after 2010, which increased the share of joint-stock companies in the MOCs population. In 2015, a decrease in the number of MOCs by 15% can be observed (probably related to changes in the waste management sector), since then the number of these units has been rather stable, with a slight upward trend (Fig. 6.1).

There are no central registers of service forms delivery in Poland. We use empirical data sources triangulation to estimate values describing the popularity of different forms among municipalities. According to the data regarding water supply and sewage as well as public transport obtained by a state-wide questionnaire (Survey 2018), the share of MOCs providing these services among other forms of service coordination is respectively

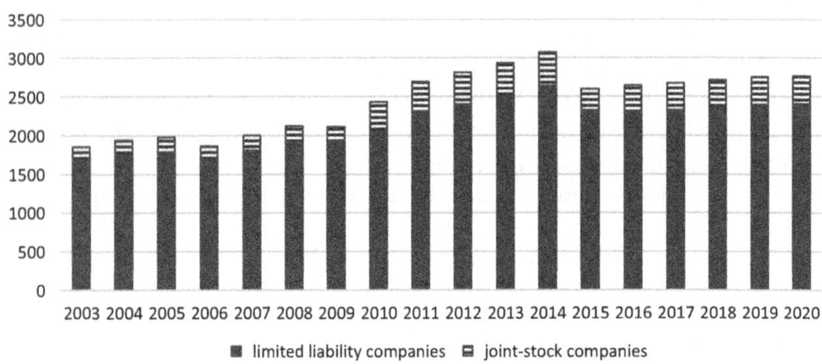

Fig. 6.1 Number of MOCs in Poland (Source: Polish Ministry of Treasury (Dolewka, 2017) and BNF (n.d.). Note: 2003–2015 data based on information on transformations and privatisation of municipal property provided by the Polish Ministry of Treasury (Dolewka, 2017); 2016–2020 data—own estimation based on data on newly established MOCs available on the website of BNF (n.d.), assuming that the average share of joint-stock companies remained at the average level from 2012 to 2015

35% and 13%. The same questionnaire study revealed that this form is not used at all in daily care services, which is a factor that indicates low usage of MOCs in social service delivery in Poland. At the same time, according to the statements of the representatives of Polish Waters (*Wody Polskie*)—the central regulator established only in 2018, mainly to control the price levels of water supply—the share of MOCs in the provision of water supply and sewage services is even greater and amounts to approximately 47% (Gniadkowski, 2018).

On average, there are several to over a dozen MOCs in each of the largest Polish cities. Provision of local services in the form of a MOC is therefore the most popular in large cities, which is also indicated by the data on the share of investments implemented by MOCs in total municipal investments (see Sect. 6.5.3). While there are usually two MOCs in smaller municipalities if this form of provision has been adopted, there is not any MOC in more than half of Polish municipal local governments (most often among the smaller ones) (National Court Register 2018).

Analysing only the data on MOCs in the water and sewage sector, we see that this form of provision is the most popular among mid-sized and large cities. By 2018, 99% of the cities with 50,000 or more inhabitants provided water and sewage services in the form of MOCs. In the group of municipalities with between 20,000 and 50,000 inhabitants, it was about 85%, but in smaller units (between 10,000 and 20,000 inhabitants) it was slightly over 40%; while in the smallest municipalities (less than 10,000 inhabitants) this percentage is below 20% (National Court Register 2018). The popularity of this form varies over time (Fig. 6.2). Increasingly, smaller municipalities decide to transform the existing form of providing water and sewage services (mainly budgetary units or budgetary enterprises) into MOCs, as indicated by the trend line in Fig. 6.2.

6.5.2 *The Most Affected Service Sectors*

A municipal company may be established to carry out public utility tasks whose purpose is the ongoing and continuous satisfaction of the collective needs of the local community through public services.[13]

[13] In Poland, it is also legal to establish municipal corporations dealing with banking, insurance, advisory, promotional, educational and publishing activities for the local government, as well as other corporations important for the development of the municipality, including sports clubs. Exceptionally, after meeting additional conditions required by the law, the municipality may establish municipal corporations of a commercial nature.

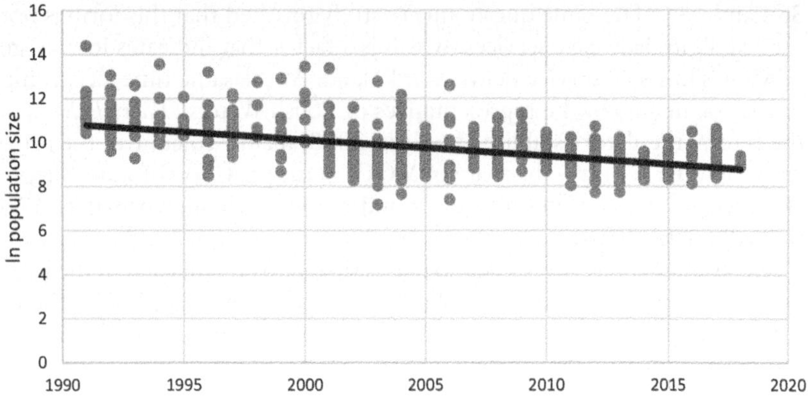

Fig. 6.2 The size of municipalities that formed MOCs in the water and sewage sector in 1990–2018 (Source: Own calculations based on data from the National Court Register (2018)). Note: Size of municipalities is measured by population after transformation with logarithmic function (N = 721)

MOCs are created by municipalities in Poland mainly to provide and organise local technical services. MOCs in Poland are present in water supply and sewage (over 46% of all MOCs), in housing (approximately 14–15%), waste management (over 10%), production and supply of electricity, gas, steam and hot water (over 10%), as well as public transport (approximately 6%), sport and tourism (approximately 5%), local economic development and promotion (about 2%) and health care (approximately 2%). The remaining corporations operate in the area of urban greenery, culture and education and others such as funeral services and animal shelters (National Court Register 2018).

MOCs operate in Poland as both single-purpose and multi-purpose organisations. The analysis of the available data allows us to conclude that at least 20% of them are multi-purpose corporations, most often in small and medium-sized municipalities. Most often also, one company combines the provision of water and sewage services and municipal waste management (approximately 75% of multi-purpose MOCs is related to the provision of these two local services). While multi-purpose MOCs are usually found in smaller towns, single-purpose MOCs most often operate in large cities.

6.5.3 Management and Finances

In terms of average employment, MOCs operating in the water and sewage, public transport, waste management and heating sectors are similar (approximately 60–70 employees per company on average), while companies operating in other sectors are slightly smaller (housing, approximately 30 employees per company; sports and tourism, 38; and green areas and road maintenance, 36) (National Court Register 2018).

Among the arguments in favour of providing services in the form of a MOC, the issue of more effective implementation of public investments is often raised (Gołaszewski, 2019). The survey data collected over the years by the local government magazine *Wspólnota* shows that investments expenditures carried out by MOCs constitute:

- 24%–25% of total expenditures allocated to investments by municipalities in big cities (cities with county status, mean for the years 2017–2019)
- 19% of total expenditures allocated to investments by municipalities in medium-sized cities (mean for the years 2014–2016)

We do not know what share of municipal investments is generated by MOCs in small towns and rural municipalities, but there is no doubt that this share is lower than in big and medium-sized cities.

Investment expenditures are often financed with the use of repayable instruments. Another argument for establishing MOCs in Poland is gaining more flexibility of local borrowing policies. The debt incurred by MOCs—which are separate legal entities—does not count against the legal debt limits for local governments, even if in practice it is hard to imagine that municipal government does not take any responsibility in case of MOC insolvency. The results of the *Wspólnota* surveys also provide information on to what extent municipal debt is the debt generated by MOCs. On average, in the years 2014–2019, in big cities (cities with county status, $N = 66$), the share of MOCs' debt in municipal debt was 25% (40% in regional capitals, 11% in other big cities). We do not have exact data for smaller municipalities, but we expect that this share was much lower.

The highest value of the share capital is held by MOCs operating under the conditions of a natural monopoly: water and sewage (EUR 4.3 million on average) and heating (EUR 2.1 million on average). The owners' contribution is slightly lower at the disposal of municipal housing corporations and local transport companies (on average about EUR 1.5 million per company), as well as waste companies (EUR 1.2 million) (National Court Register 2018). An analysis of the profitability of MOCs in the largest Polish cities in three sectors (water and sewage, local transport, waste management) shows that waste companies are in the best and transport firms in the weakest financial condition (Knade et al., 2014).

The results regarding the share of debt and investments of MOCs in the finances of municipalities indicate the important role that MOCs play, not only in the process of providing services, but also in building public infrastructure.

6.6 Ownership of MOCs and MOCs in Inter-municipal Cooperation[14]

Most of the MOCs are corporations owned by a single municipality, but there are also corporations in which a municipality holds more than 50% of the share, as well as corporations co-owned by more than one local government (inter-municipal corporations). The analysis shows that approximately 86%–88% of all analysed MOCs are 100% owned by one municipality. Thus, companies owned by two or more local governments and mixed capital companies (with private capital) are only less than 12–14% of MOCs (National Court Register 2018; Survey 2018). The popularity of inter-municipal corporations can be exemplified by the value of the water-sewage services sold by corporations owned by a single municipality and inter-municipal corporations in 2013—it was respectively about EUR 1.5 billion and EUR 0.275 billion (Swianiewicz, 2015).

The owner is not always a determinant of the range of a MOCs operation area—some of them expand beyond the borders of the municipal owners and offer services to the neighbouring municipalities based on the public procurement law. This modus operandi can be found in large cities offering services to municipalities in the cities' functional areas on the basis of a contract of agreement (see Sect. 6.2). Moreover, among Polish MOCs, structures exist which we call 'double-deckers'—these are MOCs launched by inter-municipal unions; actually 25% of operating unions co-own a MOC. The owner of the MOC is an inter-municipal union that was

[14] This part is based on the results of outcomes of the research project: "Inter-municipal cooperation—forms, scale, motives, mechanisms, outcomes—comparison of European countries" (DEC-2015/19/B/HS4/00119).

founded by several municipalities. It is a shift of inter-municipal cooperation from the public to the private law domain. And those MOCs can also offer services to neighbouring municipalities. There are also MOCs in which one party is a municipality and the other is a different MOC, a MOC founded by two inter-municipal unions, and one MOC launched by Polish municipalities together with a German inter-municipal union[15] (National Court Register 2014).

According to the estimated data, there were about 1600 corporations owned by one municipality and 160 corporations owned by at least two municipalities, thus, about 9% of the total number (National Court Register 2014). Among those 160 corporations, we decided to include also those which had ownership of other, non-territorial government actors, provided that their share was lower than 50%.

In addition, cross-sectoral cooperation postulated by Voorn et al. (2017) understood as public-private co-ownership appears relatively rare; we detected only a few cases. The vast majority of inter-municipal corporations' shareholders are public authorities: territorial governments and/or their unions (in total 130 cases, 71 among them being owned only by units of the local level). We have also noticed only one but very interesting case of meta-cooperation, where an inter-municipal company is co-owned by two separate inter-municipal unions, as well as 9 cases where an inter-municipal company is co-owned by a municipal company. Thus, even within only 160 identified cases, we observe diverse multi-layered ownership structures[16] (National Court Register 2014).

Moreover, inter-municipal corporations are the most significant form of institutionalised cooperation. However, in the general image, the share of institutional forms based on inter-municipal cooperation bodies in public service provision is not high. All inter-municipal corporations, regardless of their thematic area of operation, reported total sales of PLN 2.51 billion (ca. EUR 0.60 billion), which is 1.62% of all municipal expenditure (Swianiewicz et al., 2016), whilst diverse inter-municipal cooperation forms account for only about 3% of financial flows related to the

[15] This company was established in 1994 on the initiative of local authorities of two cities: Guben in Germany and Gubin in Poland (the so-called divided city), with the financial support of both central governments and the European Union, and is an example of successful cross-border cooperation (Musiał-Karg, 2009).

[16] However, the registry includes also an enigmatic category of "other shareholders" that is not specified.

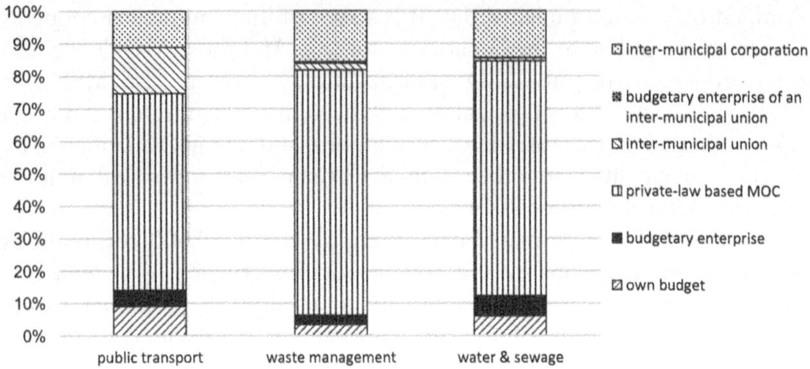

Fig. 6.3 The share of diverse service delivery legal forms according to service sector in 2012 (Source: Lackowska et al., 2019)

performance of tasks by local governments (Swianiewicz et al., 2016; Łukomska & Szmigiel-Rawska, 2019) (see Fig. 6.3).

In the framework of the services mentioned in Fig. 6.3 (public transport, waste management, water & sewage), their financial share varies from slightly more than 10% in the case of water and sewage up to over 20% in the case of local public transport. This brings us to the conclusion that the importance of specific cooperation forms varies according to service sector. The policy areas mentioned in Fig. 6.3 are also the same ones that most inter-municipal corporations focus on (see Table 6.1).

6.7 Conclusions and Prospects for the Future

As a rule, MOCs in Poland are used by local governments to shift some of their endeavours to the private sector, which is an important function of this form of service delivery in Europe in general (Tavares, 2017; Tavares & Camões, 2010; Voorn et al., 2019). Most of Polish MOCs are 100% owned by one municipality, which shows that this form is rarely a tool for public-private partnership in Poland and more often a means to expand the range of management strategies beyond those enabled by public law. In a way, however, it is also a tool to reach for additional resources—for capital throughout a debt and human resources since labour law is more flexible in the private than in the public sector.

Table 6.1 Fields of activity of inter-municipal corporations in Poland in 2014

Main thematic area	*Number of corporations*	*Share of corporations (%)*
Water supply & wastewater	53	33.1
Waste management	40	25.0
Public transport	16	10.0
Housing	10	6.3
Local economic development and promotion	10	6.3
Gas & energy	8	5.0
Education & training	2	1.3
Sport & tourism	6	3.8
Environment protection	0	0
Road infrastructure	0	0
Culture	0	0
Other	17	10.7

Source: Own elaboration based on data from National Court Register (2014) and Swianiewicz et al. (2016)

MOCs in Poland were planned as a tool to market and privatise local services. It was assumed that the share of private capital in the local service provision sector would increase over time. MOCs were firstly created in the largest cities and then smaller and smaller territorial units have been transforming their budgetary enterprises into corporations. It was expected that in this way the management of services by MOCs would be a technocratic and apolitical process (Aziewicz, 1994, 1998). However, these expectations turned out to be at least partially naive. MOCs are not free from politicisation, as evidenced, for example, by the fact that shortly after the change of local authorities as a result of local elections, we can observe changes in the positions of executive directors in MOCs (Swianiewicz & Kurniewicz, 2018; Swianiewicz et al., 2019). Instead of de-politicisation and increased effectiveness of more technocratic management, in practice, municipal companies have been created to benefit from specific legal regulations allowing VAT refunds, increasing borrowing capacities of cities, or more flexible human resources management.

The share of debt and investments of MOCs in the finances of municipalities indicate that MOCs play an important role not only in the process of providing services, but also in building public infrastructure. A very interesting characteristic of the Polish MOCs set is also an occurrence which we call 'double-deckers'—MOCs owned by inter-municipal unions.

MOCs in Poland have been lately a subject of an ongoing discussion on transparency and democratisation of this form of public management. A major amendment to the Act—Code of Commercial Companies—is now under consideration to enforce better corporate governance. The proposed changes to the law are to affect the activity and position of the supervisory board, which will gain new powers and responsibilities. It seems that the proposed changes are aimed at strengthening the position of the MOCs' owners and the supervisory boards towards executive boards and directors. As a result, MOCs may become even more dependent on their owners and more politicised than before. This, in turn, may lead to increasingly moving away from the primary reasons for establishing MOCs in Poland, that is, service provision depoliticisation through marketisation and privatisation.

References

Aziewicz, T. (1994). *Prywatyzacja usług komunalnych w Polsce [Privatisation of municipal services in Poland].* The Gdańsk Institute for Market Economics.

Aziewicz, T. (1998). *Gospodarka rynkowa w usługach komunalnych [Market economy in municipal services].* The Gdańsk Institute for Market Economics.

BNF. (n.d.). *Baza gminnych spółek komunalnych [Database of municipal companies].* Accessed March 17, 2021, from https://www.bnf.pl/katalog/baza/baza-gminnych-spolek-komunalnych

Chyb, N. (2015). Nieprawidłowości w funkcjonowaniu spółek komunalnych poza sferą użyteczności publicznej – analiza problemu [Irregularities in the operation of municipal companies outside the public utility sphere – an analysis of the problem]. *Samorząd Terytorialny, 9*, 5–14.

Dolewka, Z. (2017). Efektywność form organizacyjnych w realizacji zadań publicznych w samorządzie terytorialnym [Efficiency of organizational forms in a realization of public tasks in local government]. *Przedsiębiorczość i Zarządzanie, 11*, 57–71.

Gniadkowski, A. (2018, May 19). Wszystko jedno jak, byle ceny nie wzrosły [No matter how, as long as prices do not rise]. *Wspólnota, 10*, 12–15.

Gołaszewski, M. (2019, February 23). Finansowanie inwestycji w spółkach komunalnych [Financing of investments in municipal companies]. *Wspólnota, 4*, 44–49.

Heinelt, H., Magnier, A., Cabria, M., & Reynaert, H. (Eds.). (2018). *Political leaders and changing local democracy: The European mayor.* Palgrave Macmillan.

Knade, Ł., Sośnicka, A., Goska, H., & Klupczyński, M. (2014). *Kondycja finansowa spółek komunalnych w Polsce [Financial condition of municipal companies in Poland].* Raport CURULIS. Accessed March 19, 2021, from https://www.curulis.pl/pliki/wiedza/20141030_raportspolkikomunalne_v13.pdf

Lackowska, M., Swianiewicz, P., & Picej, A. (2019). Komercjalizacja współpracy międzygminnej? Rola spółek międzygminnych w dostarczaniu usług publicznych na tle innych form współpracy samorządowej [Commercialisation of inter-municipal cooperation? The role of inter-municipal companies in providing public services against the background of other forms of municipal cooperation]. *Prace i Studia Geograficzne, 64*(3), 69–91.

Ladner, A., Baldersheim, H., Hlepas, N., Keuffler, N., Navarro, C., Swianiewicz, P., & Steyvers, K. (2019). *Patterns of local autonomy in Europe*. Palgrave Macmillan.

Łukomska, J., & Szmigiel-Rawska, K. (2019). Inter-local relations and trans-scaling through finance in Poland. *Journal of Economic Policy Reform, 22*(2), 184–201.

Musiał-Karg, M. (2009). Współpraca transgraniczna w miastach podzielonych na przykładzie Słubfurtu i Gubien [Cross-border cooperation in divided cities on the example of Słubfurt and Gubien]. In S. Konopacki (Ed.), *Polska pięć lat w Unii Europejskiej [Poland five years in the European Union]* (pp. 169–186). Ibidem.

National Court Register. (2014). Database with data from the Polish National Court Register obtained through research projects conducted at the the University of Warsaw, Department of Local Development and Policy (grant agreement numbers: UMO-2016/23/B/HS4/03148 and UMO-2015/19/B/HS4/02898).

National Court Register. (2018). Database with data from the Polish National Court Register obtained through research projects conducted at the the University of Warsaw, Department of Local Development and Policy (grant agreement numbers: UMO-2016/23/B/HS4/03148 and UMO-2015/19/B/HS4/02898).

NIK. (2016). *Realizacja zadań publicznych przez spółki tworzone przez jednostki samorządu terytorialnego [Implementation of public tasks by companies established by local government units]*. NIK.

Rodrigues, M., Tavares, A. F., & Araújo, J. F. (2012). Municipal service delivery: The role of transaction costs in the choice between alternative governance mechanisms. *Local Government Studies, 38*(5), 615–638.

Survey. (2018). Database with responses from representatives of Polish municipalities to a survey conducted as part of a research project conducted at the University of Warsaw, Department of Local Development and Policy (grant agreement number UMO-2016/23/B/HS4/03148).

Swianiewicz, P. (1992). Local democracy in Poland: Is progress being made? *Policy and Politics, 20*(2), 87–99.

Swianiewicz, P. (1997). Local services in Poland in the wake of public provision. In G. Stoker & D. Lorrain (Eds.), *The privatisation of urban services in Europe* (pp. 168–188). Pinter.

Swianiewicz, P. (2007). Changing forms of urban government in Central and Eastern Europe. In R. Hambleton & J. S. Gross (Eds.), *Governing cities in a global era urban innovation, competition and democratic reform* (pp. 93–112). Palgrave Macmillan.

Swianiewicz, P. (2015). *Water and sewage management sector in Poland – the role of local governments*. Unpublished report for Ministry of Regional Development and Infrastructure in Georgia solicited by the Polish Embassy in Tbilisi.
Swianiewicz, P. (2017). Urynkowienie, prywatyzacja i rekomunalizacja. Formy dostarczania lokalnych usług publicznych w opiniach burmistrzów krajów europejskich [Marketisation, privatisation and re-municipalisation. Forms of delivery of local public services in the opinion of mayors of European countries]. *Samorząd Terytorialny, 5*, 11–26.
Swianiewicz, P., Gendźwiłł, A., Krukowska, J., Lackowska, M., & Picej, A. (2016). *Współpraca międzygminna w Polsce: związek z rozsądku [Inter-municipal cooperation in Poland: A relationship of convenience]*. Scholar.
Swianiewicz, P., & Kurniewicz, A. (2018). Cykl polityczny w opłatach za lokalne usługi publiczne w Polsce [The political cycle in tariffs on local public services in Poland]. *Studia Regionalne i Lokalne, 2*(72), 56–77.
Swianiewicz, P., Kurniewicz, A., & Kalcheva, D. (2019). The political budget cycle in earmarked taxes for local public services: A comparison of Poland and Bulgaria. *Journal of Comparative Policy Analysis: Research and Practice, 21*(5), 463–480.
Tavares, A. F. (2017). Ten years after: Revisiting the determinants of the adoption of municipal corporations for local service delivery. *Local Government Studies, 43*(5), 697–706.
Tavares, A. F., & Camões, P. (2010). New forms of local governance: A theoretical and empirical analysis of municipal corporations in Portugal. *Public Management Review, 12*(5), 587–608.
Voorn, B., Van Genugten, M., & Van Thiel, S. (2017). The efficiency and effectiveness of municipally owned corporations: A systematic review. *Local Government Studies, 43*(5), 820–841.
Voorn, B., Van Genugten, M., & Van Thiel, S. (2019). Multiple principals, multiple problems: Implications for effective governance and a research agenda for joint service delivery. *Public Administration, 97*(3), 671–685.
Żabski, Ł. (2017). Instytucje nadzoru właścicielskiego nad spółkami samorządowymi [Institutions of the owner's supervision of local government companies]. *Prace Naukowe Uniwersytetu Ekonomicznego we Wrocławiu, 493*, 190–202.

CHAPTER 7

Private Law, Public Control: Municipally Owned Corporations in Slovakia

Emília Sičáková-Beblavá and Matúš Sloboda

7.1 Introduction

The corporatisation of public services provisions is a hybrid between hierarchical and market-based governance models (Fratini et al., 2012). According to Wollmann (2016), in the early 1970s service provision was largely public/municipal sector based. New Public Management (NPM) guided modernisation in the 1990s, and the public/municipal sector dominance was, to a large extent, replaced by privatised service provision. However, a 'comeback' of public/municipal sector provision has been observed in the past decade (Wollmann, 2016). This phenomenon is called 're-municipalisation' (Moldenæs & Torsteinsen, 2017). In this regard, corporatisation as a research topic is attracting increasing attention because it is becoming a more common vehicle for delivering services. Municipal corporatisation is a rising trend in Europe, North America,

E. Sičáková-Beblavá • M. Sloboda (✉)
Faculty of Social and Economic Sciences, Institute of Public Policy, Comenius University, Bratislava, Slovakia
e-mail: emilia.beblava@fses.uniba.sk; matus.sloboda@fses.uniba.sk

M. Van Genugten et al. (eds.), *Corporatisation in Local Government*, https://doi.org/10.1007/978-3-031-09982-3_7

Canada, and Australia (Aars & Ringkjøb, 2011; Andrews et al., 2020; Citroni et al., 2013; Grossi & Reichard, 2008; Tavares, 2017) and we see a variety of forms and types of municipal corporations (Van Genugten et al., 2020). The research done by Tavares (2017), Andrews et al. (2020) and Voorn et al. (2020) expands on the understanding of causes and effects of the trend of corporatisation. Despite such widespread studies of municipal corporations in Western Europe and North America, there remain gaps in the literature concerning the nature of these trends in Central and Eastern Europe.

Within this context, the aim of this chapter is to explore municipally owned corporations (MOCs) in Slovakia from the perspective of service characteristics, institutional regulatory settings, and financial conditions. MOCs are defined as structurally separated from their owner local government unit(s) and with independent corporate status (legal autonomy); managed by an executive board appointed primarily by the municipal owners (managerial autonomy) with majority public ownership (Voorn et al., 2017).

To fulfil our goal, we synthesise the already conducted research in the area with our own research findings. As for the literature overview related to corporatisation on the local government level in Slovakia, we have investigated the existing literature on MOCs from various perspectives and time periods, and used different data sources.

Our research findings are based on expert interviews[1] and quantitative analysis. We have collected data about all MOCs with complete financial records in Slovakia ($N = 719$). This unique data source (Finstat.sk) has not been used in previous research in Slovakia. Finstat.sk is the finstat.sk portal, a private web portal that scrapes public data on financial records, business purpose(s), and names of CEOs and executive boards about public and private firms and corporations. This database allows us to operationalise the variables of legal form, size in terms of employees, revenues, and business purpose(s). We also used data collected by the Slovak Governance Institute (SGI) (2017b) on the members of the MOC executive board in

[1] Five interviews were conducted with prof. Gabriela Korimová, PhD. (University of Matej Bel in Banska Bystrica), assoc. prof. Gabriela Vaceková, PhD. (Charles University in Prague), assoc. prof. Miroslav Beblavý, PhD. (ESPRI Institute, Bratislava), Boris Strečanský (PhD candidate, FSES CU), Michal Piško (TIS) and Jana Červenáková (Association of cities and towns).

the 50 largest local government units in the period between 2010 and 2016.

Regarding terminology, we use the term 'local government unit' (LGU) as a synonym for local government or municipality. We distinguish between a public law corporation (formed/controlled by LGU based on public law) and a private law corporation (formed under Commercial Code, shareholding companies, and limited liability companies).

The chapter is divided into nine parts and conclusions. The next part provides the context of the local self-government system in Slovakia. This is followed by a description of the legal status of MOCs. The fourth part presents the trends in the use of MOCs, and we later analyse factors that may determine types of MOCs. We then look at the governance of MOCs from the perspective of autonomy and accountability. The last two parts explore decision-making processes and the politicisation of MOCs. The chapter ends with concluding remarks.

7.2 The Context of Local Self-Government and Legislative Framework in Slovakia

Since 1990, public sector reforms have been implemented in Slovakia and the establishment of a new democratic model of public administration has taken place. The former three-level system of national committees, in which state power and administration, as well as part of local self-government, was concentrated, was abolished in 1990 (Nemec, 2018). Adopting the Act 369/1990 on Municipalities was a cornerstone for the further formation of a modern and decentralised local government system. State administration was separated from local elected self-government. However, the LGUs were weak in terms of formal competences as well as abilities and resources to perform tasks. The system was highly politicised, and due to the non-transparent system of financing, municipal leaders depended on good relations with the government if they wanted extra resources for the development of their LGU.

The largest local self-government reform after 1990 occurred during the first Mikuláš Dzurinda government (1998–2002). In 1999, the new position of Plenipotentiary of the Slovak Government for Public Administration Reform was formed. Viktor Nižňanský was appointed as the responsible for developing the strategy for decentralisation and public sector reform. The decentralisation reform aimed at (a) territorial reform,

(b) institutional reform, and (c) public administration reform (fiscal and functional). During 2002–2004, more than 400 competences, as well as assets and possessions, were transferred to LGUs (Neubauerová, 2003). According to Nemec (2018), the reforms transferred a massive set of responsibilities to local and regional self-government; however, this transfer lacks sufficient fiscal decentralisation. The second Mikuláš Dzurinda government (2002–2006) designed and implemented fiscal decentralisation, as well as some additional changes in the territorial structure of state administration bodies. In 2005, the second phase of fiscal decentralisation was launched and focused on budgeting regulations, public and local administration, local taxes, and the collection and redistribution of other fees (Žárska & Kozovský, 2008). No other significant reforms in local self-government have been undertaken since the Dzurinda governments.

There are eight higher territorial units (counties) and 2927 LGUs—cities, towns, and villages in Slovakia. Although LGUs are formally equal, there are significant differences between them. According to Swianiewicz et al. (2017), the average size of a territorial unit in Slovakia is one of the smallest in Europe, consisting of only around 1900 inhabitants. The extent of decentralisation of competences, finance, and political power is thus largely determined by the LGU's ability to perform different tasks. Empirical research confirms that larger LGUs allow a more radical decentralisation of competences (Swianiewicz et al., 2017). The European Charter of Local Self-Government confirms that the Slovak local self-government system is very close to its principles and that LGUs are equipped with a large set of competences and responsibilities (Council of Europe, 2016).

The Act on Municipalities and the Commercial Act define the legal framework related to the forming and operation of MOCs owned by LGU. The Act on Municipalities also enables LGUs to create separate legal entities in various forms. They can create organisations ruled under the public law; examples are budgetary organisations (BOs) and contributory organisations (COs). They can also establish MOCs based on private law, such as limited liability companies or shareholding companies.

The MOCs, as separate legal entities, were formed in Slovakia either by transforming already existing organisations under public law since 1990 or by the decision of LGU to create a new MOC. The established legal framework allowed LGUs to create new, legally separate MOCs under the above-mentioned Commercial Act. The ownership interest of LGUs in an

MOC is not limited—LGUs can hold 100% assets in a corporation, less, or can set up co-ownership by several LGUs.

Furthermore, other acts also regulate the operation of MOCs, such as the Freedom of Information Act and the Public Procurement Act. The reason is that MOCs established under private law are hybrid organisations that stand between commercial firms and government agencies (Kickert, 2001). The motivation behind the introduction of private sector organisational forms into the realm of self-government was the expected benefit in effectiveness and public sector governance (Preker & Harding, 2003) through decreasing bureaucracy and higher flexibility.

7.3 Legal Status of MOCs

The Slovak legislation allows for various organisational forms of MOCs. The Slovak LGUs use various forms of cooperation that are summarised in Table 7.1. They may be established under both private and public law. As for the public law organisational forms, budgetary organisations (BOs) and contributory organisations (COs) (subsidy-based organisations) are the possibilities. Private law, on the other hand, enables four organisational forms: shareholding companies, limited liability companies, non-profit organisations providing public service, and cooperatives.

According to the legislation, a BO is formed by one owner (LGU) and is connected to the LGU budget, by which it is fully financed. No additional revenue is allowed for a BO. A CO can also be owned by only one owner and is expected to primarily gain its revenue through the provision of its services. The founder may provide a budgetary transfer to balance the possible difference between its expenditures and revenue. The founder of both CO and BO selects a statutory representative of the organisation.

Shareholding companies or limited liability companies can be formed based on the Commercial Act. They can be formed by LGUs with full or partial ownership. Non-profit organisations that provide public services are based on private law and must be registered under the register of the Slovak Ministry of Interior. They can have various areas of interest, such as the development of cultural and spiritual values, the environment, human rights, health and social care, or education.

Table 7.1 Summary of organisational forms (MOCs) with LGU involvement

Types of legal organisational forms on the local level	*Standard forms (100% ownership of LGU)*	*Hybrid forms (100%–67% ownership of LGU)*	*Hybrid forms (Less than 67% ownership of LGU)*	*Hybrid forms (several organisations)*
Public law organisations/ corporations	Budgetary organisations	–	–	Public-private partnership (concession law)
	Contributory organisations	–	–	Joint municipal office
Private law organisations/ corporations[a]	Shareholding company	Shareholding company with up to 33% of shares owned by private actors.	Shareholding company with more than 34% of assets owned by private actors.	Shareholding company owned by several LGUs.
	Limited liability company	Limited liability company with private partner owning up to 33%.	Limited liability company with private partner owning more than 34% of assets.	Public-private partnership (forming daughter company that is privatised).
	Non-profit organisations	–	–	–

[a]These organisations can also be classified as a social enterprise

7.4 Trends in the Use of MOCs: Preference for Flexibility and 100% Ownership

Local representatives prefer managerial control over MOCs. Furthermore, the trend over the past ten years shows that LGUs prefer 100% ownership relatively more than ever before. Table 7.2 provides an overview of various ownership shares, as well as BOs and COs. The vast majority of MOCs (79%) are fully owned by LGUs. In addition, LGUs own more than 50% of all assets in another 8% of MOCs. This can be explained by financial (e.g. the possibility of taking loans) and managerial flexibility (e.g. in wage policy) provided by this legal form. In relation to wage flexibility, the motivation can also be clientelist, to nominate politically affiliated individuals with better wage possibilities.

Figure 7.1 illustrates the emergence of MOCs on a yearly basis as a share of the number of MOCs established in a particular year, as well as

Table 7.2 Type of ownership by age of MOCs

	<3 years	*<10 years*	*<15 years*	*<20 years*	*>20 years*	*All*
	Share % (N)					
Less than 50 % owned by LGU	0.0% (0)	4.5% (7)	5.4% (15)	6.3% (25)	6.9% (17)	6.6% (42)
50.1%–99.9% owned by LGU	4.3% (2)	3.2% (5)	6.4% (18)	7.4% (29)	8.6% (21)	7.8% (50)
100% owned by LGU	95.7% (45)	89.7% (140)	86.1% (241)	83.8% (330)	71.0% (174)	78.8% (504)
BO + CO	0.0% (0)	2.6% (4)	2.1% (6)	2.5% (10)	13.5% (33)	6.8% (43)

Source: Based on data from the Finstat.sk (2021) database containing all MOCs with complete financial records and year of establishment

the total number of MOCs (1990–2019). In terms of corporatisation at the local government level, we can identify two specific time periods. The first is the period after the Velvet Revolution and the formation of the independence of the Slovak Republic. The second is the period of administrative, fiscal, and territorial reform.

As for the first period (1990–1995), the emergence of corporations at the local government level relates to the fact that during the socialist period, private law corporations were prohibited. The change of the economic and political regime enabled the emergence of private law corporations. In 1990, local self-governments were formed as a part of the first phase of public administration reform. Buček (2015) suggests that LGUs used many opportunities to obtain property previously owned by the state in this period. The competences from the state level were gradually decentralised to the local level by the Act on Municipalities. After the split of Czechoslovakia, the reorganisation of the public sector occurred with the formation of new competences for LGUs.

The first Mikuláš Dzurinda government (1998–2002) initiated large reforms related to territorial decentralisation in 2000–2001. Functional and administrative decentralisation was implemented by the second Dzurinda government (2002–2006) in 2002. It consisted of transferring competences from the state to the local level. This reform was followed by new regulations on budgeting and tax system reform. Fiscal decentralisation was finalised in 2005 and 2006. According to Malíkova et al. (2013), these reforms were incremental changes in the public sector and the introduction of NPM. The data indicate that since 2001 (potential early effects of reform initiatives) to 2008 (potential delayed effects), the largest increase of newly founded MOCs was recorded (about 37% of all MOCs were founded in this period). It is a larger share of newly founded MOCs than in any other eight-year period. This effect was boosted by the strong economic growth between 2004 and 2008 that significantly improved the asset situation of local self-government (Buček, 2015). Figure 7.1 also suggests that for the past 20 years, public law corporations (BOs and COs) have been crowded out by the formation of private law corporations. This may be due to the growing complexity of tasks in which delivering requires more flexible forms of management.

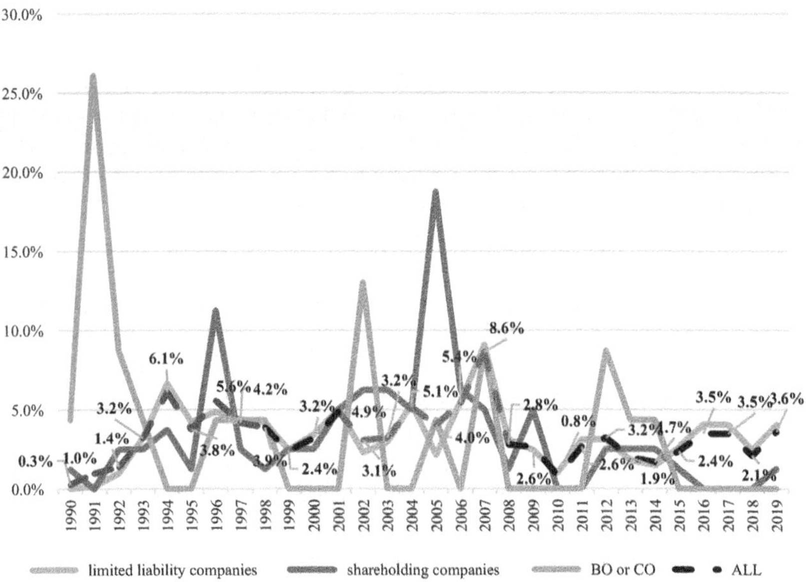

Fig. 7.1 The emergence of MOCs since 1990 (Source: Based on data from the Finstat.sk (2021) database that contains all MOCs with complete financial records). Note: The black dashed line represents the ratio of newly founded corporations (all legal forms). The red dashed line is the period (2001–2008)—2002–2004 transfer of competences; 2004 tax system reform; 2005 fiscal decentralisation. The violet dashed line represents the period of 1990 (after the Velvet revolution) and the independence of the Slovak republic (1993) and the first years after it (1994–1996)

The Finstat.sk (2021) database registers in total 4696 MOCs which were established in approximately half of LGUs (45%) in Slovakia. Larger LGUs provide more public services, and therefore they tend to utilise MOCs more often for public service delivering than smaller LGUs. This relatively large number of MOCs in Slovakia can be explained by the education sector, when each school (kindergarten, primary, and secondary grammar school) is registered as a public law corporation, predominantly as BO. The majority (57%) of MOCs (except schools) was founded after the year 2000.

7.5 Size, Type, and Economic Sectors of MOCs

The legal form may be determined by the size of MOCs in terms of revenues and the number of employees. More than half of all shareholding companies reported revenues greater than one million euros in 2019. This share is more than four times smaller for limited liability companies. The data also indicate that budgetary and contributory organisations usually provide fewer complex services on a smaller scale and, therefore, are also smaller than private law corporations in terms of yearly revenues.

The LGUs in Slovakia have a strong preference for MOCs established under private law, predominantly limited liability companies. Public law corporations (BOs and COs) represent only 9% of the corporations formed by LGUs. The data also indicate the relationship between legal form and the size of corporations. MOCs with less than 50 employees are more likely to have the form of a limited liability company than any other legal form. Most limited liability companies have less than ten employees. Larger MOCs, with more than 50 employees, are relatively more often shareholding companies (35%) or BOs/COs (33%) than limited liability companies (4%).

Moreover, the data suggest that smaller LGUs prefer limited liability companies relatively more often than larger LGUs. The occurrence of BOs and COs increases with the size of LGUs. However, public law organisations are rarely used by LGUs. They are usually formed to provide cultural and educational services. Therefore, public law organisations are used relatively more often in larger LGUs which have more of these facilities than smaller LGUs. Larger LGUs tend to consider the establishment of shareholding companies significantly more often than smaller LGUs. Four out of five MOCs, which have a form of shareholding companies, operate in the largest LGUs above 20,000 inhabitants. Smaller LGUs have limited capacity of human and financial resources, and therefore the management of shareholding companies is for them more challenging in comparison to limited liability companies.

MOCs can provide various types of (public) services—from waste collection and disposal management, transport and construction, energy supply, real estate, media, agriculture and forestry, healthcare and education. Approximately half of all MOCs operate in the agricultural and forest sector, tourism and gastronomy, real estate, or energy and mining. According to the Finstat.sk (2021) dataset, MOCs are most active in the sector of agriculture and forestry (see Fig. 7.2). The forest area represented 41% of total land area, and approximately half of forest area is managed by non-state actors such as private corporations, the church, LGUs, and local communities (FAO, 2020). The median size of LGUs that operate in this

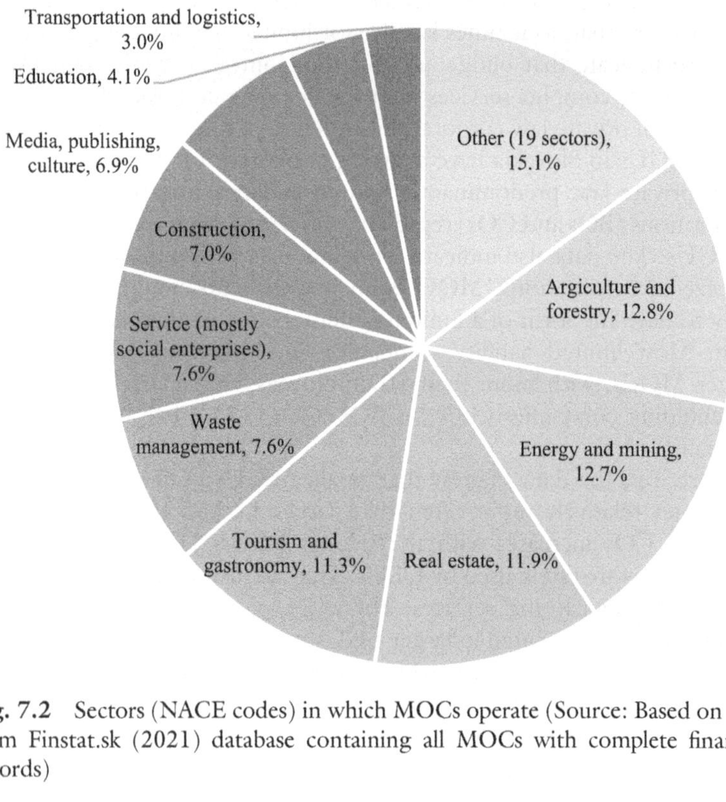

Fig. 7.2 Sectors (NACE codes) in which MOCs operate (Source: Based on data from Finstat.sk (2021) database containing all MOCs with complete financial records)

sector is 2000 inhabitants, which indicates that this type of operation (predominantly as limited liability companies) is very common in smaller LGUs. Similarly, the sector of tourism and gastronomy (e.g. accommodation, operation of sports facilities, and sport clubs) is relevant for smaller LGUs that establish limited liability companies to operate thermal baths. Larger LGUs tend to manage sports clubs (predominantly football clubs) as MOCs.

The real estate sector is more relevant in larger LGUs which have more assets to manage (e.g. renting municipal housing or rental of commercial space). One in eight LGUs uses MOCs in the sectors of energy and mining (mostly sewerage, heat and water supply). In both sectors, LGUs still prefer a form of limited liability company; however, we observe a growing share of shareholding companies (20%) in this area. The higher the total assets, the more likely the MOC takes the form of a shareholding company.

There are two possibilities for inter-municipal cooperation in Slovakia—horizontal (collaboration on service provision) and vertical (the service provision of MOCs owned by an LGU to other LGUs). The former type of cooperation is relatively more utilised than the latter. In terms of horizontal cooperation, it is quite common that several (usually smaller) LGUs form a joint municipal office (JMO) to organise the provision of selected services. However, in comparison to MOCs, JMOs are almost exclusively formed to perform competences transferred to LGUs from the state. This is mainly the agenda of construction offices, education, road maintenance, and environment. The provision of these services is significantly regulated in terms of standards and processes, which limits space for innovation. Hence, MOCs are more often utilised in areas of original competences of LGUs, such as transportation, forestry, real estate, energy sector, or tourism and gastronomy. Joint corporations are used relatively more often in the energy and waste management sectors. Joint corporations occur in the situation where a MOC is owned by a larger LGU, and it provides services to smaller and adjacent LGUs. For example, the local waste management corporation owned by the middle-sized LGU of Hlohovec provides services not only in Hlohovec but also in the microregion Handlova, in seven other LGUs and villages for 25 thousand inhabitants. However, the establishment of a joint corporation in which two or more LGUs are shareholders is relatively rare and represents only about 3% of all MOCs. These joint corporations operate mainly in water supply and sewerage (43%), waste management (26%).

About 8% of all MOCs provide specific types of services, and many have a special status of a social enterprise. The legal framework that enabled the formation of social enterprises was adopted in 2005. To be registered as a social enterprise by the Ministry of Labour of the Slovak Republic, a company must employ disadvantaged job applicants, at least 30% of net revenue must be used for new employment and improving of labour conditions, and the company must be registered in the registry of social enterprises. The status of a social enterprise is defined very narrowly with the principal goal of preparing the long-term unemployed for the open labour market. This limits the potential contribution of social enterprises to social services and community development (Strečanský & Stoláriková, 2012). According to Placek et al. (2021), of all transition economies, Slovakia was the first that promoted social enterprises through pilot projects and legislative changes. The Slovak government approved eight pilot projects in 2008. However, these projects caused negative reactions as the rules for recruiting new employees were not adhered to in several pilot cases (Placek et al., 2021). In 2018, the new act on social enterprises came into force and currently there are about 250 registered social enterprises in Slovakia. Very often, social enterprises operate in areas of construction, wholesale and retail, agriculture and forestry, accommodation and catering, gardening, education, health care and social services, and laundry services (Gregorová & Svidroňová, 2020).

Generally, MOCs are single purpose in terms of orientation in service delivery in one specific sector. However, most of them have officially registered more subjects of business that fall into one particular sector. For instance, MOCs in the sector of tourism and gastronomy are a typical example of various subjects of business (e.g. rental, cleaning services, and retail). On the other hand, sectors such as waste management, transportation, health care, or education require very specific subjects of business and limit room for subjects that are less related to the sector.

Public-private partnerships are usually not used within the LGUs in Slovakia. The only sector that established a special form of this partnership is water management. Before 1989, there were three water companies in Slovakia that operated throughout the country under the control of the Slovak Ministry of Agriculture. Since 2001, those companies have been transformed to 14 MOCs, as shareholding companies. The shares were allocated to the LGUs according to the number of citizens. Some of those corporations later formed their 'daughter' corporations that are responsible for the operation of the water infrastructure and water supply. Some of those daughter corporations were privatised and from that perspective they can be defined as a special form of public–private partnership.

7.6 Autonomy of MOCs: The Essential Role of the Municipal Council

The key legislation necessary for autonomy and accountability and public oversight of the local private law corporations is based on several national laws: Act on Municipalities 369/1990, Act on the Capital City of the Slovak Republic Bratislava 377/1990, Municipal Asset Act 138/1991, Public Procurement Act 343/2015, Act on Execution of Work of Public Interest 552/2003, Freedom of Information Act 211/2000, and Act on Measures Related to Reporting on Antisocial Activities 307/2014.

Furthermore, the decision-making of MOC managers is limited by several tools in three areas:

- Formalised rules
- Financial constraints
- Organisational constraints

One of the rules defined by central regulations is the Public Procurement Act that regulates proceedings for the purchasing of services or tangible and intangible assets in private law and public law corporations. State legislation regulates personnel policy, selection proceedings, hiring, and wage policies. That applies also to private law MOCs with ownership by LGUs of at least 67%. There are special rules related to private law MOCs with more than 67% of public ownership[2] in terms of autonomy. These MOCs have stricter regulations of selection procedures, provision of property declarations for certain positions in management, ethical duties (e.g. prohibition on accepting gifts or other benefits in connection with the performance in his/her position in management, or duty of confidentiality), and limits for other business activities.

Financial issues (getting loans, making long-term investments, changes in the budgets) are not constrained by state regulations in the case of private law MOCs. However, the municipal council has an important role in setting the degree of autonomy of the MOC in which it is a majority owner. The municipal council can regulate this via decisions of the council

[2] Based on the Act on the Performance of Work in the Public Interest (§ 127).

(e.g. selection of members in executive boards, by-law of companies owned by the LGU) in case of private law corporations, or via internal regulations and norms in case of public law corporations. The decision approval of the municipal council is necessary also in the case for organisational issues (e.g. reorganisation, mergers, sale of assets, and cooperation with private businesses).

Shareholding companies have a more complicated decision-making structure that contains a general assembly (formed by shareholders, if 100% owned by one municipality, it is the only shareholder), executive and supervisory boards. The executive board is accountable to the supervisory board. The main role of supervisory boards is to supervise the executive board, and the Commercial Code defines the set of basic duties for supervisory boards in shareholding companies. However, the general assembly can broaden the scope of the rights and duties of the supervisory board. Unfortunately, there is no research available that would provide insight if that were the case in the Slovak shareholding companies formed by LGUs.

Limited liability companies have similar governing bodies—they consist of a main statutory and executive body (CEO), executive board (board of directors), and general meeting (in corporations fully owned by LGUs represented by mayors). According to the Commercial Code, the two-tier system is optional for limited liability companies. The reason is that companies with this legal form are on average small in terms of number of employees and revenues. Each body has different roles and functions, and they are set in the MOC articles. The general assembly has a key role in decision making about a wide range of issues such as selection of members of executive and supervisory boards, budget, investments, strategies and development plans, organisational structure, and discussion about internal documents (regulation, standards) which are approved by the executive board.

The autonomy of the MOC is thus limited in all legal forms and mainly in a case of 100% ownership by LGU(s), which is the most prevalent case in Slovakia. This is due to (at least) two reasons. The first reason is that the municipal council selects the CEOs in MOCs and in the case of a shareholding company, the council also selects members of executive and supervisory boards. The second possible reason is that managerial autonomy is constrained by regulation applied at the central level (regulation of procurement and personnel policy). Regarding setting objectives of MOCs, local self-governments have not adopted the system that is common at the central government level, where the ministries sign the contracts (defining objectives and activities) with their BOs and COs (e.g. Ministry of Culture, 2021) on a yearly basis. Coordination in this manner is more often performed through personal and informal channels at the local and regional level, and MOCs have defined more general objectives in their establishment status, and setting goals is not usually formalised on a yearly basis. However, there is a lack of empirical data in this field.

7.7 Accountability Regimes: Corporate Governance Codes Are Positive Deviations

Regarding access to information about local private law corporations, the Freedom of Information Act obliges them to inform about the administration of public resources and state, county, or municipal assets. Many MOCs claim that public resources are only subsidies from the state budget or from EU funding and refuse to provide information. Management of a MOC uses to claim that it needs to protect their activities against their competitors, who could easily access delicate information (Černá & Kohoutková, 2019). In this context, Riapošová and Dančíková (2014) evaluated how responsive local private law corporations are to providing information in Slovakia. Research indicates that annual reports are easily publicly available. On the contrary, the CVs of the representatives are hardly accessible. The MOCs refused to provide CVs of their representatives in 75% of the cases. Furthermore, MOCs were less responsive to providing information than state corporations. They also suggest that in some cases local private law corporations simply were not aware of the official legal obligations and proceedings defined in the law related to management of information inquiries (Riapošová & Dančíková, 2014).

Accountability mechanisms (transparency and communication) have been investigated by TIS in the 100 largest Slovak corporations within the Index of MOCs Development. This index was calculated for 2012, 2015, and 2019. Regarding transparency and communication out of the total possible score (100), data from the year 2019 show that the overall transparency average score of Slovak corporations is rather poor (43%) (TIS, 2020). According to Černá and Kohoutková (2019), there are significant obstacles to openness and public oversight. For example, MOCs in Slovakia do not publicly assess the fulfilment of performance criteria with respect to the subject of their business activities. They also do not publish the results of the selection procedures on their websites. Additionally, there is almost no information available on the salaries, bonuses, and other benefits of MOC managers. The weak part is also identified in Access to Information Policy and Public Procurement. Černá and Kohoutková (2019) also suggest that MOCs in Slovakia seem to be the least transparent in areas of property sales and lease policy and ethics infrastructure (e.g. if they have ethics code devoted to issues such as conflict of interest resolution, hospitality rules, rules for sponsoring/donations). According to TIS (2020), the transportation company of the city of Košice, the second largest city in Slovakia, was the most transparent MOC in Slovakia, reaching 81%. The least transparent was the housing company of the middle-sized town Nové Mesto nad Váhom (6%).

MOCs are governed by laws depending on their legal form. There is no unified complex corporate governance code in MOCs in Slovakia. However, some rules have been developed for decision-making areas that can serve as good practice.

One of the examples is innovation in purchasing goods, and services work through e-auctions. Several MOCs voluntarily started to allocate contracts using e-auctions years before it became obligatory for the state, LGUs, counties and public organisations (including MOCs) to purchase commonly available goods, services, and construction work through the electronic contracting system (Piško, 2018). Ethical standards are also developed in some MOCs on a voluntary basis. An ethical code has been developed, for example, by the housing company in Košice, the second largest city in Slovakia, and the Public Transport Company in Bratislava. However, no analysis of its efficiency is available. Another example of good practice is the Public Transport Company Bratislava that publishes all information about subsidies or gifts to third parties and projects which have been supported by the company (Piško, 2018). There are also attempts to define additional rules for selecting governing bodies in local private law corporations. An example is the City of Bratislava (2019), which has developed and applied specific rules and opened competition in the process of selecting governing bodies.

7.8 The Selection of CEOs in MOCs: The Political Cycle Matters

The selection of the CEO is carried out by the municipal council. Regulations at the national level do not explicitly require an open and formalised selection procedure when selecting the CEO. However, the central government defined standards for the selection of CEOs in state corporations in 2011. This Government Resolution required conducting a prior formalised selection procedure before making public appointments. In addition, it defined educational requirements (university-level education). These standards are not legally binding for LGUs. However, they can be adapted to the local government context, because each LGU can choose how to select public managers. Therefore, the appointment and selection of CEOs in MOCs is in the hands of the municipal council and mayor. The municipal council can decide to open and formalise the selection procedure if there is political will or public pressure to do so.

The selection of CEOs (and public appointments in general) is perceived negatively by Slovak citizens. TIS and research agency Focus conducted a survey on the recruitment process in local government organisations in 2007, in which 51% of respondents perceived the recruitment process as one of the most corrupt decision-making areas (ŠípoŠ, 2012). TIS launched a benchmarking system on transparency of public corporations in 2010 (see the previous part), and since then this benchmark has encouraged LGUs to conduct a prior formalised selection procedure.

In fact, LGUs have two options concerning the selection procedure of CEOs: (a) utilising a formally structured selection procedure or (b) providing a direct political nomination and appointment by local political leadership. The former may take the form of a public hearing. In either case, the final decision and approval of a candidate are always made by the municipal council.

Sloboda and Sičáková-Beblavá (2020) and the SGI (2017a) investigated the selection procedures of CEOs to MOCs. The former research analysed the sample of 100 largest municipalities, and the latter analysed the sample of 50 largest municipalities. When selecting CEOs to MOCs, politicians prefer direct political nomination without transparent selection procedures. According to SGI (2017a), only one out of three CEOs was selected through a formally structured selection procedure. Sloboda and Sičáková-Beblavá (2020) found out that the share of transparent selection procedures is 45%. Šípoš (2012) argues that political parties consider inter-organisational public appointments to MOCs to be part of the party's personnel policy.

Concerning politicisation, the data indicate that approximately one out of seven CEOs held a political office in a municipal council at the time of the selection process. However, this type of selection proceeding does not have a statistically significant influence on the selection of CEOs with previous political experience (Sloboda & Sičáková-Beblavá, 2020). Moreover, data do not suggest a statistically significant difference between these two approaches of CEO selection in relation to previous managerial experience from the private sphere and university education. Approximately, nine out of ten CEOs in MOCs have had previous managerial experience, and approximately half of the CEOs have had previous experience in the private sphere (Sičáková-Beblavá & Sloboda, 2017). Although local politicians prefer direct nomination of CEOs instead of a formally structured selection procedure, the meritocratic approach and functional politicisation seem to be more prevalent than in party patronage in Slovak municipalities. This suggests that formalising the selection process may lead to recognition of the principle of merit in public appointments (Sancino et al., 2016).

The municipal council also has the competence to select members of executive boards. To analyse executive boards, we use the data collected by SGI (2017b) and a sample of 400 MOCs in the 50 largest municipalities in Slovakia (2006–2014). It allows the investigation of politicisation but does not provide information about the background (education, previous work experience) of members of executive boards.

Shareholding companies are on average larger than limited liability companies in terms of number of employees and revenues. Therefore, they also have larger executive boards. This may be one of the reasons why the share of municipal councillors in executive boards in shareholding companies is 1.5 higher than in limited liability companies. On average, one in three members of the executive boards of shareholding companies is a member of the city council. The composition of executive boards is significantly affected by the election cycle. Approximately 80% of all changes in the executive boards occurred within one year (365 days) after the election. Newcomer mayors make 90% of all changes in executive board members in this period of one year after election (SGI, 2017b).

Politicisation may be a strategy to secure and obtain political support for mayors. This may be even more important for mayors without political affiliation who won the election as independent candidates. The data suggest that mayors without political affiliation (independent) tend to nominate (and councils appoint) city councillors to executive boards by 10% more likely than mayors who ran for mayoral office as political party or coalition candidates (SGI, 2017b). Independent mayors may have weaker political support in the council than mayors who ran for office together with candidates for councillors under the same political party or coalition. Positions in executive boards can serve as one of the possible ways to secure political support.

7.9 Municipal Corporatisation as a Political Issue

Corporatisation itself is not a salient political issue in local government; however, the private law corporations owned by LGUs are usually publicly discussed (a) when the private law corporation is sold to private investors; (b) when the management and executive board are selected, especially after local election; and (c) in relation to their spending, public procurement, and subsidy granting.

Examples related to the first publicly discussed issue are water companies. The infrastructure of the water companies is usually owned by several LGUs and the shares are distributed according to the population. Three out of 20 water companies operating in Slovakia have formed their daughter/subsidiary companies with the aim of operating in the provision of water services. Some water companies have been privatised, and the privatisation of water operation services is usually publicly discussed, especially because privatisation has been for a long time related to corruption misuse and scandals (Sičáková-Beblavá et al., 2011).

Management and board selection are usually publicly discussed before and after local elections. Before local elections, candidates who run for mayoral office use to propose policies towards depoliticisation and strengthening of professionalisation in the management of public companies (Vallo, 2018). Media and political opponents as well as anti-corruption NGOs pressure the political leadership after local elections to scrutinise the selection processes and its outcomes. The index on transparency and openness of MOCs, developed by TIS, is usually published before local elections. There are several indicators, for example, on the personnel policy and the public procurement procedures, because MOCs are obliged to follow public procurement legislation (TIS, 2020). TIS's findings usually receive significant media attention, and some findings also become a salient political issue (e.g. the finding about expensive cars rented by Bratislava Water Company (TIS, 2019)).

Politicisation of MOCs is a salient issue in election campaigns. As already illustrated in the previous section, the composition of executive boards is affected by the electoral cycle, and the new political leadership tends to replace representatives in MOCs. A relevant example in this regard is the political newcomer mayor of Bratislava, Matúš Vallo, who announced changes in the selection procedures of members of executive boards and CEOs of MOCs. In less than three months after his appointment, the city council of Bratislava approved new rules for the selection of members of executive boards. The rule applies to all MOCs with full or majority management control by the city (Bratislava City Council, 2019). It defines the selection procedures in three phases: (a) questionnaire and CV submission, (b) interview, and (c) the roasting of a candidate by the selection commission. Furthermore, it specifies selection criteria for education (university degree), management experience of at least three years, sector experience, past results of the candidate's work, integrity (conflict of interest), and the quality of the candidate's presentation on MOC management. This example of good practice is rare in Slovakia. Most LGUs do not have transparent criteria for selection procedures when selecting members of executive boards. However, a small number of LGUs have formal rules for the selection of CEOs (e.g. the city of Pezinok for the selection of CEOs of contributory organisations (City of Pezinok, 2019)).

7.10 Conclusions

Together with the economic and political transformation at the central level in Slovakia, LGUs transformed the modes of service provision and shifted from public law organisations to private law organisations. The data suggest that, for the last 20 years, public law corporations (BO and CO) have been crowded out by the formation of private law corporations. LGUs prefer full control and 100% ownership of MOCs. This is relatively more common in the case of a limited liability company than in a shareholding company. Nine out of ten (88.3%) limited liability companies are fully owned by LGU. This occurs in approximately half of the cases of shareholding companies. This can be very likely because shareholding companies are generally larger in terms of number of employees and revenues than limited liability companies and very often provide more complex services, which may require more know-how and private sector capital. However, this interpretation requires more exploration.

Data also show that LGUs in Slovakia rarely establish shareholding companies as they represent only 12% of all private law companies. Limited liability companies are on average significantly smaller in terms of number of employees and revenues, which can indicate fewer complex operations and a smaller demand for the utilisation of more sophisticated management processes used in shareholding companies.

LGUs have several tools that can be applied to control operations in MOCs. Control is greater when the municipality is the sole (100%) owner of the MOC. This chapter has shown that local representatives tend to prefer a large majority in MOCs, approximately one in ten MOCs is 100% owned by a LGU. This suggests that local representatives prefer flexibility, which private law corporations offer, and to maintain control over MOCs via selection of management so that the LGU can influence operational and strategic decisions.

MOCs provide various types of (public) services; however, the most prevalent sectors are waste collection and disposal management, agriculture and forestry (maintenance of local forests), real estate (housing and renting), energy supply (water, heating), tourism and gastronomy (thermal baths), and social services. Water supply and waste collection are often areas in which LGUs cooperate when a MOC provides services for adjacent LGUs, or several LGUs own shares in a MOC (e.g. water companies).

In relation to internal governance, there are several competences that LGUs can exercise to promote accountability and transparency. It is important to point out that these competences can be used for professionalisation of MOCs, but very often also misused for politicisation. There are some good practices emerging to increase professionalisation in LGUs. However, research suggests that most LGUs do not have transparent criteria for selection procedures when selecting members of executive boards.

To get a better and more reliable picture that would allow a deeper understanding of corporatisation on the municipal level in Slovakia, further quantitative and qualitative research is needed. The potential research problems to investigate relate to understanding the reasons behind deciding what legal form will be used when establishing MOCs, the impact of accountability mechanisms, the personnel policy of the corporations including the effects of wage flexibility, or freedom to decide what selection procedure will be applied.

Acknowledgment This work was supported by the The Slovak Research and Development Agency under the grant (APVV-18-0435) Behavioral Interventions in Local Government: Increasing the Efficiency of Local Public Policies.

References

Aars, J., & Ringkjøb, E. H. (2011). Local democracy ltd: The political control of local government enterprises in Norway. *Public Management Review, 13*(6), 825–844.

Andrews, R., Ferry, L., Skelcher, C., & Wegorowski, P. (2020). Corporatization in the public sector: Explaining the growth of local government companies. *Public Administration Review, 80*(3), 482–493.

Bratislava City Council. (2019). *Materiál na rokovanie mestského zastupiteľstva v Bratislave. [Material for the City Council meeting].* Accessed January 10, 2021, from https://zastupitelstvo.bratislava.sk/data/att/40200.pdf

Buček, J. (2015). Municipal property during the post-socialist transition in Slovakia. In J. Buček & A. Ryder (Eds.), *Governance in transition* (pp. 275–307). Springer.

Citroni, G., Lippi, A., & Profeti, S. (2013). Remapping the state: Inter-municipal cooperation through corporatisation and public-private governance structures. *Local Government Studies, 39*(2), 208–234.

Černá, S., & Kohoutková, A. (2019). *Transparentnosť Městských společností: Příklad 5 dopravních podniků v ČR. [Transparency of municipal companies: An example 5 transport companies in the Czech Republic].* Oživení, o.s.

City of Bratislava. (2019, June 27). *Mestské podniky budú mať nových šéfov. [City businesses will have new bosses].* Accessed August 8, 2020, from https://bratislava.sk/sk/sprava/mestske-podniky-budu-mat-novych-sefov

City of Pezinok. (2019). *Zásady výberu riaditeľov mestských organizácií Mesta Pezinok: Popis výberového konania. [Principles of selection of directors of municipal organizations of the City of Pezinok: Description of the selection procedure].* Pezinok.

Council of Europe. (2016). *Local and regional democracy in the Slovak Republic.* Monitoring report – Slovak Republic. Council of Europe.

FAO. (2020). *Global forest resources assessment 2020: Report Slovakia.* FAO.

Finstat.sk (2021). *Database of companies.* Accessed January 10, 2020, from https://www.finstat.sk/

Fratini, C. F., Brown, R. R., Elle, M., Jensen, M. B., & Mikkelsen, P. S. (2012). *Corporatization of the water sector: Implications for transitioning to sustainable urban water management* (228–235). Proceedings of the 7th International Conference on Water Sensitive Urban Design.

Gregorová, B. A., & Svidroňová, M. M. (2020). *Analýza o stave sociálneho podnikania na Slovensku. [Analysis of the state of social entrepreneurship in Slovakia].* BRESE Interreg Europe.

Grossi, G., & Reichard, C. (2008). Municipal corporatization in Germany and Italy. *Public Management Review, 10*(5), 597–617.

Kickert, W. J. M. (2001). Public management of hybrid organizations: Governance of quasi – autonomous executive agencies. *International Public Management Journal, 4*(2), 135–150.

Malíkova, L., Jacko, T., & Stanova, L. (2013). *New public management a Slovensko: podoby a aplikácia princípov [New public management and Slovakia: forms and implementation of principles].* Vydavateľstvo Univerzity Komenského.

Ministry of Culture. (2021). *Kontrakty na rok 2021 uzatvorené medzi MK SR a rozpočtovými a príspevkovými organizáciami v zriaďovateľskej pôsobnosti MK SR. [Contracts for 2021 concluded between the Ministry of Culture of the Slovak Republic and budgetary and contributory organizations in the founding competence of the Ministry of Culture of the Slovak Republic].* Accessed December 5, 2021, from https://www.culture.gov.sk/ministerstvo/organizacie-ministerstva/kontrakty/rok-2021/

Moldenæs, T., & Torsteinsen, H. (2017). Re-politicisation as post-NPM response? Municipal companies in a Norwegian context. *Local Government Studies, 43*(4), 512–532.

Nemec, J. (2018). Public administration reforms in Slovakia: Limited outcomes (why?). *NISPAcee Journal of Public Administration and Policy, 11*(1), 115–134.

Neubauerová, E. (2003). *Finančné aspekty decentralizácie verejnej správy. [Financial aspects of public administration decentralization].* Ekonóm.

Piško, M. (2018). *The good practices on transparency in Slovak enterprises owned by public sector.* Transparency International Slovensko.

Placek, M., Vacekova, G., Svidronova, M., Nemec, J., & Korimova, G. (2021). The evolutionary trajectory of social enterprises in the Czech Republic and Slovakia. *Public Management Review, 23*(5), 775–794.

Preker, J. M., & Harding, A. (2003). *Innovations in health service delivery: The corporatization of public hospitals.* World Bank.

Riapošová, Ľ., & Dančíková, Z. (2014). *Analýza vymožiteľnosti infozákona v štátnych a mestských firmách. [Analysis of the Enforceability of the Information Law in State and Municipal Companies].* Transparency International Slovensko.

Sancino, A., Grossi, G., & Sicilia, M. (2016). Between patronage and good governance: organizational arrangements in (local) public appointment processes. *International Review of Administrative Sciences, 82*(4), 785–802.

SGI. (2017a). *Kto riadi mestské firmy. [Who governs the city companies].* Accessed March 10, 2020, from https://www.governance.sk/kto-riadi-mestske-firmy/

SGI. (2017b). *Členovia orgánov a všeobecné data o mestských firmách. [Members of Boards in City Companies – dataset]*. Accessed February 12, 2020, from https://www.governance.sk/o-mestskych-firmach-a-ich-problemoch/clenovia-organov-a-vseobecne-data-o-mf/

Sičáková-Beblavá, E., Šipoš, G., & Kurian, M. (2011). Korupcia a protikorupčná politika na Slovensku 1989 - 2010. [Corruption and anti-corruption policy in Slovakia 1989 - 2010]. *Forum Historiae, 5*(2), 157–197.

Sičáková-Beblavá, E., & Sloboda, M. (2017). Party patronage in local-government companies Slovakia. *Proceedings of the 21st International Conference Current Trends in Public Sector Research, 1*, 345–352.

ŠípoŠ, G. (2012). Recruitment policy. In G. ŠípoŠ (Ed.), *Good governance in local government* (pp. 45–48). Transparency International Slovensko and InŠtitút pre dobre spravovanú spoloČnosť.

Sloboda, M., & Sičáková-Beblavá, E. (2020). Effects of formalized procedures for selection of CEOs in municipally owned enterprises. *Journal of Economics, 68*(5), 520–538.

Strečanský, B., & Stoláriková, K. (2012). Social economy and social enterprises in Slovakia. *Civil Szemle, 9*(4), 87–100.

Swianiewicz, P., Gendźwiłł, A., & Zardi, A. (2017). *Territorial reforms in Europe: Does size matter?* Centre of Expertise for Local Government Reform.

Tavares, A. (2017). Ten years after: Revisiting the determinants of the adoption of municipal corporations for local service delivery. *Local Government Studies, 43*(5), 697–706.

Transparency International Slovensko. (2019, September 8). Ktoré verejné firmy taja autá svojich manažérov? [Which public companies keep their managers' cars secret?]. *SME Blog*. Accessed December 10, 2020, from https://transparency.blog.sme.sk/c/516321/ktore-verejne-firmy-taja-auta-svojich-manazerov.html

Transparency International Slovensko. (2020). *Hodnotenie firiem za rok 2019. [Evaluation of companies in 2019]*. Accessed November 3, 2020, from https://firmy.transparency.sk/

Vallo, M. (2018). *Plán Bratislava. [Bratislava Plan]*. Accessed October 15, 2020, from https://issuu.com/teamvallo2018/docs/issue_planb_05-2018_165x240mm

Van Genugten, M., Van Thiel, S., & Voorn, B. (2020). Local governments and their arm's length bodies. *Local Government Studies, 46*(1), 1–21.

Voorn, B., Van Genugten, M., & Van Thiel, S. (2017). The efficiency and effectiveness of municipally owned corporations: A systematic review. *Local Government Studies, 43*(5), 820–841.

Voorn, B., Van Genugten, M., & Van Thiel, S. (2020). Performance of municipally owned corporations: Determinants and mechanisms. *Annals of Public and Cooperative Economics, 91*, 191–212.

Wollmann, H. (2016). Public and social services in Europe: From public and municipal to private provision—and reverse? In H. Wollmann, I. Koprić, & G. Marcou (Eds.), *Public and social services in Europe: From public and municipal to private sector provision* (pp. 313–334). Palgrave Macmillan.

Žárska, E., & Kozovský, D. (2008). *Teoretické a praktické aspekty fiškálnej decentralizácie. [Theoretical and practical aspects of fiscal decentralization]*. Ekonóm.

PART III

Central Federal European Countries

CHAPTER 8

Municipally Owned Corporations in Austria: High Popularity, Low Transparency

Sanja Korać and Iris Saliterer

8.1 Introduction

This chapter looks at a context where economic activities at the local government level via municipally owned corporations (MOCs) are explicitly rooted in the constitution, and therefore are popular vehicles for the provision of public services, but also for inter-municipal cooperation. However, comprehensive overviews of MOCs regarding their size, sectors, or industries, municipal equity, as well as governance issues are nonexistent in literature. This appears to be the result of only limited reporting requirements to the statistical office, limited budgeting and accounting reporting requirements, and a lack of public corporate governance codes

S. Korać (✉)
University of Klagenfurt, Klagenfurt am Wörthersee, Austria
e-mail: korac@uni-speyer.de

I. Saliterer
University of Klagenfurt, Klagenfurt am Wörthersee, Austria

University of Freiburg, Freiburg, Germany
e-mail: iris.saliterer@vwl.uni-freiburg.de

M. Van Genugten et al. (eds.), *Corporatisation in Local Government*, https://doi.org/10.1007/978-3-031-09982-3_8

or guidelines for the local level. In the following sections, the authors will look at the context and legal framework for municipal economic activity, trends in the popularity of MOCs across different regions in Austria, as well as the public discourse around MOCs in general and around governance issues in particular. Legal forms, types, sectors, and size of MOCs are presented in Sect. 8.5, before managerial authority and governance structures are discussed in Sects. 8.6 and 8.7. Concluding remarks are provided in Sect. 8.8.

8.2 The Administrative Context for Municipal Economic Activity

Austria is a federal state that consists of the central (or, federal) government, 9 state governments (or, federal provinces; *Länder*), and 2095 local governments (municipalities).[1] There exists no legal distinction between different types of local governments, but a certain status, that is, 'statutory city' (*Statutarstadt*), 'urban municipality' or 'city' (*Stadtgemeinde*), and 'market town' (*Marktgemeinde*) points to (historical or formal) rights awarded to different local governments. The average population size of Austrian municipalities is 3336[2] (excluding Vienna), and ranges from 42 inhabitants in the smallest municipality (Gramais), to 1,908,104 inhabitants in the largest municipality (Vienna). The latter, however, is a specific case insofar as it is both a municipality as well as a state government (*Land*).

While the central government has been described as holding the financial reins in the multi-tier system,[3] financial interdependence that is mirrored in the rules of the Fiscal Equalisation Law (*Finanzausgleichsgesetz FAG*, regularly re-negotiated for a period of four years) and fragmented distribution of powers between the administrative levels account for strong subnational levels. State governments are vested with extensive legislative and executive powers particularly in the policy fields of economic affairs, environmental protection, social welfare, health, and education (Egger-Peitler & Höllerer, 2018, p. 17).

[1] The administrative tier of districts (in total, 99) is integrated in the state government and as such represents no independents territorial authority.

[2] Own calculation based on data of Statistik Austria (2020).

[3] Compared to other federal states in the EU for instance, Austria's central government expenditures may be judged as relatively high (Egger-Peitler & Höllerer, 2018).

8.2.1 *Municipalities and Municipal Functions*

Municipalities, the smallest and nearest-to-citizen units in the state system, are guaranteed a substantial degree of autonomy through the principle of subsidiarity and the constitutional right to self-government (Art. 116 B-VG). In their own sphere of influence, that is matters that exclusively or mostly concern the local community within its geographical boundaries, municipalities are not subject to directions from upper levels of government (Art. 118 B-VG). This touches mainly upon the municipalities' functions and services in the area of public welfare, elderly care, public transport, sanitation, planning and zoning, roadworks, school infrastructure, and utilities. However, to ensure lawfulness in the municipalities located in their province, state governments have supervisory rights, the right to information, and the right to repeal and approve local ordinances. In addition to the own sphere of influence, there also exists a transferred sphere of influence where tasks are delegated to local governments and the mayor acts as the executive body for federal as well as respective state government laws (see also Loizidou & Cools, 2011).

The Austrian constitution provides for local government economic activities in the sense that local governments may possess property or assets, and may own municipal enterprises or corporations (Art. 116 B-VG). This explicit permission may be one of the key factors explaining the popularity of MOCs. The constitution, however, also sets clear boundaries to the economic activity of municipalities: the economic activity must (1) be essential to addressing the demand by citizens located in the respective municipality, and (2) remain in a reasonable proportion to the capacity of the municipality and the demand by citizens. As a consequence, MOCs may be understood as the long arm of the state that is used for the delivery of services in the public interest; and probably therefore, MOCs have been less disputed than state-owned enterprises at the federal and state level from a legal perspective (see Kahl, 2019, p. 402 ff.).

8.2.2 *The Legal Framework for Municipal Economic Activity*

Several legal provisions allow for, but also limit municipal economic activity in Austria. Given that municipalities have statutory duties as part of the politico-administrative system, their economic activities must be limited to activities and tasks that will not harm or circumvent their statutory duties or core tasks. Furthermore, MOCs under private law are only allowed when no legal provisions for service delivery under public law (or through the core administration) exist (Baumgartner & Fister, 2019, Rz 3.30). In practice, for services in the area of public utilities (e.g. water, sewer, energy, and waste), a municipality may choose between all legal forms under private law as well as public law.

The already-mentioned constitutional principle of municipal self-government, on the one hand, allows 'free asset management' for municipalities, including the right to utilise all instruments of private law not only for the purpose of governance but also for the commercial purpose of achieving profits. On the other hand, the same article highlights that this right must be exercised within the boundaries of basic law, or, general federal and state laws. From a practical perspective, the equality principle is one of the most important basic law provisions that limits municipal economic activity. MOCs that deliver services which citizens depend on must treat citizens equally, irrespective of, for example, their gender, their socio-economic or religious background (Art. 7 B-VG). The dependence on services emerges mainly from a monopoly of the municipally owned corporation (MOC) in the context of public utilities (e.g. water, sewer). In this case, the MOC has an obligation to contract. If a MOC is in no monopoly position, the obligation to contract exists only if it would breach the municipality's obligation for equal treatment (Baumgartner & Fister, 2019). Additionally, in situations where a MOC is in a competitive position (with one or more privately owned corporations), competition laws limit municipal economic activity to prevent harm to competition. The latter is mainly achieved through the prohibition of cross-subsidies,[4] which have been subject to criticism by and ruling of the European Union for several years and in several industries (see e.g. European Regulators Group for Postal Services, 2019, Regulation (EC) No 1370/2007).[5]

While the aforementioned legal provisions set boundaries for municipal economic activities, there also exist some phrasings in municipal budget ordinances that may be rather supportive of the latter: they call for an efficient management of municipal assets (and therefore a MOC), which includes preserving the assets in an undiminished manner and managing it

[4] Cross-subsidies in this context describe the practice that funds yielded in a regulated sector (or through core administrative activities) are used to support activities in an unregulated (competitive) sector.

[5] More general provisions in the European law (mainly from a competition perspective) are beyond the scope of the present chapter. For a more detailed discussion see Kahl, 2019, pp. 407–421.

to achieve an—as large and durable as possible—earning.[6] Additionally, according to the financial constitution (*Finanzverfassung*), the federal and respective state government must authorise certain levies in municipalities. In theory, this may be an impetus for municipal corporatisation, where the owner of the corporation (in this case, the municipality) has higher flexibility in setting fees and prices for services.

8.3 Trends in Municipal Economic Activity

Municipalities in Austria have utilised MOCs to deliver certain services, in particular public utilities and public transport, for decades. As such, the local level differs from the national level where several large-scale formal privatisations have been carried out in the 1990s, and material privatisation had dominated the political agenda of (a centre-right coalition) federal government in the 2000s (see e.g. Bischof, 2020). The main reason for the differing picture may not lay in a particular resistance to privatisation by municipalities, but rather in the functions or tasks that municipalities fulfil, of which many tend to be considered as core public tasks by Austrian citizens. As an example, in over 90% of municipalities, water supply is organised by municipal providers. Among those municipalities that have privatised water supply, the majority have done so mainly only formally, keeping control over the service via MOCs (see Verband Kommunaler Unternehmen Österreichs, 2021).

Over the last five years, there have been incremental as well as rather substantial changes in the number of MOCs. The total number of MOCs for the years 2016–2019 ranges between the low 2000s, but for the years 2020 and 2021 is in the low 4000s (2016: 2159; 2017: 2157; 2018: 2239; 2019: 2196; 2020: 4186; 2021: 4110). As suggested by the data,[7] the notable increase between 2019 and 2020 seems to be rooted in an increased tendency to use MOCs as a vehicle for inter-municipal cooperation. These MOCs are mainly operating under public law (see also Sect. 8.3).

Another picture emerges when looking only at MOCs operating under private law: the total number of MOCs that are listed in the business register (*Unternehmensregister*) or in the register of (non-profit) associations

[6] The earnings may, however, also be interpreted as 'value' including social value (see Baumgartner & Fister, 2019, Rz 3.29).

[7] Data for 2020 obtained via Statistik Austria (2021), data for 2016–2019 obtained via internet archives sites of Statistik Austria.

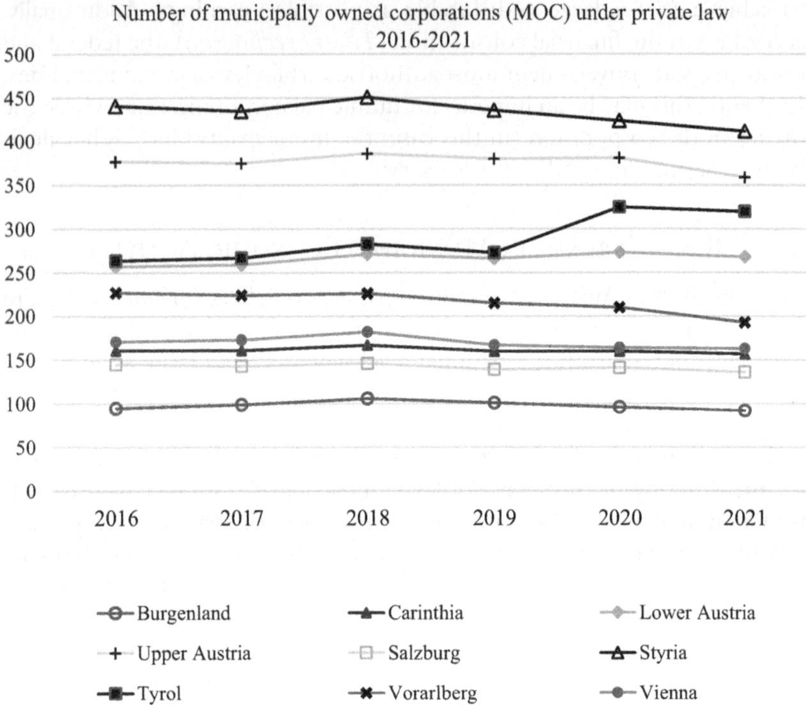

Fig. 8.1 Number of MOCs operating under private law, 2016–2021 (Source: Authors' own illustration based on data of Statistik Austria, 2021)

(*Vereinsregister*)[8] remained in the lower 2000s between 2016 and 2021. Interestingly, there are some differences across the nine states: a downward trend is observable in Styria (*Steiermark*), Vorarlberg (*Vorarlberg*), and Upper Austria (*Oberösterreich*) over the past five years, while there is a notable increase in MOCs in the state of Tyrol (*Tirol*) between 2019 and 2020 (see Fig. 8.1).

When considering the ratio of MOCs to the number of municipalities within a state, there are some differences worth noticing. Excluding

[8] Note that this is a purposeful selection of municipally owned corporations under private law and that it thereby omits legal forms under public law, particularly entities of inter-inter-municipal cooperation for specific services, e.g. inter-municipal school cooperations, inter-municipal registry office, inter-municipal planning.

Vienna, where one municipality (see the description of the administrative status of Vienna as a state and a city above) owns around 170 corporations, one state (Vorarlberg) shows more than twice the MOCs than municipalities (2.25), one state (Tyrol—*Tirol*) shows a balanced ratio of around 1 (1.03), three states (Salzburg, Carinthia—*Kärnten*, and Styria—*Steiermark*) show a ratio of more than 1 (1.19, 1.22, and 1.51 respectively). Only three states (Lower Austria—*Niederösterreich*, Burgenland, Upper Austria—*Oberösterreich*) show a ratio below 1 (0.46, 0.57, and 0.86 respectively). Interestingly, the variance in the numbers of MOCs thus does not seem to be linked to the number of municipalities in a state. Similarly, it does not seem to be linked to the number of larger municipalities (with a population of more than 10,000) in a state. While Lower Austria, for instance, has 26 municipalities with more than 10,000 inhabitants, the ratio of MOCs to municipalities is 0.46. In Carinthia (*Kärnten*), only seven municipalities reach the threshold of 10,000 inhabitants, but the ratio of MOCs to municipalities is 1.21. In Vorarlberg, where 10 municipalities have a population over 10,000, the ratio is 2.25. The number of MOCs also does not seem to be related to a possible demand to cover a larger area: while again, Lower Austria is the largest state geographically, it ranges in the middle on the average number of MOCs (266). Vorarlberg, geographically the second smallest state, is comparable to Lower Austria on the average number of MOCs (216) (see Table 8.1).

8.3.1 MOCs in Public Discourse

Given the strong principle of local self-government in Austria, MOCs tend to remain a local political issue, and seldom are on the broader political agenda. A search of press releases of the association of MOCs since the late 1990s shows a focus on efficiency, sector integration, digitalisation, cyber security, and sustainability (Austria Presse Agentur, 2021). Usually, privatisation efforts are likely to trigger public discourse in Austria (see the remarks on privatisation at the national level above), and so do re-municipalisation efforts. In more recent years, there have been some re-municipalisation activities, mainly in the city of Vienna (for the following examples, see Furtner et al., 2019, pp. 112 ff.). Between 2007 and 2015, the Viennese public transport corporation (*Wiener Linien GmbH & Co KG*) has taken over several bus routes that previously had been operated by private corporations. However, at the same time, the amount of bus route kilometres operated by private corporations increased due to a general increase in bus routes in the area of

Table 8.1 Key figures on municipalities, MOCs, and states

State	*Municipalities*	*Municipalities with >10,000 inhabitants*	*Average No. MOCs under private law (2016–2021)*	*Ratio No. MOCs under private law/ municipalities*	*Size in km²*
Burgenland	171	1	98	0.57	3965
Carinthia	132	7	161	1.22	9537
Lower Austria	573	26	266	0.46	19,180
Upper Austria	438	13	376	0.86	11,983
Salzburg	119	7	142	1.19	7155
Styria	286	13	433	1.51	16,399
Tyrol	279	8	289	1.03	12,648
Vorarlberg	96	10	216	2.25	2602
Vienna	1	1	170	170	415

the city of Vienna. The same corporation, *Wiener Linien GmbH & Co KG*, took over the security service in public transport from a previously commissioned private service provider in 2017 (after only one year of operation by the private service provider). In a similar service area, the Viennese public utility company (*Wiener Stadtwerke*) replaced a private corporation in managing 30 public garages in Vienna and Lower Austria. In the culture sector in 2013, a Viennese municipal corporation organised as a non-profit (club/association) (*Theaterverein Wien*), added the *Theater an der Gumpendorfer Straße* to its independent theatres. The respective theatre had been previously organised as a private club, owned by two individuals. In the tourism and leisure sector, a public infrastructure corporation of the city of Innsbruck took over a cable car company (*Patscherkofelbahn*) in Tyrol in 2014. The latter had previously been sold to a private company in 1996. In most cases, high operating costs or a lack of investment funds have been the reason for re-municipalisation. While it is likely that some of the cases have sparked political debate in the respective municipalities, the cases have not played a notable role in the media and have been covered mainly in regional outlets at the time of tender or sale.

However, in the midst of a government crisis in 2021,[9] a scandal at the federal government's holding (managing all state-owned enterprises at the

[9] The then-chancellor Kurz was placed under investigation on suspicion of corruption.

federal level) drew public attention towards state-owned enterprises by highlighting shortcomings in personnel acquisition and applicant selection, and the practice of awarding all powers to a single representative. As a consequence, the civil society and non-governmental organisations have called for increased transparency and clear governance guidelines in all "state-affiliated" enterprises.[10] In particular, Transparency International has pointed at the risks of "tailoring" a job posting to desired candidates, installing controllable members to hearing committees, informal instructions to personnel consulting firms, and skewed negotiations with first-ranked but undesired candidates (see Transparency International Austria, 2021).

While possible shortcomings in the transparency of MOCs mainly remain under the radar, more recently, a few focused audit reports have led to increased media attention to governance issues particularly in MOCs under private law. Two audit offices have conducted audits of MOCs in four mid-sized cities (9500–55,000 inhabitants) (see Landesrechnungshof Salzburg, 2021; Rechnungshof Österreich, 2021a, 2021b), showing (1) a lack of equity management, strategic management, and standardised monitoring, management accounting, and risk management, (2) a lack of the four-eyes-principle, (3) opacity in service exchange, (4) (prohibited) cross-subsidisation, (5) a lack of transparent hiring processes and payment guidelines and caps for top management positions, and (6) conflicts of interest due to the mayor or top administrators acting as members of the board or the supervisory board. While the audited local governments' number of MOCs did not exceed 17, the issues do not seem to be resolved in larger local governments. Only recently (November 2020), the capital of Vienna (with 170 MOCs) has announced efforts to develop a public corporate governance code, comprising provisions on the rights and duties of the owner, the interaction between management and supervisory bodies, transparency and reporting obligations, compensation, equal treatment and promotion of women, and controlling and auditing.

For MOCs under public law, media interest seems to be low, even though inter-municipal cooperation in the form of public corporations seems to have increased during the last two years.

Also during the COVID-19 pandemic, MOCs did not receive particular attention in the public or in the media. Only MOCs in the area of leisure (indoor and outdoor swimming pools) and culture (theatres,

[10] All enterprises where any government level (federal, state, local) has direct or indirect equity.

museums, city guides), which have been affected by the responses to the COVID-19 pandemic (closings of tourist sites, cultural and leisure facilities), have been in a (publicly only little noticed) debate of granting financial assistance by the federal finance ministry.

8.4 Legal Status of MOCs

MOCs in Austria can operate both under public and under private law. MOCs under public law refer to (1) public-law institutions (*Anstalten*), a legal form that is often found with museums or government offices such as the statistical office, (2) foundations (*Stiftungen*), a legal form that is known due to the broadcasting company ORF, and (3) public corporation (*Körperschaften*), a legal form often selected for statutory professional associations (see Kahl, 2019, pp. 424 f.). These legal forms are rather prevalent at the federal level, which is also mirrored in the provided examples. However, public corporations are often found also at the municipal level, mainly with the case of inter-municipal cooperation (municipal associations).

The legal forms under private law differentiate between partnerships, where (at least in the case of one partner) there is practically no limitation of liability, and corporations, where liability is limited to a certain amount of general capital or stock capital raised to set up the respective corporation. The legal form partnerships (*Personengesellschaften*), and here particularly the form of general partnership (*Offene Handelsgesellschaft/ Offene Gesellschaft*) which generally does not provide for a limit of liability, but also the status of partner with unlimited liability in a limited partnership (*Komplementär* in *Kommanditgesellschaft*) have been viewed with much scepticism, and literature has argued for an avoidance of these legal forms (see the debate mentioned in Kahl, 2019, p. 426) due to their potentially unlimited damaging impact on the municipal budget (in case of insolvency of bankruptcy of the partnership). Nevertheless, a view of the legal forms used by municipalities for their corporations in 2021 shows that they are (still) used in practice, even though they account for a fraction of legal forms used. The data on MOCs listed either in the business register (*Unternehmensregister*) or in the register of (non-profit) associations (*Vereinsregister*) (i.e. MOCs operating under private law) show 3 general partnerships operating in 2021. In addition, there exist 130 limited partnerships. The data from the statistical office do not show which part in the partnership (i.e. partner with limited liability or partner with unlimited liability) is played by the municipality.[11] However, an unrestricted participation (and thus liability) of municipalities in partnerships should no longer occur due to the requirements in the Stability Pact 2012 (see Korac & Saliterer, 2019, p. 14). Thus, cases where the municipality is the partner with unlimited liability will be declining.

8.4.1 *Trends in Legal Forms*

Figure 8.2 provides an overview of the total number of municipally owned (or, municipally controlled) corporations that are either classified as units of the General Government (here: local government), or as units that are Market Producers. The differentiation between Market Producers and General Government goes back to the classification of sectors according to the European System of Accounts (Eurostat, 2010). The category of General Government is defined as comprising entities that are non-market producers, are financed by compulsory payments made by entities belonging to other sectors, and entities that are principally engaged in the redistribution of national income and wealth. For the purpose of the present chapter, the focus lies on the sector classified as S.1313 (local government). The category of Market Producers focuses on the sector of non-financial corporations (S.11) as well as financial corporations (S.12), both being independent legal entities and market producers, but recognised as public producers, public corporations, or public quasi-corporations. For Fig. 8.2, only entities that are classified as units in S.11 and S.12 but are being controlled by municipalities have been included in the data.

The data show that the larger part of MOCs are non-market producers (i.e. general government). Here, the entities are mainly organised as limited liability companies (private law) (35%) or as public corporations (here explicitly inter-municipal cooperation; other public corporations are assigned to the category 'other') (32%). The smaller part is found with clubs/associations (non-profits) (11%), or in mixed forms (here explicitly limited partnership and limited company, and club/association and limited partnership). Note that only one joint stock company is found in the non-market producers category.

Market producers are mainly organised as public corporations (here explicitly inter-municipal cooperation) (43%). This is insofar little surprising

[11] Answering this question would require an in-depth search of the business register and as such lay beyond the scope of the present chapter.

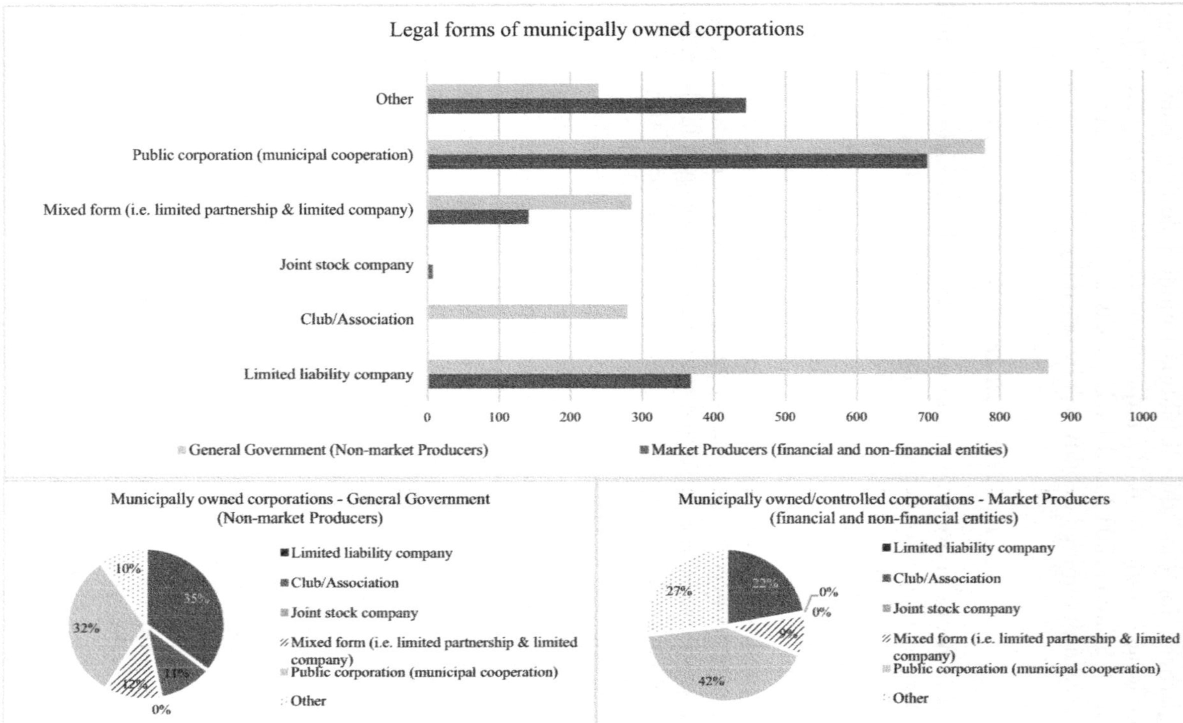

Fig. 8.2 Legal forms of MOCs in 2021—comparison of municipally owned/controlled corporations categorised as Market Producers and as General Government (non-market producers) (Source: Authors' own illustration based on data of Statistik Austria, 2021)

as this category contains largely inter-municipal cooperation in the area of utilities (water, sewage, waste), an area of public services that has been considered suitable for inter-municipal cooperation particularly for smaller municipalities in order to reach economies of scale on the one hand. On the other hand, this area of public services usually can sustain itself (cover at least 50% of operating costs through prices). Other dominant legal forms for market producers are limited liability company (22%), and less so mixed forms (here explicitly limited partnership and limited company, and club/association and limited partnership) (9%). Joint stock companies again are used only seldom (n = 7), and there is only one club/association found in the category of Market Producers. The large proportion of MOCs that cannot be assigned to any one of the mentioned legal forms is notable (27%). While this may be due to missing indication of legal forms, this figure may also mirror the limitation of the analysis method used.[12]

8.5 Purpose, Sectors, and Types of MOCs

Traditionally, state-owned enterprises have been active in various sectors and areas like the infrastructure sector (utilities and transport), but also in cultural (theatres, museums) and social services (job placement, elderly care). The intensity of activities in these areas vary, however, across the administrative levels. Federally owned corporations mainly address infrastructure like road construction and maintenance, railways (*ASFINAG*, *ÖBB*), postal services (*Post AG*), industry management (many of the corporations in the *ÖBAG* group) and real estate management (of federally owned land as well as buildings like university or school buildings—*BIG*), but also cultural services (museums); states' (*Länder*) owned corporation mainly provide utility services (electricity and gas) and financial services (banking, insurance). MOCs provide for a wide array of services such as utilities (electricity, gas, water, sewage, waste), financial services (municipal savings banks), infrastructure (ski lifts, cable cars), social services (sheltered workshops, elderly care, public housing), cultural services (theatres), but also health and sanitary services (animal carcass disposal, stockyards, funeral services) (see also Kahl, 2019, p. 424).

[12] For the overview provided in Fig. 8.2, data obtained from the Austrian Statistics Office have been analysed with filter functions as well as the search function in Microsoft Excel. This method is satisfactory if legal forms are indicated clearly, but has limitations in case of typographic errors or differently provided indications of legal forms.

8.5.1 *MOCs as a Vehicle for Cooperation*

Inter-municipal cooperation has been explicitly permitted in the constitutional right to self-government, and municipalities have used the vehicle of MOCs for this purpose for decades, as mentioned above. Nevertheless, a notable increase can be observed between 2019 and 2020. The reasons for this cannot be discerned at this stage, but it can be assumed that increasing fiscal squeezes in municipal budgets may have fostered institutionalised inter-municipal cooperation.

A view of the data on MOCs under public law reveals that most of the MOCs that are a vehicle for inter-inter-municipal cooperation (760 out of 867) are non-market producers in the area of schools, public health/sanitation, planning/zoning, financial services/special funds/tax and fee collection, and registry services. In contrast, market producers are found in the area of water and sewage services and public transport (107 out of 867) (Statistik Austria, 2021).

While the Austrian statistical office (*Statistik Austria*) provides data on state-owned corporations where government (at the federal, state, or the local level) owns more than 50% and thus has a controlling position over those corporations, state-owned corporations where governmental entities have a blocking minority are not included in the figures. Earlier contributions have already reached limits in their attempt to report the status quo of states and MOCs in Austria, concluding that no robust data is available (see Reichard, 2016, p. 13 f.). A complete overview of MOCs with an indication of (1) the amount or extent of shares owned by the respective municipality, and (2) the amount or extent of shares owned by other state or private sector partners would require manually searching for the information in municipal equity holdings reports (if publicly available), or requesting data from 2095 municipalities directly, which goes beyond the scope of the present chapter.

8.5.2 *Size and Activities of MOCs*

A closer look at MOCs' size and area of activity reveals a diverse picture. As there exists no detailed list that would allow a complete overview of MOCs in these aspects, the authors purposely selected 36 corporations that are not representative for, but may give an impression of the overall sample. The selection aimed to include MOCs of different legal forms and located in different states as well as in smaller but also larger municipalities. The corporations' size is reflected in its equity, since data on employees and the annual turnover mainly are not publicly available.

While the cost-free publicly available information on equities ranges between €0 (in case of corporations with unlimited liability), ca. €70, the low thousands, and double-digit million figures, for several of the selected corporations, there was only the ratio or share of equities available (provided in % with no information on the total capital). Only seldom is such information provided on the corporations' website—even in case of seemingly large corporations (e.g. water or gas utility suppliers for mid-sized municipalities). There is, however, a tendency of MOCs in the utilities area being rather large (with a capital of several million euros), probably not least due to high investments required, and MOCs being likely to keep with the minimum of capital required by law according to the respective legal form (in particular, limited liability company: €35,000[13]). However, even though the minimum capital for joint stock companies is €70,000, the selected cases of this legal form showed a capital of more than one million euro.

MOCs mainly serve a single sector. Those operating under private law provide, for instance, real estate management services, cultural and tourism services, regional development services, financial services, funeral services, fairs and event services, airports, swimming pools, social services, and public housing. It is rather the corporations in the area of utilities (water, sewage, electricity, heating) that are multi-purpose corporations. MOCs under public law almost exclusively seem to serve only one sector, e.g. old town conservation (if owned by one municipality), but also water, public transport, sewage, tax and fees collection, public health/sanitary services, school infrastructure/school building maintenance, registry services and planning/zoning services (if owned by more than one municipality; i.e. inter-municipal cooperation).

8.6 Managerial Autonomy in MOCs

Municipalities are required to monitor the business activities of their MOCs. A municipality needs to ensure that its MOCs work to maximise the common good, ensure the provision of public services, and increase the quality of life and sustainability. This may stand in contrast to the

[13] The exception to this are limited liability companies in different sectors in Vienna, where the corporations have a capital of at least €100,000 but go up to more than one million.

commercial goals that a corporation operating under private law pursues, and has therefore fuelled the debates on MOCs struggling to find balance between democracy (=safeguarding the interests of the owner, i.e. the interests of the citizens of the municipality) and efficiency (=entrepreneurial autonomy). To tackle this possible trade-off, a municipality's strategy/vision/mission statement must be reflected in the MOC's objectives, and interests and information between the owner (municipality), the citizens as indirect owners, the supervisory board (if applicable, see below), and the board of directors or the management need to be transparent. However, municipal influence in a MOC's business matters will be limited by the respective legal form chosen for a MOC, as will be explained below.

8.6.1 Limitations of Managerial Autonomy

Managerial autonomy in Austrian MOCs first depends on the respective legal form under which the corporation operates. While at a first glance it may be assumed that top management in MOCs operating under public law will have stronger ties with policy makers and the administration, MOC practice in Austria draws a different picture. Municipal organisation regulations provide that the mayor represents the municipality in all matters. The mayor therefore has unrestricted, autonomous powers in the municipality's economic activities. The municipal council must be consulted only on the establishment of the MOC, on capital increases, important asset transfers, changes to a MOC's tasks, and matters of fundamental importance to the municipality.[14] As such, the mayor assumes the role of the owner representative in a MOC, and (in case of non-existing governance regulations) is free to fill top management and supervisory positions in a MOC at own discretion. For MOCs with a legal form under private law and with limited liability, two bodies are usually key to a MOC's managerial autonomy, and thus also its limitation—the executive board and the supervisory board.

The executive board is entrusted with the management of the company, following the principle of due diligence and the best interest of the company, the owner, the employees and the public interest. Executives or managers, however, are bound by the object and purpose of the corporation (which often mirrors a public interest), and also need to ensure that the corporation operates in a legally compliant, efficient, expedient, and

[14] These matters are not defined in more detail.

economic way. The executive board develops the strategic direction of the company (i.e. basic entrepreneurial decisions within the framework defined by the object and purpose of the company, such as opening new business areas, investment and financing) within the framework of the legal and statutory requirements and within the framework of any requirements of the owner and the supervisory board.

A supervisory board is common, but its existence is subject to the distinct legal form (obligatory in joint stock companies), and the capital stock as well as the number of employees. The supervisory board regularly monitors the management of MOCs and advises on fundamental matters. More precisely, it monitors the compliance with the principles of legality, economic efficiency, expediency, and economy in management decisions; the compliance with the purpose of the company in management decisions; the development of performance; the risk management and internal control system; and the implementation of the resolutions of the supervisory board. The supervisory board must also *a priori* approve any significant changes in business activities, fundamental changes in the net assets, financial position or results of operations, or in the risk structure of the corporation. In these cases, the consent of the supervisory board must be obtained if the respective law (applicable to the legal form of the corporation) does not provide for consent. Consent is not required if changes are made on the basis of a resolution or instruction of the owner or shareholders (since the liability of the supervisory board is excluded in this case).

There are only few detailed reports on staffing of management or the executive board as well as the supervisory board in Austrian MOCs (see the remarks in Sect. 8.3.1). These cases show that in practice, management positions are filled with top administrators from the municipality, fulfil the MOC's management role and their administrative role in parallel. At the same time, representatives of the municipality tend to assume several management roles, e.g. in a MOC holding as well as its subsidiaries, in parallel. More importantly, however, mayors (the sole representatives of the owner) assume roles in the supervisory board, which lead to conflicts of interest. As a consequence, even if top management positions are filled with individuals not affiliated with the municipality, the composition of the supervisory board (in particular, the share of seats filled by politicians or civil servants representing the administration), may limit managerial autonomy in MOCs.

8.6.2 Steering and Monitoring

Questions of steering and monitoring of MOCs appear to be answered as diverse as the general picture of MOCs presents itself. As mentioned above, MOCs that operate under private law with limited liability, but do not reach a certain capital and employee threshold, are not obliged to operate with a two-tier board system. Thus, where corporations operate under public law and under a one-tier board regime, steering and monitoring may be more immediate, and often powers are bundled at the mayoral position. However, where MOCs follow corporate governance codes, the delineation of responsibilities between management and the supervisory body (if applicable) presents itself very clearly.

While the federal level has introduced a public corporate governance code in 2012, the code is only binding for corporations owned by the federal government. The sub-national governments are invited to orient themselves on the federal code, but are not obliged to do so. Some states (Tyrol, Salzburg) and municipalities (Innsbruck) have used the federal public corporate governance code as a model for their own codes. The capital Vienna seems to embark on a similar path, announcing the development of a Vienna Public Corporate Governance Code (see Sect. 8.3.1).

MOCs organised as joint stock companies orient themselves on (1) the Austrian corporate governance code for publicly listed companies in the private sector, even though they are not listed and do not have to comply with the latter (e.g. *Wiener Stadtwerke Holding AG*), or on (2) sector-specific corporate governance codes (e.g. non-profit building/housing associations) (e.g. *Neue Heimat*).

While corporate governance codes set rules on certain business aspects, e.g. prohibit the provision of loans to certain groups (e.g. members of the executive board or the supervisory board), there are no regulations on where a state or MOC may get loans, which size they need not exceed, which long-term investments may be made and how, and whether and how budgets may be shifted. Furthermore, if labour issues such as hiring and firing or setting wages, and organisational issues such as re-organisation, sale of assets, and cooperations/partnerships, do not constitute fundamental changes to the corporation, executives and managers are not limited by corporate governance codes in their decisions. Such scenarios would usually be regulated in 'equity guidelines' (*Beteiligungsrichtlinien*). However, the authors could not conclusively infer whether municipalities in Austria have equity guidelines as none are publicly available via websites. Due to mentions of such guidelines in reports of audit institutions, at least larger municipalities seem to have established equity guidelines that are used for steering their MOCs. However, as these are not easily available to citizens, the question remains whether these guidelines serve the purpose of accountability towards the (indirect) owner—the municipality's citizens.

In practice, strategic management of MOCs—in terms of prioritising the company's goals or systematically implementing strategic municipal goals seems to be rather the exception. Often, financial planning and financial targets seem to be more important to the municipal owners. Also, equity guidelines are seldom and definitions of general rights and responsibilities of actors may mainly be found in statutes, rules of procedure and the reporting system, or, ultimately are communicated by political actors in supervisory board meetings. This picture has been painted in practitioner-oriented publications already more than ten years ago (see Biwald et al., 2008), and it appears that not much has changed, at least from an outside or citizen perspective. If equity guidelines exist, they are more likely to serve as internal administrative regulations that guide an administrative representative in their role as supervisory board member.

8.6.3 *Accountability*

Accountability and transparency regimes and mechanisms, again, depend on whether the municipally owned corporation in question orients itself towards any corporate governance code or no such guidelines exist. In the first case, there are clear rules on when the executive board needs to inform the supervisory body (and therefore, indirectly, the municipality) or the owner, and how this information needs to be communicated.

According to the (for municipalities, non-binding) public corporate governance code, the executive board and management must immediately inform the supervisory body or—if none has been established—the shareholders of all significant events that are of material importance for assessing the company's situation and development (e.g. events relating to planning, business development, risk situation, and risk management; significant changes in the economic environment; and deviations from the established plans and objectives).

To inform indirect owners (citizens), information related to the corporation, i.e. the corporate governance report, annual financial statements or other financial statements and, if applicable, the management report and a non-financial report or a non-financial statement, must be made available on its website. Only competing companies are exempt from this obligation if it may lead to a competitive disadvantage. The general approach here is that shareholders and third parties are informed primarily by the company's annual financial statements/management report or consolidated financial statements/group management report.

The disclosure of the compensation of the members of the executive board and the supervisory board, on the other hand, requires the consent of the persons concerned.

To ensure compliance with law, regulations, and guidelines in internal operations, companies with more than 30 employees or annual sales of more than one million euros and corporate groups are required to establish internal audit units that perform internal audits on the basis of generally accepted international auditing standards.

For corporations that do not follow any corporate governance code, accountability and transparency would be regulated in equity guidelines, which, unfortunately, are not publicly available.

8.7 Governance Structures in MOCs

MOCs operating under a legal form with unlimited liability typically have corporate governance structures of only one tier. Those operating under limited liability, and in particular, larger limited liability companies, operate with two-tier boards. Here, the law provides for two tiers if certain prerequisites are met[15]:

- The share capital exceeds €70,000 and the number of shareholders exceeds 50.
- The number of employees exceeds 300 on average.
- The corporation controls or is controlled by other corporations based on a direct participation of more than 50% and the number of employees of the companies together exceeds 300 on average.
- The company is the general partner of a limited partnership and the number of employees in its company and in the company of the limited partnership together exceeds an average of 300.
- The bodies representing the employees of a company resulting from a cross-border merger have the right to elect or appoint some of the members of the supervisory board or to recommend or reject their appointment.

[15] The listed prerequisites are not exhaustive. See § 29 GmbH-Gesetz.

Extant literature on board compositions, in particular, political affiliations of board members, has analysed state-owned corporations with ownership by the federal state (see Meyer et al., 2018). State-owned corporations at the local level, and therefore MOCs, to the best of the authors' knowledge, have not been analysed yet. Therefore, we cannot provide general information on the composition of the supervisory board with regards to the ratio of politicians, civil servants, economists/external experts, employee representatives and others in this chapter.

The authors, however, selected specific MOCs, utility providers, to gain a first glance of the supervisory board composition. For each of the nine states, one utility provider has been selected for the sample. In a first step, this would be utility providers for the state capital. However, not every state capital has a general utility provider. In two states,[16] no general utility provider exists and the services seem to be split between more specialised, smaller corporations. In one state,[17] the state capital has no general utility provider, so the authors selected the next biggest municipality, where, however, no information could be found for the supervisory board online. Thus the authors selected the third biggest municipality and analysed its utility provider's supervisory board. In another state, one general utility provider exists, but no information is publicly available on whether there exists a supervisory board.[18] In this state, there is no general utility provider in the next biggest municipalities either. Again, the services seem to be provided by more specialised corporations.

The selected cases show a diverse approach to the composition of utility provider supervisory boards across municipalities (see Fig. 8.3). The board size ranges between 8 and 13 persons. While in some corporations, all of the mentioned groups are represented (politicians, civil servants, economists/experts, employee representatives) (Bregenz, Schwaz, Vienna), other corporations operate with only some of the groups represented in the supervisory boards (Graz, Linz). Interestingly, in the case of Graz, the administration seems to be indirectly represented in the Graz utility provider's supervisory board: three of the board members are part of the executive or management team of another municipal corporation (here,

[16] Burgenland, Salzburg.

[17] Tyrol.

[18] Further, there is no publicly available information on the capital of the corporation and the authors therefore could not discern whether there is a legal obligation to operate with a two-tier board or not.

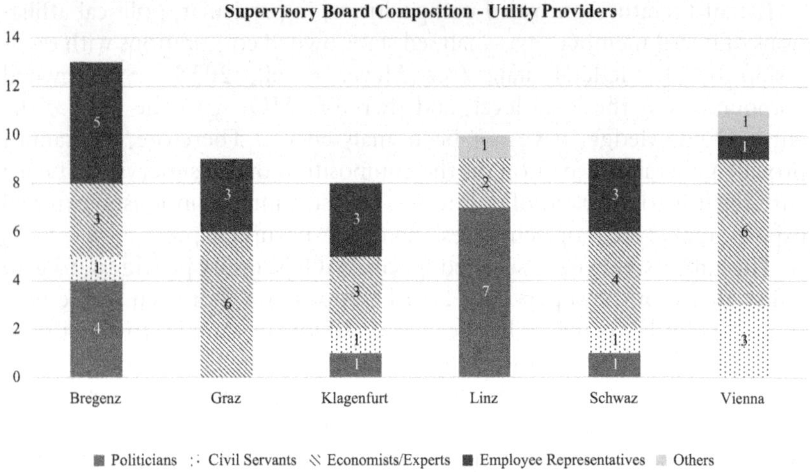

Fig. 8.3 Supervisory board composition of six municipal utility providers across Austria

the municipal holding), and the other three board members are part of the executive or management team of a state corporation. The case of Vienna is a peculiar one—not only because of its size given that the corporation serves the nation capital and therefore around a fifth of the Austrian population. Four of the six economists/expert members of the supervisory board are part of the executive or management team of another MOC (here, the subsidiary companies in the area of public transport, energy, or grids). The group of 'others' often refers to persons with a background in particular chambers (chamber of commerce, chamber of labour).

8.8 Conclusion

In Austria, MOCs have traditionally been popular vehicles for the provision of public services, and in recent years more increasingly also for inter-municipal cooperation. This popularity may stem from the explicit constitutional provision, the higher flexibility for municipalities in setting fees and prices for services (without authorisation of the federal and the respective state government), and, in the case of inter-municipal cooperation, also from increasing fiscal squeezes in municipal budgets. While MOCs provide a wide array of services, most MOCs serve a single sector. The notable exceptions are MOCs providing utilities (e.g. water and sewer, electricity, waste).

Comprehensive overviews of Austrian MOCs regarding their size, sectors or industries, municipal equity, as well as governance issues are, however, non-existent in literature, and the Austrian context shows shortcomings in MOCs' transparency from several points of view. First, limited reporting requirements to the statistical office lead to the fact that publicly obtainable data are of unsatisfactory quality for the purpose of this chapter. Most Austrian municipalities are small and medium-sized and offer no or only limited information on MOCs on their websites.

Second, the general reporting requirements for municipalities are limited. While the budgeting and accounting reforms in 2020 and 2021 have brought about higher standards in financial (and non-financial) reporting for municipalities, the changes referred to the core administrative activities, and only to a limited extent to reporting on investments and equity. Some MOCs bear unlimited liabilities for their owning municipality, but these remain mainly invisible to citizens. This limited data also accounts for the authors being able to provide only spotlights of the status quo of MOCs in this chapter, with clear limitations and caveats in the data provided.

Third, due to legal provisions, mayors represent municipalities in all matters. They have therefore unrestricted autonomous powers in the municipalities' economic activities and assume the role of the owner representative in MOCs. Together with the fact that only few municipalities have corporate governance codes or publicly available equity guidelines, this unearths noteworthy shortcomings in MOCs' personnel policies, and equity and risk management in general. The scandal at the state-owned enterprise holding at the federal level as well as a few focused audit reports of MOCs in four medium-sized cities have increased media and civil society attention towards governance issues. Against the background of the strong self-governing principle, however, it remains to be seen whether the public pressure will spread across different municipalities and translate to obligatory equity guidelines and public corporate governance codes in the near future.

References

Austria Presse Agentur. (2021). *Verband kommunaler Unternehmen Österreichs – VKÖ [Austrian Municipal Corporation Association – VKÖ].* Accessed March 23, 2021, from https://www.ots.at/pressemappe/6880/verband-kommunaler-unternehmen-oesterreichs-vkoe

Baumgartner, G., & Fister, M. (2019). Bundesverfassungsrechtliche Grundlagen der kommunalen Wirtschaftstätigkeit [Federal constitutional foundations of municipal economic activity]. In G. Baumgartner (Ed.), *Recht der kommunalen Wirtschaftstätigkeit* (pp. 69–121). Manz.

Bischof, D. (2020). *Grassers Schatten über Schüssels Ära [Grasser's Shadow over Schüssel's Era].* 09 12 2020, 20:00, Update 10 12 2020, 11:22. Wiener Zeitung. Accessed July 6, 2021, from https://www.wienerzeitung.at/nachrichten/politik/oesterreich/2084863-Grassers-Schatten-ueber-Schuessels-Aera.html

Biwald, P., Mitterer, K., & Parzer, P. (2008). *Organisation und Steuerung kommunaler Daseinsvorsorge. Formen der Leistungserbringung – Beteiligungsmanagement [Organisation and management of municipal services. Forms of service provision - Equity management].* KDZ.

Egger-Peitler, I., & Höllerer, M. A. (2018). *Public administration characteristics and performance in EU28: Austria.* European Commission.

European Regulators Group for Postal Services. (2019). *ERGP Report on the cross-subsidisation.* ERGP.

Eurostat. (2010). *European System of Accounts ESA 2010.* Eurostat and European Commission.

Furtner, A., Halber, S., Kaya, S., Terzic, L., Wülbeck, L., & Scheucher, R. (2019). *Rekommunalisierung in Europa [Remunicipalisation in Europe].* Österreichische Gesellschaft für Politikberatung und Politikentwicklung.

Kahl, A. (2019). Öffentliche Unternehmen [State-owned enterprises.]. In M. Holoubek & M. Potacs (Eds.), *Öffentliches Wirtschaftsrecht. Volume II* (pp. 399–454). Verlag Österreich.

Korac, S., & Saliterer, I. (2019). Stellenwert und Steuerung kommunaler Wirtschaftstätigkeit – Möglichkeiten und Herausforderungen [Status and control of municipal economic activity - opportunities and challenges]. In G. Baumgartner (Ed.), *Recht der kommunalen Wirtschaftstätigkeit* (pp. 1–33). Manz.

Landesrechnungshof Salzburg. (2021). *Beteiligungen der Stadtgemeinde Zell am See im Gesundheitswesen [Shareholding of the municipality of Zell am See in the health care sector].* Landesrechnungshof Salzburg.

Loizidou, I., & Cools, M. (2011). *Local and regional democracy in Austria. The Congress of Local and Regional Authorities.* Council of Europe.

Meyer, R. E., Höllerer, M. A., & Leixnering, S. (2018). A question of value (s): Political connectedness and executive compensation in public sector organizations. *International Public Management Journal, 21*(3), 477–500.

Rechnungshof Österreich. (2021a). *Beteiligungen der Stadt Krems an der Donau und der Stadtgemeinde Leonding [Shareholding of the city Krems an der Donau and the municipality Leonding].* Reihe Niederösterreich 2021/9, Reihe Oberösterreich 2021/6 [Lower Austria Series 2021/9, Upper Austria Series 2021/6]. : Rechnungshof Österreich.

Rechnungshof Österreich. (2021b). *Landeshauptstadt St. Pölten [State Capital St. Pölten].* Reihe Niederösterreich 2021/3 [Lower Austria Series 2021/3]. : Rechnungshof Österreich.

Reichard, C. (2016). Gemischtwirtschaftliche Unternehmen im europäischen Vergleich [Mixed economy Companies in European comparison]. *Zeitschrift für öffentliche und gemeinwirtschaftliche Unternehmen, 48*, 10–24.

Statistik Austria. (2020). *Bevölkerungszahl 31.10.2019 gemäß § 10 Abs. 7 FAG 2017 Gebietsstand: 1.1.2020 [Population 31 10 2019 according to § 10 Abs. 7 FAG 2017, Territorial Status 1 1 2020].* Accessed July 7, 2020, from http://www.statistik.at/web_de/statistiken/menschen_und_gesellschaft/bevoelkerung/volkszaehlungen_registerzaehlungen_abgestimmte_erwerbsstatistik/bevoelkerungsstand/index.html

Statistik Austria. (2021). *Einheiten des öffentlichen Sektors gemäß ESVG Stand März 2021 [Public sector entities according to ESA 2010 as of March 2021].* Accessed April 15, 2021, from https://www.statistik.at/web_de/statistiken/wirtschaft/oeffentliche_finanzen_und_steuern/oeffentliche_finanzen/oeffentlicher_sektor/index.html

Transparency International Austria. (2021). *Mehr Transparenz bei der Besetzung von Top Positionen in staatsnahen Unternehmen [More Transparency in filling top positions in state-affiliated corporations].* Accessed November 18, 2021, from https://www.ots.at/presseaussendung/OTS_20210708_OTS0085/mehr-transparenz-bei-der-besetzung-von-top-positionen-in-staatsnahen-unternehmen

Verband Kommunaler Unternehmen Österreichs. (2021). *Wasser. Die kommunale Siedlungswasserwirtschaft [Water. Municipal Water Management].* Accessed November 18, 2021, from http://www.vkoe.at/verband/wasser/

CHAPTER 9

Corporatised Public Service Provision of Local Governments in Germany: A Key Topic for UN-SDGs and Promising Public Corporate Governance Developments

Ulf Papenfuß

9.1 Context of Local Governance and Corporatised Public Service Provision

Germany is a federal state that consists of the federal government, 16 states (*Länder*) and 11,455 local authorities, including 107 county-free cities, 294 counties and 11,054 municipalities belonging to a county (Ruge & Ritgen, 2021). Germany is a characteristically constitutional state with a parliamentary democracy comparable to that of other countries. The local level plays a strong administrative and political role in the German system (Kuhlmann et al., 2021; Reichard & Schröter, 2021). The right to local self-governance has a longstanding history and is part of

U. Papenfuß (✉)
Zeppelin University, Friedrichshafen, Germany
e-mail: ulf.papenfuss@zu.de

M. Van Genugten et al. (eds.), *Corporatisation in Local Government*, https://doi.org/10.1007/978-3-031-09982-3_9

Article 28 (2) of the Basic Law providing municipalities the right to shape all matters of the local community.

In principle, local government is the operational level responsible for implementing programmes and laws from the federal and state levels (Kuhlmann et al., 2021; Reichard & Schröter, 2021; Ruge & Ritgen, 2021). Local governments are usually entrusted by states with the performance of federal and state laws in one of two ways: (1) either the state transfers tasks to the local governments and thus transforms them into municipal tasks, or (2) the local governments perform state tasks as external tasks and thus act on behalf of the state. This framework explains the largely decentralised administration in Germany (Kuhlmann et al., 2021; Reichard & Schröter, 2021; Ruge & Ritgen, 2021). In addition to compulsory tasks, local governments also provide voluntary tasks.

Local governments account for 30% of public service personnel in Germany. This high percentage reflects the special importance of local governments, which deliver most public services in direct contact with citizens. State personnel only account for a higher percentage of public service personnel due to the numerous public servants working in schools, universities, police and courts. The central budgets of the local governments cover roughly one-third of public expenditure, excluding social security. Moreover, there are special budgets for local governments which base on public expenditure as well (Ruge & Ritgen, 2021).

The distinction between counties and municipalities is important for understanding the structure of local self-government bodies in Germany (Kuhlmann & Wollmann, 2019). Due to their limited size and/or administrative power, municipalities and cities are usually not able to fulfil all tasks of the local community on their own. For this reason, they are incorporated into a county. When municipality is referred to in the following, also cities are meant.

Each state has municipal laws and county laws that primarily regulate the organisational rights of municipalities and counties (i.e. local constitutional law). Local governments have elected representative bodies (i.e. municipal council or city council). Citizens usually elect the head of a local administration (i.e. the mayor) directly (Reichard & Schröter, 2021). As in many other countries that follow the "classical" continental European administrative system and its traditions (Kuhlmann & Wollmann, 2019), municipalities in Germany, in general, have a sophisticated implementation level of public sector reforms (Kuhlmann et al., 2021).

Municipally owned corporations (MOCs) are enterprises that are under the control of a municipality either by majority ownership by one or more municipalities or otherwise by exercising an equivalent degree of control (Grossi et al., 2015; OECD, 2015; Papenfuß, 2020a). Corporatised public service provision means that a public service of a public authority is provided by a corporate organisational form under the control of the government. Corporatisation is the process by which governments convert an existing public service into a majority-owned corporate entity or create a new service (Andrews et al., 2020; Papenfuß & Schmidt, 2021b). Corporatised public service provision and corporatisation can be an "excellent example of the systemic or corporate public entrepreneurship" (Andrews et al., 2020, p. 482).

It is very important not to mix up corporatised public service provision and corporatisation with commercialisation and profit-seeking. A decision can be made in favour of a corporatised form striving for more effective and efficient public service provision, but this does not necessarily imply a stronger focus on profit or financial goals (Expert Commission G-PCGM, 2022; Papenfuß, 2020a; Papenfuß & Schmidt, 2021b). Corporatised public service provision is an organisational form for service provision and an alternative to the provision of public services by the administration on the one hand, or contracts of the administration with private partners or total private service provision on the other hand (Andrews et al., 2020).

Regarding the establishment opportunities of MOCs, the municipal laws of the state include requirements for municipalities. A municipality may establish or may participate in the establishment of a MOC in a legal form under private law or gain a share of an existing enterprise in a legal form only if (1) this action has an important public interest, (2) this public interest cannot be better and more economically achieved with other means, and (3) the municipality ensures an appropriate influence on the relevant corporate bodies that is secured in the statutes of the MOC or in some other way. In addition, (4) this economic activity must be in reasonable proportion to the municipality's capacity in terms of its nature and extent. Plus, (5) the municipality must choose a legal form that limits its own liability to a certain amount. The municipality cannot assume losses of an indefinite or unreasonable amount. Finally, (6) the municipality must ensure that the annual financial statements and management reports are prepared and audited according to the German Commercial Code for large enterprises (Papenfuß & Schmidt, 2016). At appropriate intervals, the municipality should examine the extent to which the economic activity complies with legal conditions and requirements (Expert Commission G-PCGM, 2022).

9.2 Relevance of MOCs and Trends

According to the statistics currently available from the German Federal Statistical Office, there were 16,634 MOCs in 2019 (Federal Statistical Office, 2022a). Regarding the percentage of state-owned enterprises at all government levels, 87.5% were MOCs at the local level, 10% were majority-owned by the states, 1.5% by the federal government and 0.9% by social security funds. In 2009, there were 13,258 MOCs, representing a 21% increase in the past ten years (Federal Statistical Office, 2022a). They have generated total profits of €609 billion with around €583 billion spent on expenses.

Empirical studies at the local and municipal levels in Germany have shown that the number of employees in MOCs and comparable independent organisational forms is as high as the number of employees in administration and often even higher (Papenfuß & Keppeler, 2020). In 2019, MOCs had 1,215,375 employees, accounting for 50.3% of public sector employees on the local level (Federal Statistical Office, 2020). MOCs made 54% of public investments. The debts located in MOCs often exceed the debts of the administration. In 2016, these debts amounted to 56% of the total municipal debt (Bertelsmann Foundation, 2013, 2019).

With regard to the international discussion on re-municipalisation, there is some evidence for the energy sector. From 2007 to 2012, municipalities and municipal companies undertook more than 160 concessions. One study reports that 72 newly founded municipal energy utilities emerged from 2005 to 2015 (Friedländer et al., 2021).

9.3 Legal Forms of MOCs

In Germany, MOCs can operate in private or public legal forms. Table 9.1 displays the numbers in the classification categories of the federal statistical office (Federal Statistical Office of Germany, 2022c). The most widespread legal form is the limited liability company (*Gesellschaft mit beschränkter Haftung*) with 9911 MOCs which have legal and managerial/financial independence (Papenfuß & Keppeler, 2020). The second common legal form are the 3283 in-house corporations (*Eigenbetriebe*) which have managerial/financial independence but no legal independence. In the

Table 9.1 Legal forms of MOCs

Legal form	*MOCs*		
	2009	*2014*	*2019*
Limited liability companies	7568	7995	9911
In-house corporations	3624	3446	3283
General partnerships and limited partnerships etc.	442	571	1276
Special purpose associations	1095	1108	1111
Other private-law legal forms	279	311	539
Other public-law legal forms	250	351	514
Total	13,258	13,782	16,634

Source: Federal Statistical Office of Germany (2022c)

comparatively small group "other private-law legal forms" the legal form joint-stock corporations (*Aktiengesellschaft*) is the more frequently discussed form. Limited liability companies are dominant, because unlike joint-stock corporations, they allow the public shareholder to exert strong influence on corporate strategies, business plans and daily operations through statutes, shareholder meetings and shareholder instructions. In the group "other public-law legal forms" public institutions and foundations under public law (*Anstalt und Stiftung des öffentlichen Rechts*) play an important role which have managerial/financial independence and legal independence. The 1111 special purpose associations are inter-municipal cooperations of several local governments for a joint fulfilment of public services with legal and managerial/financial independence. Inter-municipal cooperation also exists in the form of other legal forms such as limited liability companies with several local governments as shareholders, but special purpose associations are more common for inter-municipal cooperation.

Between 2009 and 2019 the share of the legal form "limited liability company" in the total number of MOCs increased from 57.1% to 59.6%; the share of in-house corporations decreased from 27.3% to 19.7%. In an overall view, the numbers indicate a trend towards legal forms with more legal and managerial independence.

For the debate, it is important to stress that the decision on "private legal form" or "public legal form" of a MOC conceptually is not related to a focus on profit or financial goals. There might be tendencies, but a MOC in a public legal form can be more profit-oriented than in a private legal form. Very informative for many research fields is to classify MOCs in profit-making forms (i.e. generating revenues for both business activity and disbursements to the public budget) and not profit-making forms (i.e. competing for grants/subsidies from the governmental budget to ensure their public service delivery) independent of the legal form as conceptually stressed in the current corporatisation debate (Papenfuß & Schmidt, 2021b).

9.4 Policy Sectors of MOCs and Organisational Characteristics

In Germany, MOCs provide a wide range of services. Table 9.2 outlines the number of MOCs in different sectors and their sales revenues in each sector. The sectors are shown sorted by the highest value for the number of MOCs for 2019. Regarding the number of MOCs in 2019, the sectors with the largest share are "Water supply, waste disposal, pollution abatement" (22%), "Energy supply" (14.8%) and "Housing" (13%). In terms of revenue, "Energy supply" (56%), "Health and social care" (11.6%) and "Water supply, waste disposal, pollution abatement" (9.2%) have the largest shares. In comparison between 2009 and 2019, for instance, the data show a strong increase in the number of MOCs for "Energy supply" and "Housing" and a reduction for "Water supply, waste disposal, pollution abatement". In some sectors, the number of MOCs and revenues have developed in the same direction; in single sectors, such as "Water supply, waste disposal, pollution abatement", the numbers have decreased, and the revenues have increased.

The data and tables underline that MOCs are crucial to the state and society as well as the prevailing debate on the United Nations' Sustainable Development Goals (SDGs). With regard to Sustainable Development Goal (SDG) 7 "Affordable and clean energy", the number and size of MOCs in the energy sector show their crucial importance to ensure access to affordable, reliable, sustainable and modern energy for all. A lot of services for SDG 7 are provided by MOCs and not by administrations or private companies. This is also the case for SDG 6 "Water and Sanitation", to ensure availability and sustainable management of water for all. Moreover, MOCs provide a substantial part of services which are essential for SDG 10 "Reduced Inequalities" in several sectors, such as social care. For this reason, performance, accountability and equity of MOCs is central to achieve SDG 10. The number of MOCs in the sector housing make

Table 9.2 Number of MOCs in different sectors and their revenues

	Number of MOCs			*Revenue of MOCs*		
Year	*2009*	*2014*	*2019*	*2009*	*2014*	*2019*
Water supply, waste disposal, pollution abatement	3753	3720	3669	25,699	28,001	34,025
Energy supply	1341	1628	2469	129,196	165,327	207,984
Housing	1647	1642	2166	11,221	11,826	16,209
Freelance, scientific and technical services	965	1097	1589	4429	5060	4563
Health and social care	1165	1134	1265	27,928	32,774	43,002
Art, entertainment and recreation	809	814	943	1207	1494	2848
Other commercial services	467	531	820	3262	4558	6659
Public administration, defence, social security	1055	1032	739	4618	4581	3866
Public transport and storage	692	674	728	8370	8463	11,916
Provision of financial and insurance services	178	241	554	18,188	18,659	24,719
Provision of other services	264	278	388	1273	1163	1700
Construction	291	284	335	1965	2119	2003
Education	216	263	335	534	666	1312
Information and communication	212	227	330	4425	5208	7342
Hospitality and catering	104	114	164	391	502	745
Trade, maintenance and repair of motor vehicles	31	31	62	310	2408	1224
Manufacturing industry	34	33	37	277	272	241
Agriculture, forestry and fishing	25	30	34	42	51	68
Mining and quarrying	9	9	7	321	277	310
Total	13,258	13,782	16,634	243,656	293,410	370,738

Source: Federal Statistical Office of Germany (2022a, 2022b)

them fundamental to realise SDG 11 "Sustainable Cities and Communities" regarding affordable rental prices and living space. Next, the achievement of SDG 3 "Good Health and well-being" strongly depends on MOCs because many hospitals, nursing homes and social care organisations are MOCs. For the climate targets formulated by politicians to reduce CO_2 emissions and to realise climate neutrality, it is obvious that MOCs in the areas of public utilities, public transport and housing and many more areas, emit a high proportion of the total amount of CO_2, making a reduction in these company groups particularly important. In addition, MOCs as policy instrument are often assigned a role model function for the private sector in order to achieve overriding political goals. Finally, good governance, accountability, performance, corruption prevention and trust of MOCs and their coordinated interaction with administrations are crucial to realise SDG 16 “Strong institutions” in the public administration debate on powerful and trustworthy public institutions. Regarding digital transformation as a trigger for strong institutions, it is crucial that many municipalities or MOCs with subsidiaries have established so-called digital MOCs which should organise and support digital transformation also in the administration and the whole municipality group. Moreover, many municipalities have shared service centres for digital transformation in MOCs, providing service for the administration.

Notably, the official statistics in Germany, such as those from the Federal Statistical Office, do not provide any data on how many MOCs on average have been established in different city size classes. To enable a better understanding of the situation in German municipalities, Fig. 9.1 displays the data from an own unique large-scale study (Papenfuß et al., 2018). This study analysed MOCs in private and public legal forms in all 386 municipalities with a population of over 30,000 as well as all 294 counties and identified over 5500 MOCs. The study manually collected all relevant and available aggregate holding reports from municipalities websites. An aggregate holding report is a report to the citizens and policy makers on a MOC’s service and investments (Papenfuß et al., 2019). The evaluation addressed all direct (first-degree) and indirect majority (second- or third-degree; at least 50% majority) MOCs. Some municipalities administer and control their MOCs with a unit in the core administration and directly hold the shares of these companies, whereas other municipalities outsource

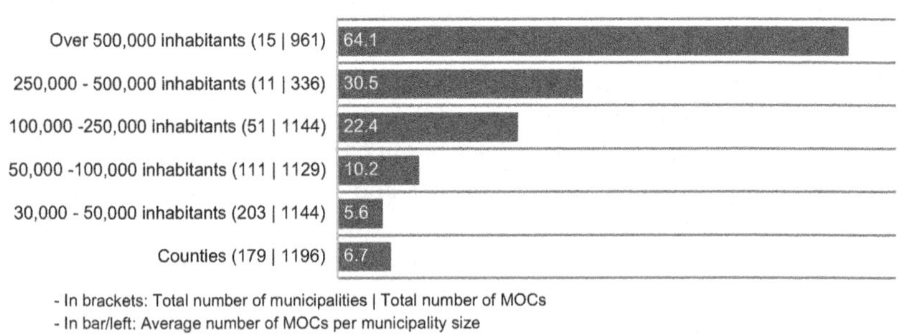

Fig. 9.1 Average number of MOCs in municipalities in Germany

these tasks to a holding management company. MOCs are direct MOCs if they are direct subsidiaries of a holding management company that is specifically responsible for their control and management. The data reflect the best comparison possible for the sample, regardless of the different institutional approaches. The study calculated the participation rate for indirect subsidiaries as commonly done by taking direct and indirect shares in parent, subsidiary and sub-subsidiary companies into account. Figure 9.1 displays the average number of MOCs per municipality.

As shown in Fig. 9.1, large municipalities tend to have more MOCs than smaller cities, and there is a significant increase between every municipality class with, on average, 64 MOCs in the biggest municipalities and on average 30 MOCs and 22 MOCs in the next size categories. These numbers additionally depict the high relevance of MOCs for each municipality to provide public services and the need for coordinated service provision with the administration. In many bigger municipalities, more than 70% of public employees work in MOCs. However, the data underline the relevance of MOCs, also for small municipalities. For instance, a public utility in a small municipality may have five subsidiaries with a direct or indirect majority ownership of the municipality. Five MOCs in a municipality with 30,000 inhabitants should also be seen in comparison to the size of the administration; often, a large proportion of public investments goes beyond MOCs and more public employees work in MOCs instead of the administration. This implies a need for sufficient democratic control, accountability and good governance in the context of MOCs also in smaller municipalities.

It should be stressed that Fig. 9.1 contains only numbers identified using the described methodology. In addition, some MOCs in the form of inter-municipal cooperation have more than one municipality as a shareholder and do not have more than 50% of their shares owned by one municipality. Furthermore, some enterprises have a municipality as a relevant minority shareholder.

The statistical offices do not provide data on organisational public-private partnerships and inter-municipal cooperation. According to another study on organisational public-private partnerships in 2011, the capital cities and five largest cities in each of the sixteen German states maintained a total of 255 direct (first level) organisational public-private partnerships (Papenfuß, 2013c). On average, this means 3.1 organisational public-private partnerships per municipality. Moreover, there were 389 indirect organisational public-private partnerships as subsidiaries of other MOCs.

9.5 Autonomy and Public Corporate Governance of MOCs

Autonomy is a crucial feature of MOCs, and it is often an important reason behind their establishment (Grossi et al., 2015). In Germany, MOCs differ greatly with respect to the autonomy that they are granted, both formally and in practice. The conceptual goal of corporatisation is to provide public services in an effective and efficient manner by making use of the strengths of MOCs. In comparison to public service provision with the administration, MOCs, amongst others, provide more managerial and financial autonomy, specific professionalism, faster strategy and decision-making more, more public entrepreneurship, more specialisation and better personnel recruitment/development opportunities (Krause & Van Thiel, 2019; Papenfuß, 2020a; Papenfuß & Schmidt, 2021b). In comparison to other service provision alternatives, such as contracting with private partners, MOCs can provide a stronger focus on public services and offer better planning and control opportunities. It is crucial to find the right balance between autonomy, managerial flexibility and political control regarding the goals of the municipality (Grossi et al., 2015; Krause & Van Thiel, 2019; Papenfuß, 2020a, 2020b). In Germany, some municipalities already have a quite good autonomy balance, in other municipalities there are excessive attempts of political interference. In the context of MOCs, the governance culture between municipalities differs substantially.

In the debate on autonomy, public corporate governance provides an important framework. Since around 2000, the term "public corporate governance" has become well established in Germany, Austria and Switzerland as a synonym for corporate governance of state-owned enterprises and MOCs (Austrian Federation, 2017; Expert Commission G-PCGM, 2022; Federal Ministry of Finance, 2020; Steiner et al., 2014; Papenfuß, 2020a, 2020b).

9.5.1 *Public Corporate Governance*

While the international academic debate has discussed concepts and terms such as corporate governance, public governance, public sector governance and public service governance, these concepts and terms do not specifically focus on corporate governance and the management of public authority organisations with independent economic management, such as MOCs. The term "public corporate governance" is more precise because the combination of the words "corporate" and "public" makes it possible to specifically address all public organisations with independent economic management in a differentiated manner. Although the term has seldom been used in international journals, it is now on the rise (Austrian Federation, 2017; Expert Commission G-PCGM, 2022; Federal Ministry of Finance, 2020; Papenfuß, 2020a, 2020b; Papenfuß & Schmidt, 2021a, 2021b; Steiner et al., 2014). Public corporate governance is the legal and factual regulatory framework for control, supervision and management of public organisations with independent economic management. Public corporate governance also includes steering, managing and supervising the behaviour of relevant stakeholders (Papenfuß, 2020a, 2020b).

Public corporate governance relates to both (1) the external control and supervision of organisations with independent economic management by the political bodies of a municipality and the core administration and (2) the internal management undertaken by independent organisational entities. Moreover, public corporate governance deals with the design of all components of the local government governance system and hence to a large extent with the core administration (e.g. the corporation management unit) and respective political authorities (e.g. the municipality council, mayor).

Public corporate governance can be understood as a synonym for "corporate governance of MOCs". However, the term "public corporate governance" more effectively conveys that the core administration and the political system are central parts in this area (Papenfuß, 2020a, 2020b). The word "corporate" specifies public organisations with independent economic management (Papenfuß, 2020a, 2020b).

9.5.2 *Legal Requirements Regarding Autonomy, Strategy Development, Goal Setting and Monitoring*

From a conceptual perspective, the local government should establish a holistic sustainable strategy for a municipality and its MOCs. As a shareholder, the local government should define the object of a MOC's purpose as the first strategic orientation. It should be derived from the local government's superordinate strategic objectives with regard to the public mandate of the MOC in its statutes (Expert Commission G-PCGM, 2022; Papenfuß et al., 2019). The legally demanded important public interest should be illustrated with performance and impact objectives, financial objectives and concrete sustainability objectives (Expert Commission G-PCGM, 2022). The authorised representatives of the local government in the MOCs bodies should work towards ensuring that the management body (executive directors) develops the MOC strategy based on the shareholder objectives, coordinates it with the supervisory body and adopts it in the shareholders' meeting (Expert Commission G-PCGM, 2022). In practice, the development of local governments' owner objectives is especially challenging and the executive directors have to fill the gap or use it in case of non-existing or unclear objectives.

The local government exercises both its rights as a shareholder in the shareholders' meeting. As a shareholder, the local government should examine whether to establish an optional supervisory board. In Germany, a supervisory board is optional until a MOC's size exceeds 500 employees. Afterwards, it becomes required by law. The supervisory board is appointed by the local government. If no supervisory board is established, the shareholders' meeting should assume its tasks instead. If a supervisory board is set up, the guiding principle behind it should be to ensure that responsibilities are very clearly divided between the shareholders' meeting and the supervisory board. Unclear responsibilities between shareholders' meeting and supervisory board are a crucial governance problem in practice.

The administration of the local government should ensure the establishment of effective shareholdings management for all MOCs of the local government and provide this entity with adequate human and material resources in terms of both quality and quantity (Expert Commission G-PCGM, 2022). Many municipalities already have an organisational unit with qualified personnel, in many others, in particular smaller municipalities, there still is a severe lack of administrative capacity.

The supervisory board regularly supervises and advises the management body on the management of the MOC. It must be involved in decisions of fundamental importance to the MOC. In daily life, it is often difficult for the mayor and administration to achieve "eye-to-eye level" with the executive director.

The management body manages the daily operations of the MOC. The management body is obligated to conduct the MOC's business in accordance with its statutes and the resolutions of the shareholders' meeting and supervisory body. In general, executive directors have quite a lot of autonomy, but there are also cases of strong political influence and political issues outside the official governance processes.

9.5.3 *Public Corporate Governance Codes for MOCs*

In the overall conception of autonomy and public corporate governance, public corporate governance codes (PCGCs) are crucial instruments that can cover all relevant governance fields (Expert Commission G-PCGM, 2022; Federal Ministry of Finance, 2020; OECD, 2015; Papenfuß, 2020a, 2020b; Papenfuß & Schmidt, 2021a; Steiner et al., 2014). In Germany, PCGCs are developed by local governments and approved by the responsible political body (e.g. a municipal council). PCGCs are intended to summarise the basic characteristics of the public corporate governance system and regularly address occurring governance questions, ambiguities and legal gaps. A public corporate governance code (PCGC) prescribes regulations for the management and supervision of MOCs and should contain internationally and nationally recognised standards of responsible governance. They define goals, responsibilities, duties, rights, instruments and processes for various areas. Empirical studies have shown that PCGCs can enhance the governance and control of MOCs (Papenfuß & Schmidt, 2021a; Papenfuß & Wagner-Krechlok, 2022; Steiner et al., 2014).

In Germany, roughly 55 local governments have established PCGCs since 2005, and several more are in the process of doing so. Although the basic concept and structure of these PCGCs are the same all over Germany, there are crucial differences and deficits in their formulation (Papenfuß & Schmidt, 2021a; Papenfuß & Wagner-Krechlok, 2022; Papenfuß, 2013a, 2020a).

Since 2001, there has been a corporate governance code for listed enterprises in Germany, which is regarded as a crucial instrument in the private sector (Aguilera & Cuervo-Cazurra, 2004; Cuomo et al., 2016; Haxhi & Van Ees, 2010). However, compared to the corporate governance codes for listed enterprises, there are numerous special features and requirements in the context of MOCs. For example, the regulatory field owner must be completely differentiated regarding the political bodies involved and many specific processes in the political-administrative system. In numerous other fields, specific regulations tailored to the situation are also required due to the constitutive public purpose of MOCs, politicians in supervisory boards and information processes with the administration and so on (Expert Commission G-PCGM, 2022; OECD, 2015; Papenfuß & Schmidt, 2021a).

As in corporate governance codes for listed enterprises in the private sector, the underlying so-called "comply-or-explain" principle differentiates PCGCs from other regulatory instruments. The management body (executive directors) and the supervisory board (directors) must declare annually as part of the published corporate governance statement that the recommendations of the PCGC have been and continue to be complied with or which recommendations have not been or are not being applied and why not. Deviations from the recommendations must be justified in a comprehensible manner (Expert Commission G-PCGM, 2022; Papenfuß, 2020a).

The comply-or-explain principle is used in many corporate governance codes for listed companies and is applied in many countries (Aguilera & Cuervo-Cazurra, 2004; Cuomo et al., 2016; Expert Commission G-PCGM, 2022; Papenfuß, 2020a). Due to the freedom of choice and flexibility it allows (Cuomo et al., 2016; Expert Commission G-PCGM, 2022; Papenfuß, 2020a), PCGCs can formulate governance standards for MOCs that differ, for instance, in size, legal form, etc.

As already realised by several, but not all, German public authorities, the responsible actors should ensure that the establishment and transparent publication of the declaration of compliance is anchored in the MOC's statutes or by resolution in the shareholders' meeting to realise the idea of the "comply-or-explain" principle. The "comply-or-explain" principle explicitly allows deviation from recommendations with regard to the specific situation. A deviation from a recommendation should not be understood as a "deficiency". In justified cases, it is an expression of good public corporate governance. In practice, a full understanding of the "comply-or-explain" principle, a "lived deviation culture" and the proper interpretation and use of declarations of compliance is of salient importance (Expert Commission G-PCGM, 2022; Papenfuß, 2020a). Some municipalities and MOCs already provide quite good declarations of compliance in a transparent manner, others still show severe shortcomings. In particular, there are still important deficits regarding the understanding of the "comply-or-explain" principle and the flexible opportunities to deviate from PCGCs in justified cases.

Owing to their compliance flexibility, PCGCs can provide more precise and far-reaching requirements for governance and control than inflexible laws. Typically, laws can only regulate standard cases that do not occur frequently in practice. Therefore, laws necessarily leave regulatory gaps and loopholes that PCGCs can compensate for. PCGCs do not restrict the freedom of MOCs to make decisions, which, for good reasons, has been strengthened. The developments around PCGCs in Germany could perhaps be used as a driver for additional developments in other countries and on international policy-making levels.

9.5.4 German Public Corporate Governance-Model Code

Because of identified deficits in the established PCGCs of local governments and avoidable duplication of work in Germany, a high-profile expert commission developed the German Public Corporate Governance-Model Code (G-PCGM) in an integrative and transparent process, and published the G-PCGM in German as well as in English language[1] (Expert Commission G-PCGM, 2022). The G-PCGM strives to support local governments and public authorities on other government levels as well as individual actors to further strengthen public corporate governance. The approach of the expert commission, including the consultation process, and resulting G-PCGM could be of interest to many countries in the future debate on the governance and control of MOCs.

The development of the G-PCGM was based on a nationwide consultation procedure with the broad participation of actors from the public sector. In regular further future consultations, the expert commission invites practitioners and scholars to submit comments on the G-PCGM. The expert commission considers these comments and publishes them on their website. A regular international exchange of expert commissions that deal with PCGCs in their countries would be promising to contribute to good governance in the field of MOCs.

9.5.5 Organisational Element Shareholdings Management in Administrations

Another important issue in the debate on the autonomy and influence of the municipality in the context of MOCs is the organisational model for shareholdings management. Most German public administrations have an organisational element known as shareholdings management. As mentioned previously, the administrative management of the public authority should ensure the establishment of effective shareholdings management for all MOCs of the local government and provide it with adequate human and material resources in terms of both quality and quantity. However, the organisational model and the quality and quantity of personnel differ substantially between cities. In some cities, shareholdings management is located at the top of the administration at the mayor's level. In other

[1] See webpage www.pcg-musterkodex.de/home-englisch/

cities, it is in the financial department (*Kämmerei*). Some cities have MOCs with the public authority as the 100% shareholder, the latter fulfilling the task of conducting shareholdings management.

9.6 Board Structure and Board Members

In Germany, the corporate governance system is organised based on a two-tier board system. The management board, which is composed of the executive directors, handles the day-to-day management of the enterprise. The supervisory board, which contains the non-executive directors, is involved in decisions of fundamental importance, supervises and advises the members of the management board. The management board is of special relevance because of its greater competencies and operational influence in the German two-tier system. In the following, the chapter outlines some data on governance issues which are strongly discussed in many countries as well as in the international scientific debate.

9.6.1 Supervisory Boards: Size, Composition, Pay and Representation of Women

The members of supervisory boards are politicians, members of the public administration, external business experts and the representatives of trade unions. There are currently no representative data on the size and composition of the supervisory boards of MOCs in Germany. However, an empirical study from 2013 on the biggest cities in Germany can still convey the structure of the situation (Papenfuß, 2013a, 2013b). On average, a supervisory board had 10.4 members. However, depending on the city, this ranged from an average of 8.1–12.5. It is striking that, on average, the cities with higher populations had smaller supervisory boards than those with lower populations. This indicates that political representation may be given greater importance in some cities than others.

The overall average proportion of politicians on supervisory boards in the assessed cities was 46.8%, but the results ranged widely between cities. For example, the proportions in Stuttgart (75.5%) and Munich (70.6%) were considerably higher than those in Berlin (23.4%), Hamburg (27.6%) and Dortmund (35.6%). Only around 16% of all supervisory board members were sorted into the business/external category. The proportion of business/external members at the time of the study ranged from 28.5% in Berlin to 6.3% in Dortmund (Papenfuß, 2013a, 2013b).

In addition, there were substantial differences in supervisory board's pay between municipalities. The overall average pay for all members of a supervisory board together was around €17,900, but this number varied on average from €36,000 in some cities to €2,100 in others. The average compensation for an individual supervisory board member also ranged from approximately €3,500 to €200 (Papenfuß, 2013a, 2013b). Supervisory board's pay still strongly depends on the size and sector of a MOC. In big public utilities, some supervisory board members can receive around €5,000 to €7,000 per year, but in many smaller MOCs, the members only receive €2,000 or less per year.

Regarding the representation of women on the supervisory boards of MOCs, a study illustrated that 30.5% of the members of the MOCs' supervisory boards in the sixteen German state capitals were women in 2018. Compared to 2014, this represents only a slight increase of 0.9%. Furthermore, there were big differences in representation between cities (FidAR, 2018).

9.6.2 Executive Directors and Executive Boards

As in other board systems and countries, executive directors are particularly influential and responsible for day-to-day management in Germany. They have the most power and strong influence on strategic decisions and service provision (OECD, 2015; Papenfuß & Schmidt, 2021b). In Germany the mayor is the key decision-maker in terms of appointing and paying executive directors, accompanied by the administration and municipal council. There is high flexibility in the appointment processes and recruitment can address the whole labour market (Papenfuß & Schmidt, 2021b).

Professional Backgrounds of Executive Directors and Their Pay This section presents data from an own study that identified majority-owned corporations in all 183 German cities with over 50,000 inhabitants, using these cities' shareholdings reports (Papenfuß & Schmidt, 2022). First, corporations with direct or indirect second-degree majority ownership by a city (at least 50% majority) were included, while dissolved or merged corporations were excluded. Second, the available 2013–2017 annual financial statements of these MOCs were obtained from the company register, which is a national repository of corporate reports. Third, all personalised pay data of the full-time executive directors were collected from the annual financial statements, cities' shareholdings reports and executive-director pay databases for German public corporations. The study sample was composed of 510 executive directors employed in 291 MOCs associated with 64 German municipalities from 2013 to 2017. On average, a MOC had 2.1 executive directors, and around 60% of these MOCs had only one executive director.

In the sample, 52.4% of the executive directors were private-sector switchers: 23.3% with executive director experience and 29.0% with experience below the executive director level and one or more previous jobs at any hierarchical level below the executive director level in the private sector. 12.5% of the executive directors were politicised. Here, 5.9% were former political mandate holders, meaning that they had held a professional party office (e.g. mayor or minister), served on a city council, in regional parliament or on a cabinet of ministers. In contrast, 6.7% had become visible as party members without holding a political mandate. Moreover, the sample indicated general linear career patterns in one sector, with only 4.9% of executive directors having experience in MOCs, the private sector, public administration and the party-political context as politicians.

Furthermore, executive director pay has become a key issue in the governance and political control of MOCs under the close scrutiny of public audit agencies, the media, the political sphere and the general public (Papenfuß & Schmidt, 2021b). Appropriate pay is an especially important issue for MOCs in Germany, as fairness and equity are pertinent public values to which public-sector organisations should adhere (Keppeler & Papenfuß, 2021; Papenfuß & Schmidt, 2016). The mean executive director pay of the total panel was €211,000 (maximum of €984,000). The highest average executive director pay levels were in municipal utilities (€283,000) and public hospitals (€264,000), while social services (€98,500) had the lowest levels (see also Papenfuß & Schmidt, 2016).

Moreover, recent political, social and media discussions in Germany have focused on vertical pay dispersion, drawing comparisons between executive directors at the highest organisational level and the average employee (Keppeler & Papenfuß, 2021). Vertical pay dispersion is of high relevance for research and practice in the public sector, and an important issue for future comparative research, as equity is a pertinent public sector value. Vertical pay dispersion means differences in pay levels across organisational levels (Keppeler & Papenfuß, 2021). One empirical study investigated the manager-to-worker pay ratios in Germany and introduced the issue into the debate on international scientific public management (Keppeler & Papenfuß, 2021). The numerator of the ratio represents the average total pay of the executive director team members, while the denominator represents the average employee pay, excluding the pay of the executive directors' team members and the board. The average total pay of the executive directors' team members was calculated by summing the executive directors' annual salaries, bonuses, other annual compensation and long-term incentive pay-outs and then dividing the result by the number of executive directors in the organisation (as given in the MOC's annual report). Overall, the data collection led to a sample of 1076 manager-to-worker pay ratios for 337 MOCs in 68 German municipalities aggregated over a five-year period. The mean manager-to-worker pay ratio was 3.17. The results diverged between sectors: the mean ratio for hospitals was 4.48, 3.87 for public transport, 3.80 for public utilities and 2.62 for nursing and social services (Keppeler & Papenfuß, 2021).

Transparency of Executive Director Pay A large-scale study on executive directors from 2018 provided representative findings on pay disclosure for 5543 MOCs in all 386 German municipalities with a population of more than 30,000 and all 294 counties (Papenfuß et al., 2018). At the municipal level, the person-related pay disclosure was 16.2%. Among the 413 local governments, four municipalities had a 100% rate of person-related pay disclosure, thus demonstrating the feasibility of the transparency requirements. Six municipalities had a person-related disclosure rate of at least 75%. Twenty-five local governments achieved a disclosure rate between 50% and 75%. Of the 413 governments, 43 had a disclosure rate between 25% and 50%, whereas 87 had a disclosure rate of more than 0% and less than 25%. A total of 248 local governments (60% of the 413 local authorities) had a personal disclosure rate of 0%. The differences can be explained by the fact that some transparency laws for MOCs are only applicable in some federal states and only some local governments have PCGCs.

Representation of Women as Executive Directors Regarding the representation of women as executive directors, there is only one longitudinal empirical study with several follow-up studies which has provided comparative findings between German municipalities on the status quo and developments in the representation of women as executive directors over a couple of years (Papenfuß et al., 2021). This study analysed the MOCs of 69 municipalities. This study included the city states, capital cities of the states and the four most populated municipalities in each state. This approach ensured a nationwide and regionally balanced selection of local governments across all federal levels.

In 2021, the proportion of women was 19.5%, a decrease of 0.2 points compared to the previous year. Notably, there were considerable differences between municipalities. In 12 municipalities, the representation was over 30%. In 17 municipalities, it was below 10% (Papenfuß et al., 2021). Women continue to be much more frequently represented in health and social services (31.8%) and hospitals (25.5%) than in many other sectors. The lowest proportion of women was in the digitalisation and information technology sector (1.9%). Between 2018 and 2021, the overall proportion of executive director positions held by women increased by 1.5 points. Compared to 2018, there were some significant increases in 31 municipalities and some significant decreases in 16 municipalities. The representation stagnated in many other municipalities (Papenfuß et al., 2021).

9.7 Conclusions

In Germany, with regard to the outlined data, MOCs are of particular importance to the big questions of the modernisation of the state and public administration, the SDGs, sustainable city development, digital transformation and the equality of living conditions entail. In the past ten years, the number of MOCs has increased by 21% to 16,634 MOCs, which indicates a trend towards further increasing relevance.

Many pertinent organisations have stressed that the implementation of overriding political goals, such as the UN-SDGs, require reform developments not only at the international and national levels, but also at the local level. For Germany, the data on MOCs underline that several SDGs cannot be adequately achieved without a sufficient performance, equity, good governance, accountability, corruption prevention and trustworthiness of MOCs such as SDG 7 "Affordable and clean energy", SDG 6 "Water and Sanitation", SDG 10 "Reduced Inequalities", SDG 11 "Sustainable Cities and Communities" and SDG 3 "Good Health and well-being".

Due to this relevance, the prevailing governance deficits in the context of MOCs are all the more important. However, besides these shortcomings, the empirical data also show promising developments which could support reform processes in German municipalities and other countries. As in other German-speaking countries, "public corporate governance" is a well-established term in Germany, and offers potential for the international debate. Furthermore, quite a lot of PCGCs public corporate governance codes have been established by local governments since 2005, which are central governance instruments for MOCs. These developments could perhaps be used as a driver for additional developments in many other countries and on international policy-making level.

High-performance public service provision, equity and accountability of MOCs, as well as the integrated governance of administration and MOCs in the context of corporatised public service provision, are extraordinarily important topics for the so-called big questions of our time and for research in different disciplines. Moreover, MOCs are valuable research objects and provide a fruitful theoretical context in the middle between administration and the private sector, whose exploration is promising to enhance our overall theoretical understanding of many theoretical issues in overarching scientific debates.

References

Aguilera, R. V., & Cuervo-Cazurra, A. (2004). Codes of good governance worldwide: What is the trigger? *Organization Studies, 25*(3), 415–443.

Andrews, R., Ferry, L., Skelcher, C., & Wegorowski, P. (2020). Corporatization in the public sector: Explaining the growth of local government companies. *Public Administration Review, 80*(3), 482–493.

Austrian Federation. (2017). *Bundes Public Corporate Governance Kodex 2017 [Federation's Public Corporate Governance Code]*. Austrian Federation.

Bertelsmann Foundation. (2013). *Kommunaler Finanzreport - Einnahmen, Ausgaben und Verschuldung im Ländervergleich [Municipal finance report - Revenue, expenditure and debt comparison among federal states]*. Bertelsmann Foundation.

Bertelsmann Foundation. (2019). *Kommunaler Finanzreport [Municipal finance report]*. Bertelsmann Foundation.

Cuomo, F., Mallin, C., & Zattoni, A. (2016). Corporate governance codes: A review and research agenda. *Corporate Governance: An International Review, 24*(3), 222–241.

Expert Commission G-PCGM. (2022). *German public corporate governance-model code (G-PCGM)*. Version as of 14 March 2022. https://doi.org/10.13140/RG.2.2.26454.52800.

Federal Ministry of Finance. (2020). The federation's public corporate governance code. In *Principles of good corporate governance and active management of federal holdings*. Federal Ministry of Finance.

Federal Statistical Office. (2020). *Finanzen und Steuern – Personal des öffentlichen Dienstes [Finances and taxes – public service personnel]*. Fachserie 14, Reihe 6. Statistisches Bundesamt (Destatis).

Federal Statistical Office. (2022a). *Öffentliche Fonds, Einrichtungen und Unternehmen: Deutschland, Jahre, Ebenen des öffentlichen Bereichs, Wirtschaftsabschnitte 2014 – 2019 [Public funds, institutions, and enterprises: Germany, years, government levels, economic sections 2014 – 2019]*. Accessed February 15, 2022, from https://www-genesis.destatis.de/genesis//online?operation=table&code=71811-0001&bypass=true&levelindex=0&levelid=1649772105795#abreadcrumb

Federal Statistical Office. (2022b). *Bilanz: Deutschland, Jahre, Ebenen des öffentlichen Bereichs, Wirtschaftsabschnitte 2014 – 2019 [Balance sheet: Germany, years, government levels, economic sections 2014 – 2019]*. Accessed February 15, 2022, from https://www-genesis.destatis.de/genesis//online?operation=table&code=71811-0007&bypass=true&levelindex=0&levelid=1649772105795#abreadcrumb

Federal Statistical Office. (2022c). *Öffentliche Fonds, Einrichtungen und Unternehmen: Deutschland, Jahre, Ebenen des öffentlichen Bereichs, Rechtsform 2014 – 2019 [Public funds, institutions and enterprises: Germany, years, government levels, legal form 2014 – 2019]*. Accessed February 15, 2022, from https://www-genesis.destatis.de/genesis//online?operation=table&code=71811-0003&bypass=true&levelindex=0&levelid=1649772105795#abreadcrumb

FidAR. (2018). *Public women-on-board-index (Public WoB-Index)*. FidAR – Frauen in die Aufsichtsräte.

Friedländer, B., Röber, M., & Schaefer, C. (2021). Institutional differentiation of public service provision in Germany: Corporatization, privatization and re-municipalization. In S. Kuhlmann, I. Proeller, D. Schimanke, & J. Ziekow (Eds.), *Public administration in Germany* (pp. 291–308). Palgrave Macmillan.

Grossi, G., Papenfuß, U., & Tremblay, M. (2015). Corporate governance and accountability of state-owned enterprises: Relevance for science and society and interdisciplinary research perspectives. *International Journal of Public Sector Management, 28*(4), 274–285.

Haxhi, I., & Van Ees, H. (2010). Explaining diversity in the worldwide diffusion of codes of good governance. *Journal of International Business Studies, 41*(4), 710–726.

Keppeler, F., & Papenfuß, U. (2021). Understanding vertical pay dispersion in the public sector: The role of publicness for manager-to-worker pay ratios and interdisciplinary agenda for future research. *Public Management Review*. https://doi.org/10.1080/14719037.2021.1942531

Krause, T., & Van Thiel, S. (2019). Perceived managerial autonomy in municipally owned corporations: Disentangling the impact of output control, process control, and policy-profession conflict. *Public Management Review, 21*(2), 187–211.

Kuhlmann, S., Proeller, I., Schimanke, D., & Ziekow, J. (2021). *Public administration in Germany*. Palgrave Macmillan.

Kuhlmann, S., & Wollmann, H. (2019). *Introduction to comparative public administration. Administrative systems and reforms in Europe* (2nd ed.). Edward Elgar Publishing.

OECD. (2015). *OECD guidelines on corporate governance of state-owned enterprises*. OECD.

Papenfuß, U. (2013a). *Verantwortungsvolle Steuerung und Leitung öffentlicher Unternehmen – Empirische Analyse und Handlungsempfehlungen zur Public Corporate Governance [Responsible management and control management of state-owned-enterprises - empirical analysis and recommendations on public corporate governance]*. Springer Gabler.

Papenfuß, U. (2013b). Aufsichtsräte öffentlicher Unternehmen: Städtevergleich zu Konzeptionen und Governancepraxis [Supervisory boards of state-owned enterprises: City comparison on conceptions and governance practice]. *Public Governance, Sommer*, 16–18.

Papenfuß, U. (2013c). Organisatorische public private partnerships: Bestandsaufnahme, Entwicklungsmuster und Forschungsperspektiven [Organisational public-private partnerships: Inventory, development patterns, and research perspectives]. *dms – Der Moderne Staat – Journal for Public Policy, Law and Management, 6*(2), 361–370.

Papenfuß, U. (2020a). Corporate governance of state-owned enterprises: Conceptualization, challenges and perspectives for the public corporate governance field. In L. Bernier, P. Bance, & M. Florio (Eds.), *The Routledge handbook of state-owned enterprises* (pp. 433–444). Routledge.

Papenfuß, U. (2020b). Public corporate governance. In H. K. Anheier & T. Baums (Eds.), *Advances in corporate governance: Comparative perspectives* (pp. 220–248). Oxford University Press.

Papenfuß, U., & Keppeler, F. (2020). Does performance-related pay and public service motivation research treat state-owned enterprises like a neglected Cinderella? A systematic literature review and agenda for future research on performance effects. *Public Management Review, 22*(7), 1119–1145.

Papenfuß, U., & Schmidt, C. (2016). Pay for performance in German state-owned enterprises: Evidence and reflection for organizational success research with undistorted and "right" data. *Corporate Ownership & Control, 13*(2), 336–350.

Papenfuß, U., & Schmidt, C. (2021a). Understanding self-regulation for political control and policy-making: Effects of governance mechanisms on accountability. *Governance, 34*(4), 1115–1141.

Papenfuß, U., & Schmidt, C. (2021b). Personnel governance of corporatized public services: Effects of executive resources and corporation forms on turnover. *Public Administration*. https://doi.org/10.1111/padm.12752

Papenfuß, U., & Schmidt, C. (2022). *Valuation of sector-switching and politicization in the governance of corporatized public services. Governance*. https://doi.org/10.1111/gove.12721

Papenfuß, U., & Wagner-Krechlok, K. (2022). Diffusion of governance standards in public corporate governance codes: Measurement framework and three countries comparison. *Corporate Governance: An International Review*. https://doi.org/10.1111/corg.12494

Papenfuß, U., Schmidt, C., & Keppeler, F. (2018). *Vergütungstransparenz-Ranking 2018: Offenlegung der Top-Managementvergütung öffentlicher Unternehmen im Vergleich von Kommunen, Ländern und Bund [Pay-transparency ranking 2018: Disclosure of top management pay of state-owned enterprises in comparison of local, state and federal governments]*. Zeppeling Universität.

Papenfuß, U., Schmidt, C., & Schoneweg, L. (2021). *Frauen in Top-Managementorganen öffentlicher Unternehmen – Ein deutschlandweiter Städtevergleich [Women as executive directors of state-owned enterprises - A Germany-wide comparison of cities]*. Zeppelin Universität.

Papenfuß, U., Steinhauer, L., & Friedländer, B. (2019). Clearing the fog for an overall view on state-owned-enterprises: Quality of aggregate holdings reporting by public administrations in 12 countries. *International Review of Administrative Sciences, 85*(1), 116–136.

Reichard, C., & Schröter, E. (2021). Civil service and public employment. In S. Kuhlmann, I. Proeller, D. Schimanke, & J. Ziekow (Eds.), *Public administration in Germany* (pp. 205–223). Palgrave Macmillan.

Ruge, K., & Ritgen, K. (2021). Local self-government and administration. In S. Kuhlmann, I. Proeller, D. Schimanke, & J. Ziekow (Eds.), *Public administration in Germany* (pp. 123–141). Palgrave Macmillan.

Steiner, R., Raess Brenner, K., & Saxenhofer, A. (2014). Effects of public corporate governance guidelines at the subnational level in Switzerland. *Yearbook of Swiss Administrative Sciences, 5*(1), 139–161.

CHAPTER 10

Corporatisation in Swiss Local Government

Claire Kaiser, Reto Steiner, and Jana Machljankin

10.1 Introduction and Context

In Switzerland, corporatisation at the municipal level has been ongoing since the late 1990s, yet the literature on the topic is limited. We aim to close this gap by discussing the trend towards corporatisation in Switzerland and the unique characteristics of Swiss municipally owned corporations (MOCs), including their legal status, distribution by industry sector, degree of autonomy, and board structure.

To this end, we analysed official cantonal documents as well as the relevant literature. In particular, the chapter draws on the results of our own empirical studies, such as a study on public corporate governance at the local tier of government conducted in nine major Swiss cities of 50,000 inhabitants or more (Steiner et al., 2020) and a comprehensive study conducted periodically since 1988 among Swiss municipal secretaries (Steiner et al., 2021).

For a better understanding of the context, we present a brief overview of the municipalities of Switzerland and how they are embedded in the Swiss political system.

C. Kaiser • R. Steiner (✉) • J. Machljankin
ZHAW School of Management and Law, Winterthur, Switzerland
e-mail: claire.kaiser@zhaw.ch; reto.steiner@zhaw.ch; jana.machljankin@zhaw.ch

M. Van Genugten et al. (eds.), *Corporatisation in Local Government*, https://doi.org/10.1007/978-3-031-09982-3_10

As constituent elements of the Swiss Confederation, each of the 26 cantons consists of municipalities (*Gemeinden*), of which there are currently 2148 (as of 1 January 2022) (Swiss Federal Statistical Office, 2022). Subject to the laws of the respective canton, the municipalities can select an appropriate structure and administrative organisation, raise taxes, and independently perform any tasks not already provided by the cantons or the federal government (Linder, 2021; Steiner et al., 2021). The cantons also delegate specific tasks to their municipalities (Friederich et al., 1998).

According to the European Local Autonomy Index, the autonomy of Swiss municipalities is the highest in Europe, especially in financial matters and decision-making authority (Ladner et al., 2019). This autonomy is guaranteed constitutionally and enshrined in cantonal law (Swiss Federal Constitution, Art. 51 (1)), which also specifies the degree of freedom the municipalities enjoy (Steiner et al., 2021).

The municipal landscape of Switzerland is relatively heterogeneous and fragmented. Compared to other countries, it was reasonably stable over a long period. Between 1850 and 1990, the number of municipalities decreased only slightly from 3203 to 3021. However, around 1990, municipal mergers started to gain importance as a reform strategy. More than one-fourth of Swiss local governments have disappeared in the past 30 years, nearly all of them voluntarily. Given the many mergers between municipalities currently under consideration, this development is likely to continue.

The Swiss municipal landscape can be described as relatively small-scale by international comparison. According to the Swiss Federal Statistical Office (2021), the median size of a Swiss municipality in 2020 was 1556 inhabitants. Although more than one-third (37%) have fewer than 1000 inhabitants, almost half of the Swiss population (47%) lives in cities with a population of 10,000 or more. Only 10 Swiss cities have more than 50,000 inhabitants.

10.2 Forms of MOCs

In Switzerland, MOCs may be established either under private or public law. According to this main differentiation, the different legal forms are described in the following paragraphs.

10.2.1 MOCs Under Private Law

The two most relevant legal forms under Swiss private law in the context of municipal corporatisation are companies limited by shares (*Aktiengesellschaften*) and cooperatives (*Genossenschaften*) (Steiner et al., 2020). Further possibilities are private foundations (*privatrechtliche Stiftungen*), limited liability companies (*Gesellschaften mit beschränkter Haftung [GmbH]*), and associations (*Vereine*), all of which are briefly discussed in this section.

Companies Limited by Shares The company limited by shares *(Aktiengesellschaft or AG)* (Art. 620 et seqq., Swiss Code of Obligations) is one of the most important organisational forms of municipal corporatisation. The share capital is divided into smaller units (shares). The shareholders are primarily capital providers and participate in the decision-making process based on their share of the capital. Shareholders can be one or more municipalities, but also other shareholders from the private sector. Such companies are referred to as *gemischtwirtschaftliche Unternehmen*. Shareholders are not personally liable for the company's liabilities. The share capital must be at least CHF 100,000 (EUR[1] 100,000). This organisational form is primarily chosen for tasks in a competitive environment (e.g. an internet provider). Prescribed bodies are the general meeting of shareholders, the board of directors, and the auditors. The board of directors has extensive powers and corresponding responsibilities. The organisation and financial affairs (including the protection of creditors) of companies limited by shares are regulated in detail under federal law (Art. 60 et seqq., Swiss Code of Obligations; Steiner, 2002).

Cooperatives According to the Swiss Code of Obligations, a cooperative *(Genossenschaft)* is a corporate entity consisting of an unlimited number of persons or commercial enterprises. It primarily aims to promote or safeguard the economic interests of its members by way of collective self-help, or it is established for charitable purposes (Art. 828 (1)). Its economic activities can be for-profit or non-profit. To establish a cooperative, at least seven members must be involved. The cooperative is established after its articles of association have been approved and entered in the commercial register (Art.

[1] The conversion rate as of 15 March 2022 was applied for conversion from CHF to EUR throughout this chapter.

830). The general assembly is the highest governing body (Art. 879 (1)). A cooperative can oblige its members to make periodic contributions (Art. 832 (3)). While the number of members is not finite, there is no legal right to join a cooperative. The legal equality of all members is characteristic of the cooperative (Art. 854). They all have one vote at the general assembly regardless of their possible capital participation (Art. 828 et seqq.; Steiner, 2002). This aspect is often criticised when several municipalities of different sizes establish a cooperative or when private individuals participate.

Private Foundations Foundations may be established under private or public law. A private foundation is an entity that is legally independent and endowed with assets for a particular purpose (Swiss Civil Code, Art. 80). There are many similarities between private foundations *(privatrechtliche Stiftungen)* and public foundations *(öffentlich-rechtliche Stiftungen)* (see Sect. 10.2.2). However, one significant difference is that in foundations under private law, the founding body cannot dissolve the foundation or change its purpose.

Limited Liability Companies A limited liability company (*Gesellschaft mit beschränkter Haftung or GmbH)* is incorporated with its own legal personality regulated under the Swiss Code of Obligations (Art. 772). Its nominal capital must amount to at least CHF 20,000 (EUR 20,000) (Art. 773). It can be established by one or more natural persons or legal entities, or other commercial enterprises (Art. 775). The articles of association must contain information regarding the business name, seat, and object of the company, the amount of nominal capital, the number and nominal value of the capital contributions, and the form of external communications.

Associations An association *(Verein)* can have a political, religious, scientific, cultural, charitable, social, or another non-commercial purpose. Associations acquire their legal personality as soon as their intention to exist as a corporate body is apparent from their articles of association (Swiss Civil Code, Art. 60). The law allows them extensive freedom in terms of organisation, making them suitable for flexible solutions. The general assembly and the board of directors are prescribed as organs. In addition, one-fifth of the members of an association have the right to call an extraordinary general meeting (Swiss Civil Code, Art. 64; Steiner, 2002). As with a cooperative, all members have equal voting rights, which can create problems in the event of a conflict if members are unequal in size.

10.2.2 MOCs Under Public Law

Public Corporations In the context of municipal corporatisation, MOCs organised as ***public corporations (öffentlich-rechtliche Anstalten)*** are especially relevant. These are organisational entities that are fully government owned, mostly legally independent, and have their own management structure (Steiner & Huber, 2012a, p. 192). A public corporation is regulated by its own, dedicated municipal law and fulfils specific public tasks that have been outsourced to it by municipal law (Häfelin et al., 2020).

Public corporations are reasonably autonomous in their organisational decision-making powers (see Häfelin et al., 2020; Steiner, 2002).

We can distinguish between legally ***independent*** and ***dependent public corporations*** (Häfelin et al., 2020). Independent public corporations have their own legal personality under public law. A legal person acting in its own name has rights and obligations. It can, therefore, dispose of its assets and be held liable for its actions, although a municipality might provide for subsidiary state liability. Independent public corporations are also often called ***municipal enterprises***, which is imprecise because, as stated above, municipal enterprises can be created under public or private law (Steiner, 2002).

On the other hand, dependent public corporations have no legal personality, no legal capacity, and they do not own any assets, nor can they be held liable. Their assets belong to the entity on which they are dependent (i.e. the municipality) (see Häfelin et al., 2020).

Independent public corporations make it easier for municipalities to establish participating structures and buy (part of) other companies. In addition, business transactions become more transparent. A possible disadvantage might be the organisational and financial effort it takes for a municipality to monitor the activities of an independent public corporation. However, supervision is necessary and even if a public corporation is independent, the municipality remains liable (see Friederich, 1999, p. 500 et seq.; Steiner, 2002). A further disadvantage of such entities is the lack of a democratic structure. In these institutions, decisions are made by the management body rather than the voters or a legislative body. If a municipality decides to outsource a municipal task by establishing a municipally owned corporation (MOC) in the form of a public corporation, the fulfilment is thus, to some extent, withdrawn from the process of democratic participation (Canton of Aargau, 2019). On the other hand, service standards can still be enforced through performance contracts between a municipality and a public corporation.

Municipal Associations A municipal association (*Gemeindeverband or Zweckverband*) is formed by two or more municipalities to perform municipal tasks they have in common (see Steiner, 2002; Häfelin et al., 2020) such as water supply or waste disposal. It has a membership structure with individual municipalities as members; private individuals and private companies are excluded. The political municipality serves as a role model for this legal entity as the municipal association is also sovereign, with its own executive (management) and legislative ("voters" are the municipalities), and subject to supervision by the cantonal government (see Friederich, 1997, p. 7).

Municipal associations may be ***single-purpose*** (e.g. just wastewater treatment) or ***multi-purpose*** (various municipal tasks) (see Müller, 1999, p. 55). In addition, they can fulfil both autonomous (e.g. operating a theatre) and non-autonomous (e.g. sewage treatment) municipal tasks. Because municipal associations are subject to democratic participation, decision-making can be lengthy.

A potential disadvantage of a municipal association is that it may act like a monopoly. Citizens in the member municipalities are generally obliged to use the service provided by the municipal association, and the price is often determined unilaterally by the association (see Schedler, 1996, p. 120).

Public Foundations A public foundation (*öffentlich-rechtliche Stiftung*) is an entity that is legally independent and endowed with assets for a particular purpose (Swiss Civil Code, Art. 80). It can be defined as an administrative unit with a foundation charter that is subject to public law, usually has a legal personality, and fulfils a public task using its endowments (Häfelin et al., 2020).

A foundation carries out the wishes of its founder or founding body. It is easy to set up and only needs one body, namely a board of trustees (see Friederich, 1997, p. 8). The board of trustees appoints external auditors (Swiss Civil Code, Art. 83b). State authority supervises the foundations (Swiss Civil Code, Art. 84). A change in purpose or the dissolution of a foundation requires a decision by the supervisory authority or founding body and is rare. Foundations are, therefore, suitable for long-term, consistent tasks because they guarantee continuity regarding the purpose (see Müller, 1999, p. 63; Steiner, 2002).

10.2.3 Most Common Types of MOCs

Although there is no systematic overview of the types of MOCs in Swiss municipalities, a recent empirical study on public corporate governance by Steiner et al. (2020) yielded some valuable data concerning the distribution of MOCs in the major Swiss cities, from which we have drawn the following conclusions.

Of the MOCs of larger cities, 76% are companies limited by shares (*Aktiengesellschaften*). The main reason for this preference is that the energy sector dominates the participation portfolios of these cities. Since this market was liberalised in the late 1990s, electric power plants and utility companies usually take the form of companies limited by shares. Only 18% of MOCs are cooperatives (*Genossenschaften*), while public corporations (*öffentlich-rechtliche Anstalten*) are even less common. The proportion of public-law institutions is significantly higher among municipalities and smaller cities with up to 20,000 inhabitants, as half of all intermunicipal MOCs, for example, are structured in this way (see Sect. 10.3.5). In the case of smaller municipalities, the desire for more influence and closer ties to the municipality probably plays a significant role.

We need to keep in mind that dependent institutions (*unselbstständige Anstalten des öffentlich-rechtlichen Rechts*) provide many public services at the municipal level under public law. Because they do not keep their own accounts, it is contested if they can be considered as MOCs. Examples include the Zurich transport network (*Zürcher Verkehrsverbund*) and the St Gallen municipal utilities (*Stadtwerke St. Gallen*) (Steiner et al., 2020).

10.2.4 Legal Provisions for Setting Up an MOCs

In general, municipalities in Switzerland provide services within departmental units. Pursuant to cantonal legislation, they can, however, also transfer specific tasks to MOCs and/or other third parties. In doing so, they must ensure that the task they have delegated is implemented in a lawful and appropriate manner.

There are many reasons why a Swiss municipality decides to outsource a municipal service. It may want to (a) increase a utility's entrepreneurial, organisational, financial, and personal autonomy, (b) focus more on its core tasks, (c) increase its performance measurement, and (d) change the assignment of responsibilities (Canton of Aargau, 2019). Whenever one or several of these goals become a priority, the municipal government may establish a MOC.

A transfer of tasks occurs when a municipality permanently outsources one or several tasks to a legal entity under public or private law. The municipality might set up a new legal entity or give a task to an existing legal entity owned by the municipality, several municipalities, or private co-owners.

Due to Switzerland's federalist system, the 26 Swiss cantons have the right to regulate MOCs themselves through cantonal legislation. Various cantonal constitutions regulate the transfer of public tasks to MOCs. For an overview of the regulations for establishing MOCs in the 26 cantons of Switzerland, we analysed the cantonal constitutions and the existing cantonal laws on municipalities.[2] Only the results with an explicit legal basis based on official documents were considered without examining the legal intricacy of individual cases. Specifically, we investigated the existence of regulations on the transfer of tasks in general and regulations for setting up MOCs, either independently or jointly with other municipalities. We were also interested in details such as the requirements of statutes and other legal provisions (e.g. the involvement of the electorate or the approval by the cantonal government).

Overall, the extent to which the concept of the transfer of public tasks to MOCs is provided for by the cantons and the municipalities varies greatly. Of the 26 Swiss cantons, only two, Obwalden and Appenzell Innerrhoden, have no law on municipalities that regulates MOCs. In the other cantons, the legal provisions to set up MOCs are usually laid down in both the cantonal constitution and the law on municipalities. Therefore, at least a general legal provision for regulating the transfer of tasks can be found in almost all sub-national legislations. For 21 of the 26 Swiss cantons, the transfer of public tasks is explicitly regulated by law, either by outsourcing the tasks permanently to an institution with the responsibility to plan, control, and execute them (i.e. by creating a MOC) or by outsourcing tasks to third parties based on a service contract. Although most cantons allow for the creation of MOCs under public or private law, circumstances vary. For some cantons, the amendment or introduction of comprehensive provisions for establishing MOCs under public law is relatively new (Ticino, Bern and Aargau). Other cantons have no such provisions, or only in a limited way, especially concerning the establishment of MOCs, either individually owned and independent or in the form of a

[2] Laws on municipalities regulate the basic framework of the municipal organisation, the fulfilment of tasks, cantonal supervision, and other matters.

joint initiative under public law (Appenzell Innerrhoden, Obwalden, Vaud, Valais, Neuchâtel, Geneva and Jura). Some cantons seem to explicitly (and exclusively) regulate the establishment of MOCs under private law that are of general interest to the public (Neuchâtel and Jura). About half of the cantons allow their municipalities to cooperate with other municipalities in performing specific tasks by establishing joint MOCs under private law (Fribourg, Valais and Geneva, among others).

Most cantons (21 of 26) have legislation that stipulates the content of statutes for creating joint MOCs in the form of a municipal association (*Zweckverband*; see Sect. 10.2.2). Less than half have municipal laws with explicit regulations concerning statutes for independent MOCs in the form of a public corporation (*öffentlich-rechtliche Anstalt*; see Sect. 10.2.1). In the canton of Basel-Landschaft, on the other hand, municipal law only mentions the need to regulate such statutes, but not what the individual components of these statutes are.

In most cantons (19 of 26), the establishment of independent or joint MOCs under public law is subject to approval by the cantonal government (*Regierungsrat*). By contrast, in the canton of St Gallen, municipalities do not need the canton's explicit authorisation to establish a MOC under public law, provided they notify the competent cantonal authority. The same applies to municipalities in the canton of Bern wishing to establish a joint MOC in the form of a municipal association (*Gemeindeverband*; see sect. 10.2.2). If, however, the establishment of a joint MOC affects intercantonal relationships, most municipal laws require the approval of the cantonal parliament (Lucerne and Thurgau).

In Switzerland, the electorate is the highest body of a municipality, so most cantons have mandatory regulations regarding the direct democratic participation rights of those entitled to vote in matters concerning independent MOCs or participation in joint MOCs. In 22 of the 26 cantons, establishing a new MOC requires voters to decide on tasks to be assigned, the legal form of the responsible body, the organisation, and the financing. In addition, special regulations apply in some cantons where voters can express their will in the municipality's general assembly (Basel-Stadt, Fribourg, Valais and Aargau). The general assembly consists of the voting population and is, therefore, a direct democratic political organ. In the canton of Neuchâtel, voters are represented by the general council (*Generalversammlung*), which is the municipality's legislative authority, and the population only votes on the establishment of MOCs under private laws that are in the public interest.

Our overview shows that Swiss municipalities are limited by legislation in their possibilities concerning the setting up of MOCs. Due to the federal nature of the Swiss political system, the municipalities use different frameworks and are bound by different circumstances regarding the establishment of MOCs. However, there seems to be a recent trend towards more regulation concerning the establishment of MOCs. This trend does not extend to the French-speaking cantons in western Switzerland (Geneva, Jura, Neuchâtel and Vaud), however. One reason for this could be the different political culture of these cantons and their preference for a more centralised approach (i.e. in the Napoleonic tradition) (Bach et al., 2017), making them more hesitant to outsource government activities so there is less need for regulation.

10.3 Trends of Municipal Corporatisation

10.3.1 The History of MOCs

At the national tier of Swiss government, the concept of agencification, in particular the establishment of federal government agencies, and the establishment of public enterprises first appeared in the 1990s. At the cantonal and local tiers of government, corporatisation in the form of public law entities had already started some decades before for specific tasks, gaining momentum in the 1990s. At the municipal level, first movers were services such as water supply, sewage treatment, and waste disposal (Steiner & Huber, 2012a, p. 195). A trend towards corporatising such task-based agencies into new organisational entities in the form of MOCs under private law could be observed in the 1990s (Schedler, 2003). In fact, by that time, approximately two-thirds of Swiss municipalities (of more than 3000 inhabitants) held shares in companies limited by shares (Schedler, 2003). However, local services are still mainly provided by the municipalities themselves (Portela, 2020). Incidentally, due to the aforementioned cultural differences between the language regions, MOCs are more common in the German-speaking part of Switzerland than in the French-speaking cantons (Wicht, 2016).

10.3.2 Trend in the Use of MOCs

Data concerning trends in the use of MOCs in Swiss local government are scarce. To find evidence of the development of corporatisation in municipalities, we decided to examine developments in the number of staff working in municipal public bodies (i.e. MOCs) and in the municipalities' departmental units. The source of this data is a survey conducted periodically since 1988 among Swiss municipal secretaries *(Gemeindeschreiber and Gemeindeschreiberinnen)*, who are asked about the performance, reforms, and political system in their respective municipality (Steiner et al., 2021). In this context, the municipalities were also asked about the number of staff working in MOCs and in their departmental units.

Table 10.1 shows the workforce in MOCs in 2009 and 2017 according to population size. To put these figures into context, the workforce in departmental units of the municipality is also shown. In 2017, the average number of staff in the smallest municipalities (up to 249 inhabitants) is two, both in the municipalities' departmental units and in their MOCs (which are, however, rare in small municipalities). In municipalities with fewer than 5000 inhabitants, these numbers remain below 20. Larger municipalities with 5000–9999 inhabitants have around 50 people working either in their departmental units or MOCs. Smaller cities (10,000–19,999 inhabitants) employ 95 people in their MOCs. Larger cities (20,000 inhabitants or more) have up to 825 people employed in this way.

To find a possible trend, we were interested not only in the absolute workforce numbers in the municipal public bodies but also in the

Table 10.1 Workforce in MOCs and municipalities' departmental units in 2009 and 2017

Municipal size (population)	*Average number of employees in 2017*		*Average number of employees in 2009*		*Change from 2009 to 2017, in %*	
	Departmental units	*MOCs*	*Departmental units*	*MOCs*	*Departmental units*	*MOCs*
-249	2	2	2	1	+2	+49
250–499	3	3	2	2	+12	+39
500–999	3	4	3	3	+3	+21
1000–1999	5	7	5	5	+7	+33
2000–4999	17	20	12	17	+41	+17
5000–9999	50	56	40	34	+26	+62
10,000–19,999	142	95	135	88	+5	+8
20,000–	1227	825	1332	464	-8	+78

Source: Steiner et al. (2021)

development of these staff numbers between 2009 and 2017. Overall, we found that there has been an increase both in municipalities' departmental units and MOCs, albeit this is more pronounced in the latter. The largest increase in staff numbers in MOCs can be observed in large cities (+78%), followed by large municipalities (5000–9999 inhabitants; +62%) and the smallest municipalities (up to 249 inhabitants; +49%). Overall, these figures point to a trend towards more corporatisation in Swiss municipalities. Consequently, in around 2010, there was again a clear trend towards more MOCs. This trend may be related to the fact that at the federal level, network industries such as postal services, railroads, and telecommunications were spun off into companies in 2008 and 2009. This also influenced the development at the municipal and cantonal levels.

10.3.3 MOCs by Policy Sector

This section examines the policy sectors in which MOCs are most prevalent. Most of the results discussed below are based on the empirical public corporate governance study mentioned above (Steiner et al., 2020), which categorises public tasks according to the following policy sectors: culture, sport, and leisure; education; energy; financial services; health and social services; housing; IT; primary economy; traffic and transportation; water and waste management; and other services.

An analysis of nine Swiss cities with more than 50,000 inhabitants (see Fig. 10.1) shows 249 MOCs in 2012. (In the case of two or more of these nine cities owning the same MOC, which is relatively rare, it was counted twice.) In 7% of all MOCs, the cities were the sole owners. In most cases, therefore, there are several co-owners, usually nearby municipalities or private co-owners. In 72% of all MOCs, the individual cities are only minority owners. MOCs were mainly found in the energy sector (23%), closely followed by the traffic/transportation sector (22%) and culture, sport, and leisure (20%). Due to the market orientation in these sectors, it is not surprising that MOCs are especially common among municipal utilities. Furthermore, MOCs can also be found in the housing (11%), water and waste management (5%), and health/social services sectors (4%). Financial services (4%), the primary economy sector (3%), education (1%), and IT (1%) are the sectors with the least number of MOCs. Other industries make up for the remaining 7%.

There are considerable differences between Swiss cities in terms of the number of MOCs. With 64 MOCs, Lausanne has by far the largest portfolio; Geneva with only eight MOCs is in last place. Due to the

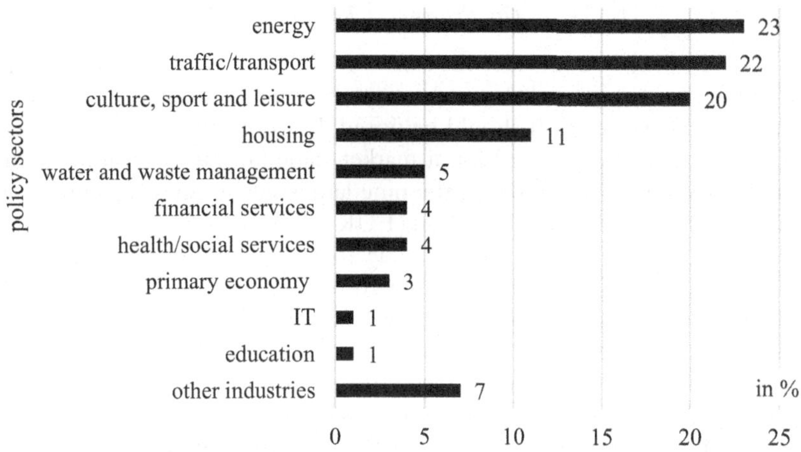

Fig. 10.1 MOCs according to policy sector in percentage (Source: Steiner et al., 2020, p. 37)

composition of the portfolios, different priorities can be identified. In Lausanne, investments in the housing sector form the largest group with a share of 27%. In Lucerne and Bern, it is the culture, sport, and leisure sector, with shares of 44% and 29%, respectively. The cities of Zurich, Biel, St Gallen, and Winterthur have an above-average share of energy providers. In Lugano, the traffic/transportation sector dominates with 47%. Geneva focuses on investments in the traffic/transportation (38%) and financial services sectors (37%).

In another study examining utility services (i.e. electricity, water, natural gas and biogas, heating, mobility, and telecommunications) in medium-sized cities, it could be shown that the number of municipalities participating in utilities is heterogeneous and varies depending on the type of utility, with more than half of them (55%) serving between one and 10 municipalities (Portela, 2020).

Finally, a survey by the canton of Zurich (2019, p. 6) shows the emergence of 14 municipal corporations and 11 inter-municipal agencies between 2005 and 2019. The municipal corporations consist of utilities (water and electricity supply), retirement homes and nursing homes, municipal pension funds, and one non-profit organisation for asylum seekers. The newly created inter-municipal agencies are retirement and nursing homes, sewage and waste disposal, and social services.

10.3.4 The Financial Volume of MOCs

In the following, we consider the size of MOCs in Switzerland according to the financial volume (balance sheet total), again according to the 2020 survey by Steiner et al. It should be noted, however, that a large number of MOCs are not accounted for at market value but rather at nominal or reminder values. The MOCs of the nine largest Swiss cities account for a financial volume of CHF 1.8 billion (EUR 1.7 billion).

To put this figure into context: The total expenditure of these Swiss cities in the year under review amounted to CHF 10.2 billion (EUR 9.8 billion). The energy sector clearly dominates with a financial volume of CHF 1.3 billion (EUR 1.2 billion), accounting for 72% of the total value of all MOCs. 11% is attributable to traffic/transportation with CHF 206 million (EUR 198 million), 8% to financial services with CHF 150 million (EUR 144 million), 5% to housing with CHF 96 million (EUR 92 million), and 2% to culture, sport, and leisure with CHF 43 million (EUR 41 million). The other industries account for less than 2% in terms of financial volume.

The portfolios of the different cities also vary in terms of their financial volume. In 2012, the portfolio of the city of Zurich, with a total value of CHF 536 million (EUR 516 million), accounted for 30% of the aggregated financial volume of the portfolios of all cities. The value of the Lugano portfolio ranked second at CHF 358 million (EUR 345 million) (20%). Finally, some 20% (CHF 351 million [EUR 338 million]) of the value of the total portfolio of all nine cities is attributable to the financial volume of the MOCs of the city of Lausanne.

10.3.5 MOCs and Inter-municipal Cooperation

Inter-municipal cooperation (IMC) is an important phenomenon in Switzerland at the local level. This form of service provision has increased considerably over the last few years (Steiner et al., 2021, p. 124). Most cantons have legal provisions on IMC and the creation of joint MOCs (see Sect. 10.2.4). However, except for a few cantons (e.g. the canton of Zurich), cantonal law rarely mentions public corporations *(öffentlich-rechtliche Anstalten)* in connection with IMC. If two or more municipalities establish an independent public corporation, the same regulations are necessary in all participating municipalities and the public enterprise is founded and supported by all of them. However, such solutions are relatively complicated due to the coordination effort required and, thus, relatively rare (Steiner, 2002).

For IMC, we can distinguish the organisational forms of public-law entity (*öffentlich-rechtliche Körperschaft*), private law entity (*privatrechtliche Körperschaft*), and contract (*Vertrag*), where the agency of one municipality performs a task for several municipalities. In the survey among Swiss municipal secretaries mentioned earlier (Steiner et al., 2021), respondents were asked about the organisational forms of their IMCs. Half of all IMC ventures in Switzerland are organised as public-law entities (50.6%), one-third is organised by contract (32.1%), and 17.3% are private law organisations. Overall, cooperation with other municipalities has become more important. Results of the 2021 survey by Steiner et al. show: For the 2005–2009 period, nearly 75% of municipalities indicated that they had increased their use of IMC.

10.4 Managerial Characteristics of Swiss MOCs

To have a better understanding of the characteristics of MOCs in Switzerland in terms of their operations, we have identified and analysed the main managerial aspects.

10.4.1 Autonomy of MOCs

According to the categorisation of Steiner and Huber (2012b), the autonomy of organisational state entities (including MOCs) has five aspects: technical, financial, organisational, personnel, and management autonomy.

Technical autonomy means having the competence to define a strategy and the operational conditions. Financial autonomy refers to full liability concerning revenues, costs, and investments. An organisational unit with organisational autonomy can establish its organisation, processes, project organisation, and job profiles. Personnel autonomy includes the recruitment of staff, wage-setting, staff appraisals, and personnel development. Finally, management autonomy includes management principles, internal communication, and leadership in conflict and crisis situations.

The degree of autonomy that an MOC has is based on its legal form. For the considerations that follow, we rely on the work of Häfelin et al. (2020). Despite its lack of a legal personality, an institution can be highly autonomous. On the other hand, institutions with a legal personality can lose some or all of their autonomy.

A MOC in the form of a public corporation *(öffentlich-rechtliche Anstalt)* is autonomous when it has a relatively large amount of administrative independence, meaning the freedom to make decisions subject to municipal regulations. Within the legal framework, MOC management can decide how to fulfil the tasks assigned to it. In particular, it has the right to regulate organisational issues and the relationships between the institution and its users. Concerning these issues, it can also take legal action and issue institutional (legal and administrative) ordinances.

The legal form of a public corporation offers the municipalities a great deal of freedom concerning its specific design. When establishing such a MOC, the municipality can decide how much influence it wants to exert. In the canton of Zurich, for example, the level of autonomy is regulated by means of a corporation decree *(Anstaltserlass)* (see also Sect. 10.4.4 below). The general idea is for the influence of the responsible municipality and the autonomy of the MOC to be subject to the specific requirements of the task in question.

The autonomy of MOCs under private law is governed by the Swiss Code of Obligations. In the case of companies limited by shares (*Aktiengesellschaften*), the influence of the municipality only extends to the election of the board of directors by the general assembly of the municipality's representatives. The general assembly also approves the accounts. As owners, municipalities can formulate an owner's strategy for their MOC and monitor compliance via the general assembly. Finally, the municipality can sign a performance agreement with a MOC.

10.4.2 Organisational Structure of MOCs

MOCs in Switzerland always have a two-tiered organisational structure. All MOCs require a governing body, usually a board of directors (*Verwaltungsrat*). Mostly, they install a second tier such as a management board (*Geschäftsleitung*), which is subordinate to the first body. As a rule, the board of directors is responsible for the MOC's strategic management, the management board for its operational management. The members of the management board are salaried employees. The corporation decree *(Anstaltserlass)* determines the number of board members and the organ that elects the board of directors (usually the municipal council or a general assembly).

The main tasks of a MOC's board of directors, which are not delegable, include decisions on the budget and annual accounts, the financial and task plans, and the annual report. The board must also decide on performance agreements with the responsible municipality, define the corporate strategy, adopt essential internal law (e.g. organisational regulations for the board of directors, staff regulations, and tariffs), conclude important contracts, and make major financial decisions as well as employ members of the management board.

The corporation decree (*Anstaltserlass*) issued by the municipality determines how many members the board of directors should have (usually at least three). As a rule, they are appointed by the municipal council or a general assembly, which also appoints the board's president. The board members are individuals with a suitable professional background. They usually serve for four years.

10.4.3 Oversight of MOCs

Public corporate governance is a conceptual framework that provides an overview of the steering and monitoring of MOCs. One purpose of public corporate governance is the regulation of supervision and control (Steiner et al., 2014, p. 140). Still, at the same time, it should also provide guidance for roles and ensure the autonomy of the executive directors regarding the interventions of supervisory boards (i.e. politicians).

While corporate governance guidelines are standard in many cantons for canton-owned MOCs, they are not yet that common in Swiss municipalities. There are such guidelines in the cantons of Zurich and Aargau. The following refers to the canton of Zurich, which serves as a role model for how MOCs are supervised in Switzerland.

According to a handbook on institutions in the canton of Zurich (Canton of Zurich, 2019), when a task is transferred to an MOC, it can be managed in a more entrepreneurial manner. There is more flexibility, decision-making processes are simplified, and decisions are depoliticised. At the same time, the municipality remains responsible for ensuring that the task is fulfilled. In other words, the municipality has a warranty obligation (*Gewährleistungspflicht*), and the MOC is subject to the supervision of the responsible municipality.

Oversight is usually the responsibility of a municipality's executive council (*Gemeinderat*). In some cases, the cantonal parliament also has an oversight function. Examples of supervision activities for a public corporation (*öffentlich-rechtliche Anstalt*) include large investments or expenditures by the MOC. In an IMC, the MOC is supervised by all participating municipalities. Those rights of influence as well as the way in which they are exercised by the participating municipalities are regulated in a corporation contract *(Anstaltsvertrag)*.

There are several supervisory instruments with which a municipality can oversee a MOC. For example, it elects the MOC's management board, defines the owner strategy, and approves service agreements. Furthermore, the responsible municipality receives the MOC's budget, annual accounts, annual report, and finance and task plan *(Finanz- und Aufgabenplan)*. It also appoints the controlling body and receives the audit report. The municipality can secure any further rights of influence in its decree, such as approval of the MOC's budget and annual accounts or the purchase and sale of real estate by the MOC.

In the case of a company limited by shares under private law *(privatrechtliche Aktiengesellschaft)*, the municipality performs its duties through the general assembly, where it is limited to electing the board of directors, electing the auditing body, and approving the budget. In addition, the municipality can determine the owner's strategy, with which it tells the MOC what it expects from its investment.

10.4.4 Decision-Making Concerning Human Resources, Finances, and Organisational Issues

The personnel of MOCs founded under public law is usually governed by public law (*Personalverordnung*), which takes precedence over any regulations issued by the MOC. As a result, disputes between an employer and a staff member are subject to Swiss administrative procedural law. In the case of MOCs under private law, the personnel law under the Swiss Code of Obligations applies. Often, in the case of larger companies, collective labour agreements are concluded.

The corporation decree specifies how a MOC finances its operations. It dictates, for example, whether the MOC can levy fees itself or whether fees are funded through service payments by the municipality. In the case of a foundation, the amount of the endowment capital is also regulated in the decree. Similarly, capital is needed in the starting phase after establishing a MOC. This capital contribution can also take the form of real estate. In the case of companies limited by shares under private law, the rules of the Swiss Code of Obligations apply.

The establishment of a MOC, as well as its tasks and internal organisation, is also regulated in the corporation decree mentioned above. These tasks must be clearly defined and cannot be provided by means of blanket authorisation for further tasks. Finally, the decree also specifies the exact scope and the specifications concerning delivery for the task to be provided.

Even in the case of MOCs such as public corporations *(öffentlich-rechtliche Anstalten)* that otherwise are independent, citizens in most cantons vote on its corporation decree at the ballot box and approval by the cantonal parliament is needed (see also Sect. 10.2.4).

10.5 Conclusions

In Switzerland, there was broad political consensus for about 20 years starting in the 1990s that outsourced companies are a desirable organisational form for the performance of government tasks. There are competitors or at least a high demand for customer orientation. This attitude was triggered by the New Public Management discussion, which had also gained a foothold in Switzerland. In addition, the market for previously purely governmental tasks, especially in network industries, opened up throughout Europe. Governmental service providers had to be made fit in the face of emerging competitors.

Since municipal services in Switzerland are provided to a large extent at the municipal and cantonal levels, MOCs experienced a veritable boom. This development continued into the 2010s. Only recently have there been reservations about further outsourcing of services. The reasons may be that most tasks have already been outsourced to competitive providers. Furthermore, after a series of events involving market upheaval, mismanagement, global tension, and a global pandemic, there is a renewed call for a strong state. By definition, MOCs have a relatively high degree of autonomy, making political intervention more difficult.

Considering the financial volume managed by MOCs at the municipal level, these legally independent organisations are politically relevant. In addition, citizens react quickly to quality problems in their services. Therefore, politicians need regulations that are as detailed and specific as possible, show the scope and limits of the MOCs' autonomy, and assign a precisely worded supervisory function to politics. However, there is always tension because entrepreneurial action and political control can undoubtedly lead to contradictions. For example, a public company must raise prices to ensure its survival, but politicians have little interest in price jumps if there is a risk that they might be held responsible by citizens.

By international comparison, Swiss municipalities enjoy a stable equilibrium between the autonomy granted to MOCs and their political supervision. As a rule, boards of directors are primarily appointed based on their professional competencies rather than their allegiance to a political party. The companies have a great deal of scope in developing their tasks, and their financial autonomy is also high. At the same time, with clear legislation and oversight by the government and parliamentary commissions, the governance of MOCs is taken seriously. Municipal ownership strategies and public corporate governance guidelines in the form of soft law are becoming increasingly important. Especially the larger cities are pioneers in this area, while the smaller municipalities have some catching up to do as they often lack the experience and resources for effective supervision. The cantons are called on to set minimum standards and ensure that the municipalities perform their supervisory role vis-à-vis the MOCs.

These findings on MOCs are symptomatic of the municipal level in Switzerland. Municipalities have a high degree of autonomy compared to the rest of Europe, with an openness to the market economy and precise regulation in the Weberian tradition. At the same time, they operate in a consensus-oriented society. There is a lack of economy of scale and even professionalism, especially among smaller and medium-sized municipalities.

If we dare to look into the future, then consolidation can probably be assumed. New MOCs can be expected primarily for selected new government tasks. In the case of existing MOCs, the focus will be on achieving an even better balance between regulation and the level of autonomy and supervision granted. As it has in the past, this development may be triggered by incidents attracting a lot of media attention ("scandals"). Another driver might be criticism from strictly private companies that MOCs are moving into business areas that compete with the private sector and that the tasks assigned by law are being interpreted more and more broadly by the MOCs.

References

Bach, T., Van Thiel, S., Hammerschmid, G., & Steiner, R. (2017). Administrative tradition and management reforms: A comparison of agency chief executive accountability in four continental Rechtsstaat countries. *Public Management Review, 19*(6), 765–784.

Canton of Aargau. (2019). *Leitfaden Selbstständige öffentlich-rechtliche Gemeindeanstalten [Guide to independent municipal institutions under public law]*. Departement Volkswirtschaft und Inneres.

Canton of Zurich. (2019). *Handbuch Anstalten [Handbook of institutions]*. Direktion der Justiz und des Innern.

Friederich, U. (1997). Rechtsformen interkommunaler Zusammenarbeit [Legal forms of intercommunal collaboration]. *Information der Dokumentationsstelle Raumplanungs- und Umweltrecht*, 1–10.

Friederich, U. (1999). Aufgaben [Tasks]. In D. Arn, U. Friederich, P. Friedli, M. Müller, S. Müller, & J. Wichtermann (Eds.), *Kommentar zum Gemeindegesetz des Kantons Bern* (pp. 449–533). Schulthess.

Friederich, U., Arn, D., & Wichtermann, J. (1998). *Neubildung politischer Gemeinden im Kanton Schaffhausen. Überlegungen zu einer optimalen Gemeindegrösse und zu Vor- und Nachteilen von Gemeindefusionen [New formation of political municipalities in the Canton of Schaffhausen. Considerations concerning municipality size and the benefits and drawbacks municipality mergers]*. Mimeo.

Häfelin, U., Müller, G., & Uhlmann, F. (2020). *Allgemeines Verwaltungsrecht [General administration law]* (8th ed.). Dike.

Ladner, A., Keuffer, N., Baldersheim, H., Hlepas, N., Swianiewicz, P., Steyvers, K., & Navarro, C. (2019). *Patterns of local autonomy in Europe*. Springer.

Linder, W. (2021). *Swiss Democracy: Possible solutions to conflict in multicultural societies*. Palgrave Macmillan.

Müller, M. (1999). Allgemeine Bestimmungen [General provisions]. In D. Arn, U. Friederich, P. Friedli, M. Müller, S. Müller, & J. Wichtermann (Eds.), *Kommentar zum Gemeindegesetz des Kantons Bern* (pp. 1–68). Stämpfli.

Portela, C. A. (2020). Urban utilities and opportunities for the private sector in local energy services in Switzerland. *Competition and Regulation in Network Industries, 21*(2), 193–218.

Schedler, K. (1996). *Ansätze einer wirkungsorientierten Verwaltungsführung [Approaches of impact-oriented administration]* (2nd ed.). Haupt.

Schedler, K. (2003). Local and regional public management reforms in Switzerland. *Public Administration, 81*(2), 325–344.

Steiner, R. (2002). *Interkommunale Zusammenarbeit und Gemeindezusammenschlüsse in der Schweiz [Intercommunal cooperation and municipal mergers in Switzerland]*. Haupt.

Steiner, R., & Huber, E. (2012a). Switzerland. In K. Verhoest, S. Van Thiel, G. Bouckaert, & P. Laegreid (Eds.), *Government agencies: Practices and lessons from 30 countries* (pp. 191–202). Palgrave Macmillan.

Steiner, R., & Huber, E. (2012b). *Autonomiegrad der Organisationseinheiten des Bundes [The degree of autonomy of the federal government's organisational units]*. KPM-Schriftenreihe No. 47. Center of Competence for Public Management.

Steiner, R., Ladner, A., Kaiser, C., Haus, A., Amsellem, A., & Keuffer, N. (2021). *Zustand und Entwicklung der Schweizer Gemeinden. Ergebnisse des nationalen Gemeindemonitorings 2017 [State and development of Swiss municipalities. Results of the National Municipal Monitoring 2017]*. Somedia.

Steiner, R., Raess Brenner, K., & Saxenhofer, A. (2014). Effects of public corporate governance guidelines at the subnational level in Switzerland. In *Jahrbuch der Schweizerischen Verwaltungswissenschaften 2014* (pp. 139–161). Schweizerische Gesellschaft für Verwaltungswissenschaften.

Steiner, R., Saxenhofer, A., Kaiser, C., & Raess Brenner, K. (2020). *Die Public Corporate Governance der Schweizer Kantone und grösseren Städte - eine empirische Analyse [Public corporate governance in the Swiss cantons and larger cities - An empirical analysis]*. KPM-Schriftenreihe No. 58. Center of Competence for Public Management.

Swiss Federal Statistical Office. (2021). *Ständige Wohnbevölkerung nach Alter, Kanton, Bezirk und Gemeinde, 2010-2020 [Permanent resident population by age, canton, district and municipality, 2010-2020]*. Accessed March 21, 2022, from https://www.bfs.admin.ch/bfs/de/home/statistiken/bevoelkerung/stand-entwicklung/bevoelkerung.assetdetail.18344310.html

Swiss Federal Statistical Office. (2022). *Amtliches Gemeindeverzeichnis der Schweiz. Gemeindestand [Official municipal directory of Switzerland. Status of municipalities]*. Accessed January 21, 2022, from https://www.bfs.admin.ch/bfs/de/home/grundlagen/agvch.html

Wicht, P. (2016). *Organizational choices in the delivery of local public services in Switzerland: A cultural perspective*. University of Lausanne.

PART IV

Napoleonic Countries

CHAPTER 11

Municipally Owned Corporations in France: An Emerging Tool of Public Engineering

Gwenaël Leblong-Masclet

11.1 Introduction

A total of 1332 companies, representing 15 billion euros turnover and 62,097 employees (Fédération des EPL, 2020a, 2020b): the volume of activity of municipally owned corporations (MOCs) remains modest in France (on average: 46 employees, 11 million turnover for each MOC). To compare, the total local public expenditure represents 223 billion euros, for 35,054 municipalities, 101 departments and 18 regions, employing nearly 2 million people (French Local Affairs Ministry, 2021). But through three recent waves of decentralisation (1982: local autonomy law/2003: local financial autonomy constitutional affirmation/2015: regions and metropoles' reinforcement), MOCs bear witness to the vitality of local action.

11.1.1 The Context of Decentralisation in France

French decentralisation features a three-level territorial structure: the "regions", in particular in charge of economic development and regional

G. Leblong-Masclet (✉)
Brest Métropole, France

M. Van Genugten et al. (eds.), *Corporatisation in Local Government*, https://doi.org/10.1007/978-3-031-09982-3_11

transport, and more recently the planning of environmental transitions, which nonetheless remain "political and financial dwarfs" (Pasquier, 2021); the "departments", always questioned about their relevance have acquired expertise in social matters, and in particular in the most rural areas (Cukierman, 2020); and finally, the "municipalities", marked by their close proximity to inhabitants, but also part of a process of strengthening inter-municipal cooperation, particularly in dense urban areas, now set up as *métropoles* with extended powers.

Local public action remains popular with the French, who show strong confidence in local public institutions (Cheurfa & Chanvril, 2019). Local authorities, with more than two-thirds of civil public investment, also are essential to economic vitality and in particular to the economic cushioning of crises. Besides their local policies, they retain an important role in a balanced territorial development, whether it is to activate "agglomeration economies" (research, higher education, innovation) or to ensure territorial equity (local health policies, fight against medical deserts, inter-urban transport, etc.).

11.1.2 Recent Development of MOCs

A small number of French MOCs were created at the beginning of the twentieth century, or at the end of World War II (WWII), for example, local energy monopolies, but the past 15 years have considerably accelerated the development, a result of the 2010–559 law about Development of the Local Public Societies. In this context, 60 *Entreprises publiques locales* (EPL, i.e. Local public companies), as MOCs are called in France, were created in 2019–20, with 150 more in the pipeline (Fédération des EPL, 2020a, 2020b). Importantly, MOCs are now regarded as an additional tool of territorial engineering, marked by hybridisation between the public interest and entrepreneurial flexibility (La Gazette des Communes, 2019).

This chapter will first present the trends in the development of MOCs and then the reasons which today drive the use of MOCs, before focusing on their governance, in which the presence of the municipality remains essential. Finally, the chapter will conclude, using concrete examples, by discussing municipalities' efforts to organise the strategic steering of MOCs, in order to strengthen the coherence and effectiveness of local public action.

11.2 Trend in the Use of MOCs in France: A Recent Re-structuring of the Institutional System

The recent nature of the development of MOCs can be explained, in a historical approach, by the French preference for recourse to sectoral public institutions of the "public establishments" type. But recent developments in case law have more recently led to reconsideration of the nature of local public action, around three types of private law-based MOCs.

11.2.1 Historical Approach

The first MOCs in France appeared in Alsace Moselle, then belonging to Germany, in 1895, finding their source of inspiration in the German *Stadtwerke* (Fédération des EPL, 2020a, 2020b). The experience was transposed into French national law in 1926, then promoted under the major reconstruction law of October 28, 1946, and the Monnet plan 1947–53. In 1953, there were still only 20 MOCs in operation, but there were 300 in 1963, then 650 in 1979, notably opening up in the land use planning sector. The slow emergence of MOCs is also influenced by a policy, from the 1990s, of liberalisation of large public services in networks (train, energy, etc.), generally formed around large national companies owned by the State, and which have gradually experienced a process of entrepreneurialism or even privatisation (Herzog, 1997).

Public Industrial Establishments Rather than Corporatisation Until recently, the impact of MOCs in France was relatively limited; French law restricted them to a "mixed economy system", where the public shareholding was limited to 40%, then to 65% after 1955. Indeed, public municipal services were largely maintained in the field of public law: "public establishments" are still fully controlled agencies, with public legal personality. Otherwise, the system found flexibility, in a famous decision of the Court of Conflicts (1921), West African Commercial Company, and known as the "Eloka ferry case". In this case, the judge considered a distinction between "administrative public services" (e.g. sport or cultural public services) on the one hand and so-called industrial and commercial public services (e.g. water, public transportation) on the other. Regarding the latter, the judge pronounced that the administration operated the service "under the same conditions as an ordinary industrialist", thereby placing the employees under private law (except the accounting and director chief officer). The "Public establishments" nevertheless remained under public jurisdiction.

The possible forms of public establishments are numerous and varied, allowing a municipality either to empower a service (e.g. a sanitation service) or to organise a partnership with other public structures through a third-party institution. In the field of research, and later in every other field, French law also allows public–private cooperation through the status of "Public Interest Groups" (*Groupements d'intérêt public*); they nevertheless must pursue non-profit activities of general interest, such as health, research, economic development, and digital services. Moreover, local authorities can also act in the non-profit sector by creating associations or NGOs, or in the social and solidarity economy through participation in cooperative societies of collective interest (SCICs). In the latter case, municipal shareholding necessarily remains in the minority leading to a minor control of the bodies. Therefore, this option remains relatively marginal for the time being.

What is obvious is the institutional system's appetite for facilitating numerous public structures, each in charge of a sectoral policy, requiring coordination needs. This strategy has therefore been traditionally favoured over the full corporatisation of public services. Throughout the twentieth century, local public entrepreneurship was therefore limited to the restricted purpose of associating private shareholders to a general interest mission. It was not until 1983 that the public shareholding could be increased to 80%.

European Court Law and Recent Corporatisation After 2006, the status of MOCs took off again and their number increased. Facing the European case law (especially the consequences of the Teckal case), the Parliament agreed to experiment with new 100% public shareholding companies, *Sociétés publiques locales*, initially in the urban development sector. These corporations address the European "in-house" criteria and can avoid competitive public procurement processes, through three main features: a 100% public shareholding, an economic field specially dedicated to the public shareholder field of competencies, and an "analogous control", as if it could be a shareholder inner unit. This model has been generalised in 2010, as described further by Delion and Durupty (2010).

11.2.2 Since the 2010s: Three Different Types of Private Law-Based MOCs

MOCs are now structured around three legal forms: *Sociétés d'économie mixte* (SEM), *Societés publiques locales* (SPL) and *Sociétés d'économie mixte à opération unique* (SEMOP). The three legal forms are all private law based (Table 11.1), nevertheless SPL belongs 100% to public shareholders. While the notion of MOCs has been widely considered from a managerial and institutional lobbying perspective, the legal construction remains much more fragmented. Thus, the General Code of Local Authorities (CGCT) devotes separate chapters to SEM, then SPL, and finally SEMOP. SEM and SPL are multi-purpose, and SEMOP, single-purpose companies. The legal approach of these three forms remains distinct in particular regarding the conditions of their creation.

SEM: A Private Company with Mix Private and Public Shareholding *Sociétés d'économie mixte* (SEM), meaning "mixed economy companies", remains the most used legal form. These MOCs are limited companies under

Table 11.1 Three different types of MOCs in France: comparative approach

	SEM	*SPL*	*SEMOP*
Existing since...	1946	2006 (as an experiment); 2010	2014
Number	887	417	28
Shareholding	Mix public and private	100% public (at least two public shareholders)	Shared between a public authority and a private partner
Status	Private law limited company	Private law limited company	Private law limited company
Development	Long term	Recent and fast since the 2010s	Very recent, modest
Contracting with the local authority	As for private companies, procurement rules apply	In-house	Through the founding process
Competence	Own development	Only in the field of the shareholders' competencies	Restricted to the partnership project
Territory	No limit	Local shareholders' territory	Project territory

commercial law, characterised by a mixed shareholding between the public (between 50% and 85% of the capital) and the private sector. They can develop their own activities and markets, but cannot encroach on "in-house" services, so they must respond to public procurement processes, even when dealing with their public shareholders. Local authority shareholders hold more than half of the votes in the governing bodies for SEMs, and the Chairman and the Chief Executive Officer are appointed by the company's governing bodies. Local authorities are thus able to control the orientation of the company through its corporate governance, and through an annual report of the Municipal Council, and contracts reports. A total of 887 of the MOCs in France have the status of SEM, that is, roughly 65%. SEMs have also set up 409 subsidiaries.

Concerning SEMs, the CGCT sets out in article L1521-1 the following possibility for local authorities or their groups, "within the framework of the competences which are recognised to them by the law, (to) create mixed economy corporations which associate them with one or more private persons and, possibly, with other public persons to carry out development, construction operations, to operate public services of an industrial or commercial nature, or for any other activity of interest general; when the object of local semi-public companies includes several activities, they must be complementary".

SPL: A 100% Public Shareholding Company *Societés publiques locales* (SPL), meaning "public local companies", are also legal structures of commercial law, but are characterised by a 100% public capital, held by at least two local authorities. Their legal purpose is to act only for their public shareholders, in their field of competencies and on their territory, so they are typically considered to be "in-house" corporations. The governing bodies are entirely made up of elected representatives from the public shareholders, with the Chairman and Chief Executive Officer appointed by the governing bodies. SPLs are prohibited from creating subsidiaries and from taking shareholdings in other companies. There are currently 417 SPLs in operation.

According to article CGCT L1531-1, SPLs required total control of shareholding by local authorities, as well as the exclusion of activities on behalf of their shareholders. At least two public entities are needed to constitute an SPL. Importantly, public establishments of inter-communal cooperation (EPCI, metropoles for example), developed since the 1990s, can be shareholders, jointly with their parent municipalities. Nevertheless, the question of competences has been raised: as an EPCI has its own competencies, distinct from the municipalities, can a common SPL operate in both their fields of competence? After some judicial procrastination, the Parliament settled this issue in 2019 with an approach favourable to the creation of SPLs, but these debates bear witness to a legal framework that remains to be stabilised.

SEMOP: A Private/Public Company Dedicated to a Single Partnership Operation Sociétés d'économie mixte à opération unique (SEMOP) is a more recent legal form of MOC permitted by a July 1, 2014, law that completes the MOC range with a so-called mixed-economy company with a single operation. It allows a municipality to launch a specific public procurement model, dedicated to choosing a private shareholder that will enter in the SEMOP and then operate a public delegation contract. In this case, the local authority defines the company's mission, sets the governing rules and enters a joint venture with a private operator. SEMOPs belong to at least two shareholders: a local authority and a private economic operator. The SEMOP's existence is then limited to the sole purpose of carrying out a specific mission, and it is automatically dissolved at the end of the contract. Subsidiaries and equity investments are prohibited. The reference public shareholder is to represent between 34% and 85% of the holdings; so the other shareholders, including the operator shareholder, must represent between 15% and 66% of the holdings. A SEMOP corporation is limited to work for its local public owner and on its territory. At least 34% of the votes are held by local authority officials in the governing bodies of the SEMOP. Presidency of the board of directors or of the supervisory board is legally entrusted to an elected official. There are currently 28 active SEMOPs in France.

SEMOPs are still relatively marginal because Article L1541-1 of the CGCT strictly regulates recourse to this legal form of MOC: it establishes the principle of competition between the potential private shareholder and limits the company to a single object. This unique object cannot be modified throughout the duration of the contract. The definition of MOCs, as having a unique scope including SEM, SPL and SEMOP corporations, is rather a doctrinal construction and often reflects operational reality rather than a legal entity. Beyond the strict perimeter of the definition of MOCs, in accordance with that used in the literature, whereas SEMs have a long history, the development of SPLs and SEMOPs represent a recent extension of the range of engineering tools. Table 11.1 gives a summary of the three types of private law-based MOCs.

11.2.3 Diverse Fields of Activity

The MOCs National Association (*Fédération des EPL*) analyses the areas of activity of its members as follows: "Today, MOCs lead actions in various fields. Tourism, culture, recreation and planning are predominant. Sectors such as housing and real estate or mobility confirm their importance" (Fédération des EPL, 2020a, 2020b). As environmental policies are developing at the local level, MOCs also develop in the field of energy, environment, networks, and economic development. As "Swiss army knives" of local authorities, 65% of these companies are committed to a strategy of developing complementary activities, according to the National Association, "with the aim of investing in new segments of their traditional markets, developing synergies between the various public services, but also in order to improve the overall profitability of the company" (Fédération des EPL, 2020a, 2020b). Thus, 339 MOCS operate in tourism, leisure and culture, 300 in development, 237 in the environment and networks, 173 in accommodation and real estate, 143 in economic development, 81 in mobility and 59 in the field of personal services (Fédération des EPL, 2020a, 2020b).

11.3 Reasons for Municipal Authorities to Use MOCs

After having identified the diversity of the legal forms of MOCs in France, it is useful to question the reasons which may lead local authorities to favour the use of different types of MOCs. The development of "in-house" status has resulted in a strong advantage of SPLs, which operate as private companies under the control of local authorities, while avoiding procurement rules. Secondly, the process of corporatisation fits, paradoxically, in a process where MOCs can be considered as a tool of monopolistic public interventionism, and a commitment to transparency and democratic control; third reason, the structuring of a MOC allows municipalities to explore new organisational strategies.

11.3.1 Escaping Public Procurement Rules: A Motivation for the Transformation of SEMs into "In-house" SPLs

In terms of institutional flexibility, the SPL, as we have already said, aims to and is supposed to escape public procurement rules. The objective set by Parliament for creating the legal form of SPL was to get as close as possible to EU "in-house" procurement law (Rouveyran & Ricci, 2013). It should be noted, however, that the Public Supreme Court has not made an assessment regarding the principles of in-house status. Thus, while the control of the public shareholding, as well as a focus on only missions entrusted by the public shareholders, fulfil two of the three essential criteria for setting up an SPL, the notion of "similar control" remains a key dimension in the ability to act in-house (Sée, 2013). This control also allows the public authority to influence the company in a decisive way, for example by appointing the majority of the members of the company's board of directors, according, for example, to the Brixen judgement of the ECJ, October 13, 2005.

Consequently, the configuration of institutional relations between the public shareholder and the company are determining factors in the selection of one form of MOC rather than another. The relative stabilisation in French law relating to in-house rules has led, over the past decade, to the transformation of many SEMs into SPLs, through two main approaches. The first consisted of the outright transformation of the pre-existing SEM into an SPL, through the withdrawal of private shareholders. The second consisted of the structuring of an SPL, mirroring the pre-existing SEM, with the latter maintaining the competing activities and the former concentrating on internal services, in a general context of sharing support and management functions between the two entities.

11.3.2 Public Control of Monopolistic Services?

The movement that has structured the development of MOCs in France over the past decade is the attention paid to strengthening public management of large local network services, such as water distribution and waste management. Under the effect of various objectives, which can range from the search for strengthened citizen control, financial transparency, to the search for increased competition or to the transformation of local economic models, many local authorities have mobilised MOCs to take over their operational perimeter services previously entrusted to large international groups.

The political choice made in Rennes (210,000 inhabitants, west of France, Brittany, left-wing led since 1977), concerning its drinking water production and distribution service, is an example of this public intervention strategy: "After 130 years of management by the company Veolia Water, the city of Rennes has decided not to renew the contract ending on March 31, 2015. Three possibilities were studied for water management: public service delegation (DSP) to a private operator, a municipal service to be created, or building a local municipally owned company (...)" (Collectivité Eaux du bassin rennais, n.d.). Then, The City of Rennes conducted in 2011 and 2012 an evaluation of the method of management to be implemented, and in January and February 2013, the Municipal Council and the Union Committee of the Water Collectivity agreed to the creation of a Local Public Corporation (SPL) in charge of their public drinking water distribution and production services. This new structure was intended to:

- increase their public control over the management of water services;
- pool their operating resources;
- open up the possibility for the water services of other communities to join the SPL (Collectivité Eaux du bassin rennais, n.d.)

This choice marks the "desire to strengthen the control of their public service" in terms of drinking water (Collectivité Eaux du bassin rennais, n.d.). According to the local authority, "it is also a choice of reason which is part of the logic of pooling costs and the possibility of opening up to other communities for the benefit of the user and his purchasing power" (Collectivité Eaux du bassin rennais, n.d.). The local public company is also considered to be the vector of enhanced citizenship on the environmental theme, by involving all stakeholders in the City (communities, associations, corporations, etc.) in water management.

11.3.3 MOCs Enable Local Authorities to Explore New Organisational Strategies

In France, MOCs are continually increasing the tools available to the territorial decision-maker to strengthen their modalities of action. Thus, the diversity of tools now available (community services, SEM, SPL, associations) allows the municipality to use the appropriate tool for each public policy, in different models and economic contexts. Diversifying the range of structures at their disposal allows local decision-makers to gain in agility and efficiency, usually through three very different models:

- Public–public partnership, for example through an SPL, allows two or more local authorities to share common skills, for the benefit of entrepreneurial intervention, including in competitive fields. The Rennes water distribution service, mentioned above, is an example of this: the association with the production function of all the municipalities in the watershed has been a factor in strengthening democracy and multiplied action.
- Public–private partnership, through SEM or SEMOP, now makes it possible to rebalance power between public and private sector operators. It also facilitates entry into competitive markets. In the management of tourism or leisure activities, for example, the development of entrepreneurial know-how allows a territory to gain autonomy and to relocate the decision centres. Moreover, driven by the general interest, the SEM has a broad decision-making capacity, including outside the scope of traditional economic rationality. The local authority integrates its own economic ecosystem, through a commercial law vehicle, for the benefit of endogenous growth.
- Private–private partnership: through the subsidiaries of its SEMs, the community can now work directly and on an equal footing with private companies. As a result, shareholder pacts become a local public tool for promoting public purposes. Nevertheless, this strategy implies a high level of control by the municipality over the MOC. It therefore raises questions about the modalities of this control and the conditions of governance.

11.4 Governance and Operation

The governance and operation of MOCs in France can be analysed from four perspectives. First is the legal framework prescribing the conditions of control. Second is the role of the local authority as the reference shareholder for a MOC. Third is the dual control of the municipality—that of the shareholder and that of the principal. And, finally, four is the implications of a high level of control for the legal situation relating to conflicts of interest.

11.4.1 *Conditions of Control by Public Authorities*

The legal framework is relatively similar for SEMs, SPLs and SEMOPs with regard to the conditions of control by public authorities. Firstly, the essential acts of relationship between the municipal owner and its corporation remain the strict responsibility of the municipal deliberative assembly, which has regular control over the activities of the company. Secondly, the deliberations of the board of directors or of the supervisory board and of the general assemblies are systematically communicated within the 15 days following their adoption to the representative of the Central State, who exercises control of the financial interests, in connection with the regional financial chambers (*Chambres régionales des comptes*).

Nevertheless, the day-to-day operation of the corporation is quite flexible. Like an ordinary private company, a MOC can choose its own corporate governance model, whether a one-tier or two-tier board. The shareholder agreement drives the governance, general principles and way-of-acting of the company, through the jurisdiction of common Commercial Law. Thus, in its report "The inadequacies of the legal and accounting framework for MOCs" (2017), the Court of Auditors (*Cour des Comptes*) called for a better articulation of public and commercial law in relation to public corporations, in order to strengthen public control over MOCs' decision-makers.

11.4.2 *Predominance of the Public Reference Shareholder*

According to the Cour des Comptes the share capital of the SEMs belonging to local authorities represented, in June 2016, a total amount of 4.3 billion euros. This capital has the dual characteristic of being both rarely paid in the form of dividends and composed of illiquid shares. The share capital was held 62% by local authorities and their groups and 38% by other shareholders. "The diversity of shareholders is very relative: while the other shareholders may indeed be private shareholders, there are also other legal persons governed by public law, i.e., in practice, other local semi-public companies, the Caisse des Dépôts et Consignations, the consular chambers or public housing offices" (Cour des Comptes, 2017, p. 7).

Despite the development of inter-municipal cooperation since 1999, municipalities remain the main reference shareholders of local SEMs (36%), ahead of inter-municipal cooperation establishments (EPCI) (27%), departments (20%), communities with special status (10%) and the regions (7%). On the other hand, inter-municipal cooperation entities are the main shareholders of SPLs, to the tune of 43% against 29% for the municipalities, 21% for the departments, and 7% for the regions.

The opportunity to strengthen the role of minority shareholders in French MOCs has been greatly debated (Brameret, 2017). Often driven by the desire to contribute to the general interest of the community, they take an influential approach, which can sometimes be decisive in the strategic choices of the local authority. In its aforementioned report, the Court gives priority to strengthening the information of the deliberative assembly on the decisions of the MOCs, in particular by reinforcing the alert role of the auditor.

11.4.3 The Double Control of the Municipal Owner

The public owner's control of MOCs in France is twofold: shareholder control over the corporate purpose and the management of the MOCs on the one hand, and contract control on the other (Brameret, 2011). In its role as reference shareholder, the public owner is required to determine the *raison d'être* of the MOCs. Thus, unlike a traditional private company, the very DNA of the MOCs will be marked by its contribution to the general interest and to the public policies promoted by the municipality (Uguen, 2015). As such, the MOC fully plays its role of operator, in a conception that places the local authority in a position of "strategic holding entity of public interests". This specific shareholder relationship comprises three levels:

- the political project carried by the executive, often common, between the community and its company, which must bear witness to a vision of the territory and of a project to which the MOC will thus contribute;
- the quality of the relationship between the director of the SEM, bearer of a strong entrepreneurial capacity, and the general manager of community services, a key player in the strategic management of the community;
- finally, the maturity of the understanding by community services, including trade unions, of the usefulness of a MOC, which is not positioned in competition with public services, but in a complementary approach, in economic fields allowing it to develop new markets, for the benefit of the territory's public players.

A former director of SEM testifies as follows: "The autonomy of the director of MOCs is very wide on a daily basis. But the most difficult experience for me was a municipality where the will of elected officials failed to dispel the municipal teams' mistrust of SEM. As soon as this is perceived as a threat, a tool for privatisation, the system of complementarity malfunctions. It is therefore essential to work on the managerial culture of both the SEM and the community so that the actors can understand each other" (interview for this chapter, 2021).

Likewise, control of the MOCs' strategy also allows the public manager to acculturate to entrepreneurial models: MOCs enable the development of new know-how, and a better understanding of commercial ways-of-thinking. The fluidity of careers (still to be improved) between management position in the local authority services and in the MOCs direction, is one way to develop local skills. Relationships between MOCs directors, or between them and the general management team of the parent municipalities, often remain informal, and the common interest is roughly embodied in the practice if not the principles of governance. Nevertheless, it is widely recognised that the use of institutional structures to facilitate this alignment more effectively could improve the management of public affairs.

11.4.4 *MOCs, Law and Ethics: Towards New Regulations?*

The strong control of MOCs by local authorities has led national authorities, and in particular the Court of Auditors, to recommend changes in two areas. The first concerns the control of remuneration. The second consists in questioning the risks of conflict of interest for elected officials, who are representatives of the local community and also key decision-makers within MOCs, private companies. This last point underlines the need for legal clarification about the duties of elected officials who serve on MOC boards, making it possible to reassure them of their responsibilities and to protect the public interest during the process of corporatisation.

Enforcing Remuneration Control? Strengthening control over MOCs' decision makers' remuneration is one of the main recommendations of the French Court of Auditors: "If the general code of local authorities retains, in addition to provisions of the Commercial Code, a set of measures aimed at ensuring the control of local public enterprises, certain shortcomings, linked to their recent development, have been brought to light", assures the Court (Cour des Comptes, 2017, p. 10). Remuneration and benefits of all kinds should be better controlled (Broussole, 2020): the deliberative assemblies of local authorities are competent to set, by express and prior deliberation, the maximum amount of remuneration or special benefits that may be received by the elected representatives who represent them at the meeting within the company and the nature of the functions which justify them. "But there are no official statistics on the average amount of remuneration and other special benefits provided by local public enterprises. In addition, in the silence of the law, the provisions of the Commercial Code are applicable" (Cour des Comptes, 2017, p. 10).

According to the Court, "uncertainties persist, in particular for the function of Chairman and Chief Executive Officer" (Cour des Comptes, 2017, p. 11). In terms of public law, it is useful for elected officials to be a member of the management bodies for MOCs, and possibly the management bodies of any subsidiaries owned by MOCs. However, because "their salaries and benefits of any kind in these subsidiaries are not subject to any supervision by the communities", the Court remains concerned about the potential abuses of power and position that go along with being a company director.

Strengthening the Protection of Elected Officials in the Face of the Risk of Conflict of Interest? According to many observers, the legal framework for MOCs in France needs to be stabilised in order to better take into account the purpose of general interest MOCs. This could help to protect elected officials against an overly bureaucratic analysis of the risk of conflicts of interest. During the course of recent case law, the analysis of ethical and criminal risks within MOCs has been greatly expanded. Thus, in its last annual report, the SMACL (first municipality insurance company) noted a 32% increase in criminal proceedings against local elected officials during the 2014–20 mandate, compared to the previous mandate (SMACL, 2020, p. 14). These figures testify to an increasing and potentially unwelcome juridification of public life.

The administrative judge has often had a comprehensive appreciation of the notion of the elected representative's personal interest. From this definition of the conflict of interest, three central elements emerge which call local elected officials to special attention. First of all, the notion of interference. Little known to jurists, it means that the exercise by an elected official of his functions must be disrupted, concerned or even influenced by an interest other than that of his chosen community. Then there is the existence of conflicts between public interests. Thus, a recent article warned that: "While the prevention of situations of conflict between a public interest (its mandate) and a private interest (a personal financial interest, for example) hardly poses a problem in principle, the existence of a conflict between two public interests (two functions for example) is more problematic, insofar as this situation implies that there could be a conflict between two functions or mandates aimed at satisfying the general interest. Finally, the notion of appearance is particularly dangerous for elected officials" (La Gazette des Communes, 2020).

The assessment of conflicts of interest is reinforced by the development, with an indisputable focus on transparency, of the new ethical framework applicable to elected officials and agents. Thus, the High Authority for the Transparency of Public Life (HATVP), in the second version of its ethics guide published in February 2021, clarifies its position concerning the risk of illegal taking of interest by elected representatives representing their community within external organisations, including MOCs. Note that the publication of this second guide marks a strengthening of the HATVP doctrine, without prior consultation to our knowledge with the stakeholders (Haute Autorité pour la transparence de la vie publique, 2021, p. 28).

According to the latest ethics guide, a systematic conflict of interest occurs when a local elected official, even in the exercise of his or her elective functions, performs administrative functions in a private organisation, SEM, SPL, SCIC or associations. This means that he cannot participate in voting, and should not attend meetings, formal or informal, concerning the private organisations in circumstance in which he or she represents the community. In other words, with a few examples:

- A local authority President is in systematic conflict when he chairs an SEM or an SPL and at risk of conflict of interest or favouritism when he attends a point concerning the arbitration of a decision likely to impact the MOC.
- A Deputy President in charge of Planning, if he wants to protect himself against a conflict of interest, can no longer legitimately exercise functions within the territorial SEM of planning.
- A Deputy President in charge of Economic Development in a Region could no longer participate in the governance of an economic development agency.

Given the apparent differences between administrative law and criminal law relating to the appointment of elected officials to MOC boards, the question arises how can those officials effectively represent public interests in a private but publicly owned corporation? It would probably be useful for the Law in the near future to be concerned with protecting local elected representatives in order to build balanced solutions, which guarantee ethics but are mindful of the role of the local elected representative.

11.5 Conclusion: MOCs a Source of Strategic Intensification for Local Authorities?

As a synthesis, MOCs developed in France through two waves (after WWII and in 2010) and, recently, as a consequence of the European law: French institutions are adapting to a new environment, securing their traditional social mechanisms through wide public sector and services, and facing new stakes. MOCs are opening new windows, in both public–public and public–private cooperation fields. A total of 1332 MOCs now represent a 15 billion total turnover, and 62,000 employees. The "average" French MOC is then a modest but efficient enterprise, with 46 employees but 11 million turnover. These private limited companies are acting in many sectors of public interest, tourism, leisure, culture, urban development, environment and networks, mobility, economic development and so on. Whatever their legal status (SEM, SPL, SEMOP), MOCs remain under double monitoring by the local authority: shareholder monitoring and contract management. This institutional system enables a strong managing autonomy on a daily basis but also strong governance control by public shareholders.

If the subject of the management of local public organisations is now widely discussed in France, the place of MOCs within the country's institutional structure remains a little covered subject. Often approached from the legal and financial point of view (i.e. control method, management control, off-balance sheet risk), or even in the field of economic action of the municipalities, MOCs are rarely analysed by researchers as a tool of strategic management for municipalities, departments or regions.

MOCs are absent from the Romain Pasquier "Dictionary of territorial policies" (Pasquier et al., 2020), a reference work in political science, but also from the David Carassus "Driving local public policies" (Carassus, 2020), which compiles all the management tools available to the local decision-maker. Public Management research might progress in analysing MOCs and their data. The role of MOCs in the local public ecosystem is nonetheless a source of strategic intensification and could be viewed as a shift for the local authorities that could nowadays be positioned as a "strategic holding of public interests". While there are a few metropolises that can testify to the usefulness of such an organisational strategy approach, important questions remain about its application in the French context.

The first issue is managerial: how is it possible to develop tools for a strategic alignment between the community and its MOCs? Two notable experiences point towards the need to develop a governance code and strategy to achieve such alignment. The first one, carried out in Grenoble Agglomeration (South East, 445,000 inhabitants, Alpes) in 2010, aimed to establish a governance charter. This common guidance document was defining the objectives and resources of each MOC, and the City's expectations. The second experiment, launched about ten years ago in Brest Metropole (Brittany, West of France, 210,000 inhabitants) and called *Maison Commune* meaning "Common Home", also consists of setting up a strategic project shared between the community and its ten operators (Zignani, 2016).

The Brest approach relates to the second issue of the usefulness of establishing a common culture between the community and its operators. Beyond the application of strategic management tools, the Brest approach aimed at identifying a base of common values, serving as a common thread for action by MOCs (Jarjaille, 2021). The "Common Home" approach adopted by the municipality was structured around three practices:

- a collective strategic dialogue process, carried out in 2014, which involves Brest Metropole and the operators, jointly;
- a charter, a reference document, signed by all of them defining shared values and testifying to the collective expression of a shared interest;
- a strategic roadmap for each operator, which structures the strategic positioning of the City as a majority shareholder, and enables elected officials to make the link between public policies and the intervention of operators. This roadmap, aligned with the term of office, recalls the strategic objectives and organises the reporting.

The second issue for French MOCs in which future research will also take an interest is the question of relevant territorial scales. By opening up the possibility of public engineering that goes beyond the limits of a municipality's own territory, MOCs are strengthening the emergence of a metropolitan governance regime, which increasingly institutionalises the interdependencies and reciprocity between densely populated urban areas and the surrounding rural communities. So, there are many exploration avenues to reinvent local public action for the twenty-first century.

References

Brameret, S. (2011). *Les relations des collectivités territoriales avec les sociétés d'économie mixte locales: Recherche sur l'institutionnalisation d'un partenariat public-privé [The relations of local authorities with local semi-public companies: Research on the institutionalization of a public-private partnership]*. Paris: LGDJ Editions.

Brameret, S. (2017). *Faut-il une réforme des entreprises publiques locales? [A reform of MOC is needed?]*. La Semaine Juridique – Administrations et Collectivités Territoriales, LexisNexis, 419.

Broussole, Y. (2020). Des sociétés d'économie mixte locales insuffisamment contrôlées [SEM: Lack of control]. *Gestion and Finances Publiques, 3*, 29–33.

Carassus, D. (2020). *Le pilotage des politiques publiques locales [Driving local public policies]*. Berger-Levrault Editions.

Cheurfa, M., & Chanvril, F. (2019). *2009–2019: La crise de la confiance politique [2009–2019, Crisis of political trust]*. Sciences Po Cevipof.

Collectivité aux du bassin rennais. (n.d.). *Une gestion publique de l'eau [Public water management]*. https://www.eaudubassinrennais-collectivite.fr/qui-sommes-nous/gestion-publique-eau/. Accessed 10 September 2021.

Cour des Comptes. (2017). *Les insuffisances du cadre juridique et comptable des EPL [The shortcomings of the legal and accounting framework of MOCs]*. Cour des Comptes.

Cukierman, C. (2020). *Rallier les citoyens, relier les territoires: Le rôle incontournable des départements [Rallying citizens, connecting territories: The essential role of departments]*. Rapport d'information n° 706 (2019–2020). Paris: French Senate.

Delion, G., & Durupty, M. (2010). Chronique du secteur public économique [Chronicle of the economic public sector]. *Revue Française d'Administration Publique, 136*, 1045–1053.

Fédération des EPL. (2020a). *L'histoire de la féderation: Histoire des EPL, les dates [History of the national association: History of MOCs, dates]*. https://www.lesepl.fr/federation/histoire/histoire-des-epl-les-dates/#:~:text=1895%20Apparition%20en%20Alsace%20Moselle,%C3%A0%2040%25%20de%20leur%20capital.&text=Un%20pic%20sera%20atteint%205%20ans%20plus%20tard%20avec%201%20529%20Sem. Accessed 10 September 2021.

Fédération des EPL. (2020b). *Les chiffres clés. L'ampleur du mouvement des EPL en France [Key indicators. The scale of the EPL movement in France]*. https://www.lesepl.fr/le-mouvement/chiffres-cles/. Accessed 10 September 2021.

French Local Affairs Ministry. (2021). *Les collectivités locales en France [Local authorities in France].* https://www.collectivites-locales.gouv.fr/files/files/dgcl_v2/DESL/colloc2020/cl_en_chiffres_2020_web.pdf. Accessed 10 September 2021.

Haute Autorité pour la transparence de la vie publique. (2021). *Guide déontologique II:Contrôle et prévention des conflits d'intérêts [Ethics Guide II: Control and prevention of conflicts of interest].* Paris: HATVP.

Herzog, P. (1997). Quel avenir pour les entreprises publiques ? [What future for public enterprises?]. In P. Herzog (Ed.), *Reconstruire un pouvoir politique: Dialogue pour gouverner en partenaires* (pp. 90–102). La Découverte.

Jarjaille, I. (2021, July 1). Toutes les entreprises publiques locales pilotées à la manière d'une holding [MOCs managed like a holding company]. *La Gazette des Communes.* https://www.lagazettedescommunes.com/751644/toutes-les-entreprises-publiques-locales-pilotees-a-la-maniere-dune-holding/?abo=1.

La Gazette des Communes. (2019). *Entreprises publiques locales: Gare à l'emballement [MOCs: Beware of the hype].* https://www.lagazettedescommunes.com/dossiers/entreprises-publiques-locales-gare-a-lemballement/. Accessed 10 September 2021.

La Gazette des Communes. (2020, September 30). *Prévenir de manière concrète les conflits d'intérêts des élus locaux [Concretely prevent conflicts of interest of local elected officials].* https://www.lagazettedescommunes.com/698391/prevenir-de-maniere-concrete-les-conflits-dinterets-des-elus-locaux/?abo=1.

Pasquier, R. (2021, June 1). *Le pouvoir des Régions est parfois assez résiduel [The power of the Regions is sometimes quite residual], Le Telegramme.* https://www.letelegramme.fr/bretagne/romain-pasquier-le-pouvoir-des-regions-est-parfois-assez-residuel-01-06-2021-12759382.php.

Pasquier, R., Guigner, S., & Cole, A. (2020). *Dictionnaire des politiques territoriales [Dictionary of territorial policies].* Presses de Sciences Po.

Rouveyran, T., & Ricci, N. (2013). Les contrats passés par les SPL [Contracts by MOCs]. *Revue Contrats Publics, 131*, 46–49.

Sée, A. (2013). Les sociétés publiques locales et le droit de la mise en concurrence [MOCs and competition law]. *Contrats Concurrence Consommation*, LexisNexis, 2, 38.

SMACL. (2020). *Le risque pénal des élus locaux et des fonctionnaires territoriaux [Penal risk of local representatives and civil servants].* Annual public report. Paris: SMACL.

Uguen, B. (2015). Inventer de nouveaux outils métropolitains [Inventing new metropolitan tools]. *Revue Française de Finances Publiques, 129*, 163.

Zignani, G. (2016, December 23). Les outils juridiques doivent être utilisés pour servir des objectifs concrets [Legal tools must be used to serve concrete objectives]. *La Gazette des Communes.* https://www.lagazettedescommunes.com/477376/les-outils-juridiques-doivent-etre-utilises-pour-servir-des-objectifs-concrets/.

CHAPTER 12

Municipally Owned Corporations in Greece: Historical Evolution and the Current Situation

Athanasia Triantafyllopoulou and Theodore N. Tsekos

12.1 Local Government in Greece

According to article 101 of the Greek Constitution, the management of local affairs belongs to local self-government. The common legislature may provide for local government levels and determine the scope of responsibilities of each level. It is noteworthy that until 1994 a distinction existed between exclusive and shared competences of local government. As "exclusive competences" were qualified, mainly, activities related to

A. Triantafyllopoulou
Department of Business and Public Administration, University of the Peloponnese, Athens, Greece

T. N. Tsekos (✉)
Department of Business and Public Administration, University of the Peloponnese, Athens, Greece

Institute of Political Research, National Centre for Social Research, Athens, Greece
e-mail: t.tsekos@go.uop.gr

M. Van Genugten et al. (eds.), *Corporatisation in Local Government*, https://doi.org/10.1007/978-3-031-09982-3_12

infrastructure building, water supply, irrigation projects, leisure projects (parks, squares) and so on. As "shared" (between the central and local government) responsibilities were considered activities of a social nature such as the establishment of nurseries, retiring and nursing homes, hospitals and cultural activities (Sotirélis, 2002). This distinction was abolished in 1994 (n.2218) and a "presumption of general competence" is provided in favour of the local self-government for all kinds of local affairs. The provision was included in the Constitution during the 2001 revision.

Legislation on local government provided for the establishment of municipal companies as early as the first decades of the twentieth century and the local self-government took advantage of this opportunity over time. Special laws allowed municipalities to set up municipally owned corporations (MOCs) for water management and energy production in the 1920s (Triantafyllopoulou, 2008).

In addition to these special laws that allowed the establishment of corporations by municipalities, general provisions authorised the cooperation of local government with private corporations and cooperatives under several legal forms for different purposes (mixed corporations for service provision, municipal cooperatives for water management and energy production and municipal corporations for industrial production and commercial purposes).

In 2010 a law (3852/2010) provides for two levels of local self-government: the first tier which consists of municipalities and the second tier which consists of regions. Currently there are 332 municipalities and 13 regions.

The number of local authorities of the first tier was formed after three administrative reforms since the formation of the New Greek State. In particular, a law of 1832 provided only for municipalities. The first reform took place in 1912 (Law DNZ) establishing two different entities, municipalities (over 10,000 inhabitants) and communities, as the first level of local government. The prerequisites for the recognition of a settlement as an administratively independent community (at least 300 inhabitants, financial autonomy and the operation of a primary school) were quite reduced and thus contributed to the establishment of a large number of communities, resulting in the creation of 5600 municipalities and communities (Makrydimítris & Pravíta, 2012).

Although both the 1912 Act and relevant laws adopted later provided for voluntary mergers, such mergers did not take place. In 1997, the first compulsory amalgamation was implemented (Law 2539/1997), which resulted in 1033 municipalities and communities (901 municipalities and 102 communities). In 2010, after the Memoranda of Understanding (MoU) between Greece and the institutions of the European Union and the International Monetary Fund and the undertaking by Greece to reduce public spending (Tsekos & Hlepas, 2018) a second compulsory amalgamation took place (Law 3852/2010), which initially resulted in 325 municipalities and finally, after an amendment in 2018 (Law 4555) providing for the creation of more municipalities in the island areas, 332 municipalities where established.

A second level of local government was introduced for the first time in 1994 after several legislative attempts (1896, 1926, 1986, 1990). Law 2218/1994 provided for 51 prefectural[1] self-governments. In 2010 (Law 3852) compulsory amalgamation was foreseen for the local self-governments of the second level and, thus, prefectural self-governments were replaced by 13 regions.

According to the Constitution, local self-government benefits from a "presumption of competence" in the exercise of all kinds of local affairs. The legislation, however, lists restrictively specific areas of responsibility for both first and second tiers of local government. Such areas of responsibility of the first level of local government are economic development, social protection, environmental protection, culture, sports, education, employment and civil protection as well as the proper overall functioning of cities and settlements. To the second level of local self-government belong the tasks of regional development, spatial and health planning. In addition to the responsibilities that are characterised by the legislation as local, the central administration agencies and other public bodies have the competence to delegate their own responsibilities to the local government, accompanied by the corresponding funding.

Local authorities are elected by direct, secret and universal suffrage every four years. Their main governing bodies are: (a) the municipal and

[1] The prefectures (nomarchies) have been geographical-administrative subdivisions of the Greek political-administrative system since 1833, initially as a deconcentrated state body. Similar levels exist in several other countries such as France, Italy and Japan. The prefecture corresponds approximately to the level of the county for the Anglo-Saxon countries. In 1994 the state Prefecture was abolished and was replaced by the Prefectural self-government, as a second level of local self-government, with an elected Prefect and Prefectural Council. A total of 51 Prefectures were established. Their population was on average 250,000 people but with large variations from about 300–400,000 the largest to 20–30,000 the smallest. They were abolished in 2010 and replaced by regions.

regional council, respectively for the first and second level of local self-government, which are also the decision-making bodies for local policy issues and deal with every matter concerning the municipality or the region, (b) the mayor and the regional governor (secretary general of the region) who are the top executives that implement the decisions of the municipal and regional councils, and (c) elected committees among the municipal and regional councillors that are responsible for specific policy areas, namely the Executive Committee (for general matters), the Economic Committee and the Quality of Life Committee.

The local government hires its own personnel, according to its organisational regulation which defines the structure of the administrative units as well as the job positions and staff qualifications.

It also has the capacity to cooperate on the basis of specific regulations with other public agencies, the social and the private sector as well as to establish legal entities under the public or private law and to delegate to such entities specific responsibilities to achieve more efficient management of local policies.

Special regulations allow the establishment of companies by the local government, as legal entities under private law, either with the municipalities and regions as a sole partner or with the participation of other natural and legal persons under public or private law (Articles 252 et seq. of the Code of Municipalities and Communities, Law 3463/2006) (Triantafyllopoulou, 2009).

Local government has fiscal autonomy, but no financial independence. Funding comes chiefly from the central government (more than 60% of total funding), which allocates financial resources taking into account the population, area, planned projects and services of each local government as well as the specific needs of urban, mountainous and island municipalities.

The state administration exercises control over the legality of the decisions of the collective (councils) and single-member (mayors, vice-mayors, regional governors and vice-governors) administrative organs of the local self-government, without, however, hindering their policy initiative, according to a constitutional provision. The legality control is exercised currently by the Coordinator of the Decentralised Administration, which is a regional state body.

Financial control over local government is exerted by the Court of Auditors, which is entitled to exercise checks and controls on the purpose and the objectives of local government expenditure.

The complicated relationship between central and local government (Hlepas & Getimis, 2011) has generated several problems, mainly regarding the scope of responsibilities, the control of operations and the sources of funding of the local government.

12.2 Historical Trends Regarding Corporations in Greek Local Government

The Code of Municipalities and Communities of 1954 (L.D. 2888/1954) reintroduces and confirms that municipalities and communities have the competence to set up companies or participate in companies set up by other natural or legal persons with the object of carrying out projects to serve citizens. The MOCs are under the control of the municipal or community council, which votes on their budget; they have their own cashier service and their account is audited by the Court of Auditors. The establishment of such MOCs is done by royal decree, following a decision of the municipal or community council, which justifies the necessity of setting up the MOC (Kirollýtis, 1983).

In implementation of this legislative decree, MOCs were established in the field of transport, water supply, sewerage, and radio broadcasting, but also industrial and commercial corporations were created in the primary and secondary sectors of the economy.

The same legislative decree of 1954 provides for the establishment of Small Local Government Corporations that are a special kind of municipal or community agencies operating outside the main body of the local government's administrative services, even though they are managed by the municipal or community council and the income and expenses that stem from their operations, are registered in a special account of the municipal or communal budget.

A 1980 law (1065/1980) gave local governments the possibility of setting up MOCs under the form of either municipal and community corporations or *Sociétés Anonymes* (SAs).

Such MOCs operate under the private law as business sector entities, and it is explicitly stated in the law that their personnel are governed by the general provisions of labour law and not by the civil service regulations. Businesses are established by presidential decree following a decision of the municipal or community council. For the participation of the local self-government in the SAs, the elaboration of an economic-technical study is required. The object of the MOCs, both the municipal-community and the SAs, is the execution of projects and the financial exploitation of these projects, as well as the provision of services.

12.2.1 *Water Supply and Sewerage Companies (DEYAs)*

During the same period, Law 1069/1980 on the establishment of Water Supply and Sewerage Companies (DEYAs) was issued. The DEYAs are established by a decision of the municipal council and the issuance of a presidential decree. Currently, after an amendment of the above-mentioned law, DEYAs are instead created by decision of the Head of the Decentralised State Administration. Besides water supply and sewerage management, the scope of these companies is expanded to include district heating and waste management activities. While these companies operate under private law, the Supreme Administrative Court (Council of State), (decision number 103/1991) due to their responsibilities of public interest, classifies these companies as a hybrid between private and public sectors.

DEYAs are governed by a board of directors appointed by the municipal council and consist of elected representatives of the municipality, representatives of a local body and citizens with knowledge in this field, as well as a representative of the employees, if more than ten staff members are employed.

The budget and report of the company is approved by the municipal council. Audit is exercised by the Court of Auditors. Between 1980 and 1998, 70 DEYAs were registered.

Today approximately a similar number of municipal water and sewerage companies are still operating and although attempts were made to privatise the two largest of them, in Athens and Thessaloniki metropolitan areas (respectively 4 million and 1 million inhabitants), this was not achieved, and all of them still remain under public control.

12.2.2 *MOCs under the socialist government*

In 1984, under a socialist government for the first time in the country's political history, a new law (1416/1984) introduces a number of different types of local self-government corporations. Without the explicit abolition of the regulations existing at that time, but through their adaptation to the new regime, the involvement of the local government in the local economy and development becomes much more extensive and substantial.

The following categories of MOCs are foreseen by the law:

1. "Pure" municipal corporations. They are governed by a board of directors which consists of nine to eleven members and is appointed by the municipal council with the following composition: at least two municipal councillors, representatives of local civil society organisations, a staff representative if more than ten people are employed and representatives of residents or citizens who have expertise on the business object. The president and vice president of the corporation are appointed by the city council. A general manager may be hired under private contract.
2. Inter-municipal corporations created by at least two municipalities (and/or communities). They are governed by a board of directors, similar to that of pure municipal corporations. In addition to the board of directors, there is also an inter-municipal body, as a quasi-assembly of the partners.
3. *Sociétés Anonymes* (SAs or public limited companies) established jointly with cooperatives and operating under private law. Local governments (municipalities and communities) participate in the share capital with a percentage of 51% and cooperatives (of any form) with 49%. Public participation is also possible (of a maximum of 20%). During the first period of implementation of the law and for 5 years companies of this form were exempted from taxation, provided that the board of directors included two members nominated by the government. This provision was abolished in 1997 (Law 2459/1997) (Tátsos, 2004).
4. SAs with broad citizen participation ("popular basis companies") operating under private law. The main difference with the normal SAs is the composition of the share capital: the local government (municipalities and communities) retain 35% of it and together with the participating cooperatives can retain 51% while 49% is distributed among individual shareholders, each of whom cannot hold more than 2%. Companies of this type during the first application of the law and for two years from their establishment are exempt from income tax. The regulation was also abolished in 1997 (Law 2459/1997).

5. Joint-stock companies: this form of public limited companies includes two sub-categories: (a) SAs in which municipalities and communities hold the entire share capital unless the state participates, holding a maximum of 20%—companies of this type are exempt from tax for two years from their establishment; and (b) SAs where municipalities and cooperatives hold 51% of the capital while the rest is distributed amongst shareholders without individual limit.
6. Mixed economy companies: according to Law 947/1979, municipalities are given the right to participate jointly with other public entities in mixed economy companies for land development purposes.

In 1997, when the "pure" municipal corporations were subjected to the civil service status for staff recruitment, some municipalities on their own initiative and without any specific legal provision established civil non-profit companies through natural persons of the political influence of each mayor. The establishment of such entities was based on the stipulation of the civil code for companies without legal personality and was used in order to circumvent the staff hiring restrictions imposed by the civil service recruitment procedures.

Law 3463/2006 limited the purpose of MOCs in the fields of culture and the provision of social services. In other words, it prohibited the creation of companies for commercial purposes, as a result of which there was no longer any interest from municipalities to establish companies which could not generate income and allow the profitable management of municipal property (Triantafyllopoulou, 2009).

12.2.3 *Prefectural Corporations*

After the establishment of the second tier of local self-government in 1994 (n.2218), the creation of the following types of prefectural corporations was foreseen by the law:

1. "Pure" prefectural corporations are created by a decision of the prefectural council, with a business plan based on the results of economic and technical study that is a precondition for the establishment of the company.
2. Pure inter-prefectural corporations are created by two or more prefectural self-governments with the same conditions that apply to the pure prefectural corporations.

3. The prefectural corporations have by law the possibility to participate in public limited companies with cooperatives, SAs with broad citizen participation companies ("popular basis companies") as well as joint public limited companies, according to the above-mentioned.
4. Civil non-profit companies: the law on prefectural corporations of this form does not extend to a detailed regulation of conditions, but refers to a presidential decree, which was not issued.

12.2.4 "Special Purpose" Corporations

The term "special purpose" is used in the Greek legal order to denote the regulation of a distinct activity that is not already listed in a wider category of related activities. Therefore, special regulations provided for the establishment and operation of several types of corporations and activities of "special purposes" with specific business objectives.

1. Radio broadcasting companies and companies for the provision of cable television services: The possibility of granting a radio station licence to local governments is provided by a law of 1987 (Law 1730), amended in 1995 (Law 2328), 1998 (Law 2644) and 1999 (Law 2778). The last act stipulates that local authorities may set up companies to provide radio and television services and legalises all pre-existing companies, which operated without a licence. A total of 24 municipal broadcasting corporations have been established.
2. Public passenger transport companies. From the very beginning in 1832, the local government was given the exclusive responsibility of the local public transport. However, in order to exercise this competence, which is constantly re-introduced in the laws for the primary local self-government (the most recent is the Code of Municipalities and Communities of 2006 [Law 3463/2006]) the issuance of a Ministerial Decision is required, in order to regulate details. This Ministerial Decision has never been issued until today, but neither does it seem that the municipalities put much pressure on its issuance.

   Instead, the Greek state since 1973 (Law 102/1973) granted, exclusively for 20 years the urban and inter-city lines, to syndicated schemes named Joint Bus Operation Funds (KTEL) which had been established in each prefecture. In 2001 a new law (Law 2963) provides for the conversion of the Joint Bus Operating Funds into public limited companies with a participation in their capital of up to

40% of the local government. In practice the local government, with a couple of exceptions, has not exercised this right, probably because municipalities are cautious in engaging in a competence which can prove to be complex and costly. In addition to road passenger transport, there have been attempts to involve island municipalities in maritime transport. In particular, shipping companies were created by the municipalities of two Aegean islands (Chios and Kalymnos). Both attempts failed.

3. Gas distribution companies. The Public Gas Company SA, which was established in 1952 (Law 2234), had the possibility to create local gas distribution companies in the form of public limited companies with the exclusive rights of gas distribution systems in a specific area with a limit of calorific capacity of 100 gigawatts. Local self-government could participate in such gas distribution companies with a percentage of 49%. In 2002 (Law 2992) the possibility of local government participation was abolished.
4. Joint-stock companies. A 1984 law (Law 1416) allowed local governments to participate by buying shares in already operating public limited companies or joint ventures and consortia.
5. Groups of economic purpose. Local governments were given the opportunity in 1983 (Law 1338 as amended by the provisions of Law 3613/2007) to participate in trans-European joint ventures in order to utilise European funding tools and programmes. These joint ventures, as long as they are based in Greece, operate as non-profit companies with a maximum of 20 members that may come from all member states of the European Union.
6. Social protection units. According to the provisions of Law 2072/1992, a special category of corporations is foreseen for delivering social services in cooperation with local governments. These activities take place in the context of the policies pursued by the Ministry of Health and Welfare, on condition that they are financed by European programmes. Such units operate under the legal form of civil non-profit companies.

12.2.5 *Local Government Corporations in Total*

By 1998, about 1000 companies in almost all sectors of the economy had been set up under the different legal forms provided by the abovementioned legislation at the two levels of local government

(Triantafyllopoulou, 2008). Table 12.1 shows the number of local government corporations by sectors and branches of economic activity.

For the same period (2000), the financial performance, that is the total revenues and net profits of the municipal companies, is shown in Table 12.2 (in euros) (Triantafyllopoulou, 2008).

Given that in the same year the GDP of Greece amounted to 157 billion euros, we notice that the total activity of municipal enterprises did not exceed 0.30% of the above GDP. However, since for the same year the total public funding of the local government amounted to about 3.2 billion euros, the turnover of municipal enterprises, that is around 15% of the above amount, is not negligible.

Table 12.3 shows the legal forms of total 1455 companies in 2002 (Triantafyllopoulou, 2008).

Table 12.1 Local government corporations by sectors and branches of activity

Sector/branch	*Number of local government Corporations*
Primary sector	33
A. Agriculture-livestock-forestry	12
B. Fisheries	7
C. Mines-quarries	14
Secondary sector	128
A. Manufacturing	29
B. Electricity supply	9
C. Construction	90
Tertiary sector	815
A. Wholesale and retail trade	6
B. Operation of hotels-restaurants	54
C. Transport and communications services	38
D. Credit institutions	1
E. Real estate management	186
F. Education	77
G. Health and social welfare services	124
H. Other services	329
Total	976

Table 12.2 Revenue and net profits of local government corporations

Sector	*Income of the municipal corporations*	*Sectoral income as % of the total municipal corporate income*	*Profits*	*Profits as % of the sectoral municipal corporate income*
Primary sector	8,659,593	1.91%	583,005	6.7%
Secondary sector	119,620,791	26.40%	-8,697,580	-7.3%
Tertiary sector	324,819,673	71.69%	-21,628,784	-6.7%
Total	453,100,057		-29,743,359	-6.56%

Table 12.3 Local government corporations (including MOCs and prefectural corporations) according to their legal form

Legal form	*Number of corporations*	*Percentage*
"Pure" local government corporations	**1089**	74.8
Pure municipal corporations	999	67.64
Pure community corporations	30	2.03
Pure inter-municipal	30	2.03
Pure joint municipal and community corporations	1	0.07
Pure prefectural corporations	26	1.76
Pure corporations established by local association of municipalities and communities	3	0.20
Sociétés Anonymes	**221**	14.83
SAs	218	14.62
Joint public and private ventures	2	0.14
Public limited sports company	1	0.07
Other corporate forms	**5**	0.34
Limited liability companies	4	0.27
Limited partnerships	1	0.07
Civil non-profit companies	**140**	9.48
Total	**1455**	100

Of these, 73% were municipal and community corporations (first tier of local government), while 25% were prefectural (second tier of local government) and 2% were mixed municipal and prefectural corporations.

It is also noteworthy that several of these companies fell into inactivity, that is, although formally they remained in operation and retained their board of directors they did not engage in any kind of productive or commercial activity and that in an increasing percentage from 19% in 1997 to 36% in 2002.

12.3 The Political Background

It is clear that MOCs in Greece spread out, mainly, in the 1980s after the rise of the Socialist Party in power, a political development that triggered profound changes in the local self-government. The programmatic priorities of the Socialist Party (Panhellenic Socialist Movement—PASOK), including the extensive transfer of policy-making at the local level, the enhancement of citizens' participation and the boost of social economy (third sector organisations, or TSOs, social corporations and cooperatives), contributed, in parallel, to the assignment of a significant number of additional responsibilities to the local self-government. The institutional changes of this period, related to the expansion of MOCs, not only emphasised the developmental role of local government, but also emphasised its character as a participatory institutional framework (Tsekos & Triantafyllopoulou, 2016).

During the same period, several institutional and operational tools were developed to facilitate and support the new roles and activities undertaken by the local government, mainly through MOCs. The most important of these are the following:

- The "program contracts" between the local self-government, the public sector agencies and the social sector corporations (Law 1416/1984) for the management of development projects and the provision of services. With the institution of programme contracts, the local government took initiatives for the execution of development projects, mainly in the field of culture and social protection, but also the utilisation of wealth-producing resources within the administrative boundaries of local government organisations.
- The "development associations" are supra-local associations with compulsory participation of the municipalities that aim at the elaboration and implementation of local and regional development programmes. The proposals of the development associations must be taken into account by the central government when drawing up the national development programme, which thus acquires a bottom-up design character. From 2006 (Law 3463) onwards, however, the

development initiative of the municipalities is limited and the bottom-up nature of the national planning is overturned as the law stipulates that the municipalities must comply with the political priorities of the central government.

Using the above-mentioned legal framework, local authorities had the opportunity to set up corporations for both the exploitation of assets and the provision of services to citizens. MOCs were strengthened through tax exemptions and their flexible operating status. The rules of private law under which the corporations operated helped the local government to get access to financing on market terms and to manage their human resources in a flexible manner. Especially the local and regional development corporations strengthened the character of the local self-government as a development institution. They were established in almost all regions and fulfilled their mission as "technical and scientific support of local government". At that time and before the creation of the development companies, the municipalities did not have the opportunity, due to legal restrictions and bureaucratic procedures, to hire the necessary high-level scientific staff for the implementation of the programmes and initiatives of European funds. The development companies hired such staff on market terms and provided consulting and technical support to the municipalities.

The staff of MOCs during this period amounted to 22,522 people (28% basic education, 42% secondary education, 30% tertiary education), while 83% of them were on indefinite and fixed-term employment contracts and the rest were hired under project contracts.

However, there is another side to the coin. In an environment of political patronage like the one prevailing in the Greek political system, the flexibility offered by the legislation on MOCs to local political staff could only be used to strengthen their political influence. MOCs could employ staff without the procedural standards and controls of the public recruitment system while no legal requirements obliged them to purchase goods and services through public tender processes. Additionally, local governments could enter into contracts with MOCs without tenders and could thus transfer public money directly to them. Finally, the boards of directors of these MOCs offered a pool of jobs that could be used to reward political supporters and clients. The whole situation favoured clientelist practices (Tsekos & Triantafyllopoulou, 2016).

The rise to power of the Conservative Party (New Democracy) in 1990 interrupted to some extent the dynamics of MOCs. The new government expressed the accumulated dissatisfaction of private companies at the local level due to the competition from MOCs mainly in the public and municipal procurement of goods and services. In the construction sector, private contractors had reacted because local government projects were undertaken by the relevant MOCs. Other entrepreneurs, who had expressed interest in utilising the assets of the local government, reacted because the MOCs had taken over their utilisation. In addition, there were political reactions. MPs elected in provincial constituencies, competed with municipal councillors for local political support, mainly in terms of influence on public recruitment, a clientelist attitude that is observed over time in Greek society. All the above generated a political *momentum* leading to policies which contributed to the diminution of the role of MOCs and even to the suspension of the operation of several of them.

In 1993 the Socialist Party returned to power. Putting into effect the European policy on vocational training, the socialist government legislated for the establishment of vocational training centres by the local government either in the form of MOCs or in cooperation with the public and social sectors.

In 2004 the Conservative Party took over the government again and re-implemented a policy of reducing the role of MOCs. In 2006, new legislation has completely changed their status with new regulations, which are still in force today, with only minor changes.

12.4 The Current Situation

In 2006 a new Code of Municipalities and Communities (Law 3463) was introduced. Among its provisions are regulations for the local self-government corporations that abolish the "pure" municipal corporations and the SAs of both the first and the second level of local self-government. Existing companies are obliged to adapt to the new regime, provided that no commercial activities are carried out by them.

12.4.1 Types of MOCs and Regional Corporations

In particular, it is provided that the following kind of municipal and regional corporations can be created:

1. Public Benefit Corporations (PBCs) that can be established by a municipality (communities were abolished since 2010) in the fields of (a) culture, sports and education (b) social protection and solidarity and (c) environmental protection excluding parks and open spaces management, recycling and so on, which are considered to be the responsibility of the municipal administration.
2. Municipal water supply and sewerage companies (DEYAs) continue to operate.
3. Development SAs established by regions—only one per region in which the regional self-government holds more than 51% of the share capital.
4. Municipalities do not have the possibility to establish SAs, after 2010, but they can participate in development companies established by the regions.
5. Development Organisations of Local Self-government aiming at the management of European funds and acting as financial intermediaries of state aid actions. They operate as SAs and can be established by local governments and associations of municipalities with a total percentage of 51%, as well as the Regional Development Funds, the Central Union of Municipalities, and the Networks of local self-government organisations. They are governed by a board of directors, which is elected by the assembly of partners.

The local government, according to the current regime (3852/2010), has the possibility to establish legal entities under public law and to grant them specific responsibilities in the social and cultural sector. Their establishment is made by decision of the municipal or regional council, and after the approval of the decision by the supervisory body, the decision is published in the Government Gazette. Legal entities under public law operate as public administrative agencies.

Municipalities and regions are also authorised by the same law to establish legal entities under private law. Their establishment is made by decision of the municipal or regional council and a presidential decree published in the Government Gazette.

There is a limit of two legal entities under public or private law per municipality or region: one in the field of social services and another one for cultural activities. From this limit of two legal entities are excluded those established under public law for the management of port funds, in those cases where this responsibility has been transferred to the municipality, as well as municipal legal entities that manage private donations, bequests and legacies. Cities with a population of more than 300,000 residents are authorised to operate in total four legal entities, two under public law and two under private law.

At the end of the day, given that the local government, obliged to act through legal entities under public law or PBCs that also operate as public, can no longer make the most of the flexibility of MOCs operating under market rules.

12.4.2 Provisions for Existing MOCs Following the 2006 Legislation

The 2006 law provided for the adaptation of MOCs to the new regulations in particular.

At that time, the existing "pure" municipal corporations had to adapt to the new regime and become PBCs, given that they would not include commercial activities in their mission. They did, however, have the opportunity to break up their businesses and set up a PBC and a commercial SA. A deadline was granted for such a conversion firstly until 31 December 2007 and then following several extensions until 31 December 2010. In the event of non-adjustment within that period, the "pure" municipal corporations would automatically be dissolved.

The SAs that operated upon the entry into force of the new law, with all kinds of businesses, and the "special purpose corporations" as well, had the possibility to remain in operation. However, they were not able to hire additional staff.

The legislation of 2006 and in particular the obligation to convert "pure" municipal corporations into PBCs, operating as public agencies, and the prohibition of their commercial purpose led to the drastic reduction of their number. Today there are about 60 PBCs and 29 development SAs.

12.5 The Evolvement of the Legal and Business Status of MOCs

The status of MOCs has been a matter of high importance to the legislators for a long time. The corporations during the early period (until 1954) did not differ from the legal entities under public law in terms of their organisational and operational modalities, as already mentioned, while they were not undertaking, in essence, any business risk. After 1954, with the establishment of joint-stock companies, MOCs have begun operating according to the market rules.

12.5.1 *Staff and Procurement*

In the 1980s, the "pure" municipal corporations and the SAs of the local authorities are legaly excluded from the public sector (article 51, par. 2 of Law 1892/1990), classified as legal persons under private law and operate according to the market rules. The corporations are exempted from the public procurement process, and their employees are hired by decisions of the corporation's board of directors without any other formal procedure. This management scheme is introduced in order to guarantee a flexible regime for better utilization of the local governments' assets so to generate revenue, and strengthen their budget.

The private legal status of MOCs has been changed by several acts. The first reform took place in 1994 (Law 2229/1994) regarding the project execution process. With the new regulations, MOCs (and regional corporations) are obliged to implement their projects following the procedures required for public works.

At the same time, the procedure for service procurement is changing. The central administration, referring to the directive 92/50/EEC (the directive was adapted to the Greek legislation in 2007 with PD 60/2007) obliged MOCs to follow the procedure of public service contracts.

The European Union, in order to protect competition and to prevent the selection on political criteria of suppliers providing goods, works, or services to public authorities, issued directive 92/50/EEC which mandated that public procurement should be done through tender procedures. The public bodies referred to in the directive as "contracting authorities" are the state and local authorities, bodies under public law and associations consisting of one or more of the above entities (Manunza, 2003).

The criteria for designating a body as an entity governed by public law are the following: firstly to be created in order to meet specific needs of general interest and not having commercial purposes, secondly to have a distinct legal personality, thirdly to be financed for the most part by the state, the local authorities or other public law bodies, otherwise their management to be subject to control exercised by these authorities, or more than half of the members of their board of directors to be appointed by the state, by the regional or local authorities or by other bodies governed by public law.

Based on the above provisions of the directive, the MOCs did not meet the criteria for inclusion in the status of public bodies/contracting authorities because, being of a commercial and/or industrial nature, the law did not allow for subsidies from local governments or other public bodies and did not provide for a supervisory or management board for businesses. The only criterion, which applied, but merely to "pure" corporations, was the appointment of the board of directors. On the contrary the management board of the municipal SAs resulted from an election by the shareholders and therefore cannot be considered a political appointment.

Therefore, for their sole purpose, most MOCs should be excluded from public procurement procedures. However, the view of the Greek public administration was, on the contrary, that MOCs are contracting authorities and therefore obliged to follow the respective procedures of the public tenders.

In 1997, the staff recruitment system was partially changed with the enactment of a relevant law (Law 2527/1994). With the new provisions, candidates for positions that require compulsory and secondary education qualifications are recruited through the civil service recruitment procedures. Candidates for positions that require higher education qualifications are hired directly by the board of directors, in accordance with the terms of the staff regulations drawn up by each company. In 2002 the regime of 1997 is amended again (with Law 3051/2002), and the recruitment of staff becomes part of the public administration recruitment process with the exception of the scientific personnel with increased qualifications, which is still recruited according to the procedure defined in the corporation's staff regulation.

An issue arose during this period with the top management staff, which was considered by the law as general administrative staff and, therefore, MOCs had to hire with the procedure of public servants' recruitment. However, following a relevant decision of the Supreme Personnel Selection Council (Independent Authority for the control of the recruitment process of the public sector), top managers continued to be hired by the board of directors in accordance with the staff regulations of each corporation.

The operation of PBCs follows the provisions of the public sector. In particular, the rules of public procurement (Law 4412/2016) are applied for the execution of projects, the execution of procurement and the assignment of services, and are subject to financial control by the Court of Auditors, like any public body. The staff of these companies is also recruited following the public servants' recruitment procedure without exception.

With regard to development SAs, the law is tossing and turning between the status of private and public law. The staff of the development SAs is hired according to the provisions applying to the public employees while the procedure of public procurement is also utilised, when they carry out state-financed programmes, whereas in case their projects are self-financed and for commercial activities, the provisions of private law are followed.

In terms of organisation, PBCs set up internal regulations which provide for staff positions and qualifications, disciplinary issues and the relationships between employees and the corporation's management.

12.5.2 *Planning, Budget and Supervision*

The planning and financial budget of PBCs is drafted by the board of directors of the company and approved by the municipal council. The city council exercises oversight over PBCs through their budget, as well as financial control through the appointment of auditors. The Coordinator of the Decentralised Administration and the Court of Auditors may also request financial control.

12.5.3 *Board of Directors and Director General*

The boards of directors of the local self-government companies are formed in a different way when it comes to SAs (public limited companies) and differently in the case of PBCs.

Sociétés Anonymes The board of directors of the SAs is elected by the general assembly of the shareholders. Given that the local government retains a majority of the shares, the management of the SAs can be fully controlled by the representatives of the local government (and in practice by the municipal majority). However, usually in the Articles of Association of the Company, a clause is included for the appointment of a minority on the board of directors, in accordance with the legislation on public limited companies, so that all shareholders or groups of shareholders can be represented. There are many cases where the board of directors results from the consent of the shareholders so that, regardless of the percentage in the share capital, the composition of the board of directors comes with the agreement of all shareholders.

Still this legislative provision that stipulates for a majority of the local self-government in the board of directors prevented frequently private companies from participating in local self-government SAs.

The Articles of Association of the companies usually provide for the election of the chairman of the board of directors and the assignment of specific responsibilities to him, as well as the hiring of a director general after a public announcement and according to specific qualifications stated in the personnel regulations of each company. However, there are several cases in which both roles of chairman of the board and director general are performed by the same person.

The members on the board of directors usually come from the municipal or regional council or are the legal representatives of the shareholders-collective bodies, regardless of their formal qualifications. The selection of a director general usually requires formal qualifications, for example, higher education degree, preferably in economics, with a working experience mostly from the private sector.

It is observed that, where the roles of the president of the board and the director general coincide, the holder is usually a councillor, member of the majority in the municipal or regional council. He often pursues a low-profile management strategy limited to the purely formal operations of the company. On the contrary in cases where the management of the company was assigned to non-elected persons with high qualifications, recruited after a public announcement and given substantial responsibilities, they developed initiatives, gained the trust of the councillors unrelatedly to their political affiliation and led the company to play an essential role in the local economy and development. On the contrary, if the elected officials, after a change of majority, tried to replace managers who had achieved significant business results, the companies either performed poorly or even became inactive.

The "Pure" Corporations and PBCs The board of directors of the "pure" corporations (1984–2006) and the PBCs (2006–present) is appointed by the municipal council, which appoints both the chairman and the vice-chairman of the board. At least 2 members of the board of directors (their total number ranges from 5 to 11 members) are municipal or regional councillors, one member comes from a local association and one member is a staff representative. The other members are local citizens or residents who are familiar with the business.

The above composition of the boards is rarely respected. Usually, more representatives of the municipal or regional councils are appointed while the representatives of the local associations are also in practice councillors that are involved in public associations, cooperatives, unions and so on. Even the citizens or residents with expertise in the business area are often selected amongst councillors.

The chairman and the vice-chairman of the board of directors can receive compensation if the company's financial situation allows it. The company's director general can be hired by the board of directors, after an announcement and according to the qualifications defined in the company's regulations.

Currently the scope of PBCs is limited as they only implement programmes funded by the European Union and/or national resources and, thus, the responsibilities of the directors general are limited to project management, in accordance with the regulations of the European Funds.

What is interesting is that there is a constant questioning of the municipal character of SAs and PBCs. There is pressure from the staff of the companies themselves to turn them into either fully private or purely public companies. The first case concerns companies that are still commercially active, as in the case of renewable energy production, which seek greater flexibility and independence from political control. Pressures for conversion to public enterprises and application of the status of permanent civil servants to their staff come from PBCs. Responding to these requests, the current government introduced a new piece of legislation (Law 4674/2020), providing for a new type of entities similar to the development SAs, labelled Development Organisations of the Local Self-Government, legally operating as public limited companies but managed according to the procedures of public agencies, with shareholders municipalities or regions and/or regional associations of municipalities. The same law stipulates the possibility to turn development SAs into Development Organisations of the Local Self-Government.

12.6 Concluding Remarks

MOCs have played an important role in Greece, having gone through many stages. In the early stages of their emergence, during the interwar period and during the 1950s, they were assigned by law responsibilities and activities that were related to the mission of local government but were not easy to carry out by the municipal services. Businesses in this first period, which is schematically defined between 1950 and 1980, had an operational character and role. Municipal water supply and sewerage companies but also some in energy production, radio and so on are typical examples for this period. Since the 1980s when the Socialist Party first came to power, the responsibilities of local government have been significantly strengthened (Hlepas, 2010). This development has also contributed to the expansion and strengthening of the role of MOCs. Their number increased dramatically and they developed a wide range of activities from social and personal services, culture and sports to manufacturing, tourism, construction and real estate. The prevailing political ideas at the time saw municipal and regional corporations as a key tool for local development. An important factor pushing for the proliferation of the corporations was the fact that since the mid-1990s the European Union has pursued a policy of restricting state aid and strengthening competition. Municipalities and regions have set up new development companies in order to be eligible to join European funding programmes on competitive terms. These complex political dynamics have led to equally complex institutional solutions, giving rise to a wide range of legal forms for MOCs and regional corporations.

This exceptional growth of MOCs and regional corporations between 1980 and 2000 had two facets. On the one hand, corporations provided local government with important tools to play a more substantive role in local and regional economic and social development (Getimis, 2021). On the other hand, operating within a strong framework of political patronage, corporations offered local political staff the opportunity to manage valuable clientelist resources in the form of staff appointments and assignments of procurement contracts. The clientelist utilisation of MOCs corrupted the efficiency and the quality of their operations and outcomes and, in the long run, undermined their role.

At the same time, the expansion of MOCs generated some strong reactions, mainly from two directions. First, the political staff of the central government (MPs, ministers, etc.) did not view in a positive light the strengthening of the political capital of the local elected staff (municipal and regional councillors, mayors, regional governors, etc.) facilitated through the control of the corporations. In addition, the local small and medium enterprises, mainly in the field of tourism, construction and real estate, confronted in a very negative way the competition of the corporations and the privileged relations they had with the municipalities and regions, mainly in the field of public procurement. Thus, constant pressures were exerted to limit their role and number. Pressures were heard from the conservative governments that passed successive laws to reduce the number and business areas of the municipal and regional corporations.

Finally, MOCs and regional corporations have been losing more and more flexibility in recent years, both because the European funding framework reduces the margins in order for them to get direct outsourcing of public procurement contracts and because the central government has limited their ability to hire staff directly without going through the publicity and competition procedures of the public service recruitment system. They thus lose their clientelist usefulness and worth.

References

Getimis, P. (2021). Local state-society relations in Greece. In F. Teles, A. Gendźwiłł, C. Stănuş, & H. Heinelt (Eds.), *Close ties in European local governance: Linking local state and society* (pp. 165–180). Palgrave Macmillan.

Hlepas, N. K. (2010). Incomplete Greek territorial consolidation: From the first (1998) to the second (2008–09) wave of reforms. *Local Government Studies, 36*(2), 223–249.

Hlepas, N. K., & Getimis, P. (2011). Impacts of local government reforms in Greece: An interim assessment. *Local Government Studies, 37*(5), 517–532.

Kirollýtis, N. (1983). Meléti gia tin istorikí exélixi tis epicheirimatikís drastiriótitas tis topikís aftodioíkisis [Study on the historical development of the business activity of the local self-government]. *Epitheórisi Topikís Aftodioíkisis*, Noémvrios-Dekémvrios, 2–47.

Makrydimítris, A., & Pravíta, M. H. (2012). *Dimósia Dioíkisi [Public Administration]*. Ekdóseis Sákkoula.

Manunza, E. R. (2003). Privatised services and the concept of "bodies governed by public law" in EC directives on public procurement. *European Law Review, 28*(2), 273–282.

Sotirélis, G. (2002). *I Metarrýthmisi tis Topikís Aftodioíkisis. Proklíseis kai prooptikés metá tin syntagmatikí anatheórisi [The Reform of Local Government. Challenges and prospects after the constitutional revision]*. Ekdóseis. Proskínio.

Tátsos, N. (2004). *Dimosionomikí apokéntrosi. Theoría kai práxi [Fiscal decentralisation. Theory and practice]*. Ekdóseis Typothíto-Dardanós.

Triantafyllopoulou, A. (2008). *Epicheiríseis ton organismón topikís aftodioíkisis. Nomikó kathestós kai stoicheía epicheiríseon apó to 1833 éos símera [Local Government Corporations. Legal status and business data from 1833 until today]*. S.I. Zacharopoulos.

Triantafyllopoulou, A. (2009). O thesmós ton epicheiríseon tis aftodioíkisis katá ton kódika dímon kai koinotíton (n.3463/2006) [The institution of self-government enterprises according to the Code of Municipalities and Communities (Law 3463/2006)]. *Dioikisi kai Politeia*, Melétes ar. 40. Athens: Ekdóseis Ant.N. Sákkoula.

Tsekos, T. N., & Hlepas, N. K. (2018). Greek municipalities before and during the austerity era: Imposed policies, local resistances and unsuccessful reforms. In A. Lippi & T. Tsekos (Eds.), *Local public service in times of austerity across Mediterranean Europe* (pp. 49–71). Palgrave Macmillan.

Tsekos, T. N., & Triantafyllopoulou, A. (2016). From municipal socialism to the sovereign debt crisis: Local services in Greece 1980–2015. In H. Wollmann, I. Koprić, & G. Marcou (Eds.), *Public and social services in Europe* (pp. 135–149). Palgrave Macmillan.

CHAPTER 13

Municipal Corporatisation in Italy

Giuseppe Grossi and Simone Cocciasecca

13.1 Introduction

In Italy, there has been a long history of state involvement in economic activities (Allini et al., 2016), through several institutional trends, such as public-public collaboration, public-private partnerships and contracting out, but mainly through corporatisation (Argento et al., 2010). Since the early 1990s, in Italy the corporatisation of public bodies has indeed become a prominent phenomenon, especially at the local level and in the domain of public services (Profeti et al., 2012).

Following the wave of New Public Management (NPM), the belief in the supremacy of private sector solutions has been a major argument supporting the transformation of governmental entities into separate corporations, since there is still the belief that single-purpose and

G. Grossi (✉)
Economic Analysis and Accounting Division, Nord University, Bodo, Norway

Department of Business, Kristianstad University, Kristianstad, Sweden
e-mail: giuseppe.grossi@hkr.se

S. Cocciasecca
Department of Management and Business Administration, University of Chieti and Pescara, Pescara, Italy

M. Van Genugten et al. (eds.), *Corporatisation in Local Government*, https://doi.org/10.1007/978-3-031-09982-3_13

business-like public sector organisations may be more effective than large bureaucratic bodies (Grossi & Reichard, 2008). Other arguments supporting this institutional trend are external factors, such as (1) the European Union (EU) pressure towards increased competitiveness of the public sector by deregulating public service sectors and by eliminating local monopolies and (2) the ongoing fiscal pressure on municipalities that encourages to hide their liabilities by allocating partly to their corporations (Bremeier et al., 2006).

This chapter presents an updated description of municipally owned corporations (MOCs) in Italy in terms of administrative context (Sect. 13.2), the historical developments in Italy (Sect. 13.3), the possible public and private legal forms (Sect. 13.4), organisational characteristics (Sect. 13.5), their managerial autonomy (Sect. 13.6), and board structure and composition (Sect. 13.7). Finally, we analyse the empirical results and draw some conclusions about possible future trends.

13.2 Local Government Context

The Italian local government system consists of 107 provinces and about 7900 municipalities, each with an average of about 7500 inhabitants.

Provinces are responsible for transport services; environmental protection and control; supervision of fishing and hunting activities; rural and urban planning; professional education; and high school building maintenance. Municipalities are responsible for the delivery of services, such as public order and public safety; the management of municipal roads and public buildings; water management; waste disposal; local public transport; child education; services for the disabled, elderly and children; municipal policing; recreational services; libraries; cemeteries; and the management of critical issues related to natural disasters. In 2018, local governments in Italy had an overall degree of revenue autonomy (own revenues out of total resources) of 56%, which is just above the EU average (53%) (source: https://portal.cor.europa.eu/divisionpowers/Pages/Italy-Fiscal-Powers.aspx).

Municipalities can manage public services directly (*in economia*), in contracting out, or through institutions (institutions) without separate legal personally, or MOCs (Grossi & Reichard, 2016). Direct provision is possible in the case of modest size or where the characteristics of the service mean that it is not appropriate to establish a company, and provision can take place through the administrative offices. Contracting out (*concessione*) to external entities (non-profit and private organisations) is possible when the provision of the service requires equipment, professionalism or economic resources that the municipality is unable to guarantee. MOCs in Italy can have different legal forms, which will be dealt with in more detail in the specific section on legal status; however, the most present are:

- *Special undertakings* (*azienda speciale*) and *consortia* (*consorzio*) for the management of services without economic relevance, which are services structurally uneconomic, potentially unprofitable, and therefore private market is unable or not interested in providing those services;
- *Joint-stock companies* (*Società per azioni*) totally or partially owned by local governments for medium/large-scale activities (min. Equity: €120,000);
- *Limited company* (*Societa' a responsabilitaà limitata*) totally or partially owned by local governments for small-scale activities (min. Equity: €10,000).

For services without economic relevance, the legislation appears quite flexible and enables local governments to select directly, without public tendering, the possible providers: institutions, special undertakings or consortia, or totally owned companies (so-called in-house providers), such that (1) local government owns all the shares and is also able to exercise analogous control, such as the control over internal services, and (2) the company carries out the most important part of its business within the territorial area of the controlling local government and, in the case of cultural and recreational services can be assigned to associations or foundations made up, or participated in by, the local government.

For services with economic relevance, municipalities should select as providers companies regulated by private law (joint-stock companies or limited companies). According to the legislation, this means: (1) a company with public, private or mixed ownership selected through a public tender; (2) a company with mixed public and private ownership in which the private partner is selected through a public tender; or (3) one company totally owned by the local government (so-called in-house provider with the same previously mentioned conditions).

National legislation is characterised by uncertainty, as a result of political discussion and disagreement on the possible ways to provide local public services. Currently, the main area of disagreement concerns the opportunity of involving private partners with financial and professional resources in collaborative agreements with local governments.

13.3 Trends in Corporatisation

In Italy, the municipalisation process began in the early 1900s, following the industrialisation and growing urbanisation processes that characterised the country around the end of the nineteenth century, when it became necessary to regulate the management of local public services (Pischel, 1972). The first legislation approved by parliament in 1903 (Act no.103, so-called *Legge Giolitti*) introduced the possibility of providing public services (such as gas, water, urban transport and electricity, and other services) directly or through corporations (so-called *azienda municipalizzata*). The growing diffusion of corporatisation contributed to the urban development and modernisation of services in large and medium cities, especially in the northern regions (Citroni et al., 2016). Therefore, in this phase, local governments were able to finance their treasuries with the large revenues connected to the management of the services and, on the other hand, to respond to problems fed by the processes of increasing urbanisation in the country (Spadoni, 2003).

In the last century, public service provision was mainly dominated by direct and indirect municipal management, and it is only since the 1990s that new reforms have been introduced in three main phases:

- 1990–2000: A *New Public Management Phase* with a process of real emancipation of the municipal company began, aimed at growing independence and responsibility and introducing more managerial principles and business-like models, with a decision-making system and regulation more oriented towards efficiency and economy. The legislative reform first of all provided the local government with a wider range of management models of the public services: to the traditional direct management, new models like the institution, the special undertaking, the joint-stock company and the limited liability company have been added (Tessarolo, 2001). In addition, the principle of managerial autonomy of MOCs was re-introduced, reducing the power of control by local governments and thus allowing a high level of managerial discretion (Serbassi, 1999).
- 2000–2010: This was a *Hybrid Phase* with many uncertainties due to a lack of both stable legislation and political commitment at the central

level. The conflicting views were promoting different values and roles of public and private actors in the provision of public services at the local level. From one side, there was strong support from some political parties to introduce privatisation and liberalisation through compulsory competitive tenders, while, from another side, there was strong political resistance to introducing competition in public sectors characterised historically by the strong dominance of municipalities and MOCs to protect and safeguard pre-existing local interests (Citroni et al., 2016). This phase was characterised by hybrid reforms that allowed the local government to go on to use traditional models (such as direct management and in-house provision) and new models (based on competitive tenders for the selection of a company with public, private or mixed ownership or a private provider in the case of mixed ownership). The effect of these reforms was a strong and uncontrolled diffusion of managerial forms. In 1995, there were 22 joint-stock companies owned by local governments (Spadoni, 2003); currently, in Italy, there are 1707 companies with majority ownership (more than 50%) held by local governments (Ministry of Finance, 2020).

- 2011 to present: The *Austerity Phase* was characterised by the introduction of reforms and a review of public sector shareholdings, with the aim of rationalising the corporations and shareholdings held by local government. These reforms were considered necessary because Italy has a large number of corporations owned by local government, many of which operate inefficiently in sectors with high barriers to competition. With the aim of reducing the large number of local government-owned corporations and thereby increasing competition and public sector efficiency, the Consolidated Law on State Owned Enterprises (part of the *Reform* the Minister of Public Administration) was enacted in mid-2016. It included existing fragmented legislations and defined qualitative and quantitative criteria for the establishment, acquisition and retention of shareholding in State Owned Enterprises (SOEs). These criteria include local governments ensuring a direct link with the institutional goals of the public sector, that is, that they provide services of public interest in a cost-effective and financially sustainable manner (Ministry of Finance, 2020). Major rationalisation criteria have promoted the following managerial forms to provide local public services (L. 190/2014[1]):

[1] Law 190/2014. Provisions for the preparation of the annual and multi-year budget of the State.

- Companies that are not considered essential to the pursuit of the municipalities' institutional purposes;
- Companies that do not have employees or have more directors than employees;
- Companies that perform similar activities to those carried out by other publicly owned companies or by instrumental public agencies, which according to legislation are public bodies that pursue public purposes, to which they are bound by constraints;
- Companies whose average turnover, over the last three years, is less than a certain threshold;
- Companies that have been loss-making for four out of the five preceding years;
- Companies that need to contain operating costs.

These reforms and reviews of public sector shareholdings led to a rationalisation of corporations and shareholdings held by local governments. According to the last annual reports of the Italian Ministry of Economy (2020), from a peak, reached in 2013, of over 6000 local government shareholdings in companies (regardless to the % of ownership), we are witnessing a gradual reduction year on year to around 4000 entities in 2018, the last available year. Figure 13.1 graphically shows the rationalisation tendency emerging in Italy over the last decade.

According to the law, all public sector organisations (including local governments) were obliged to carry out an Extraordinary Review of their

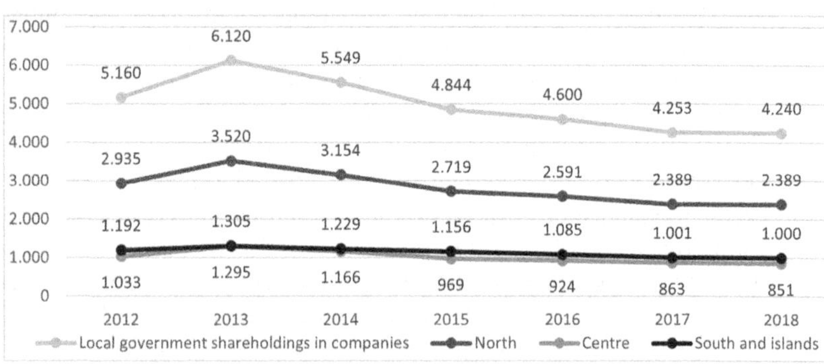

Fig. 13.1 Rationalisation of corporations and shareholdings held by Italian local governments (Source: Ministry of Economy 2020). Note: Data includes all the local Italian shareholdings, regardless of the % held

shareholdings by September 2017, identifying those investments that should be rationalised and completing the rationalisation by September 2018. However, the rationalisation deadline was later postponed until the end of 2021 for those companies that had been profitable on average over the three years before the Extraordinary Review. The law established annual progress reviews, monitored directly by the Ministry of Economy and Finance (MEF), with the support of the Competition Authority and a sanction system linked to the prerogatives of the Court of Auditors (Ministry of Finance, 2020).

In conclusion, according to the latest report from the Ministry of Economy (2020), there are actually 1707 local government-owned enterprises in Italy, in which a municipality holds at least 50% of the ownership. They are divided into 54% in the north, 22% in the centre and 23.5% in the south and islands. Over 75% of them arose from the 1990s onwards; specifically, the most prolific decade was the 2000s with 754 new companies, about half of the entire population of MOCs.

13.4 Legal Status

To provide public services, local governments created different types of legal entities (public and private) in which they participate totally or partially (Grossi & Reichard, 2008; Argento et al., 2010). More details about their diffusion are provided in Table 13.1.

Table 13.1 Legal status of MOCs in Italy

Legal status		%
Limited liability company[a]	822	48.15
Joint-stock company[a]	396	23.20
Foundation[a]	150	8.79
Special undertaking	116	6.80
Consortium	45	2.64
Institution[b]	39	2.28
Limited liability consortium company[a]	38	2.23
Public entity	32	1.87
Other non-corporate legal status	28	1.64
Association[a]	20	1.17
Cooperative[a]	11	0.64
Joint-stock consortium company[a]	10	0.59
Total	1707	100.00

Source: Ministry of Economy 2020

Note: [a]Private legal status; [b]not a MOC

Since the 1990s, local governments in Italy have experienced a severe reduction in financial resources, coupled with a significant increase in their competences and tasks (Profeti et al., 2012); in this context, the recourse to private-law companies instead of in-house mechanisms for service provision brings some advantages:

- it grants mayors greater ease of human resource management, as well as an easier interface with banks and with the market in general, including the possibility of developing public-private partnerships (Profeti et al., 2012);
- it opens the opportunity to increase debt outside the limits of the stability pact (Citroni et al., 2012);
- it helps to avoid or shift the blame to managers for policy errors or unsatisfactory services in the context of poor financial resources (Christensen & Pallesen, 2001).

13.4.1 Private Legal Forms

Private legal forms (limited companies and joint-stock companies) have grown rapidly over the last 20 years and now dominate the organisational landscape of Italian local government-owned enterprises (Ministry of Finance, 2020).

A limited company (*società a responsabilità limitata—srl*) can have a majority public or private shareholding and is regulated by private law. Limited companies provide the same services as joint-stock companies. The limited company form is only available for small-scale enterprises with a minimum equity of €10,000, which cannot be divided into shares to be traded on the stock exchange. A joint-stock company (*società per azioni—spa*) can also have a majority public or private shareholding. Joint-stock companies are supposed to be financially independent, but, in several cases, the local government owners have to cover their losses. They are usually created to provide greater variety of services (water, waste disposal and transportation) but are sometimes also used for public works and town planning and development activities, as well as for the provision of cultural and social services (social work, shelters for the homeless, home care, elderly care, care of disabled people, social rehabilitation). The joint-stock company is considered more attractive than other organisational forms, as it offers more flexibility and easy access to the financial markets through the stock exchange (Grossi & Reichard, 2008; Argento et al.,

2010). This phenomenon occurred in the largest cities that created large conglomerates in the utility sectors through mergers and acquisitions.

Foundations (*fondazione*) and associations (*associazione*) are also regulated by private law and are owned either totally or partially by local governments. They are often financially dependent on local government grants and are created to provide cultural and social services. A cooperative (*cooperativa*) is a private law-regulated organisation owned by several individuals who are interested in cooperating for solidarity and mutual reasons rather than for profit, and are responsible to manage social, cultural, sport and recreational services (Argento et al., 2010; Grossi & Reichard, 2008).

13.4.2 Public Legal Forms

Public legal forms (institutions, special undertakings and consortia) are less used by Italian local government than in the past. Three forms can be distinguished:

An institution (*istituzione*) is an organisation which is owned by a local government, without its own legal status. Even if it has managerial and accounting autonomy, it is financially dependent on local government grants. Institutions are usually created in order to provide social and cultural services (libraries, museums, theatres and cultural events) (Argento et al., 2010; Grossi & Reichard, 2008). Even when fully owned by the local government, institutions cannot be considered MOCs, as are not legally independent with a separate legal form.

A special undertaking (*azienda speciale*) is an organisation which is owned by a local government and which, unlike an institution, has its own legal status. Even where it, too, has managerial and accounting autonomy, it is also financially dependent on local government grants. Special undertakings have been created to provide a great variety of services (public transport, public car parks, management of public building and infrastructure, water services, waste collection and disposal, road maintenance, parks and gardens). Many are currently being transformed into private legal forms (limited and joint-stock companies).

A consortium (*consorzio*) is owned by more than one local government. It has the same organisational structure as a special undertaking and provides the same kinds of services in a broader territorial area (Argento et al., 2010; Grossi & Reichard, 2008). Consortia are traditional forms of intermunicipal collaborations.

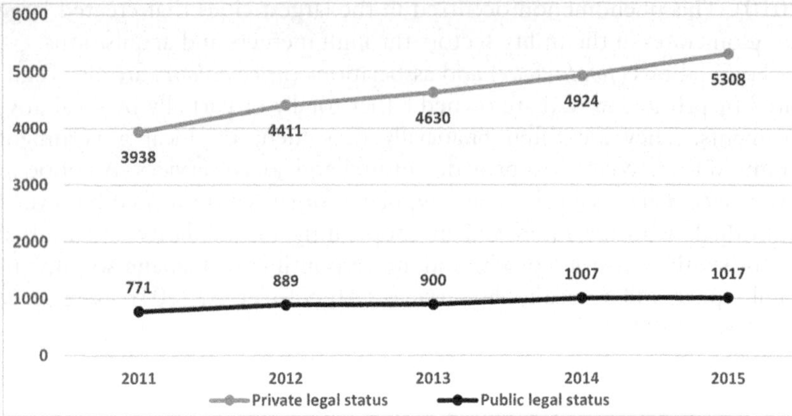

Fig. 13.2 Legal status of Italian MOCs (Source: Ministry of Economy 2020). Note: Data includes all the local Italian shareholdings, regardless of the percentage held

The legal status most represented by Italian MOCs is undoubtedly private legal status, with more than 5300 corporations (almost 84% of the total), while public legal status is held by 1017 companies. Both types of MOCs have had a general increase in the last five years (2011/2015); however, due to its greater numbers than public status, private status has shown more evident growth, concluding in 2015 with over 1300 MOCs compared to 2011. This trend is connected to the fact that in Italy joint-stock companies are entitled to register with the stock exchange and thus, gain access to financial market. MOCs with private legal forms are in missed public–private ownership (Argento et al., 2010; Grossi & Reichard, 2008). Figure 13.2 graphically shows this trend in the use of private and public legal status in the Italian MOCs during the last years.

13.5 Organisational Characteristics

Over two-thirds of the MOCs belong to small municipalities of less than 50,000 inhabitants. In terms of size, micro-enterprises dominate, considering both the number of employees and the annual turnover. Local government corporations with less than ten employees in fact number 966,

Table 13.2 Overview of MOCs in Italy

Geographical location	*No.*	*%*	*Year of establishment*	*No.*	*%*
North	922	54.01	Later than 2010	163	9.55
Centre	383	22.44	2000–2009	754	44.17
South and islands	402	23.55	1990–1999	381	22.32
Employees			1980–1989	39	2.28
Above 250	68	3.98	1970–1979	27	1.58
50–249	229	13.42	1960–1969	23	1.35
10–49	443	25.95	Before 1959	37	2.17
Less than 9	966	56.59	Missing data	283	16.58
Missing data	1	0.06	Population of the municipality		
Turnover (in € millions)			Over 100,001 inhabitants	307	17.98
Above 50	33	1.93	50,001–100,000	232	13.59
10–49.9	157	9.20	10,001–50,000	707	41.42
2–9.9	422	24.72	5001–10,000	207	12.13
Less than 2	827	48.45	1001–5000	209	12.24
Missing data	268	15.70	Less than 1000 inhabitants	45	2.64

Source: Ministry of Finance (2020)

over half of the population, while those with less than €2 million of turnover total 827. Large corporations in terms of employees (i.e. with over 250 individuals) are less than 4%, while in terms of turnover (i.e. with over €50 million) represent less than 2% of the population. Table 13.2 summarises this information in greater detail.

MOCs are active in several sectors. The majority (almost 34%) are active in building construction and development and operate particularly in the utility sectors (waste management, supply of water, electricity and gas) (more than 20%) and general ancillary and financial services (19%) but also in social services (11%), education and culture (around 10%), sport and recreational services (around 4.5%), and environmental services (around 0.5%). Table 13.3 summarises the subdivision of local government corporations by economic sectors. Most corporations are single-purpose, but multiple-purpose corporations do exist in Italian local government, especially in the utilities. The MOCs active in the utilities are often owned by several municipalities and provide public services in a regional geographical area. MOCs with private legal forms (joint-stock companies and limited liability companies) are new forms of inter-municipal collaborations.

Table 13.3 MOCs per service sector

Sector	*No.*	*%*
Building construction and development	577	33.80
Utilities (waste, water, electricity and gas)	357	20.91
General administration and finance services	326	19.10
Social services	192	11.25
Education and culture	171	10.02
Sport, leisure and health	76	4.45
Environment and agriculture	8	0.47
Total	1707	100.00

Source: Ministry of Finance (2020)

13.6 Managerial Autonomy

In this section, we deal with the theme of autonomy in Italian MOCs. We have analysed the managerial autonomy regarding how they make their own decisions in service delivery, who sets goals and objectives for MOCs and who monitors them, the presence of accountability regimes (e.g. transparency) and how particular issues such as labour and financial issues are managed.

13.6.1 *Decision-Making*

In terms of decision-making autonomy, the Local Government Act (LGA) establishes that local government-owned corporations are an instrumental body of the local government, with their own legal identity, entrepreneurial autonomy and own statute, approved by the city or province council. Local government-owned corporations' management is also required to conform to the general accounting principles for private sector companies. The LGA also establishes that the institutions are also instrumental bodies without their own legal personality of the local government for social and cultural services, with management autonomy; moreover, their accounting systems are also required to conform to the local government.

The local government should define in advance the managerial objectives for which the owned companies must aim, according to qualitative and quantitative parameters, and organise a suitable information system, aimed at defining (1) the financial relationships between the owner local government and the company, (2) the accounting, management and organisational situation of the company, (3) the service contracts, (4) the quality of services and (5) the compliance with the law on public finance. Based on the 2011 accounting reform of local authorities (D.Lgs. 118/2011[2]), the local government must periodically monitor the performance of unlisted companies, analyse the deviations from the defined objectives and identify the appropriate corrective actions, also with a specific focus on possible financial losses. The overall results of the local government-owned companies are included in the consolidated financial statements compiled annually by the local government.

The 2012 reform intended to strengthen the internal control system of local governments (D.Lgs. 174/2012[3]). Particularly, with respect to the previous regulations, it established the direct involvement of the most important organisational figures, in terms of responsibility, present in local government, such as the general city or province manager and also the service managers. Each local government should identify appropriate strategies, tools and methodologies, in order to outline their own internal control system and ensure the legitimacy, regularity and correctness of administrative actions. Local government should define the internal control system which aims to:

- monitor the effectiveness, efficiency and affordability of administrative actions, in order to optimise, even with timely actions, the relationship between objectives and results achieved, as well as between resources used and the results of the owned corporations;
- evaluate the adequacy of decisions made when implementing plans, programmes and other tools for determining the policy direction, in terms of consistency between the results achieved and the objectives of the owned corporations;
- ensure regular control of the financial balances of the relevant management and cash management to achieve the public finance objectives determined by the internal stability pact, through the coordination and the supervision activities on the part of the finan-

[2] Legislative Decree 118/2011. Provisions on the harmonisation of accounting systems and budget formats of the Regions, local authorities and their bodies, pursuant to articles 1 and 2 of the law of 5 May 2009, no. 42.

[3] Legislative Decree 174/2012. Urgent provisions on the finance and functioning of local authorities, as well as further provisions in favour of the areas hit by the earthquake in May 2012.

cial service manager, as well as the control activity of the service managers;

- verify, through the control of management objectives, the preparation of consolidated financial statements and the effectiveness, efficiency and affordability of the external management bodies of the public body;
- ensure the quality control of the services provided, both directly and through external providers, with the use of methodologies to satisfy external and internal users.

The same 2012 reform (D.Lgs. 174/2012) also established that the local government should create a control system over the unlisted owned companies. These controls are implemented by the local government's own structures, which are responsible for ensuring the appropriate corrective actions. The external auditors of the local governments are also responsible for auditing the institutions if they are without their own legal identity. The statute of the special undertakings provides for a specific auditing body and separate forms of management control.

The control system of the local government plays a central role in controlling owned companies through periodic evaluation of their performance (Corte dei Conti, 2018). Successful performance of the owned corporations is also based on their corporate governance, so that the management and the overall results of local government corporations are constantly monitored, as they also affect the finance of the local government themselves. In this regard, measures should be introduced to overcome possible conflicts of interest between the local government and the company, through the systematic control of the degree of achievement of the objectives, in terms of the cost-efficiency, effectiveness and quality of the services provided and also with respect to possible benchmarks (Corte dei Conti, 2018).

13.6.2 *Transparency*

Transparency is one of the general principles of the activity and organisation of the public sector in general. Publicly owned companies at both the central and local levels are required to ensure the highest level of transparency regarding the use of their resources and the results obtained (D.Lgs. 175/2016[4]). Subsequently, a disclosure obligation was also introduced

[4] Legislative Decree 175/2016. Consolidated law on publicly held companies.

regarding the communication of data, information and documents held to the local government's corresponding database (L. 241/1990[5]); this communication must also take place on the institutional website, in the "Transparent Administration" section (D.Lgs. 97/2016[6]). Finally, in the case of non-disclosure or incomplete publication of data relating to investee entities, the local government is prevented from disbursing sums of any title to the defaulting company, with the exception, however, of payments that the administrations are required to provide as an object of contractual obligation for services provided to them (D.Lgs. 33/2013[7]).

13.6.3 Human Resource

In terms of labour issues, local governments that decide to outsource a service are required to adopt the necessary decisions to reduce and recalculate the staffing. In fact, the outsourcing of a service must be implemented by the body within a programme of reorganisation measures capable of also ensuring, in the context of a general reduction in current expenditure, a reduction in personnel costs, as a result of activities no longer carried out within the local government (Corte dei Conti, 2016). The supervision of the actual implementation is delegated to the auditors of the local government and to the other internal control departments; they are also required to report the savings resulting from the adoption of measures relating to organisation and to personnel. Local government should monitor salaries of employees of the owned companies (Corte dei Conti, 2014).

In terms of new recruitment, local government-owned companies should follow and respect the principles of transparency, publicity and impartiality (D.Lgs. 165/2001[8]; L. 147/2013[9]). Regarding recruitment

[5] Law 241/1990. New rules on administrative procedure and right of access to administrative documents.

[6] Legislative Decree 97/2016. Review and simplification of the provisions on the prevention of corruption, advertising and transparency.

[7] Legislative Decree 33/2013. Reorganisation of the regulations concerning the right of civic access and the obligations of publicity, transparency and dissemination of information by public administrations.

[8] Legislative Decree 165/2001. General rules on the organisation of work employed by public administrations.

[9] Law 147/2013. Provisions for the preparation of the annual and multi-year budget of the State.

constraints, local governments should set the objectives of rationalising and reducing costs related to owned companies; therefore, they must consider both any provisions that prescribe prohibitions or limitations on the hiring of new personnel and any provisions also expected by the sector in which each corporation operates (Corte dei Conti, 2019).

13.6.4 Finance

In financial terms, MOCs should be included in the consolidated financial statement of the local government and are monitored by the local government on specific expenditures (consultancy, public relations, conferences, exhibitions, advertising and sponsorships) (L. 196/2009[10]). For certain product categories (e.g. electricity, gas, fuel, telephony), companies, if fully publicly owned, directly or indirectly, are required to obtain supplies through the conventions or framework agreements made available by Consip Ltd, the national SOE which manages the purchases of the public administration (D.Lgs. 95/2012[11]). In general, the contribution to the achievement of financial objectives by special undertakings, institutions and companies directly or indirectly owned by the local government should be monitored according to the criteria of affordability and efficiency (Corte dei Conti, 2019).

13.7 Board Structure and Composition

In the traditional Italian model of corporate governance, the shareholders' assembly appoints the body invested with management functions, as well as the body that carries out supervisory functions. Therefore, its role remains intact as the strategic corporate body in which partner interests (public and/or private) are represented. Italy follows a one-tier concept: the board of directors consists of external and internal members and is the body exclusively accountable to the shareholders' assembly. This board has simultaneous executive and supervisory functions. Board members are usually appointed by the local government and, in the case of a mixed public–private corporation, also by the private owner (Grossi & Reichard, 2008). The representation of local government in the board of directors

[10] Law 196/2009. Accounting and public finance law.

[11] Legislative Decree 95/2012. Urgent provisions for the revision of public spending with invariance of services to citizens.

of Italian MOCs is often proportional to its participation in the equity, but there are also cases of golden share mechanisms.

The general discipline provides that, if the State or other public sector entities (such as local governments) have shares in an unlisted joint-stock company, the statute may grant them the right to appoint board members, or members of the supervisory board, and auditors in a number proportional to their participation in the share capital (Civil Law); however, it is forbidden to appoint local government employees to the boards of directors of publicly owned companies (D.Lgs. 175/2016). Regarding the eligibility requirements, members of the administrative and control bodies of publicly owned companies must fulfil the requirements of integrity, professionalism and autonomy established by decree of the Prime Minister, on the proposal of the Minister of Economy and Finance (D.Lgs. 175/2016). Generally, the board of directors of publicly controlled companies is made up of a sole director. However, for reasons of organisational adequacy but always considering the need to contain costs, the shareholders' meeting of the publicly controlled company may order that the company be administered in different ways: (1) by a board of directors composed of three or five members, (2) by a two-tier system, consisting of a management board and a supervisory board, or (3) by a one-tier system, consisting of a board of directors.

Regarding remuneration, specific remuneration ceilings are applied both to the remuneration of directors vested with particular offices in unlisted companies directly and indirectly owned by a local government and to the all-inclusive annual remuneration of employees of these companies. The determination of the remuneration is established firstly by dividing the companies into different categories, according to their complexity, on the basis of specific parameters concerning turnover, investments and number of employees; subsequently, a salary cap for the remuneration of the directors is assigned to each category. Still on the subject of remuneration and with a view to containing it, a 30% reduction in the remuneration of administrators in local government corporations who have achieved a negative financial result in the three previous years has also been established. The supervision of all these limitations is the responsibility of the local government and, in the event of violation of these restrictions, the executive directors and responsible managers of the company are liable, by way of tax damage, for the salaries and fees paid by rule of the contracts.

Currently there are 5795 representatives (board members, chairs, chief executive officers and unique administrators) of 1600 companies owned by Italian local governments (data on members are available for 1600 companies out of a total of 1707) (Ministry of Economy 2020).

Board members amount to 3950, mainly concentrated in the north of the country (2544 directors, 64.4% of the total), followed by the centre of the country (761, 19.3%) and the south with islands (645, 16.3%). In terms of gender diversity, there are 1361 women members (34.5% of the total), while male directors are prevalent, with 2589 representatives (65.5%). Lastly, regarding remuneration, the majority of board members have an unpaid appointment (2811 directors, 71.1% of the total), while only 28.8% of members (1139 representatives) receive a wage, equal to €17,925 on average.

Chairs of the boards of Italian MOCs number 1259: 762 in the north (60.5%), 261 in the centre (20.7%) and finally 236 in the south and islands (18.8%). The male presence is more pronounced, with 1077 chairs (85.5%), compared to only 182 female counterparts (14.5%). A slight majority of chairs receive a wage (655 individuals, 52% of the total), which is equal to €21,174 on average; the remaining 604 chairs (48%) are unpaid.

There are 483 unique administrators, of whom 254 are appointed in an MOC located in the north of the country (52.6%), 113 in the centre (23.4%) and finally 116 in the south and islands (24%). This category of representatives displays the least gender diversity among all the types of representatives of Italian MOCs: 92% of chairs are male, specifically 446 individuals, while only 37 chairs are female (8%). Lastly, regarding remuneration, the majority of chairs hold a paid appointment (400 individuals, 82.8% of the total) equal to €21,667 on average, while only 17.2% of them (83 representatives) act free of charge.

The final category of representatives of Italian MOCs is CEOs. They number 103: 65 in the north (63.1%), 24 in the centre (23.3%) and finally 14 in the south and islands (13.6%). Even in this case, male presence dominates, with 91 male CEOs (88.3%) and only 12 female (11.7%). The majority receive a wage (90 CEOs have a remunerated office, 87.4% of the category), which is equal to €46,260 on average; only 13 CEOs (12.6%) have an unpaid appointment. Table 13.4 summarises this information in greater detail.

13.8 Conclusions

In Italy, there has been a long history of state involvement in economic activities (Allini et al., 2016); since the early 1990s, the corporatisation of public bodies has become a prominent phenomenon, especially at the

Table 13.4 Overview of local government representatives in Italian MOCs

Role	*North*		*Centre*		*South and islands*		*Male*		*Female*		*Paid*		*Free*		*Wage (average in €)*
	#	%	#	%	#	%	#	%	#	%	#	%	#	%	
General representatives	3625	62.5	1301	22.5	869	15	4203	72.5	1592	27.5	2233	38.5	3562	61.5	/
Board members	2544	64.4	761	19.3	645	16.3	2589	65.5	1361	34.5	1139	28.8	2811	71.2	17,925
Chairs	762	60.5	261	20.7	236	18.8	1077	85.5	182	14.5	604	48	655	52	21,174
Sole administrators	254	52.6	113	23.4	116	24	446	92.3	37	7.7	400	82.8	83	17.2	21,667
CEOs	65	63.1	24	23.3	14	13.6	91	88.3	12	11.7	90	87.4	13	12.6	46,260

Source: Ministry of Finance (2020)

local level and in the public services domain (Profeti et al., 2012). In this chapter, we presented an updated description of municipal corporatisation in Italy in terms of context, trends, legal status, background characteristics, autonomy of professional managers, and board structure and composition.

Firstly, it emerged that the main drivers for Italian municipalities to create corporations are (1) to improve their local public services' supply conditions; (2) to attract private partners and financial sources in the offering of services and in the realisation of infrastructure investment, especially in the south; and (3) to realise economies of scale by corporatising and merging smaller entities. However, factors such as political discussion and disagreement on the possible ways to provide local public services make national legislation uncertain, especially regarding the survival of the direct management of public services and the difficulties of involving private partners with financial and professional resources in collaborative agreements with local governments.

Secondly, it emerged that, due to the large number of corporations owned by local government, many of which operate inefficiently in sectors with high barriers to competition, Italy has recently faced a period of reforms and review of public sector shareholdings. The aims of these national reforms were to (1) rationalise the corporations and shareholdings held by local governments, (2) reduce the MOCs and, thereby, (3) increase competition and efficiency of public service delivery. Thanks to these reforms, from a peak of over 6000 local government shareholdings in companies reached in 2013, Italy is witnessing a gradual reduction to around 4000 entities in 2018 (Ministry of Finance, 2020).

Thirdly, to provide public services, Italian local governments can still create different types of legal entities (public and private) with different types of ownership (total or partial/mixed public and private). However, private legal forms (specifically, limited companies and joint-stock companies) have grown rapidly over the last 20 years and now dominate the organisational landscape of Italian MOCs, mainly because they can (1) grant an easier interface with financial institutions and with the market in general, (2) allow debt to develop outside the limits of the stability pact (Citroni et al., 2012) and, finally, linked with the political aspect, (3) allow politicians to distance themselves from potentially unpopular activities in the context of poor financial resources, thus avoiding responsibility and shifting the blame for policy errors or unsatisfactory services on to professional managers of MOCs (Christensen & Pallesen, 2001; Fiorina, 1986).

Fourthly, in terms of characteristics, Italian MOCs are quite recent entities (over 75% of them arose from the 1990s onwards), concentrated in the north of the country and mainly belonging to small municipalities of less than 50,000 inhabitants that often represent forms in inter-municipal collaboration. They are micro-enterprises, in terms of both employees and annual turnover, active in several sectors, mostly with a single purpose: from building construction and development to utility sectors (waste, water, electricity and gas), to social services.

Fifthly, on the one hand, Italian legislation grants relevant autonomy to MOCs, since they are considered an instrumental body of the local government, with their own legal identity and managerial and legal autonomy; on the other hand, it is, however, the local government that has to define in advance the managerial objectives for which the owned companies must aim, according to qualitative and quantitative parameters; moreover, the most important local public managers (e.g. city or province managers or service managers) are directly involved in planning and monitoring the performance of the MOCs.

Sixthly, in respect of MOCs' board structure, in Italy it is the shareholders' assembly that appoints the body invested with management functions, as well as the body that carries out supervisory functions; therefore, board members are usually appointed by politicians of the local government, following a one-tier concept: the board consists of both external/professional and internal/political members and the is body exclusively accountable to the shareholders' assembly. Moreover, in general, the board of directors of Italian MOCs is made up of a sole director, even where, for reasons of organisational adequacy but always considering the need to contain costs, the shareholders' meeting of the publicly controlled company may order the company to be administered in different ways.

Given the growing fiscal pressures on the Italian local governments on the one hand, and the mixed experiences of MOCs, it seems likely that the diffusion of MOCs will decline but remain an important part of the municipal landscape. Local governments face a challenge to increase their ability to plan, manage and control the external delivery of local services for which they are responsible.

References

Allini, A., Manes Rossi, F., & Hussainey, K. (2016). The board's role in risk disclosure: An exploratory study of Italian listed state-owned enterprises. *Public Money & Management, 36*(2), 113–120.

Argento, D., Grossi, G., Tagesson, T., & Collin, S. O. (2010). The 'externalisation' of local public service delivery: experience in Italy and Sweden. *International Journal of Public Policy, 5*(1), 41–56.

Bremeier, W., Brinckmann, H., & Killian, W. (2006). *Public Governance kommunaler Unternehmen: Vorschläge zur politischen Steuerung ausgegliederter Aufgaben auf der Grundlage einer empirischen Erhebung [Public governance of municipal enterprises: Proposals for the political governance of outsourced tasks based on an empirical survey]*. Düsseldorf: Hans-Böckler-Stiftung.

Christensen, J. G., & Pallesen, T. (2001). The political benefits of corporatization and privatization. *Journal of Public Policy, 21*(3), 283–309.

Citroni, G., Lippi, A., & Profeti, S. (2012). *Governi privati: Le società partecipate dei comuni strumento e arena del governo locale [Private Governments: The investee companies of the municipalities, instrument and arena of the local government]*. Rubbettino.

Citroni, G., Lippi, A., & Profeti, S. (2016). Local public services in Italy: Still fragmentation. In H. Wollmann, I. Kopric, & G. Marcou (Eds.), *Public and social services in Europe: From public and municipal to private sector provision* (pp. 103–117). Palgrave Macmillan.

Corte dei Conti. (2014). *Sezione regionale di controllo per la Lombardia – Delibera 28/2014/PAR [Regional control section for Lombardy – Resolution 28/2014/PAR]*. CdC.

Corte dei Conti. (2016). *Sezione delle autonomie – Computabilità degli incarichi dirigenziali conferiti nel tetto di spesa stabilito dall'articolo 9, comma 28, del d.l. 31 maggio 2010, n. 78 [Autonomy Section – Computability of managerial appointments conferred in the expenditure ceiling established by Article 9, paragraph 28, of Legislative Decree May 31, 2010, n. 78]*. Rome: CdC.

Corte dei Conti. (2018). *Gli organismi partecipati dagli enti territoriali – Osservatorio sugli organismi partecipati/controllati da comuni, città metropolitane, province, regioni e relative analisi – Relazione 2018 [Organisations owned by local authorities – Observatory on participating/controlled bodies by municipalities, metropolitan cities, provinces, regions and related analyses – 2018 Report]*. Rome: CdC.

Corte dei Conti. (2019). *Gli organismi partecipati dagli enti territoriali e sanitari [Organisations owned by local and health authorities]*. CdC.

Fiorina, M. P. (1986). Legislator uncertainty, legislative control, and the delegation of legislative power. *Journal of Law, Economics and Organization, 2*(1), 33–51.

Grossi, G., & Reichard, C. (2008). Municipal corporatization in Germany and Italy. *Public Management Review, 10*(5), 597–617.

Grossi, G., & Reichard, C. (2016). Variance in the institutions of local utility services: Evidence from several European countries. In H. Wollmann, I. Kopric, & G. Marcou (Eds.), *Public and social services in Europe: From public and municipal to private sector provision* (pp. 297–312). Palgrave Macmillan.

Ministry of Finance. (2020). *Rapporto sulle partecipazioni delle Amministrazioni Pubbliche – Dati 2017 [Report on the shareholdings of public administrations – 2017 data]*. Roma: MEF.

Pischel, G. (1972). *L'azienda municipalizzata [The municipal company]*. Cispel.

Profeti, S., Lippi, A., & Citroni, G. (2012). Private government "with" public money? Municipal corporations and local utilities in six Italian regions. *IPSA Congress*. Madrid.

Serbassi, L. (1999). *Guida al contratto di servizio nei servizi pubblici locali [Guide to the service contract in local public services]*. D'Anselmi.

Spadoni, B. (2003). *I servizi pubblici locali. Dalla municipalizzazione alla liberalizzazione [Local public services. From municipalisation to liberalisation]*. http://www.dirittodeiservizipubblici.it/articoli/articolo.asp?sezione=dettarticolo&id=20. Accessed 27 April 2022.

Tessarolo, C. (2001). *Servizi pubblici locali, in Guida normativa [Local public services, in Normative guide]*. CEL.

CHAPTER 14

Municipal Corporatisation in Portugal: From Mania to Depression

António F. Tavares and Pedro J. Camões

14.1 Introduction

The Portuguese local government system is a dual-tier system, including both a municipal and a sub-municipal level. Article 236 of the Portuguese Constitution establishes two categories of local governments: municipalities and parishes (*freguesias*). Both types of local governments operate with elected executive and deliberative decision-making bodies and possess financial and administrative autonomy (Tavares & Camões, 2021). Mayors are directly elected as heads of the winning list, and the winning party or coalition is always part of the government. Mayoral powers are derived from executive competences assigned by law and the mayor allocates portfolios among the elected members of the executive, thereby securing a strong influence over executive decision-making (Mendes & Camões, 2008). The executive body has also a specific set of competences

A. F. Tavares (✉) • P. J. Camões
Research Centre in Political Science, School of Economics and Management, University of Minho, Minho, Portugal
e-mail: atavares@eeg.uminho.pt; pedroc@eeg.uminho.pt

M. Van Genugten et al. (eds.), *Corporatisation in Local Government*, https://doi.org/10.1007/978-3-031-09982-3_14

assigned by law and beyond those allocated to the mayor. Confirming this strong mayor status, "Portuguese mayors can only be removed through a judiciary process and not through a political process (recall election or vote of non-confidence by the council)" (Tavares & Camões, 2021, p. 247).

In Portugal, municipally owned corporations (MOCs) are established as legal persons under private law, and named municipal, inter-municipal or metropolitan, depending on who exercises the dominant influence: a single municipality, two or more municipalities or an association of municipalities, or a metropolitan area, respectively. Only municipalities or associations of municipalities are legally allowed to set up municipal corporations. The competence to approve MOCs rests on each municipality's deliberative body—the municipal assembly—after proposal by the local executive. The strong authority over the executive as well as the fact that most Portuguese mayors are "locally born and bred and therefore have extensive knowledge of their communities, as well as many formal and informal contacts with their citizens" (Elcock, 2008, p. 808), gives the mayor the credibility and legitimacy required to secure the approval of the proposal from the assembly. In the case of inter-municipal or metropolitan corporations, all the municipal assemblies must approve their creation.

The local corporate public sector (LCS) includes all forms of organisations involving a majority of public capital, namely municipal corporations, stock companies, public foundations and cooperatives (Tavares & Camões, 2010). MOCs will be the primary focus of this chapter, with the other forms of corporatisation mentioned sporadically to establish comparisons.

According to Portuguese law, MOCs are defined as companies in which local authorities exercise dominant influence due to the verification of one of the following requirements: (a) ownership of the majority of the capital or of the vote; (b) right to appoint or remove the majority of the members of the executive board or supervisory body; and (c) any other form of management control. This definition relies primarily on who holds the power rather than on the ownership of share capital.

The first MOC created in Portugal was the *EPUL-Empresa Pública de Urbanização de Lisboa* (Lisbon's Public Company of Urbanisation) established on December 31, 1971, with legal status approved by Law-Decree 613/71, December 31. After the restoration of democracy in Portugal, in April 1974, Law-Decree 260/76, Law 79/77 and Law-Decree 100/84 allowed local executives to establish MOCs approved by the municipal assembly. Few municipalities took advantage of this organisational form, primarily due to the absence of a national legal framework defining the mode of delegation of powers to these companies. In a legalistic system, dominated by a "what is not explicitly permitted is forbidden" mindset, local governments did not risk creating MOCs that might be deemed illegal. As a result, MOCs were rarely used until the late 1990s.

Three pieces of legislation have defined the Portuguese LCS between the late 1990s and the present day. The Municipal, Inter-municipal and Regional Corporations Act of 1998 was the first (highly permissive) legislation that allowed the extensive creation of municipal corporations and almost no limiting criteria. Before the 1998 Law, the provision of municipal level services was primarily the responsibility of in-house bureaucracies and the MOC form was rarely employed. However, the widely shared perception that the rigidity of administrative law was hampering improvements in the efficiency, effectiveness and quality of public services led to a search for alternative service delivery modes capable of instilling corporate management values and practices in local public service provision. The 1998 legislation provided additional discretion in personnel and financial management by allowing the transfer of in-house service production to MOCs. In the early stages of local corporatisation, many services initially provided in-house were moved to newly created MOCs by transferring of both the services and the workforce to these organisations.

As early as 2001, the political debate began focusing on yearly public deficits and the rising of Portuguese public debt. The uncontrolled expansion of MOCs was regarded by politicians at the national level, the media and the public as one of the main causes of this crisis in public finances. This perception was largely exaggerated as local public spending represented less than 10% of total public spending. However, the media explored the few instances where MOCs were associated with corrupt practices, poor management and political cronyism (also known in Portugal as *jobs for the boys*). Against this backdrop, Law 53-F/2006, December 29, curbed the expansion in the LCS by imposing stricter formation criteria to discipline the initial boom. This legislation tightened the legal requirements municipalities must fulfil in order to create companies, particularly criteria of rationality and added value, the need for technical studies of economic viability, and the mandatory establishment of contracts between the MOC and the participating municipal entities, all of which had not been included in the previous legislation (Batalhão, 2015;

Livro Branco do SEL, 2011). The 2006 legislation delimited the functional areas by explicitly preventing the creation of municipal companies to perform activities of "an exclusively administrative nature" or "predominantly commercial purpose".

In 2011, the crisis of sovereign debt forced the Portuguese government to reach out for financial help that materialised in the signing of the Memorandum of Understanding (MoU) with a triad of international organisations (EU Commission, IMF and European Central Bank). As part of the financial bailout, the Portuguese government committed itself to impose further restrictions on the creation and operation of these entities. The LCS was a primary target in the reform of local administration aiming at the rationalisation and adaptation of local government. The MoU was very specific regarding the fulfilment of the commitments assumed regarding the LCS. It mainly focused on the elaboration of an evaluation report, the application of new, more restrictive limits on indebtedness, the enactment of a new regulatory legal framework for the creation and operation of the LCS, a temporary suspension in the creation of new MOCs and the strengthening of the monitoring powers of Central Administration. The Green Document of the Reform established four goals for the LCS: adapting the number of entities to the local context of each municipality; delimiting the strategic sector in which the LCS operates; adjusting the object and activities of the LCS to the attributions and competences of the municipalities; and restricting contributions by the municipalities in the LCS' own revenues.

Law 50/2012, August 31, sought to implement these principles and discipline in the creation, operation, monitoring and dissolution of MOCs. The most noticeable consequence of the MoU, and Law 50/2012 in particular, was the imposition of financial conditionalities that, if not fulfilled, would impose the mandatory dissolution of MOCs. The implementation of these criteria led to a mass extinction of MOCs, as we describe below in the trends section. It is worth emphasising that the evolution in the use of MOCs in Portugal has been largely determined by the degree of permissiveness of the legal framework. As legislation became more and more stringent, the number of new companies diminished and many have closed due to the stricter rules.

This chapter describes the Portuguese LCS, including its legal framework, trends in expansion and retrenchment, organisational characteristics, autonomy features and MOC board structure. After this introduction, the second section presents the overall trend in municipal corporatisation in Portugal. The third section defines the legal status and organisational forms adopted as part of the LCS. The fourth section provides detailed characteristics of LCS organisations, including their size, purpose and policy sector in which they operate. Next, we describe the main governance features of these organisations, with particular attention to their levels of financial, personnel, and public procurement autonomy, accountability regime, and monitoring and auditing practices. The sixth section provides some information regarding the structure of governing boards and characteristics of the executive director. The seventh section concludes.

14.2 Trends in Municipal Corporatisation in Portugal

Portugal experienced a substantial expansion in the LCS at the turn of the century, mainly due to the enactment of the Municipal, Inter-municipal and Regional Corporations Act of 1998. According to official data, 269 out of 308 Portuguese local governments (approximately 88%) invested capital in public and private corporations. The rise in these forms of service delivery occurred through the accelerated growth of the LCS demonstrated by the increase in number of municipal corporations from 49 in 1998 to 136 in 2001 (see Table 14.1) and stock companies with connections to local governments from 143 in 1999 to 187 in 2001 (Almeida 2001; Tavares & Camões, 2010).

According to the White Paper of the Local Corporate Sector (Livro Branco do SEL, 2011), of the 392 MOCs of all types existing at the time, only 68 (about 17%) were created during Law 53-F/2006, of December 29, with the vast majority of MOCs created or starting operation between 2000 and 2006, under Law 58/98, of 18 August. According to Batalhão (2015), this concentration coincided with the incentives provided by the Community Support Framework III (2000–2006), which included incentives to the corporatisation of the institutions managing co-financed projects. Table 14.1 displays the number of MOCs showing the steep rise in new MOCs between 1998 and 2006, followed by a slower increase until 2011.

Regarding the motivations for the creation of MOCs, Tavares and Camões (2007) found that municipalities with greater financial autonomy (less dependence on central government transfers) were more likely to adopt MOCs in search of improved productive efficiency. Their result

Table 14.1 Evolution of municipal corporations in Portugal, 1998–2020

Year	*# MOCs*	*# New MOCs*	*# Dissolved MOCs*
Until 1998	49	49	0
1999	74	25	0
2000	109	35	0
2001	136	27	0
2002	152	16	0
2003	173	21	0
2004	198	25	0
2005	236	38	0
2006	261	25	0
2007	282	21	0
2008	290	8	0
2009	301	11	0
2010	310	9	0
2011	312	8	6
2012	268	2	46
2013	239	0	29
2014	193	0	46
2015	168	0	25
2016	157	0	11
2017	147	2	12
2018	140	1	8
2019	140	5	5
2020	135	2	7

Source: Camões and Rodrigues (2020) and Fernandes et al. (2020)

Note: Data refers to December 31st of each year and only to 100% publicly owned MOCs

concerning the effect of ideology was corroborated by their subsequent study (2010), showing that the creation of MOC was preferred by right-wing governments. Da Cruz and Marques (2011) calculate total factor productivity (PTF) of ten Portuguese MOCs, in order to assess their performance and compare it with that of the in-house bureaucratic model. The research found very negative results for the MOC model and concluded that the intended benefits were not achieved in Portugal. The authors argue that several causes may have contributed to this effect, but political patronage in appointing the CEOs of these companies and the lack of technical competence were, presumably, two of the most significant.

By 2011, the LCS was an important public issue subject to significant political debate and criticism. According to Mafra (2013), in their attempt to solve efficiency and performance problems caused by the rigidity of administrative law, local governments over-relied on MOCs as private law entities to escape it, leading to inadequate coordination between entities, waste of public resources and deficient service provision to citizens. MOCs were operating in important sectors at the municipal level, without appropriate democratic control by the voters. Managerial positions in the companies opened opportunities for political influence, with companies becoming a source of "jobs for the boys". Furthermore, in a few instances, mayors were accumulating functions as Chief Executive Officers of MOCs, which raised concerns regarding illicit accumulation of salaries as well as conflicts of interests in the exercise of public functions (Mafra, 2013, see also Camões, 2015).

The overall negative performance and public image of MOCs led to their inclusion in the local government reform package enacted as a result of the 2011 financial bailout. The new legal framework approved in 2012 required the dissolution of MOCs when at least one of the following four criteria is present in the previous three years: (a) sales and services rendered during that period do not cover at least 50% of total expenses for the respective financial years; (b) the contributory weight of operating subsidies is greater than 50% of its revenues; (c) the value of the operating result minus the value of amortisations and depreciations is negative; (d) the net result is negative. The fourth column in Table 14.1 shows the number of dissolved MOCs per year. Starting in 2012, the number of MOCs was reduced by 155 in the four years that followed, from a high of 312 to 157 MOCs in 2016.

Camões and Rodrigues (2020) investigated the determinants of dissolutions beyond the financial bailout and find that the likelihood of a MOC being terminated increases when they are multi-purpose and receive a larger proportion of their revenues from local government grants. In addition, MOC dissolution tends to occur when their parent local government has a high level of indebtedness. They conclude that "the global financial crisis increased the awareness of the financial dimension of political choices" (p. 7) and the response strategy by local politicians was to close MOCs, even if facing unpopularity associated with the reduction of services.

14.3 Legal Status of Portuguese MOCs

Municipal corporations are set up as separate corporate entities, "at arm's length" of the local government and operate under commercial (private) law and, complementary, under public corporate sector law. There is no public-law equivalent to MOCs, even though a few municipalities in Portugal run municipal enterprise funds. This later form is a separate budgetary fund employed to report an activity for which a fee is charged to users for goods or services. Municipal enterprise funds are not legally separate entities, but they have an executive board appointed by the local government to manage a specific activity (typically utilities), which makes them "corporate-like". They share some similarities with municipal enterprise funds in the United States, namely the reliance on user fees and charges, the use in utilities sectors, and the separation from the general fund as part of governmental accounting procedures (Molinari & Tyer, 2003; Rubin, 1988; Stumm, 1996). However, municipal enterprise funds in Portugal are subject to consolidation in municipal accounts and follow public law and public accounting rules, therefore departing from the financial practices and operating rules characterising private businesses as well as MOCs.

According to Oliveira (2001), the first LCS legislation (Law 58/98, of August 18) introduced private law to local government activities, since municipal, inter-municipal or metropolitan companies remain under the domain of local public entities, but operate under private law as defined by the legal framework at the national level. In Portugal, it is generally accepted that MOCs were an attempt to improve financial management, relax public procurement rules and circumvent civil service laws and their implications for personnel management, contract agreements and organisation (Tavares & Camões, 2010). The LCS appeared as a middle-of-the-road strategy between in-house production and contracting out to the private sector (Leavitt & Morris, 2004), aimed at reforming municipal management and improving the quality and effectiveness of local service provision (Tavares & Camões, 2007).

Two monitoring institutions are primarily responsible for auditing MOCs' accounts and their relationships with their parent local governments. The Court of Accounts (*Tribunal de Contas*) is a judicial branch organisation that inspects and evaluates the legality and conformity of public budgeting and spending practices, producing decisions valid for all public organisations, including MOCs. The General Inspection of Finances

(*Inspecção Geral de Finanças*) is a central government organisation in charge of auditing the legality of public budgeting and contracting practices.

The MOC model is clearly dominant in the LCS in Portugal. Nevertheless, local governments are allowed to participate in the capital of private stock companies as minority shareholders as well as create foundations, cooperatives and private law associations, all of which operate under private law. In 2018 there were 95 of these minority shareholder participations active, mostly in the areas of investments and economic infrastructures (20%), education (18%), tourism (13%), and solid waste and sewer (12%) (DGAL, 2018). Cooperatives and foundations have been far less used models of organisation and the information available is very scarce (Fernandes et al., 2020).

14.4 Organisational Characteristics of Portuguese MOCs

The overwhelming majority of MOCs in Portugal are 100% owned by municipalities, either as single owners or as joint owners (inter-municipal MOCs). Table 14.2 presents the number of MOCs by share. The latest data from 2021 indicated that 135 MOCs (about 78%) were entirely owned by public sector organisations. Sixteen MOCs were mixed companies, with at least 75% of the shares owned by public sector organisations, whereas in 23 companies (13%) the share of public ownership varied between 50 and 74%. Strictly speaking, 39 companies can be considered institutional public–private partnerships (Da Cruz & Marques, 2011), as they involve at least some share of private capital investments.

Most MOCs are directly owned in the majority or totality by a single municipal government. The latest data included in Table 14.3 indicates that 143 companies were included in this group. In very few cases, they

Table 14.2 Number of municipal corporations by share

Type	*2021*
Pure public (100%)	135
Mixed 75–99%	16
Mixed 50–74%	23

Source: DGAL (February 2021)

Table 14.3 Number of municipal corporations by type

Type	*Type/mode of participation*	
	Direct	*Indirect*
MOCs	143	6
Inter-municipal MOCs	24	2
Municipal Enterprise Funds	23	0

Source: DGAL (February 2021)

are indirectly owned by other entities dominated by the municipality, for example, other MOCs. The remaining types included 24 inter-municipal MOCs directly owned by several municipalities and 23 municipal enterprise funds. The numbers of MOCs by type have remained relatively stable in recent years and no dramatic changes are expected in the near future.

The 1998 legal framework led many municipalities to convert into MOCs several services with an "industrial profile" previously produced by in-house bureaucracies. At first, these transformations occurred primarily in the sector of utilities, including water supply, solid waste collection, drainage of wastewater, urban public transport and low voltage electrical power distribution. Soon, however, many other services were converted, often without proper cost-benefit analysis. Despite the lack of economic or managerial rationales, many MOCs were created to operate outside the market and produce only for one customer, created by that same customer (Oliveira, 2001).

The case of Portugal clearly shows that MOCs were created frequently to provide services in functional areas in which their suitability was inadequate. After the approval of Law 50/2012, the presence of MOCs was limited to specific functional areas of activity. Now, companies can pursue activities within the scope of municipal functions, namely the management of services of general interest or the promotion of local and regional development. Services of general interest require universality and continuity of the services to be provided, the satisfaction of the basic needs of the citizens, the promotion of local and regional economic and social cohesion, and the protection of service users, without jeopardising economic efficiency and respecting the principles of non-discrimination and transparency. In practice, this includes water supply, solid waste collection and street cleaning, drainage of wastewater, urban public transport management and inspection of urban public parking, management of collective infrastructures and provision of services in the areas of education, teaching and professional training, social welfare, culture, health and sport, and distribution of low voltage electrical power.

MOCs targeting the promotion of local and regional development aim to enhance economic growth, the development of local strengths, the elimination of asymmetries, and the strengthening of economic and social cohesion, while respecting the same principles stated above. The promotion of local and regional development includes the maintenance and conservation of urban infrastructure and urban management, urban renewal and rehabilitation and management of built heritage, management of social housing, electrical power production and urban and rural development at the inter-municipal level. The current distribution of MOCs by activity sector is included in Table 14.4 and shows a clear prevalence of MOCs for delivering the services of general interest described in the previous paragraph.

This delimitation of functional areas was intended to prevent non-commercially viable MOCs from operating and Law 50/2012 was able to accomplish this goal, perhaps even better than expected, as described in the trends section. However, subsequent amendments to the Law excluded the application of some dissolution criteria to MOCs operating in the areas of education and professional training, culture and social welfare, in order to prevent their closure. This case-by-case approach suggests that trying to fit the MOC model to services for the "wrong" reasons produces companies that lack financial and commercial viability (Tavares, 2017).

Table 14.4 Number of corporations by activity sector

Sector	*Total*
Culture and sports	29
Education	8
Municipal infrastructure	15
Industrial production	11
Public works	10
Tourism	2
Urban mobility	13
Water and sewer	51
General administration	36
Total	175

Source: DGAL (February , 2021)

Currently, by focusing on efficiency and effectiveness, MOCs can become more attractive to private investors. Operating in highly profitable sectors without competition, some companies were partially bought by private investors and converted into mixed companies. This raises some concerns regarding the lack of democratic legitimacy because their leaders are not elected (Lidström, 2017); however, as long as the majority of capital remains in the hands of the local authorities, public responsibility is partially ensured through the appointment of the board of directors by local government(s) (Leavitt & Morris, 2004). No systematic evidence exists in Portugal concerning the privatisation of MOCs, but the limited evidence presented in Table 14.2 suggests that several MOCs were partially bought by private companies, but always below the 50% threshold of shares.

14.5 The Governance of Portuguese MOCs

According to the national legal framework, Portuguese MOCs are set up to rely on revenues derived from user fees, are governed by an appointed executive board, and have independent corporate status (including the right to own property and the right to sue and be sued) (Tavares & Camões, 2007). The three members of the MOC executive board, including the president, are elected by the company's general assembly. As the main shareholder, the local government executive designates its representatives in the general assembly and provides strategic guidance and quantified goals to the MOC's executive board. In practice, the local executive *de facto* controls the executive board. A statutory auditor appointed by the municipal assembly of the enacting government certifies each company's financial yearly report.

Formally, MOCs are subject to financial control by the General Inspectorate of Finance and the Court of Auditors designed to assess the legality, economy, efficiency and effectiveness of their management. To this end, companies must adopt adequate internal control procedures to guarantee the reliability of accounts and financial information. The companies must also ensure the balance of the operating accounts, presenting balanced annual results.

Since the inception of Law 58/98, the explosive growth in the number of MOCs was plagued by multiple poor governance practices and abuses. Figueiredo (2012, p. 11) synthesises two reports by the Inspectorate-General of Finance and the Court of Auditors reporting the main problems and points of contention associated with the LCS during the first decade of expansion in MOCs. In general, MOC performance was not assessed based on criteria of economy, efficiency and effectiveness. The problems are too many to mention, but mostly relate to accountability. Municipalities failed to monitor appropriately the pursuit of objectives by MOCs, signed management contracts that did not establish quantified targets to be reached, signed programmatic contracts with MOCs not subjected to a minimum set of rules on the granting of operating subsidies, and transferred assets to companies without a set of conditions safeguarding the public interest. All these practices resulted in a lack of transparency of the financial flows from municipalities to MOCs and the inability to secure accounting autonomy of the respective financial flows. Moreover, loans and borrowing by MOCs were not subject to specific rules, which led to the accumulation of operating deficits that inevitably had to be covered by the municipalities.

The relationship with the private sector was also marred by lack of transparency. The choice of private partners frequently failed to respect competition and transparency rules, and there was a disproportionate volume of guarantees provided by the municipalities to financial operations undertaken by third-party creditors of companies. Furthermore, there are reports of the transformation of municipal companies into private companies without a legal regime for reversing the exploration and control of public goods to the municipalities. Lastly, the auditors noted the absence of sanctions, namely of a non-administrative nature for non-compliance with the legal regime of MOCs.

The financial bailout acted as an external shock to bring about significant changes to these practices, as many MOCs were simply dissolved because of the draconian performance criteria described in the trends section. The initial excesses gave way to new imperatives of transparency and impartiality. In general, Portuguese MOCs are not required to turn profits, but, as a common rule, they are required to adopt balanced budgets. One of the most innovative aspects of Law 50/2012 concerns the regime of financial consolidation, according to which the parent local governments take on the responsibility of maintaining balance budgets in the companies' accounts. In the case of imbalances, the net debt and loans of the companies are included in the calculation of the net debt of the participating municipal entities. If the annual operating income plus financial charges are negative, a financial transfer by the parent local government(s) is mandatory, in proportion to the equity interest, aimed at achieving a balance in MOC accounts. In cases of financial losses, the Law also demands that the main shareholders prevent companies from contracting new financial responsibilities, and tracks the evolution of the indebtedness of the entities of the LCS to make sure they comply with the limits established for the financial balance of the municipality until the effective rebalancing is reached. Thus, accounting practices must now identify all financial flows between MOCs and the participating entities (transparency in financial relations), as well as the principle that any financial contributions from participating entities must be defined by contract. In addition, companies are subjected to competition rules. They have to follow public procurement laws when searching for private partners to invest and obey by national and EU competition regulations.

The creation of new MOCs or the participation of municipalities in the capital of private companies is now subject to ex-ante inspection by the Court of Auditors. The companies must be registered in the commercial registry and their statutes shared with the Court of Auditors, the General Directorate of Local Governments and the Attorney General's Office. The monitoring and control of MOCs is also done through the special duties of information of these companies to the municipalities and of these to the General Directorate of Local Governments, through the complete and timely submission of projects of activity plans, annual budget projects, investment plans, annual accountability documents, quarterly budget execution reports, among others. Failure to comply with these duties implies the dissolution of the MOC executive body.

14.6 Board Structure and CEOs of Portuguese MOCs

One of the least explored aspects of municipal corporatisation is the structure and composition of the boards of MOCs. Ground-breaking work was done by Papenfuß et al. (2018) and sought to investigate gender diversity and CEO wages in MOCs in Germany and the Netherlands. Other work has focused on the profile of CEOs, as well as the composition and practices of the executive and supervisory boards of MOCs in the Netherlands (Voorn et al., 2018a, b). Unfortunately, so far no similar studies have been conducted in Portugal. As a result, it is not possible to determine the sociodemographic profile of Portuguese CEOs, the public *versus* private sector background or the level of technical training and political experience.

By law, we know that only one out of the three members of the MOC executive board can be paid a full-time wage. Exceptionally, two board members can receive full-time wages if a company's average annual profits in the previous three-year period exceed five million euros. The law requires the names, curricula and wages of the members of the governing board to be publicised on each company's website, but it is currently unknown whether this transparency requirement is fulfilled by the MOCs.

The wage of the member of the executive board is capped by law at the full-time wage of the local executive councillors. Anecdotal evidence suggests that, very often, the CEO of a municipal company is the mayor of the parent local government. However, s/he is forbidden by law to accumulate salaries for both functions and typically foregoes the CEO salary, as it is legally capped at a lower level than the mayor's remuneration.

14.7 Conclusion

This chapter addressed the role of the local corporate public sector in delivering public services in Portugal. After the large-scale expansion of the sector during the first decade of the twenty-first century, the bailout that followed the financial crisis led to a significant retrenchment over the last decade. This recent trend in Portugal contrasts with other countries, such as the UK (Andrews et al., 2020; Ferry et al., 2018) or Sweden (Bergh et al., 2018, 2021), where the sector expanded in recent decades, in a trend that preceded the crisis (Voorn et al., 2018a, b). The Portuguese case is helpful to illustrate two important points regarding the adoption of new forms of service delivery. First, the adoption of MOCs was seen as panacea for the excessive red tape surrounding decision-making in local bureaucracies. In the attempt to circumvent stringent administrative, financial and civil service laws, and public procurement rules, municipalities turned to corporatisation as a solution to achieve flexibility and specialisation in the daily management of service delivery activities. As is often the case, the initial enthusiastic adoption was followed by disenchantment. Citizen criticism combined with news reports of corruption practices and lack of transparency led to a tapering off in the creation of new corporations. However, it took an external shock—the financial bailout—to initiate a downward trend in municipal corporatisation. The last decade was characterised by the termination of close to 200 companies and the internalisation of many services they were providing.

The international literature reports several studies investigating the efficiency and effectiveness of MOCs (see Voorn et al., 2017 for a review). Yet, no comparable studies could be identified for Portugal. The only studies in the Portuguese context are based on a handful of cases conducted almost a decade ago. Focusing primarily on mixed MOCs, they report the existence of goal conflicts and negotiation problems between shareholders due to the "multiple principals" phenomenon (Da Cruz & Marques, 2012; Marques & Berg, 2011; see also Voorn et al., 2019). Both the decisions to adopt and to terminate MOCs were undertaken without proper technical studies required by law to shape the decision. Given the oscillations in popularity of the MOC model in Portugal, it is perhaps surprising for an outsider that there is yet to be a comprehensive study about the efficiency and effectiveness of the sector. Portuguese researchers can use as a possible template the recent study conducted in Sweden by Bergh et al. (2021) investigating the association between the use of MOCs and local government performance in terms of citizen satisfaction, business climate, and corruption levels. The time has arrived to expand research on Portuguese MOCs to investigate these important correlates.

The evidence regarding the characteristics of existing MOCs in Portugal is still scarce. We know a lot about their legal status and organisational characteristics, but less about governance rules and performance, and even less about the structure and composition of their governing boards. Similarly, the sociodemographic profile, educational background and prior employment of their CEOs are also unknown. These significant gaps in our knowledge require the collection of systematic data, both primary and secondary, to achieve a better understanding of the sector.

Acknowledgements The authors acknowledge the Research Centre in Political Science (UIDB/CPO/00758/2020), University of Minho/University of Évora supported by the Portuguese Foundation for Science and Technology (FCT) and the Portuguese Ministry of Education and Science through national funds.

References

Andrews, R., Ferry, L., Skelcher, C., & Wegorowski, P. (2020). Corporatization in the public sector: Explaining the growth of local government companies. *Public Administration Review, 80*(3), 482–493.

Batalhão, C. J. (2015). *As empresas municipais S.A. ("S" de Sociedades "A" de Anómalas): A aplicação do CIRE [Municipal corporations S.A. ("S" of societies "A" of anomalous): The application of the CIRE]*. Braga: Associação de Estudos de Direito Regional e Local (AEDREL).

Bergh, A., Erlingsson, G. Ó., Gustafsson, A., & Wittberg, E. (2018). Municipally owned enterprises as danger zones for corruption? How politicians having feet in two camps may undermine conditions for accountability. *Public Integrity, 21*(3), 320–352.

Bergh, A., Erlingsson, G. Ó., & Wittberg, E. (2021). What happens when municipalities run corporations? Empirical evidence from 290 Swedish municipalities. *Local Government Studies*. https://doi.org/10.1080/03003930.2021.1944857.

Camões, P. J. (2015). A evolução da atividade empresarial local e das participações locais. [The evolution of the local corporate public sector and local holding companies]. In A. F. Tavares, L. de Sousa, N. Ferreira da Cruz, & S. Jorge (Eds.), *A reforma do poder local em debate* (pp. 165–170). ICS.

Camões, P. J., & Rodrigues, M. (2020). From enthusiasm to disenchantment: An analysis of the termination of Portuguese municipal enterprises. *Public Money & Management, 41*(5), 387–394.

Da Cruz, N. F., & Marques, R. C. (2011). Viability of municipal companies in the provision of urban infrastructure services. *Local Government Studies, 37*(1), 93–110.

Da Cruz, N. F., & Marques, R. C. (2012). Mixed companies and local governance: No man can serve two masters. *Public Administration, 90*(3), 737–758.

DGAL. (2018). *Relatório sobre a monitorização do setor empresarial local [Report on the monitoring of the local public sector]*. Direção Geral das Autarquias Locais (DGAL).

DGAL. (2021). *Lista de empresas locais [List of municipal corporations]*. http://www.portalautarquico.dgal.gov.pt. Accessed 10 February 2021.

Elcock, H. (2008). Elected mayors: Lesson drawing from four countries. *Public Administration, 86*(3), 795–811.

Fernandes, M. J., Camões, P. J., & Jorge, S. (2020). *Anuário financeiro dos municípios portugueses 2019 [2019 Financial municipal yearbook]*. OCC.

Ferry, L., Andrews, R., Skelcher, C., & Wegorowski, P. (2018). New development: Corporatization of local authorities in England in the wake of austerity 2010–2016. *Public Money & Management, 38*(6), 477–480.

Figueiredo, V. L. F. (2012). *O setor empresarial local e as implicações da adoção do sistema de normalização contabilística no apuramento do endividamento municipal [The local corporate sector and the implications of adopting the accounting standardization system in the calculation of municipal indebtedness]*. (Doctoral dissertation). Lisboa: ISCAL.

Leavitt, W. M., & Morris, J. C. (2004). In search of middle ground: The public authority as an alternative to privatization. *Public Works Management & Policy, 9*(2), 154–163.

Lidström, A. (2017). Public authorities and intermunicipal cooperation in a European context. *Urban Affairs Review, 53*(2), 403–409.

Livro Branco do SEL. (2011). *Livro branco do sector empresarial local [White paper on the local corporate public sector].* http://www.portalautarquico.dgal.gov.pt. Accessed 8 April 2021.

Mafra, J. M. R. (2013). *O regime jurídico da atividade empresarial local e das participações locais – A função de fiscalização [The legal framework for local corporate activity and local holding companies – The oversight function].* Revisores e Auditores.

Marques, R. C., & Berg, S. (2011). Public-private partnership contracts: A tale of two cities with different contractual arrangements. *Public Administration, 89*(4), 1585–1603.

Mendes, S., & Camões, P. J. (2008). Party politics and local government coalition formation in Portugal. In D. Giannetti & K. Benoit (Eds.), *Intra-party politics and coalition governments in parliamentary democracies* (pp. 69–85). Routledge.

Molinari, J., & Tyer, C. (2003). Local government enterprise fund activity: Trends and implications. *Public Administration Quarterly, 27*(3/4), 369–391.

Oliveira, A. C. (2001). Empresas municipais e intermunicipais: Entre o público e o privado [Municipal and inter-municipal corporations: Between public and private]. *Revista de Administração e Políticas Públicas, 2*(1), 126–136.

Papenfuß, U., Van Genugten, M., De Kruijf, J., & Van Thiel, S. (2018). Implementation of EU initiatives on gender diversity and executive directors' pay in municipally-owned enterprises in Germany and The Netherlands. *Public Money & Management, 38*(2), 87–96.

Rubin, I. S. (1988). Municipal enterprises: Exploring budgetary and political implications. *Public Administration Review, 48*(1), 542–550.

Stumm, T. J. (1996). Municipal enterprise activities as revenue generators: A different view. *American Review of Public Administration, 26*(4), 477–488.

Tavares, A. (2017). Ten years after: Revisiting the determinants of the adoption of municipal corporations for local service delivery. *Local Government Studies, 43*(5), 697–706.

Tavares, A. F., & Camões, P. J. (2007). Local service delivery choices in Portugal: A political transaction costs framework. *Local Government Studies, 33*(4), 535–553.

Tavares, A. F., & Camões, P. J. (2010). New forms of local governance: A theoretical and empirical analysis of municipal corporations in Portugal. *Public Management Review, 12*(5), 587–608.

Tavares, A. F., & Camões, P. J. (2021). Portugal: Elections and voting in a dual-tier local government system. In A. Gendźwiłł, U. Kjaer, & K. Steyvers (Eds.), *Routledge handbook of local elections and voting*. Routledge. Forthcoming.

Voorn, B., Van Genugten, M., & Van Thiel, S. (2017). The efficiency and effectiveness of municipally owned corporations: A systematic review. *Local Government Studies, 43*(5), 820–841.

Voorn, B., Van Genugten, M., & Van Thiel, S. (2018a). *Respondentenrapport "Verbonden Partijen in Nederland 2018" [Respondents report survey "Municipally owned corporations in the Netherlands 2018"]*. Institute for Management Research.

Voorn, B., Van Thiel, S., & Van Genugten, M. (2018b). Debate: Corporatization as more than a recent crisis-driven development. *Public Money & Management, 38*(7), 481–482.

Voorn, B., Van Genugten, M., & Van Thiel, S. (2019). Multiple principals, multiple problems: A framework for effective governance and a research agenda for joint service delivery. *Public Administration, 97*(3), 671–685.

CHAPTER 15

Corporatisation in Spanish Local Government: Governing the Diversity

Germà Bel, Marc Esteve, Juan Carlos Garrido-Rodríguez, and José Luis Zafra-Gómez

15.1 Introduction

Local governments have explored a panoply of organisational arrangements to implement their public services (Andrews et al., 2015; Esteve et al., 2013; Van Genugten et al., 2020). In the case of Spain, we have seen over the last decades an increase in new organisational forms departing from classic direct provision options often used at the municipal level. These organisational forms have encompassed two important changes. On

G. Bel (✉)
Universitat de Barcelona, Barcelona, Spain
e-mail: gbel@ub.edu

M. Esteve
University College London, London, UK
e-mail: marc.esteve@ucl.ac.uk

J. C. Garrido-Rodríguez • J. L. Zafra-Gómez
Universidad de Granada, Granada, Spain
e-mail: jcgarrido@ugr.es; jlzafra@ugr.es

M. Van Genugten et al. (eds.), *Corporatisation in Local Government*, https://doi.org/10.1007/978-3-031-09982-3_15

the one hand, local governments have implemented different ventures to collaborate with private sector providers. On the other hand, they have also created new organisational forms, such as corporations, to implement some of the postulates of the New Public Management trend that influenced the Spanish administration quite heavily. One common organisational form used under these reforms has been municipally owned corporations (MOCs). As Bel et al. discuss, 'public corporations are thought to deliver public services efficiently, either by developing more managerial flexibility (given that they operate under general or corporate law), establishing their working conditions or by operating outside traditional political bureaucratic structures' (Bel et al., 2022, p. 232).

Research on MOCs has recently focused on disclosing the potential benefits that this organisational form has over traditional procurement models (see, for example, Tavares & Camões, 2010; Torsteinsen & Van Genugten, 2016; Voorn et al., 2017), and the determinants of their adoption across local governments (Andrews et al., 2020; Da Cruz & Marques, 2011; Tavares, 2017; Voorn et al., 2020). However, MOCs seem to entail multiple challenges that could hinder their performance. Da Cruz and Marques (2012), for example, warn that those corporations with private sector participation post managerial challenges that could significantly decrease their performance. In a similar vein, Voorn et al. (2019) argue that one of the main challenges of MOCs is their governance. In particular, the authors suggest that corporations have multiple principals, and this creates coordination problems in the MOC. While there have been some recent attempts to study the governance of corporations (Voorn et al., 2020), little is known yet on how their governance influences their performance (Ferry et al., 2018; Voorn et al., 2017).

While there is some evidence on various characteristics of MOCs from different countries, such as Portugal, the UK or the US, among others, we do not have a comprehensive review of these organisational forms in most OECD countries. In the present chapter, we will focus on describing the use and the nature of MOCs in Spain. We think that the Spanish context is particularly suitable to analyse these organisational forms for several reasons. First, in the last decade, there have been a lot of research works analysing the effects of the New Public Management on the externalisation of Spanish public services as a source of getting better results and benefits (Bel & Warner, 2008; Pérez-López et al., 2015, 2018; Plata-Díaz et al., 2014, 2019; Zafra-Gómez et al., 2016, among others). At the same time, we have also seen a strong trend to analyse the effects of remunicipalisation or bringing back services that were outsourced in the past, as the costs or benefits were less effective than expected (Campos-Alba et al., 2021). While multiple studies have provided empirical evidence looking at some specific organisational forms, there is a lack of studies analysing multiple organisational forms in the Spanish context. Hence, in this chapter, we will explore the different arrangements that are currently used in Spanish municipalities to implement public services.

The chapter is structured as follows. Firstly, we will discuss the institutional and regulatory framework of Spain, and how that limits the types of organisational forms that can be used to implement public services. Then, we will review the legal characteristics of Spanish MOCs. Next, we provide a radiography of the current state of MOCs in Spain, discussing their use and main characteristics. Finally, we conclude by discussing organisational and decision-making process in MOCs in Spain.

15.2 Institutional and Regulatory Framework

The territorial organisation of Spain was originally established in the Spanish Constitution of 1978. Its configuration is based on three tiers: central government, regional governments, and local governments. Regional governments delegate some regulatory and supervisory powers to local governments, which are established in each regional constitution (*Estatutos de Autonomía*). However, local governments operate under the principle of autonomy with respect to other executive governmental tiers, and their basic powers are established in the Law 7/1985, of 2 April, which regulates the basis of the Local Regime (LBRL, hereinafter).

The LBRL establishes the basis for local autonomy, which is organised in two different tiers: municipalities and provinces (which, in the case of the Canary and the Balearic Islands, are island councils). The number of municipalities in Spain is 8131, including 47 peninsular provinces, 3 insular provinces and 2 autonomous cities—Ceuta and Melilla—, located in Northern Africa. Most of these are very small: in 2020, 6827 municipalities (84% of the total) had fewer than 5000 inhabitants, whereas 888 municipalities (11%) had between 5001 and 20,000, and only 416 municipalities (5%) had more than 20,000. Hence, the average population per municipality is low: 5836, which is relevant regarding the issue of scale economies in local public services. This distribution of municipalities according to their population is relevant as well because the LBRL establishes a different menu of public services that must be compulsorily

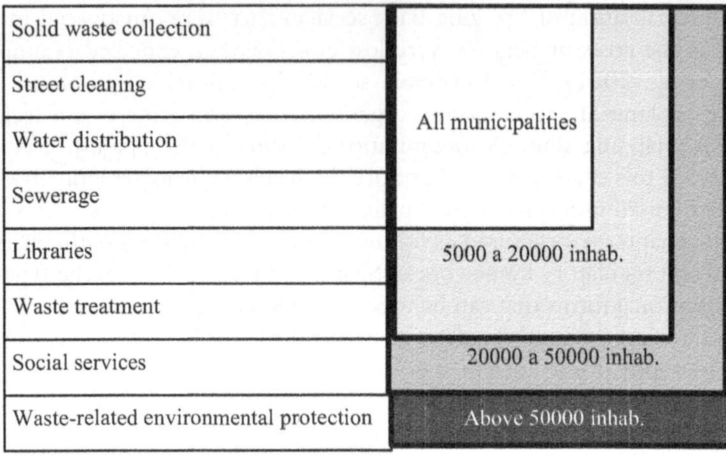

Fig. 15.1 Services that are compulsory depending on municipality population

provided by each municipality depending on their size, as shown in Fig. 15.1.

Municipal governments in Spain are formed based on local elections, which are regulated in the Organic Law 5/1985, of the general electoral regime (LOREG, hereinafter). The members of the municipal council are elected on a proportional basis in an election based on party lists. In the first meeting of the municipal council after the election, the city councillors elect the mayor. If any candidate obtains more than half of the votes in the city council, that candidate is the elected mayor. If no candidate obtains such support, the head of the party list that obtained the most votes in the municipal elections automatically becomes the mayor. The government of the municipality is formed by members of the city council appointed by the mayor to take responsibility for the different areas to be managed.

Whereas the rules for municipal government formation are homogeneous all over Spain, the rules for government formation in the upper local government, provinces or island councils, are much more diverse. The general case is that of indirect election of provincial councils based on the results that each party obtained in the municipal election in the municipalities of the province. In six provinces (Asturias, Cantabria, La Rioja, Madrid, Murcia and Navarre) that form uni-provincial autonomous regions, the regional government has absorbed the power of the provincial governments, so there is no local provincial government. The councils of three Basque Country provinces (Araba, Bizkaia and Gipuzkoa) and the island councils are formed through direct elections. In all cases, the respective councils elect the president of the institution.

Finally, it is worth to mention another layer within local government that exists in several regions, and most notably in Aragon and Catalonia, where counties (*comarcas*) have been formally instituted as an administrative jurisdiction by respective regional laws. The counties operate at an intermediate scale, between municipalities and provinces. County governments in Aragon and Catalonia have been very effective in promoting inter-municipal cooperation for local services delivery (Bel & Costas, 2006; Bel et al., 2014). County governments are constituted through indirect elections, like most provincial governments.

15.3 Legal and Organisational Status of MOCs

The regulation of functional decentralisation for local service provision, under which local governments establish corporations for the delivery of public services, is based on the LBRL and subsequent legislation that develops the principles contained in that law. Three forms of local corporatisation can be distinguished: (1) Autonomous Organisation (OA, hereinafter), (2) Business Public Entity (EPE, hereinafter) and (3) Local Commercial Company (SML, hereinafter; whose capital belongs to the local entity). The main difference between the three is whether they operate under administrative or under commercial law, and the degree of operational autonomy from the local government.

OAs operate under administrative law and enjoy some operational autonomy (functional decentralisation). Related to arm's-length bodies (ALB), in which organisations hold varying degrees of structural and legal autonomy, as classified in Van Genugten et al. (2020), OAs integrate ALB Types 1 and 2. The different organisational forms that exist within public law can be grouped into one category, which is the public agencies. Some examples of public agencies are municipal councils, local administrative boards, official chambers, department assemblies, the senate and many others. These agencies are forms of governance used to deliver public services and operate under public law (administrative law), as they are run entirely by government. They are also used by local authorities in a process of corporatisation to develop MOCs.

EPEs and SMLs correspond to ALB Type 3 in Van Genugten et al. (2020). EPEs operate under private law and enjoy some operational autonomy, although—as in the autonomous bodies—the decision-making process in their executive boards is subject to administrative law, rather than commercial law. SMLs are much more frequent than EPEs, and they fully operate under private law and enjoy wide operational autonomy. The main organisational forms that exist within private law are fully MOCs, mixed MOCs with minority public ownership and mixed MOCs with majority public ownership. Thus, these organisational forms can collaborate with the private sector in different ways when delivering public services. Some of these organisational forms operating under private law are public foundations, public corporate entities or official chambers of Commerce, Industry and Navigation. Regarding public foundations, these are private law entities despite being publicly owned and called public foundations. They operate under the jurisdiction of commercial/civil law and are non-profit organisations that are created for the achievement of general interest purposes. Public corporate entities are also private entities, but their capital is mostly public. These different organisational forms have the ability to formalise private contracts and thus operate under private law in matters of contracting.

15.4 The Dynamics of Local Corporatisation

Pressure aimed at improving performance of public services triggered in Spain (as in many other countries) local government reform, to better serve the needs of citizens and to create public value as a result. Searching for ways to better implement these services, many local governments resorted to contracting out of public services, which was a preeminent policy in the last decades of the past century (Bel, 2006). Management reform in those municipalities where retaining public production was the choice intensified by the beginning of the current century, and corporatisation of public services has been a relevant tool (Mur, 2011).

Through this process, policymakers have turned to two main organisational forms, as discussed above. On the one hand, they have created MOCs to deliver public services, which operate under private law and are thought to deliver these services efficiently, given that they fall under the jurisdiction of commercial law. And on the other hand, we have also seen an increase in the number of autonomous organisations and public agencies that while they can also be considered MOCs, they operate under the public law, are more distant to political interference and are more managerial oriented. This pattern resulted in an intense growth in the number of local public entities and commercial companies (public firms) in Spain in the first decade of this century (Mur, 2011, pp. 140–143): while a total of 467 public firms existed in 1998, in 2008 the figure had grown up to 1233 (of which 82.6% were municipal). The number of public firms kept growing in the following years.

Following the Great Recession, a very relevant—for our purpose—law was passed in 2013: the Law 27/2013, for rationalisation and sustainability of the Local Administration (LRSAL hereinafter), which disrupted the trend so far observed. The LRSAL modified the LBRL by introducing some preference criteria and several requirements regarding the modalities of functional corporatisation (Martínez-Alonso Camps, 2018, p. 82): both the forms of EPE and of SML have a subsidiary nature with respect to OAs. The first two can only be used when it is conclusively proven that they are more sustainable and efficient than OAs, for which the criteria of economic profitability and investment recovery must be considered.

Furthermore, the LRSAL determined the suppression of MOCs that were suffering a financial imbalance (in most cases, resulting in the service being reinternalised or suppressed). In addition, more recently restrictions have been established on the freedom of decisions regarding remuneration and employment contracts. And the Law 19/2017 of Public Sector Contracts (LCSP, hereinafter) did in practice equate the regulation for contracting with third parties to those rules established for production of public services under administrative law.

Due to all these changes, the number of MOCs has decreased since 2013, as figures in Table 15.1 show. The reduction in the number of MOCs has been more intense in the case of autonomous bodies (OA), presumably because of the compulsory suppression of those with financial

Table 15.1 Number of local MOCs after LRSAL was passed

Month–year	*OA*	*EPE*	*SM*	*Total*
July 2013	1250	56	1590	2896
May 2016	1048	55	1496	2599
July 2018	944	57	1464	2465
February 2021	832	56	1367	2255
Change July 2013–February 2021 (%)	–33.4%	0.0%	–14.0%	-22.1%

Source: based on Martinez 2018, p. 85; Ministry of Finance (2021)

unbalance, followed by commercial companies (SM), which have been those most affected by reduction of operational freedom regarding labour contracting and contracting with third parties.

Despite the changing patterns that corporatisation has followed in Spain in the last two decades (an upward trend in the first decades of the century and a decreasing trend in the second one), it has never been a relevant issue either in the public debate or in the political discussion—not even when the LRSAL was passed in 2013, forcing the suppression of many corporations. This law was passed within the context of measures promoted by the central government and legislator under the so-called agenda for modernisation of the public sector. The stated aim was to reduce costs associated with service delivery by subcentral governments, but other parallel measures in the domain of economic policy and administration have more prominence in the public and political debate.[1] It is worth adding that, so far, no ex-post evaluation has been conducted to assess the efficacy of these reforms affecting organisational forms for public delivery, and it is far from clear that a more cost-efficient provision of public services has been achieved.

15.5 The Current Structure of Local MOCs: A Radiography

In this section, we provide a detailed description and analysis of the composition of the local MOCs in Spain. We obtained data for a total of ten services and examined the different forms of provision used in relation to corporatisation in a sample of 1257 Spanish municipalities. In relation to the services included in this study, we consider the following: waste collection; waste treatment; sewerage; street cleaning; environmental protection; water management; public library; social services; sports facilities; and public transport. It is worth noting that these ten services concentrate almost all MOCs in Spain. Therefore, representativeness of the full population of services is extremely high.

[1] An exception to the low impact on public and political debate on corporatisation exists in the region of Catalonia, where political controversy about the expansion of corporatisation of Health services instead of preserving traditional in-house production has been intense. However, management of health services in Spain depends on regional governments rather than local governments, and therefore this debate goes beyond the scope of this contribution. Bel and Esteve (2022) provide detailed information on the organisational structure of health services across Spanish regions.

Furthermore, thanks to the richness of the database we have available, we can go beyond country-level analysis, thus we provide information at regional level. This is relevant in countries such as Spain, where in many cases the regional legislators and governments have some legislative and executive powers related to locally provided public services.

Data were obtained from the Ministry of Finance, more specifically from the Department of Regional and Local financing, and also from the database of the Effective Cost of the local services, from the same Ministry. A singular and relevant characteristic of both databases is that they include the management form of production, allowing us to observe the situation of each of the services. The raw data from the available databases needed some transformation to ensure precise and robust results. In that regard, the database had to be cleansed as not every municipality publishes the information correctly, which forced us to remove several municipalities. Furthermore, it was necessary to classify the different management forms into the groups that we intend to analyse, because the Spanish legislation allows a wide variety of legal forms to produce the service, but their essential characteristics can be very similar.

It is important to consider two additional remarks when going through the information in our database. Table 15.1 presented information on the number of existing MOCs. Tables 15.2, 15.3 and 15.4 provide a different type of information, based on the number of municipalities that use MOCs. Therefore, a MOC appears several times when it is used to articulate inter-municipal cooperation (one each time a municipality in the database provides that information). If we take into account that OAs are, by far, the most frequent form of corporation involving inter-municipal

Table 15.2 Percentage of municipalities using each type of corporation, by population of the municipality

Inhabitants	*OA*	*EPE*	*Mixed firm with government majority*	*Mixed firm with private majority*
<1000	88.27%	2.79%	8.94%	0.00%
1001–5000	77.44%	10.44%	12.12%	0.00%
5001–20,000	66.97%	19.00%	14.03%	0.00%
20,001–50,000	23.21%	40.18%	32.14%	4.46%
>50,000	14.68%	39.45%	41.28%	4.59%
Total	55.47%	24.61%	18.75%	1.16%

Source: based on data from the Ministry of Finance (2021)

Table 15.3 Frequency of type of corporations by region (municipalities using each type of corporation: selected services)

CCAA	*OA*	*EPE*	*Mixed firm government majority*	*Mixed firm private majority*
Andalusia	47.03%	21.49%	29.33%	2.15%
Aragón	50.00%	37.95%	9.64%	2.41%
Asturias	43.86%	48.25%	7.89%	0.00%
Balearic Islands	34.09%	65.91%	0.00%	0.00%
Canary Islands	55.03%	19.53%	20.71%	4.73%
Cantabria	91.74%	4.13%	4.13%	0.00%
Castile La Mancha	80.00%	10.85%	9.15%	0.00%
Castile León	67.17%	12.12%	20.71%	0.00%
Catalonia	55.42%	12.92%	30.78%	0.88%
Extremadura	61.97%	25.35%	9.86%	2.82%
Galicia	82.18%	9.24%	7.26%	1.32%
Madrid	73.09%	13.90%	13.00%	0.00%
Murcia	13.70%	17.81%	68.49%	0.00%
Navarre	50.00%	50.00%	0.00%	0.00%
La Rioja	63.64%	0.00%	36.36%	0.00%
C. Valenciana	46.81%	26.38%	23.40%	3.40%
Basque Country	27.31%	42.56%	28.11%	2.02%
Total Spain	55.47%	24.61%	18.75%	1.16%

Source: based on data from the Ministry of Finance (2021)

Note: The autonomous cities of Ceuta and Melilla are not included. In these two cities very few corporations exist, and these are only OA Ceuta, and only EPE in Melilla

cooperation, it is no surprise that frequency of OAs is higher when considering the number of municipalities using OAs (Tables 15.2, 15.3 and 15.4), than when considering the number of actually existing OAs (Table 15.1). The opposite happens with the MOCs of commercial forms, which much more frequently than OAs operate only in the municipality that owns the corporation.

Second, it is important to bear in mind that EPE has a different meaning in Table 15.1 and in our database. In Table 15.1 the distinction between EPE and SM was based on whether the decision process in the board of directors was subject to administrative law or commercial law, which places one subset of fully government-owned firms in EPEs and another subset in SMs. That information was not recollected by the Ministry of Finance, as the procedure followed the criteria set in the LBRL when creating the database that we have been able to use. Hence, the

Table 15.4 Percentage of corporations by type of local public service (municipalities using each type of corporation

Service	*OA*	*EPE*	*Mixed firm government majority*	*Mixed firm private majority*
Water services	38.58%	3.15%	55.12%	3.15%
Sewerage	34.57%	3.70%	56.79%	4.94%
Libraries	37.78%	62.22%	0.00%	0.00%
Social services	75.60%	23.60%	0.80%	0.00%
Sports facilities	2.63%	93.42%	3.95%	0.00%
Street cleaning	30.00%	23.33%	46.67%	0.00%
Environmental protection	77.19%	1.75%	21.05%	0.00%
Waste collection	77.70%	2.03%	20.27%	0.00%
Public transport	56.25%	2.08%	37.50%	4.17%
Waste treatment	88.62%	0.00%	10.57%	0.81%
Total	59.94%	17.84%	21.10%	1.12%

Source: based on data from the Ministry of Finance (2021)

database includes information on the percentage of government ownership in the firm-type forms (fully or partially) owned by governments (which, as such, always operate under commercial law). Therefore, our data structure differentiates between:

- OAs and (EPE + Mixed Firms—the latter jointly owned by government and private investors) regarding under which type of law the corporation operates; and
- (OAs + EPE) and Mixed Firms, regarding whether governments have full or partial control of the corporation (and further distinguishing when partial control is associated to a majority in ownership).

15.5.1 MOCs and Population of Municipalities

Table 15.2 shows the frequency of different type of corporatisations by range of municipalities' population. The distribution of corporatisation forms is very similar for the municipalities with less than 20,000 inhabitants: the most frequent forms of corporatisation are the autonomous organisms (*mancommunities* and consortia). Both organisms are aimed to channel cooperation for the delivery of public services, but two relevant differences exist between them (Barrero Rodríguez, 2002): First, *mancommunities* can be formed only by municipalities, whereas consortia can also include other administrations different from municipalities, and even private partners.[2] Second, while consortia tend to be single-service tools, *mancommunities* often provide several services in the member municipalities.

In contrast, in more populated municipalities the most frequent forms of corporatisation are company firms. As population increases, public firms and mixed companies gain more importance, being the most frequently used forms in the largest municipalities.

The frequency of mixed firms with private majority is marginal in Spain, and only reaches some relevance in the largest municipalities (>20,000 inhabitants). In this regard, it is worth noting that there is no unanimous agreement on whether mixed firms where the government has a minority of shares are to be considered MOCs. In the case of Spain, the legislation can entitle governments to exert control on the firm even when holding a minority of shares (e.g. appointing the CEO). Therefore, we think it is appropriate to keep this type of firm within the MOC form.

15.5.2 MOC Across Regions

Given the territorial diversity and relevant administrative decentralisation in Spain, it is interesting to see whether there is a unique pattern of type of corporatisations across Spain or if, on the contrary, regional differences are relevant. Table 15.3 shows the frequency of type of corporation in each region.

Data in Table 15.3 show that OA is the dominant form in most regions, with special incidence in Cantabria, Galicia and Castilla-La Mancha. Public firms are especially frequent in the Balearic Islands, Navarre and Asturias. Finally, mixed firms—usually with a government majority—reach the highest figures in Murcia, Catalonia, La Rioja, Basque Country and Comunitat Valenciana. This is consistent with a higher frequency of contracting out in these last regions, found for solid waste and water services in Bel (2006), which would define an institutional environment more prone overall to private participation in the delivery of public services.

[2] Although this type may also include other local government levels, for the sake of simplicity we call them MOCs as well.

15.5.3 MOCs and Local Public Services

Moving now from jurisdictional to sectorial observation of corporatisation, Table 15.4 presents the distribution of frequencies of type of corporations in the ten local services that we have analysed in detail, which are those in which corporatisation is more frequent, by far. Indeed, by looking at figures for total percentage of type of corporation, it can be clearly observed that—even if several services are not included in the table—the distribution of frequencies is virtually equivalent to that obtained in the previous tables, where all data in our database for all services was taken into account. Maximum discrepancy is less than half a percentage point for OAs, and even lower differences are found for EPEs and mixed firms.

A clear divide can be observed between type of services and prevalent type of MOC. Services related to environmental management of solid waste (waste treatment, waste collection and environmental protection) show the highest frequency of OAs. This is due to the fact that economies of scale on volume are particularly relevant for those services, and OAs are used to organise cooperation among municipalities, particularly those of smaller dimension. This interpretation is consistent with robust but more partial evidence from previous studies that have analysed choices of production form of local services in Spain, most frequently related to solid waste management in specific regions—Aragon, Catalonia and Galicia—(e.g. Bel & Costas, 2006; Bel & Fageda, 2010; Bel et al., 2014; Bel & Miralles, 2003; Bel & Mur, 2009) or for overall Spain (e.g. Pérez-López et al., 2018; Plata-Díaz et al., 2014; Zafra-Gómez et al., 2013).

EPEs are particularly frequent in those services where physical fixed facilities are more important, as these services are coproduced by citizens when using those facilities: public libraries and sport services. In these cases, OAs have limited relevance—particularly in the case of sport facilities—and mixed firms are just marginal, regardless of the government holding a majority or a minority of the firm ownership. Instead, those services in which physical networks (different from fixed facilities) are more important and economies of density tend to be more relevant than economies of volume, show a stronger association to mixed firms as type of corporatisation, usually under governmental majority. That is the case of street lighting and especially of water-related services (water distribution and sewerage), which could be related to the relevance of asset specificity, sunk investments and consequent funding requirements (Bel et al.,

2022; Zafra-Gómez et al., 2016), although historical patterns in the water distribution sector in Spain might have played a role as well (Bel, 2006).

MOCs in Spain tend to be single-purpose, unlike other countries where multi-purpose MOCs are more common, such as Italy (e.g. Garrone et al., 2013). When corporatisation affects different services within a jurisdiction, it is frequent to have different corporations for those different services.

The size of MOCs in Spain is very diverse. We can find very large municipal firms at one end of the spectrum, such as Transports Municipals de Barcelona, a fully public firm that is responsible for collective transportation services in the metropolitan area of Barcelona (see Albalate et al., 2012; Bel & Rosell, 2016), and whose expenses in 2019 were 1.01 billion euro and its labour force 7896 employees (TMB, 2019). At the other end of the spectrum, there exist a myriad of OAs formed by a few small municipalities that engage in joint delivery of services with relevant scale economies, such as waste collection and management. Public firms of small dimension also exist in small municipalities, though these are less frequent than OAs, and mixed firms of small dimension are much more exceptional.

15.6 Organisational and Decision-Making Process in MOCs

Regarding operational autonomy and legislation under which they operate, a sharp divide must be made between autonomous organisations (OAs) and commercial firms (be these fully owned by the government or mixed with a majority of government-shareholding). OAs are the type of corporation used by most municipalities (even if the number of existing public enterprises is higher), because consortia and—especially—*mancommunities* are used as a vehicle for inter-municipal cooperation. Instead, public firms tend to have a municipal stand-alone character, with the noteworthy exception of metropolitan areas, where they are also used for cooperative purposes.

15.6.1 Autonomous Organisations

Mancommunities and consortia follow the guidelines established by the municipal councils of the member municipalities, as well as the statutes with which they were formed. OAs have an assembly, which is formed by representatives of the member municipalities, and an executive board elected by the Assembly. The executive board is formed by a president (typically the mayor of a member municipality) and several elected officials of other member municipalities. A manager is appointed for the management of day-to-day operations. OAs deliver services strictly within the range of services established in their statutes, and the quality of services delivered tends to be a primary goal.

According to the administrative nature of OAs, employees have the condition of public employees, and labour regulations and relations are determined by administrative law, being similar to those applying to member municipalities. The primary responsible for organisational decisions is the president of the OA, although decisions on some specific issues can be made by the OA Assembly. OAs do not have taxing powers, and their funding comes crucially from payments made by member municipalities and subsidies received from supra-municipal governments. Within the legal framework applying to all public administration units in Spain, the OA executive board is empowered to take financial decisions regarding long-term investments, loans and so on.

Monitoring of OA is conducted at three different levels: first, by the member municipalities; second, by the regional governments, which hold some power related to local administrations in Spain; third, by the central government, at a more general level and mainly for strict financial purposes. Furthermore, transparency laws affecting public administrations have gained importance in Spain in recent years, so that an increasing degree of publicly available information useful for social monitoring exists.

OAs don't usually have a corporate governance code, probably because their governance is heavily regulated by administrative law. This type of regulation generally imposes constraints and restricts freedom of operation of all administrations, thus including OAs.

15.6.2 Government-Owned Firms

Government-owned firms, either public firms or mixed firms with majority of government-shareholding, also have a double tier of governance bodies: an assembly of shareholders and an executive board, which is appointed by the Assembly. The executive board tends to be formed by elected officials of the municipality(ies) that owns the firm, and by appointed representatives, usually also coming from the political sphere. In this case, however, technical echelons have more relevance than in OAs, particularly in the largest public firms. For instance, the objectives of the entity are decided by the board of directors, based on information and proposals coming from the executive manager and the managing team. Decisions on service delivery are made by the board of directors (with fewer constraints than in OAs) and are implemented by the managerial structure. Concerns with efficiency tend to be more relevant in this type of corporation.

Government-owned firms have a commercial legal nature, so their operation develops under commercial law. Employees in public firms do not have the condition of public servants, and labour regulations and relations are determined by general labour regulations law, similar to those governing the private sector. The primary responsible for organisational decisions is the board of directors—where the position of the president is not as preeminent as it is in OAs. In the same way, the board of directors is also the primary responsible for decisions with respect to financial issues (long-term investments, loans, etc.) and labour, and an important role is played by the managerial team to implement them. In this regard, the bigger the firm, the higher the relevance of the managerial structure.

Monitoring of government-owned commercial firms is partially different from that of OAs. Public firms (both majority and fully owned by government) tend to conduct internal financial auditing, for which external auditors can be contracted, and the results obtained are submitted to the Shareholders Assembly, which is the first instance of monitoring, still intra-firm. Further than the own firm's bodies, additional monitoring activity is conducted by the municipal governments that hold shares, and supra-municipal supervisory institutions (both regional and central). Similar to OAs, transparency laws affecting public administrations have resulted in increasing volumes of information on the public firms being released. In this case, however, because these corporations operate under commercial law rather than administrative law, more conflicts with private data protection issues have emerged; or at least, these have been claimed by some municipal governments as reasons to limit the publicity of financial firms and personal data of their top managerial employees.

Corporate governance codes are only a recent concern for public firms in Spain. Two of the largest municipal/metropolitan firms in Spain, such as *Empresa Municipal de Transportes de Madrid* SA and *Transports Municipals de Barcelona* SA, only had a corporate governance code available in 2017 and 2020, respectively. Other firms of lower dimension are currently in the process of creating their own governance codes (e.g. *Aigües d'Argentona*), thus this process seems to be expanding.

Public firms enjoy managerial freedom for day-to-day operations, as well as financial ones, although monitoring of financial accounts has always been strictly structured (whether strictly implemented or not, it is difficult to say). In the last ten years, however, an increasing trend to limit national laws and regulation issues related to financial decisions and the contracting of personnel has limited freedom of management. In addition, the high degree of bureaucratic formalism—traditional in Spain (due to its French administrative tradition and Civil Law legal origin)—has exuberantly increased further in recent years: proceduralism, paperwork and red tape are on the rise. This is commonly seen by managers of public firms (and for anybody managing anything) as restrictions and rigidities that heavily damage the ability of public firms to operate efficiently.

Furthermore, we have also observed some significant informal governance mechanisms that have a strong influence on the management of both forms of MOCs in Spain. The most significant one is how the top public sector representatives are chosen to fulfil their roles in the upper echelons of the managerial teams of MOCs. While, in theory, these profiles are chosen based on their expertise and skills, in practice we have seen very high levels of patronage. Because these profiles are politically appointed, having a strong affinity with the governing party is a must in most, if not all, top managerial appointments. Spain has a long-standing tradition of patronage in public administration appointments (see Ballart, 2007), and this seems to extend further to MOCs—as it also happens in other European countries (Ennser-Jedenastik, 2014).

15.7 Conclusion

Governments have relied on the use of MOCs for a very long time. However, MOCs can have multiple organisational characteristics, and these are very contingent to each country implementing them (Van Genugten et al., 2020). This chapter has reviewed the use of MOCs across local governments in Spain. First, it has described the institutional and regulatory framework of Spain. Interestingly, the Spanish context offers three different forms of MOCs: (1) OA; (2) EPE; and (3) SML (whose capital belongs to the local entity). While these three corporation forms show many similarities, we have discussed how their main difference is that local autonomous organisations operate under administrative law, whereas public entities and commercial companies both operate under private law.

The distinction between these last two forms is that Local Commercial Entities may have higher levels of operational autonomy.

Spain saw an intense growth in the use of MOCs at the beginning of the century (Mur, 2011), and until 2013, the year in which legal reforms passed disincentivising—and even penalising—MOCs. While Spain has multiple examples of the three types of corporations across public services, the evidence provided in this chapter does show a strong tendency to use autonomous organisations for inter-municipal cooperation, so much so that more than half of municipalities using MOCs in Spain do so with this organisational form. This trend is even more pronounced in specific regions. It is also important to note that MOCs seem to be used in both simple and complex public services, as they are widely used in public services such as waste treatment and collection, social services, environmental protection, and libraries. As empirical evidence begins to emerge, we will be able to distinguish the efficiency and efficacy effects of implementing public service via MOCs, instead of using more traditional procurement mechanisms (such as direct provision). Moreover, future studies should also disentangle how the private participation in Spanish MOCs influences their performance.

References

Albalate, D., Bel, G., & Calzada, J. (2012). Governance and regulation of urban bus transportation: Using partial privatization to achieve the best of two worlds. *Regulation & Governance, 6*(1), 83–100.

Andrews, R., Esteve, M., & Ysa, T. (2015). Public–private joint ventures: Mixing oil and water? *Public Money & Management, 35*(4), 265–272.

Andrews, R., Ferry, L., Skelcher, C., & Wegorowski, P. (2020). Corporatisation in the public sector: Explaining the growth of local government companies. *Public Administration Review, 80*(3), 483–493.

Ballart, X. (2007). The study of public management in Spain. An interdisciplinary and ill-defined terrain. In W. Kickert (Ed.), *The study of public management in Europe and the US* (pp. 203–221). Routledge.

Barrero Rodríguez, C. (2002). Los conceptos de Mancomunidades y Consorcios: Necesidad de delimitación y diferenciaciones [The concepts of Mancommunitites and Consortia: Delimitations and differentiations]. *Revista Andaluza de Administración Pública, 45*, 81–120.

Bel, G. (2006). *Economía y política de la privatización local [Economics and Politics of Local Privatisation]*. Marcial Pons.

Bel, G., & Costas, A. (2006). Do public sector reforms get rusty?: Local privatization in Spain. *Journal of Policy Reform, 9*(1), 1–24.

Bel, G., & Esteve, M. (2022). Resilient managed competition during pandemics: Lessons from the Italian experience. *Health Economics, Policy and Law, 17*(2), 220–223.

Bel, G., Esteve, M., Garrido, J. C., & Zafra-Gómez, J. L. (2022). The costs of corporatisation: Analysing the effects of forms of governance. *Public Administration, 100* (2), 232–249.

Bel, G., & Fageda, X. (2010). Empirical analysis of solid management waste costs: Some evidence from Galicia, Spain. *Resources, Conservation & Recycling, 54*(3), 187–193.

Bel, G., Fageda, X., & Mur, M. (2014). Does cooperation reduce service delivery costs? Evidence from residential solid waste services. *Journal of Public Administration Research and Theory, 24*(1), 85–107.

Bel, G., & Miralles, A. (2003). Factors influencing the privatisation of urban solid waste collection in Spain. *Urban Studies, 40*(7), 1323–1334.

Bel, G., & Mur, M. (2009). Intermunicipal cooperation, privatization and waste management costs: Evidence from rural municipalities. *Waste Management, 29*(10), 2772–2778.

Bel, G., & Rosell, J. (2016). Public and private production in a mixed delivery system: Regulation, competition and costs. *Journal of Policy Analysis and Management, 35*(3), 533–558.

Bel, G., & Warner, M. (2008). Does privatization of solid waste and water services reduce costs? A review of empirical studies. *Resources, Conservation and Recycling, 52*(12), 1337–1348.

Campos-Alba, C. M., De La Higuera Molina, E. J., Pérez-López, G., & Zafra-Gómez, J. L. (2021). Drivers of contracting back in local governments: analysing efficiency, opportunistic political cycles, political corruption and financial factors. *Journal of Economic Policy Reform, 24*(3), 347–360.

Da Cruz, N. F., & Marques, R. C. (2011). Viability of municipal companies in the provision of urban infrastructure services. *Local Government Studies, 37*(1), 93–110.

Da Cruz, N. F., & Marques, R. C. (2012). Mixed companies and local governance: No man can serve two masters. *Public Administration, 90*(3), 737–758.

Enner-Jedenastik, L. (2014). The politics of patronage and coalition: How parties allocate managerial positions in state-owned enterprises. *Political Studies, 62*(2), 398–417.

Esteve, M., Boyne, G., Sierra, V., & Ysa, T. (2013). Organizational collaboration in the public sector: Do chief executives make a difference? *Journal of Public Administration Research and Theory, 23*(4), 927–952.

Ferry, L., Andrews, R., Skelcher, C., & Wegorowski, P. (2018). New development: Corporatization of local authorities in England in the wake of austerity 2010–2016. *Public Money & Management, 38*(6), 477–480.

Garrone, P., Grilli, L., & Rousseau, X. (2013). Management discretion and political interference in municipal enterprises: Evidence from Italian utilities. *Local Government Studies, 39*(4), 514–540.

Martínez-Alonso Camps, J. L. (2018). Los debates sobre los servicios públicos locales: Estado de la cuestión [The debates on local public services: State of the art]. *Revista Catalana de Dret Públic, 57*, 72–96.

Ministry of Finance. (2021). *Base de datos general de entidades locales [General database of local entities]*. https://serviciostelematicosext.hacienda.gob.es/sgcief/BDGEL/aspx/default.aspx. Accessed 18 February 2021.

Mur, M. (2011). Una aproximación al sector público empresarial local [An approximation to the local business public sector]. *Revista Española de Control Externo, 13*(38), 135–156.

Pérez-López, G., Prior, D., & Zafra-Gómez, J. L. (2015). Rethinking new public management delivery forms and efficiency: Long-term effects in Spanish local government. *Journal of Public Administration Research and Theory, 25*(4), 1157–1183.

Pérez-López, G., Prior, D., & Zafra-Gómez, J. L. (2018). Temporal scale efficiency in DEA panel data estimations. An application to the solid waste disposal service in Spain. *Omega, 76*, 18–27.

Plata-Díaz, A. M., de la Higuera-Molina, E. J., Garrido-Rodríguez, J. C., & Zafra-Gómez, J. L. (2019). Contracting Out and Social Services: Responses to the Austerity Machine, Financial Condition and Political Parties. *Administration & Society, 51*(6), 951–990.

Plata-Díaz, A. M., Zafra-Gómez, J. L., Pérez-López, G., & López-Hernández, A. M. (2014). Alternative management structures for municipal waste collection services: The influence of economic and political factors. *Waste Management, 34*(11), 1967–1976.

Tavares, A. F. (2017). Ten years after: Revisiting the determinants of the adoption of municipal corporations for local service delivery. *Local Government Studies, 43*(5), 697–706.

Tavares, A. F., & Camões, P. J. (2010). New forms of local governance: A theoretical and empirical analysis of municipal corporations in Portugal. *Public Management Review, 12*(5), 587–608.

TMB. (2019). *Pressupost de TMB 2019 [Budget of TMB 2019]*. Transport Metropolitans de Barcelona.

Torsteinsen, H., & Van Genugten, M. (2016). Municipal waste management in Norway and the Netherlands: From in-house provision to inter-municipal cooperation. In S. Kuhlmann & G. Bouckaert (Eds.), *Local public sector reforms in times of crisis* (pp. 205–220). Palgrave Macmillan.

Van Genugten, M., Van Thiel, S., & Voorn, B. (2020). Local governments and their arm's length bodies. *Local Government Studies, 46*(1), 1–21.

Voorn, B., Van Genugten, M. L., & Van Thiel, S. (2017). The efficiency and effectiveness of municipally owned corporations: A systematic review. *Local Government Studies, 43*(5), 820–841.

Voorn, B., Van Genugten, M., & Van Thiel, S. (2019). Multiple principals, multiple problems: Implications for effective governance and a research agenda for joint service delivery. *Public Administration, 97*(3), 671–685.

Voorn, B., Van Genugten, M., & Van Thiel, S. (2020). Performance of municipally owned corporations: Determinants and mechanisms. *Annals of Public and Cooperative Economics, 91*(2), 191–212.

Zafra-Gómez, J. L., López-Hernández, A. M., Plata-Díaz, A. M., & Garrido-Rodríguez, J. C. (2016). Financial and political factors motivating the privatisation of municipal water services. *Local Government Studies, 42*(2), 287–308.

Zafra-Gómez, J. L., Prior, D., Plata-Díaz, A. M., & López-Hernández, A. (2013). Reducing costs in times of crisis: delivery forms in small and medium sized local governments' waste management services. *Public Administration, 91*(1), 51–68.

CHAPTER 16

Corporatisation in Local Government: The Case of Turkey

Evrim Tan and Irmak Özer

16.1 Context

Turkey is a unitary state with two tiers of administration: the central government and the local government. The state administration is apportioned into 81 provinces, which are headed by an appointed governor. The governor is the highest-ranked representative of the central government in provinces, and its main function is to be a medium between locality and the central authority. Provinces are subdivided into districts, which are headed by appointed district governors (*kaymakams*). Governors and district governors hold more supervisory (e.g. inspection, monitoring) role in local affairs, whereas local governments are responsible for service provisions. Local governments in provinces are governed by elected authorities. The principal local government is the municipality. Local

E. Tan (✉)
KU Leuven, Leuven, Belgium
e-mail: evrim.tan@kuleuven.be

I. Özer
Middle East Technical University, Ankara, Turkey

M. Van Genugten et al. (eds.), *Corporatisation in Local Government*, https://doi.org/10.1007/978-3-031-09982-3_16

governments are administratively categorised according to their area of jurisdiction and the vested autonomy in public services. The four types of local governments are metropolitan municipalities, municipalities, special provincial administrations (SPAs) and village administrations.

As of 2020, 94.4% of the Turkish population lives in municipalities (Turkish Statistical Institute, 2021). Following the municipal amalgamations in 2014, the number of municipalities in Turkey has decreased gradually from 2954 to 1398 (Turkish Statistical Institute, 2021). Thirty metropolitan municipalities have particular jurisdictional powers and structures different from the rest of municipalities. Metropolitan municipalities were established in 1984 for larger urban areas where the population exceeds 750,000 inhabitants. In contrast to other municipalities, metropolitan municipalities have two tiers of administration in which the metropolitan administration (second tier) is vested with the responsibility of coordinating the district municipalities (first tier). Nonetheless, all municipalities share the same responsibilities on public service provision.

The second type of local government, SPAs, is responsible for the provision of services in rural areas outside the jurisdiction of municipalities. SPAs are established following the French *département* system. Similar to the French *département* system, originally the relationship between SPAs and the central government was left ambiguous, and for long, the status of SPAs as local government has been contested given the central government's direct control of the decision-making processes (Tan, 2019). Following the legislative changes in 2003–2005, the governor's discretion in SPA's decision-making processes has been reduced and the autonomy of SPA has been strengthened. SPA has an elected provincial council, but the governor is the official head of SPA. The actual decision-making power is vested in the provincial council, whereas the governor's role in decision-making processes is rather regulatory. Village administrations are another form of local government established in small communities in rural areas. An elected alderman's council and an elected *muhtar*[1] govern them. Although villages are recognised as public organisations subject to the Law on Villages (issued in 1924), they are not allocated financial sources to carry out their own services. Therefore, all public services in villages are delivered by SPAs. The regulative framework for each type of local government is defined by separate laws.

[1] *Muhtar* is a person appointed by way of election by the residents of that village or neighbourhood to carry out the legal affairs of the village or neighbourhood.

Ownership of corporations by the local government is not a recent phenomenon in Turkish public administration. The first examples of corporations that provide public services can be traced back to the 1850s. The first legal clause that grants local authorities to engage in commercial activities through the ownership of corporations is mentioned in 1580-coded Municipality Law[2] in 1930. This clause granted municipalities a *carte blanche* to engage in commercial activities in any area deemed necessary. Nevertheless, the 1930s were also the period when *étatism* was adopted as part of the development strategy. This period marks a peak point of centralism in Turkish public administration both in terms of policy planning and also in economics (Tan, 2019). Therefore, it is pertinent to interpret this clause as part of the state's entrepreneurial role in the private sector domain rather than an enhanced discretion granted to local government. In these years, municipal enterprises are established in public and goods transport services (Yaprak, 2019). The scope of these enterprises has expanded in the following decades into additional sectoral areas such as construction and housing (Yaprak, 2019). In the 1980s, interventionist policies were replaced by neoliberal politics. The legal changes in 1994 opened the door to the privatisation of municipally owned corporations (MOCs), and the establishment of new MOCs has been put under the discretion of the central government (Yaprak, 2019). Even though municipalities had the right to establish and run MOCs, they were required to get the Ministerial Cabinet's permission for such a formation. These policies continued in the following years to break up the monopolies of municipalities in certain services areas (e.g. natural gas distribution) until the overhaul of all Turkish local government legislations in the period of 2003–2008. This period marks a broad reform in the Turkish local government imbued with the New Public Management principles (Tan, 2014). Through the new legislation, both municipalities and SPAs, as well as local government unions, are granted by law to form and own corporations. However, there is not a single piece of legislation that regulates MOCs. For instance, while the Metropolitan Municipality Law permits the establishment of municipal limited liability companies, corporations and limited liability partnerships, the Municipality Law does not include any prescriptive clauses. However, an opinion piece published by the

[2] Article 19 grants municipalities the same commercial rights entitled to privately owned corporations for the delivery of public services required at the locality (Yaprak, 2019).

Ministry of the Interior in 2018,[3] clarifies limited liability companies and corporations are permissible company forms for the municipal ownership for areas with a population higher than 50,000 inhabitants. For the areas with a lesser population and for the local government unions with less than 35 employees, only limited companies are recognised as permissible forms.

MOCs can be established only within the service provision areas delegated to municipalities by law.[4] MOCs can either be established by municipalities or be owned through an endowment.[5] The conditional endowments are subject to the approval of the municipal assembly, whereas unconditional endowments can be carried out with the approval of the mayor (Yaprak, 2019). The establishment of a MOC requires the approval of the decision by the municipal assembly and following the 696-coded decree law in 2019 requires the approval of the Presidential Cabinet. Nonetheless, the existing legislation is not prescriptive in certain forms of corporatisation and the approval of the Presidential Cabinet is interpreted as not necessary for the acquisition of corporations through endowments (Yaprak, 2019) or derivative ownership through MOCs (Demirbaş et al., 2017). For these forms of corporatisation, the municipal assembly's decision is deemed sufficient.

16.2 Trends

Despite the relatively long past of MOCs in Turkey, the public data on MOCs is scarce and scattered across different government databases. One public source is the Presidency of Strategy and Budget[6] established following the 2017 constitutional referendum and the succeeding overhaul of the Turkish government from a parliamentary system to an executive presidency. In this database, public personnel information of MOCs is preserved, but no financial data about MOCs can be found. Another database belongs to the Ministry of Treasury and Finance (MTF), preserving budget data of only affiliated entities but not the rest of the MOCs. The third source of public data is the performance reports published by the Court of

[3] Art. 3 of Ministry of Interior decision no: 85373441-250-E.1075.

[4] Art. 70 in the law no 5393-Municipality Law and Art. 26 in law no 5126-Metropolitan Municipality Law.

[5] Art. 38 in the law no 5393-Municipality Law.

[6] The databases of the former Ministry of Development and the budget directorate of the Ministry of Finance merged within the new administration.

Accounts (CoA), which is legally responsible for auditing MOCs.[7] However, the performance reports on MOCs are limited[8] and precede only until 2012. These reports contain the most comprehensive information about MOCs, but they rely on the self-declaration of municipalities, and our inquiry with CoA officials suggests that it is not certain of the total number of MOCs in Turkey.

Acknowledging these limitations, we have compiled a new dataset on MOCs from the aforementioned governmental sources as well as by tracing the publicly available information found on the websites of municipalities. Based on this dataset, as of 2020, there are a total of 489 MOCs in Turkey.[9] Through these sources, we were able to collect information about the equity shares owned by municipalities, partnership structure, accountability mechanisms, foundation year, legal status, service areas, board structure, compositions of the supervisory and executive board. However, personnel data and financial data, including the salary structures, are mostly kept discreet. As of 2019, only 24 corporations share financial information about their revenues and expenditures in publicly available sources.

Figure 16.1 presents the MOCs in Turkey according to their year of foundation. The findings show that there is an upward trend in the foundation of new MOCs from 2010 onward, both for metropolitan municipalities and other municipalities. In the decade following 2009, the total number of MOCs in Turkey has almost doubled with a steep increase in the number of corporations owned by both metropolitan and other types of municipalities.

The only publicly available data about the personnel numbers of MOCs is kept as aggregate data in central government sources. Figure 16.2 presents the change in the active public personnel numbers employed in municipalities and MOCs. The blue column indicates the total public personnel employed in municipalities, municipality unions and the affiliated

[7] Art. 4 in law no 6085-Court of Audit Law (enacted in 2010) states that all public entities and their affiliated entities and corporations are subject to the public auditing laws.

[8] According to the CoA reports, since 2012, more than 300 corporations that are registered as MOC in municipality performance reports have never been audited.

[9] We acknowledge that some MOCs listed in our database might be in the process of dissolution. However, our inquiry at CoA suggests that dissolution of MOCs often takes a few years and therefore, we infer that this database represents the closest to the list of active MOCs in Turkey.

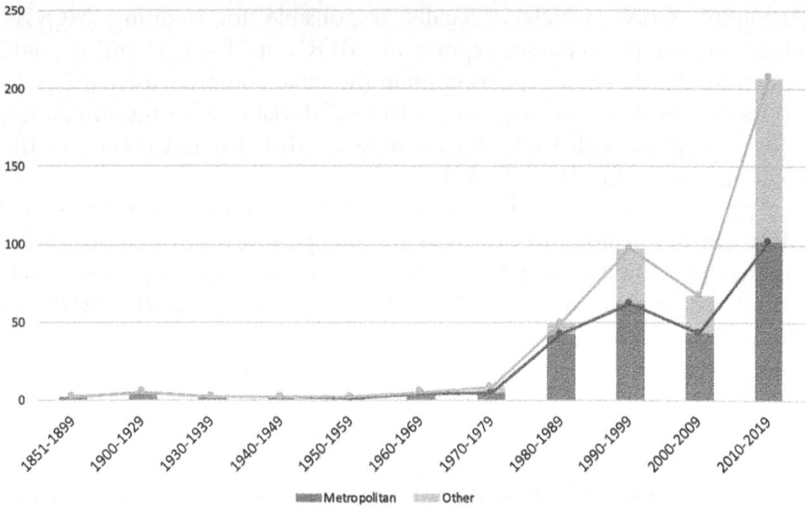

Fig. 16.1 MOCs in Turkey according to the year of foundation

entity[10] of municipalities. The orange column indicates the number of public personnel employed in MOCs. The trend in public personnel numbers indicates from 2015 onwards, the public personnel employment in MOCs has risen steeply and currently the public personnel employed in corporations double the personnel employed in municipalities, affiliated entities and municipal unions. We expect this steep rise after 2015 to be closely related to the 696-coded presidential decree that came into force in 2017 and enforced all subcontracted personnel contracted for municipal services to be employed as public personnel in owned corporations. This decree specifically aimed for the employment of workers that were employed in continuous tasks for municipalities in areas such as garbage collection, gardening and other maintenance services. Those municipalities without a previously owned corporation are recommended to open new corporations to provide such services. Consequently, with the decision of the Presidential Cabinet in March 2018, 845 new MOCs were

[10] In our research, we categorised affiliated entities as MOCs whose corporate status is legislated by public law. Affiliated entities are headed by the mayor, but they are independent organisations with a separate budget from the municipality. In this database, the personnel number of affiliated entities, municipalities, and their unions are registered cumulatively.

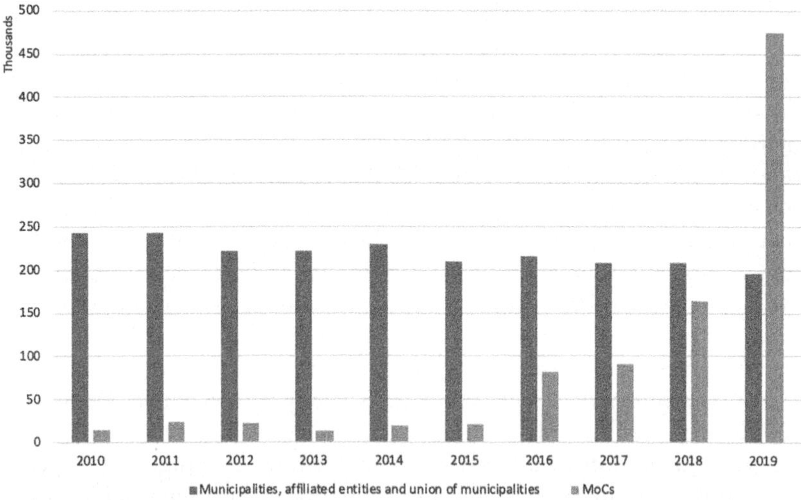

Fig. 16.2 Personnel employment in MOCs and local government (Source: Turkish Presidency of Strategy and Budget, 2021)

established. Figure 16.2 shows a clear divergence between the trends of public personnel employment in municipalities and MOCs. While the public personnel employment in municipalities, affiliated entities and their unions follows a decreasing trend, the weight of MOCs in public personnel employment has increased abruptly, accommodating more than two-thirds of all public personnel employed currently in the Turkish local government.

16.3 Legal Status

The local government laws are prescriptive that all local governments and their associations can establish corporations and hold shares in corporations for public service delivery. However, these laws are not prescriptive about the legal scope nor the status of these corporations. In the absence of a clear legal definition of MOCs, the jurisprudence of administrative courts and the practices of public entities have been suggestive of the legal status of MOCs. Consequently, the legal status and thus the obligations of MOCs according to public law have been subject to wider debates among public law and public administration scholars.

The first group of scholars (e.g. Gözler, 2018; İsbir, 2017; Zabunoğlu, 2012) considers MOCs as a public sector organisation. In this reading, a MOC is recognised as the extension of municipalities in public service provision—a right granted upon them through respective legislation, and thereby MOCs are subject to public law. The second group of scholars (e.g. Sevgili Gençay, 2018; Özdemir, 2011; Kavruk, 2005), on the contrary, considers MOCs as private sector organisations, emphasising the fact that they are established according to the clauses of Commercial Law, and they are for-profit organisations. The third group of scholars (e.g. Ulusoy, 2017; Demirkaya, 2010; Tortop, 1998; Dilbirliği, 1995) considers MOCs as *sui generis* organisations with attributes to both public and private law, yet without any consensus on their legal status. For instance, while Ulusoy (2017) recognises their legal status both as private and public, Demirkaya (2010) does not include them in either of the categories, calling them unique organisational entities. In another reading, Dilbirliği (1995) posits that MOCs should be treated as private entities concerning public auditing regulations, even though they use public money through the ownership of municipalities and their personnel falls under the scope of the Public Pension Fund.

The confusion about the legal status of MOCs is not limited only to the academic circles. For instance, a public inquiry in 2009 by the general directorate of population and citizenship affairs asks the Ministry of Interior (MoI) to clarify whether MOCs are public sector organisations by law (Yaprak, 2019). In the answer, MOCs are interpreted as private sector organisations notwithstanding the percentage of shares held by municipalities.[11] This interpretation consequently suggests that MOCs should be exempted from public auditing regulations. Nonetheless, in the Law of Court of Accounts enacted in 2010, MOCs are recognised as public sector organisations falling under the purview of CoA.

Similarly, the legal inquiries[12] to the Court of Cassation (CoC) and Council of State about their legal status suggest that up until 2011, the Courts interpreted MOCs as not public sector organisations regardless of the percentage of share held by municipalities. However, it seems like this view has changed following the Law of the Court of Accounts. In a suit for damage against the Ankara Metropolitan Municipality, the prosecutor

[11] Ministry of Interior, No: B.05.0.M.A.H. 0.01.01.00/6546-45,150, Date: 12 March 2009.

[12] A list of legal decisions published by these Courts can be found in Yaprak (2019: 55–57).

of CoC interpreted owning a majority share brings executive responsibilities such as designating the members of the executive board, and thereby the libellee MOC becomes an extension of the municipality.[13] This creates a liability to the municipality against the claimants, albeit the MOC operates under private law. This legal interpretation suggests that in case the MOC is controlled by the majority share of a municipality, the MOC is subjected to public law.

In this given context, it is difficult to categorise MOCs in Turkey according to their public or private law status. However, the legislative framework and the jurisprudence of the Courts suggest that there are different categories of MOCs according to the executive relationships with the principal municipality. Following this logic, we have clustered MOCs in Turkey under three categories.

i. *Affiliated entities:* These entities are legally called affiliated entities of municipalities and their corporate status is 'General Directorate'. Affiliated entities are autonomous organisations outside of the municipality's organisational hierarchy. However, the full ownership of these entities belongs to the municipality, and the municipal assembly acts as the general assembly of the corporation.[14] For the moment, there are a total of 33 affiliated entities, all owned by metropolitan municipalities. Affiliated entities are established by law and their public law status is not disputed. The provision of water and sanitation services within the metropolitan municipal borders[15] is delegated to the affiliated entities. Today there are a total of 30 affiliated entities in charge of the water and sanitation services within the metropolitan municipality jurisdictional areas. The other affiliated entities are Ankara Electricity, Gas, and Bus General Directorate, Istanbul Electricity, Tram, and Tunnel Management General Directorate, and Izmir Electricity, Water, Gas, Bus and Tram General Directorate.
ii. *Majority shareholder:* In this category, municipalities control the majority share of the corporation either by direct ownership or by indirect ownership through another MOC. MOCs, whose majority

[13] Court of Disputes, Case no: 2013/1287 E., 2013/1771.

[14] Law no 2560, Art. 4.

[15] In 2014, the metropolitan municipality borders were extended to the provincial administrative borders.

share owned by municipalities, are subject to different regulations and practices concerning public laws.[16] However, the regulations are not prescriptive about the public law status of these corporations. Therefore, these corporations best fit the *sui generis* description by their legal status. By public laws, direct and indirect ownership of a corporation does not make a difference concerning the scope of public laws. The most important criterion appears to be whether the equity share owned by municipalities exceeds 50%. The indirect ownership can still create, nonetheless, certain advantages to the municipality in executive decision-making processes. For instance, the commerce law obliges all shareholder organisations in unlimited companies to be represented in the general shareholders' meeting. As such, indirect ownership may create some advantages for the municipality during the selection of the executive board. Or municipalities might find it easier to implement company acquisition decisions through the executive channels of owned corporations.

iii. *Minority shareholder:* In this category, municipalities own a share in the corporation but do not control the majority share. According to the revised articles of the Court of Accounts Law, these corporations are still considered as MOCs and within the scope of public audit provisions. However, the discretion of CoA is very limited over the finances of minority shareholder companies, and many loopholes and legal contradictions make these corporations in practice outside the scope of public law. Besides, none of the other legislations (e.g. public employment, public tenders, etc.) apply to these corporations. Therefore, these corporations act like any other profit-based organisation.

Figure 16.3 shows the distribution of MOCs according to this categorisation. Following Van Genugten et al. (2020)'s typology on arm's length bodies at the local level, whilst affiliated entities can best be categorised as Type II organisations, the rest of the MOCs fit to Type 3 entities. The most common form is a direct majority share ownership by municipalities. The findings suggest that municipalities opt for direct ownership over indirect forms of ownership. Furthermore, in about 23% of MOCs,

[16] These rules and regulations are elaborated further in Sect. 16.5.

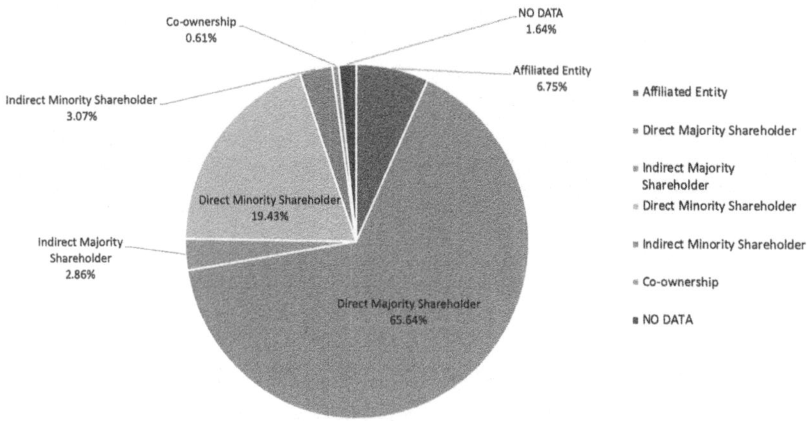

Fig. 16.3 MOCs according to the type of municipal ownership

municipalities do not own a majority share, but they are minority shareholders or equal shareholders with other public and private entities.

16.4 Background Characteristics

The service areas of MOCs in Turkey show a great variety, and excluding affiliated entities, many MOCs are active in multiple sectoral areas. As mentioned before, affiliated entities provide services in specific service areas. The majority of these entities (90%) provide water and sanitation services, and the remaining three provide services in transportation and gas distribution. Excluding the affiliated entities, Fig. 16.4 shows the sectoral outlook of MOCs. The numbers show the percentage of MOCs that are active in the given sectoral area. The majority of the MOCs (51.54%) is active in more than one sectoral area, therefore, the sum of percentages exceeds a hundred per cent. The two areas where MOCs are mostly active are social services (52.85%) and commerce (47.15%). The social services include companies that provide personnel, training and cleaning services to municipalities. This suggests that a significant share of MOCs serves the organisational needs of municipalities. Commerce and industry[17] (29.39%) are other popular areas for MOCs' activities. Commerce and industry companies are mostly established to generate additional revenues for

[17] The industry sector does not include energy provider companies.

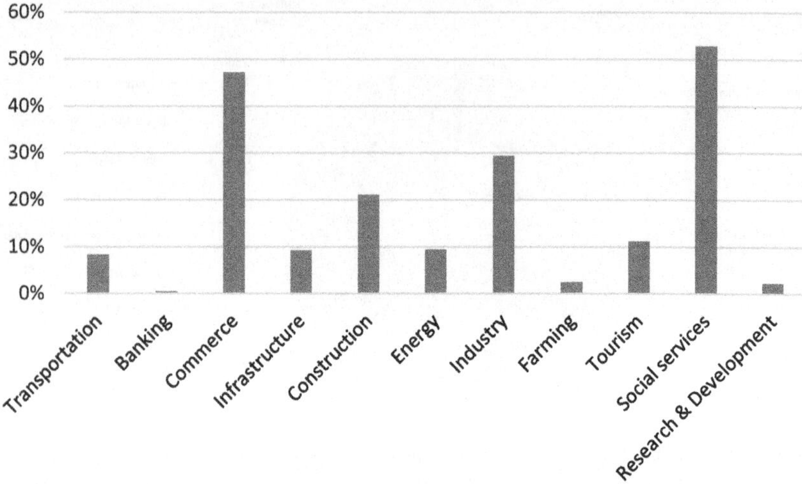

Fig. 16.4 MOCs according to sectoral areas (Affiliated entities are not included)

municipalities. By taking into account these findings, we assess that most MOCs in Turkey serve the organisational and financial needs of municipalities rather than service provision.

Most of the MOCs (57.67%) in Turkey provide services in multiple areas varying from two to six service areas. With more than half of the MOCs, the most prominent service area for multi-purpose MOCs is the commerce sector. The majority of single-purpose MOCs (55.71%) is active in social services (e.g. personnel, cleaning, training and sociocultural services). The prominence of the social service among single-purpose MOCs is related to the 696 decree law, which led to the foundation of an additional 845 MOCs to provide personnel services to the municipalities.[18]

Precisely 48.37% of MOCs in Turkey are owned solely by a municipality without any partnership. While 24.19% of MOCs do not provide any data about their partnership status, the remainder is distributed over four partnership types: public-private partnership (22.56%); a municipal partnership between at least two municipalities (2.44%); a mixed form of partnership including a municipal partnership and private shareholders

[18] Precisely 845 Municipality Personnel Corporations were founded in 2018 as a result of the 21 March 2018 dated decision of the Council of Ministers.

(0.20%); and public-public partnership (2.24%) where public sector organisations outside municipalities hold the partner status.

It is difficult to estimate the size of MOCs in Turkey, as there is limited publicly available financial and personnel data. In our dataset, there are only 35 MOCs besides affiliated entities sharing the total personnel numbers. According to the threshold conditions set by the 2018 presidential decree, 21 of these corporations can be considered as large as they employ more than 125 employees. Yet, given the weight of the public personnel employment in MOCs (see Fig. 16.1) and the share of MOCs that provides personnel services to the municipalities, we can suggest that most MOCs in Turkey are large according to the employed personnel.

16.5 Autonomy and Legislation

The data on MOCs suggest that there is a growing trend in the share of MOCs in public employment and public service provision. This growing trend is assumed to be closely related to the operational and managerial advantages of the corporate law to which MOCs are subjected. For instance, according to the Municipality Law,[19] municipalities are allowed to form private corporations for more efficient, economical and faster service provisions and to assist revenue generation. Similarly, the eighth five-year development plan emphasises the advantages of MOCs as 'cutting the red tape, benefiting from the market advantages and managerial practices in the private sector, enjoying flexible employment and wage regulations, freeing from the administrative tutelage of the central government, retrieving the public funds that normally go to private companies through tenders by the way of owned corporations, utilising local opportunities by way of facilitating local participation and mobilising local capital, and creating new employment opportunities'.

In addition to the managerial flexibility, it appears that political motivations also play a role in the establishment of MOCs. For instance, Dilbirliği (1995) suggests that municipalities establish corporations to create employment for political reasons and to leave a visible mark as a political advertising tool. Demirbaş et al. (2017) also argue that the appointment decisions to the executive board of MOCs are used as a salary boost to the personnel and thus allow a tighter control by the senior management over the executive decisions of MOCs. Similarly, in a survey conducted with

[19] Art. 70.

heads of units of MOCs, the results suggest that the autonomy of MOCs is often undermined by the political interventions and influences (Bektaş & Olgun, 2017). Some salient results about the most important of MOCs are: 'political and other interest relations heavily influence personnel employment resulting in inadequate work performance (26.3%)', 'excessive intervention of politicians in the executive decisions (21.1%)', 'the managerial attitude reminiscent of public administration impedes the dynamism of private sector (15.8%)', and 'the inadequacy of executives and personnel (10.6%)'. These results suggest that in a majority of MOCs, the political tutelage of municipalities and political parties appears to be highly influential on MOCs' operations, undermining any supposedly managerial advantage brought by the corporate law.

Besides the tutelage of political actors over the operations, MOCs are also subjected to particular public law provisions, unlike regular private sector organisations. In short, the autonomies of MOCs are regulated in the following areas with respective legal provisions.

1. *Personnel employment:* The legal provisions regulating personnel employment in affiliated entities and other MOCs differ. The affiliated entities are regulated by public law, and as such, they abide by the rules for public personnel employment and pensions. Furthermore, the personnel quota of affiliated entities is decided by the municipal assembly.[20] For the rest of MOCs, private law regulations apply in personnel employment and wage arrangements.

   However, the 696-coded presidential decree in 2017 had impacted the autonomy of MOCs whose majority ownership belongs to municipalities. Before this decree law, many municipalities were hiring subcontracted personnel through private companies, especially in areas such as parks and gardening services, garbage collection, and other maintenance services. Through this decree, subcontracting of personnel for continuous tasks in such service areas has been banned for municipalities and corporations whose majority share is owned by municipalities (Art. 83). This decree also obliges the employment of such personnel as workers according to the rules of public employment (Art. 112 and Art. 113). This decree brings flexibility to municipalities to employ the personnel in corporations whose majority share is owned by the municipality and

[20] Law no 5393-Municipality Law, Art. 49.

providing personnel services. In return, these services provided by these companies to municipalities have become exempt from the provisions of the 4774-coded Public Tender Law[21] and the VAT for the related services provided to municipalities adjusted from 18% to 1%.[22] As a consequence of the decree, the MOCs providing personnel services in social service areas have lost their flexibility and partial autonomy in terms of labour issues.

2. *Executive relationship:* Similar to personnel employment, there are different rules for affiliated entities and other corporations for their executive decisions. By law, the mayor is the head of the affiliated entity and is responsible for monitoring all financial and managerial activities.[23] The mayor appoints the executive board in affiliated entities.[24] The mayor can also approve the budget transfers between affiliated entities and metropolitan municipality.[25]

   Unlike affiliated entities, there are not many provisions in the legislative framework regulating the executive relationship between municipalities and owned corporations. 657-coded Civil Servants Law[26] states that municipalities can appoint civil servants as representatives in the general assembly and the executive board of MOCs. However, the Metropolitan Municipality Law[27] states that only the personnel employed in a managerial position in municipalities and affiliated entities can have a seat in the executive and supervisory boards of MOCs. A possible interpretation of this law is that except for the corporations owned by metropolitan municipalities, civil servants outside management can also be appointed as municipal representatives.

   Nonetheless, the legislative regulations are not prescriptive about the selection of the people to represent the municipality in MOCs. Especially, following the shift of Istanbul and Ankara metropolitan municipalities from the Justice and Development Party to opposition parties after the 2019 local elections, this legal ambiguity has become an instrument of a political struggle between the government

[21] Additional clause-20.
[22] Law no 7153, Art. 68.
[23] Law no 5126-Metropolitan Municipality Law, Art. 18.
[24] Law no 2560, Art. 7.
[25] Ibid., Art. 27.
[26] Law no 6085-Court of Audit Law, Art. 28.
[27] Law no 5126-Metropolitan Municipality Law, Art. 26.

and opposition parties. An appointment decision taken by the new mayor of Ankara to a corporation owned by the municipality has been declined for approval by the company registration bureau in Ankara. The refusal decision has been warranted to a 2019 memorandum of the Ministry of Environment and Urbanisation suggesting that the persons who will represent the municipality or its affiliated organisation in the general assembly of municipal companies must be determined by the decision of the municipal council. In the following lawsuit, the commercial court decreed in favour of the municipality, setting a precedent for other cases. However, this decision was later taken to the Court of Appeal, which reversed the decision of the commercial court obligating the municipal assembly's approval for selections to the executive board of MOCs (Haberler.com, 2021).

3. *Public auditing:* Regardless of the percentage of shares owned by the municipality, all MOCs are subject to public audits. The Court of Accounts Law had initially vested the CoA with the auditing responsibility of corporations whose majority share is owned by public sector organisations. However, following the 2016 revisions,[28] this specification has been removed from the Law and all corporations with a share owned by public sector organisations have been brought under the purview of the CoA. The public audit provisions oblige the CoA to monitor the financial and performance reports of any corporation where municipalities own equity shares. Yet, the administrative procedure of audits varies between majority and minority shareholder MOCs. By law,[29] the CoA can audit directly majority shareholder corporations. For minority shareholder corporations, the CoA can only ask for an independent auditor report.[30] In practice, however, auditing minority shareholder companies appear to be cumbersome due to the unwillingness of these corporations to cooperate due to their disagreement about the jurisdiction of the Court to audit a corporate law-bound company. Relatedly, the presidential decree in 2018[31] states that only the majority shareholder MOCs that meet two out of three threshold condi-

[28] Art.3, footnote 2.
[29] Art. 4, additional paragraph no: 14/1/2016-6661/19, ibid.
[30] Art. 4 of 6085-coded Court of Audit Law.
[31] Decree No: 2018/11597.

tions[32] in two consecutive annual budget periods are required to provide an independent auditing report. This regulative contradiction seemingly creates disputes about the legal obligations of minority shareholder corporations towards CoA. Our inquiry with CoA officials suggests that these legal contradictions have been brought to the presidential cabinet for further clarifications. Furthermore, 6012-coded Trade Law[33] obliges all corporations that require independent auditing to share the report with the corporation's general assembly. In short, both private and public law regulations provide a stricter financial control mechanism over majority ownership corporations. However, MOCs are not subject to the provisions of 5018-coded Public Financial Management and Control Law. Therefore, in case of an irregularity, the CoA cannot open a public loss case against the corporation. In these cases, the CoA can warn the corporations and ask the municipality to sell its share or close the corporation. However, within the current legislative framework, the enforcement of the Court over the corporations is limited.

4. *Public tenders:* The affiliated entities and majority shareholder corporations are subject to 4734-coded Public Tender Law[34] and 4735-coded Public Tender Contracts Law.[35] Accordingly, these corporations should abide by the public tender rules in goods and service purchases. However, article 3(g) of Public Tender Law exempts majority shareholder companies from public tender regulations for purchases that do not exceed a specific amount.[36] For 2021, this amount is set at about 19 million Turkish lira,[37] which corresponds to about 2 million euros. There are also some exemptions recognised for the corporations owned by metropolitan municipalities providing services on public transportation, construction yards, community facilities, car parks and other social service areas.[38] Moreover, article 26 of Public Tender Contracts Law recognises the

[32] The threshold conditions are the total value of assets should be at least 30 million Turkish lira (TL), total annual revenues should be at least 40 million TL, and total personnel number should be at least 125.

[33] Art 397 (2).

[34] Art. 2 (d).

[35] Art. 26.

[36] This number is revised every year by rescript.

[37] 11 March 2021, Euro/TL exchange rate.

[38] Art. 26 of 5216-coded Metropolitan Municipality Law.

discretion of the Minister of Environment and Urbanisation over affiliated entities and majority shareholder corporations on banning service providers that are found guilty according to the Law's provisions[39] from entering public tenders.

5. *Reporting:* All MOCs are obliged to keep the minutes of the general assembly meetings and prepare annual activity reports that contain financial status and the salaries and financial benefits provided to corporate managers. The reporting obligations are derived from the provisions of Trade Law,[40] as well as public auditing provisions that apply for eligible MOCs. However, salary information and financial benefits are rarely included in the publicly available activity reports. Among 489 investigated MOCs, 10.63% of MOCs provide their annual activity reports on their websites; 4.29% reported the corporate managers' salaries and 2.25% reported the overall salaries and financial benefits provided to corporate managers. Unlike other MOCs, all affiliated entities make their annual activity reports publicly available and shares the salary information of the personnel. According to the CoA officials, MOCs are reluctant to share the managers' salary information publicly. Furthermore, all MOCs are legally required to provide financial information (ledger and daybook) to the Ministry of Finance. There are two digital systems to enter the financial information that varies between affiliated entities and other MOCs. Affiliated entities are financially dependent on the national budget. Therefore, they are obliged to use the Public Expenditure and Accounting Information System. The rest of the MOCs is required to use the e-Ledger system according to the 6012-coded Trade Law. However, according to the CoA officials, MOCs have problems in using the recently developed e-Ledger system. To facilitate this transition process, the CoA provides workshops in partnership with the Union of Municipalities of Turkey.
6. *Fiscal autonomy:* The affiliated entities and majority shareholder corporations are categorised as public sector organisations in the Public Treasurership Regulation.[41] This regulation sets some restrictions on public sector organisations for saving and investing public money. For example, all public sector organisations are obliged to use their

[39] Art. 25.
[40] Art. 514.
[41] Regulation no: 810, approved in March 2019.

financial resources only through the fiscal tools provided by public banks.[42] Although these regulations do not exclude using private banks or foreign banks for the transfer of funds for service provision and tender processes, they compel MOCs to open saving accounts in public banks. Secondly, the provisions set restrictions and conditions on opening foreign currency accounts. Opening foreign currency accounts and exchanging capital into foreign currencies are specified as 'if deemed necessary and to the extent of their needs'. This vague definition gives discretion to the central government on the fiscal management of all public sector organisations. It is important to interpret these provisions within the context of the fiscal strain[43] that the Turkish government has experienced in the aftermath of the 2017 referendum. This referendum has revamped the Turkish public administration from a parliamentary system to an executive presidency.

16.6 Board Structure

The 5393-coded Municipality Law keeps affiliated entities subject to the standards set for internal[44] and external auditing.[45] Even though the decision of setting up a supervisory board is left to the discretion of the executive board, all affiliated entities have supervisory boards according to the codes set by the general assembly compatible with public standards, with independent regulations created by their general assemblies. However, there is no available information regarding the composition of supervisory boards except for the head of the supervisory board. For the rest of the MOCs, there is not a specific provision under public law for setting up a

[42] Art. 5 (2).

[43] From April 2017 until the enactment of this regulation in 2019, the Turkish lira has devalued against the euro and US dollar about 65%.

[44] According to the 5018-coded Law, article 63, internal auditing is 'an independent, objective assurance and consultancy activity to evaluate and guide whether the resources are managed according to the principles of economy, effectiveness, and efficiency to add value and improve the work of the public administration. These activities are carried out with a systematic, continuous, and disciplined approach to evaluate and improve the administrations' management and control structures and the risk management of financial transactions, management and control processes, and following generally accepted standards'.

[45] According to the 5018-coded Law, article 68, the post-expenditure external audit is carried out by the Court of Accounts for compliance with the goals and plans as set by the central government.

supervisory board. The supervision (i.e. inspection and auditing) of these MOCs falls under the 6012-coded Trade Law. According to the law, the Presidential Cabinet decides on the companies to be supervised by independent auditors.[46] The rules of supervision are set by the law. The supervisory process is carried out under the Turkish Auditing Standards, in line with the international standards, issued by the Public Oversight, Accounting, and Auditing Standards Authority. Independent supervisors have been chosen by the company's general assembly to carry out the companies' supervision.[47] The law also obliges the auditors (including independent auditors) to either be certified public accountants or be independent accountants and financial advisors/companies authorised by the Public Oversight, Accounting and Auditing Standards Authority.[48] However, there are no prescriptive provisions on the rules of establishment for a supervisory board nor its composition.

In line with this regulative framework about supervision, the number of tiers varies between affiliated entities and the rest of the MOCs in terms of board structure. Whilst all affiliated entities have two-tier boards (i.e. an executive board and a supervisory board), the majority of the remaining MOCs has a one-tier board. Among the 244 MOCs, including affiliated entities that share information about their board structure on their websites, a one-tier board structure (200) prevails over a two-tier board structure (44). A total of 217 MOCs, including affiliated entities, share information about their executive boards' composition. Among those, 92.63% contains at least one civil servant in the executive board followed by external experts (46.54%) and political party representatives (10.60%). There is no specific information, however, for 95.91%[49] of the MOCs about the composition of their supervisory board. Among the few MOCs that share information, supervisory boards with only civil servants (3.27%) are more common than those that are composed of both civil servants and external experts (0.61%) and only external experts (0.20%). As stated in the 6012-coded Trade Law, these civil servants and external experts are either certified public or independent accountants or financial advisors/companies.

[46] Law no 6012-Trade Law, article 397, additional paragraphs 4 and 5.

[47] Ibid., Art. 399.

[48] Ibid., Art. 400.

[49] This percentage includes the MOCs that share no organisational charts and those that share their organisational charts but do not provide any information about their supervisory boards' composition on their websites.

The lack of publicly available information prevents the extrapolation of reliable trends about the MOC's board structure formation in Turkey. Notwithstanding, our dataset points out that except for the affiliated entities, MOCs in Turkey opt for a one-tier board structure. While a generalisation is difficult given the scarce data, in the composition of supervisory boards, civil servants prevail over external experts. As MOCs' external auditing depends on the documents provided through the internal auditing process, the absence of a supervisory board creates further public auditing problems for the CoA.

16.7 Executive Director

Mayors are the executive director of affiliated entities.[50] The mayor's executive power over an affiliated entity is checked by the municipal assembly. For other MOCs, the executive power is divided between the head of the executive board and the general director. The head of the executive board represents the corporation, whereas the general director administers the corporation. The head of the executive board is elected by the executive board, and the main responsibility of the executive board is to oversee the activities of the corporation. However, the head of the executive board cannot request financial and administrative information outside the board meetings.[51] The general director presides over the general assembly of the company and manages the day-to-day business.

There is scarce publicly available information about the executive boards of MOCs. About 62% of investigated MOCs does not disclose any information about their executive board. For those that share information, the professional background of the head of the executive board and general directors varies exclusively in the following areas: municipality administration (15.75%), public sector (7.98%), business (7.57%) and political party (1.23%). The political affiliation of executive directors is another area with scarce information, rarely any information is shared on the website of corporations. However, based on the publicly available information on the Internet, about 8% of the executive directors are affiliated with a political party. This number just gives an estimation, it does not necessarily indicate the level of politicisation among executive directors.

[50] Law no: 2560, article 7.

[51] Law no 6012-Trade Law, article 392(5).

The salary information of executive directors is rarely shared in publicly available sources. As mentioned before, affiliated entity personnel is subject to public personnel regulations.[52] For each fiscal period, the Ministry of Finance sets a base salary for public personnel based on several criteria such as seniority and education level. For 2019, the base salary is set as 11,690 TL[53] for the general directors in public personnel status. Except for the public personnel, there is no legal limit set for the salaries of MOCs' personnel. Furthermore, executive directors do not have a fixed monthly salary. Instead, they are entitled to an attendance fee for the executive board meetings, which is decided by the corporation's general assembly. According to the available data, the highest amount earmarked for an attendance fee was 13,000 TL[54] in 2019.

16.8 Conclusion

The findings in Turkey suggest that the importance of MOCs in Turkish public administration and public sector employment have increased significantly from 2010 onwards. In one decade, the number of MOCs has doubled, and most of the employment at local government shifted to MOCs. Despite the growing importance of MOCs in the public sector, the public data about MOCs are conspicuously absent, and there are many loopholes and contradictions in the regulations. The information gap and the legal complexity surrounding the MOCs seem to be associated with several issues. First of all, the prescriptive legal code inherent in the Napoleonic public administration system (Tan, 2014) appears to mismatch with the regulatory flexibility aimed through corporatisation. Especially, this mismatch becomes more salient if a municipality shares the ownership of the corporations. These corporations operate in practice outside the purview of the auditing institutions and the transparency rules set for the public sector organisations. For instance, our inquiry at the CoA suggests that not all MOCs are aware of their responsibility towards CoA, and not all of them are willing to share their financial records. Combined with the lack of resources and enforcement mechanisms, more than 300 MOCs have never been audited by the CoA, according to the performance reports.

[52] Law no 657-Public Personnel Law and Law no 2560, article 1.

[53] According to the 2019 Euro/TL average exchange rate, this amount is about 1950 euros.

[54] According to the 2019 Euro/TL average exchange rate, this amount is about 2150 euros.

Secondly, the legal complexity appears to be augmented by the constitutional changes following the 2017 referendum. The newly created Presidential Cabinet incorporated the executive powers of the abolished Council of Ministers and the presidential decrees have become the main tools for legislative actions. Despite the heterodoxy about the juridical pre-eminence of legislations over presidential decrees (e.g. Gözler, 2019; Özbudun, 2018; Yıldırım, 2017), the deterioration of institutional checks and balances in the aftermaths of the referendum seemingly adding up to the regulative ambiguity surrounding the administrative and judicial institutions.

Thirdly, and relatedly to the former point, the control of corporations owned by the metropolitan municipalities has become a highly politicised issue following the 2019 local elections. The local election results led to the change of leadership in the metropolitan municipalities of Istanbul and Ankara to opposition leaders for the first time since the start of the Justice and Development Party (AKP) government in 2002. Presidential decrees and administrative decisions taken by the central government created stricter control mechanisms for MOCs and curbed the executive power of mayors on owned corporations in favour of municipal assemblies. The political motivation behind these legislative changes has been publicly expressed by president Erdoğan shortly after the elections implying that the political majority in the municipal assemblies of Istanbul and Ankara are controlled by the AKP members, and thereby the mayors will be 'lame ducks' (Ahval News, 2019). For instance, as mentioned earlier, the 2019 memorandum of the Ministry of Environment and Urbanisation opined that the approval of the municipal assembly is warranted for any appointment decisions to the MOCs. Despite the initial rejection by the commercial court, the appeal decision of the Court of Appeal cemented this statement that undercuts the control of mayors over the owned corporations. Furthermore, an official statement shared by the Ministry of Treasury and Finance in March 2021 requests all local government authorities to share the information of majority shareholder corporations, including the share of capital, personnel numbers and budget information with the Ministry until the end of the month (Official Gazette, 2021). We infer from our findings that MOCs in Turkey operated for long under the radar of the auditing institutions despite the regulatory changes since 2011, but only after the shift of power in key metropolitan municipalities from AKP to opposition parties, the central government has started to tighten up the financial and administrative control on MOCs. For the moment, there is an absence of publicly available information to assess the financial and political importance of MOCs for municipalities, but the political manoeuvres initiated by the central government suggest that the importance of MOCs for municipalities is more than it catches the eye. Further research to understand the politicisation of MOCs and the financial importance of MOCs for metropolitan municipalities is highly recommended to understand the beneath the surface relationships between the municipalities and their owned corporations.

References

Ahval News. (2019, April 4). *Turkey's Erdoğan calls elected opposition mayors lame ducks.* https://ahvalnews.com/ekrem-imamoglu/turkeys-erdogan-calls-elected-opposition-mayors-lame-ducks.

Bektaş, M., & Olgun, I. (2017). Belediye Şirketleri ve İştirakleri [Municipal corporations and affiliates]. In H. Ateş & M. Bıyıkoğlu (Eds.), *Belediye Yönetimi ve Kamusal İlişkiler* (pp. 225–265). Derya yayınevi.

Demirbaş, T., Çetinkaya, Ö., Güneş, V., & Bektaş, N. B. (2017). Yeni Kamu İşletmeciliği Bakış Açısıyla Türkiye'de Belediyelerin Şirket Yoluyla Hizmet Sunma Modelinin İncelenmesi [An investigation of the model of municipalities to provide services through companies in Turkey from the perspective of New Public Management]. *Journal of Administrative Sciences, 15*(30), 145–175.

Demirkaya, Y. (2010). Avrupa Birliği'nin Yerel Kamu Şirketleri Stratejisi: Türkiye'de Hukuki Yapı ve İstanbul Büyükşehir Belediyesi Uygulamaları [Local public companies strategy of the European Union: Legal structure in Turkey and Istanbul metropolitan municipality practices]. *Mustafa Kemal University Journal of Social Sciences Institute, 7*(13), 420–444.

Dilbirliği, M. (1995). Belediye Şirketleri [Municipal corporations]. *Çağdaş Yerel Yönetimler Dergisi, 4*(2), 65–80.

Gözler, K. (2018). *Mahalli İdareler Hukuku [Law of Local Administrations]* (1st ed.). Ekin Yayınevi.

Gözler, K. (2019). *Türk Anayasa Hukuku [Turkish Constitutional Law]* (3rd ed.). Ekin Yayınevi.

Haberler.com. (2021, March 15). *Danıştay son noktayı koydu! Belediye Başkanları atama yaparken meclise soracak [The Council of State put the last point! Mayors will ask the council when appointing].* https://www.haberler.com/guncel/danistay-son-noktayi-koydu-belediye-baskanlari-13995720-haberi/.

İsbir, B. (2017). *Kamu Tüzel Kişileri [Statutory bodies].* Turhan Kitabevi.

Kavruk, H. (2005). Yerel Yönetim Şirketleri [Local government corporations]. In H. Özgür & M. Kösecik (Eds.), *Yerel Yönetimler Üzerine Güncel Yazılar 1: Reform* (pp. 421–448). Nobel Akademik Yayıncılık.

Official Gazette. (2021). *Kamu İşletmelerinin Faaliyetlerinin İzlenmesi ve Raporlanmasına Dair Tebliğ [Communique on monitoring and reporting the activities of public enterprises].* No. 31418. https://www.resmigazete.gov.tr/eskiler/2021/03/20210309-7.htm. Accessed 27 April 2022.

Özbudun, E. (2018). *Türk Anayasa Hukuku [Turkish constitutional law]* (18th ed.). Yetkin Yayınları.

Özdemir, G. (2011). Belediye İktisadi Teşebbüslerinin Kuruluş Amacı, Hukuki Dayanakları ve Güncel Durum [Establishment purpose, legal basis and current situation of municipal economic enterprises]. *Selçuk Üniversitesi İİBF Sosyal ve Ekonomik Araştırmalar Dergisi, 15*(21), 59–80.

Sevgili Gençay, F. D. (2018). Belediye İktisadi Teşebbüslerinin Hukuki Statüsü [Legal status of municipal economic enterprises]. *Türkiye Barolar Birliği Dergisi, 134*, 153–176.

Tan, E. (2014). Towards a managerial state: Turkey's decentralization reforms under the AKP government. In C. Conteh & A. S. Huque (Eds.), *Public sector reforms in developing countries: Paradoxes and practices* (pp. 124–138). Routledge.

Tan, E. (2019). *Decentralization and governance capacity: The case of Turkey.* Palgrave Macmillan.

Tortop, N. (1998). Yerel Yönetimler ve Küçük ve Ortak Ölçekli İşletmeler [Local governments and small and medium sized enterprises]. *Çağdaş Yerel Yönetimler, 7*(1), 72–73.

Turkish Presidency of Strategy and Budget. (2021). *Budget data on public employment.* https://www.sbb.gov.tr/kamu-istihdami/. Accessed 27 April 2022.

Turkish Statistical Institute. (2021). *Adrese dayalı nüfus kayıt sistemi sonuçları [Address-based population registration system results].* https://data.tuik.gov.tr/Bulten/Index?p=Adrese-Dayali-Nufus-Kayit-Sistemi-Sonuclari-2020-37210. Accessed 27 April 2022.

Ulusoy, A. (2017). *Türk İdare Hukuku, Genel Esaslar ve İdari Teşkilat [Turkish administrative law, general principles and administrative organisation]* (Vol. 1). Yetkin Yayınları.

Van Genugten, M., Van Thiel, S., & Voorn, B. (2020). Local governments and their arm's length bodies. *Local Government Studies, 46*(1), 1–21.

Yaprak, N. (2019). *Belediye İktisadi Teşebbüslerinin Hukuki Niteliği* [Legal character of municipality-owned enterprises]. (Doctoral Thesis). Istanbul: Istanbul University Faculty of Social Sciences.

Yıldırım, T. (2017). Cumhurbaşkanlığı Kararnameleri [Presidential decrees]. *MÜHFHAD, 23*(2), 13–28.

Zabunoğlu, Y. K. (2012). *İdare Hukuku [Administrative Law].* Yetkin Yayınları.

PART V

Nordic Countries

CHAPTER 17

Municipally Owned Corporations in Denmark: Historical Continuity and Contemporary Complexities in a Local State-Centred Reform Trajectory

Andrej Christian Lindholst

17.1 Introduction

This chapter provides an overview and interpretation of Danish municipalities' historical and contemporary use of corporate and corporate-like organisational forms—which can be defined broadly as municipally owned corporations (MOCs)—with the aim to contribute to a comparative understanding of country-specific trajectories (Moynihan, 2006; Torsteinsen, 2019). Danish municipalities have used corporate and corporate-like organisational forms as specialised vehicles for delivery of public services for many decades. Different 'arm-length' governance arrangements characterise the various organisational forms, including indirect political and bureaucratic controls mediated through boards of

A. C. Lindholst (✉)
Department of Politics and Society, Aalborg University, Aalborg, Denmark
e-mail: acl@dps.aau.dk

M. Van Genugten et al. (eds.), *Corporatisation in Local Government*, https://doi.org/10.1007/978-3-031-09982-3_17

directors, and executive boards that link strategic and political objectives with operational day-to-day management. The main organisational forms include inter-municipal communalities, single or jointly owned municipal companies with limited liability, and companies with shared public–private ownership. The purposes for their use are diverse and include activities within alternative education, regional tourism, utilities (e.g. waste management, energy and central heating, and water services), fire services, health (e.g. dental services) and transport (e.g. airports, harbours and bus services). Overall, MOCs provide alternatives to other well-known service delivery arrangements such as contracting out, private non-profit (self-governing) institutions, user-owned cooperatives, public–private partnerships (PPPs), inter-municipal collaborations and in-house provision.

Higher-level government bodies, including EU institutions and the Danish central government, have partly regulated and directed the use of MOCs through a mix of general and sector-specific policies and legislation. Administrative structures and institutional rules and norms, however, bestow Danish municipalities with substantial competencies and autonomy in how they organise service delivery, and otherwise similar municipalities may differ significantly in their use of MOCs. In addition, the rationales for MOCs derive from a mix of their comparative (dis) advantages, general reform ideas—notably from the New Public Management (NPM)—and their incorporation into a long-standing state-oriented reform model, ideological differences and political compromises, sector-specific particularities and developments, and the general structure of the Danish public sector.

Key debates on the contemporary use of MOCs and their future are mainly taking place between experts and administrative and political actors, and touch upon governance issues such as how to exercise political and administrative controls, support good corporate governance, ensure diversity and equal gender representation in management, and measure performance. Ideological preferences sometimes underline the debates at the national level and frame the strategic purposes for using MOCs differently—notably, preferences differ regarding the use of MOCs as a permanent and stable arrangement for service delivery, versus as a transitory organisational form supporting a broader privatisation strategy. These debates are associated with multiple innovations that gradually mature and improve the use(s) of MOCs.

The chapter's main argument is that the use of MOCs in Denmark is best viewed in light of the considerable delegation of competencies and autonomy to the municipal level, multiple sector-specific developments taking place within a multilevel governance framework, and a dominant orientation towards (local) state-centred reform trajectories infused with pragmatism rather than ideology. Given that the use of MOCs retains responsibilities and ownership in the hand of municipalities, this may furthermore be interpreted as the emergence of expression of a modified and flexible local Neo-Weberian State (NWS) model that (also) relies on indirect controls through an increasingly complex number of governance arrangements and organisational forms. Curiously, the continued and widespread use of MOCs has attracted much less scholarly and political-administrative attention than related alternative organisational forms such as public–private partnerships (PPPs) and contracting out-alternatives characterised by profit-motivated investments and private sector involvement. This lack of attention is also a contrast to the research on the widespread formation and privatisation of state-owned corporations at the central government level in the 1990s (e.g. Christensen & Pallesen, 2001; Greve, 2000). Publicly available statistics on MOCs are furthermore limited.[1]

The chapter draws on existing literature, review of political-administrative debates, and publicly available statistics and data sources, and is organised in the following sections: The next section, 'National Context and Reform Trajectories', provides a review of key characteristics of the Danish context, the organisation of the public sector and the general reform agenda in Denmark. Section 'MOCs in Denmark' provides an overview of and key data for the main organisational forms of MOCs in Denmark. Section 'Governance of MOCs' highlights key challenges and debates as they are occurring among experts, politicians and administrators. Lastly, 'Conclusions' wraps up the chapter and provides key takeaways.

17.2 National Context and Reform Trajectories

Considering that ambiguities and context shape local interpretation and adoption of general reform doctrines (Moynihan, 2006), the historical and contemporary use of MOCs in Denmark can hardly be understood

[1] The limited availability of public statistics has also been confirmed in personal communications with Denmark's national statistical bureau (Danmarks Statistik) and The Danish Business Authority (Erhvervsstyrelsen).

without an appreciation of the politico-administrative institutions and public sector reform trajectories.

In comparison, Denmark is a small and densely populated country characterised by an advanced economy, low income inequality, and a large and well-functioning tax-financed public welfare system (OECD, 2021). The Danish political-administrative system is characterised as a constitutionally regulated consensus-oriented democracy with substantial delegation of responsibilities from the national level to a two-tier local government system (OECD, 2018). A structural reform enacted in 2007 reduced the number of regional authorities (upper-tier) from 13 to 5 and the number of municipalities (lower-tier) from 271 to 98. Danish municipalities are multi-purpose and enjoy comparatively high levels of autonomy, including the right to collect taxes, set service levels and organise service delivery (Ladner et al., 2016). The Danish Constitutional Act's §82 guarantees the general principle of local self-governance, while the Danish Municipal Act regulates the competencies of municipalities in further detail. Central government authorities provide legal supervision of municipalities and monitor whether their activities comply with existing laws. Annual agreements between the central government and the Danish Local Government Association regulate the general expenditure, service priorities and investment levels among local governments. The local city council in each municipality and its elected councillors hold overall administrative and financial responsibilities for the entire municipal organisation. Key municipal competencies include primary education, childcare, eldercare, integration of refugees and immigrants, environmental protection, utilities, waste management, assistance to the unemployed, local economic development, urban planning and development, and culture and sports.

Reform trajectories in Denmark are often characterised and debated as an expression of modernisation rather than marketisation (Greve, 2006; Lindholst & Hedegaard, 2019), an NWS model (Pollitt & Bouckaert, 2017), a Nordic administrative tradition (Kuhlmann & Wollmann, 2019), and, most recently, a layered and complex hybrid that combines the content from multiple 'big' reform models (Greve et al., 2020). These characteristics emphasise the use of various reform instruments to modify and reinforce a dominant bureaucratic organisational structure into what sometimes is described as a friendlier and more efficient bureaucracy (Pollitt & Bouckaert, 2017). The trajectories also tend to keep the state (rather than markets or civic society) as the central actor for economic and social development, as well as reinforce traditional democratic and administrative institutions and their legitimacy through professionalisation of administrative staff and employees, customer and service-orientation, and development of a performance and evaluation culture. These trajectories furthermore take place on the backdrop of an administrative tradition defined by the rule of law, a unitary-decentralised political-administrative structure with strong local governments, an open and transparent administrative culture with high accessibility and freedom of information for citizens, high levels of citizen participation and user involvement, and a strong civic self-organisation (Kuhlmann & Wollmann, 2019).

The use of MOCs and the wider use of semi-autonomous agencies operating at arm's length of government bureaucracies for large-scale reform purposes is historically and conceptually associated with the NPM reform model and a strong emphasis on market-based logics and business-like management practices (Moynihan, 2006; Verhoest, 2018). However, in the Danish context, the use of MOCs—as shown in the next sections—also represents a continuation of existing pre-NPM governance arrangements and forms that have a less radical emphasis on market-based logics and business-like practices and retain a dominant role for local governments in terms of ownership and responsibilities for public services. In this perspective, their continued use and renewal may be interpreted as an evolution or expression of a modified NWS or post-NPM state-centred model where ownership, responsibilities, and political and bureaucratic controls are working through additional and more indirect and autonomous forms—in contrast to more direct—but nonetheless remain in the hands of the (local) state.

17.3 MOCs in Denmark

According to the Danish Constitution's §82, the municipalities' right to govern their internal affairs and responsibilities is regulated by law and under supervision by the central state. A complex set of regulations including the Municipal Act, the Local Authority Mandate and several sector-specific laws provides the legal mandate for municipalities' rights to organise different types of service delivery and activities through various corporate-like organisational forms (Olesen, 2015). Central state authorities have responsibilities for overseeing the use of different forms for MOCs within different services. State authorities (The Danish Appeal Board/Authority) are responsible for supervision and control of legal compliance as well as approval of municipal participation in and use of municipal communalities and companies (but excluding ‘small’ companies with limited staff and/or turnover as defined by the Danish Auditor Act). Beyond outright privatisation and contracting out, the main alternatives to in-house organisation are inter-municipal communalities and different variations of municipally owned limited liability companies with single and joint ownership and jointly owned public–private companies. From a governance perspective, the differences in legal framework and regulation constitute a set of possible benefits and drawbacks. Table 17.1 provides an overview of key differences between main alternatives that involve direct or indirect municipal ownership for activities.

Table 17.1 Comparison of municipal service provision by in-house organisations, communalities and companies

Issue	*In-house organisation*	*Inter-municipal communality*	*Municipal company*
Activities	Only municipal activities	Only municipal activities	Only municipal activities
Ownership	A single municipality	Two or more municipalities	One or more owners (public and/or private)
Competitive tendering?	Not required (in-house rule)	Not required (in-house rule)	Normally not required (in-house rule)
Employment relations (staff)	Employed by the municipality	Employed by the communality	Employed by the company
Owner governance tools	City-council decisions and administrative instructions (day-to-day management)	Articles of association, right to instruct board members	Articles of association, general meeting, owner strategy, legally binding agreements (contracts)
Financial liability	Unlimited	Solidarity (unlimited)	Limited to capital contribution
Law	Public: Legal status as public authority. Public law including administrative law, public record act	As in-house organisation, but some exceptions can be granted in individual cases	Independent legal status. Private law with exceptions if authorised by special law and/or the public record act
Authority tasks	Yes	No, unless authorised by special law	No, unless authorised by special law
Legal forms	Part of the municipality (which is an independent juridical body)	§60 companies	Limited companies, Law 548-companies, 40/60-companies under special law (e.g. water sector)

Source: Adapted from ØIM (2014)

From a legal perspective, the choice of organisational form involves consideration of a complex set of laws and regulations that defines how each form can be organised and managed. In general, the legal and regulative framework differs for the various organisational forms and involves public and private law in varying degrees. A main rule is that municipalities cannot participate in or carry out activities whose purpose is commercial (i.e. profit-oriented), and/or distort (private) market competition, unless this is mandated under a special law. Municipalities are generally allowed to engage only in activities that are of internal use and benefit for their citizens. Thus, the scope of municipal engagements in companies with shared public–private ownership is limited. It follows from the Local Authority Mandate that, as a main rule, municipalities can participate in corporate organisational forms (companies) under four general conditions (Olesen, 2015). First, (other) legal regulations must not hinder that a task is provided by an entity outside the municipality. Second, the company may only undertake tasks the municipality has authority to do itself. Third, the municipality must not control the company directly, and an arm-length relation must exist between the owning municipality and the company's strategic and operational management bodies. Fourth, the company must not have a profit-oriented purpose.

Special regulation within some sectors allows for some exceptions to the main rule. For example, sector-specific regulation within the water sector gives municipalities the right to participate in so-called 40/60 companies with shared public–private ownership and a for-profit purpose in special circumstances where the strategic purpose is (international) export of services and products based on technologies embedded in municipal services and know-how. Sector-specific regulation also has great influence on the use of municipally owned corporations. In some cases, new regulation provides municipalities with greater choice over different organisational forms. A new Danish harbour law enacted in 1999, for example, allowed for new corporate and corporate-like forms with delegation of greater autonomy and more competencies for the purpose of enhancing Danish harbours' commercialisation and competitiveness in a European perspective. By 2020, of the 63 members of the Danish Harbour Association, 25 harbours were organised within the municipal organisation, 26 as municipal self-governed, 7 as municipally owned limited liability companies and 5 with other forms. In other cases, new regulation limits the choice to a particular organisational form. For example, a national agreement on waste management and circular economy in 2020 required the formation of several new municipal companies with limited liability as part of a political plan to privatise activities within the municipal waste management sector.

17.3.1 *Inter-municipal Companies (§60 Communalities)*

The right for Danish municipalities to establish and participate in formal inter-municipal co-operations, where ownership is shared between two or more municipalities, is authorised by the Local Government Act's §60. These §60 communalities work mainly under public law and allow municipalities to delegate responsibilities for limited activities into a company structure with shared public ownership. The act does not allow private partners to participate. Historically, most MOCs with shared ownership in Danish local governments are established as §60 communalities. Communalities enable regional authorities and municipalities in Denmark to provide different types of services jointly through a formal arrangement which guarantees a degree of arm-length relationship between owners and daily activities. The deeper rationale is commonly to exploit scale economies and/or sustain a competent and skilful service provision (Lundtorp, 2000). An almost paradigmatic and internationally unique case for this rationale is found in the historical development within utilities in Denmark. Denmark has combined local production of electricity with the development of district heating systems since the 1950s. The combined production has allowed Danish municipalities to exploit surplus energy from electricity production in district heating systems and create some of the most energy-efficient systems in the world. Technological innovations and development of increasingly larger capacities for production and transportation within district heating and electricity have sustained the economic rationale for the establishment—and later mergers—of smaller communalities into increasingly fewer and larger communalities from the 1950s until the late 1990s. However, EU policies enacted and transposed into national laws in the early 2000s required a disaggregation of main functions (production facilities, transport infrastructure and distribution) to promote liberalisation and competition within the energy sector and have resulted in the dismantlement of large multi-divisional communalities (Lindholst, 2021).

For 2020, the Danish national authorities reported the existence of 82 regional and municipal communalities in accordance with criteria for organisational size defined by the Danish Auditor Act. Regional authorities were involved in only five communalities providing similar public transport services across Denmark. Table 17.2 provides an overview of the number and service types that the municipalities have organised as communalities.

Reflecting historical figures, municipalities mostly use communalities within utilities, including various forms of waste management and energy. Historical figures also indicate a greater number of communalities among lower- and upper-tier local governments in the 1990s and the beginning of the 2000s. About 225 communalities were reported with municipal participation for 1998 (and 245 for 2003), with higher numbers and the greatest economic importance within utilities (waste and energy) and transport (Strukturkommissionen, 2004, p. 441). These figures need to be interpreted in the context of the earlier administrative structure with

Table 17.2 Self-reported communalities in Denmark by 2020

Service	*Number*	*Notes*
Utilities	30	Communalities within utilities are typically large, have many owners and combine waste and heating services. A few communalities provide specialised services including dangerous waste management and biogas.
Fire and ambulance services	20	Also include coastal lifeguard services.
Transport	14	Five communalities are regional with joint regional and municipal ownership. Transport also includes three airports, four ferry services and two harbours.
Health	7	Includes dental services and supplies.
Education	2	Very small and specialised communalities, for example, school ship for disadvantaged youth.
Food services	2	Joint provision of meals for municipal institutions.
Nature areas	5	Mostly small communalities managing and/or providing local nature experiences. One larger communality promotes outdoor tourism.
IT	1	Communality providing IT services for two municipalities.
Public space	1	Communality providing street and park maintenance and works for two municipalities.

Source: Ankestyrelsen (2020)

271 municipalities (and 13 regional authorities) in place before the enactment of the structural reform in 2007. A rough comparison shows no or little change in the average number of communalities per municipality between the decades (approximately 0.82/0.89 communalities per municipality in 1998/2003 versus 0.84 in 2020). Some sector-specific developments are nonetheless notable. For example, municipal communalities dealing with tax services were common before 2007, but these disappeared when the structural reform centralised tax services to the state level.

Public law provides Danish municipalities with substantial freedom to organise the governance structure of communalities in different ways. In some cases, communalities may be organised with a structure, including an owner assembly with representatives from the owner municipalities as highest authority, an administrative board, and an appointed professional management team with responsibilities for implementation of strategic objectives and day-to-day management. In other cases, a communality may be organised with only an administrative board as a single governance body. The board composition typically includes elected local politicians as key representatives. In case of an ownership structure with many owners, only politicians from the largest municipalities are included. Also, in some cases the boards include outside professionals (e.g. individuals with private sector experience), representatives from other public authorities (e.g. police directors in fire services), and employee representatives. However, communalities represent only one form for organising inter-municipal cooperation. Danish municipalities often perceive the formal demands for organising and managing joint activities in a communality as too bureaucratic and inflexible. Thus, Danish municipalities have been historically and are presently engaged in a high number of different inter-municipal collaborative activities for a vast range of purposes (KL, 2018; Strukturkommissionen, 2004, pp. 434–439).

Politically and administratively, it was expected that the importance of communalities would decrease after the structural reform in 2007, which merged 271 municipalities into 98. However, current administrative debate centres upon why their importance has held steady, or even increased, since the reform (Steno, 2021). One likely explanation voiced is that the fewer and larger municipalities have improved their managerial and legal competencies and ability to exploit and evaluate the benefits of inter-municipal collaborations and communalities. New policy issues such as business development in a globalised world, the delegation of new responsibilities (e.g. specialised social services) from upper-tier to lower-tier governments, and the content of new national sector policies (e.g. the waste management reform in 2020), have also sustained a continued use of communalities.

17.3.2 *Municipal Companies*

Compared to the use of commonalities, the use of a limited liability company represents a stronger manifestation of the arm-length principle, including the organisation of activities within an independent juridical entity. The use also represents a stronger reliance on private law within a public sector context. The Danish Companies Act regulates how formal governance structures should be organised and is stricter that the legal framework for MOCs operating under public law (see section on inter-municipal communalities). The stricter regulation specifies, for example, the required content of the articles of the association, and competencies of governing bodies including the general meeting and the governance structure. The Danish Companies Act allows public companies to adopt two alternative structures in what can be regarded as an extended one-tier governance structure based on a clear hierarchy between the governing bodies (Hansen, 2009). Both structures work under the general meeting that represents the highest authority in the company. The general meeting, for example, elects members of the board of directors or the supervisory board. Companies are furthermore required to undergo annual external financial audits. The first option specifies a structure where the company is managed by a board of directors and an executive board. The board of directors is responsible for overall, financial and strategic management and appoints the executive board, which it also oversees. The executive board has responsibilities for day-to-day management. The second option specifies a structure for public limited companies where the company is managed by an executive board appointed by a supervisory board. The supervisory board has responsibilities for the financial management and oversees the executive board. The executive board has responsibilities for overall and strategic management as well as day-to-day management. Employees are entitled to be represented in the governance structure in larger companies (defined by an average of at least 35 employees within the three preceding years).

The use of municipal companies with limited liabilities ranges from smaller operations with a single municipal owner to large jointly owned operations organised in a multi-divisional structure (a group with a parent company controlling multiple subsidiaries) and governed through a complex ownership structure. However, some municipalities are also single owners of complex multi-divisional groups with several subdivisions and multiple activities. Greater Copenhagen Utility (HOFOR) is an example of a large multi-divisional company with a multiple ownership structure operating within utilities with subdivisions for heating, energy and water. The company is non-profit and its vision is to create sustainable towns and cities by providing green, safe, and clean water and energy solutions. The company is Denmark's largest within its service areas with more than 1400 employees, an annual turnover of about €700 million (2020 figures), and—within water services alone—more than one million customers located across 15 municipalities. The ownership structure is complex and ranges from a single-owner municipality for some parts to 15 for others. However, the by far largest municipality (Copenhagen) dominates the ownership throughout all subdivisions.

Publicly available data for utilities (Forsyningstilsynet, 2019) indicate that a Danish municipality in 2018 typically was the single owner of about 3–4 companies and participated in about 2–3 jointly owned companies. The data indicate the existence of 299 companies with a single municipal owner and about 80 jointly owned companies. The number and type of companies and the extent of a company's operations vary greatly within these figures. For example, the data indicate that out of the 98 Danish municipalities, 60 (equal to 61%) are engaged in one or more companies as single owner, 77 (79%) are engaged in a jointly owned company, and only 7 (7%) are not engaged in any MOC. Furthermore, some municipalities are mainly engaged in jointly owned companies while others mainly rely on companies as single owner. Denmark's largest municipality—Copenhagen, with about 640,000 inhabitants (2021)—represents the most extreme example with its engagement in 46 MOCs within utilities alone, of which only two are solely owned by the municipality. Most of Copenhagen's neighbouring municipalities are participating in these MOCs through joint ownership. The dominant and widespread use of jointly owned companies reflects similar rationales to those driving the use of communalities, where municipalities appear to exploit economies of scale and sustain competencies within specialised services such as water treatment or waste management.

Some companies or company-like organisational forms are established under special law such as The Business Promotion Act. A total of six intermunicipal companies, 'business houses', were established under the Act as independent juridical entities with the purpose of promoting business affairs and innovation in Denmark. All Danish municipalities finance these proportionally to their population size. The business houses are managed through a board of directors with responsibilities for day-to-day operations. Municipal owner committees with strategic responsibilities appoint the board, which includes representatives from city councils, the business sector and knowledge institutions. Annual performance contracts are implemented to guide and monitor activities.

17.3.3 Public Companies with Private Participation

Danish law allows local governments (municipalities and regions) under specific circumstances to participate in jointly owned public–private companies with commercial purposes. The current legal framework for public–private companies was enacted by the Danish parliament on 1 January 2007 with Law 548 and later amendments (law on municipalities' performance of tasks for other public authorities and municipalities and regions' participation in companies). Some companies with shared public–private ownership are still regulated by earlier laws by dispensation (e.g. Law 383 and 384). The framework's main purpose is to promote public–private cooperation in markets where only public providers are present and possibilities for contracting out are limited. In reality, the law only allows public authorities to participate in commercial activities in conjunction with the dissemination of public know-how to private companies. Thus, establishment of L548 companies appears to be a privatisation strategy for transferring activities from the public to the private sector. In the political and administrative language, L548 companies are sometimes framed as a part of the agenda for promoting public–private partnerships (e.g. Regeringen, 2011).

L548 companies work under private law, including the Danish Companies Act, and have status as independent legal entities. Public–private companies can be organised under different corporate forms with limited liabilities (e.g. joint-stock company or limited liability company/public and private limited companies) and must involve a minimum of 25% private participation in terms of capital contribution and voting rights at the general meeting. In addition, the law limits the maximum allowed turnover generated from sales to other municipalities or regions to 50%.

Historically, the number of companies with private involvement appears moderate. Sixty-four companies with private participation were registered

Table 17.3 Local government companies in 2013 with shared public–private ownership

Sector	*Companies in 2013 (number)*
Housing	2
Utilities (gas/energy/heating)	15
Business development	6
Leisure	6
Cloth services	2
Transport	4
Other purposes	29
Total	64

Source: Erhvervsstyrelsen (2014, p. 55)

for 2013 by the Danish national authorities across different service sectors (Erhvervsstyrelsen, 2014). An overview is provided in Table 17.3. The figures appear to be an increase in comparison with self-reported figures for the 1990s where approximately 50 companies with private participation were registered in total, and no more than 20 companies were found to be in operation for a single year (Strukturkommissionen, 2004).

17.3.4 *Other Types of Public Ownership*

Several additional public ownership structures exist that represent either important alternatives to or variations of MOCs. The general feature of these is that they represent a wider range of organisational forms that are democratically governed and that do not rely on for-profit private ownership.

First, municipalities are jointly involved in specialised activities through *indirect* ownership. One example is the IT-procurement company Kombit A/S. The company is 100% owned by the Danish Local Government Association on behalf of its members (all Danish municipalities) and offers joint IT-procurement services supporting innovation and digitalisation of the Danish public sector. Board members are locally elected politicians, typically mayors from different municipalities, who represent the interests of the owners (municipalities). The rationale for the company is to provide Danish municipalities a better bargaining position against large and globally oriented IT-service providers. Second, some municipalities are strategically involved in a few companies with shared ownership with central state authorities (Finansministeriet, 2018). Companies providing large-scale infrastructure such as regional transport (e.g. airports) or urban development in the capital region are examples of this ownership mix where the rationale is driven by mutual local, regional and national interests. Third, cooperatives based on shared user ownership—or membership—are very common within energy supply. Cooperatives represent a democratic form of ownership and control over activities where all users hold voting rights at the general assembly. These cooperatives represent an alternative to MOCs that maintains a public or democratic ownership structure but without government involvement. Most of these are small and locally based. However, they may also be very large and offer regional coverage. The cooperative 'Share' [*Andel*, in Danish], for example, became in 2020—after a fast expansion through several takeovers and sell-offs from state companies—owned by about 400,000 users (or 'members') and is responsible for delivery of about 40% of all electricity in Denmark. The cooperative is organised with a group structure with several subdivisions, including activities within energy production (e.g. wind turbines), digital infrastructure, software development, smart energy systems and infrastructure for electric vehicles.

17.4 Major Governance Challenges

Several governance issues appear pertinent to highlight in relation to the current and future use of MOCs in Denmark. The contemporary debates bear resemblance with earlier debates on the use of central state-owned companies and issues emerging within a 'grey zone' where public and private governance logics overlap (Greve, 1997, 2000). The issues include, for example, remuneration of board members and top managers, the extent of political and bureaucratic control, and the degree of transparency and public accountability.

17.4.1 Strategic Purpose

Different strategic purposes drive the use of MOCs in different sectors. The dominant and historical strategic purpose envisions MOCs as a stable and effective organisation form for providing different public services. The alternative strategic purpose envisions MOCs as a transitory organisation form—an intermediate step towards full privatisation. This alternative strategic purpose resembles much of the logic that drove developments at the state level in the 1990s (e.g. Christensen & Pallesen, 2001). This alternative purpose was enacted in 2020 in a new national political agreement on a climate plan for a green waste sector and circular economy where substantial parts of municipal waste management were envisioned to shift to the private sector through contracting out and privatisation. Formation of MOCs with limited liabilities was included as a stepping stone towards later privatisation by enabling better external market-based and financial assessment of assets. Thus, national politics may in some cases circumvent local competencies and autonomy and devise a less local state-centric reform trajectory.

17.4.2 Corporate Governance

Ongoing administrative debates in the 2010s on the governance of MOCs have centred on several key issues, and expert groups and sector associations have developed common guidelines on good corporate governance.

Gender issues and the general composition of boards in MOCs have been debated parallel to wider debates on board composition and the competencies of privately owned Danish companies. In general, diversity in board composition is perceived as an advantage. Diversity is generally believed to bring in complementary skills and multiple perspectives as a way of avoiding the pitfalls of 'group thinking'. Barriers to diversity and ways to overcome these are also part of the debates (DST, 2019). However, no public data are available for the composition of boards or management teams in MOCs. Anecdotal evidence from some municipal sectors indicates an extreme gender bias. Informal reports from annual gatherings in the water sector, for example, describe virtually all participants as elderly males with a background in engineering. More generally, women are systematically underrepresented in management positions within the public and private sectors, and this underrepresentation is more pronounced for higher management positions compared to lower (DST, 2019). In the public sector, the share of women in top management is 30.8%, compared to 48.1% in middle management. These figures should furthermore be interpreted in consideration of the fact that about two-thirds of those employed in the public sector are women (DI Analyse, 2018). Available survey-based data from the late 2000s for the municipal level show that while 64% of all employees are women, only 43% of those employed in top management positions are women (Madsen et al., 2010). However, the balance is moving in the direction of a more even gender distribution. The share of women in management positions in the public sector has increased substantially in the 2010s, from 34.5% in 2010 to 43.7% in 2017 (DST, 2019).

A special debate in the context of MOCs relates to the benefits and drawbacks of politicians' membership on boards. The salient question here is whether locally elected politicians can provide sufficient business and management competence on the board. Survey-based data from the 2000s show that about 80% of board members in MOCs are locally elected politicians (including ordinary politicians and mayors), 10% are municipal employees and 10% are external representatives (ISM, 2006, p. 178).

A special governance issue relates to the relationship between owners (normally represented by the city council) and the strategic and operational management of MOCs. As a consequence of the arm-length principle for MOCs enacted by public and private law, administrative debates have centred upon how strategic governance can be improved through more indirect means and controls so that activities are aligned with the city council's interests. In the 2010s, for example, guidelines were developed for so-called ownership strategies. These strategies—or 'soft law'—constitute a key governance tool and complement the legal requirements of 'hard law'. A survey from 2018 (KL, 2019) indicated that a vast majority (85%) of municipalities had developed ownership strategies for utilities in either a sector-specific or general form. The survey found that most strategies were sector-specific, while a few municipalities relied on a general strategy for all their companies. The survey also found that municipalities used sector-specific strategies in all sectors, including multi-utilities, water, waste, central heating, fire services and harbours. The municipalities stated that the explicit purposes for the development of strategies were (in prioritised order) to (a) strengthen the ownership-role or 'owner visibility' and define the framework for action, (b) support appointed council members in company boards, (c) support communication and transparency for the public and (d) prevent and address earlier problems. Furthermore, the key regulatory purposes were to (a) clarify objectives for finance and development of values, (b) make transparent the roles and responsibilities of the municipality and the companies/company, (c) integrate attention to the municipalities' wider policies in the company's strategy (e.g. city planning, climate policies and social responsibilities), and (d) ensure effectiveness and accountability in the companies' operations. Nearly one-half (44%) stated that the ownership strategy was the most important tool in the strategic management of companies. However, ownership strategies were widely supplemented with several complementary tools, of which the most important included (a) ongoing informal dialogue, (b) participating and voting in the general assembly and (c) provision of management information.

Soft law for MOCs also encompasses sector-specific guidelines for good corporate governance. The trade association for water management, for example, has issued principles for good corporate governance in utilities owned by municipalities (DANVA, 2017) with reference to national and international developments and experiences. These principles offer detailed recommendations for how good corporate governance can be organised and implemented with regard to the relationship between a municipality and a MOC as well as the roles and responsibilities of the MOC's governing bodies. More generally, such guidelines represent schemes for maturation and professionalisation of corporate governance within a Danish context, and informal benchmarks for good practices.

Criteria for salaries and remuneration of board members and staff are well-regulated and relatively strict for inter-municipal communalities operating under public law (SIM, 2016b). Size and criteria for salaries and remuneration, need, for example, to be approved by state authorities with respect to legality and expediency. Collective agreements between the Danish Local Government Association (for employer) and trade union (for employees) are also in place (including top managers) that regulate salaries and terms of employment. Criteria for salaries and employment terms for employees in MOCs operating under private law follow guidelines for (central) state-owned companies and appear more liberal than for MOCs operating under public law. Salaries and employment terms for MOCs operating under private law, for example, should be competitive and able to attract qualified staff (SIM, 2016a). Danish municipalities can locally enact more specific criteria for salaries and employment terms through, for example, articles of the association and ownership strategies. Despite the relatively well-regulated framework, the size of salaries and remuneration of board members and top managers in MOCs are recurrently publicly debated. Cases reported and criticised in the national media show that, due to their responsibilities as board members and chairs of MOCs, some mayors and chief executives receive a higher income than the Danish Prime Minister does. In a response to such criticism, The Danish Association for Local Governments has issued guidelines for what is prudent and legally allowable regarding salaries for high-ranked managers (KL, 2017).

17.4.3 Performance

MOCs commonly work under soft financial constraints and do not operate in markets with direct competition on either the demand or supply side. In many cases, MOCs serve a natural monopoly or operate in markets with very limited competition or high entrance costs. Additionally, user fees finance services provided by most MOCs, such as those operating within public utilities. In consequence, debates about cost and quality levels are recurrently emerging in conjunction with debates about alternative ways of organising services. These alternatives notably include privatisation with full transfer of responsibilities and assets to private for-profit ownership. To address such concerns, national benchmarking systems have been established within some sectors. National benchmark systems within water management established under the Danish Water Sector Act, for example, provide annual performance information for water companies on indicators related to health, security of supply, energy, climate and environment, and also provide input for central authorities' calculation of effectiveness compared to cost levels and regulation of individual performance targets.

17.4.4 Public Accountability

While in many cases MOCs are organised under private law, the Danish Public Record Act regulates access to information in companies with majority public ownership. Historically, public access to internal information about publicly owned companies operating under private law has been very limited. However, revisions of the act in the 2010s have expanded public access to internal information. Overall, debates have centred on balancing concerns for effective market-based operations and demands for public and democratic accountability (Mortensen, 2015).

Political-administrative debates about public and democratic accountability of MOCs have occurred on an ongoing basis since the 1990s and have typically been framed in arguments about the pros and cons of several organisational alternatives including in-house provision, contracting out and privatisation (Lundtorp, 2000; Strukturkommissionen, 2004). However, little systematic knowledge is available about the use and governance of MOCs at aggregate levels and—except for some sector-specific reports (e.g. Transport-, Bygnings- og Boligministeriet, 2018)—there is a general lack of public evaluation and independent research. This finding is at odds with the logic of an NWS model where evaluation and learning are perceived as critical for improved accountability and efficiency. In consequence, the contemporary use of MOCs can be argued to represent not only a grey zone between public and private sector logics, but also a cloaked zone for grander large-scale scrutiny and wider political-administrative deliberation about reform trajectories.

17.4.5 *Commercialisation and Export*

Concerns for commercialisation and international export of Danish know-how and technologies have in some sectors promoted the use of public–private companies. Lack of supportive legal regulation and lack of awareness of possibilities have been seen as barriers to economic growth. Developments in the Danish water sector provide one example. In 2015, the Danish export of water technologies and know-how amounted to about DKK 15 billion in a growing international market. Key elements of the know-how and technologies are available in public water companies operating under the Danish Water Act. The Water Act was revised in 2016 in order to enable better exploitation of market opportunities. The revision clarified capital requirements and expanded the range of possible activities for public–private companies allowed under the act (Deloitte, 2016). This issue relates to a wider debate about prospects for export of know-how and technologies associated with the Danish public sector.

17.5 Conclusions

MOCs with various forms and purposes have been widely used in Denmark for decades and predate the reform doctrines of the NPM. Their contemporary use represents a historical continuity with added complexities. The use varies in substantial degrees across local governments and sectors. Some municipalities rely on only a few MOCs, or none at all. Others rely mostly on MOCs with a single ownership, while others rely on MOCs with joint ownership. MOCs are most important within utilities, where communalities and limited liability companies are the dominating forms. User-owned cooperatives also appear as a predominant alternative that rely on a public non-profit ownership rather than private for-profit ownership. The variations may best be viewed in light of the substantial competencies and autonomy delegated to the local government level in the Danish politico-administrative system. However, the variations and trajectories are also partly shaped by higher-level policies that regulate local choice to varying degrees. Examples include the liberalisation and commercialisation of the energy sector due to EU regulations enacted in the 2000s, the liberalisation and commercialisation of municipal harbours through enactment of new national legislation in 2012, and the statutory demand for corporatisation of municipal waste management enacted in 2020 as part of new national policies promoting sustainability and a circular economy.

In this chapter, it is argued that the steadily more complex and mature use of MOCs within and across different sectors supports an understanding of the dominant trajectory as the emergence or expression of a modified NWS or (local) state-centred reform model. In this trajectory, local governments retain responsibilities and ownership for service delivery, continue to take on a leading role for societal and economic developments and—in contrast to reliance on direct intra-organisational controls—manage activities indirectly through arm-length inter-organisational political and bureaucratic controls.

It is evident that it is increasingly important to address the challenge of how to master governance in the grey zone between public and private sector logics. Key debates in recent years are indicative of a widespread awareness of the challenges and the need to address these. Accordingly, the challenges have been addressed by innovation of new inter- and intra-organisational governance tools and controls, such as soft law and performance measures, owner strategies, and the awareness of the need for greater diversity in board compositions. In some cases, national law supports—if not prescribes—the development of governance tools, as in the case of performance measures within water management.

Curiously, political-administrative debates and developments mostly address questions of accountability and improved governance at the intra-organisational (e.g. corporate governance and composition of executive boards) and inter-organisational (e.g. ownership strategies) levels, and less so at the systemic or the aggregate level. Issues related to, for example, the overall impact on local democratic processes are touched upon in debates, but not followed by evaluations or systematic scrutiny. From the viewpoint of an NWS model, this may be a major blunder, as the legitimacy and effectiveness of a performance- and result-oriented public organisation can be argued to depend on systematic evaluations, transparency and political-administrative learning processes.

References

Christensen, J. G., & Pallesen, T. (2001). The political benefits of corporatization and privatization. *Journal of Public Policy, 21*(3), 283–309.

DANVA. (2017). *Kodeks for god selskabsledelse i kommunale forsyningsselskaber [Code of good corporate governance in municipal utilities].* Dansk Affaldsforening, Dansk Fjernvarme og Danske Vandværker.

Deloitte. (2016). *Vejledning om oprettelse og drift af 40/60-selskaber i vandsektoren [Guidance on the establishment and operation of 40/60 companies in the water sector].* Erhvervsstyrelsen.

DI Analyse. (2018). *Bestyrelsesformænd: Vi skal have flere kvindelige topledere [Chairman of the Board: We need more female top executives].* Dansk Industri.

DST. (2019). *Kvinder i ledelse [Women in management].* København: Danmarks Statistik.

Erhvervsstyrelsen (2014). *Redegørelse om kommuners og regioners deltagelse i erhvervsdrivende selskaber mv. [Statement on municipalities 'and regions' participation in commercial companies, etc.].* : Erhvervsstyrelsen.

Finansministeriet. (2018). *Statens Selskaber 2018 [The states' companies 2018].* Finansministeriet.

Forsyningstilsynet. (2019). *Liste over Kommunernes energiselskaber [List of municipal energy companies].* Forsyningstilsynet.

Greve, C. (1997). *Styring og demokratisk kontrol af statslige aktieselskaber [Governance and democratic control of state-owned corporations].* Københavns Universitet.

Greve, C. (2000). *Statens virksomheder: Aktieselskabsdannelse og privatisering i 1990erne [State-owned companies: Joint-stock company formation and privatization in the 1990s].* Jurist- og Økonomiforbundets Forlag.

Greve, C. (2006). Public management reform in Denmark. *Public Management Review, 8*(1), 161–169.

Greve, C., Ejersbo, N., Lægreid, P., & Rykkja, L. H. (2020). Unpacking Nordic administrative reforms: Agile and adaptive governments. *International Journal of Public Administration, 43*(8), 697–710.

Hansen, J. H. (2009). The Danish green paper on Company Law reform – Modernising Company Law in the 21st century. *European Business Organization Law Review, 10*, 73–95.

ISM. (2006). *Rapport fra udvalget vedrørende de styringsmæssige relationer i forholdet mellem kommunalbestyrelser og kommunale selskaber [Report from the committee regarding the governance relations in the relationship between municipal councils and municipal companies].* København: Indenrigs- og Sundhedsministeriet.

KL. (2017). *Vejledning om ansættelse, aflønning og forhold ved afskedigelse af direktører og andre chefer for fælleskommunale §60-selskaber [Guidance on employment, pay and conditions for dismissal of directors and other leaders of joint municipal §60 companies]*. Kommunernes Landsforening.

KL. (2018). *De samarbejdende kommuner [The collaborating municipalities]*. Kommunernes Landsforening.

KL. (2019). *Resultater af spørgeskemaundersøgelse om kommunernes ejerstrategier i forsyningssektoren [Results of a questionnaire survey on the municipalities' ownership strategies in the supply sector]*. Kommunernes Landsforening.

Kuhlmann, S., & Wollmann, H. (2019). *Introduction to comparative public administration: Administrative systems and reforms in Europe* (2nd ed.). Cheltenham: Edward Edgar.

Ladner, A., Keuffer, N., & Baldersheim, H. (2016). Measuring local autonomy in 39 countries (1990–2014). *Regional & Federal Studies, 26*(3), 321–357.

Lindholst, A. C. (2021). Addressing public-value failure: Remunicipalization as acts of public entrepreneurship. *Journal of Economic Policy Reform, 24*(3), 380–397.

Lindholst, A. C., & Hedegaard, T. F. (2019). Den befolkningsmæssige legitimitet af markedsgørelse som reformprojekt for den danske offentlige sektor [The public legitimacy of marketisation as reform project for the Danish public sector]. *Nordisk Administrativt Tidsskrift, 96*(2), 47–68.

Lundtorp, S. (2000). *Kommunalt Samarbejde: Hvorfor og hvorfor ikke? [Municipal Cooperation: Why and why not?]*. Kommunernes Landsforening.

Madsen, M. B., Holt, H., Bruun Johansen, A., & Kløft Schademan, H. (2010). *Kvinder og mænd i den offentlige sektor: Karrieremønstre, lederønsker og ledermuligheder [Women and men in the public sector: Career patterns, leadership aspirations and leadership opportunities]*. SFI.

Mortensen, B. O. G. (2015). Offentlighed om offentlig ejede virksomheder i Danmark [Publicity about publicly owned companies in Denmark]. *Nordisk Administrativt Tidsskrift, 92*(1), 5–23.

Moynihan, D. P. (2006). Ambiguity in policy lessons: The agencification experience. *Public Administration, 84*(4), 1029–1050.

OECD. (2018). *Key data on local and regional governments in the European Union*. OECD.

OECD. (2021). *OECD data*. www.data.oecd.org. Accessed 15 March 2021.

ØIM. (2014). *Notat om retlige rammer for fælles løsninger for kommunalt samarbejde [Memorandum on legal framework for common solutions for municipal cooperation]*. Økonomi- og Indenrigsministeriet.

Olesen, K. N. (2015). Hjemmel for offentlig markedsaktivitet [Legal authorization for public market activity]. *Nordisk Administrativt Tidsskrift, 92*(1), 24–43.

Pollitt, C., & Bouckaert, G. (2017). *Public management reform: A comparative analysis – into the age of austerity*. Oxford University Press.

Regeringen. (2011). *Strategi til fremme af offentlig-privat samarbejde [Strategy for promoting public-private partnerships]*. Økonomi- og Erhvervsministeriet.

SIM. (2016a). *Bedre styringsmuligheder i forsyningssektorerne [Better governance in the utilities sectors]*. Social- og Indenrigsministeriet.
SIM. (2016b). *Vejledning om kommunale fællesskaber [Guidance on municipal communities]*. Social- og Indenrigsministeriet.
Steno, M. (2021). Udvidet samarbejde kræver bedre ledelse [Expanded collaboration requires better leadership]. *Kommunen.dk, 64*(4), 26–27.
Strukturkommissionen. (2004). *Strukturkommissionens betænkning nr. 1434: Bind 1–Hovedbetænkningen [Structural Commission report No 1434: Volume 1 – Main report]*. Indenrigs- og Sundhedsministeriet.
Torsteinsen, H. (2019). Debate: Corporatization in local government—The need for a comparative and multi-disciplinary research approach. *Public Money & Management, 39*(1), 5–8.
Transport-, Bygnings- og Boligministeriet. (2018). *Ekspertudvalget om havneloven: Anbefalinger [Committee of Experts on the Port Act: Recommendations]*. Transport-, Bygnings- og Boligministeriet.
Verhoest, K. (2018). Agencification in Europe. In E. Ongaro & S. Van Thiel (Eds.), *The Palgrave handbook of public administration and management in Europe* (pp. 327–346). Palgrave Macmillan.

CHAPTER 18

Municipal Corporatisation in the Netherlands: A Vehicle for Inter-municipal Cooperation

Bart Voorn and Marieke Van Genugten

18.1 Introduction

The Netherlands is a typical example of a country with high municipal corporatisation, of which inter-municipal corporatisation makes up a large part (Torsteinsen & Van Genugten, 2016). For this reason, municipal corporatisation is of great importance in the Netherlands, and the use of municipally owned corporations (MOCs) has become increasingly studied by various Dutch scholars (Gradus & Budding, 2020; Klok et al., 2018; Schipper, 2021; Voorn et al., 2017, 2018a, 2018b, 2019, 2020a, 2020b).

In this chapter, we tell the tale of municipal corporatisation in the Netherlands. One of the main sources of this chapter is a survey sent out to directors of all MOCs in 2017 (Voorn et al., 2020a). In addition, we

B. Voorn (✉) • M. Van Genugten
Institute for Management Research, Radboud University, Nijmegen, The Netherlands
e-mail: bart.voorn@ru.nl; marieke.vangenugten@ru.nl

M. Van Genugten et al. (eds.), *Corporatisation in Local Government*, https://doi.org/10.1007/978-3-031-09982-3_18

make use of other data from our own research and studies from various other Dutch scholars on this theme.

This chapter is organised as follows. We first discuss the context of the Dutch local government system and the trend of municipal corporatisation. Next, we delve deeper into the topics of legal status, organisational characteristics, autonomy and internal governance. Finally, we discuss some salient issues for Dutch local corporatisation in the conclusion.

18.2 Context

Corporatisation in Dutch municipalities takes place within a specific institutional setting (Kuhlmann & Wayenberg, 2016). In terms of local government system, the Netherlands can be characterised as a decentralised, unitary country. Decentralisation refers to the transfer of tasks and responsibilities to subnational governments. Yet at the same time, the Dutch unitary institutional system results in a centrally imposed coherency and coordination. This means that although Dutch local governments have a high degree of autonomy and a broad scope of responsibilities (comparable to other Nordic countries), they can only do their job by relying quite heavily on central government (similar to the continental-Napoleonic tradition) (John, 2001; Lidström, 1996). This dependency on central government is reinforced by the fact that local governments' financial autonomy is relatively low.

This unitary but decentralised local government system creates a specific Dutch local government context. While the scale of municipalities in the Netherlands has increased substantially in previous decades, with the average municipality now having around 50,000 inhabitants, municipalities' dominant role in public service provision leads them to organise many tasks cooperatively, particularly through corporations sharedly owned and governed with other municipalities (Ministry of the Interior and Kingdom Relations, 2021; Schaap, 2019; Voorn et al., 2020a).

Also relevant as Dutch local government context is that the Netherlands has a dualistic municipal system, where legislative power is exercised by the municipal council, and executive power is exercised by the council of mayor and aldermen. Aldermen are given portfolios, much like ministers in a cabinet. This contextual factor too affects corporatisation in the Netherlands, in the sense that it determines the governance arrangement: individual aldermen are responsible for the governance of MOCs that fit their specific portfolio. They then report to, and are (to a lesser or greater extent) monitored by, the municipal council.

The legal context is relevant as well. Dutch law, for the most part, is lenient in allowing corporatisation. MOCs can be founded in several ways, for many different sectors, and are for this reason particularly heterogeneous (Voorn, 2020). What law applies to them—public (administrative) law or private (commercial) law—depends on their legal status.

First, municipalities are free to found associations, foundations and various types of enterprises for the delivery of public services, and these are governed by the Dutch Civil Code (*Burgerlijk Wetboek*)—Dutch private (commercial) law. These private-law MOCs can be employed by municipalities with few restraints set by lawmakers. Corporatisation in private commercial law is frequently chosen by municipalities because it tends to be the most flexible option for founding MOCs. Private law sets few organisational restraints, for example with respect to board structure (see Sect. 18.7). Lastly, MOCs under private law are very flexible in terms of their ownership, and so are frequently used for the purpose of public-private partnership or inter-municipal cooperation. In sum, private law offers a flexible way for municipalities to corporatise local service delivery, allowing for many forms of organisation for MOCs.

Next, *exclusively* for inter-municipal corporations, since 1950 there exists also a public-law form under the Joint Arrangements Act (*Wet gemeenschappelijke regelingen*), which is in many ways more rigid than the private law. For some services, such as public health and safety, use of this public-law form is mandatory; for others, the law dictates that the private-law form can be chosen if there are strong public interest arguments for this. Public law offers greater labour protection for employees, and dictates among others board structures, voting procedures, and some other rules for public accountability. Perhaps the most critical of these rules is that public law mandates that municipalities elect a 'daily board' comprised of aldermen for daily oversight of the MOC, and releases aldermen on this 'daily board' from being bound to decisions by their own municipal councils. This encourages inter-municipal consensus-building, but also creates a conflict of interest for aldermen, trapped between their municipality's local interest and the common good, that highly complicates and substantially muddles their roles and responsibility (Voorn & Van Genugten, 2021). In practice, we observe some techniques used by lawmakers to avoid the stringent rules under Dutch public law; for instance, executive management is often shifted to an outside executive director, who effectively takes up many of the tasks ascribed to the 'daily board'. We also observe that public-law MOCs are sometimes just entities on paper, that supervise one or a number of private-law subsidiaries where the actual service delivery takes place. Summarising, public law also offers a path towards corporatisation for municipalities, but only for the purpose of inter-municipal cooperation, and it sets various additional restraints for the purpose of accountability. We discuss the distinction between public and private law in more detail in Sect. 18.4.

18.3 Trend

While local corporatisation as an overall trend is quite recent, MOCs have existed in the Netherlands for much longer than this century (some MOCs were founded as early as 1936 [Voorn et al., 2018a, 2018b]). Many of these long-standing MOCs are inter-municipal MOCs. Already at the end of the 1970s and early 1980s, the interest in contracting out and inter-municipal cooperation in Dutch municipalities increased (Torsteinsen & Van Genugten, 2016). Fiscal stress, a growing number of tasks, and core-task discussions in local councils induced municipalities to find alternative ways of providing public services to improve the efficiency of policy implementation, and to reduce costs to answer to the need to achieve cutbacks (Hendriks & Tops, 2003; Van Thiel, 2004). Small municipalities in particular expected to gain economies of scale by cooperating with other municipalities. The most frequently used form of cooperation was the inter-municipal public-law MOC, although the private-law MOC began to emerge at the end of the century (Torsteinsen & Van Genugten, 2016). Unfortunately, empirical evidence on the number of MOCs in this period is lacking.

It appears that the majority of local corporatisation in the Netherlands occurred in the 2000s. Gradus and Budding (2020) recently studied trends in the refuse collection sector, and, using time series data for every year from 1999 to 2014, they found that the frequency of the use of MOCs for the delivery of refuse collection services increased from about 6% of services in 1999 to just over 30% in 2010, after which numbers stabilised. The authors conclude that "similar to some other European countries, the Netherlands face a trend toward municipality-owned firms and corporatisation" (p. 557). Voorn et al. (2018a, 2018b, 2020a) make similar findings in a descriptive study of all MOCs in the Netherlands. They find that the average age of Dutch MOCs is 17 years, which points to their relatively recent founding.

There is not yet any direct evidence what underlies this trend of local corporatisation. At least one important driver is the decentralisation of tasks by national government. In many cases decentralisation is accompanied with a call or obligation to cooperate inter-municipally in the form of a corporation, or municipalities feel the need to collaborate with other municipalities because of a lack of administrative capacity (Raad voor het Openbaar Bestuur, 2021; Schaap, 2019). An additional reason may be the fear of amalgamation. By collaborating with other municipalities and putting services at arm's length municipalities hope they will be able to continue service delivery to their citizens without having to amalgamate and losing their autonomy and local identity (Herweijer & Fraanje, 2011). It is also possible that the trend of corporatisation at the local level largely mimics a similar trend occurring at the national level (Van Thiel et al., 2020), and there is also evidence of cross-municipality policy learning (Voorn et al., 2018a, 2018b). Gradus and Budding (2020) considered various causes for corporatisation in the waste collection sector, but found many possible causes to be insignificant. The only relevant significant determinant seemed to be the number of seats held by the VVD (the largest Dutch right-wing party) in the municipal council, which encourages corporatisation; a larger number of seats for left-wing parties appeared to be an obstacle to corporatisation. Corporatisation may thus be at least partly ideological. Beyond this, we still lack actual empirical evidence of the determinants of this recent corporatisation trend in the Netherlands.

In sum, although corporatisation is not a new phenomenon at the local level in the Netherlands, corporatisation in the Netherlands appears to have been mostly a trend in the first decade of the century, after which the trend towards it seems to have slowed significantly. Causes are still mostly unknown, although national policies related to decentralisation and the lack of administrative capacity of municipalities are clear incentives. There is also provisional evidence that politics matters, with corporatisation more preferred by right-wing than by left-wing parties. Overall, corporatisation remains a salient political issue, with corporatised entities responsible for rather substantive policy such as welfare services, infrastructure-building, (youth) care and COVID-19 vaccinations.

18.4 Legal Status

As mentioned in Sect. 18.2, both private law and public law offer options for corporatisation for municipalities. However, public law comes with many added rules. In the face of these added rules, the question remains why municipalities choose the public-law option in the first place—after all, these rules can also be implemented under private law, for instance, through statutes or governance codes.

The reason for this can be found in Dutch law. Critical in Dutch law as it applies to MOCs is the Municipalities Act (*Gemeentewet*), the law that dictates municipal behaviour, which clearly establishes rules for municipalities: private-law MOCs are to be used only when they are "considered particularly appropriate for advancing a specific public interest" (*"bijzonder aangewezen worden geacht voor de behartiging van een bepaald openbaar belang"* [article 160, Municipalities Act]). Thus, Dutch national lawmakers have effectively ordered municipalities to use the public-law option for corporatisation in most cases. Dutch parliamentary history suggests that a key reason for this mandate is that the public-law option should better clarify and protect roles and responsibilities, organisational structures, governance, democratic control and transparency in the context of corporatisation (Tweede Kamer, 1988/89, p. 106). Arguably, the law has failed in this purpose.

Over time, many private-law MOCs have been founded for the purpose of corporatisation (Voorn et al., 2018a, 2018b, 2020a). This has led to some debate among Dutch legal scholars, academic researchers and practitioners about the legality of municipalities' current approach to corporatisation, where corporatisation through private law appears increasingly prominent, despite the lawmaker's clear preference for the public-law form. On one side, renowned legal scholar Zijlstra (2019, nr. 277) writes that "as far as I can see, there is no area in administrative law in which the government so consistently and brazenly violates the law as here" ("*[e]r is voor zover ik kan zien geen terrein van staats- en bestuursrecht waar de overheid zó consequent en zonder gêne het recht schendt als hier*"). On the other hand, some research suggests that Dutch public law may be so stifling of effective decision-making that the trend towards it should not be considered surprising (Voorn, 2020), and in particular that the rigidity of public law prevents solutions to various collaborative governance problems in inter-municipal corporatisation that have together become known as the multiple principal problem (Voorn et al., 2019). It may actually obscure rights and responsibilities, for instance by creating a conflict of interest for aldermen on the board. And it is also arguably undemocratic, given aldermen's ability to vote against the interests of their own municipal councils, and given the fact that voting rights in these public-law MOCs do not reflect the populations of the participating municipalities.

It is thus not surprising that over 60% of all MOCs in the Netherlands today are based in private law (see Table 18.1).

One key determinant of the legal status (and thus applicable law) of MOCs is service sector. For MOCs operating in services such as general and financial services, environmental services, social affairs, and security and health, public-law organisations are the dominant organisational form (Voorn et al., 2020a). These are particularly sectors where the Dutch national government has desired inter-municipal cooperation; in many cases, it has encouraged or demanded the use of the public-law form. Among private-law forms, enterprises are mostly used for MOCs with economic and development tasks, sports and well-being, and infrastructure and refuse collection tasks, most of which are services that require substantial investments (Voorn et al., 2020a), and foundations are used particularly in the education and culture services: more than half of the MOCs in this service sector are foundations.

Schipper (2021) adds to this research by looking at two classifications of service characteristics: measurement complexity and investment specificity. He finds that public-law organisations are used particularly often when service complexity increases, likely because more complex services are often more political, and so municipalities may be hesitant to leave these services in the hands of more autonomous directors of private-law organisations. Meanwhile, enterprises based in private law are used often for 'simple' (low-complexity) services, likely because of easier governance and lesser political service nature. Schipper (2021) also finds that when

Table 18.1 Legal statuses of MOCs in the Netherlands

Corporate status	N	%
Public-law organisation	309	38.7
Enterprise *(private law)*	279	34.9
Foundation *(private law)*	189	23.7
Association *(private law)*	22	2.8
Total	799	100

Source: adjusted from Voorn et al. (2020a)

services require more specific investments, municipalities are likely to outsource them to enterprises, while low-specificity services are more often given to foundations. This can be explained by the fact that services with more specific investments, such as refuse collection, are easier to leave to private markets and may also yield larger benefits from business-like service delivery.

Beyond this, Voorn et al. (2019) suggest that one core reason for the use of private-law corporatisation is the avoidance of the governance problems that can occur in public-law corporations when the public regulations are too rigid to solve collective action problems (the multiple principal problem).

18.5 Organisational Characteristics

Looking at the organisational characteristics of MOCs in the Netherlands, we observe a large variety in terms of service sector, ownership, size and single-/multi-purpose MOCs. We discuss these characteristics subsequently in this section.

MOCs are used across many different service sectors. Voorn et al. (2018a, 2018b, 2020a) compared the use of MOCs across eight different sectors, finding them to be ubiquitous (Table 18.2). Some sectors stand out. One sector is 'Social affairs and employment' (19.8%). Services in this

Table 18.2 MOCs per service sector

Sector	*Total (%)*
General and finance	6.2
Economy and development	15.3
Infrastructure and refuse collection	14.1
Nature and agriculture	13.6
Education and culture	11.3
Social affairs and employment	19.8
Sports and well-being	9.6
Security and health	10.2
Total	100

Source: adjusted from Voorn et al. (2020a)

Note: these percentages are based on self-classification in a survey of MOCs; this table does not show the whole population of MOCs in the Netherlands but rather a subset of 177 of 799 MOCs sector have been decentralised to local government and are often organised inter-municipally (Ministry of the Interior and Kingdom Relations, 2021). Another sector is 'Economy and development' (15.3%) which focusses on issues that often require a regional approach for which municipalities establish inter-municipal MOCs (Ministry of the Interior and Kingdom Relations, 2021) or require the participation of private partners, for example for development projects, for which municipalities establish joint MOCs with private partners.

This takes us to the ownership of MOCs. In the Netherlands, MOCs are inter-municipally owned in nearly three-quarters of cases (Voorn et al., 2020a). This is a high number compared to other countries. The average number of municipality-owners per joint MOC is ten municipalities (PROOF Adviseurs/KWINK Groep, 2020). More than 20% of municipalities' budget goes to public-law joint MOCs (Raad voor het Openbaar Bestuur, 2021). The number of employees of public-law joint MOCs is 47.012 in 2019 (by way of comparison, municipalities employed 153.668 employees in 2019) (Boer, 2021). Enterprises and foundations are used in equal proportions for inter-municipal cooperation, while public-law MOCs are used exclusively for inter-municipal cooperation, as Dutch legislation does not allow for single-owned public-law MOCs. Enabling inter-municipal cooperation is thus a prime reason for corporatisation in the Netherlands (Voorn & Van Genugten, 2021). Incidentally, inter-municipal cooperation is increasingly taking place without establishing a MOC (Ministry of the Interior and Kingdom Relations, 2021).

Only 13% of Dutch MOCs involve public-private partnerships (Voorn et al., 2018a, 2018b, 2020a). Internationally, this is a low number. Public-private partnerships mostly appear in the sectors 'Infrastructure and refuse collection' and 'Economics and development', much like in other countries involving development projects for housing or business parks.

Looking at the size of MOCs we also observe large variation. There are MOCs with budgets of under a million euros and less than ten employees, and MOCs with thousands of employees and a budget of nearly a billion euros. Table 18.3 divides MOCs into three similarly sized groups according to their budgets and number of employees. Noticeably, public-law MOCs are on average substantially larger than private-law MOCs, both in terms of budget and number of employees.

Most MOCs are single-purpose. However, multi-purpose MOCs do exist as well. One type of multi-purpose MOCs is public-law-based regional collaborations (the former city regions or quasi-regional

Table 18.3 The size of MOCs

Budget size	*N (%)*	*Number of employees*	*N (%)*
Small (<4mln)	60 (33.9%)	Small (<16)	59 (33.3%)
Medium (4mln–17mln)	58 (32.7%)	Medium (17–125)	59 (33.3%)
Large (17mln>)	59 (33.3%)	Large (126>)	59 (33.3%)
Total	177 (100%)	Total	177 (100%)

Source: adjusted from Voorn et al. (2020a)

Note: these percentages are based on self-classification in a survey of MOCs; this table does not show the whole population of MOCs in the Netherlands but rather a subset of 177 of 799 MOCs

governments (Hulst et al., 2009) which often are active in the domains of economic development, labour, spatial planning, housing, public transport and energy (Ministry of the Interior and Kingdom Relations, 2021; Schaap, 2019). Another type of multi-purpose MOCs are shared municipal service organisations (*ambtelijke fusies*) in which municipalities merge the complete civil services of all participating municipalities (often two to four) into one separate shared municipal service organisation (Herweijer & Fraanje, 2011). This shared municipal service organisation is charged with the provision of all local tasks to the participating municipalities. The first one was established in 2008, and in 2021, 16 shared municipal service organisations exist. In addition, MOCs occasionally team up together; for instance, in many cases the public health MOCs (*GGD*) are in the same building as the Safety Regions (*Veiligheidsregio*) or youth care organisations (*Jeugdzorg*), so collaboration between MOCs with different tasks does occur as well.

18.6 Autonomy

Autonomy is a key feature of MOCs and is often an important reason why MOCs are established. However, MOCs can differ greatly with respect to the autonomy they have, both formally and in practice. Voorn et al. (2018a, 2018b, 2020a) asked directors of MOCs to describe their level of managerial and financial autonomy (cf. Verhoest et al., 2004). In this section, we first describe these two forms of autonomy. Second, we discuss the steering relationship between owner-municipalities and MOCs, which is illustrative of the level of autonomy MOCs have in practice.

Dutch MOCs have a high degree of managerial autonomy which means that they themselves can make decisions on human resource and financial management. In particular, Voorn et al. (2018a, 2018b, 2020a) show that MOCs have control over temporary personnel policy (e.g. the ability to freely hire temporary and external personnel) and over longer-term policy (such as decisions on hiring new personnel, on wages, lay-offs and promotions). Many MOCs also have control over labour agreements and pension arrangements, although MOCs' control over these is substantially less. Their autonomy with respect to financial management is evidenced by MOCs' ability to make decisions about purchasing material and ICT, as well as setting tariffs and shifting funds between budgets for personnel and material (Voorn et al., 2018a, 2018b, 2020a). However, MOCs have substantially less freedom in taking loans and in shifting budgets between years. In addition, the freedom to invest and to participate in other companies is even more rare (Voorn et al., 2018a, 2018b, 2020a). Private-law MOCs have substantially more managerial autonomy—in particular with respect to human resource management—than public-law MOCs (Voorn et al., 2018a, 2018b, 2020a).

Next to managerial autonomy, Voorn et al. (2020a) also studied the financial autonomy of MOCs, which refers to the extent to which a MOC depends on municipal funding or own revenues for its financial resources (cf. Verhoest et al., 2004). They show that MOCs are frequently dependent on municipal funding (accounting for on average of 47.9% of their budgets), but also receive funding through tariffs to users (15.9%) or tariffs to municipalities (9.5%). Sometimes, MOCs receive funding from other actors (7.2%) or receive different income (including subsidies, 19.5%) (see also Table 18.4) (Voorn et al., 2020a). There are large differences between different types of MOCs in this respect. Public-law MOCs are most dependent on municipal budgets, while enterprises are clearly less dependent, and obtain more funding from tariffs and other sources (Voorn et al., 2020a).

Apart from these forms of autonomy, the level of autonomy highly depends on how municipalities set up their steering relationship with MOCs. Important issues in this respect are goal-setting, reporting on performance, and informal ways of steering.

The overall goal of a MOC is set by the founders (mostly municipalities) of a MOC and is laid down in founding documents or statutes. This overall goal is often translated in performance indicators which are included in policy documents, (quasi-)contractual agreements between municipalities and MOCs, or in subsidy documents (Voorn et al., 2018a, 2018b, 2020a). MOCs appear to have much say in what performance indicators are set. In

Table 18.4 Financial resources of MOCs

Financial resources	*Unweighted average*	*Public-law organisation*	*Enterprise*	*Foundation*
Budget municipalities	47.9%	**62.7%**	*27.1%*	50.4%
Tariffs for users	15.9%	4.7%	**30.2%**	13.4%
Tariffs for municipalities	9.5%	12.5%	6.9%	8.6%
Budget (other public sector)	5.9%	8.9%	2.1%	5.6%
Budget (private parties)	1.3%	1.7%	1.5%	0.5%
Other	19.5%	*11.9%*	**32.2%**	21.5%
Total	100%	100%	100%	100%

Source: adjusted from Voorn et al. (2020a)

Note: these percentages are based on self-classification in a survey of MOCs; this table does not show the whole population of MOCs in the Netherlands but rather a subset of 177 of 799 MOCs

almost half of the cases, performance indicators are formulated jointly, while in the majority of cases, MOCs take the lead in formulating them (sometimes after consulting their municipality-owners). Comparatively, private-law MOCs have more control over setting performance indicators than public-law MOCs (Voorn et al., 2018a, 2018b, 2020a).

This is confirmed in a qualitative study which shows that strategic initiative is mostly on the side of MOCs (Voorn et al., 2020b). This can be explained by three factors. First, the longer MOCs exist, the more they take over goal-setting from the municipalities. In other words, increasing distance over time between municipality and MOCs causes increasing information asymmetries and shifts the goal-setting role to the corporation. Second, the lack of continuity on municipality side, in particular in the board of mayor and aldermen and the municipal council, leads to increasing initiative on the side of MOCs. Third, the existence of multiple principals, in case of joint MOCs, leads to diversity and/or free riding in goal-setting, which in turn results in much autonomy in goal and performance indicator setting for MOCs.

An additional way for municipalities to steer MOCs is to gain insight into the actual performance through reporting. MOCs appear to report extensively to municipalities (Voorn et al., 2018a, 2018b, 2020a). The majority of MOCs report between 3 and 6 times per year to municipalities. Almost three-quarters of MOCs report more often than once a year. Interestingly, public-law MOCs report more often to municipalities than private-law MOCs. This may be explained by the obligations laid down in the Joint Arrangements Act on reporting to the municipal councils of the owner-municipalities. MOCs report on different types of performance indicators: 71.8% of MOCs report on performance indicators related to financial results, 61.6% on performance indicators tied to quality of service delivery, and 41.2% on indicators related to other societal effects (Voorn et al., 2018a, 2018b, 2020a). These societal effect indicators are often sector- or service-dependent: for example, economic development organisations report on investment climate, while youth care organisations report on quality of care and in- and outflow rates in youth care. Only 9% of MOCs do not use and report on performance indicators. A qualitative study on this topic shows that in case no performance indicators are used, the budget is often used as a steering instrument (Voorn et al., 2020b). Multiple reasons underlie the limited use of performance indicators, including ideological reasons (performance indicators may bring underlying problems in MOCs to light, which is not necessarily in the political interest of their responsible aldermen), capacity problems (municipalities after corporatisation may not have the necessary in-house expertise to oversee the MOCs), and bureaucratic culture (corporatisation in many cases does not lead to an immediate switch away from previous, non-performance-based, in-house governance mechanisms) (Voorn et al., 2020b).

What is more, even when performance indicators exist, many executive directors of MOCs do not believe that how they perform on these indicators actually has consequences (Voorn et al., 2018a, 2018b, 2020a). The majority of the executive directors expect neither benefits if they perform well (92.7%) nor negative effects such as sanctions if they perform poorly (76.8%). The only consequence they expect is a firm conversation with their municipality-owners (Voorn et al., 2020b).

In addition to these formal ways of steering, municipalities use informal ways of steering as well. One such informal steering mechanism is the communication between the municipal civil services and MOCs. Communication appears to be frequent (Voorn et al., 2018a, 2018b, 2020a). Most MOCs (67.7%) communicate with municipal civil servants on a weekly basis; the large majority (89.2%) has contact at least on a monthly basis. Furthermore, public-law MOCs communicate the most with local civil servants; half of these MOCs even have contact on a daily basis. The nature of this communication varies. It is often about operational affairs, but evaluative and strategic affairs are also regularly discussed.

A complicating factor in joint MOCs, leading to a high level of autonomy, is the multiple principal problem (Voorn & Van Genugten, 2021). At least two governance problems can be observed. On the one hand, the problem of free riding, which means that some municipality-owners rely heavily on steering and monitoring behaviour of other, mainly larger, municipality-owners. On the other hand, duplication of governance, meaning that municipality-owners all have their own individual wishes and agendas and often do not align these, giving MOCs autonomy to formulate their own goals and agenda (Voorn & Van Genugten, 2021).

All in all, Dutch MOCs have a lot of autonomy. This can be explained by a lack of capacity and knowledge on municipality side and resulting information asymmetries between MOCs and municipalities, a lack of service measurability, a bureaucratic culture and political factors (Voorn et al., 2020b). This has important negative consequences for the democratic legitimacy of MOCs (Van Genugten et al., 2020), a topic that has been receiving more and more attention from local councils, experts and national government (Peters & Castenmiller, 2020), resulting in pending amendments to the law on public-law MOCs (the Joint Arrangements Act) and calls for more systemic measures (Raad voor het Openbaar Bestuur, 2021).

18.7 Internal Governance

In this section, we turn to the internal governance of MOCs, namely board structure and the executive director in particular. These topics are still understudied in the Netherlands. Apart from descriptive data about board structure, there is no empirical data and research available on this topic.

18.7.1 Board Structure

In the Netherlands, both public-law and private-law MOCs typically have a two-tier board with an executive and a non-executive (supervisory) board. In general, the supervisory board supervises and advises the executive board and is involved in strategic decisions. In practice, almost three-quarters of MOCs have a supervisory board (Voorn et al., 2018a, 2018b, 2020a). Although both public and private law mandate the presence of a supervisory board, private law is more lenient and does not set very strict requirements about what this supervisory board actually looks like, so composition and tasks of supervisory boards can vary. Dutch private law also offers the option of a one-tier board that includes supervisory and executive board members on the same board, which is occasionally used. Public law mandates that municipalities elect a 'general' and 'daily board' comprised of politicians. As these boards nearly always hire an outside executive director, in practice this 'general' and 'daily board' function as a supervisory board (Voorn & Van Genugten, 2021).

The composition of the boards in MOCs differs: in private-law MOCs, the executive board and supervisory board consist of professionals or volunteers with specific expertise, while in public-law MOCs, the supervisory board consists of politicians (as representatives of the owner-municipalities) and the executive board consists of professionals. Thus, there is a difference in how owners are represented in the governance structure of a MOC. In private-law MOCs, owners are represented in the shareholders' meeting, while in public-law MOCs they are represented in the 'general board'. The frequency of owners' meetings also varies per type of MOC. Typical shareholders' meetings in private-law MOCs occur once or twice a year, while the owners' meeting of public law MOCs meets much more frequently, between four and six times per year (Voorn & Van Genugten, 2021).

Some Dutch MOCs adhere to governance codes. In the Netherlands, these governance codes are sectoral codes. Governance codes differ between sectors, but they are all derived from the Dutch commercial code for listed companies (Tabaksblat code) (Papenfuß et al., 2018). This governance code first of all includes regulations on checks and balances within organisations and in particular, between the supervisory board and executive board. Furthermore, rules about transparency, integrity and diversity of the supervisory board are included, as well as regulations about appointment, tenure and remuneration of executive board members (Papenfuß et al., 2018). Examples of sectoral codes relevant for MOCs are healthcare organisations, primary and secondary schools, and cultural organisations. These sectoral governance codes have a 'comply-or-explain' rule, but the codes are not legally binding. In cases where there is no sectoral code, some larger private-law MOCs voluntarily adhere to the Tabaksblat code—for example, MOCs in the utilities sector—or they have their own company governance code, usually derived from the Tabaksblat code. Public-law MOCs do not have a governance code if there is no sectoral code (Papenfuß et al., 2018).

18.7.2 Executive Director

As described in the previous subsection, all MOCs have an executive board responsible for the daily management of the MOC. Executive boards tend to be very small, often limited to a single executive director (Papenfuß et al., 2018; Voorn et al., 2018a, 2018b, 2020a). This is particularly the case for public-law MOCs and enterprises. In 67.4% of these MOCs, there is a single executive director (Voorn et al., 2018a, 2018b, 2020a). In other private-law MOCs, such as foundations and associations, daily control is more divided. In 74.4% of foundations and associations, the executive board consists of multiple executive directors.

These executive directors are demographically not very diverse. Relatively few boards feature women or members with a non-Dutch background (Papenfuß et al., 2018; Voorn et al., 2018a, 2018b, 2020a). In background and expertise, the executive boards of MOCs are more diverse. Board members often have public sector backgrounds (67.8%), but backgrounds in the private (49.7%) and non-profit sectors (26.4%) also often feature on executive boards (Voorn et al., 2018a, 2018b, 2020a). Regarding expertise, many boards feature management backgrounds, service sector knowledge, and expertise in finance. Comparatively, public-law MOCs often have much service sector knowledge, and enterprises less so. Foundations often feature financial experts in their boards, but they have access to less management expertise when compared to public-law MOCs and enterprises. Note that although at an aggregated level boards are to some extent diverse, at individual board level they are not, as many boards only have one single executive director.

Taking a closer look at the function of executive director, it appears that more than half of the executive directors work full-time for MOCs (58.8% of MOCs) (Voorn et al., 2018a, 2018b, 2020a). Directors in public-law MOCs work full-time the most, and directors of foundations the least. This is likely strongly correlated with organisation size, but may also relate to the fact that directors of public-law MOCs and enterprises are most likely to be monetarily compensated for their work, while this is less likely to be the case for directors of foundations (Voorn et al., 2018a, 2018b, 2020a).

All sector governance codes require that the remuneration of executive boards is disclosed in the annual report. Since 2013 this obligation is also laid down in a law, which caps the remuneration of top civil servants at the level of minister salaries. The law holds for MOCs as well (Papenfuß et al., 2018).

18.8 Conclusion

Municipal corporatisation in the Netherlands appeared to be a trend at the start of this century that has since levelled out. In that sense, the trend in the Netherlands has mimicked that of many other countries in and outside Europe. Moreover, just as elsewhere, this trend has created a very heterogeneous plethora of MOCs, appearing in many different sectors, shapes and sizes, and with various types of board structures, manager backgrounds and sectoral governance codes.

However, local corporatisation in the Netherlands has its own intricacies and in some ways plays out differently from elsewhere. In particular, the Dutch unitary and decentralised government system has brought much corporatisation for the purpose of inter-municipal cooperation. Moreover, the specific workings of Dutch public law, as well as the priority given to public-law organisations for the purpose of inter-municipal cooperation, create a unique Dutch legal context for corporatisation that municipalities and MOCs must navigate.

This interplay between public and private law in the Dutch context creates some peculiarities in how Dutch municipalities have operated when it comes to municipal corporatisation. In particular, the stringency of Dutch public law has created some collaborative governance problems for governing MOCs. Municipalities have tried to circumvent these problems in various ways, including turning to private-law organisations in cases where that choice was legally debatable, and by setting up hybrid structures, for instance by having a public-law organisation on paper which then governs private-law subsidiaries. It can be debated whether current legislation is the best way forward.

This altogether has led to a range of governance challenges, and above all it has led to very autonomous MOCs. Performance management appears to be limited in Dutch MOCs, for reasons that range from improper political incentives, limited in-house governance capacity, and persistent bureaucratic culture. Moreover, executive directors of MOCs do not actually expect too many consequences for failure. From a governance perspective, this all is problematic. Fortunately, this deficiency in 'formal' governance is offset at least in part by much informal steering. On the whole, however, MOCs are very autonomous, which has upsides but also offers some risk, particularly in light of what appears to be suboptimal governance procedures.

One aspect of Dutch municipal corporatisation that we continue to know less about is the internal governance of MOCs. We know that the expertise of executive directors is mixed and that, demographically, diversity is still lacking in terms of board composition: boards of MOCs continue to be dominated by primarily the stereotypical old white males. But we know much less about how board members are appointed, and how boards and MOCs function internally. Future research can still shed light on these aspects of Dutch local corporatisation.

In conclusion, local corporatisation in the Netherlands is both different from and similar to local corporatisation in many other countries. The main distinct features of Dutch local corporatisation are their inter-municipal nature and the particular interplay between public and private law, which create a unique context for Dutch municipalities and MOCs to navigate. Local corporatisation in the Netherlands appears to be here to stay, but in terms of governance there is still much to be learned—and done.

References

Boer, A. (2021, April 2). Gemeente zit in zóveel samenwerkingsverbanden dat niemand ze meer controleert: 'Ondemocratisch en ernstig' [Local governments are involved in so many inter-municipal cooperations no one scrutinises them anymore: 'Undemocratic and serious']. *De Gelderlander.*

Brown, T. L., & Potoski, M. (2005). Transaction costs and contracting: The practitioner perspective. *Public Performance & Management Review, 28*(3), 326–351.

Gradus, R., & Budding, T. (2020). Political and institutional explanations for increasing re-municipalisation. *Urban Affairs Review, 56*(2), 538–564.

Hendriks, F., & Tops, P. (2003). Local public management reforms in the Netherlands: Fads, fashions and winds of change. *Public Administration, 81*(2), 301–323.

Herweijer, M., & Fraanje, R. (2011). *Samen werken aan bestuurskracht [Collaborating for administrative capacity].* Kluwer.

Hulst, R., Van Montfort, A., Haveri, A., Airaksinen, J., & Kelly, J. (2009). Institutional shifts in inter-municipal service delivery: An analysis of developments in eight Western European countries. *Public Organization Review, 9*(3), 263–285.

John, P. (2001). *Local governance in Western Europe.* Sage.

Klok, P. J., Denters, B., Boogers, M., & Sanders, M. (2018). Intermunicipal cooperation in the Netherlands: The costs and the effectiveness of polycentric regional governance. *Public Administration Review, 78*(4), 527–536.

Kuhlmann, S., & Wayenberg, E. (2016). Institutional impact assessment in multilevel systems: Conceptualising decentralisation effects from a comparative perspective. *International Review of Administrative Sciences, 82*, 233–254.

Lidström, A. (1996). *Kommunsystem i Europa [Local government in Europe]*. Publica.

Ministry of the Interior and Kingdom Relations. (2021). *Staat van het bestuur [State of the administration]*. Ministry of the Interior and Kingdom Relations.

Papenfuß, U., Van Genugten, M., De Kruijf, J., & Van Thiel, S. (2018). Implementation of EU initiatives on gender diversity and executive directors' pay in municipally-owned enterprises in Germany and The Netherlands. *Public Money & Management, 38*(2), 87–96.

Peters, K., & Castenmiller, P. (2020). Kaderstellen en controleren door de gemeenteraad: een zware opgave [Legislation and scrutiny by the local council: A difficult task]. *Bestuurswetenschappen, 74*(2), 10–33.

PROOF Adviseurs/KWINK Groep. (2020). *Inventarisatie regionale samenwerkingsverbanden decentrale overheden 2020 [Inventory regional collaborations decentralised authorities 2020]*. Den Haag: PROOF Adviseurs/KWINK Groep.

Raad voor het Openbaar Bestuur. (2021). *Droomland of niemandsland? Uitgangspunten voor het besturen van regio's [Dream land or no man's land: Principles for governing regions]*. Raad voor het Openbaar Bestuur.

Schaap, L. (2019). *Lokaal bestuur [Local government]*. Convoy.

Schipper, E. W. (2021). *Externe verzelfstandiging door Nederlandse gemeenten: Gemeentelijke dienstverlening op het grensvlak tussen publiek en privaat [Agencification by Dutch municipalities: Municipal service provision at the interface between public and private]*. (Master thesis). Nijmegen: Radboud Universiteit.

Torsteinsen, H., & Van Genugten, M. (2016). Waste management in the Netherlands and Norway – From in-house provision to inter-municipal cooperation. In S. Kuhlman & G. Bouckaert (Eds.), *Local public sector reforms in times of crisis: National trajectories and international comparisons* (pp. 205–220). Palgrave.

Tweede Kamer. (1988/89). *Nieuwe bepalingen met betrekking tot provincies (Provinciewet) [New provisions relating to provinces (Province Act)]*. Kamerstukken II 19836, nr. 9.

Van Genugten, M., Van Thiel, S., & Voorn, B. (2020). Local governments and their relationship with arm's length bodies. *Local Government Studies, 46*(1), 1–21.

Van Thiel, S. (2004). Quangos in Dutch government. In C. Pollitt & C. Talbot (Eds.), *Unbundled government: A critical analysis of the global trend to agencies, quasi-autonomous bodies and contractualisation* (pp. 167–183). Routledge.

Van Thiel, S., Van Genugten, M., & Voorn, B. (2020). Principals and agents: The relationship between governments and state-owned enterprises. In L. Bernier, M. Florio, & P. Bance (Eds.), *The Routledge handbook of state-owned enterprises* (pp. 322–335). Routledge.

Verhoest, K., Peters, B. G., Bouckaert, G., & Verschuere, B. (2004). The study of organisational autonomy: A conceptual review. *Public Administration Development, 24*, 101–118.

Voorn, B. (2020). *When politics meets professionalism: The characteristics and performance predictors of municipally owned corporations.* (Dissertation). Nijmegen: Radboud University.

Voorn, B., & Van Genugten, M. (2021). Dealing with multiple principals in at arm's length organisations: A qualitative study of Dutch municipally owned corporations. *Public Administration.* https://doi.org/10.1111/padm.12746.

Voorn, B., Van Genugten, M., & Van Thiel, S. (2017). The efficiency and effectiveness of municipally owned corporations: A systematic review. *Local Government Studies, 43*(5), 820–841.

Voorn, B., Van Genugten, M., & Van Thiel, S. (2018a). *Respondentenrapport vragenlijstonderzoek "Verbonden partijen in Nederland 2018" [Respondents report survey "Municipally owned corporations in the Netherlands 2018"].* Institute for Management Research.

Voorn, B., Van Genugten, M., & Van Thiel, S. (2019). Multiple principals, multiple problems: A framework for effective governance and a research agenda for joint service delivery. *Public Administration, 97*(3), 671–685.

Voorn, B., Van Genugten, M., & Van Thiel, S. (2020a). The features of Dutch municipally owned corporations. In B. Voorn (Ed.), *When politics meets professionalism: The features and performance predictors of municipally owned corporations* (pp. 113–138). Institute of Management Research.

Voorn, B., Van Genugten, M., & Van Thiel, S. (2020b). Performance management in municipally owned corporations: Explanations for use and non-use. In B. Voorn (Ed.), *When politics meets professionalism: The features and performance predictors of municipally owned corporations* (pp. 183–205). Institute of Management Research.

Voorn, B., Van Thiel, S., & Van Genugten, M. (2018b). Debate: Corporatisation as more than a recent crisis-driven development. *Public Money & Management, 38*(7), 481–482.

Zijlstra, S. E. (2019). *Bestuurlijk organisatierecht [Administrative organisation law].* Wolters Kluwer.

CHAPTER 19

Corporatisation in Norwegian Local Government

Jan Erling Klausen and Harald Torsteinsen

19.1 Introduction

During the last decades, municipally owned companies (MOCs) have become an increasingly prevalent feature of the Norwegian local government sector. Municipalities use MOCs to carry out a wide range of tasks and services, predominantly 'technical' tasks such as power supply, fire protection, waste services and water provision, but also functions related to culture, education and health care. In recent years, establishment of new MOCs seems to have levelled off, partly due to increasing ideological and party-political division over management-inspired reforms in the public sector. Although MOCs are commonly seen as an effective and efficient

J. E. Klausen
Department of Political Science, University of Oslo, Oslo, Norway
e-mail: j.e.klausen@stv.uio.no

H. Torsteinsen (✉)
Department of Social Sciences, UiT The Arctic University of Norway, Tromsø/Harstad, Norway
e-mail: harald.torsteinsen@uit.no

M. Van Genugten et al. (eds.), *Corporatisation in Local Government*, https://doi.org/10.1007/978-3-031-09982-3_19

way of organising public task execution, several studies suggest that MOCs raise concerns over democratic accountability and control. Although the municipal council is ultimately responsible for the full range of the local government's tasks and responsibilities, MOCs often operate more than one arm's length removed from their political owners.

19.2 Context

Norway is a unitary state with two levels of subnational government, which together constitute local government. Following a recent structural reform (Klausen et al., 2021), there are now 356 municipalities (local) and 11 counties (regional). Units at both tiers are led by elected councils. Local governments enjoy comparatively high levels of autonomy (Ladner et al., 2016). Local and regional politicians mostly represent national political parties, which implies a high degree of political integration between the three levels of government (Sellers et al., 2020). Most Norwegian municipalities are organised according to the aldermen principle, in which the political executive committee (*Formannskap*) is composed of representatives from all or most political parties in the municipal council (Jacobsen, 2020). The chief executive officer (CEO) (*Kommunedirektør* or *rådmann*) is hired by the municipal council (*Kommunestyre*), and this person is accountable to the council for the entire municipal administration, including the municipal service-providing entities. The municipalities of Oslo and Bergen as well as three counties (Nordland, Troms and Finnmark, and Viken) are organised as parliamentary systems. The city (or county) government is the executive and relies on support from the majority of the elected city (or county) council.

Norway is a universalist social democratic welfare state (Esping-Andersen, 1990) and belongs to the highly decentralised group of northern/central European local government systems (Hesse & Sharpe, 1991; Schwab et al., 2017). Consequently, local governments oversee a very broad range of tasks and services, most of which are mandatory by law. Currently, local and county government expenses equal 17.5% of GDP (OECD, 2022). Measured by share of public consumption, local government stands for approximately 34.1% (OECD, 2022). The local governments are funded mainly by local taxation (39%), government grants (45%) and various fees and charges from service users (13%).

Norway is not a member state of the EU. Norway is, however, a party to the agreement on the European Economic Area (EEA) and hence a full member of the internal market. Consequently, all EU directives, regulations and court rulings that are deemed relevant for the single market apply to Norway.

All 356 municipalities have non-differentiated competencies which means that even the smallest municipalities are obliged by law to provide the same range of services as the largest ones. Service provision is subject to extensive legal regulation and supervision by the central government, gradually transforming the local governments into agents of the state (Goldsmith & Page, 2010, p. 255), especially regarding welfare service provision. In addition to the mandatory tasks, local governments may take on new tasks at their own initiative. While the Local Government Act (LG Act) mandates a few key organisational elements, local governments are largely allowed to decide on their own organisation.

Most local governments produce the largest share of their services in-house. Between 85% and 100% of local governments incorporate kindergartens, primary education, institutionalised and home-based care services, water and sewage, upkeep and maintenance in their own organisation (Monkerud et al., 2016, pp. 93–95). Inter-municipal cooperation is however also widespread. Between 50% and 85% of local governments provide waste management, auditing, emergency rooms, crisis centres, fire protection and IT services in cooperation with neighbouring municipalities, through a variety of cooperative arrangements (Jacobsen, 2014). Additionally, a notable share of local governments purchase services such as road maintenance, kindergartens, maintenance of municipal buildings and infrastructure from private sector providers. The use of market-based steering mechanisms including competitive tenders, pay-per-unit systems, public–private partnerships, benchmarking and free user choice increased rapidly since the early 2000s, but in recent years the growth of such mechanisms seems to have levelled off (Monkerud et al., 2016).

MOCs can be legally established in three ways as:

1. A limited liability corporation (AS) based on the private law Limited Companies Act (AS Act)
2. An inter-municipal corporation (IKS) mandated by the public law Inter-Municipal Companies Act (IKS Act)
3. An in-house municipal company (KF) according to Chap. 9 of the Local Government Act (LG Act)

These forms align with the typology of arm's length bodies presented in Van Genugten et al. (2020): KF as Type 1, IKS as Type 2 and AS as Type 3. We include the KF as a MOC because both formally and in practice it is considered and treated as such in the Norwegian context.

Municipalities may also join into cooperative arrangements (SA) based on the Cooperatives Act.[1] The SA is mostly used for organising kindergartens (536), waterworks (420) and community centres (130). Although this form is prevalent in local government, comprising 1186 entities all together in 2008, there is to our knowledge practically no research available (Breen et al., 2008). Therefore, we will not explore the SA companies further.

Finally, municipalities may set up foundations. Since foundations are self-owning, independent bodies operating beyond municipal control, we will not include this form in this chapter.

While AS and IKS are legally autonomous entities, the KF is a semi-autonomous hybrid organisation, politically integrated but administratively separated. Contrary to the AS, an IKS can only be owned by municipalities, counties or other inter-municipal companies. Nonetheless, the IKS is in many ways quite like the AS (Høivik, 2005). A board appointed by the owner assembly (*general assembly* in the AS, *assembly of representatives* in the IKS and *municipal council* in the KF) oversees the corporation, and the MOC manager is accountable to the board. A mandatory ownership agreement in the IKS corresponds to the articles of association in the AS. One key difference between AS and IKS is that IKS owners take on unlimited proportional liability. Moreover, IKS shares are not transferrable. The distribution of shares is laid down in the ownership agreement. IKS ownership can only be changed by unanimous decision among the owners (IKS Act §26). Dissolution of an IKS necessitates agreement among the owners and must be sanctioned by the ministry (IKS Act §32).

If a local government wants to co-own a corporation with private owners, the limited liability AS is the only form available. According to §1–1 in the Partnership Act,[2] local governments cannot establish or participate in an unlimited liability partnership, general or limited, with private co-owners.

[1] *Lov om samvirkeforetak (Samvirkelova).*

[2] *Lov om ansvarlige selskaper og kommandittselskaper (Selskapsloven).*

19.3 A Brief Note on Data

The empirical basis for this chapter is mainly taken from extant studies (particularly Bjørnsen et al., 2015; Klausen & Winsvold, 2021; Opedal et al., 2012; Ringkjøb et al., 2008). While these publications offer rich evidence about MOCs in Norway's local government sector, they are based on statistics dating from 2014 and earlier. We have, consequently, supplemented and updated the empirical material by collecting statistics from the Norwegian Register of Business Enterprises, Brønnøysundregistret.[3] Due to varying methodologies, there are some minor deviations between the newly collected data and extant studies.

19.4 Trends

Although MOCs are not a completely new phenomenon in the Norwegian local government sector, the growth of MOCs during the last couple of decades has been strong and comprehensive, organising a widening range of local services. The prevalence of MOCs is now such that it changes our conception about what local government essentially is, and what its functions should be. It seems reasonable to assume that the surge of MOCs may impair democratic accountability. Thus, corporatisation is not only a question of finding practical solutions to public service delivery, but also an issue of how to preserve local democracy, including how to renew it. The New Public Management (NPM) legacy of public sector reform, advocating strict separation of politics and administration, makes the issue of local democracy imminent when applied to externalised local service provision through corporatisation (Aars & Ringkjøb, 2011). Although corporatisation in Norwegian local government may be interpreted as a result of international reform trends like NPM, the growth of MOCs certainly also reflects considerable pragmatism in responding to internal needs, challenges and ideas. As Norwegian municipalities metaphorically are carrying the welfare state on their backs, a role assigned by the national government, the number, range, and complexity of tasks designated to the local government sector have over the last 60 years grown to challenge the capacity and competence of a large share of the local governments. In this situation, corporatisation has emerged as an attractive solution for

[3] All domestic and foreign enterprises operating in Norway are obligated by law to register key information with the Register of Business Enterprises.

meeting this challenge by increasing the municipalities' managerial capacity over a growing range of tasks, especially within the technical sector.

During the last 25 years, MOCs have become increasingly prevalent in the local government sector. In the period 2011–2014, approximately 2900 corporations were operational, distributed in this way according to their company form (Bjørnsen et al., 2015; Opedal et al., 2012):

- 2418 limited liability companies (AS)
- 254 inter-municipal companies (IKS)
- 224 in-house companies (KF)[4]

Although the number of AS has grown continuously since the mid-1990s, the growth accelerated after the turn of the new millennium. The growth of AS then levelled off in the period 2011–2014 (Bjørnsen et al., 2015) however, before starting to grow again after 2018 (see Fig. 19.1).

The IKS and KF forms of MOC were introduced in 2000. The number of IKS rose sharply during the first years after its introduction, partly because already existing inter-municipal cooperative arrangements were formalised, but within a few years the growth slowed down. Following the

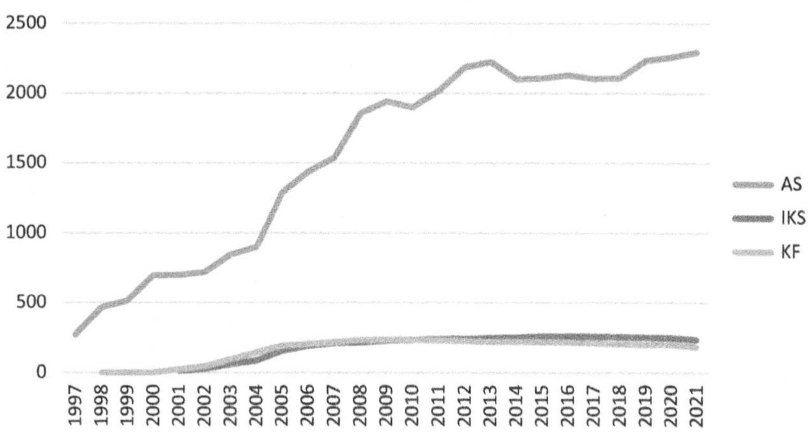

Fig. 19.1 Number and legal form of MOCs, 1997–2021 (Source: The Register of Business Enterprises, 2021)

[4] Of these, 11 were owned by counties, and in 2021 this was reduced to 7.

structural reform of 2020, the number of IKS dropped somewhat from approximately 260 in 2015/2016 to 236 entities in 2021 (whereof 7 are under liquidation).

As could be expected, the number of KF rose as well after 2000. It reached 216 units in 2006, and by 2021 the number had decreased to 185.

Figure 19.1 illustrates the trends of corporatisation in Norwegian municipalities since 1997.

Figure 19.1 shows that almost 85% of Norwegian MOCs are limited companies (AS). What these curves do not show, is the considerable overlap that exists between the companies. For instance, all three MOC types may hold subsidiaries, usually organised as AS. Raw data on these patterns is available, but it would require a separate research project to analyse and bring them to light. Therefore, as of today, the prevalence of this overlap appears to make the picture of corporatisation rather complex and opaque.

19.5 Legal Status

Norwegian MOCs may be established under both public and private law. The most prevalent form of MOCs, the AS, is a private law entity regulated by the general AS Act,[5] while the IKS is a public law company under the IKS Act.[6] As these forms hold separate legal personality, they seem to align with the segregated hybrid type organisation described by Skelcher and Smith (2015, p. 440) as "[f]unctions oriented to different logics … compartmentalised into separate but associated organisations". In contrast, the KF is not legally separated from its owner municipality, thereby resembling the segmented hybrid form, defined by Skelcher and Smith (2015, p. 440) as "logics … compartmentalised within the organisation". The KF is a public law entity regulated by the LG Act,[7] which applies to all political and administrative bodies in municipalities and counties.

The LG Act contains provisions that authorise municipal control with MOCs. The municipal control committee (LG Act, chapter 23) and audit agency (LG Act, chapter 24) have the mandate to monitor and control the activities of all companies in which the municipality holds ownership interests. However, the control committee may only demand access to information from limited companies if they are 100% publicly owned.

[5] *Aksjeloven*.

[6] *Lov om interkommunale selskaper.*

[7] *Kommuneloven*.

Further, public laws like the Public Administration Act[8] and the Freedom of Information Act[9] have some validity for MOCs, and always if they make decisions concerning individual citizens, business firms or organisations.

Norway's membership of the EU single market through the EEA agreement entails several restrictions on local governments' dealings with corporations that they own. The agreement contains provisions forbidding public support to all types of companies. These provisions are of special relevance for the IKS form because of its unlimited liability clause. EU regulation has also influenced other parts of Norwegian legislation relevant for MOCs. Most notably, the Public Procurement Act[10] and the Competition Act[11] contain provisions by which municipalities and their MOCs must abide. Local governments are in general required to issue public tenders for specific tasks, instead of issuing the task in question directly to a corporation owned by themselves. Exceptions from this rule apply only if (a) the corporation is under the full control of the local government, and (b) the corporation's activities predominantly comprise tasks and services mandated by the corporation's public owner(s).

As mentioned in Sect. 19.4 on 'Trends', approximately 85% of the MOCs are AS whereas approximately 9% hold the IKS form. That leaves approximately 7% for the in-house companies (the KF form). Some modifications apply, though. First, as almost all 356 Norwegian municipalities are co-owners of one or more IKS, our conception of how prevalent the three organisational forms are, may be extended by considering the proportion of municipalities involved. For instance, between 85% and 93% of Norwegian municipalities provide their waste services through intermunicipal arrangements, primarily IKS companies (Monkerud et al., 2016, p. 93; Torsteinsen & Van Genugten, 2016, p. 213). Second, many IKS and some AS own (or co-own) several subsidiaries, usually organised as limited companies, a practice motivated by, among other things the need to separate monopoly and commercial activities. Thus, the mixing of organisational forms within the framework of one overarching enterprise structure, usually an IKS or an AS, should be considered when presenting numbers of prevalent forms. Even a KF may own or co-own AS

[8] *Forvaltningsloven.*

[9] *Offentleglova.*

[10] *Anskaffelsesloven.* See also Directive 2014/24/EU of the European Parliament and of the Council of 26 February 2014 on public procurement and repealing Directive 2004/18.

[11] *Konkurranseloven.*

subsidiaries, and although this is not common, it illustrates the hybrid character of corporatisation in Norwegian local government. However, access to information about these enterprise structures is not readily available. Finally, many municipalities hold minority share positions in various AS companies, sometimes side by side with private shareholders. If most shares are owned by private interests, the companies are no longer counted as public companies in public statistics, and it would require extensive and detailed investigation to find out how many and to what extent municipalities are involved in such companies. Consequently, cross-ownerships, use of enterprise structures and the holding of minority positions in private limited companies make the analysis of prevalence of MOC forms more complicated and opaquer than a simple counting exercise could envisage.

19.6 Background Characteristics

MOCs are used for several purposes. The most recent survey, based on data from 2014, reports on the distribution of AS and IKS among different classes of activity (Bjørnsen et al., 2015). Note that AS may be owned by one municipality in full, by a consortium of local governments, or by private as well as public sector owners. Unfortunately, the data does not allow distinction between such differences in ownership structure, which means we do not know how many AS count as instances of corporate inter-municipal cooperation. The distributions are reported in Tables 19.1 and 19.2.

Further, the number of employees presented in the tables indicates the size of the two MOC forms. In all, 41,959 were employed in AS and IKS in 2014. Not all MOCs are actual enterprises with employees, however. Limited corporations (AS) are sometimes established as a way of organising the ownership of municipal buildings, such as the city hall.

The KF form is primarily used within the following services (numbers indicate entities): property management (47), culture and sport (46), and harbour management (44). To a lesser extent we find KFs working with local business development (17) and energy production/distribution (15). The total number of employees was 6120 in 2011 (Opedal et al., 2012). Thus, measured by the number of employees, Norwegian MOCs constitute almost 10% of the local government sector.

Finally, most Norwegian MOCs are single-purpose entities. However, that does not prevent them from running several activities within their

Table 19.1 Distribution of AS among classes of activity, 2014

	Enterprises (N = 2418)	*Employees (N = 35,627)*
Electricity, gas-, steam- and hot water supply	22.7%	27.0%
Property management and related services	20.6%	2.6%
Employment training, adapted work	16.3%	22.3%
Business development, electronic communications, other technical or scientific service provision	8.5%	6.0%
Roads and communications	8.0%	21.0%
Building and construction, including planning, regulation and technical services	6.9%	8.5%
Culture, leisure, tourism	6.6%	3.8%
Water, sewage and waste services	5.3%	5.2%
Residual category	2.7%	1.1%
Kindergartens, education, health and care services	2.3%	2.4%

Source: Bjørnsen et al. (2015)

Table 19.2 Distribution of IKS among classes of activity, 2014

	Enterprises (N = 354)	*Employees (N = 6332)*
Water, sewage and waste services	22.9%	27.9%
Administrative services	19.8%	9.1%
Fire protection	18.4%	29.7%
Culture and education	15.0%	12.9%
Technical services, building and construction, other	9.9%	4.6%
Health and care services	9.0%	12.1%
Harbour management	3.4%	2.2%
Electricity, gas and hot water supply	1.7%	1.6%

Source: Bjørnsen et al. (2015)

enterprise structure, but then usually tasks associated with their main purpose. For example, a waste service IKS may take care of both household waste and industrial waste, or an AS operating in the cultural sector may encompass both a cinema and a concert hall.

19.7 Board Structure

Norwegian MOCs typically have one-tier board structures. There is one exception, though. AS companies with more than 200 employees are obliged to establish a supervisory board (*bedriftsforsamling*) with 12 members, of which 2/3 are appointed by the owner assembly while 1/3 are chosen by the employees (AS Act §6–35). However, few, if any, MOCs of the AS type are of this size, not least because in such cases it is quite common to opt for an enterprise structure comprising two or more smaller AS companies. Thus, for all practical purposes the one-tier board is the relevant board structure for all three types of Norwegian MOCs.

KS, which is the interest and employer organisation for all 356 municipalities and 11 counties in Norway, has developed its own corporate code for owners' and MOCs' corporate governance (KS, 2020). The report first describes and explains what corporate governance is, which company forms are available and the legal foundations of forms and ownership control. Finally, the report presents a corporate governance code consisting of 21 recommendations, especially relevant for the KF, IKS and AS forms of MOCs. It also seems that the KS report has been somewhat influenced by the OECD guidelines on corporate governance of state-owned enterprises (2015). In addition, many municipalities introduce and discuss supplementary recommendations in their ownership reports, often based on local or mediated experiences.

We do not have data indicating new trends in the board structure of Norwegian MOCs. Although several and repeated recommendations have been voiced to 'purify' boards of local politicians, even by some politicians themselves, we have little information substantiating if and to what extent this is happening.

19.8 Autonomy

Autonomy may be defined as the delegated capacity of an organisational entity to make and implement decisions without (too many) constraints from the authority centre on the exercise of those capacities. The more the authority restricts the entity's exercise by structural, political, legal, financial or interventionist measures, the less the actual autonomy becomes (Verhoest et al., 2004; Berge & Torsteinsen, 2021b). Corporatisation may be seen as a type of delegation (Overman, 2016) that formally gives organisational entities more autonomy than in-house integrated entities have.

The introduction of MOCs in municipal service provision signifies hiving-off entities from the traditional political-administrative chain of command that (ideally) characterises local government, thereby replacing direct, vertical, hierarchical steering with indirect, horizontal, contractual-resembling governance. According to Ringkjøb et al. (2008), corporatisation thus implies "fragmentation of democratic power" (ibid. p. 49). This constitutes the general context within which MOC managers exercise their authority.

Generally, Norwegian MOCs, including their managers (or CEOs), enjoy extensive manoeuvring space. Research indicates that too little constraint may be more usual than too much constraint (Klausen & Winsvold, 2021; Opedal et al., 2012; Ringkjøb et al., 2008). However, although most MOCs are legally autonomous and operate at arm's length from their owners, their independence is politically conditioned. They constitute entities of a local government governance system, which implies that their owners may expel their boards, change their organisational form, and even re-municipalise them, that is, re-integrate them into the municipal organisation. In practice, MOC managers usually exercise their authority and make their decisions without much interference from their owners (Aars & Ringkjøb, 2011; Bjørnsen et al., 2015, p. 150; Ringkjøb et al., 2008), almost as if the MOCs *were* independent organisations. Case studies indicate that corporatisation leads to de-politicisation, illustrated by municipal councils giving ownership reports scarce attention (e.g. Torsteinsen & Bjørnå, 2012). Further, the political steering of municipal service provision becomes significantly weaker when it is corporatised compared to in-house provision (Berge & Torsteinsen, 2021a; Bjørnsen et al., 2015, p. 150). In addition, the municipal CEO does not have any formal authority in steering the companies, not even the in-house KFs. Despite limited owner steering, the freedom of MOCs and their managers is conditioned, and it may be influenced in various ways.

First, the selection of organisational form involves politically choosing specific structural and legal frameworks, which both enable and constrain managerial autonomy. The KF model, for instance, is more embedded politically in the owner organisation than the IKS and the AS forms. In a KF, the municipal council serves as its owner assembly, for example by appointing its board. As with AS and IKS, a KF is placed outside the municipal CEO's chain of command, except for one situation; the CEO may require the KF board to halt the implementation of a decision until the municipal council has had a chance to consider its economic consequences. However, municipal CEOs seem reluctant to utilise this control mechanism and consequently it is seldom put into practice (Opedal et al., 2012). Further, the IKS form means the company has two or more owners, a feature that may create inter-owner contradictions and coordination problems (Tavares & Feiock, 2018; Voorn et al., 2019). As the number of owners grows, these problems may be exacerbated, even to the extent that transaction costs may exceed scale economy benefits (Blåka, 2017; Sørensen, 2007). The implication may be that in order to reduce these costs, owners choose to intervene less with IKS operations, thus unintendedly enhancing the IKS' autonomy. In this way, an IKS may even become more autonomous than an AS-type MOC, especially if the AS is owned by a single municipality. During the last decade, the EFTA Surveillance Authority (ESA) has repeatedly criticised Norway for using the IKS form for commercial activities. Since this form implies that owners hold unlimited responsibility for the company's economic obligations, ESA claims that this is in breach with EU competition regulation, because it gives the IKS unfair competitive advantages equivalent to illegal state support (The Nordic Competition Authorities, 2016). Despite several years of discussions and investigations, Norwegian authorities have so far not been able to amend the IKS Act. Instead, IKS enterprises have sought to meet the criticism from ESA by separating commercial and monopoly activities through separating accounts or through creating subsidiaries organised as AS companies, thereby upholding the autonomy of the IKS.

Second, legal regulations may also influence the manoeuvring space of MOCs and their managers. In Sect. 19.5 on the MOCs legal status, we described general laws relevant for MOCs' organisational designs, operational practices, obligations, limitations and so on. In addition, laws and provisions on sectors and services describe the specific tasks that municipalities are responsible for and may assign to either in-house entities or MOCs, for example, water supply, sewage services, waste management, harbour management, fire protection, health care and employment training. Although these laws authorise numerous regulations and provisions, they leave considerable space to MOC managers for exercising professional and managerial discretion (Ringkjøb et al., 2008).

Third, municipalities may enhance or circumscribe MOCs' autonomy through financial means. Doing so is especially straightforward for KFs, where the municipal council decides on the KF's budget. When establishing an IKS, municipalities must set up a corporate agreement (IKS Act §4) defining, among other things, how much the company can invest or take up in loans without the explicit approval of its owners. Further, irrespective of organisational form, monopoly services like water supply and sewage services and household waste collection and treatment are financed according to the full cost recovery (FCR) principle. Users including citizens, organisations or businesses, pay fees decided annually by the municipal council(s). These fees are supposed to cover 100% of the total costs associated with providing the specific service, including depreciation of investments. Cross-subsidisation between services and organisational entities is illegal. A side effect of the FCR principle seems to be insufficient maintenance and renewal of infrastructure, especially within water and sewage services (Norsk Vann, 2021, p. 3). This happens despite explicit suggestions from service providers, stating that investments are necessary. However, a case study indicates that when service provision is corporatised, investment projects are easier to implement. Consequently, corporatisation seems to enhance the service provider's financial autonomy compared to service entities organised in-house (Berge & Torsteinsen, 2021b). Nonetheless, since municipal councils are reluctant to rise fees too much or too fast for fear of public protests, financial limits associated with FCR services will always exist.[12]

Finally, MOC autonomy may also be circumscribed by owners' desire and need for strengthening their budgets by taking dividends from their commercial companies. Municipalities have been particularly eager to reap dividends from hydroelectricity production, a sector where local government ownership is at approximately 50%. The AS model dominates this sector, split between subsidiary companies for grid (monopoly) and production (competition). A few years ago, when hydroelectricity production was extremely profitable, municipalities and counties could extract as much as 90%—sometimes more—of the MOCs' surplus as dividend.[13] This practice reduced the MOCs' autonomy for developing long-term strategies and for implementing necessary maintenance and renewals.

National laws and provisions regulating local service provision, define purposes, goals and so on for each single service, and the extent of details seems to have increased over the years (e.g. Difi, 2010; Fimreite, 2003; Indset et al., 2012; Reichborn-Kjennerud & Vabo, 2016). For some

[12] The maintenance lag within for instance infrastructure of municipal water supply and sewage services has been calculated to be 390 billion NOK (Kommunal Rapport, 19 June 2019).

[13] See, for example, Teknisk Ukeblad (TU), 18 November 2013.

public services, EU regulation has influenced national goal setting significantly, for example within waste management (Torsteinsen & Van Genugten, 2016). Further, when establishing a MOC, the owner—or owners, for an IKS—has to formulate a founding document. The AS and the IKS laws require the most comprehensive documents (§2–1 and §4, respectively), while the LG Act confines itself to describing basic provisions for a KF. All municipal councils involved have to pass the founding document for an IKS and for an inter-municipal AS. In addition, the owners' corporate assemblies must do the same. The founding documents must include the companies' goals and objectives, although these may be formulated in rather general terms, giving MOCs considerable manoeuvring space. As companies develop, their activities may deviate somewhat from what has been stated in the founding document. Usually, the MOCs themselves initiate revisions of the document to align with practice and they also develop their own long-term strategies and short-term action plans. Finally, the LG Act of 2018 requires that municipalities must produce ownership reports at least once every election period (§26–1). Before 2016, less than 50% of Norwegian municipalities made any such reports (Monkerud et al., 2016). Now, these reports must contain the municipality's principles for ownership governance, a review of all companies in which the municipality holds ownership (or other) interests, and statements explaining the purpose of these ownership (and other) interests. Some local governments decide on ownership strategies for each individual corporation in their portfolio. The quality and frequency of ownership reports vary between municipalities, so does the political attention municipal councils give them.

Studies show that municipalities mainly govern their MOCs through owner assemblies and founding provisions. In addition, they may influence the companies more indirectly by strategically appointing board members and by defining the content and quality of the services that the companies are supposed to deliver (Ringkjøb et al., 2008, p. 52). In some municipalities, the CEO ensures that MOC documents are routinely scrutinised in order to give advice to the politicians involved in governing the MOCs (Klausen & Winsvold, 2021). The main trend, however, seems to be that Norwegian municipalities are rather weak and passive owners (Ringkjøb et al., 2008, p. 55).

19.9 Monitoring

The formal monitoring of MOCs rests on two pillars, the municipal and the corporate pillars, respectively.

Governing and oversight of MOCs reside largely with four municipal actors: The council, the mayor, the control committee and the municipal auditors (Fig. 19.2). First, the ***municipal council*** decides on the establishment of MOCs, their articles of association and their legal corporate forms. The council carries the superior political authority and responsibility for the municipality's ownership positions and its service provision. Thus, the municipal council cannot organise away its responsibility through corporatisation. The ownership report of the municipality and the annual reports from the MOCs are important documents in this respect. Information from owner assembly meetings and board meetings communicated by the mayor or appointed local politicians may reach the executive committee of the municipal council and maybe also the council itself, but these communication channels are often informal and occasional. Second, the ***mayor*** carries a special responsibility since she or he is the municipality's legal representative. Accordingly, the owner assembly of MOCs is appointed by and usually composed of the mayor (wholly owned AS) or the mayors of the municipal owners (inter-municipal companies, IKS or AS).[14] Because the mayor signs the companies' annual documents, the mayor bears full responsibility for ensuring adequate monitoring of the MOCs. Sometimes the mayor may involve the municipal administration in assisting him or her in monitoring the MOCs. This function can be placed with the municipal CEO, with a special staff unit, or distributed with different municipal departments. Consequently, this function may be divided between several administrative entities, making the control fragmented, incoherent and occasional. As late as 2016, nearly 90% of the municipalities did not have administrative units specialised for ownership management and control (Monkerud et al., 2016). In local governments organised by the parliamentary principle (Oslo and Bergen), the city government is responsible for monitoring MOCs.[15] Based on authority

[14] Sometimes, other local politicians may be appointed members of the owner assembly. This happens if a municipality owns many companies, thus overwhelming the capacity of the mayor, or if a larger municipality holds several seats in the assembly of an IKS, thus necessitating the appointment of additional members.

[15] Local Government Act, chapter 10. Three of 11 counties have chosen the parliamentary model: Nordland, Troms og Finnmark, and Viken.

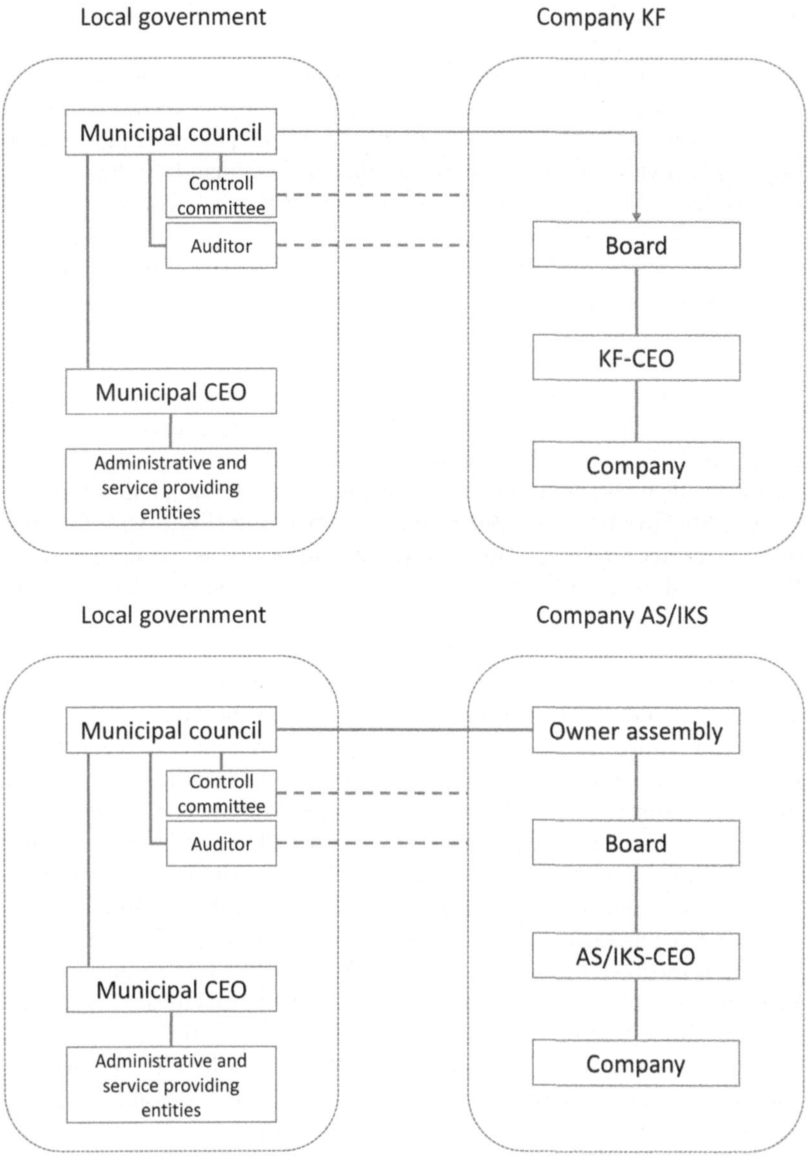

Fig. 19.2 Relations of authority, appointments and accountability. Note: dashed lines indicate monitoring and control

delegated from the city council, each member of the city government is responsible for corporations that fall under their individual portfolios. Third, all municipalities are required to establish a ***control committee***, composed of local politicians, and appointed by the council.[16] The committee serves as 'the eyes and ears' of the municipal council, monitoring the decisions and activities of the municipal administration, including the management of the municipality's owner interests in MOCs. The committee must prepare an inspection plan at least once every election period, listing which MOCs to control, and the plan must be passed by the council. Further, the committee holds a wide mandate to require information, to investigate and to attend meetings in owner assemblies. By law, the committee has unlimited access to whatever information deemed necessary for supervision, and it is required to prioritise administrative auditing according to presumed risk and significance (§23–3). The committee reports directly to the council. The control committee shall have its own secretariat, which by law needs to be organised independently from the municipal administration. Fourth, the ***municipal auditors***, cooperating closely with the control committee, have very much the same authority as the committee.[17] Finally, local governments commonly use several non-mandatory monitoring instruments (Bjørnsen et al., 2015). Mayors, municipal CEOs and professional managers commonly meet with MOC managers and board members in the period between owner assemblies, in order to exchange information and discuss corporate strategy and performance.

The corporate monitoring system comprises three elements (Fig. 19.2). First, ***the owner assembly***, which usually meets once or twice a year, is the superior authority of the IKS and the AS-type MOCs. For the KF MOC type the municipal council plays this role, which underlines the hybrid character of this sort of company (politically integrated, administratively autonomous). Second, apart from deciding on the MOC's annual documents, a key function of the owner assembly is to appoint ***the board***, which de facto is the main monitor of a MOC (Tricker, 1995). Most board members still seem to be local politicians, earning their seats in the usual post-election 'horse-trading' of positions (Bjørnsen et al., 2015). In line with company law, the board oversees the MOC on behalf of the owners. In addition to taking care of the owner's interests, the board is also supposed to cooperate with the MOC manager in developing the company (Van

[16] *Kontrollkomite*. Local Government Act, chapter 23.

[17] *Kommunerevisjon*. Local Government Act, chapter 26.

Thiel, 2015). Sometimes, the balance between control and cooperation may become difficult to uphold, for example, if board members let themselves be co-opted (Selznick, 1949), thus identifying themselves more with the company than with their municipal owner or owners. Case studies indicate that some local politicians, who have been appointed as board members, may operate as mouthpieces for the company when they enter the municipal council or the executive committee (Berge & Torsteinsen, 2021b; Torsteinsen & Bjørnå, 2012). While some find this combination of roles highly problematic and claim that boards should be 'professionalised', that is, only include non-political experts, others argue that politicians on the boards promote informal information sharing and mutual understanding, beneficial for corporate autonomy and democratic control. Nonetheless, in a survey, local politicians mention appointment of board members as a relatively important way to control companies (Ringkjøb et al., 2008, p. 52), and sometimes municipalities even instruct their board members how to vote in board meetings (Bjørnsen et al., 2015, p. 128). Finally, the IKS and AS companies are annually controlled by ***auditors*** engaged by their own boards, and the results are communicated through the annual reports, which are also distributed to the owners.

19.10 Accountability

In the former section, we described how introducing MOCs into Norwegian local government service provision meant setting-up a corporate monitoring system in addition to the municipal one already in existence. This two-pillar system has implication for the construction of formal accountability regimes. Bovens (2007, p. 450) defines accountability in a narrow sense as "a relationship between an actor and a forum, in which the actor has an obligation to explain and to justify his or her conduct, the forum can pose questions and pass judgment, and the actor may face consequences". Schillemans (2011) has elaborated this definition by describing three phases of account giving: the information, discussion and consequence phases.

Within the municipal pillar, multiple forums and actors may be identified, linked together in a hierarchical chain of governance. The ultimate forum is of course the citizens, calling the municipal council to account through local elections every fourth year, but also through the political discourse going on between elections. At the next level, the municipal council is the forum whereas the municipal administration (including service-providing entities) is the actor. Both in practice and according to the LG Act, the actor that is formally accountable to the council is the municipal CEO. This follows from his or her position as the supreme leader of the whole municipal administration, and the council may not even intervene in his/her exercise of staff management (§13–1). Thus, at this third level, the municipal CEO is the forum while all subordinate managers are the actors called to account.

Within the corporate pillar the owner assembly is the forum at the first level, while the board is the actor required to give account. At the next level, the MOC's top manager serves as the actor vis-à-vis the board now operating as the forum, and finally, the top manager serves as the forum to whom subordinate managers must give account. This chain of accountability relations is commonly referred to as corporate governance (Berle & Means, 1933; Tricker, 1995). It is the corporate sector counterpart to the system of accountability relations found in public sector representative government as outlined above (Klausen & Winsvold, 2021). One extant study found that deficient understanding of corporate governance and the rather complex chain of accountability relations between the council and the MOC is an important impediment for control over MOCs by elected councillors (Bjørnsen et al., 2015).

Consequently, the accountability linkage between the municipality and the IKS and the AS types of company is the owner assembly, the council as the forum and assembly as the actor. In practice, however, politically appointed board members may also be called to account by the municipal council, for example, in terms of not being re-appointed. Although at odds with codes of corporate governance (KS, 2020), this practice is not unusual, neither in Norway nor abroad (Van Thiel, 2015). When it comes to the KF form of MOC, the accountability linkage between the municipal council and the company is tight and direct through the board. However, as the council plays two roles vis-à-vis the board, both as the owner assembly for the KF and as the supreme political authority for the whole municipal organisation, the relationship may be characterised as hybrid and thus somewhat opaque.

19.11 The MOC Executive Director

We do not have any data describing if and to what extent the decision-making authority of MOC managers is restrained. To acquire this type of data a separate study would have to be made. Some data has been collected in case studies, mostly as supplementary information to another research focus (e.g. Berge & Torsteinsen, 2021b; Renå, 2013). Beyond that, our impression is basically made up of stories presented in the media.

Concerning labour issues, in some cases corporatisation may be motivated by the need to recruit expertise that is attractive in the private market and therefore used to salaries above negotiated municipal tariffs. This has been documented in a couple of municipalities in western and southern parts of Norway (Berge & Torsteinsen, 2021b), but we have no data indicating how prevalent this phenomenon is. These case studies also show that MOC managers are reluctant to set wages higher than necessary for attracting specialised engineers, in order to avoid tensions between the company and its owner. Consequently, public ownership may have a disciplinary effect on MOC managers' decision-making.

As to financial issues, founding documents often decide limits for the aggregated size of loans and liabilities that the company may take, and these limits are regulated over time. This issue is especially important for the IKS, for which the owners carry unlimited responsibility, and for the KF, whose budget is (usually) integrated into the overall municipal budget. Nonetheless, several cases uncovered by media show that some managers may have wide manoeuvring space, sometimes with serious consequences. In a research article Renå (2013) has analysed three cases of economic misgovernance in municipal companies, including two KFs and an AS. One of his most interesting findings was that the municipalities' own control regimes were not able to discover the crimes being committed. Instead, the scandals were uncovered by investigative journalists in one of Norway's largest newspapers, *Aftenposten*. Similar scandals have recently been uncovered by Norway's leading business newspaper, *Dagens Næringsliv*. These examples indicate that municipal owners of MOCs do not always exert sufficient economic control.

Finally, to what extent the decision-making power of MOC managers is restrained when it comes to organisational issues, will probably appear in founding documents, employment contracts, laws or elsewhere. In a legal analysis, comparing the IKS and the AS forms, Høivik (2005) concludes that the top managers have approximately the same manoeuvring space in both. However, if usual restraints on selling public property apply, the municipal councils will have to be involved if the economic and strategic values exceed certain limits.

19.12 Conclusion

During the last 25 years, corporatisation has become a prominent feature of Norwegian local government. Although growth in the number of MOCs has levelled off since 2013–2014, we have seen a slight increase since 2018. Approximately 85% of the MOCs are organised as private law limited liability companies (AS) while the remaining entities are public law inter-municipal (IKS) and in-house companies (KF). These forms align with Type 3, Type 2 and Type 1 respectively in Van Genugten et al.'s (2020) typology of arm's length bodies. The prevalence of corporate forms is especially high within 'hard' services, for example, energy supply, waste management, property management and fire protection, but it is also used within some 'soft' services, for example, employment training, administrative services and culture and education. However, measured by the number of employees, MOCs constitute almost 10% of local government employment (KS, 2022). This implies that although MOCs are important within 'hard' services, they play a minor role within the dominating welfare services of the municipalities, that is, education, kindergartens, health and social services, which account for almost 90% of all municipal employees.

Although some local governments have made distinct progress towards advancing democratic accountability of MOCs, the local government sector overall is still marked by deficient corporate governance—not least because exercising indirect governance is challenging for lay part-time local politicians, lacking sufficient competence and capacity to do so. In addition, the municipal CEO's role in governing MOCs, even in-house KFs, has been limited and unclear, and many of them have felt side-lined in this respect. Thus, the introduction and rapid growth of MOCs seem to have uncovered an institutional gap in terms of local government failing to develop public corporate government mechanisms and practices to keep up with this development (Klausen & Winsvold, 2021). With the new LG Act (2018), however, national government has made a small step towards filling this gap by ordering the municipalities to prepare an ownership report at least once every four years.

References

Aars, J., & Ringkjøb, H.-E. (2011). Local democracy LTD. The political control of local government enterprises in Norway. *Public Management Review, 13*(6), 825–844.

Berge, D. M., & Torsteinsen, H. (2021a). Corporatization in local government – Promoting cultural differentiation and hybridity? *Public Administration*. https://doi.org/10.1111/padm.12737.

Berge, D.M., & Torsteinsen, H. (2021b). Governance challenges of different institutional logics and modes of organising: A Norwegian case study of municipal water supply. *Local Government Studies*. https://doi.org/10.1080/03003930.2021.1942853.

Berle, A. A., & Means, G. C. (1933). *The modern corporation and private property*. Palgrave Macmillan.

Bjørnsen, H. M., Klausen, J. E., & Winsvold, M. (2015). *Kommunale selskap og folkevalgt styring gjennom kommunalt eierskap. [Municipal companies and democratic governance through municipal ownership]*. NIBR.

Blåka, S. (2017). Does cooperation affect service delivery costs? Evidence from fire services in Norway. *Public Administration, 95*, 1092–1106.

Bovens, M. (2007). Analysing and assessing accountability: A conceptual framework. *European Law Journal, 13*, 447–468.

Breen, T., Løvik, A., & Moe, G. (2008). *Samvirke innen offentlige tjenester. Pleie og omsorg [Cooperatives within public services. Social care]*. FOU-prosjekt 074024. Oslo/Skjetten: KS-FOU and Det Kgl. Selskab for Norges Vel.

Difi. (2010). *Statlig styring av kommunen – Om utviklingen i bruken av juridiske virkemidler på tre sektorer [National government's steering of the municipality – On the development of legal measures in three sectors]*. Oslo: Difi-rapport 2010:4.

Esping-Andersen, G. (1990). *The three worlds of welfare capitalism*. Polity Press.

Fimreite, A. L. (2003). Velferdsstat og lokaldemokrati – uforenelige størrelser? [Welfare state and local democracy – incompatible phenomena]. *Norsk statsvitenskapelig tidsskrift, 19*(3), 334–358.

Goldsmith, M., & Page, E. (2010). Conclusion. In M. J. Goldsmith & E. C. Page (Eds.), *Changing government relations in Europe: From localism to intergovernmentalism* (pp. 247–260). Routledge.

Hesse, J. J., & Sharpe, L. J. (1991). Local government in international perspective: Some comparative conclusions. In J. J. Hesse (Ed.), *Local government and urban affairs in international perspective* (pp. 603–621). Nomos.

Høivik, K. (2005). Interkommunalt selskap eller aksjeselskap? [Inter-municipal company or limited company?]. *Lov og rett, 44*(9), 531–549.

Indset, M., Klausen, J. E., Møller, G., Smith, E., & Zeiner, H. H. (2012). *Likeverdighet mellom stat og kommunesektor [Equality between state and local government]*. NIBR/Telemarksforskning.

Jacobsen, D. I. (2014). *Interkommunalt samarbeid i Norge: Former, funksjoner og effekter [Inter-municipal cooperation in Norway: Forms, functions and effects]*. Fagbokforlaget.

Jacobsen, D. I. (2020). *Perspektiver på Kommune-Norge – en innføring i kommunalkunnskap (2. utgave) [Perspectives on Norwegian local government – An introduction]*. Fagbokforlaget.

Klausen, J. E., Askim, J., & Christensen, J. (2021). Local government reform: Compromise through cross-cutting cleavages. *Political Studies Review, 19*(1), 111–126.

Klausen, J. E., & Winsvold, M. (2021). Corporate governance and democratic accountability: Local state-owned enterprises in Norway. *Journal of Public Policy, 41*(1), 161–184.

Kommunal Rapport. (2019). 19 June Edition.

KS. (2020). *Anbefalinger om eierskap, selskapsledelse og kontroll [Recommendations about ownership, corporate governance and control]*. KS folkevalgtprogram 2019–2023. Oslo: KS.

KS. (2022). *Statistikk om kommuneansatte [Statistics about municipal employees]*. Oslo: KS. https://www.ks.no/nye-kartregioner/norge-i-tall/statistikk-om-kommuneansatte/. Accessed 11 April 2022.

Ladner, A., Keuffer, N., & Baldersheim, H. (2016). Measuring local autonomy in 39 countries (1990–2014). *Regional & Federal Studies, 26*(3), 321–357.

Monkerud, L. C., Indset, M., Stokstad, S., & Klausen, J. E. (2016). *Kommunal organisering 2016. Redegjørelse for Kommunal og moderniseringsdepartementets organisasjonsdatabase [Organization of local government 2016.* Report from the Ministry of Local Government and Modernization's database]. Oslo: NIBR.

Norsk Vann. (2021). *Effektivisering = organisering + teknologi + metodikk under forutsigbare rammebetingelser [Norwegian water improvement = organization + technology + methods within predictable regulative frames]*. Sluttrapport. Hamar: Norsk Vann.

OECD. (2015). *OECD guidelines on corporate governance of state-owned enterprises, 2015 edition*. Paris: OECD.

OECD. (2022). *OECD fiscal decentralization database. Consolidated government expenditures as percentage of GDP (Table 4 1970–2020)*. Paris: OECD.

Opedal, S., Blomgren, A., & Tennås Holmen, A. K. (2012). *Kommunale foretak – konsekvenser for folkevalgt styring og lokaldemokrati [Municipal companies (type 1) – Consequences for popular rule and local democracy]*. IRIS.

Overman, S. (2016). Great expectations of public service delegation: A systematic review. *Public Management Review, 18*(8), 1238–1262.

Reichborn-Kjennerud, K., & Vabo, S. I. (2016). Extensive decentralisation – But in the shadow of hierarchy. In J. Ruano & M. Profiroiu (Eds.), *The Palgrave handbook of decentralisation in Europe* (pp. 253–272). Palgrave Macmillan.

Renå, H. (2013). Når kontrollen svikter – En studie av tre korrupsjonssaker i norsk kommunesektor [When control fails – A study of three cases of corruption in Norwegian local government]. *Norsk statsvitenskapelig tidsskrift, 29*(4), 279–308.

Ringkjøb, H.-E., Aars, J., & Vabo, S. I. (2008). *Lokalt folkestyre AS. Eierskap og styringsroller i kommunale selskaper [Local democracy Ltd. ownership and governing roles in municipal companies]*. Rokkansenteret Rapport 01/2008. Bergen: University of Bergen.

Schillemans, T. (2011). Does horizontal accountability work? *Administration & Society, 43*(4), 387–416.

Schwab, C., Bouckaert, G., & Kuhlmann, S. (Eds.). (2017). *The future of local government in Europe. Lessons from research and practice in 31 countries*. Nomos.

Sellers, J. M., Lidström, A., & Bae, Y. (2020). *Multilevel democracy. How local institutions and civil society shape the modern state*. Cambridge University Press.

Selznick, P. (1949). *TVA and the grass roots. A study in the sociology of formal organization*. University of California Press.

Skelcher, C., & Smith, S. R. (2015). Theorizing hybridity: Institutional logics, complex organizations, and actor identities: The case of nonprofits. *Public Administration, 93*(2), 433–448.

Sørensen, R. J. (2007). Does dispersed public ownership impair efficiency? The case of refuse collection in Norway. *Public Administration, 85*(4), 1045–1058.

Tavares, A. F., & Feiock, R. (2018). Applying an institutional collective action framework to investigate intermunicipal cooperation in Europe. *Perspectives on Public Management and Governance, 1*(4), 299–236.

Teknisk Ukeblad. (2013). 18 November Edition.

The Nordic Competition Authorities. (2016). *Competition in the waste management sector – Preparing for a circular economy*. http://www.konkurransetilsynet.no/globalassets/filer/publikasjoner/nordiske-rapporter/nordic-report-2016-waste-management-sector.pdf. Accessed 29 September 2017.

The Register of Business Enterprises. (2021). *Database*. Brønnøysund.

Torsteinsen, H., & Bjørnå, H. (2012). Agencies and transparency in Norwegian local government. *Scandinavian Journal of Public Administration, 16*(1), 5–25.

Torsteinsen, H., & Van Genugten, M. (2016). Municipal waste management in Norway and the Netherlands – From in-house provision to inter-municipal cooperation. In G. Bouckaert & S. Kuhlmann (Eds.), *Local public sector reforms in times of crisis: National trajectories and international comparison* (pp. 205–220). Palgrave Macmillan.

Tricker, B. (1995). Corporate governance – A subject whose time has come. *Corporate Governance: An International Review, 3*(4), 187–188.

Van Genugten, M., Van Thiel, S., & Voorn, B. (2020). Local governments and their arm's length bodies. *Local Government Studies, 46*(1), 1–21.

Van Thiel, S. (2015). Boards of public sector organizations: A typology with Dutch illustrations. *International Journal of Public Sector Management, 28*(4/5), 322–334.

Verhoest, K., Peters, G. B., Bouckaert, G., & Verschuere, B. (2004). The study of organisational autonomy: A conceptual and methodological review. *Public Administration and Development, 24*(2), 101–118.

Voorn, B., Van Genugten, M., & Van Thiel, S. (2019). Multiple principles, multiple problems. A framework for effective governance and a research agenda for joint service delivery. *Public Administration, 97*(3), 671–685.

CHAPTER 20

Municipally Owned Corporations in Sweden

Anna Thomasson

20.1 Introduction

Sweden is a country that has a long tradition of municipally owned corporations (MOCs). The first examples of the use of MOCs in Sweden can be traced back to as early as the late nineteenth century (Meyer et al., 2013). Swedish local governments have a large degree of autonomy and discretionary power. Among other things, this means that they (with few exceptions) are free to choose how to organise public service provision. One of the solutions that have gained traction in Sweden is the MOC. The use of MOCs for the provision of public services is thus widely spread among Swedish municipalities. Corporations are thus a common feature in public service provision in Sweden and can be found in smaller as well as larger local governments. The size and scope of the MOCs also varies greatly and range from large energy companies with financial results of several million Swedish crowns that provide services on a larger market, to smaller single-service corporations in rural areas.

A. Thomasson (✉)
School of Economics and Management, Lund University, Lund, Sweden
e-mail: anna.thomasson@fek.lu.se

M. Van Genugten et al. (eds.), *Corporatisation in Local Government*, https://doi.org/10.1007/978-3-031-09982-3_20

Despite the long tradition of using MOCs for public service provision and the fact that they manage and are responsible for central infrastructure, Sweden has experienced several cases of corruption in which MOCs had a central role (e.g. see Amnå et al., 2013). In response to this, the regulatory framework has been revised over the years to strengthen the local governments control over their corporations. The effects have, however, not been as anticipated, and several issues remain unsolved.

The long tradition of using MOCs in Sweden combined with the fact that the solution is widespread and common makes Sweden an interesting country to study. Especially in the light of corporate scandals and problems with corruption. In this chapter we will therefore describe more in depth the use of MOCs in Sweden as well as how and why the regulation regarding the governance of MOCs has developed over time.

20.2 Context

According to the Swedish Municipal Act (SFS[1] 2017: 725), there are two types of local governments in Sweden: regional authorities and municipalities. Sweden has 21 regional authorities and 290 municipalities. Regional authorities span over a larger geographical area than municipalities, and their main responsibilities are health services, hospitals, primary care and dental care. Swedish municipalities, on the other hand, are responsible for a vast number of public services such as elderly care, schools, childcare, recreation area, urban planning and infrastructure, including water, sewage, waste management and public housing. Besides the above-mentioned services, it is also common for Swedish municipalities to provide services that are not a public responsibility and for which private alternatives exist, including central heating, broadband and electricity.

Regional authorities and municipalities are governed by an assembly. Members of the assembly are elected in general elections every fourth year. Thereafter, they elect members to committees and boards[2] of the municipality or regional authority as well as to boards and committees of other organisations that are fully or partly owned by the municipality or regional authority. Based on the goals and budgets decided by the council, it is the committees and boards that are responsible for political governance of the public services provided by the municipality or regional authority.

[1] *Svensk Författningssamling* (Collection of Swedish Regulations).

[2] The Swedish titles of these bodies are ***kommunala styrelser*** and ***nämnder***.

Regional authorities and municipalities are thus both considered local governments and are subjected to similar rules and regulations regarding how to organise and provide for public services. According to the Swedish Municipal Act (SFS 2017: 725), local governments in Sweden have a large degree of autonomy and discretionary power to determine how to organise public service provision. This includes the right to determine the size of the municipal income tax, level of fees as well as how to allocate tax money and how to organise service provision. Different options are available to them besides the in-house solutions; specifically, local governments can choose to either outsource service provision to private contractors or set up a MOC responsible for service provision. Local governments in Sweden can also choose to provide for public services in collaboration with other local governments. One way to establish an inter-municipal collaboration is by establishing a jointly owned liability company.

Hence, local authorities in Sweden are (with a few exemptions) free to corporatise public service provision (SFS 2017: 725). The exemptions relate to services that require an exercise of authority. In addition, local governments can only set up MOCs if the services provided by the corporation can be argued to have a public relevance, and there is no unfair competition with private sector providers.

20.3 The Use of MOCs in Sweden

The use of MOCs to provide public services has a long history which predates New Public Management (NPM) by many years. The first examples of the use of corporations by local governments in Sweden can be traced back to as early as the late nineteenth century (Meyer et al., 2013). As early as 1924, the Swedish Government requested an investigation regarding the character of the business conducted by municipally (or as it was referred to then town-owned) owned corporations (SOU,[3] 1924). It is difficult to say how and why Swedish municipalities started to corporatise public services in the first place. One likely explanation is the long tradition of close collaboration between the public and private sectors in Sweden (Child, 1936; Marklund, 2009). Another is that several of the services that today are considered as being a public sector responsibility in

[3] *Statens Offentliga Utredningar* (Public investigations ordered by the Swedish national government).

Sweden had their origins in private sector initiatives such as the provision of water and sewage services (Hansson & Collin, 1991; Malmer, 2003).

In the 1960s and 1970s, with the expansion of the public sector and the development of the social welfare state, the use of the corporate model became widespread in Sweden (Hansson & Collin, 1991; Meyer et al., 2013). The model experienced a further boost in the middle of the 1980s with the marketisation that followed in the wake of NPM (Erlingsson et al., 2018). All in all, since the 1960s, the use of MOCs has gradually become more and more popular. The number of corporations owned by Swedish local governments is, according to the last update by Statistics Sweden, 1979 corporations (www.scb.se). Out of these, 1836 were owned by municipalities and 143 by regional authorities. As there are 290 municipalities in Sweden, 1836 MOCs mean that, on average, each municipality owns 6.3 corporations. The ownership of MOCs is however not that evenly distributed among the municipalities. There are several municipalities that own over ten corporations and some that own more than 20, while other municipalities have only a few or even none.

The number of corporations owned by municipalities has increased dramatically during the last decades. As illustrated in Fig. 20.1, from 606 corporations in 1973 to 1686 in 2018 and the number continues to

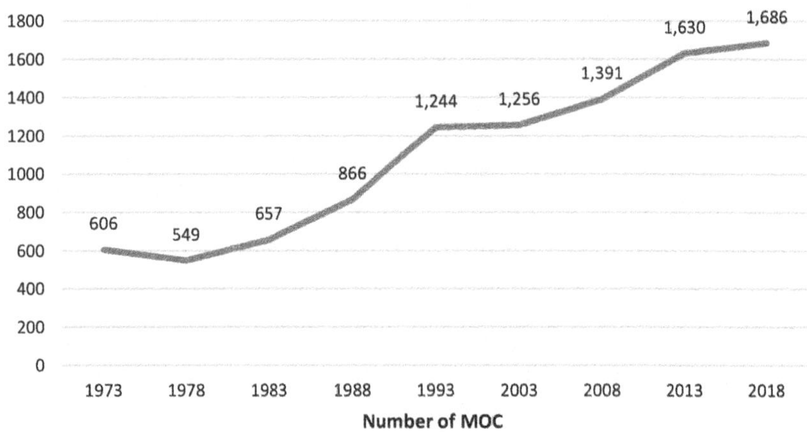

Fig. 20.1 The number of MOCs, 1973–2018 (Source: Erlingsson & Thomasson, 2020, p. 15). Note: The numbers refer to corporations where municipalities own more than 50% of the shares

increase. There is no apparent explanation to this increase, besides a continuing interest for more market-oriented solutions combined with an increase in inter-municipal collaborations. The corporation is a common way for municipalities that collaborate to organise joint service provision.

Due to the long tradition of MOCs in Sweden, corporatisation has been neither a public nor a political controversial issue (Bergh et al., 2021). Corporatisation is, however, due to the spread and the high number of corporations owned by local governments in Sweden, an important feature of Swedish local governments. MOCs thus play an important role in public service provision in Sweden (Bergh et al., 2021; Erlingsson & Thomasson, 2020). According to Statistics Sweden,[4] 56,762 people were employed by MOCs in 2019. In the same year the total turnover of MOCs amounted to 229,467 million Swedish crowns.

20.4 Legal Status

In Sweden, there is only one form of MOC, and it is subjected to public as well as private law (Kastberg, 2020).[5] When it comes to private law, all limited liability corporations in Sweden are, regardless of ownership and size, subjected to the same legislation, namely the Swedish Company Act (SFS 2005: 551). MOCs in Sweden are also subject to the Municipal Act (SFS 2017: 725) and depending on type of service provision, there are special regulations for public service provision. For example, water and wastewater management as well as the management of household waste are public monopolies and as such subjected to a specific set of regulations. The focus here, however, will be on the combination of the Municipal Act and the Corporate Act and how that influence the governance of MOCs in Sweden.

Roughly, one can say that the Municipal Act states how and when local governments can corporatise public services as well as set up the terms and conditions for the relationship between the municipality as the owner and the corporation. For example, in the Municipal Act, it is stated that the municipal board has an obligation to monitor the corporation that the municipality owns. In addition, when a municipality hands over the

[4] Statistics Sweden (Statistik myndigheten) (2019), www.scb.se

[5] One should note here that Swedish municipalities can also form foundations, but they are not considered corporations and are subjected to a completely different set of legislation and considered a legal form on its owned and therefore not addressed here.

responsibility of a public service to a fully owned corporation, the municipal assembly is obliged to determine the municipal purpose of the corporation and includes that in the articles of association. The articles of association also have to contain a section stating that decisions that are of greater importance or fundamental to the nature of the services provided by the corporation are to be made by the municipal assembly (SFS 2017: 725). The municipal assembly is also obliged to appoint board members, auditors and secure transparency. Similar rules apply to corporations that are only partly owned by the municipality,[6] but they should be applied proportionally in relation to the number of shares owned by the municipality and the specific circumstances of the shared ownership (SFS 2017: 725).

Corporations owned by local governments in Sweden are, as stated above, subjected to the same legislation as are corporations listed on the stock exchange. The Swedish Company Act (SFS 2005: 551) provides a framework for the corporate governance of limited liability corporations. Consequently, MOCs in Sweden have a similar corporate governance set-up as do private sector corporations.

MOCs in Sweden are thus subjected to both public and private law, and there is no specific corporate form for corporations owned by local government. What has been provided here is a brief description of how MOCs fall under public and private law. However, in practice the lines are not that clear and there is an overlap between private and public law, which creates uncertainties and ambiguities when it comes to the governance of MOCs (Kastberg, 2020). For example, MOCs have two sets of auditors: charted accountants as stipulated by the Corporate Act, responsible for auditing the financial status and a municipal audit (political appointed laymen), focusing on how the service provided by the corporation complies with the overall goals for the municipality decided by the municipal assembly. The role of auditors will be developed further under the section "Accountability, Transparency and Monitoring".

[6] This applies also in situations where the municipalities own less than 50% of the shares.

20.5 Organisational Characteristics

20.5.1 *The Characteristics of MOCs*

MOCs in Sweden vary in size from larger ones to smaller ones. However, it all depends on how size is measured, in terms of the number of employees or annual turnover, for example. When it comes to the number of employees, size depends on, among other things, the type of service provided, but also the size of the municipality. Similarly, if the focus is on size in terms of annual turnover, corporations in sectors with a large infrastructure or fixed assets have a different turnover than service-oriented corporations. It is fair to say, however, that in terms of size, the Swedish MOC is a diverse group. Table 20.1 shows in which services MOCs can be found in Sweden as well as the size of each group of services.

A vast majority of the MOCs can be found within the sector of real estate and related services. A total of 56% of all MOCs in Sweden can be found within that sector. Real estate in this case refers to public housing and public buildings. The latter refers to buildings built for and used by public services providers, for example, schools, nursing homes, public baths and sports arenas. The second largest category of corporations is corporations within the sector of energy and environment. Twenty-six per cent of all MOCs in Sweden can be found within this sector. Examples of

Table 20.1 Service provided by MOCs in Sweden, number of employees per service and annual turnover in 2019

Service	*Number of corporations*	*Number of employees*	*Annual turnover (million Swedish crowns)*
Electricity, gas, heating, waste management and water supply	465 (25.3%)	19,470	107,212
Hotel and restaurants	23 (1%)	477	1972
Transport and communication	164 (9%)	6183	13,076
Real estate and corporate services	979 (53%)	21,048	93,080
Education, health care and social services	21 (1%)	2640	2494
Others	184 (10%)	6944	11,633
Total	1836	56,762	229,467

Source: Statistics Sweden 7 December 2020[a]

[a]Statistics Sweden (Statistik myndigheten) 7 December 2020, www.scb.se

services provided by corporations within this sector include district heating, electricity and gas, waste management, and water and sewage services. The third most common type of corporations is corporations operating in the transport sector and/or communication and information sector. Eleven per cent of the MOCs can be found within this sector. Other sectors where MOCs can be found are culture, health, education, restaurants, agriculture, defence, mining and financial services. All in all, even though three sectors clearly dominate, MOCs can thus be found in a range of different sectors in Sweden. In addition, it is most common for MOCs to be single-purpose corporations, that is, providing just one service, for example, waste management, water supply or heating. Although multi-purpose corporations exist, especially what is referred to as multi-utilities,[7] single-purpose ones are more common.

20.5.2 *The Use of MOCs for Inter-municipal Collaborations and PPP*

It is common for Swedish municipalities to cooperate, especially with other municipalities. Public-private partnerships are rare in Sweden, and there are only a few. Inter-municipal cooperation of different kinds is, on the other hand, common and occurs in various services areas. Municipalities in Sweden can choose to cooperate either through formal agreements of different kinds or by establishing a jointly owned organisation for service production. For the latter, three different solutions are available: one solution is to enter into a formal agreement where one municipality (the host) acts on behalf of another municipality (Mattisson & Ramberg, 2015). Another solution is to form a statutory joint authority, which has the same juridical power as a municipality, but is formed by and owned by municipalities (Mattisson & Ramberg, 2015). And finally, the third option is to establish a jointly owned MOC. The specific form chosen by municipalities depends on the type of service and tradition. Specifically, when it comes to services in the real-estate, energy and environmental sector, the MOC is the most common solution as well as the statutory joint authority. However, there are no exact figures available that can tell us exactly how common it is. What can be said is that inter-municipal collaboration is a growing trend, which is likely to mean that we will see more jointly owned

[7] Multi-utility companies are companies that provide two or more infrastructure- or technical services. For example, water, electricity, central heating and waste.

MOCs in Sweden in the future, especially in the sectors of energy and environment.

20.6 Autonomy

The goals and objectives of MOCs are pursuant to the current legislation and existing regulations, including the Municipal Act, decided by the municipal assembly. Thus, it is a fixed, stepwise process starting with the municipal assembly deciding on the overall goals and objectives of the municipality. Each service-providing unit within the municipality as well as the corporations are then expected to, with point of departure in the overall objectives of the municipality, develop objectives for their specific service. There is, however, a difference between the corporations and other service-providing units within the municipality. The municipal assembly decides on ownership directives that are specific for each corporation owned by the municipality. Those directives are supposed to include the goals and objectives of the corporation. The objectives are often developed in collaboration with the board and the executive director of the corporation and the members of the municipal board.[8]

Besides deciding on the directives, the municipal assembly is also obliged to decide on the Articles of Association when the corporation is formed. The Articles of Association state the overall purpose of the corporation and should also, according to the Municipal Act, clearly state the purpose of the municipal ownership of the corporation and define the public purpose of the corporation.

Executive directors are then responsible for developing and implementing the corporation's strategy in collaboration with the board and other managers of the corporation, taking into consideration the objectives and goals stated in the ownership directives. This responsibility is clearly stated in the Company Act. It is thus also the board together with the executive director that has the main responsibility for the overall performance of the corporation. In practice, this means that the board, the executive director and the managers of the MOC generally are free to make decisions

[8] The municipal board and the municipal assembly are comprised of politicians. Both their composition reflects the outcome of the general election. The municipal board constitutes the executive power in the municipality, while the municipal assembly is equivalent to the parliament on the national level.

regarding employment and wages, investments, how to organise the operations as well as with whom the corporation is to collaborate.

There are, however, certain limitations to the autonomy. One limitation, as mentioned above, is that the corporation, according to the Municipal Act, is obliged to include the municipal assembly in all decisions that are of major importance to the corporation. What this means exactly is not clarified in the legislation and thus subjected to individual interpretations. However, those aspects likely to be considered decisions of major importance are larger investments, mergers and sales of assets. Generally, the Articles of Association or the ownership directives (or both) also address the degree to which the corporation has the right to make financial decisions. Often, there is a cap on the level of investments that the executive director and/or the board are free to decide on their own, before needing to raise the issue with the assembly. Another limitation is that MOCs are obliged to comply with the policies and decision made by the municipal assembly. In practice, this means that if the municipal assembly decides upon HR policies, environmental policies or goals, or any other type of policy, the corporation is obliged to comply with them in the same way as any other service-providing unit within the municipality. The general trend within Swedish municipalities is an increasing focus on corporate governance issues. The degree to which municipalities take interest in and monitor their corporation is thus increasing. In addition, municipalities in Sweden are increasingly aware of and interested in developing policies related to HR, sustainability and equal treatment. There is currently no code of conduct in place with which the MOCs are obliged to comply. The Swedish Association for Local Authorities and Regions has developed a code of conduct for MOCs, but it is merely to be regarded as a policy and a recommendation.

20.6.1 Accountability, Transparency and Monitoring

The municipal board is the unit, which, according to the Municipal Act, is responsible for monitoring the corporations (fully or partly) owned by the municipality. This responsibility also includes evaluating and if necessary, initiating a revision of the existing ownership directives. The Municipal Act also stipulates that the municipal assembly is to appoint directors to the board, representatives to the general annual meeting as well as at least one internal auditor. According to the Swedish Municipal Act, members of the assembly are obliged to appoint at least five auditors to an audit committee (Chaps. 3, §4, §9 and Chap. 9, §1–2). In practice, members of the audit committee are nominated by and among members of the political parties with seats in the municipal assembly. This means that the auditors elected are politicians and laymen with different political affiliations (Thomasson, 2018). Hence, they can be described as internal auditors. However, the politician-appointed auditors are not allowed to occupy seats on any other committee or board within that municipality (Municipal Act, Chap. 4, §6). The member of the audit committee works for and reports to the assembly. The main purpose of the internal audit is to ensure performance and compliance with current legislation as well as with the overall goals and objectives for the municipality decided by the assembly. The internal auditors also have the responsibility to ensure that financial resources are used in an efficient, correct and fair manner (Municipal Act, Chaps. 9–11).

MOCs in Sweden are not only subjected to public law but also to private law. Thus, they are required to have a chartered accountant that audits the financial performance of the corporation. According to the Company Act, the chartered accountant shall be appointed by representatives at the general annual meeting. Consequently, since MOCs in Sweden are subjected to public as well as private law, they have two types of auditors. Laymen and politically affiliated auditors are appointed by the municipal assembly as well as a chartered accountant that according to the Company Act is appointed by the annual general meeting. This politicisation of the audit process has however been subject for debate (Thomasson, 2018; Tagesson & Eriksson, 2011). Questions have been raised to what extent politically affiliated and appointed auditors are willing and able to scrutinise their political peers (Thomasson, 2018). One of the more prominent persons that openly and repeatedly have criticised the current system is the former head of the Swedish National Audit Office and a current member of the board of Transparency International, Inga-Britt Ahlenius (2017, 2018).

To summarise, MOCs in Sweden are more closely and regularly monitored and evaluated by the municipal board. In addition, the corporations are audited by two types of auditors: laymen auditors report to the municipal assembly and chartered accountants report to the general annual meeting. However, since it is the municipal assembly that appoints representatives to the general annual meeting as well as decides upon the ownership directives, it is the municipal assembly that according to the Municipal Act has the overall responsibility when it comes to monitoring MOCs. In practice, however, the level of knowledge and degree of interest that members of the assembly have in the MOCs vary from one municipality to another. Studies show, for example, how members of the municipal assembly only have a vague perception of the number and type of corporations owned by the municipality (Erlingsson et al., 2018; Thomasson, 2017). One possible reason for this could be that politicians governing are laymen and thus not well acquainted with all types of services or regulations, which might make it difficult for them to fully grasp the concept of corporate governance. Another possible reason is the scope of the task of local governments. Local governments in Sweden are, regardless of size, responsible for a wide range of different services. To have extensive knowledge about all these services might be difficult as a member of the municipal assembly. Yet another possible explanation is the arm's length distance between MOCs and the municipal assembly. MOCs have a great autonomy and are therefore not always as visible in the assembly as are services provide in-house.

Besides the mechanisms in place to secure accountability, transparency in the Swedish public sector is generally high. All government and government agencies in Sweden must comply with the "principle of public access to official documents".[9] This principle provides Swedish citizens the right to study official documents. Moreover, it is incorporated into one of the fundamental laws, the Freedom of the Press Act. In addition, it applies not only to government agencies but also to MOCs. Hence, according to this principle, all MOCs in Sweden are obligated to give citizens access to official documents when requested. Based on a more recent study, compliance with this regulation is generally good in government agencies as well as in MOCs, and there is no apparent difference between corporations and government agencies when it comes to adhering to this principle (Erlingsson & Wittberg, 2020).

20.7 Board Structure

MOCs in Sweden typically have one-tier boards. Generally, the boards of MOCs are made up of politicians nominated by the political parties and appointed by the municipal assembly. Often, the union appoints employee

[9] In Swedish, it is called "*Offentlighetsprincipen*". The translation of the name of the principle is from the official website of the Swedish Government: The principle of public access to official documents - Government.se (archive.org).

representatives to the board, but not always. The composition of the board generally reflects the outcome of the election, with the governing majority holding the position of chairperson and the minority holding the position of deputy chairperson. However, boards of corporations owned by several municipalities are the exception. For these corporations, the board comprises politicians from the different municipalities, and there is no clear political majority. Even though a majority of the MOCs in Sweden have boards consisting of politicians, it is not true for all corporations. There are corporations that have a combination of politicians and people with other backgrounds on the board. In those cases, it is often external experts that are invited due to identified specific needs to include such expertise on the board. There are also examples of corporations that only have civil servants from the municipality on the board. In the end, the decision regarding the composition of the board is a political one and is decided by the municipal assembly and stated in the Articles of Association. In cases where the board consists of other members than politicians, the decision is a result of careful consideration of the need for specific competence on the board.

To elect politicians as board members has, like the system with politically appointed and affiliated auditors, been criticised (Bergh et al., 2021; Erlingsson et al., 2018; Thomasson, 2017). Reasons why this politicisation of the board function has been criticised are multiple. The first reason is that it blurs the line of responsibility, and it is an example of where the overlap between private and public law creates uncertainties and ambiguities (Kastberg, 2020), in this case for the board members. When elected officials are appointed by their peers to become member of the board of MOCs, the line between the role of politician and that of board member becomes blurred. As a politician, one is expected to voice opinions and follow the political ideas of the party one represents. As a board member, however, the politicians are supposed to focus on what is in the best interest of the corporation, which not necessarily is in line with the ideas of the political party they represent.

Secondly, it is common for politicians in Swedish municipalities to simultaneously have several different assignments during one term of office. It is thus possible that a politician occupies a seat in the municipal assembly or on the municipal board at the same time when he or she also is on the board of one or several of the corporations in the municipality (Bergh et al., 2021; Erlingsson et al., 2015). This is problematic, since the municipal board together with the municipal assembly plays a key role in the governance of the MOCs. The municipal board, for one, is in the Swedish Municipal Act given a specific role to supervise and govern the corporations that are fully or partly owned by the municipality. The municipal assembly is, however, the body that has the overall responsibility for how MOCs are managed in the municipality. The municipal assembly, for example, has the right to discharge the board of a MOC if there is evidence for mismanagement. It is quite common that politicians, who are members of the municipal assembly or of the board of the municipality, also are appointed board members of a MOC. The possibility to occupy seats on the board of the MOC and on the municipal board or municipal assembly at the same time is problematic, as it means, in practice, that the politician in question is governing and supervising him- or herself. As a result, this reduces transparency and increases the risk of corruption (Bergh et al., 2021; Erlingsson et al., 2015). As there is no regulation prohibiting politicians to occupy several seats at the same time, there is nothing that hinders this practice. In fact, it is quite common. One reason why it is common could be the difficulty to recruit politicians, especially in smaller local governments. To have politicians occupying several seats is thus in many cases a practical solution. Besides being a practical solution, interviews with politicians in local governments reveal how it is considered convenient to have a member of the municipal board on the board of a MOC (Thomasson, 2017, 2019). It is considered convenient as it gives the corporation direct access to the executive power in the local government (Thomasson, 2017, 2019).

Various examples of corruptive behaviour involving MOCs are a strong argument for why there is a need to discuss this issue further. One of the largest scandals in Sweden involving MOCs and the board member of these corporations is perhaps the one in Gothenburg (Amnå et al. 2013). Gothenburg is the second largest city in Sweden and the city with the highest number of MOCs, and it is therefore perhaps not strange that this scandal attracted a lot of attention. The Gothenburg case is unfortunately not the only one. Misconducts have been revealed in relation to MOCs in other local governments as well. One example is a scandal in Östersund involving the local football team, and others are Norrköping and Sundsvall. These scandals, and the fact that they involve board members and CEOs of MOCs, are arguments for why there is a need to further discuss the composition of the boards of these corporations. The Swedish case thus shows that having politicians instead of professionals on the board of MOCs is no guarantee for increased transparency or a way to compensate for the loss of direct hierarchical control over incorporated services (Van Thiel, 2015, p. 322). On the contrary, there is a risk that the distance shrinks too much resulting in a loss of accountability.

This is further complicated by an inherent problem in the Swedish system which is that the election of board members is not based primarily on competence or aptitude, but based on the relationship between members of the political parties that nominate candidates for the board of corporations (Thomasson, 2017). Further, there is no debate in the municipal assembly prior to that decision regarding the composition of the board. Instead, the assembly accepts the nomination from the parties without discussion. Thus, in practice, all appointments are decided by the inner group of active and influential politicians within each political party, politicians that themselves hold seats in committees and on boards (Thomasson, 2017).

Thirdly, and related to what was described under the second argument, problems in securing accountability and transparency are yet another reason why the politicisation of the board of MOCs has been criticised (Erlingsson & Thomasson, 2020; Erlingsson et al., 2015). To have service providers, like corporations, operating outside the municipal organisation, means that besides securing accountability between elected politicians and citizens accountability, this accountability also needs to be secured between elected politicians and the corporations (Grossi & Thomasson, 2015). This requires special attention or there is a risk for an accountability gap due to difficulties in securing transparency, when it comes to the relationship between the municipal board and the corporation (Grossi & Thomasson, 2015). The Swedish system, where politicians occupy seats on the board of corporations while they are members of the assembly or the municipal board, contributes to this (Bergh et al., 2021; Erlingsson et al., 2015; Thomasson, 2017).

20.8 Executive Director

Executive directors of MOCs in Sweden have different backgrounds. Some have their professional background in the private sector, others in the public sector, and yet another group has experience from working in both sectors. There is thus not a typical profile. However, normally they have some prior experience of leadership or a more prominent role in either the private or the public sector. Little over a decade ago, it was more common to recruit people with a background in the private sector for the role of executive director. However, this trend is no longer that apparent.

The role is generally not politicised. Instead, it is often compared to the role of the executive director in a private corporation. The reason for this might be the fact that executive directors in MOCs, like their peers in private corporations, have the same obligations and responsibilities based on how the role is defined and described in the Company Act.

The information regarding the salaries of executive directors is public. There is no legal maximum; however, there are ethical aspects that need to be considered. Also, from time to time, the salaries of executive directors and leading civil servants are published in local newspapers and compared. This tendency among local newspapers to make comparisons of salaries on a regular basis has had a dampening effect on the salaries paid to executive directors.

20.9 Current Issues Related to Municipal Corporate Governance in Sweden

Even though MOCs historically have not attracted a lot of attention, things have gradually come to change (Bergh et al., 2021; Erlingsson & Thomasson, 2020). For example, in 2010, Swedish journalists investigated how a larger city in Sweden governed their MOCs. The city was, then, and still is, the municipality with the highest number of MOCs in Sweden (Statistics Sweden 2021[10]). The investigation revealed mismanagement and suspicion of corruption, failure to comply with the Law of Public Procurement as well as bribery in relation to the corporations. Accordingly, the investigation led to a total of ten officials and politicians being prosecuted and to an evaluation of the corporate governance system (Amnå et al., 2013).

In the aftermath of the major scandal involving MOCs in Gothenburg, there was an upsurge in the interest in MOCs. The focus was especially on issues related to transparency and accountability, resulting in an amendment of the Municipal Act (SFS 2017: 725) with the goal of increasing the responsibility of the municipal board when it comes to the governance of corporations. The ramification of this scandal is, however, not limited to changes in the legal framework, but it has also shed light on how municipalities work with corporate governance issues. Despite this, the issue of

[10] Statistics Sweden (Statistik myndigheten) (2021), www.scb.se

securing accountability is still problematic. In this chapter, several reasons for that have been given. Among these, perhaps the politicisation of the audit process and of the role of the board is the most problematic ones. The problem that the politicisation of these two processes generate and the risk for corruption that they generate has not yet been addressed by the legislators.

References

Ahlenius, I.-B. (2017, February 21). *Kommunerna behöver oberoende revision [The municipalities need an independent audit]*. Göteborgs Posten.

Ahlenius, I.-B. (2018, March 6). *"Sverige behöver en ny kommunallag" ["Sweden needs a new Municipal Act"]*. Dagens Nyheter.

Amnå, E., Czarniawska, B., & Marcusson, L. (2013). *Tillitens gränser: Granskningskommissionens slutbetänkande [The boarders of trust: Final comments from the audit commission]*. Granskningskommissionen i Göteborgs stad.

Bergh, A., Erlingsson. G., & Wittberg, E. (2021). What happens when municipalities run corporations? Empirical evidence from 290 Swedish municipalities. *Local Government Studies.* https://doi.org/10.1080/03003930.2021.1944857.

Child, M. W. (1936). *Sweden the middle way: The story of the constructive compromise between socialism and capitalism*. Penguin Books.

Erlingsson, G., Fogelgren, M., Olsson, F., Thomasson, A., & Öhrvall, R. (2015). Att bolagisera kommunal verksamhet: Implikationer för granskning, ansvarsutkrävande och demokrati? [Corporatisation of local government service provision: Implications for audit, accountability and democracy]. *Statsvetenskaplig tidskrift, 117*(4), 555–582.

Erlingsson, G., & Thomasson, A. (2020). *Kommunala bolag [Municipally owned corporations]*. Studentlitteratur.

Erlingsson, G., Thomasson, A., & Öhrvall, R. (2018). Issues on transparency, accountability and control in hybrid organizations: The case of enterprises owned by local government. In A. Bonovi Savignon, L. Gnan, A. Hinna, & F. Monteduro (Eds.), *Hybridity in the governance and delivery of public services* (pp. 31–52). Emerald Publishing Limited.

Erlingsson, G., & Wittberg, E. (2020). Respekterar kommunala bolag offentlighetsprincipen? [Are municipally owned corporations applying with the principle of public access to official records]. In G. Erlingsson & A. Thomasson (Eds.), *Kommunala bolag* (pp. 111–125). Studentlitteratur.

Grossi, G., & Thomasson, A. (2015). Bridging the accountability gap in hybrid organizations: The case of Malmö-Copenhagen Port. *International Review of Administrative Science, 81*(3), 604–620.

Hansson, L., & Collin, S. O. (1991). *Kommunalt bolag? En studie av för- och nackdelar med bolagisering av kommunalteknisk verksamhet [Municipally owned corporations? A study of the pros and cons of the corporatisation of technical infrastructure in local governments]*. Svenska Kommunförbundet.

Kastberg, P. (2020). De kommunala bolagens juridiska särdrag [The legal features of municipally owned corporations]. In G. Erlingsson & A. Thomasson (Eds.), *Kommunala bolag* (pp. 29–52). Studentlitteratur.

Malmer, S. (2003). *Ett pris blir till: Om förklaringar till kommunala avgifter och taxor [The construction of a price: Explanations to the level of fees and taxes in municipal services]*. Santérus förlag.

Marklund, C. (2009). The social laboratory, the middle way and the Swedish model. *Scandinavian Journal of History, 34*(3), 264–258.

Mattisson, O., & Ramberg, U. (2015). Co-owned local government organizations: Conditions for strategy development. *Financial Accountability and Management, 31*(3), 296–286.

Meyer, L., Mårtensson, P., & Nilsson, O. (2013). *Kommunala bolag; ägarstyrning och styrelsefunktion [Municipally owned corporations: Corporate governance and the role of the board]*. Studentlitteratur.

SOU. (1924). *Kommunal Affärsverksamhet (Business in local governments)*. 1924, 42.

Tagesson, T., & Eriksson, O. (2011). What do auditors do? Obviously, they do not scrutinize the accounting and reporting. *Financial Accountability and Management, 27*, 272–285.

Thomasson, A. (2017). What about the board? Issues of transparency and accountability in board composition. In I. Lapsley & H. Knutsson (Eds.), *Modernizing the public sector: Scandinavian perspectives* (pp. 149–162). Routledge.

Thomasson, A. (2018). Politicization of the audit process: The case of politically affiliated auditors in Swedish local governments. *Financial Accountability & Management, 34*(4), 1–12.

Thomasson, A. (2019). The importance of owner relationship in shaping hybrid organizations. In S. Alexius & S. Furusten (Eds.), *Managing hybrid organizations* (pp. 129–155). Palgrave Macmillan.

Van Thiel, S. (2015). Boards of public sector organizations: A typology with Dutch illustrations. *International Journal of Public Sector Management, 28*(4/5), 322–334.

PART VI

Conclusion

CHAPTER 21

Corporatised Local Public Service Provision: Comparative Evidence from 19 Countries and Research Agenda

Bart Voorn, Rhys Andrews, Ulf Papenfuß, Harald Torsteinsen, and Marieke Van Genugten

21.1 Introduction

Municipally owned corporations (MOCs) and the services which they provide are of growing importance to the state and society in most of the countries examined in this book. In this conclusion, we offer an overview

B. Voorn (✉) • M. Van Genugten
Institute for Management Research, Radboud University, Nijmegen, The Netherlands
e-mail: bart.voorn@ru.nl; marieke.vangenugten@ru.nl

R. Andrews
Cardiff Business School, Cardiff University, Cardiff, UK
e-mail: andrewsr4@cardiff.ac.uk

U. Papenfuß
Zeppelin University, Friedrichshafen, Germany
e-mail: ulf.papenfuss@zu.de

M. Van Genugten et al. (eds.), *Corporatisation in Local Government*, https://doi.org/10.1007/978-3-031-09982-3_21

of the chapters in this book, discussing the trends, legal types, organisational characteristics, autonomy and board structure of MOCs in 19 different countries. In doing so, our aim is to contribute to cross-country understanding of local corporatisation and to pave the way for more comparative research in the future.

In the book, we define MOCs as corporations and enterprises that are under the control of a municipality either by majority ownership by one or more municipalities or otherwise by exercising an equivalent degree of control (Andrews et al., 2020; Grossi et al., 2015; Papenfuβ & Keppler, 2020; Voorn et al., 2017). The process by which governments convert an existing public service into a majority-owned corporate entity or create a new service is referred to as corporatisation (Andrews, 2020; Papenfuß & Schmidt, 2021a).

MOCs can have upsides and downsides. On the one hand, the creation of MOCs is an approach to improve the performance in public service provision by enhancing executive autonomy, flexibility, speed for action and professionalism. The political decisions to transfer public services to public corporations can have high potential for effective and efficient public service provision for municipalities and their citizens (Andrews et al., 2020; Papenfuß & Schmidt, 2021a; Van Genugten et al., 2020). On the other hand, MOCs also induce far-reaching control and governance challenges in a multilevel delegation chain (Bel et al., 2021; Papenfuß & Schmidt, 2021b; Voorn & Van Genugten, 2021). For instance, while MOCs have the potential to incorporate more business techniques in service delivery, this may not necessarily occur (Voorn et al., 2020a, 2020b). More generally, the distancing of service delivery from direct local government oversight may reduce the extent to which local government goals are set, challenging democracy, accountability and efficiency in local public service delivery (Voorn, 2020).

In the next sections, we offer a cross-country overview of corporatisation in local government based on the five categories described in each chapter: trends, legal types, organisational characteristics, autonomy and board structure. Finally, we address implications for public administration and discuss a future research agenda.

H. Torsteinsen
Department of Social Sciences, UiT The Arctic University of Norway, Tromsø/Harstad, Norway
e-mail: harald.torsteinsen@uit.no

21.2 Trends Regarding Numbers of MOCs Across Countries

In the wake of New Public Management (NPM) reforms in the 1990s, local governments in most countries began adopting a variety of arm's-length delivery models (Van Genugten et al., 2020). It is often assumed that this process marked a movement towards privatisation of local public services, driven largely by fiscal pressures (Bel & Fageda, 2007). However, as dissatisfaction with the costs of contracting out and the quality of privatised municipal services grew in many countries, the use of MOCs also came to be seen as an attractive vehicle for bringing previously contracted out services back under municipal control (Grossi & Reichard, 2008), to "mix politics and professionalism" (Voorn, 2020).

Despite the widespread and continuing impact of NPM on local governments and their service delivery choices (Kuhlmann & Bouckaert, 2016), the rate of corporatisation in local government has varied greatly across the countries surveyed in this book. Comparison of the trajectories of corporatisation for the past 20 years reported in the country chapters suggests that, at the national level, the evolution of corporatisation can be categorised into four main clusters of countries:

(i) A small group of countries in which the use of MOCs has decreased (Greece, Hungary, Portugal)
(ii) Countries in which the use of MOCs has remained comparatively stable (Canada, Denmark, Israel, Italy, the Netherlands, Spain)
(iii) Countries in which the use of MOCs has gradually increased (Poland, Slovakia, Sweden, Switzerland, Wales)
(iv) A small group of countries in which the use of MOCs has increased dramatically (England, France, Germany, Norway, Turkey)

Although the clustering of the countries by corporatisation doesn't clearly follow an easily definable pattern, evidence from this book suggests that the use of MOCs seems more likely to be declining in those Southern European countries with a Napoleonic administrative tradition than elsewhere. Greece and Portugal both observed sharp decreases in the number of MOCs being operated by municipalities. In the case of Greece, this was driven by political changes intended to strengthen state control over public services. For Portugal, the mass termination of MOCs was a direct response to the fiscal fallout from the global financial crisis. Interestingly, both Italy and Spain observed a downturn in the use of MOCs for similar reasons during the 2010s, albeit to a level of municipally owned coporation (MOC) use that was present at the end of a period of expansion in the 2000s. Following rapidly growing corporatisation in the 2000s, it stalled in the Netherlands during the 2010s. It is possible that any marginal gains in efficiency from the drive to create inter-municipal capacity across the country became exhausted, and that pressure to achieve scale economies weakened in the wake of on-going amalgamations of Dutch municipalities.

The decreasing use of MOCs in Hungary reflects efforts by the Orban administration to reduce local autonomy and consolidate central control over the state—something that has not been observed in other former Communist countries. In Canada and Israel, countries with an Anglo-Saxon administrative tradition, municipalities' use of MOCs has been largely constrained through an array of legislative and regulatory measures that underline the institutional weakness of local government in each country. In Denmark, diverging trends towards and away from corporatisation have been observed in different policy sectors, mostly as a pragmatic response to changing EU legislation, such that, overall, the use of MOCs has remained comparatively stable.

Many of the countries surveyed in the book have observed a continual increase in the number of MOCs since the turn of the century, especially those continental countries with a Federal administrative tradition (i.e. Austria, Germany and Switzerland), where MOC use is assumed to reflect a pragmatic choice in favour of corporatised service delivery. Many of the Central and Eastern European countries and Nordic countries included in the book have also observed an increase in the use of MOCs. Norway, in particular, has witnessed a dramatic upward trend in the corporatisation of local public services, largely in order to build the managerial capacity needed to meet expanded local service responsibilities. In Sweden, the use of MOCs, has occurred mostly in response to wider economic and political pressures to explore alternatives to in-house provision. In Poland and Slovakia, corporatisation represents part of wider trends towards political and fiscal decentralisation and the introduction of legal measures to facilitate greater local autonomy over service delivery choices.

In the UK, there has been an extremely rapid growth in the use of MOCs in England, partly as a result of fiscal pressures, but also in response to expanded legal powers to corporatise services, which were not extended in Wales, which has seen only modest growth in the use of MOCs, and has a more pro-state political orientation than England. In France, rapid corporatisation of many services of general interest has occurred as municipalities seek to develop new methods for achieving greater strategic control over economic development and regeneration. In Turkey, a country with something approaching a Napoleonic administrative tradition, a dramatic increase in the use of MOCs was observed following a presidential decree intended to strengthen the authority of the state by municipalising all the employees contracted to provide local public services.

The cross-country variations in corporatisation observed in the countries surveyed in the book underline the importance of comparative research to fully understand the distinctive dynamics behind reforms to the local public sector. This comparative dimension is especially important when considering national trends in how MOCs are being created, operated and monitored within countries. Nevertheless, it is possible to detect some broad common themes in the information reported in the country chapters.

Firstly, the turn towards corporate forms of service delivery in most countries has seen the use of MOCs extended to policy fields that were traditionally managed in-house by local governments, such as housing, social services, leisure and culture. Secondly, it is also apparent that MOCs are generally increasing in size and scope, with many now managing multi-million Euro budgets. Thirdly, it is clear that in many countries increased attention is being paid to managing and monitoring MOCs. The introduction of corporate governance codes, performance management systems for arm's-length entities and regulations constraining executive pay highlight the impact of debates about the need to balance democratic legitimacy and organisational efficiency in MOCs. Summarising, while we should keep in mind that cross-country corporatisation trends can be quite dissimilar, there seems to be a trend towards corporatisation in most countries.

21.3 Overview of Legal Types

We now turn to description of the different legal types of MOCs that exist between countries. Before we start our overview, it is important to emphasise that because of the many different legal and administrative traditions and specific laws across the countries described in this book, detailed cross-country comparison of legal types is particularly difficult. Therefore, description of legal types here will be limited to overarching themes, with examples from the varying countries throughout the book. Nonetheless, we can detect some common themes in legal types throughout the countries included in this book.

In this book, the researchers of all countries have particularly classified the legal types of MOCs using the classifications of Papenfuβ and Keppler (2020) and Van Genugten et al. (2020), who presented a categorisation of legal types of MOCs based on Van Thiel's typology (Van Thiel 2012) of agencies at the national level and its earlier application of Torsteinsen and Van Genugten (2016) of this to the local level. Specifically, the typologies of Papenfuβ and Keppler (2020) and Van Genugten et al. (2020) subdivide local public service delivery organisations in five legal types depending on their functional autonomy, ranging from type 0 bodies—traditional in-house delivery—that are functionally local bureaucracies to three different types of arm's-length bodies (Papenfuβ & Keppler, 2020; Van Genugten et al., 2020) to type 4 bodies, where governments have no functional ownership but only a contracting relationship.

MOCs in this context are type 2 and type 3 bodies—entities that are structurally separated from the local government but still owned by the municipality. The main distinction between these two types being whether these structurally separated entities—MOCs—are based in public law (type 2) or private law (type 3). Theoretically, these two legal types differ in two dimensions: structural and legal autonomy (Verhoest et al., 2004). Structural autonomy refers to "the extent to which the agency is shielded from influence through lines of hierarchy and accountability" (Verhoest et al., 2004, p. 105), while legal autonomy refers to "the extent to which the legal status of the agency prevents the government from altering the allocation of decision-making competencies or makes such changes more difficult" (Verhoest et al., 2004, p. 106). As a general rule, the expectation, in line with the evidence presented in this book, is that MOCs based in private law (type 3) are more autonomous than those based in public law (type 2). We now turn to describing the different legal types that exist throughout Europe, using examples from the multiple chapters in this book.

First, the evidence from this book shows that MOCs in public law exist in some countries, but not in others. For instance, in France and Hungary, the public-law form is not used, while in Greece, it is the most common type. Moreover, the exact implications of public law can differ substantially between countries. For example, in the Netherlands and in Poland, public-law MOCs can only be founded for the purpose of inter-municipal cooperation, and takes a very specific form, while in other countries the public-law form can be used also outside of the context of inter-municipal cooperation. In addition, in some countries, public-law MOCs are purely voluntary, but in others, they can be mandated by the national government. The sheer variety of public-law types throughout the countries surveyed in this book makes it difficult to typify them according to some categorisation.

Even more variety exists among the private-law legal types of MOCs in the countries surveyed for this book. We can distinguish between limited liability companies (where local governments own a majority of the shares), that exist in nearly every country, foundations and cooperatives, that exist in most countries, and associations and other types of non-profits, that may exist depending on the specific administrative traditions of the countries. Some countries seem to have more options for the founding of MOCs than others (e.g. in Italy nearly all the previously named forms are used, while in France the limited liability company is pretty much the only form employed).

More generally, the limited liability company seems to be the most utilised legal form for MOCs among the countries studied in this book, but even there, there are large differences between countries in the importance and utilisation of the limited liability company for the purpose of local public service delivery. For example, in Sweden, only the limited liability company type (AB) is used. In Spain, also only limited liability companies are used, but they exist in two forms, the Business Public Entities (EPE) and Local Commercial Companies (SML), that differ primarily in how much autonomy the corporations have. In some countries, limited companies are primarily inter-municipal (such as Italy), but in others they are primarily owned by single municipalities (such as the Netherlands). And in some countries, MOCs even primarily take the form of public–private partnerships (PPPs), such as the "Sociétés d'économie mixte" (SEM), meaning "Mixed economy companies", in France.

Furthermore, it is difficult to find many links between the possible legal types of MOCs and the different administrative traditions of countries, as in many cases even neighbouring countries can differ quite drastically from one another in the possible legal types. More interesting are the rules for founding these private-law type companies: in many countries, municipalities have to meet certain requirements in order to found them, such as the requirement that "their economic activities must be limited to activities and tasks that will not harm or circumvent their statutory duties or core tasks" (Austria) or that there must be clear evidence that this form would work better than the private-law form (the Netherlands). In other countries, founding MOCs based in private law is much less limited by legislation.

We have so far made a distinction between public-law and private-law MOCs, based on prior knowledge from the typologies of Papenfuβ and Keppler (2020) and Van Genugten et al. (2020). It is important, however, to emphasise that the evidence in the book shows that MOCs cannot be easily subdivided in all countries using this typology. For instance, the authors of the Danish chapter describe how MOCs in Denmark often take a hybrid form with degrees of legal autonomy, operating in "the grey zone" between public and private law. In Turkey, there is ambiguity in the type of law under which MOCs operate, as they are created under public law but are subject to private law, and both scholars and legal courts are in disagreement about how MOCs should be treated under the law. Next, also in Austria, Canada and Israel, public law is often also applied to private-law MOCs. Thus, in terms of legal type, the real-world is more murky than can be fully delineated under the typology of Papenfuβ and Keppler (2020) and Van Genugten et al. (2020).

When companies have both public-law and private-law type MOCs, it appears that public-law MOCs are primarily used for "hard to measure tasks", like cultural and educational services, while private-law MOCs are primarily used for services that require more flexibility, as is described well, for instance, in the chapter about local corporatisation in Slovakia.

21.4 Organisational Characteristics of MOCs

Next, looking at the organisational characteristics of MOCs in the countries surveyed in this book, we observe some interesting differences and similarities between countries in terms of service sector, ownership, single-/multi-purpose MOCs and size of MOCs.

21.4.1 Service Sectors

In general, MOCs provide a wide array of services and are active in many policy fields. One common denominator is that in all countries surveyed in this book, MOCs are used for one or more utilities, such as waste collection, water supply, waste, sewerage, public transport and energy. The use of MOCs in the field of utilities originates from their high technical asset specificity, the opportunity to exploit economies of scope and scale, and to charge user fees (Citroni et al., 2013; Tavares, 2017). In some countries, MOCs are still mainly used for utility services, while in other countries the service portfolio of MOCs has expanded to other municipal services as well. Broadly speaking, we observe three categories of countries:

i. A small group of countries with MOCs providing mainly technical services: Denmark, Poland, Spain and Sweden
ii. A small group of countries with MOCs providing a small specific set of services: Canada, Greece, Hungary and Wales
iii. A large group of more than half of the countries with MOCs providing a wide array of services: Austria, England, France, Germany, Israel, Italy, the Netherlands Norway, Portugal, Slovakia, Switzerland and Turkey

In the first quite diverse group of countries, MOCs dominate in technical services, in which service delivery highly depends on a physical network (i.e. utilities) or physical facilities (e.g. real estate, housing, libraries). Although MOCs in these service sectors are dominant, a small part of MOCs can be found in other service sectors as well.

The second group is also a small, diverse set of countries. In Canada, MOCs operate in economic development, infrastructure, housing, libraries and policing. In Wales, MOCs are only used in waste management and economic development. In Hungary, MOCs traditionally operate in infrastructure and utilities, but there is an expansion to two other fields, namely culture and leisure. In Greece, MOCs provide water services, culture and social services.

In the third group of countries, the service portfolio of MOCs follows the multifunction model which characterises municipalities in many countries (Wollmann, 2004). In these countries, MOCs are now being used for a broad array of services, such as utilities, education, culture, sports and health, building construction, economic development and general administration. MOCs in Turkey have a somewhat different portfolio, as the large variety of services mainly covers service sectors that serve the organisational and financial needs of municipalities rather than service provision.

21.4.2 *MOCs as Vehicle for Inter-municipal Cooperation and PPPs*

A second important organisational characteristic that can be used to classify MOCs is the ownership of MOCs. In a third of the countries surveyed in this book most MOCs are 100% owned by a single municipality. This is mainly the case in Anglo-Saxon and Central East European countries. One exception is the UK, where in England and Wales around 20% of MOCs are public–private partnerships (PPPs).

In other countries, especially the Central European Federal, Napoleonic and the Nordic countries, MOCs are also used as a vehicle for inter-municipal cooperation. In countries such as Austria and Sweden the number of inter-municipal MOCs is even growing. In France, all MOCs have at least two municipal shareholders, while in the Netherlands around 75% of MOCs and in Austria 34% of MOCs are jointly owned by municipalities. In the other countries no numbers are available, but in Switzerland, Italy, Spain, Portugal, Denmark, Norway and Sweden inter-municipal MOCs are a common or even widespread phenomenon as well. Important drivers are economies of scale, expertise sharing, and the prevention of (forced?) amalgamation (Bel & Warner, 2015; Citroni et al., 2013; Voorn & Van Genugten, 2021). In Germany, one of the Central European Federal countries, inter-municipal MOCs also exists, and the number seems to increase but they are a more rare phenomenon. The same is true for two Napoleonic countries, Turkey and Greece. In Greece, most MOCs are 100% owned by one single municipality.

Interestingly, in Napoleonic countries, except for Greece, MOCs are typically used for PPPs. In Turkey 23% of MOCs are used for PPPs. Approximately the same percentage, 22% of MOCs are institutional public private partnerships in Portugal. In France around 70% of private-law-based MOCs are a PPP. In Italy, PPP is mainly used for utilities, while in Spain particularly large cities have established PPPs.

21.4.3 *Single-Purpose Versus Multi-purpose*

A third organisational characteristic addressed in the different chapters is whether MOCs are single-purpose or multi-purpose. Multi-purpose MOCs are operating in multiple service sectors. In more than half of the countries surveyed in this book, MOCs are only or mainly single-purpose, operating in one service sector. These countries are Anglo-Saxon, Central

East European and Central European Federal countries: Canada, Israel, Wales, Hungary, Slovakia, Austria and Germany. Two exceptions are England, in which multi-purpose MOCs do exist, and Poland, where 20% of MOCs are multi-purpose. 75% of these MOCs combine water and sewage services. Another point worth mentioning is that in Poland, smaller municipalities more often have multi-purpose MOCs, while large municipalities have single-purpose MOCs. Although MOCs in Hungary are usually single-purpose, there are some multi-purpose MOCs in the form of holding companies with subsidiaries.

In Napoleonic and Nordic countries the picture is more divers. For example, France and Turkey have a large share of multi-purpose MOCs; in Turkey this is 58%, while in France almost all private-law-based MOCs are multi-purpose MOCs. Contrastingly, in Greece, Italy and Spain, MOCs are usually single-purpose, although in Italy some multi-purpose MOCs exist for sewage, water, waste, electricity and gas for reasons of economies of scale. In the Nordic countries Denmark and the Netherlands, both types of MOCs exist, while in Norway and Sweden MOCs are usually single-purpose.

However, it is important to emphasise that the distinction between single-purpose and multi-purpose MOCs is not straightforward, and we suggest that for future research this classification may not be as useful as it has been presented to be in earlier literature. For instance, often MOCs are organised in groups with mother companies and daughter companies, a typical case is public utility which has ten daughter companies, and they all interact with each other across sectors. The daughter companies may be single-purpose, while the public utility is multi-purpose. Moreover, there are several cross-sector activities in many single MOCs. Maybe a future approach could be to work with an understanding that a single-purpose MOC generates 80% or 90% of the activities/revenues in one sector to be seen as single-purpose MOC, and otherwise as multi-purpose MOC. Or perhaps we should move away from using this terminology and focus on describing more precisely what MOCs do.

21.4.4 Size of MOCs

Comparing the size of MOCs, the final organisational characteristic, is a difficult task due to the large variety in service sectors. Furthermore, data are often lacking or different types of data are reported (e.g. number of employees, revenues). Looking at the countries surveyed in this book, we learn most about size in terms of number of employers. This number differs a lot between MOCs in the different countries. We observe three categories of countries:

i. A small group of countries in which MOCs are typically small, often even micro-enterprises: in Hungary MOCs have less than 50 employees, in Greece the average is 22 employees, but most MOCs have less than 10 employees, and in Poland in technical sectors MOCs usually employ 60–70 employees, while other sectors are smaller.
ii. A large group in which MOCs vary from very large to quite small organisations: Austria, Denmark, England, France, Germany, Israel, Italy, the Netherlands, Slovakia, Spain and Switzerland.
iii. In Turkey, MOCs are typically large according to employed personnel. They usually have more than 125 employees.

21.5 Cross-country Comparison of Autonomy in MOCs

Next, the chapters in this book have described the autonomy that MOCs have in the various countries. Autonomy is an important characteristic of MOCs: one of the main drivers behind delegation and corporatisation in the public sector is the idea that by granting service-providing entities more autonomy they will perform better, that is to say become more effective, efficient, professional and able to deliver higher service quality. The same anticipation seems to motivate local governments when they delegate tasks to arm's-length bodies like for instance MOCs. But MOCs are not equally autonomous in all countries.

Autonomy is a tricky concept, comprising multiple features and dimensions (Ladner et al., 2016; Verhoest et al., 2004), and it may be analysed at various levels, for instance the individual, the organisational or the institutional, and also as an outcome of the interaction between levels. The level perspective indicates that autonomy is a relational phenomenon. The autonomy of the CEO of an MOC may depend on his/her relationship with the board(s) or with the owner assembly of the company. Further, the autonomy of the MOC varies with its legal corporate form or type of arm's-length bodies (Van Genugten et al., 2020), usually created and regulated by the national government. Its autonomy also varies with the type of tasks or services it provides—especially concerning activities more or less defined and monitored by national authorities—and depends on its political and administrative relationship with the owner(s). Finally, the national government may influence the autonomy of local government concerning corporatisation through legal, economic, organisational, and other formal or informal governance mechanisms, including specific provisions related to service-sector policies. The interaction between levels is dynamic and changes over time, creating varying national and local trends in corporatisation and public corporate governance.

In a comparative study of local autonomy in 39 European countries, Ladner et al. (2016) had already uncovered a pattern that very much aligns with the typology of local government used in this book. Nordic (except the Netherlands) and Central European Federal countries, including Poland, France and recently Italy, receive the highest autonomy scores, while Anglo-Saxon and some Napoleonic countries—Greece and Turkey—score lowest among the case countries in this book on an index comprising 11 features. After a conspicuous decline in local autonomy, Hungary has recently joined this group. In the middle category we find Portugal and Spain from the Napoleonic group and Slovakia from the Central East European group. Somewhat surprisingly also the Netherlands, belonging to the Nordic type, finds itself in this middle category. While the autonomy of Spanish municipalities has decreased recently, Slovakian municipalities have climbed on the autonomy ranking. Three of the eleven elements of the local autonomy index are especially relevant for the manoeuvring space municipalities have for creating and governing MOCs—organisational autonomy, policy scope and political discretion. Concerning the first feature, Denmark, Norway, Poland, and Switzerland score highest, while France scores lowest. When it comes to policy scope, the Nordic countries have a very wide range of tasks, followed by France, Germany, and Hungary, whereas in Greece and Turkey the portfolio is especially narrow. Finally, when it comes to political discretion, Finnish, German, and Swedish municipalities score highest, while Greece, Turkey, and Switzerland (!) score lowest. These findings align with conspicuous discrepancies between wide policy scope and limited political discretion observed in Austria, Denmark, France, Norway, and Switzerland, indicating strong national regulation and ambitions for creating nationwide equality through standardisation (Ladner et al., 2016).

The relevance of the Ladner et al. (2016) study for our topic is its systematic and in-depth analysis of how national regulation creates and influences the manoeuvring space for local government which in its turn lay the premises for how municipalities shape and govern their MOCs, including the autonomy they grant to their MOCs. Within this framework constructed in different ways in different countries by national and then local governments, MOCs may have various degrees of autonomy concerning operative, financial, organisational, and labour issues and setting of goals and strategies. Further, monitoring and accountability systems and practices may vary, in some cases strengthening, in other cases circumscribing autonomy.

According to the findings presented in the country chapters of this book, MOCs and their CEOs generally have considerable to high degrees of autonomy in operational, day-to-day matters, whereas it is somewhat lower when it comes to more important strategic issues. Findings also indicate that autonomy, especially concerning the last category of issues, has been reduced during the last decade. This process aligns with increasing development of monitoring and accountability regimes directed at MOCs, sometimes triggered by national authorities. We especially see this in Napoleonic countries like Portugal, Spain, and Turkey, in Israel of the Anglo-Saxon group, and in Hungary belonging to the Central East European type. In Israel and Turkey, the changes are linked to political tensions and contradictory regulations at the national level, whereas in Hungary, the national government seems to seek more centralised control generally. In Sweden, following a scandal in Gothenburg municipality in the first decade of the millennium, the control of MOCs has been strengthened through an amendment in the Local Government Act of 2017. Further, we observe that in countries belonging to the Central European Federal group, the autonomy of MOCs is high but strictly formalised and regulated, whereas in the Anglo-Saxon countries, especially England and Wales, there seem to be few formalities.

Autonomy is usually higher in private law (ALB type 3) than in public law (ALB type 1 and 2) companies (Van Genugten et al., 2020), and this observation applies to all countries described in this book. However, there are several important exemptions in single countries where autonomy in public legal forms can be higher than in private legal forms. Further, autonomy is generally higher in the Nordic and the Central European Federal countries and in some countries belonging to other groups, Canada (Anglo-Saxon), France and Italy (Napoleonic), and Poland, increasingly also Slovakia (Central East European), than in other countries.

When it comes to setting goals, founding documents passed by democratic assemblies (municipal/county/regional councils) are important in most countries. In several countries, especially those belonging to the Nordic and Central European Federal groups, these documents must contain a minimum of provisions described in national laws. They are usually stricter and more detailed for public-law than for private-law MOCs. Democratic assemblies of owner municipalities may also outline key performance indicators, strategies and set financial and other limits for their MOCs. In countries with two-tier board systems, the supervisory board also seems to play an important role in goal setting. Within these limits, corporate governance bodies (owner assemblies and boards) are usually free to define operative, and sometimes also strategic goals. In the Netherlands, strategic goals are mostly set by the MOCs' own initiatives, and this is an increasing trend. In Denmark, sector-specific national laws and strategies are important, while in Sweden, after the municipal council has decided strategies for every MOC, the municipal executive committee plays a prominent role, often in cooperation with the CEO and the board of the MOCs. In Spain and Poland, the mayor is often involved in goal setting, whereas in the UK, senior public managers play an important role. In Canada, provincial government regulates goal setting, while in Slovakia the process is informal through personal contacts, and in Turkey, political influence is growing. In Germany, the strategic goal-setting processes differ substantially between municipalities which can also be seen in the outlined and published goal-setting processes in public corporate governance codes.

Finally, when it comes to monitoring and accountability, these mechanisms and processes are often interlinked. The systems vary considerably, and some country chapters provide scarce if any information at all. In many countries, shareholders assemblies, (if present) supervisory boards and board appointments (and dismissals) play an important role. The Central European Federal and the Nordic countries seem to have the most developed regimes at the local government level. In Germany for example, municipalities often have a special administrative unit for governance of MOCs. This type of entities is also emerging in Norwegian and Swedish municipalities. In addition, reporting procedures and audit systems are extensive. Despite this and a high level of transparency, mismanagement of MOCs is not always unveiled by these formal mechanisms, and instead, the job is often done by investigative journalists. In Napoleonic countries, for example Portugal and Spain, control of MOCs is performed not only by local government but also by regional and national authorities. Transparency has been and still is a problem, especially concerning economy and remuneration, for instance in France, Portugal, and Turkey. In addition, serious regulatory contradictions hamper monitoring and accountability in Turkey. In the UK, senior public managers are mainly the ones monitoring and holding MOCs to account.

21.6 Board Structure and Corporate Governance Across Countries

Finally, regarding board structure, the chapters report a broad mix of one-tier boards and two-tier boards in the context of MOCs in many countries, although there are also many countries with mixed systems or choice opportunities. In the one-tier system, the executive directors and directors are organised in one board. In the two-tier board system, the management board, which is composed of the executive directors, handles the day-to-day management of the enterprise. The supervisory board, which contains the non-executive directors, is involved in decisions of fundamental importance and supervises and advises the members of the management board. Here, the management board with the executive directors is of special relevance because of its greater competencies and operational influence.

According to the chapters, several countries usually have a one-tier board in the context of MOCs, such as Canada, England, Greece and Sweden. Two-tier boards in the context of MOCs are usually established in countries such as Austria, Germany, the Netherlands, Poland, Switzerland and Turkey. For some countries, the chapters emphasise that it is possible to choose between various governance models, such as is the case in Hungary, Italy and Slovakia.

In nearly all countries politicians are usually represented as directors in the boards or as members in supervisory boards; however, the extent diverges between countries and also between municipalities inside countries. Often, there is a mix of appointed elected representatives and local stakeholders/experts, but the mix diverges substantially. Regarding executive directors, politicisation and proximity to party politics is a typical challenge in many countries.

All chapters report on governance deficits and lack of accountability, which have led to discussions about which models, mechanisms, instruments and processes can ensure political control of MOCs and effective, efficient and sustainable provision of public services. Several country chapters, for instance Israel, Norway, Portugal and Sweden, mention economic governance "scandals" which have put the issue of corporate governance high on the political agenda.

The chapters underline that corporate governance of MOCs is a major challenge for governments and that MOCs face severe governance problems. Looking into the chapters, there are several observable patterns. On the one hand, a lack of oversight due to passive or distant ownership by the municipality can weaken the link of MOCs and municipalities and the will to perform in the best interest of the general public (e.g. Austria, Germany, Switzerland). On the other hand, according to the chapters, MOCs suffer from undue hands-on and politically motivated ownership interference (e.g. Italy, Portugal, Spain, Turkey), leading to unclear lines of responsibility, a lack of accountability and efficiency losses in corporate operations.

The imposition of commercial laws and regulations on MOCs can create challenges in the sense that enforcement actions against entities controlled by the municipality may cause intra-governmental friction. Additional governance issues arise because MOCs operate in a dual goal system. They should fulfil a public service goal and public policy while simultaneously meet financial goals. More fundamentally, corporate governance difficulties arise because accountability for MOCs performance involves a complex chain of agents, the principals of which are remote or not easily identifiable. In summary, some especially important governance challenges are multiple and often competing goals and objectives, specific ownership structures with multiple principals, protection from competition, patronage in boards, low levels of accountability and transparency.

In the overall conception of autonomy and corporate governance of MOCs, public corporate governance codes are crucial instruments that can cover all relevant governance fields (OECD, 2015; Papenfuß & Schmidt, 2021a). Public corporate governance codes are intended to summarise the basic characteristics of the public corporate governance system and address regularly occurring governance questions, ambiguities and legal gaps. Compared to the corporate governance codes for listed enterprises, there are numerous special features and requirements. For example, the regulatory field owner must be completely differentiated, as aspects of democratic legitimacy in governance and control processes must be taken into account. In some countries there is a trend to establish public corporate governance codes, such as in Germany; many other countries also have corporate governance codes for MOCs such as Canada, Denmark, Poland, and Switzerland; single chapters, such as Spain, report on the development of corporate governance codes of single big MOCs. In most countries they are established by municipalities; single countries like the Netherlands have *sectoral* corporate governance codes for MOCs. Overall, corporate governance codes are still not widespread in many countries at the municipal level, but there seems to be a tendency to, step-by-step, establish more corporate governance codes also in the context of MOCs in order to improve the governance, accountability and performance of MOCs and to strengthen trust of citizens in the state.

21.7 Summary and Research Agenda

To conclude, MOCs have become vitally important as instruments for public service delivery at the local (municipal) level. Large empirical questions remain, such as whether they indeed contribute to local government efficiency, effectiveness, and quality, and how they can best be governed. Such questions were not the topic of this book. This book offered an overview of how municipal corporatisation occurs in many different countries, looking in particular at trends, legal types, organisational characteristics, autonomy and board structure. Our chapters demonstrate that local government corporatisation is not a singular trend, nor a trend that differs by country, but that there are both cross-country differences and similarities in how local government corporatisation occurred, and in the landscape in which MOCs today operate.

In terms of *trends*, the evidence from our chapters demonstrates that on the whole, there appears to be a recent trend towards local government corporatisation. This is especially true for countries such as England, France, Germany, Norway and Turkey, that have seen a dramatic rise in the number of MOCs used in current local public service delivery. For the bulk of countries, the corporatisation trend has been more gradual or has already taken place in the past. Lastly, there is a group of countries where corporatisation had been a trend, but which now seem to be reversing course in what one might call "remunicipalisation" (e.g. Voorn et al., 2021). Scholars have begun to systematically investigate the antecedents of corporatisation (and its reversal) within single countries (see Andrews et al., 2022), but more comparative research focused on the economic, political and institutional factors that lie behind converging and diverging reform trajectories would be valuable.

In terms of *legal types*, we have found that MOCs can function under both public and private law. In most countries, municipalities have to find either public-law MOCs or private-law MOCs, which are subject to diverging laws. Public-law MOCs can have many different shapes, and the specific content of public law as it applies to MOCs is strongly dependent on country context, to the point that we can draw few overarching lessons. Private-law MOCs are likewise diverse, but we can see some overarching themes: the limited liability company is omnipresent, with foundations and cooperatives also used in many countries, as well as a variety of types of non-profits. But perhaps the most interesting finding for future comparative research is that the distinction between public and private law is often murkier than past research suggests: at least in Austria, Canada, Denmark, Israel and Turkey, either both legal regimes apply to MOCs or it is unclear which law applies to MOCs.

MOCs throughout all countries also vary much in terms of their *organisational characteristics*. In terms of *policy sector*, many countries use MOCs in many different sectors, although some countries use them primarily or exclusively for a more narrow range of (technical) services. In terms of ownership, about one-third of countries exclusively have MOCs that are owned by a single municipality, and in two-thirds of countries MOCs are also used as a vehicle for inter-municipal cooperation and PPPs (in some countries more than others, e.g. in the Netherlands the majority of MOCs are owned by multiple actors). Next, most countries seem to have multi-purpose MOCs, although we caution against further use of this term, as even in countries where MOCs are single-purpose they are often operating within multi-purpose environments. Lastly, some countries primarily have MOCs that are small in size, like Greece, and in other countries MOCs are typically large, like in Turkey, with most countries having a very heterogeneous group of MOCs.

Next, when considering the *autonomy* of MOCs, there is again great variety in the environments in which MOCs operate in the countries surveyed. When interpreting our findings, we found a great deal of similarity with the earlier findings of Ladner et al. (2016), who measured local autonomy in 39 countries; the autonomy of MOCs seems to follow the autonomy that local governments have, particularly because of how national regulation creates and influences the manoeuvring space for local government which in its turn lay the premises for how municipalities shape and govern their MOCs, including the autonomy they grant to their MOCs. Within this framework constructed in different ways in different countries by national and then local governments, MOCs may have various degrees of autonomy concerning operative, financial, organisational, and labour issues and setting of goals and strategies. Some countries therefore have more autonomous MOCs than others. Moreover, it seems that private-law MOCs tend to have more autonomy and that board structure (and particularly the presence of supervisory boards) affects MOCs' autonomy (with those with a supervisory board being less autonomous).

Finally, in terms of ***board structure and corporate governance***, there is again much difference between the different countries. Some countries primarily use one-tier boards for MOCs, which is dominant especially in the Anglo-Saxon countries. Others primarily use two-tier boards. A subset of countries allow much freedom to municipalities for themselves to choose the board structure for MOCs. Next, corporate governance differs between countries, and especially interesting is the rise of pre-set corporate governance codes, with especially Germany paving the way. Beyond that, corporate governance very much depends on national legislation and traditions. However, the corporate governance of MOCs has still been examined empirically only to a very limited extent. The comparatively limited literature on corporate governance of MOCs has triggered recurring calls to enhance the empirical state of knowledge about the determinants and effects of corporate governance concepts and instruments.

21.8 Final Words

MOCs lie on a continuum between the core public administration and private firms, mixing politics with professionalism (cf. Voorn, 2020). Research on MOCs promises to generate valuable insights for several theoretical debates, on overriding public administration issues, for instance on performance of public services, accountability, control and trust in steering relations, competing institutional logics, public corporate governance, corruption and (de-) politicisation (Grossi et al., 2015; Klausen & Winsvold, 2019; Papenfuß, 2020; Van Genugten et al., 2020; Verhoest et al., 2012). Given the substantial parts of local government budgets they cover, MOCs may become a crucial future topic in the debate about how to achieve important public interests, such as the United Nations Sustainable Development Goals. Climate protection, reduction of poverty and unemployment, sustainable city development, digital transformation, equality of living conditions—these are all public interests that MOCs are (partially) tasked with to achieve on a daily basis.

This book has offered an overview of the different features and environments of MOCs and more. If any main lesson could be drawn from it, it would be that while there are many differences between countries, there are also some overarching lessons and opportunities for cross-country policy learning. Moreover, and more fundamentally, we have found that MOCs are vitally important instruments of local public service delivery in all countries surveyed in this book, covering large parts of municipal budgets and fulfilling a wide array of critically important public service tasks.

Beyond this, there is much that we still do not know. Are MOCs more efficient and effective in delivering local public services than other forms of service delivery, such as private organisations or local bureaucracies? What makes them most effective and democratically accountable, and particularly, what legal type, what type of ownership, what level of autonomy, and what corporate governance can contribute to this? While some research has already delved into these questions (Andrews, 2022; Bel et al., 2021; Krause & Swiatczak, 2021; Voorn, 2022; Voorn et al., 2020a, 2020b), we do not yet have a complete overview of the answers to these questions, and we strongly encourage more research into all these questions.

In that context, we hope that our cross-country overview of MOCs in many countries, and the corporatisation trends, and legal types, organisational characteristics, autonomy and board structure of MOCs, will help to make that next step towards more cross-country learning about one of the most fundamental and critical trends in modern public administration: the corporatisation of local public service delivery.

References

Andrews, R. (2020). Organizational publicness and mortality: Explaining the dissolution of local authority companies. *Public Management Review, 24*(3), 350–371.

Andrews, R. (2022). Organizational publicness and mortality: Explaining the dissolution of local authority companies. *Public Management Review, 24*(3), 350–371.

Andrews, R., Clifton, J., & Ferry, L. (2022). Corporatization of public services. *Public Administration*. https://doi.org/10.1111/padm.12848.

Andrews, R., Ferry, L., Skelcher, C., & Wegorowski, P. (2020). Corporatization in the public sector: Explaining the growth of local government companies. *Public Administration Review, 80*(3), 482–493.

Bel, G., Esteve, M., Garrido, J. C., & Zafra-Gómez, J. L. (2021). The costs of corporatization: Analysing the effects of forms of governance. *Public Administration*. https://doi.org/10.1111/padm.12713.

Bel, G., & Fageda, X. (2007). Why do local governments privatise public services? A survey of empirical studies. *Local Government Studies, 33*(4), 517–534.

Bel, G., & Warner, M. (2015). Inter-municipal cooperation and costs: Expectations and evidence. *Public Administration, 93*(1), 52–67.

Citroni, G., Lippi, A., & Profeti, S. (2013). Remapping the state: Inter-municipal cooperation through corporatisation and public-private governance structures. *Local Government Studies, 39*(2), 208–234.

Grossi, G., Papenfuß, U., & Tremblay, M. (2015). Corporate governance and accountability of state-owned enterprises: Relevance for science and society and interdisciplinary research perspectives. *International Journal of Public Sector Management, 28*(4), 274–285.

Grossi, G., & Reichard, C. (2008). Municipal corporatization in Germany and Italy. *Public Management Review, 10*(5), 597–617.

Klausen, J. E., & Winsvold, M. (2019). Corporate governance and democratic accountability: Local state-owned enterprises in Norway. *Journal of Public Policy, 41*(1), 161–184.

Krause, T. A., & Swiatczak, M. D. (2021). In control we trust!? Exploring formal control configurations for municipally owned corporations. *Journal of Public Budgeting, Accounting & Financial Management, 33*(3), 314–342.

Kuhlmann, S., & Bouckaert, G. (Eds.). (2016). *Local public sector reforms in times of crisis: National trajectories and international comparison*. Palgrave Macmillan.

Ladner, A., Keuffer, N., & Baldersheim, H. (2016). Measuring local autonomy in 39 countries (1990–2014). *Regional & Federal Studies, 26*(3), 321–357.

OECD. (2015). *OECD guidelines on corporate governance of state-owned enterprises*. OECD Publishing.

Papenfuß, U. (2020). Corporate governance of state-owned enterprises: Conceptualization, challenges and perspectives for the public corporate governance field. In L. Bernier, P. Bance, & E. Florio (Eds.), *The Routledge handbook of state-owned enterprises* (pp. 433–444). Routledge.

Papenfuß, U., & Schmidt, C. (2021a). Personnel governance of corporatized public services: Effects of executive resources and corporation forms on turnover. *Public Administration*. https://doi.org/10.1111/padm.12752.

Papenfuß, U., & Schmidt, C. (2021b). Understanding self-regulation for political control and policy-making: Effects of governance mechanisms on accountability. *Governance, 34*(4), 1115–1141.

Papenfuβ, U., & Keppler, F. (2020). Does performance-related pay and public service motivation research treat state-owned enterprises like a neglected Cinderella? A systematic literature review and agenda for future research on performance effects. *Public Management Review, 22*(7), 1119–1145.

Tavares, A. F. (2017). Ten years after: Revisiting the determinants of the adoption of municipal corporations for local service delivery. *Local Government Studies, 43*(5), 697–706.

Torsteinsen, H., & Van Genugten, M. L. (2016). Municipal waste management in Norway and the Netherlands – From in-house provision to inter-municipal cooperation. In S. Kuhlmann & G. Bouckaert (Eds.), *Local public sector reforms in times of crisis: National trajectories and international comparison* (pp. 205–220). Palgrave.

Van Genugten, M., Van Thiel, S., & Voorn, B. (2020). Local governments and their arm's length bodies. *Local Government Studies, 46*(1), 1–21.

Verhoest, K., Peters, B. G., Bouckaert, G., & Verschuere, B. (2004). The study of organisational autonomy: A conceptual review. *Public Administration and Development, 24*, 101–118.

Verhoest, K., Van Thiel, S., Bouckaert, G., & Lægreid, P. (Eds.). (2012). *Government agencies: Practices and lessons from 30 countries*. Palgrave Macmillan.

Voorn, B. (2020). *When politics meets professionalism: The characteristics and performance predictors of municipally owned corporations* (Doctoral dissertation). Nijmegen: Radboud University.

Voorn, B. (2022). Professional managers, public values? The delicate balance between corporatization and stewardship to society. *Public Management Review*. https://doi.org/10.1080/14719037.2022.2026691.

Voorn, B., Borst, R. T., & Blom, R. (2020a). Business techniques as an explanation of the autonomy-performance link in corporatized entities: Evidence from Dutch Municipally owned corporations. *International Public Management Journal*. https://doi.org/10.1080/10967494.2020.1802632.

Voorn, B., Van Genugten, M., & Van Thiel, S. (2020b). Performance of municipally owned corporations: Determinants and mechanisms. *Annals of Public and Cooperative Economics, 91*(2), 191–212.

Voorn, B., & Van Genugten, M. L. (2021). Dealing with multiple principals in at arm's length organizations: A qualitative study of Dutch municipally owned corporations. *Public Administration*. https://doi.org/10.1111/padm.12746.

Voorn, B., Van Genugten, M. L., & Van Thiel, S. (2017). The efficiency and effectiveness of municipally owned corporations: A systematic review. *Local Government Studies, 43*(5), 820–841.

Voorn, B., Van Genugten, M. L., & Van Thiel, S. (2021). Re-interpreting re-municipalization: Finding equilibrium. *Journal of Economic Policy Reform, 24*(3), 305–318.

Wollmann, H. (2004). Local government reforms in Great Britain, Sweden, Germany and France: Between multi-function and single-purpose organizations. *Local Government Studies, 30*(4), 639–665.

GPSR Compliance

The European Union's (EU) General Product Safety Regulation (GPSR) is a set of rules that requires consumer products to be safe and our obligations to ensure this.

If you have any concerns about our products, you can contact us on ProductSafety@springernature.com

In case Publisher is established outside the EU, the EU authorized representative is:

Springer Nature Customer Service Center GmbH
Europaplatz 3
69115 Heidelberg, Germany

The manufacturer's authorised representative in the EU is Springer Nature Customer Service Centre GmbH, Europaplatz 3, 69115 Heidelberg, Germany. If you have any concerns regarding our products, please contact ProductSafety@springernature.com

Printed and bound by CPI Group (UK) Ltd, Croydon, CR0 4YY
28/09/2026
02224064-0002